TARGETED KILLINGS

TARGETED KILLINGS

Law and Morality in an Asymmetrical World

Edited by

CLAIRE FINKELSTEIN
JENS DAVID OHLIN
ANDREW ALTMAN

OXFORD

UNIVERSITY PRESS

OXFORD

UNIVERSITY PRESS

Great Clarendon Street, Oxford ox2 6DP
United Kingdom

Oxford University Press is a department of the University of Oxford.
It furthers the University's objective of excellence in research, scholarship,
and education by publishing worldwide. Oxford is a registered trade mark of
Oxford University Press in the UK and in certain other countries

British Library Cataloguing in Publication Data
Data available

Library of Congress Cataloguing in Publication Data
Data available

ISBN 978–0–19–964647–0
978–0–19–964648–7 (pbk.)

Printed in Great Britain
on acid-free paper by
CPI Group (UK) Ltd, Croydon, CR0 4YY

PREFACE

The law of armed conflict has traditionally been organized around the symmetry of rules of conduct: the idea that the permissions and restrictions that govern the soldiers of one side in war are the same as for the other side, regardless of the justice of each party's *causus belli*. Thus a German and an American soldier during the Second World War have an equal right to kill one another, regardless of the moral justification for the belligerency of their respective countries. Modern warfare, however, is fundamentally asymmetrical. Instead of the traditional reciprocal form of combat, where members of sovereign states fight co-belligerents from other states, we now have a war between traditional forces of a sovereign power, on the one hand, with what might be thought of as a band of civilian outlaws, namely individuals whose aggressive designs are enacted through membership of a criminal organization instead of the military forces of a sovereign state. Thus while co-equal sovereignty—on which the *ius in bello* is premised—is symmetrical, the principles of the War on Terror are necessarily asymmetrical: we regard it as permissible to target members of Al-Qaeda, for example, but we do not accept their right to target us. Similarly, although we regard members of Al-Qaeda as permissible targets, we regard them as exempt from the protections traditionally extended to ordinary enemy combatants, such as prisoner of war status and, according to some, the right of repatriation upon the conclusion of hostilities. The asymmetrical nature of the War on Terror is captured by the concept of the 'unlawful combatant.'

The pressures of modern warfare are nowhere more visibly displayed than in the policy surrounding the Obama Administration's use of targeted killing, otherwise known as 'kill or capture' raids on individuals on the JPEL ('Joint Prioritized Effects List'). While there has been a steady increase in reliance on targeted killing as a technique of war, the willingness on the part of the Obama Administration to subject the new policy to the legal and moral examination it appears to warrant has not kept pace. Yet the expanded conception of combatant status, reflected in the 'unlawful combatant' category, depends heavily on the asymmetrical logic that the traditional law of war rejects. The most crucial question for the modern theory of war, then, is whether the transformation from symmetrical to asymmetrical conceptions of military engagement is ethically and legally defensible. Should we see the concept of unlawful combatants, and all that this view expresses, as a justifiable adaptation to the realities of modern warfare? Or should we see it as a corruption of the values of reciprocity that have for many years formed the moral core of permissible aggression in war? This is one of the most important questions the essays in this volume attempt to answer.

A second question raised by the asymmetry of modern warfare is about the line between law-enforcement and military action. Traditionally, even highly organized aggressive action on the part of civilians has fallen within the domain of law enforcement: if members of Al-Qaeda are civilians, then the correct approach to handling the threat they pose would be based on law-enforcement techniques and authority. Thus, comparable to the War on Drugs, the War on Terror might be handled under the auspices of international and coordinated domesticated police action. Once again, however, if we think of enforcement efforts against international terrorists as properly falling within the domain of law-enforcement, we should also see terror suspects as entitled to the guarantees of domestic criminals, according to which rules of evidence prohibit the use of coercive interrogation techniques and the accused has a right to a fair trial and to competent legal representation. On this view, limitations on the use of preemptive force would in all likelihood render kill or capture raids morally and legally impermissible. One can frame these important questions another way: if we are correct in thinking of terrorists as engaging in military attacks on the United States, in keeping with a reconceived view of war as asymmetrical, then what is to restrict our taking such a view of the appropriateness of military conduct in fighting terrorists on United States soil? Insofar as the targeted killing of Al-Awlaki, an American citizen, can be justified under the Law of Armed Conflict, could we not extend such justification to a comparable killing of a suspected terrorist in the United States? And if so, why not extend such treatment to key players in the War on Drugs? In what does the difference between law enforcement and military action now consist?

None of these gripping questions were present in my mind in the fall of 2010, as I rounded up the list of usual suspects, searching for one that would suit for the spring conference of the Institute for Law and Philosophy (ILP). Around that time, I happened to attend a conference, jointly organized between West Point and Columbia Law School, on War and the Rule of Law. There I encountered a number of experts in military law, several of whom were active in the Judge Advocate General Corps, and others of whom had been in active duty and who were now turning to more academic pursuits. Among the topics they discussed was the permissible use of targeted killing. Much to my amazement, these experts turned out to disagree on key issues with one another. We are, of course, all accustomed to the disagreements of high theory: while they can be pointed, and at times downright aggressive, we sometimes comfort ourselves with the thought that many such academic debates will always remain just that, exercises in high theory that rarely, if ever, make a difference to the real world. But debates about the permissible use of military force?! Here disagreement was unnerving. How could those responsible in the Department of Defense and the State Department fashion military policy if the foundations of that policy were *essentially contested*? How could life in the trenches, so to speak, continue when the guardians of key military practices had disagreements so sharp that one thought pulling the trigger permissible and another not?

The closest legal theorists seemed to me to have come to this kind of practical standoff was in the area of criminal law theory. The debates in military ethics were to my mind immediately suggestive of discussions relating to the permissible scope of justifications like self-defense, defense of others, or law enforcement. I thought, moreover, that it might be useful to address the military debate through the lens of philosophical discussions about domestic law, in keeping with a principle many scholars have written about in connection with international law generally, an idea Michael Walzer dubbed the 'domestic analogy.' At the time I thought mainly of enriching theoretical debate with a clearer understanding of the ethical issues that arose 'on the ground.' I could not have anticipated what later emerged: theoreticians with only limited knowledge of the actual workings of military operations could actually help to clarify foundational concepts in military practice, at the same time that the carefully studied practices of military conduct could shed light on the structure of ethical reflection more generally.

Soon thereafter I approached my dean, Michael Fitts, with an unorthodox idea: I would gather a number of prominent philosophers working on applied ethics, combine them with legal philosophers working on Just War Theory, and bring this group of academics together with military lawyers focused on ethical issues in war, as well as statesmen and policymakers, in the hope that this eclectic combination would generate an interdisciplinary conversation about killing in war. It was not that the topic of targeted killing struck me as so worthy in and of itself. Rather, it seemed a good vehicle for an attempted marriage between theory and practice, a chance to explore an issue in applied ethics from multiple perspectives at once. It was one of those moments: Mike responded with a look that signaled a combination of incredulity and amusement: 'You want ILP to hold a conference on *what*?!' One must understand his reaction in context, of course. At that time targeted killing was not yet prominently in the public eye; still less had it entered the realm of legal academic debate. Some military topics were beginning to creep into academic, and eventually into philosophical, consciousness. The logic and permissibility of using 'enhanced interrogation techniques' had caught philosophers' attention, and conferences on torture had sprung up in law schools around the United States. But torture was an easier case: that topic had a history in moral philosophy, in the debates about the merits of Utilitarianism versus Deontology, and a battery of familiar hypotheticals with which deontologists armed themselves against the morally questionable implications of social utility maximization. Even with the revival of torture as a topic of renewed philosophical interest, however, the idea of theorizing targeted killing seemed as absurd as attempting to theorize the relative merits of the cruise missile! Fortunately, my dean was willing to indulge the targeted killing experiment, and we prepared for what was to be one of the more unusual academic gatherings I have attended.

By the time the conference rolled around, in April 2011, it was already clear that targeted killing was more than just a pretext for combining theory and practice around issues in applied ethics. It showed itself to be a crucial, perhaps *the* crucial, issue of military ethics of our day. It turned out to be a lens through which to study the heart of modern warfare, which specializes in the use of high-level technology in selective killing operations to eliminate enemies who are at the very least intermingled with a civilian population, if not properly considered civilians themselves. Because it lies at the intersection of ethical discussions about life and death, the theory of warfare, the legitimate scope of self-defense of sovereign nations, the relation between individuals and the state, the line between the civil and the military police functions, the relation between ordinary morality and legal ethics, and finally the impact of advances in technology on modern warfare, it creates a kaleidoscope through which major shifts in our ethical and legal norms can be viewed.

This volume collects most of the papers that were presented at that April 2011 conference, plus some an additional one. Most of the papers have evolved significantly since they were first presented in April—a result of the growth in sophistication that only conversation off-the-beaten track from one's own discipline can provide. As we grappled with a new, and increasingly important, technique of modern warfare in terms often uncomfortable and unfamiliar, we all moved up the learning curve. And in that sense, the enterprise was an unmitigated success. In another, probably less important sense, it was a failure: as the depth and complexity of the issues we discussed became apparent, the hope of arriving at definitive answers to the ethical questions surrounding targeted killing diminished. But in that failure lay another kind of success: we became aware that the practice of targeted killing exposes significant complexities in the moral justification for killing in war. Hopefully, the increased sense of the difficulty of the topic lies increased hope that collective efforts like the current volume will eventually yield solutions.

A number of thanks are overdue. First and foremost, I would like to thank my dean, Michael Fitts, for first indulging, and then enthusiastically embracing, not only the Institute's work on targeted killing, but its work on applied ethics and the rule of law more generally. His generous funding of ILP, and of the conference and much of the labor on the present volume, have made what was intended as an interesting interdisciplinary foray into a project with the potential for real ethical impact. There was another source of funding for the original conference on targeted killing, and that was the Jean Beer Blumenfeld Center for Ethics at Georgia State University. I am grateful to Andrew Cohen, Director of the Center, and Andrew Altman, the Center's Director of Research, for their willingness to leap into the unknown with ILP with their generous donation to conference expenses. Next are the respective contributions of my co-editors of this volume, Jens Ohlin and Andrew Altman. While the conception for the conference may have begun at West Point, Georgia State, and the University of Pennsylvania Law School, the design and conception of the volume occurred primarily at Cornell Law School. Jens was an extraordinarily clear-sighted, energetic, and disciplined leader for me and Andrew of the original proposal to Oxford University Press. The ink had barely dried on the last-minute drafts many of us turned in for clandestine circulation among our fellow conference participants, when Jens had drafted the proposal and conceived its basic format. He was also a disciplined editor, at times a task-master, in making sure contributors, and to the best of his ability, his fellow editors stuck to our agreed upon timetables and followed through with ensuring the standards for contributions to which we had aspired. He was and is, moreover, the only true expert of international law among the three of us, and the knowledge and subtlety he brought in that area to our work on the volume was essential to its success. Finally, I should say that Jens was unstinting in the time he was willing to put into the editorial process, often bearing the laboring oar on tasks that by rights should not have been his.

Andrew Altman was involved in the project from an early stage. Not only did he agree to commit funds to the realization of the conference, but he proved a quiet but clear-sighted 'editor' of the original conference I had envisioned, helping to shape the format and list of contributors that proved invaluable to the final product. As an editor of the volume, he was also steadfast and disciplined, relentlessly exacting in his rightly high standards, and essential to the volume's polish in his detailed and penetrating editorial eye. And, of course, he bore the burden of writing the Introduction to the volume alone, an invaluable help in the middle of a busy production schedule. Perhaps needless to say, the three editors are also extremely grateful to the respective contributors to the volume. All papers are original and all underwent multiple drafts and edits. We thank the authors for the very significant time and effort they have been willing to devote to this project, and for their willingness to engage with one another, both at the April conference and in their work on their contributions in the months thereafter, to make the volume a truly interdisciplinary endeavor.

Other thanks are also due. Douglas Weck, the Academic Coordinator of the Institute for Law and Philosophy at the time of the April conference, was involved in every detail of the conception and planning of that event. Now an advanced graduate student in Penn's Joint Law and Philosophy program, Doug was able to help me to think through the conference, as well as execute so many, many of the myriad details that an undertaking of this magnitude requires. In addition, Anna Gavin, the Administrative Coordinator for the Institute, worked tirelessly to make the conference a success. No detail was too small for her watchful and dedicated attention. The current Academic Coordinator of the Institute, Chris Melenovsky, along with another Penn graduate student, Justin Bernstein, were indefatigable in working on the first round of edits when the volume came back from the Oxford University Press copy-editor. After several weeks of trying to render usage, spelling, citation format, etc consistent across a large number of participants from widely divergent contexts, Chris and Justin both looked as though they had emerged from a kill or capture raid of their own. Finally, the Faculty Support Unit of Penn Law School, as well as individuals on the library staff, provided crucial infrastructure and proofreading. For their help I am grateful to the individual members of both sets of staff, as well as to the Law School once again for its willingness to commit extensive resources once again to the realization of this project.

Claire Finkelstein
Philadelphia
December 2011

TABLE OF CONTENTS

I THE CHANGING FACE OF WAR: TARGETING NON-COMBATANTS

II NORMATIVE FOUNDATIONS: LAW ENFORCEMENT OR WAR?

III TARGETED KILLING AND SELF-DEFENSE

IV EXERCISING JUDGMENT IN TARGETED KILLING DECISIONS

V UTILITARIAN TRADE-OFFS AND DEONTOLOGICAL CONSTRAINTS

TABLE OF CASES

TABLE OF INSTRUMENTS AND LEGISLATION

U.N. RESOLUTIONS

U.N. General Assembly Resolutions

U.N. Security Council Resolutions

LIST OF ABBREVIATIONS

AQ	Al Qaeda
AUMF	Authorization for the Use of Military Force
CCR	Center for Constitutional Rights
CDM	collateral damage methodology
CIA	Central Intelligence Agency
CIL	customary international law
CRS	Congressional Research Service
DoD	Department of Defense
FBI	Federal Bureau of Investigation
FSCL	Fire Support Coordination Line
HVT	High-Value Target
ICC	International Criminal Court
ICRC	International Committee of the Red Cross
ICJ	International Court of Justice
ICTY	International Criminal Tribunal for the former Yugoslavia
IDF	Israeli Defense Forces
IED	improvised explosive device
IHL	international humanitarian law
IHRL	international human rights law
JPEL	Joint Prioritized Effects List
JSOC	Joint Special Operations Command
JTAC	Joint Terminal Attack Controller
JWT	just war theory
LOAC	law of armed conflict
NCV	noncombatant casualty value
NSA	non-state actor
OEF	Operation Enduring Freedom
ROE	Rules of Engagement
SEAL	sea, air, land
SOF	Special Operations Forces
STAR	sensitive target approval and review
TK	targeted killing
UAE	United Arab Emirates
UAVs	unmanned aerial vehicles
UCCs	Unified Combatant Commands
UN	United Nations
USCENTCOM	United States Central Command
USSOCOM	United States Special Operations Command

LIST OF CONTRIBUTORS

Andrew Altman is Professor of Philosophy and Director of Research for the Jean Beer Blumenfeld Center for Ethics at Georgia State University. He is the author of *Critical Legal Studies: A Liberal Critique* (Princeton U.P.) and co-author, with Christopher H. Wellman, of *A Liberal Theory of International Justice* (Oxford U.P.).

Kenneth Anderson is Professor of Law, Washington College of Law American University, Hoover Institution visiting fellow on national security and law, and Brookings Institution nonresident senior fellow.

Russell L. Christopher is Professor of Law at The University of Tulsa College of Law.

Claire Finkelstein is Algernon Biddle Professor of Law and Professor of Philosophy at the University of Pennsylvania, and Co-Director of the University of Pennsylvania Institute for Law and Philosophy.

Kevin H. Govern is Associate Professor of Law at the Ave Maria School of Law. He earned a J.D. from Marquette University Law School, and LL.M. degrees from The Judge Advocate General's School, U.S. Army, and from Notre Dame Law School.

Amos Guiora is Professor of Law at the University of Utah, S.J. Quinney College of Law. Guiora has a AB in History from Kenyon College and a JD from Case Western Reserve Law School.

Leo Katz is the Frank Carano Professor of Law at the University of Pennsylvania Law School.

Craig Martin is Associate Professor of Law at Washburn University School of Law. He has degrees from the Royal Military College of Canada, Osaka University, the University of Toronto, and the University of Pennsylvania, and he specializes in international law as it relates to the use of force and the laws of war, and comparative constitutional law, with an emphasis on both rights and war powers.

Colonel Mark "Max" Maxwell is the Staff Judge Advocate of U.S. Army V Corps in Wiesbaden, Germany. He is an Army Judge Advocate and holds degrees from Duke University, the University of North Carolina at Chapel Hill, and the National War College.

Jeff McMahan is Professor of Philosophy at Rutgers University. He is the author of *The Ethics of Killing: Problems at the Margins of Life (2002)* and *Killing in War (2009)*, both published by Oxford University Press.

Gregory S. McNeal is Associate Professor of Law at Pepperdine University School of Law.

Richard V. Meyer is Professor and Director of the Foreign LL.M. Program, Mississippi College School of Law and Senior Fellow, United States Military Academy at West Point Center for the Rule of Law.

Phillip Montague is Professor Emeritus, Department of Philosophy, Western Washington University.

Michael Moore is the Charles R. Walgreen, Jr., University Chair, Professor of Law and Professor of Philosophy at the University of Illinois. Professor Moore writes broadly in substantive ethics, metaethics, neuroscience, moral responsibility and criminal law, political philosophy, jurisprudence, and metaphysics, his most recent book *(Causationand Responsibility*, OUP, 2009) combining three of these interests.

Jens David Ohlin is Associate Professor of Law at Cornell Law School. He earned a Ph.D. in philosophy from Columbia University and a J.D. from Columbia Law School.

Daniel Statman is a full professor in the department of philosophy, the University of Haifa. His areas of specialization are ethics, moral psychology, the philosophy of law, and Jewish philosophy. In 2000, he served on the committee that revised the ethical code for the IDF.

Fernando Tesón is Tobias Simon Eminent Scholar at Florida State University. He has degrees from the University of Buenos Aires, the University of Brussels, and Northwestern University.

Jeremy Waldron is University Professor at New York University School of Law and also Chichele Professor of Social and Political Theory at Oxford.

INTRODUCTION

Andrew Altman

On April 15–16, 2011, some three dozen philosophers, legal scholars, and military officers gathered for a conference in Philadelphia under the auspices of the University of Pennsylvania to examine the moral and legal issues surrounding the targeted killing of suspected or known terrorists. The topic had been discussed and debated in the media, mainly in connection with the increased use of unmanned armed drones to target terrorists by the Obama administration, but also in relation to Russian policies in Chechnya and Israeli policies in the Occupied Territories and elsewhere. Critics and supporters of the targeted killings had traded arguments and counterarguments that raised complex and contested questions of fact, law, and morality. The premise of the Philadelphia conference was that the differing perspectives of moral theory, legal doctrine, and military experience could jointly shed light on those difficult questions.

Two weeks after the conference took place, U.S. Navy Seals killed the infamous leader of Al Qaeda, Osama bin Laden, in his redoubt in Pakistan, and targeted killing became a front-page topic around the globe. Although media attention to the topic has naturally diminished since the first few weeks after bin Laden was killed, targeted killing is virtually certain to remain a controversial instrument in the arsenal that states use to counter threats stemming from those non-state organizations and movements that engage in terrorism.

The questions raised by targeted killing are not going away any time soon: they are at once timely and enduring. This volume is the first appearance in print of a collection that brings together scholars from across disciplines for a sustained and reasoned discussion of these questions. In this introduction, I provide material intended to orient readers, coming as they will from a broad range of academic and non-academic backgrounds. Section I explains what is meant by "asymmetric" armed conflict and how terrorism is connected to such conflict. Section II examines the term, "terrorism," sketching and defending a concept of terrorism that informs the various contributions to this volume. Section III describes the two main approaches to assessing the legality and morality of targeted killing: the law-enforcement and the armed-conflict models. Section IV summarizes each subsequent chapter, drawing contrasts and remarking on similarities among them, and Section V offers some brief concluding thoughts.

I. Our asymmetric world

The armed confrontation between states and their enemies who employ terrorist tactics is a case of the broader phenomenon of asymmetric conflict. Such conflict is characterized by opposing sides that bring to their armed contest radically different means and methods of violence and radically divergent levels of brute firepower. Asymmetric conflict is nothing new in the history of organized human violence, but in the modern world it has typically taken the distinctive form of a conflict between the regular armed forces of states, on the one side, and the irregular forces of non-state groups and movements, on the other. The "regular" forces of a state are characterized by a strict chain of command, precisely defined roles in the command hierarchy, and conformity to the legal requirement that members wear uniforms and insignia and carry their arms openly in order to distinguish themselves clearly from civilians. The "irregular" forces of non-state groups and movements are more loosely organized, and, although they typically have something akin to a chain of command, they do not abide by the legal requirements concerning uniforms and the open carrying of arms: they seek to blend into the civilian population, rather than to distinguish themselves from it.

The armed forces of states have much greater firepower and organizational strength and more advanced technological resources than do the irregular forces that they confront, and it is this fact that partly constitutes the asymmetry between states and their irregular opponents. Additionally, the firepower and technology of a state's armed forces are supplemented by the resources of the state's intelligence agencies, which can not only provide information about their adversaries to the state's leaders, but also, in the case of the CIA at least, operate their own lethal technology.

It is in order to offset their disadvantages in firepower, technology and organizational strength, that irregular forces choose to blend into the civilian population and thus adopt a tactic explicitly prohibited by international law and constituting one of the defining features of terrorism: the deliberate killing of civilians. Thus, the leadership of Al Qaeda evidently believed that to drive the United States out of the Middle-East and to force the country to change its pro-Israel foreign policy, it needed to attack not just the Pentagon, but also the World Trade Center with its thousands of civilians. Non-state groups involved in attacks on states are not likely to take the deliberate killing of civilians off the table for another reason: the members of such groups tend to regard civilians of the adversary state as complicit in grave wrongs perpetrated by their state and as morally liable to attack for that reason. In addition, once violence is adopted as the method for accomplishing a goal, then the inclination is to ramp up the violence when it turns out that the goal has not been achieved, and civilians become tempting targets when the violence needs to be ramped up. (This tendency to ramp up violence in the absence of success is shared by state officials as well, with the U.S. war in Vietnam serving as a prime example.) In short, the asymmetric threats confronted by states in the decades ahead will almost invariably involve terrorist threats.

II. Terrorism

Much about terrorism is contested, including the very meaning of the term "terrorism" itself. And many people and state agencies have succumbed to the temptation to stretch the term for rhetorical and political purposes. For example, the FBI regards the property crimes that animal liberation and environmental groups commit to further their causes as terrorism,[1] and the Animal Enterprise Terrorism Act makes it a crime to interfere with the operation of an animal enterprise by intentionally damaging real or personal property.[2] Such bloated uses of the term "terrorism" have little to recommend them. Property crimes, even when they involve an undue risk to human life—and the so-called "terrorist" crimes of animal liberation and environment groups often involve no such risk—simply do not belong in the same moral or legal category as Timothy McVeigh's Oklahoma City bombing, much less the 9/11 attacks. The justification for the law's crude conception of terrorism is obscure, at best. It might be said that the property crimes in question and the crimes of Timothy McVeigh and the 9/11 terrorists share the feature that they are politically motivated. True enough, but one should expect terrorist crimes to involve the intention to commit violence against persons, and not just to be political in motivation.

A defensible approach would take the conceptually central cases of terrorism to be those acts undertaken with the intent (and realistic possibility) of killing in a single episode of violence a number of civilians for the purpose of advancing certain political goals by intimidating (a certain segment of) the population. Acts morally different from those undertaken with such an intent and purpose should not be counted as terrorist at all, or should be seen as peripheral instances of the concept.

The term "terrorism" and its cognates are almost always used to make a moral judgment about the acts and agents to whom the terms are applied, and it might seem to follow from that fact that, as a conceptual matter, a terrorist act is morally wrong.

---

[1] *Eco-terrorism and Lawlessness on the National Forests: Hearing Before the Subcomm. on Forests and Forest Health of the H. Resources Comm.*, 107th Cong. 107–83 (2002) (statement and testimony of James F. Jarboe, Domestic Terrorism Section Chief, Counterterrorism Division, FBI).

[2] 18 U.S.C. § 43 (2000).

But this conclusion does not follow, and it is not necessary to include a moral element as part of the very concept of terrorism. Instead, one can treat the question of whether some act is an act of terrorism as a factual question about the intent and purpose behind the act, and then proceed to judge the act as an egregious moral wrong, if the act does meet the factual conditions for a terrorist act.

It should be noted that the acts counting as central cases of terrorism, on the account I have sketched, are not limited to acts of non-state groups; states can and do engage in terrorism too. This implication helps to rebut the suspicion that "terrorism" is a term that is rhetorically loaded in favor of states and against insurgent movements, a suspicion fed by such abuses of the term as we see in the FBI's categorization of crimes. However, it might be argued that the concept of terrorism I have sketched is still tilted in favor of states over their non-state adversaries. The argument is this. States often pursue their goals with armed force that, although not deliberately directed at civilians, is used with indifference toward their lives, resulting in a substantial number of collateral deaths. Such a use of armed force can certainly be terrifying to populations, but, on my account, it would not count as terrorist. This implication seems questionable, because it might not be immediately clear what the moral difference is between a state foreseeably killing many civilians as "collateral damage" and a non-state organization killing the same number of civilians, albeit deliberately. Dead is dead. Thus, one might argue that a more even-handed account of the concept of terrorism would categorize both the state and the non-state killings as central cases of terrorism.

This argument is not entirely persuasive. A widely (though not universally) held moral view is that wrongful harms brought about intentionally are more serious wrongs than those that are brought about foreseeably but not intentionally. On that premise, the state's killings, even if wrong, would be less so than the killings of the non-state group, and the state killings would arguably count as peripheral cases of terrorism, if they counted as terrorism at all. Moreover, even if the premise is mistaken, it is still the case that persons who bring about wrongful harms intentionally bear a greater burden of blame than those who bring about such harm foreseeably but not intentionally. Treating the state and the non-state killings as central instances of terrorism would elide this difference in appropriate blame.

It should also be noted that, even if the intentional killing of civilians can be morally justified in certain extreme situations, the general moral prohibition against the intentional killing of the innocent would seem to be stricter than the prohibition against foreseeably but non-intentionally killing the innocent. The relatively greater strictness of the former prohibition is connected to the premise mentioned in the previous paragraph that intentional wrongs are more serious than non-intentional ones, and the consequence of this greater strictness is that the intentional killings of civilians by the non-state groups are more likely to be wrong in the first place than the non-intentional killings by the state. Accordingly, this consequence

4

is not chargeable to any inherent bias in my account of the concept of terrorism, but, rather, simply falls out of the different relative strength of different moral prohibitions.

III. The two models

Targeted killing is the intentional killing by a state of an individual identified in advance and not in the state's custody.[3] One can only speculate as to whether such killing would have been a topic of intense and widespread global attention had the attacks of September 11 been foiled and their perpetrators arrested. Certainly, the thousands of deaths resulting from the attacks, and the indelible images of the collapse of the Twin Towers, have shadowed any subsequent discussion of the use of targeted killing in response to the threats posed by terrorism. In the eyes of some, the events of September 11 were a wake-up call to governments around the world, demonstrating just how dangerous terrorism had become and just how inadequate to the danger the time-honored procedures and principles of investigating and prosecuting criminals before civilian courts now were. But in the eyes of others, those events did not demonstrate any such inadequacy: terrorism was a serious danger; but it called not for any substantial departure from the way that liberal states dealt with crime, but rather for better coordinated and more effective law-enforcement efforts.

These opposing ways of understanding September 11 have shaped the discussion of targeted killing by leading to the articulation of two competing models for assessing the response of governments to terrorism: the armed-conflict (or war) and the law-enforcement models. The models are not meant to be simply descriptive accounts of the current state of the law, but, at a deeper level, to provide moral frameworks for judging the actions of governments and determining what the law should be. And they lead to sharply conflicting assessments of the targeted killing by governments of suspected or known terrorists and to incompatible judgments about whether the law should ever permit such killing. The two models do not exhaust the approaches that might be taken to the issue, and several of the contributors to this volume suggest that both models are inadequate and some third way is needed. Nonetheless, the two models highlight the main questions to be addressed and provide answers that, if not beyond criticism, are plausible and widely held.

The proponents of the law-enforcement model argue that terrorism should be dealt with largely by the personnel, procedures, and standards used in responding to any kind of serious crime: police, prosecutors, timely public trials in civilian courts, warrants issued by such courts upon probable cause, and the rights to adequate legal counsel, to habeas corpus, to confront one's accusers, and to the other elements of due process of law. Some marginal modifications from ordinary criminal

---

[3] Nils Melzer, *Targeted Killing in International Law* (Oxford University Press, 2008) 3–4.

prosecutions might be justifiable, for example, if state secrets are involved in the prosecution, but the aim is to stick very closely to the idea that alleged terrorists should be dealt with in the same way that all others accused of serious crimes are treated by a well-functioning liberal state. This model pointedly rejects the idea that the targeted killing of suspected or known terrorists is morally or legally permissible, apart from situations in which the targeted individual poses an imminent (or otherwise unavoidable) threat to the lives of civilians and killing him is the only way to stop the threat from being realized. Excluding such emergency situations, the authorities are morally and legally obligated to capture the suspect and forbidden from killing him. So argue the defenders of the law-enforcement model.

The proponents of the armed-conflict model argue that the law-enforcement model is inadequate to deal with the threat of terrorism and that, instead, suspected and known terrorists should be treated as enemy combatants whose very tactics—targeting civilians—violate the laws of war and whose threat should be met, in large measure, by military means on the basis of principles appropriately applied during a time of war. On this model, a military response to terrorism is justified as a matter of national and/ or personal self-defense (and defense of others). Terrorists are not simply enemies of the states against which they conduct their attacks. They are "unprivileged belligerents," who lack the legal and moral permission to kill anyone because they do not distinguish themselves from civilians, and they are war criminals because they deliberately kill civilians. If they are captured, it is morally and legally permissible to try them in military courts and accord them a less rigorous form of due process than is found in civilian criminal courts. Additionally, on the armed-conflict model, there is no moral or legal requirement to try to capture them, and it is morally and legally permissible to target them with lethal force, even when they are not posing an imminent threat to the lives of others. There is no "last-resort" requirement on operations aimed at killing the enemy in war time: a legitimate target can be permissibly killed, even if capture would be costless. Only if and when the enemy surrenders is it then forbidden to intentionally kill him. In contrast, the law-enforcement model imposes a last-resort requirement: intentional killing is permitted only if capture is not possible and the killing is "strictly indispensable to save human life from unlawful attack."[4]

One of the notable features of the debate over targeted killing is that each side regards the other as proposing an approach that is not merely sub-optimal but unacceptable. The proponents of the law-enforcement model do not simply say that targeted killing is less than the best way to respond to terrorism; rather, they reject it as morally and legally impermissible. On the other side, defenders of the armed-conflict model insist that for a state threatened by terrorists to forego the practice, when the state has the requisite means, is an unacceptable abdication of its responsibility to its citizens.

---

[4] Ibid. at 233.

The reason why the law-enforcement advocates regard the practice as impermissible is relatively straightforward: they see targeted killings as nothing more than unjustifiable homicide by the state, in other words, as murder by the officials who plan and execute the killings. Just as it is murder for a guard to intentionally kill a suspected or known terrorist who is held in detention and posing no immediate threat to any of the captors or other detainees, it is murder for CIA personnel to intentionally kill by drone a suspected terrorist in Pakistan who is posing no immediate threat to citizens of the United States or of any other country. In both cases, the suspected or known terrorist is not, literally speaking, on a battlefield confronting U.S. or other military forces with his own lethal force. Rather, he is just like any other criminal suspect who continues to hold his human right to life unless and until he is convicted of a capital crime in accordance with due process of law. Targeted killing is impermissible because it is a violation of that right.

Moreover, advocates of the law-enforcement model argue that targeted killing cannot be justified as a matter of the right to self-defense because the relevant instances of such killing do not conform to an essential condition of rightfully exercising lethal force in self-defense, viz., that the targeted individual pose an imminent threat to human life. Bin Laden was certainly a threat to the United States and other countries, but, at the time he was killed, his threat was not on the verge of being realized. According to the law-enforcement model, then, the targeted killing of bin Laden and other known or suspected terrorists cannot be justified as a matter of self-defense.

The armed-conflict advocates contend that the absence of a demarcated battlefield only shows that traditional ways of thinking about the use of armed force are woefully obsolete when it comes to addressing contemporary terrorism. We are in "a world of new wars,"[5] and the traditional idea of war as a more or less symmetrical relation between two states (or two coalitions) whose armed forces clearly identify themselves as such and confront one another in delimited geographic regions cannot be sensibly applied to the asymmetrical relation between a state and the terrorist organizations that seek to attack it. There might be no specific battlefield on which opposing armies fight in the case of terrorism, but, the proponents of targeted killing argue, a war exists between the parties to the conflict, albeit an asymmetrical war.

Contrary to the law-enforcement model, the defenders of the armed-conflict approach argue that suspected and known terrorists are not just like other criminal suspects and not even like members of the Mafia and other organized crime enterprises. Unlike traditional organized crime, the purpose of terrorist organizations is to kill large numbers of civilians in the states that they regard as the enemy, in an effort to defeat the political will of those states. Thus, Al Qaeda attacks the United

---

[5] Daniel Statman, "Can Just War Theory Justify Targeted Killing? Three Possible Models," in this Volume, ch. 3, 110 (quoting Mary Kaldor).

States for its support of Israel and the Saudi regime, seeking to drive America out of the Middle East. Moreover, terrorist organizations are often supported by friendly governments that clandestinely provide resources such as money, forged documents, weaponry, training camps and safe haven. If a state were to forego entirely the use of targeted killing in dealing with a terrorist threat, then it would be failing to meet its responsibility to protect the lives and the political independence of its people. So argue the proponents of the armed-conflict model.

As for self-defense, advocates of the armed-conflict model reject the idea that the imminence requirement, understood as a demand to wait until an attack is just about to happen, applies to actions taken against the enemy in a time of war. When a country is at war, it is not required to refrain from lethal action until the next attack from the enemy is on the verge of occurring before launching a strike. Accordingly, on the armed-conflict model, the countries threatened by bin Laden did not need to wait until his next attack was just days away to strike at him.

IV. Summaries of the chapters

Few would argue against the claim that the targeted killing of individuals who are involved in terrorist activity is morally permissible under certain conditions, and none of the contributors to this volume argues that targeted killing is absolutely and universally prohibited by morality. Indeed, it is common ground among the contributors that such killing is morally permissible where the authorities know that a particular individual is about to deliberately trigger an explosion intended to kill many civilians and the only way to prevent the explosion is to kill the individual. But the actual practice of those governments that use targeted killing is by no means limited to such a case. The debate in this volume, and in public discussion more generally, concerns the permissibility of the practice insofar as it extends beyond the imminent-explosion type of case. Proponents of the armed-conflict model argue that the extended practice is morally permissible and that the law should also regard the practice as permissible. Defenders of the law-enforcement model can concede that, in some cases at least, the extended practice might be morally permissible, but they will argue that the legal rules should flatly prohibit any targeted killing deviating from the imminent-explosion scenario.

Mark Maxwell leads off Part I, which is devoted to exploring the question of who is permissibly targeted in asymmetric armed conflicts. He argues that the law-enforcement model unduly hampers the efforts of a state to protect its citizens against terrorist threats. Unlike most scenarios in which law enforcement can be effective, terrorists often plan their operations in safe havens outside of the jurisdiction of the states they attack and the master planners might never roam beyond those safe havens. Maxwell thinks that the United States rightly abandoned the law-enforcement model in the wake of 9/11 in favor of the armed-conflict model.

However, in Maxwell's view, the pursuit of terrorists under the law of armed conflict is only the beginning of the story. He argues that there should be revisions in that sphere of the law so that states can deal even more effectively with the threats posed by terrorist groups, because the current law gives terrorist organizations a critical advantage over the states that are trying to stop them. The advantage derives, on Maxwell's account, from the way in which the law allows terrorists to exploit a basic principle of the law of armed conflict, the principle of distinction. Under this principle, combatants are legally permitted to intentionally kill one another, but they are absolutely prohibited from the intentional killing of civilians. The legal permission of combatants to kill carries with it the legal obligation to distinguish themselves in a clear and public way from civilians: combatants must wear uniforms, carry their arms openly, and so forth. Terrorists deliberately disregard such requirements of legal armed conflict and so fail to count as combatants who have a permission to kill the enemy. So what *do* terrorists count as? Maxwell tells us that, under current international law, they count as civilians who directly participate in hostilities. Such civilians do not have full civilian immunity: it is permissible for them to be intentionally killed, but only "for such time as they directly participate in hostilities."[6] When they cease their direct involvement, even if only temporarily, they regain civilian immunity.

Because of their "now immune, now not immune" legal status, Maxwell analogizes terrorists to the moles in the children's game "Whack a Mole": the moles can be hit with a mallet but only when they pop out of their underground homes; they regain their safety as soon as they duck back down into their burrows. A clever mole is difficult to whack, and, under current international law, so is a clever terrorist. So Maxwell proposes a revision in the law that would substantially reduce the immunity currently enjoyed by terrorists. In particular, he argues that terrorists who are members of an armed group should forfeit their civilian immunity when their pattern of conduct shows that they are contributing to the military function of the group. Direct involvement in hostilities would be only one form of conduct that contributes to the military function.

Jens Ohlin constructs a normative framework that seeks to integrate elements of the law-enforcement and armed-conflict models in order to answer the question, "Who is permissibly targeted?" Discussions of the question typically proceed on the assumption that relying on law-enforcement principles to deal with terrorism would better serve the rule of law than would following the norms belonging to

---

⁶ *See* Protocol Additional to the Geneva Conventions of August 12, 1949, and Relating to the Protection of Victims of International Armed Conflicts (Additional Protocol I), adopted June 8, 1977, art. 51(3), 1125 U.N.T.S. 3.

the armed-conflict model. However, Ohlin argues that this assumption is wrong: the rule of law is better served by norms taken from the armed-conflict model and modifying them to fit the asymmetric armed conflict between the state and terrorist organizations.

Ohlin points out that terrorist threats sufficiently grave to call for targeted killings stem largely from organizations rather than from individuals acting alone. Additionally, a targeted killing is a summary killing, and, in justifying such an action, the threatened state might invoke its right to self-defense or, alternatively, its rights under international humanitarian law to attack the enemy with lethal force. But, under either justification, some suitable link must be established between the individual who is targeted and the organization that poses the threat. Clearly, it is not a sufficient link merely for the individual to have a favorable attitude toward the terrorist organization, but what, then, is sufficient? Ohlin canvasses a range of linking principles.

One intuitively attractive principle is that the targeted individual must be a member of the terrorist organization. International humanitarian law relies on a membership principle to determine who is liable to lethal attack in the context of an armed conflict: the members of the military forces of the enemy. And, as Ohlin notes, in the case of a symmetrical conflict between regular forces who wear uniforms and carry their arms openly, the membership principle has the virtue that its linking criterion is public and easily applied by both sides. However, he also points out that, in the asymmetric conflict between a state and a terrorist organization, the membership principle encounters a potentially serious problem, because terrorists make a point of not wearing uniforms or carrying their arms openly.

Moreover, civil libertarians would reject membership as a linking principle because membership is ordinarily understood as a matter of status rather than conduct. In their eyes, state coercion against an individual should be predicated on what the individual has done—that is, on his conduct, not on who he is or what groups he belongs to—that is, not on his status. A linking principle more friendly to the civil-libertarian view would require the individual to be making a contribution to the criminal acts of the terrorist organization (complicity), or, alternatively, to have made an agreement to commit such acts (conspiracy). But Ohlin is concerned that such a principle would be quite elastic in application, potentially covering a far wider range of cases than seems justifiable, and would require an intensive factual inquiry to determine whether the individual was guilty of the offending conduct.

Yet, Ohlin is prepared to go part way toward accommodating the civil-libertarian viewpoint. He modifies the membership principle so that it includes a more robust conduct element, while also making the principle suitable for dealing with terrorist organizations. In Ohlin's view, the link that makes an individual liable to a targeted killing is this: the individual has a self-declared, functional membership in an organization engaged in an armed conflict with the threatened state. Functional membership means that the individual plays a role within the organizational structure by carrying out the orders and missions given to him by his superiors and by, in turn, giving orders to those, if there are any, below him in the hierarchy. This kind of membership is a hybrid concept, incorporating elements of both status and conduct. Moreover, Ohlin argues that a principle employing the idea of functional membership would better serve the rule of law than would a purely conduct-based principle, such as the complicity or conspiracy standards. Those latter standards are more difficult to apply to the individual and to administer by state agencies than the more clear-cut principle of functional membership. Ohlin concludes that, surprisingly, the principle that contains a status element better serves the rule of law than a pure conduct-based principle. The demands of national security can thus be served in a way that is consistent with the nation's commitment to legality.

Ohlin's account of who is legitimately targeted for killing is in general agreement with Maxwell's suggested revision to the rules of war, adding rule-of-law arguments to arguments about the activities that terrorists undertake as members of an organization. Daniel Statman seeks to broaden the issue beyond terrorism, arguing that targeted killing is not only a matter of how states should address terrorist threats, but, more generally, it is a question of how states should deal with threats posed by irregular forces in asymmetric armed conflicts. He presents three interpretations of just war theory and explores the implications of each for the moral permissibility of targeted killing, whether the targets are terrorists or individuals belonging to irregular forces that do not employ terrorist tactics. On the individualist interpretation, the moral principles governing war are continuous with those governing all other conditions of human life, and the moral permissibility of killing in war derives from the right that individuals have to defend themselves against others who are personally responsible for unjust and deadly threats against them. On the collectivist interpretation, combatants have such a right of individual self-defense, but they also have a moral permission to intentionally kill enemy combatants that derives from the role that combatants play in defending their society from the collective violence of the enemy. On the contractualist interpretation, the moral permission of combatants to intentionally kill derives from a tacit agreement among states (and, potentially, armed non-state groups) to diminish the death and destruction of war by drawing a firm line that permits lethal attacks directed against enemy combatants but absolutely prohibits such attacks against civilians.

Statman argues that all three interpretations of just war theory permit targeted killing and that they even provide reasons for preferring targeted killing to other forms of armed combat. He is persuaded that targeted killing is very effective in avoiding collateral deaths and in focusing lethal force against the individuals most responsible for unjust and deadly threats. Under all three interpretations of just war theory, such effective focusing of deadly force is a substantial virtue. Moreover, none of the three interpretations provides sufficient grounds for judging persons involved in terrorism as civilians immune to permissible targeting. Statman concludes by suggesting that in this new era of asymmetric warfare, there is a strong moral case in favor of legal rules that license the targeted killing of terrorists and other irregular fighters.

Jeremy Waldron examines a proposed legal norm that would license targeted killing: "N_1: Named civilians may be targeted with deadly force if they are presently involved in planning terrorist atrocities or are likely to be involved in carrying them out in the future."[7] He expects that some readers will share Mark Maxwell's view of the terrorist threat and judge that, in light of the need of society to protect itself against terrorism, N_1 ought to replace the strict legal prohibition in both domestic law and the law of armed conflict on deliberately killing civilians. However, Waldron argues that such readers ought to be wary.

When a person moves from normative judgments about particular actions, say, the judgment that the killing of bin Laden was justifiable, to the endorsement of *norms* covering killing, the logical implications of those norms might prove troubling in ways the person did not anticipate. Exploiting this logical generality of norms, philosophers and legal thinkers sometimes use a "neutral-principles test" to evaluate the validity of a person's endorsement of a given norm: can the person consistently maintain her endorsement of the norm in light of the troublesome implication? In an analogous way, making a norm into a law can have troublesome practical implications that are not anticipated. Waldron points out that such implications flow, not just from the logical generality of norms as such, but also from the fact that *legal norms* are part of the public world and so are likely to be invoked and applied by persons who have beliefs and agendas that diverge sharply from the viewpoints of many individuals who find the norm attractive as an abstract proposition. In the case of N_1, Waldron argues, we should keep in mind that, if it were a legal norm, it could be invoked publicly by governments that are hostile to us and our liberal democratic values in order to justify their actions. He also points to the fact that governments in general have a terrible track record of abuse and misjudgment when they take their gloves off in dealing with those they judge to be terrorists. Liberal democracies have been no exception, Waldron reminds the reader.

All legal rules are subject to abuse, but Waldron argues that N_1 is especially liable to egregious abuse because it deals with deliberate killing in a context in which there is no strong and independent judiciary, or its institutional equivalent, which could impartially examine each killing *post hoc* for the purpose of judging its consistency with the norm and sanctioning those responsible in cases of a violation. Accordingly, Waldron is unpersuaded by efforts to defend N_1 by appealing to the

---

[7] Jeremy Waldron, "Justifying Targeted Killings with a Neutral Principle?," in this Volume, ch. 4, 112.

idea of self-defense as it functions in domestic criminal law, a context in which there is a strong judicial back-stop.

Moreover, Waldron argues that the legal norm absolutely prohibiting the deliberate use of armed force against civilians (while permitting its deliberate use against enemy combatants) has proved to be a crucially important part of the law of armed conflict, helping to mitigate the human devastation of war. He agrees that the norm is easy to criticize as under- and overinclusive, but philosophical nuance is not what is needed in a norm that is to do the job of restraining those who wield weapons in the heat of battle and the encompassing homicide of war. Rather, what is needed is a norm that is widely acceptable, simple to apply, and capable of being inculcated in the people who pull the trigger. The strict prohibition on the intentional killing of civilians has become anchored in both law and the ethos of military service. In Waldron's judgment, it would be reckless to experiment with loosening the prohibition in order to free state officials to kill more terrorists, and it would be philosophically misguided to think that the appropriate attitude toward human life and its deliberate destruction would be better reflected by abandoning the prohibition in favor of a norm to govern war that is more consistent with norms that we already accept for governing peace.

Waldron's contribution can be understood as meeting the arguments of Maxwell and Statman on their own turf: the ground of the law of armed conflict. Whereas Maxwell seeks to loosen the legal rules of war that restrict the targeted killing of terrorists and Statman aims to show that just war theory, under any of its main interpretations, licenses targeted killing, Waldron argues that we should hold fast to restrictive rules of war that place such killing beyond the limits of permissible conduct. Ohlin's analysis suggests that, *pace* Waldron, some terrorists are the functional equivalent of combatants, and so we can hold fast to the categorical prohibition on targeting civilians while still engaging in the targeted killing of terrorists, but Waldron might judge that the conceptual tidiness of Ohlin's approach would break down in practice, weakening a crucial legal restraint on the violence of war .

Part II picks up the issue of whether the norms of war, or the norms of domestic law enforcement, are the appropriate ones to use in deciding what the legal rules should be for regulating and restricting targeting killing. Jeff McMahan begins the section by arguing that the targeted killing of terrorists can be morally justified only in terms of self-defense or defense of others, and not on retributive grounds. The most plausible version of the defensive justification, in his eyes, holds that a terrorist is liable to the use of force when he is responsible for a threat to innocent lives and the force reasonably aims to avert that threat. On this justification, the permissibility of using lethal defensive force is not based on the terrorist's involvement with past episodes of terrorism, as would be the case in retributive justification, but, rather, on his current involvement by way of intending, planning, or

13

assisting some envisioned act of terrorism. This justification might seem to fit well with the law-enforcement model, because domestic criminal law authorizes the use of deadly force for purposes of self-defense and defense of others. However, McMahan points out that the justification in question must depart from the law-enforcement model in a crucial respect: the latter model authorizes defensive force only when the threat is imminent, while targeted killing is preventive, aimed at persons whose threat is not imminent.

Turning to the question of how the law should handle the targeted killing of terrorists, McMahan finds that, under current legal norms, terrorists must be either criminals or combatants. Although he thinks that there might be no determinate legal answer to the question of which category applies, McMahan argues that there are strong reasons to regard terrorists as criminals and to treat them under a law-enforcement model, rather than as combatants, treating them under an armed-conflict model. Terrorists deliberately violate the legal requirements for having the status of combatant, a status that carries with it the legal privilege to use lethal force. McMahan thinks that such a status is reasonably restricted to the members of forces that generally observe the legal requirements in return for getting the privilege. Moreover, McMahan contends that the law-enforcement model minimizes the chances of incorrectly identifying someone as a terrorist and consequently killing him, a fatal mistake documented in several instances of targeted killing. The model also contributes to the effective deployment of defensive force by avoiding the waste of resources involved in tracking and trying to take out the wrong people. If the law were to treat terrorists as combatants, then it would be legally permissible for them to be hunted down and killed rather than arrested and tried before a court. Aside from the greater chances for mistaken identification, legally permitting such killing would create risks for innocent bystanders and be subject to abuse by regimes that target political opponents and then defend their actions by claiming that the victims are terrorists. McMahan agrees with Waldron that this risk of abuse argues strongly in favor of a categorical prohibition on targeted killing. However, in the end, McMahan is not entirely persuaded, because terrorists, though not combatants, are not ordinary criminals either. Rather, they occupy an "intermediate" position between combatants and criminals, thus creating a situation calling for new legal norms that are intermediate between the law-enforcement and armed-conflict models. Accordingly, McMahan is likely to be more sympathetic than Waldron to Ohlin's idea that functional membership in a terrorist organization should make a person into a legally permissible target of lethal force.

Claire Finkelstein notes that the administration of President Obama has dramatically increased the number of targeted killings over that of the Bush administration, while radically reducing the number of detentions of terrorist suspects. Behind these changes in presidential policy, she detects a desire to circumvent the political, legal, and moral problems that afflicted President Bush's policy of indefinite detention. However, Finkelstein argues that the shift to targeted killing fails to deal with the underlying source of those problems, viz., the lack of fit between the laws of war, on the one side, and the nature of the armed conflict between terrorists and the states they attack, on the other. Moreover, traditional arguments from personal self-defense also fail to justify targeted killing, due to the distinctive nature of the terrorist threat. However, Finkelstein does find in the law-enforcement model certain principles of pre-emptive killing that can provide solid ground for the justification of lethal attacks on terrorists who pose a danger to a state's national security.

Finkelstein argues that efforts to justify targeted killing in terms of the laws of war confront an insuperable set of obstacles, stemming from the fact that those laws were designed for conventional war, fought by regular forces on a clearly demarcated battlefield. In the asymmetric conflict between states and terrorist organizations, however, the distinctions central to conventional war have unraveled. The laws of war license combatants to kill enemy belligerents who have not surrendered, and both the license to kill and the liability to be killed depend on the status of the soldier as a member of a regular, belligerent armed force. Civilians are not permissibly targeted. But, Finkelstein argues, the targeted killing policy deviates from the law-of-war model in several ways. The targeted terrorists are named in advance, in the manner of an assassination and in contrast to a status-based attack. Individuals on the kill list are sometimes not engaged in active combat. In the case of drone-missile killings, civilians in the CIA often operate the drones, and the use of drones means that there is no opportunity for targeted individuals to surrender when facing an imminent attack. Additionally, the clearly demarcated battlefield of conventional war has disappeared in wars between states and terrorist organizations. If Finkelstein's analysis is sound, then serious doubt is cast on approaches such as those of Maxwell and Statman, which rely, respectively on the laws of war and the closely related principles of just war theory.

Finkelstein is also skeptical of the way in which McMahan tries to show that targeted killing is a morally permissible use of defensive force. She agrees with him that principles of ordinary morality, reflected in the rules of the criminal law, can ground the permissibility of targeted killing. But Finkelstein thinks that McMahan's reliance on a principle of personal self-defense and other-defense is mistaken. She argues that the appropriate principles are to be found in a law-enforcement situation in which the police are pursuing a person suspected of a felony who is resisting arrest by fleeing from them. The police are legally permitted to use deadly force against such a suspect, as long as they believe that he poses a risk of committing a future felony and have warned him of their intent to use force should he not submit. This scenario illustrates the pre-emptive use of force, and Finkelstein emphasizes that the police are permitted to kill the fleeing individual even if his suspected felony is not a capital offense and his anticipated future felony is not imminent. She argues that an appropriately fashioned targeted killing policy would fit the requirements of justified pre-emptive killing.

Richard Meyer thinks that targeted killings now fall into a legal no-man's land between the laws of war and domestic criminal law. This legal indeterminacy means that the rights and duties of the relevant parties, including the persons who carry out the killings, but also the members of the local police forces where the killings take place, are left in a fog of legal uncertainty. In order to provide for greater certainty and to conform more closely to the demands of the rule of law, Meyer argues that it is necessary for international law to draw a sharper line than it does at present between combat during war and conduct outside of war.

For Meyer, the current legal uncertainty surrounding targeted killing derives largely from a failure to appreciate the chasm that separates the morality of ordinary life from the morality of combat. The ordinary life of the members of society is governed by moral principles that are reflected in the criminal law: individuals are prohibited from using violence against others, except in a very narrow range of circumstances in which it is explicitly authorized, such as those involving legitimate self-defense. In contrast, Meyer argues, combat is governed by moral principles discontinuous with ordinary morality and reflected, not in criminal law, but in international humanitarian law. The heart of this alternative morality is the principle that members of a regular armed force who otherwise observe the laws of war are privileged belligerents permitted to kill enemy belligerents who are members of a regular armed force, except in a very narrow set of circumstances, such as when the enemy soldier has surrendered.

On Meyer's account, the targeted killing of suspected terrorists is insufficiently regulated by law. States are using military force, but it is uncertain whether those who wield the force are privileged belligerents, because international law does not clearly provide for the situation of war between a state and a non-state organization, much less between a state and an individual. Individuals who might well be terrorists are killed. However, no evidence of their involvement with terrorism need be provided to anyone by the attacking state, the attackers are *de facto* immune from prosecution under the laws of the state where the killing takes place, and no viable legal forum exists before which the family of the victim can fairly challenge his designation as a terrorist. At the same time, Meyer agrees with Mark Maxwell that the states victimized by terrorism can legitimately complain that certain other states harbor terrorists, letting suspects melt into the population and refusing to capture them, even when their whereabouts are known to the local authorities.

In order to bring some legal order to a situation that he regards as anarchic, Meyer proposes three major changes in international law. First, privileged belligerency should be restricted to the uniformed military and militias of a state that has formally declared war. Second, the law should provide for declarations of war against non-state organizations and against individuals. Third, the International Court of Justice should be given jurisdiction to decide cases challenging any state's designation of any individual as an enemy terrorist.

Meyer's invocation of a morality of war, discontinuous with the morality of ordinary life, runs contrary to the views of Finkelstein and McMahan. Although the latter two disagree with one another on what the morality of ordinary life has to say about intentional killing, both of them reject the notion of a special morality of war that displaces ordinary morality in wartime, and both affirm the idea that intentional killing in war can be justified in terms of the moral principles that govern ordinary life. In Meyer's judgment, though, any attempt to justify killing in war on the basis of the morality of ordinary life is akin to trying to square the circle.

The theme of Part III is self-defense, and it begins with Craig Martin's account of the concept of self-defense that is part of the post-World War Two system of international law. He focuses on the *jus ad bellum* rules regulating the resort to armed force by states. Under the U.N. Charter, states are prohibited from using such force unless it is undertaken in self-defense or authorized by the Security Council. Targeted killing has been justified by U.S. officials and many commentators as legally permissible on the basis of the Charter's self-defense provision, but Martin finds such a justification wanting.

Tracing major historical developments in just war theory and in the legal rules governing the use of armed force, Martin argues that the legal permission for states to use armed force in self-defense is much narrower than the proponents of targeted killing suppose it to be. The architects of the U.N. framework consciously and explicitly sought to impose stricter limits on the use of force than the failed, pre-World War Two system had incorporated. In Martin's view, essential to the framework is the idea that self-defense does not involve the geographically unlimited right of a state to attack any and every group that threatens it, wherever the group is operating. If the group is a non-state entity, such as a terrorist organization, then attacking it will, in the modern global order of sovereign states, amount to an attack on the political independence of the state in which the organization's members are found, unless the state consents to the attack. Martin contends that, without such consent, the attack is a legally permissible exercise of self-defense only if there is a more substantial connection between the terrorist group and the state than the simple geographical presence of the group within the state's borders. Accordingly, he holds that there is no legal right of self-defense against non-state entities as such, but only against those entities insofar as there is a sufficiently strong connection between them and the state in which they are located.

Although a legal right of self-defense so understood might seem unduly constraining on states, Martin argues that the narrow scope of the right is important for limiting the scourge of war among states. And, for all its horror, terrorism has not rivaled international war in the scale of death and destruction unleashed. Additionally, Martin argues that relaxing the rules on the use of armed force would risk undoing the carefully calibrated interplay currently obtaining between *jus ad bellum* rules and the rules of international humanitarian law, determining when an armed conflict exists and regulating how it is to be conducted. Under the existing system, permissible acts of self-defense automatically bring into play the rules of humanitarian law, because what counts as permissible self-defense is aligned with what counts as an international armed conflict. However, this alignment would be thrown out of kilter were the rules of permissible self-defense relaxed in the way that is recommended by defenders of targeted killing. Martin warns that the result could be a situation in which military force is used but not legally constrained by important humanitarian provisions designed to mitigate the suffering caused by war.

Like Waldron, Martin finds that the existing rules of international law do an important job of restraining the homicidal impulses that lead to war and are manifested in war and thinks that there are grave risks in loosening those restraints. As Martin sees it, the proponents of targeted killing, especially U.S. officials, have often been too quick to justify such killing on grounds that imply sweeping changes in the law and are insufficiently attentive to those risks. He might be open to the more calibrated argument and proposals offered by Ohlin and Maxwell, but Martin insists that any acceptable change stop well short of re-establishing the lax legal rules regarding the resort to armed force found in earlier eras.

One of the elements of permissible self-defense under the criminal law is the requirement that the defender refrain from exercising defensive force until the attack against her is imminent. This requirement seems to stand in the way of justifying targeted killing on the ground of self-defense, a point noted by Jeff McMahan and Claire Finkelstein. Russell Christopher agrees with McMahan and Finkelstein on that score and develops an extended set of arguments for the abandonment of the imminence requirement.

In Christopher's view, the requirement suffers from a series of moral and conceptual problems. It has the unacceptable consequence that persons who are physically unable to respond quickly enough to defend themselves against imminent aggression are deprived of a right to effective self-defense. Many proponents of the imminence requirement respond that, based on objective evidence, it serves as a good way to sort out cases of the justifiable use of defensive force from cases of the unjustifiable use. Accordingly, the argument is often made that imminence serves as a good proxy for when it is truly necessary for a person to use defensive force to protect herself against aggression. But Christopher replies that imminence is a poor proxy for the necessity of resorting to force. There are not only situations in which defensive force is necessary prior to the point of imminence, as in the case of persons too slow to mount an effective defense if they wait until an attack is imminent; there are also situations in which defensive force is unnecessary even at the point of imminence, for example, when the aggressor has a last second change of heart and decides not to pull the trigger of the gun pointed at my head. Christopher argues that the proxy here is an inadequate substitute for the underlying moral principle.

Some proponents of the imminence requirement contend that it is not simply a proxy for the real normative criteria that distinguish justifiable from unjustifiable uses of defensive force; they argue that imminence is itself one such criterion. But Christopher responds that such arguments end up, contrary to the original intention of their advocates, relapsing into a proxy-based view of imminence.

One of the key arguments for the requirement is that it distinguishes the aggressor from the defender, with the imminence of an attack serving as the objective manifestation of aggression. But Christopher argues that imminence cannot adequately serve that function. As a strictly temporal notion that specifies a certain time period just prior to a certain use of force, imminence cannot capture what is essentially a moral distinction between aggressive and defensive force. Indeed, Christopher argues that if imminence is understood strictly in terms of time, then the imminence requirement will, paradoxically, end up treating some defenders as aggressors and some aggressors as defenders.

In Christopher's view, it is to no avail to add an action component to the temporal understanding of imminence, so that the aggressor would be the party who, within the specified "imminent" time period, first physically manifests the use of force against the other party. An action component brings with it its own problems. For example, Christopher argues that it unduly restricts the right of self-defense and unjustifiably favors aggressors by requiring defenders to wait, not only until an attack is temporally imminent, but also until the aggressors physically manifest their aggression during that period. In light of these and other problems with the imminence requirement, Christopher concludes that the requirement provides no valid ground on which to object to the permissibility of targeted killings.

Phillip Montague argues that ordinary moral principles regulating self-defense provide a justification for the targeted killing of terrorists, including the killing of those persons in terrorist groups who aid and assist the individuals who wear and trigger suicide belts or who otherwise directly kill their civilian victims. He points out that the rationale for an individual's right to kill an aggressor in self-defense rests on a principle that also grounds the right of a third-party to kill the aggressor in other-defense. Rejecting the imminence requirement along with Christopher, Montague contends that the aggressor's right to life has been forfeited if it is inevitable that the aggressor will culpably kill the victim unless someone kills the aggressor first. It is permissible for anyone, not only the intended victim, to kill the aggressor in this situation. However, in some circumstances, there are more characters in the story than simply the aggressor, the intended victim, and, possibly, a third-party other-defender. The aggressor might be deliberately enabled in his designs by an accessory. Indeed, there might be a whole raft of such culpable enablers acting jointly. The culpable enablers are not themselves aggressors, and so the paradigms of individual self- and other-defense do not apply. But killing one or more of the enablers might be necessary to prevent the aggressor from killing his victims. On the other side, the intended victims might need the assistance of a whole raft of individuals acting jointly in order that lethal aggression be prevented. It is precisely this kind of scenario, with joint action on the sides of both the aggressor and defender, that many targeted killings involve, Montague argues, and so the concept of joint action becomes crucial in showing how principles of self-defense ground the conclusion that such killings can be justifiable defensive homicides.

If culpable individuals act jointly for the purpose of bringing about the death of an individual who has a right to live, and a "closed choice" situation exists in which either the intended victim will be killed or at least one of the culpable joint actors will be killed, then, Montague argues, it is permissible for someone to kill the culpable actors in whatever number is necessary and sufficient to prevent the killing of the intended victim. Targeted killings can be justified on the basis of such a principle, which does not involve any assumption about the existence of a state of war or a special morality of war.

Part IV examines various aspects of the operational implementation of targeted killings and begins with Amos Guiora's account of how targeted killing does, and should, work on the ground. Reflecting on his experience as a legal advisor in the Israeli Defense Forces, Guiora argues that the decision-making process culminating in the official authorization of the commander on the ground to commence lethal action must be regulated and constrained by certain procedural norms, else the process will fail to reliably respect the requirements of law and morality. Guiora calls these norms "criteria," and he contrasts his criteria-based approach with "intuitionism," which he understands as the view that the final decision to proceed with lethal action should be left to the discretion of the commander on the ground. Intuitionism fails to place adequate constraints on the commander's discretion and places an excessive decision-making burden on the commander's shoulders. The commander is in good position to decide when to request a go-ahead, but the request should be reviewed by a legal advisor for approval or disapproval.

The legal advisor's job is often carried out under severe time and information constraints. Guiora argues that under such conditions, an advisor should have a checklist of questions to ask the commander. The checklist would not provide an algorithmic decision procedure for the legal advisor, but it would serve to concentrate his or her attention on the legally relevant variables so that a reasoned and defensible decision could be reliably made. In the absence of a procedure, such as a checklist, to regiment decision-making in the targeted-killing scenario, unjustifiable deviations from important rule-of-law principles—such as treating like cases alike—are bound to occur at an unacceptable rate.

Greg McNeal's contribution tackles key empirical claims made by those who criticize drone attacks against suspected or known terrorists. Among those claims is the charge that U.S. drones, particularly those operating in Pakistan, have killed many times more civilians than terrorists. The drone program in Pakistan is operated by the CIA, and it remains shrouded in secrecy. However, a lawsuit has brought to light the nature of the program in Afghanistan, operated by the U.S. military, and McNeal points to that program in order to cast doubt on the claims of drone critics.

Prior to a drone strike, McNeal tells us, the U.S. military goes through a process that involves a scientific analysis of the likely blast damage that a strike would cause and an estimation of collateral causalities from such damage. Steps are then taken to mitigate the likely damage by altering various parameters of the strike, such as time of day. On McNeal's analysis, this process is highly effective: when followed, less than one per cent of the attacks have resulted in collateral casualities. Moreover, if, notwithstanding the process of estimation and mitigation, one or more civilian casualties are expected, then the strike must be approved by the President or the Secretary of Defense, due to the potentially troubling foreign-policy ramifications of such a strike. McNeal finds it difficult to believe that the CIA program would permit attacks that are as indiscriminate as charged, even as the military's program is so discriminating, especially because potentially troublesome foreign-policy implications attend civilian death from drone strikes in both Afghanistan and Pakistan. Moreover, a high-ranking military official, the head of CENTCOM (Central Command), is responsible for the drone programs both in Afghanistan and in Pakistan, and McNeal argues that it is illogical to think that the CENTCOM commander would have radically different standards for allowable collateral casualties for the CIA program than for the military's program.

McNeal proceeds to take to task a prominent drone critic, Ellen O'Connell, for inconsistency in her use of sources, relying on a source when it supports her view of the indiscriminate nature of drone strikes but rejecting the same source when it contradicts her view. He also argues that O'Connell demonstrates a lack of familiarity with the way that the targeting process works. *Contra* O'Connell's assumptions, potential targets are tracked by the drone's camera for at least 24 hours and, in order to firmly identify the target, the information from the drone tracking is put together with intelligence from a range of human and technical sources. McNeal also charges O'Connell with having produced no evidence to substantiate her assertion that Pakistan has not consented to U.S. drone attacks on terrorists in its territory.

Kevin Govern provides a close look at the U.S. Navy Seal operation that resulted in the killing of Osama bin Laden. Code-named "Neptune Spear," the operation was chosen from options that included an air strike on the compound where bin Laden resided in Pakistan. President Obama decided that the operation would proceed without the approval or even the notification of the Pakistani government, due to a lack of confidence that Pakistani officials would maintain the secrecy of the plan. In the course of the Navy Seal's raid on the compound, three people were killed, in addition to bin Laden himself. According to a report quoted by Govern, the Seal team was intent from the start on killing bin Laden: capturing him alive was not an option. If that report is accurate, then the moral permissibility of the killing would be undermined in the eyes of some observers. However, in his contribution found in Part V of this volume, Michael Moore contends that bin Laden's killing can be justified on retributive principles: The past conduct of the Al Qaeda leader merited death as punishment. As we have seen, Jeff McMahan rejects retributivist justifications of targeted killing, but he thinks that it would not have been unreasonable for President Obama to have concluded that any considerations in favor of capturing bin Laden were outweighed by the prospect that his followers would have kidnapped and killed, one by one, American hostages, in a futile effort to win their leader's release.

Kenneth Anderson's contribution replies to a commonly voiced objection to the use of drone-fired missiles for targeted killing. The objection is that, because of its precision in killing the intended target and avoiding collateral deaths, drone technology makes the resort to armed violence too easy. Put in the economic language of efficiency: although the use of drone missiles is efficient in killing the enemy without causing the deaths of many innocent bystanders, precisely the "*in bello*" efficiency of armed drones leads to the "*ad bellum*" inefficiency of excessive resort to the use of armed force in the first place. Among the reasons offered for this supposed inefficient outcome is that the drone operators work far from the battlefield in complete safety, thus removing one of the disincentives that political leaders ordinarily have for deciding to resort to armed force.

It is clear that not all targeted killing involves drone attacks, as the bin Laden case illustrates. But Anderson points out that it is also mistaken to think that all drone strikes are targeted killings. Even though drones can and do target individuals identified in advance (so-called "high-value targets"), the technology has also been used by the U.S. military in conventional attacks against columns of Taliban, where the only relevant distinguishing feature of the victims is that they are members of the enemy force. Anderson finds it reasonable to assume that drone missiles—whether used for targeted killings or conventional attacks—are in fact more precise than alternative weapons in discriminating the enemy from civilian bystanders. He also emphasizes that this greater precision would not be possible unless ground-level intelligence were effectively integrated into the use of weapon systems: technology alone would be insufficient.

Anderson points out that it would seem that a military technology that was highly discriminating in distinguishing enemy fighters from civilians and, at the same time, provided protection for one's own forces, would be a non-controversial moral gain in the campaign to reduce the horror of warfare. Harm to civilians is more likely to occur when forces are under attack or otherwise insecure. But the drone critics argue that what appears to be a non-controversial moral gain is in fact a moral loss, because the availability of drones will make a country too willing to resort to armed force in the first place. The price of precision and force protection is, the critics argue, too much to pay due to the increased resort to armed violence.

Anderson is skeptical of various aspects of this argument. He contends that the degree of risk to the personnel of their own forces is only one of several considerations that political decision-makers take into account in determining whether to resort to armed force and that the most important considerations pertain to national security rather than force protection. The one major exception, Anderson argues, is armed humanitarian intervention, which is likely to occur more frequently with the increased force protection that drones allow. And he concedes that it is likely that, as armed drones become cheaper and more widely available around the world, there will be an increased propensity of states to use armed force, especially in discrete and limited ways, for dealing with international disagreements. But he doubts that there is any neutral standard by which one can judge that the resort to armed force has become too easy or that the total amount of armed force used in the world is inefficient, or efficient. The opposing sides in an armed conflict have competing substantive standards for judging when the resort to force is desirable, and one side's value-promoting use of drones will be the other side's value-destroying resort to armed force. Anderson points out that the idea of efficiency makes sense in a context where each side to a transaction aims to better its position in terms of some shared scale of value, such as money. Thus, bargaining produces an efficient outcome when one side buys out the other—for example, a railroad buys a farmer's right not to have his crops exposed to sparks flying off the wheels of the railroad's trains—and each side gets what it values the most. But Anderson argues that the idea of efficiency makes no sense in the context of armed conflict, where the notion that one side could buy out the other is preposterous.

Part V addresses the interplay between the desirable outcomes that targeted killings seek to achieve, such as the destruction of terrorist groups and networks and the minimization of the total killings of innocents, and the limits that moral principles place on the ways in which desirable outcomes are permissibly pursued. Fernando Tesón's contribution opens the section, arguing that terrorism is a threat that is *sui generis* and cannot be adequately addressed by either the law-enforcement or the armed-conflict (that is, what he calls the "just war") models. For Tesón, terrorism is an especially noxious and dangerous form of evil, different from ordinary crime in the extent of wrongful harm that it intentionally threatens to cause and in the non-self-interested motives that drive it. However, Tesón resists the idea that liberal states are in global war with terrorists and insists that liberal states remain true to the moral principles that underlie their institutions, even as those states fight the terrorist scourge.

Tesón regards *some* terrorists as being in a state of war with liberal states, and he believes that it is morally permissible to target those terrorists. Such terrorists are to be found in a combat context, such as exists in parts of Pakistan and Afghanistan. But terrorists in Paris or New York are outside of any combat context and cannot, consistent with sound liberal principles, be killed on sight. Rather, it is morally permissible to target them only if they have been given an opportunity to surrender and killing them is necessary to save many innocent lives. Nonetheless, because even liberal states are prone to mistake in identifying when a targeted killing is necessary and because the liberal principle of the rule of law suggests that, regardless of its possible good consequences, the practice of targeted killing would constitute a form of liberal vice, Tesón argues that there should be an absolute legal ban on targeted killing in a peacetime setting. In a final twist, he allows that the President should have the authority to suspend the ban in an emergency, as long as the suspension is publicly declared and publicly justified.

Michael Moore approaches the question of the morality of targeted killing by developing a general theoretical framework for answering questions about what morality permits, forbids, and requires. The framework consists of three levels. At the first level is the consequentialist principle that one ought to choose that action from among the alternatives that will bring about the greatest net good in the world. This principle is decisive in determining the moral status of an action across a wide range of cases, but it can be preempted by principles that belong to the second level. At that level are the deontological principles that specify "strong permissions," which allow an agent to choose an action that does not have the optimal consequences, and "strict obligations," which require the agent to perform an action that does not have the optimal consequences. The right of self-defense is a strong permission, and the prohibition on deliberately killing one innocent person in order to save, say, three other innocents is a strict obligation. Normally, such permissions and obligations are decisive when they apply to a case, but at the third level of Moore's framework is a principle that overrides those permissions and obligations in cases in which catastrophic consequences would otherwise ensue.

Using his framework, Moore constructs a decision tree that shows at what point in the deliberation process, and how, consequentialist and deontological considerations are to figure in a decision about the moral permissibility of an action. The tree is not meant to constitute an algorithm that can be mechanically instantiated, but rather as a guide for coherent and cogent moral judgment. And deploying his decision tree, Moore finds that the targeted killings of suicide bombers and those who plan and otherwise aid such bombers are easy cases of justifiable killing. Additionally, he finds that the targeted killing of non-culpable individuals can be permissible, for example, in a situation in which a terrorist organization places a bomb in the brief case of an unsuspecting person who is (unknowingly) about to set off an explosion in a crowded railway station by opening the brief case. Although the person is not in the least blameworthy, killing him in order to prevent the explosion is justifiable. Even more controversially, Moore claims that morality permits targeted killings as punishment for those terrorists whose past conduct makes them deserving of the death penalty.

Leo Katz exposes and explores some of the puzzles and paradoxes that arise from the norms that govern killing. Unlike Michael Moore, Katz does not develop a systematic moral view, but rather focuses on our normative thinking when it is in the trenches, grappling with particular scenarios and cases. He begins by imagining a scenario in which an elite anti-terrorist squad deliberately provokes a known terrorist, so that they can then beat him to the punch and kill him in self-defense, without transgressing the imminence requirement for self-defense. The criminal law and most commentators would disallow the appeal to self-defense in this kind of scenario, but Katz does not buy into their view. He believes that in some cases, agents should not be disqualified from invoking a certain defense (self-defense, necessity, duress, etc.) even if they contrived to create, for the very purpose of performing an action for which they would be otherwise liable, conditions under which the defense applies. The agents of the elite squad have deliberately created just such conditions for themselves, and Katz thinks that, paradoxically, they have a valid self-defense claim.

One might think that this kind of contrived self-defense is dubious because it seems to be on all fours with a case involving another kind of contrived defense that is clearly invalid. A man hurls himself out of a window in order to land on, and kill, a certain pedestrian on the street below and then claims that his landing on the victim was an involuntary act because he had no control of his body's fall at the moment of impact. But Katz counters that the two sorts of cases can be distinguished on the ground that the death in the case of his anti-terrorist squad was brought about by a causal chain whose links were broken by the intervening agency of the person who was killed, while the causal chain in the leaping-man case was unbroken. One might reply that the decisive factor in self-defense is the necessity of using force for self-protection and that the anti-terrorist squad did not need to use force because they did not need to provoke the terrorist in the first place. But Katz thinks that this appeal to necessity runs into the problem that the necessity of using force is always relative to the time frame in which the act of defensive force is placed. For any act of defensive force there is always some previous moment such that the act would have been unnecessary had the agent—or someone else—done something differently at that previous time. A woman has a right of self-defense against her partner's violence, even if it would have been unnecessary for her to use defensive force against him had she decided at the start of the relationship that it was too risky to pursue due to the partner's known history of violence.

Additionally, Katz argues that there are deeper reasons to think that contrived defenses cannot be easily banished: they rely on certain cyclical orderings that are entrenched in systems of normative rules. If the only way for me to avoid losing a dollar is to kill the thief who demands it, then the law says that I must hand over the dollar. So the thief's life gets preference over my money. But if I would rather get killed as a result of refusing the thief's demand than hand over the dollar, then the law says that I am permitted to refuse, in which case my money is preferred to my life. And if the thief attacks me with lethal force, the law says that I am permit-ted to kill him rather than let him kill me. Thus, we have a cyclical ordering: 1) the thief's life is preferred to my money; 2) my money is preferred to my life; and 3) my life is preferred to the thief's life. And this ordering can be exploited, Katz argues, so that, paradoxically, I am permitted to kill an aggressor in preference to giving up my money. I do this by appealing to steps 2 and 3 in order to defeat 1. Accordingly, I permissibly act so as to prefer my money over my life by telling the thief who has a gun at my head to get lost, and then I permissibly save my life by killing him when he starts to pull the trigger. Risky, to be sure, but permissible if I can carry it off.

Katz proceeds to consider a scenario involving further twists in the permissible use of lethal defensive force. The aggressive, albeit misguided, followers of a peaceable holy man are about to launch an attack against us which we are entitled to preempt with force, even though many innocent bystanders will be killed. The standard view is that it is impermissible to deliberately kill the holy man, even if doing so would so demoralize the aggressive followers that they would call off their attack. But Katz is doubtful. He argues that the case is no different in its moral essentials from one in which we permissibly redirect a trolley onto a side track, thereby kill-ing one innocent person, in order to save the lives of a number of innocents who would otherwise be run over and killed on the main track in the course of our permissibly using the trolley to strike at aggressors who are about kill us. Now just imagine that it is the holy man on the side track and that it is his followers, sur-rounded by innocent bystanders, on the main track, and the conclusion is difficult to avoid that deliberately killing the holy man in the original, trolley-free scenario is permissible.

Katz opines that these and other counterintuitive conclusions about defensive kill-ing have their source in the fact that there are multiple criteria that decisions about killing seek to satisfy. This fact makes those decisions analogous to collective deci-sions that rest on an aggregation of individual preferences, and Katz points out that, due to Arrow's theorem and other results in social-choice theory, it has long been known that collective decisions cannot entirely escape paradox and irrationality. So while Michael Moore systematically combines consequentialist and deontological criteria so that we might rationally address questions of targeted killing and other contested moral issues, Katz suggests that, when we apply any such system in the trenches, it will at some point lead us into paradox and irrationality.

V. Conclusion

The taking of human life is the most serious of matters addressed by legal and moral norms. Prohibitions on homicide are part of every legal and moral system, but, aside from pacifist moral codes, the taking of human life is permitted, under certain highly limited conditions, by every moral and legal system. It is in this zone where the general prohibition starts to give way to the highly limited exceptions that the issue of the targeted killing of terrorists arises. Does such killing fall within the prohibition? Does it fall within one of the exceptions? What is the scope of the exception that permits the use of defensive force? Are there special exceptions that apply only in the context of war? These questions are only the beginning, however. In addition, there are questions arising from the complex interplay of moral and legal principles. Should the legal principles governing targeted killing restate the applicable moral principles? If not, what should the legal principles be and why?

The foregoing questions are among those at the center of public discussion and debate about targeted killing. This volume contributes to that discussion the carefully developed thoughts of scholars from a range of backgrounds. Those thoughts are not always in harmony with one another and will not end the discussion. But it is hoped that they will help to raise it to a higher level.

Part I

THE CHANGING FACE OF WAR: TARGETING NON-COMBATANTS

1

REBUTTING THE CIVILIAN PRESUMPTION: PLAYING WHACK-A-MOLE WITHOUT A MALLET?

Colonel Mark "Max" Maxwell

Some might argue that further innovations in the laws of war are unlikely. But the international rules that are now taken for granted—say, the right of wounded soldiers to receive aid from neutral humanitarians on the battlefield—once seemed just as far-fetched.[1]

I. Introduction

When a new enlistee starts his journey in the U.S. military to become a professional warrior, he learns from the first day when he can use lethal force. It is the most important aspect of being a trained and disciplined soldier. "Lethality, if you will, is the foundation on which everything we do must be built, but lethality brings with it incredible obligations and responsibility."[2] Lethal force, as a centerpiece for every warrior, is authorized on the basis of two concepts: the right of self-defense and the right to engage a hostile force as declared by a superior authority.

The U.S. military defines the right of self-defense as "the authority and obligation to use all necessary means available and to take all appropriate actions to defend th[e] . . . unit and other U.S. forces in the vicinity from a hostile act or demonstration of hostile intent."[3] Self-defense for the American soldier hinges on the actions

---

[1] Charli Carpenter, "Fighting the Laws of War: Protecting Civilians in Asymmetric Conflict," *Foreign Affairs* (March/April 2011) 152.

[2] An Interview with Martin E. Dempsey, Prism 2, No. 1 (December 2010) 154. General Dempsey became the 37th Chief of Staff of the U.S. Army and has been selected to be the next Chairman of the Joint Chiefs of Staff in September 2011.

[3] The Chairman of the Joint Chiefs of Staff Instruction, Standing Rules of Engagement for U.S. Forces, CJCSI 3121.01A, January 15, 2000, A-3.

of others; it is based on *conduct*. It is subjective: the actions of the perceived hostile force might be benign, but from the perspective of the soldier, the action is viewed as a demonstration of hostile intent. If the soldier is reasonable in his response, then his response is justified and legal.

Contrast this right of self-defense with the right to engage enemy forces that have been declared hostile. Once declared hostile by a superior authority, enemy forces can be engaged and the soldier does *not* need to "observe a hostile act or a demonstration of hostile intent before engaging that force."[4] The declared hostile force can be engaged without the trigger of a hostile act or intent; in other words, the declared hostile force is based on *status*. It is objective: the soldier is legally permitted to engage and kill the hostile force without regard to whether the lethality is reasonable from the perspective of the hostile party's conduct.

Clearly, the delineation between conduct and status is crucial in deciding what lethal measures the soldier may take in response. In the wake of the terrorist attack on the United States on September 11, 2001 ("9/11"), and the ensuing armed conflict with terrorism, the U.S. vision of this very distinction with which soldiers are indoctrinated—conduct *vice* status—has been stood on its head. This transformation has occurred because terrorists[5] do not follow the rules imposed upon the state by the Geneva Conventions and the law of war.[6] Terrorists are an asymmetric enemy: they do not wear uniforms or identifiable insignia to distinguish themselves from civilians, and, in fact, they eschew distinction between themselves and civilians. Eschewing this distinction is intentional: terrorists know that if the United States can positively identify an individual as a terrorist, then its ability to target that individual with precision and accuracy is quite impressive. Indeed, terrorists purposely blend into the civilian population, using the population as protection, because the United States will not target a terrorist if the cost to civilians is too high. In sum, terrorists seek to look like innocent civilians and garner those protections.

The difficulty with combating an asymmetric enemy has pushed the United States toward a policy of targeted killing. Legal scholars define targeted killing as the use of lethal force by a state[7] or its agents with the intent, premeditation, and deliberation to kill individually selected persons who are not in the physical custody

---

[4] Ibid. at A-5.

[5] The term "terrorism" as used in this chapter refers to acts having four characteristics: "a fundamentally political nature, the symbolic use of violence, purposeful targeting of noncombatants, [and] carried out by nonstate actors." Audrey Cronin, *How Terrorism Ends: Understanding the Decline and Demise of Terrorist Campaigns* (Princeton University Press, 2009) 7.

[6] In this chapter, the author uses the term "law of war," but other commentators use the "law of armed conflict" or "International Humanitarian Law." The author choose "law of war" because this is the terminology used in the U.S. military.

[7] "State" is a technical legal term meaning a land mass recognized by the United Nations Charter as a member state.

of those targeting them.[8] In layman's terms, targeted killing is used to eliminate individuals the state views as a danger.[9] The U.S. policy of targeted killing has led to criticism by members of the international community because of the perception that the United States is intentionally targeting and killing civilians.[10]

Although U.S. presidents have reserved the right to use targeted killings in unique circumstances, making this option a favored method of combating terrorists raises the risk that, unless the policy regarding targeted killing is adroitly structured to deal with certain situations, the law of war could be driven in a direction that is unwise for its long-term health.

II. Roadmap

This chapter outlines how the law of war regarding targeted killing can be tailored to combat international terrorism. To accomplish this objective, the chapter grapples with the principal legal question raised by the targeting of terrorists: how can a state determine that an individual is a belligerent,[11] *vice* a civilian, and therefore a legitimate target under the law of war, just as a combatant is a legitimate target because of his status as a member of an armed force?

This chapter first provides the history of targeted killing from a U.S. perspective. It will explain how terrorism has traditionally been handled as a domestic law enforcement matter and how this approach limits the U.S. government's ability to combat terrorism. With the events of 9/11, the United States departed from this law-enforcement paradigm and handled certain terrorist organizations, like Al Qaeda and associated forces, under a law of war paradigm; that is, the United States declared war against these terrorist organizations.

While this novel policy is not ill-conceived given the global nature of Al Qaeda, there are limitations under the law of war on *how* individuals can be targeted. The law of war requires that civilians not directly taking part in hostilities be protected. The key is the *status*—in an armed conflict context, is the individual a civilian or a combatant?—an individual holds as a member of an organized armed group like

---

[8] Philip Alston, "Report of the Special Rapporteur on Extrajudicial, Summary or Arbitrary Executions: Study on Targeted Killings," UN General Assembly, Human Rights Council, May 28, 2010 (A/HRC/14/24/Add.6) 3 (hereafter, Alston UN Report). See Nils Melzer, *Targeted Killing in International Law* (Oxford University Press, 2009) 5: "the use of lethal force attributable to a subject of international law with the intent, premeditation and deliberation to kill individually selected persons who are not in the physical custody of those targeting them."

[9] Eben Kaplan, "Targeted Killings," Council on Foreign Relations Background Paper (March 2, 2006)1.

[10] At this stage of discussion, a civilian is someone who is not targetable under the law of war.

[11] A belligerent can be an individual, group, or some entity which acts in a hostile manner, such as engaging in war-like acts.

Al Qaeda. Embedded in this question is the effect human-rights norms have had upon this status debate and whether these ever-expanding norms are helpful or harmful in combating terrorism.

The chapter then explains the U.S. position that certain terrorists hold a different status than the civilian population. This position has been met with resistance from those who posit that terrorists are civilians who are taking a direct part in hostilities against the state and can be targeted only for such time as they do so.[12] A new approach within the law of war to categorize individuals as either civilians, who are not targetable, or as belligerents who are targetable because of their status is then outlined. This approach will further the cause of states in effectively combating terrorism.

This chapter concludes that while status is paramount in targeting decisions, the determination of status should be based on the individual's pattern of conduct and that pattern must be sufficient to rebut the presumption that the individual enjoys the protected status of a civilian.

III. History of targeted killing

During the Cold War, the United States used covert operations to target certain political leaders with deadly force.[13] These covert operations, like assassination plots against Fidel Castro of Cuba and President Ngo Dinh Diem of South Vietnam, came to public light in the waning days of the Nixon Administration in 1974. In response to the public outrage at this tactic, the U.S. Senate created a select committee in 1975, chaired by Senator Frank Church of Idaho, to "Study Government Operations with Respect to Intelligence Activities."[14] This committee, which took the name of its chairman, harshly condemned such targeting, referred to in the report as "assassination": "we condemn assassination and reject it as an instrument of American policy."[15]

In response to the Church Committee's findings, President Ford issued an executive order in 1976 prohibiting assassinations: "No employee of the United States Government shall engage in, or conspire to engage in, political assassination."[16] The executive order, which is still in force today as Executive Order 12333, "was issued primarily to preempt pending congressional legislation banning political

---

[12] Michael H. Hoffman, "Terrorists Are Unlawful Belligerents, Not Unlawful Combatants: A Distinction With Implications for the Future of International Humanitarian Law," 34 *Case Western Reserve Journal of International Law*, 227, 228 (Fall 2002).

[13] Tyler Harder, "Time to Repeal the Assassination Ban of Executive Order 12333: A Small Step in Clarifying Current Law," *Military Law Review*, Vol. 172 (Sumer 2002) 12.

[14] United States Senate, Report No. 94–465, "Alleged Assassination Plots Involving Foreign Leaders," Washington, D.C.: U.S. Government Printing Office, November 1975, 282.

[15] Matthew J. Machon, "Targeted Killing as an Element of U.S. Foreign Policy in the War on Terror," Monograph for the School of Advanced Military Studies, Fort Leavenworth, KS (AY 2005–06) 18.

[16] Executive Order 11905 (February 18, 1976).

assassination."[17] President Ford did not want legislation that would impinge upon his ability as Commander in Chief to decide on the measures that were necessary for national security.[18] In the end, no legislation on assassinations was passed; national security remained under the President's purview. Congress did mandate, however, that the President submit findings to select members of Congress before a covert operation commences or in a timely fashion afterwards.[19] This requirement remains to this day.

Targeted killings have again come to center stage with the Obama Administration's extraordinary step of acknowledging the targeting of the radical Muslim cleric Anwar al-Awlaki.[20] Mr. al-Awlaki is a U.S. citizen who lives in Yemen and is a member of an Islamic terrorist organization, Al Qaeda, in the Arabian Peninsula.[21] He became a spiritual confidant to and had frequent e-mail correspondence with Major Nidal Hasan, an Army psychiatrist who allegedly killed 13 people and wounded 31 more, most of whom were U.S. soldiers, during a shooting rampage on Fort Hood, Texas, in November 2009.[22] Mr. al-Awlaki also played a significant role in an attempted airliner attack conducted by Umar Farouk Abdulmutallab, the Nigerian Muslim who attempted to blow up a Northwest Airlines flight bound for Detroit on Christmas Day, 2009.[23] Mr. al-Awlaki, according to U.S. officials, is no longer merely encouraging terrorist activities against the United States; now he is "acting for or on behalf of Al Qaeda in the Arabian Peninsula (AQAP)...and providing financial, material or technological support for...acts of terrorism."[24] Al-Awlaki's involvement in these activities, according to the United States, makes him a belligerent and therefore a legitimate target.

---

[17] Machon, *supra* n. 15, 20. The word "political" has been removed from the executive order and now there is simply a ban on assassinations.

[18] Nathan Canastaro, "American Law and Policy on Assassinations of Foreign Leaders: The Practicality of Maintaining the Status Quo," *Boston College International and Comparative Review*, Vol. 26, No. 1 (Winter 2003) 11–13.

[19] The Hughes-Ryan Amendment of 1974, Pub. L. No. 93–559, Sec. 32, 88 Stat. 1804 (1974).

[20] Scott Shane, "U.S. Approves Targeted Killing of American Cleric," *The New York Times*, April 6, 2010, 6A.

[21] Shaykh Anwar al-Awlaki, "The New Mardin Declaration: An Attempt at Justifying the New World," *Inspire*, Fall 1431 (2010), Issue 2, 3. *See* Declaration of Professor Bernard Haykel, *Nasser Al-Awlaki v. Obama*, No. 10-cv-01469 (JDB), United States District Court for the District of Columbia (October 7, 2010) 3. This chapter will not discuss whether Mr. al-Awlaki can be targeted as a U.S. citizen living abroad. The proposals of this chapter will be layered on existing international law.

[22] Sudarsan Raghavan, "Cleric Says He Was Confidant to Hasan," *Washington Post*, November 16, 2009, A3.

[23] Opposition to Plaintiff's Motion for Preliminary Injunction and Memorandum in Support of Defendants' Motion to Dismiss, *Nasser Al-Awlaki v. Obama*, Civ. A. No. 10-cv-1469, U.S. District Court for the District of Columbia, filed September 24, 2010, 8 (quoting the director of the National Counterterrorism Center, Michael Leiter before the Senate Homeland Security and Government Affairs Committee on September 22, 2010).

[24] Designation of Anwar al-Awlaki as a Specially Designated Global Terrorist, pursuant to Executive Order 13224 and the Global Terrorism Sanctions Regulations, 31 C.F.R. Part 594, 75 Federal Register 43233, 43234, Number 141 (July 23, 2010).

The context of the fierce debates in the 1970s is different from that of the al-Awlaki debate. The targeted killing of an individual for a political purpose—assassination—as investigated by the Church Committee—was the use of lethal force during *peacetime*, not during an armed conflict.[25] During war, the use of targeted killing is quite common.[26] But in peacetime, the use of *any* lethal force is strictly governed and limited by both domestic law and international legal norms. The next section will explain those norms and their implications for addressing the threat posed by terrorists.

IV. The law-enforcement paradigm

Before 9/11, the United States treated terrorists under the law-enforcement paradigm; that is, as suspected criminals.[27] A terrorist was protected from lethal force so long as his or her conduct did not require the state to respond to a threat or the indication of a threat. The law-enforcement paradigm assumes that the preference is not to use lethal force but rather to arrest the terrorist and then to investigate and try him before a court of law.[28] The presumption during peacetime is that the use of lethal force by a state is not justified unless necessary to meet an unlawful threat to human life. Necessity assumes that "only the amount of force required to meet the threat and restore the *status quo ante* may be employed against [the] source of the threat, thereby limiting the force that may be lawfully applied by the state actor."[29] The taking of life in peacetime is only justified "when lesser means for reducing the threat were ineffective."[30]

Under both domestic and international law, the civilian population has the right to be free from arbitrary deprivation of life.[31] Professor Geoff Corn makes this point by highlighting that a law enforcement officer could *not* use deadly force "against suspected criminals based solely on a determination an individual was a member of a criminal group."[32] Under the law-enforcement paradigm, "a country cannot

---

[25] This is why the Church Committee focused on intelligence organizations and not the armed forces. In this chapter, the terms "war" and "armed conflict" are synonymous.

[26] W. Hays Parks, Memorandum on Executive Order 12333 and Assassination, 8 (on file with author).

[27] Greg Travalio and John Altenburg, "Terrorism, State Responsibility, and the Use of Military Force," *Chicago Journal of International Law*, Vol. 4, No. 1 (Spring 2003) 109.

[28] Judgment, *Public Committee Against Torture in Israel v. Israel*, HCJ 769/02, (2005) ISrSC, para. 22.

[29] Geoff Corn, "Mixing Apples and Hand Grenades: The Logical Limit of Applying Human Rights Norms to Armed Conflict," 1 *Journal of International Humanitarian Legal Studies* 52, 85 (2010).

[30] Ibid. at 78.

[31] The Fourth Amendment to the Bill of Rights states that "[t]he right of the people to be secure in their persons, houses, papers, and effects, against unreasonable searches and seizures, shall not be violated..." U.S. Constitution. For the international law context, see The International Covenant on Civil and Political Rights, General Assembly Resolution 2200A (XXI), 999 U.N.T.S. 171, entered into force March 23, 1976, art. 6.

[32] Corn, *supra* n. 29, 77.

target any individual in its own territory unless there is no other way to avert a great danger."[33] It is the individual's *conduct* at the time of the threat that gives the state the right to respond with lethal force.

The state's responding force must be *reasonable* given the situation known at the time. This reasonableness standard is a "commonsense evaluation of what an objectively reasonable officer might have done in the same circumstances."[34] The U.S. Supreme Court has opined that this reasonableness is subjective: "[t]he calculus of reasonableness must embody allowances for the fact that police officers often are forced to make split-second judgments. . . . about the amount of force that is necessary in a particular situation."[35]

The law-enforcement paradigm attempts to "minimize the use of lethal force to the extent feasible in the circumstances."[36] This approach is the starting point for many commentators when discussing targeted killing: "it may be legal for law enforcement personnel to shoot to kill based on the imminence of the threat, but the goal of the operation, from its inception, should not be to kill."[37] The presumption is that intentional killing is unlawful by the state unless it was necessary for self-defense or defense of others.[38] Like the soldier who acts under the authority of self-defense, if one acts reasonably based on the nature of the threat, the action is justified and legal.

However, the law-enforcement paradigm fails to consider the case of a terrorist who works outside the state that he plans to attack and is virtually immune to arrest for much of the time that he is preparing for the attack, because he is operating in an area of the world where law enforcement is weak or non-existent. Moreover, those terrorists who are the master planners of an operation might never set foot outside of such an area. The events of 9/11 demonstrated these weaknesses in the law-enforcement paradigm and led the United States to rethink its approach to terrorism.

V. The law of war paradigm

In the wake of 9/11, President Bush requested Congress to give him authorization to go to war with the architects of these attacks, namely the members of Al Qaeda. The Congress, seven days after these horrific events, gave the President

---

[33] Gabriella Blum and Philip Heymann, *Law and Policy of Targeted Killing, Laws, Outlaws, and Terrorists: Lesson from the War on Terrorism* (Boston, MIT Press, 2010) 10.

[34] Thomas D. Petrowski, "Use-of-Force Policies and Training: A Reasoned Approach," 71 *F.B.I. Law Enforcement Bulletin*, No. 10 (October 2002) 26.

[35] *Graham v. Conner*, 490 U.S. 386, 396–7 (1989).

[36] Alston UN Report, 23.

[37] Ibid. at 5.

[38] Alston states that a "State killing is legal only if it is required to protect life (making lethal force *proportionate*) and there is no other means, such as capture or non-lethal incapacitation, of preventing that threat to life (making lethal force *necessary*)." Ibid. at 11.

the Authorization for the Use of Military Force (AUMF) to use all military force against those:

> nations, organizations, or persons [the President] determines planned, authorized, committed, or aided the terrorist attacks that occurred on September 11, 2001, or harbored such organizations or persons, in order to prevent any future acts of international terrorism against the United States by such nations organizations or persons.[39]

For the first time in modern U.S. history, the country was engaged in an armed conflict with members of an organization, Al Qaeda, *vice* a state. The United States' legal justification to use force, which includes targeted killings, against Al Qaeda, the Taliban, and associated forces is two-fold: the law of war and self-defense.[40]

In armed conflict, the rules of when an individual can be killed are starkly different than in peacetime. Now that the United States is in an armed conflict with Al Qaeda and associated forces, designated terrorists who are members of those groups may be targeted and killed because of their *status* as enemy belligerents. That status is determined by the President under the AUMF. Unlike the law-enforcement paradigm, the law of war requires neither a certain conduct nor a reasonable amount of force analysis to engage belligerents. In armed conflict, it is wholly permissible to inflict "death on enemy personnel irrespective of the actual risk they present."[41] Killing enemy belligerents is legal unless specifically prohibited; for example, enemy personnel out of combat like the wounded, the sick, or the shipwrecked.[42] A situation of armed conflict negates the law-enforcement presumption that lethal force against an individual is justified only when necessary. If an individual is an enemy, then "soldiers are not constrained by the law of war from applying the full range of lawful weapons..."[43] The soldier is told by the state that an enemy is hostile and may engage that individual without any consideration of the threat currently posed. The enemy is declared hostile; the enemy is now targetable. But this logic assumes the target is not a civilian who is specifically protected.

---

[39] Authorization for the Use of Military Force, Pub. L. 107–40, 115 Stat. 224 (2001), sec. 2(a).

[40] The Obama Administration has addressed this justification in two forums: filings in federal court in the case of *Al-Awlaki v. Obama*, Civil Action No. cv 10–1469 (December 7, 2010) (this civil case brought by the father of American cleric Anwar al-Awlaki's—spelled Al-Awlaki in court filings—was dismissed for lack of standing, among other rationale, but included the position of the U.S. Government to target Mr. al-Awlaki's son being premised on the concept of self-defense) and the statements of Administration officials. (Harold Koh, Legal Advisor to the Department of State, "The Obama Administration and International Law," Keynote Speech at the Annual Meeting of the American Society of International Law (March 24, 2010)).

[41] Corn, *supra* n. 29, 94.

[42] Convention for the Amelioration of the Condition of Wounded, Sick, and Shipwrecked Members of the Armed Forces at Sea, August 12, 1949, 6 U.S.T. 3217, 75 U.N.T.S. 85.

[43] W. Hays Parks, "Direct Participation in Hostilities Study: No Mandate, No Expertise, and Legally Incorrect," *New York University Journal of International Law and Politics*, Vol. 42 (Spring 2010) 780.

VI. The development of the law of war

At the center of the Geneva Conventions and its Additional Protocols is its "cardinal"[44] rule, the principle of distinction: "The parties to the conflict must at all times distinguish between civilians and combatants."[45] This principle provides that attacks against civilians are prohibited.[46] Civilians are defined in the negative as "all persons who are not members of State armed forces or organized armed groups of a party to the conflict are civilians and, therefore, entitled to protection against direct attack unless and for such time as they take a direct part in hostilities."[47] A civilian has the greatest protection under the law of war: states are obligated to never make civilians the object of attack,[48] thereby restricting the use of lethal force by the armed forces of any state.

In international armed conflict, the only status other than civilian is that of combatant. A combatant is defined in Article 43 of the First Protocol on International Armed Conflict as a member of "[t]he armed forces of a Party to a conflict," and armed forces are defined to include "all organized armed forces, groups and units which are under a command responsible to that Party of the conduct of its subordinates, even if that Party is represented by a government or an authority not recognized by an adverse Party."[49] The commentary to Article 43 emphasizes that only members of the armed forces are combatants: "all members of the armed forces are combatants, and only members of the armed forces are combatants."[50] Combatants are granted the right to directly participate in hostilities.[51] The combatant can be targeted and killed as a measure of first resort.

A further restriction on lethal force is precision: the requirement that the killing be as precise as militarily possible. Optimally, the combatant is the only one harmed.

---

[44] Advisory Opinion on the Legality of the Threat or Use of Nuclear Weapons, ICJ Reports 1996, 226, 257.

[45] *The Public Committee Against Torture in Israel v. Israel*, Judgment of the Supreme Court, A. Barak for the Court (December 11, 2005) para. 23.

[46] Protocol Additional to the Geneva Conventions of August 12, 1949, and Relating to the Protection of Victims of International Armed Conflicts, art. 48 and art. 51(2), December 12, 1977, 1125 U.N.T.S. 3 (hereafter Protocol I); Protocol Additional to the Geneva Conventions of August 12, 1949, and Relating to the Protection of Victims of Non-International Armed Conflicts, art. 13(2), December 12, 1977, 1125 U.N.T.S. 609 (hereafter Protocol II). The additional protocols have not been ratified by the United States, but the articles discussed in this chapter are considered customary international law.

[47] Nils Melzer, International Committee on the Red Cross, Interpretive Guidance on the Notion of Direct Participation in Hostilities under International Humanitarian Law, adopted on February 26, 2009, International Review of the Red Cross, Vol. 90, No. 872 (December 2008) 1002 (ICRC Guidance).

[48] ICJ Use of Nuclear Weapons, 257.

[49] Protocol I, art. 43(1).

[50] Commentary to Additional Protocol I, 515.

[51] Protocol I, art. 43(2).

Precision is predicated on the principle of distinction, which makes civilians immune to direct attack.[52] But distinction blurs when non-state actors conduct asymmetric warfare against a state.[53] When a belligerent—someone who is taking hostilities against the state—is not wearing insignia or uniform and is also blending into the civilian population, then precision becomes extremely difficult. The *obligation* of a belligerent is to "comply with the rules of international law applicable in armed conflict... "[54] If the combatant, like a terrorist, fails to comply with these rules, then he could forfeit the protections of combatant immunity; that is, the protection of a person immune from prosecution for war-like acts before capture.[55] But, in targeting a belligerent, the assumption is that the state knows that the belligerent, who looks like a civilian, is hostile. The price a belligerent pays for non-compliance is simply a loss of combatant immunity; the state, on the other hand, must now track a threat in an asymmetrical environment where the protection of the civilian population, which is the state's obligation, is in the balance.

The development and increasingly common use of precision weaponry produces—or at least intends to produce—a direct benefit of reducing collateral civilian deaths related to such attacks. When such attacks occur outside an area of traditional combat operations, such as an urban area, this reduction of civilian deaths has evolved into an expectation: the capability of using precision munitions produces a presumption that the point of doing so is to "clearly discriminate between military and civilian targets and... to limit civilian casualties."[56] Precision enhances the protection of civilians. Modern weaponry and targeting capabilities continue to push states toward an end state with no collateral damage. But this push is unrealistic if either there is no delineation between innocent civilians and the individual doing the state harm, or the delineation is not grounded in a legal structure that allows the state to target those who are doing it harm. Precision relies on the vitality of the principle of distinction.

VII. Non-international armed conflict and civilians taking a direct part in hostilities

In non-international armed conflicts, the principle of distinction is in doubt because the definitional delineation between combatants and civilians is absent

---

[52] Protocol I, art. 51(1).

[53] M. Cherif Bassiouni, "The New Wars and the Crisis of Compliance with the Law of Armed Conflict by Non-State Actors," 98 *Criminal Law* 711 (2009).

[54] Protocol I, art. 44(2).

[55] Ibid., art. 44(4).

[56] Anthony H. Cordesman, "The Gaza War: A Strategic Analysis" Center for Strategic and International Studies, February 2009, available at <http://csis.org/files/media/csis/pubs/090202_gaza_war.pdf> accessed November 3, 2011.

in the Second Protocol of the Geneva Conventions, which governs the protection of victims of non-international armed conflicts.[57] In fact, the term "combatant" does not appear in the Second Protocol. Some commentators take the view that if a conflict is not international in character, then "there is no such thing as a 'combatant.'"[58] According to this logic, since no other status exists, everyone is a civilian in non-international conflicts.

During the 1974–77 Diplomatic Conference of the Second Protocol, there was a draft definition of who takes the status of being a civilian: "anyone who is not a member of the armed forces or of an organized armed group."[59] This definition, however, "was discarded along with most other provisions on the conduct of hostilities in the last minute effort to 'simplify' the Protocol..."[60] The principle of distinction is in effect eviscerated without delineation between civilians and belligerents who are conducting hostilities in non-international armed conflicts.[61]

If "no delineation" is the starting place, it follows then that states in non-international armed conflicts are obligated to give every individual the protection of a civilian. If the only status that exists is that of a civilian, states must presume that every individual "shall not be the object of attack."[62] The state can only target and kill civilians "for such time as they take a direct part in hostilities."[63]

Under this theory, civilians can be targeted by the state under limited or specific circumstances, but two important requirements must be met. First, the ability to target civilians is restricted by a specific time constraint of "for such time;" that is, while the civilian is taking a direct part in hostilities. Second, the targeting is based on *conduct*; that is, only if the civilian is taking "a direct part in hostilities." For a soldier, non-international armed conflict is a perpetual world of self-defense where the soldier is responding to hostile intent or a hostile act. In this world, no individual can be declared per se hostile by the state and thereby targeted because of *who* they are; instead, because the only status is that of a civilian, an individual can be targeted only for the particular duration in which he is performing the specified *acts*.

A third requirement that is gaining traction within the international community is proportionality. Since all individuals hold the status of civilian, other than those

---

[57] Although, as noted by Professor Geoff Corn, the term "combatant" does appear in the commentary of art. 13.

[58] Alston UN Report, 19.

[59] Draft Art. 25(1). O.R., Vol. XV, 320 (CDDH/215/Rev. 1).

[60] ICRC Guidance, 1003–04.

[61] Geoffrey Corn and Chris Jenks, *Two Sides of the Combatant COIN: Untangling Direct Participation in Hostilities from Belligerent Status in Non-International Armed Conflict* (forthcoming)(unpublished manuscript on file with author).

[62] Protocol II, art. 13(2).

[63] Ibid., art. 13(3).

then directly participating in hostilities, this third requirement is the obligation of honoring the principle of proportionality regarding the targeted individual. Put in terms of the individual: "a civilian taking a direct part in hostilities cannot be attacked at such time as he is doing so, if a less harmful means can be employed."[64]

As for the second requirement, "States tend to address direct participation issues in a case-by-case fashion."[65] The Israeli Supreme Court did exactly that—in the words of Professor Schmitt, "tending towards exemplification rather than explication"—in its seminal case of *The Public Committee against Torture in Israel v. the Government of Israel* (hereafter, the Targeted Killing Case):

> Against the background of these considerations, the following cases should also be included in the definition of taking a "direct part" in hostilities: a person who collects intelligence in the army, . . . ; a person who transports unlawful combatants to or from the place where the hostilities are taking place; a person who operates weapons which unlawful combatants use, or supervises their operation, or provides service to them, be the distance from the battlefield as it may.[66]

The time-window requirement also presents a difficult question of interpretation. The Israeli Supreme Court noted that "[w]ith no consensus regarding the interpretation of the wording 'for such time,' there is no choice but to proceed from case to case."[67] Again, it discussed examples of what constituted "for such time:"

> On the one hand, a civilian taking a direct part in hostilities one single time, or sporadically, who later detaches himself from that activity, is a civilian who, starting from the time he detached himself from that activity is entitled to protection from attack. . . . On the other hand, a civilian who has joined a terrorist organization which has become his "home," and in the framework of his role in that organization he commits a chain of hostilities, with short periods of rest between them, loses his immunity from attack "for such time" as he is committing the chain of acts.[68]

The ambiguity of the time-window requirement makes combating terrorists extremely complex. It puts a premium on actionable intelligence. The state must collect evidence in a timely fashion proving that a certain civilian is performing or intending to perform a hostile act that could allow him to be targeted.[69] The level of proof needed to determine what qualifies as a lawful military objective, like a civilian taking a direct part in hostilities, must be reasonable.[70] In the state's

---

[64] Targeted Killing Case, para. 40.
[65] Michael N. Schmitt, "Deconstructing Direct Participation in Hostilities: The Constitutive Elements," 42 *New York University Journal of International Law and Policy* 697, 705 (Spring 2010).
[66] Targeted Killing Case, para. 35.
[67] Ibid., para. 39.
[68] Ibid.
[69] Blum and Heymann, *supra* n. 33, 7.
[70] Geoffrey Corn, "Targeting, the Reasonable Commander, and the Missing Quantum of Proof Component," 5 (forthcoming).

targeting process, the central question is: does the intelligence support targeting this person?[71]

If the targeted civilian was a combatant, that is, a permissible object of attack, then "no attempt to capture the enemy or warn the enemy in advance is necessary before shooting to kill."[72] Simply put, there is no proportionality test required for a combatant. In the words of law of war scholar W. Hays Parks, "soldiers are not constrained by the law of war from applying the full range of lawful weapons against enemy combatants..."[73]

Yet since a terrorist holds the status of a civilian in a non-international armed conflict, there are commentators who contend an additional layer of complexity exists, namely, that proportional force is required vis-à-vis the targeted terrorist; that is, "the weapon which could be expected to employ the least injury ought to be employed."[74] Proportionality in this regard was addressed by the European Court of Human Rights in 1995.[75] The *McCann* case stems from British agents intentionally killing three Irish Republican Army (IRA) terrorists in Gibraltar. The British authorities had a shoot-to-kill policy when it came to certain IRA operatives. The Court in *McCann* "held that the counter-terrorist operation had not been planned and controlled so as to minimize, to the greatest extent possible, recourse to lethal force and, therefore, amounted to a violation" of the right to life.[76] The Israeli Supreme Court cited and followed this proportionality rule in its own Targeted Killing Case.

The Israeli opinion is arguably more narrow and thereby does not impose a rule of proportionality when handling all civilians taking a direct part in hostilities, because the military operations before the Court were limited to threats within Israel and the territories immediately proximate to Israel, for example, Judea, Samaria, and the Gaza Strip (referred to as the *area*).[77] Therefore, any ruling could be read through the lens of the laws of belligerent occupation. Under this legal regime, with the army controlling an area of operation, "arrest, investigation, and trial are at times realizable possibilities."[78] Like the *McCann* case, proportionality is embedded into this legal landscape since the option of capture or less lethal means is possible, given that the area of operation is controlled by the state. The Israeli

---

[71] Declaration of Jonathan Manes, The Joint Targeting Definitions and Process, *Nasser Al-Awlaki v. Obama*, No. 10-cv-1469 (JBD)(October 8, 2010) 10.

[72] Blum and Heymann, *supra* n. 33, 7.

[73] Parks, *supra* n. 43, 780.

[74] Ibid., 786 (citing Pictet's argument during the 1974–1977 Diplomatic Conference).

[75] European Court of Human Rights, *McCann and Others v. The United Kingdom*, ECHR 385 (1995).

[76] Nils Melzer, *supra* n. 8, 23 (citing ECtHR, *McCann* case, Secs. 150, 194, 213f).

[77] Parks, *supra* n. 43, 789.

[78] Targeted Killing Case, para. 22.

Supreme Court, however, does not restrict its ruling to only occupied territories. The Court does exactly the opposite: it explicitly expands the ruling beyond the laws of belligerent occupation to encompass all international armed conflicts:

> [T]he international law regarding international armed conflict....includes the laws of belligerent occupation. However, it is not restricted only to them. This law applies in any case of an armed conflict of international character—in other words, one that crosses the borders of the state—whether or not the place in which the armed conflict occurs is subject to belligerent occupation. This law constitutes a part of *iue in bello*.[79]

The Targeted Killing Case does not explicitly address non-international armed conflict, because the Court found the conflict in the *area* to be international in flavor. The reality is that the Court's holding has equal weight in the non-international context. The reasons are simple: to argue that civilians in non-international armed conflict are entitled to less protection than those in an international conflict, from a legal perspective, is counter to the weight of authority, and from a commonsense perspective, would be difficult to fathom.

This added requirement of proportionality makes targeting a terrorist all the more difficult. Assuming the Israeli holding is now the legal standard, then to target a terrorist, regardless of where the terrorist poses a threat, the state must do three separate but intertwined analyses: whether the civilian is taking a direct part in hostilities; whether the attack on the civilians would be during such time as the civilian is taking a direct part in hostilities; and whether lesser means like capture are viable. This added requirement of using the least force possible makes combating terrorism, regardless of what a state calls it, look very similar to the law-enforcement paradigm. It is the terrorist's *actions* at the time of the threat that give the state the right to respond with force. And the responding force, if lethal, must be reasonable; that is, lesser force or capture is not feasible. This means any armed conflict where the actors are not combatants converts into a law-enforcement action.

The International Committee of the Red Cross (ICRC) recently advanced this argument in its Interpretive Guidance on the Direct Participation in Hostilities. The ICRC articulates a use-of-force continuum[80] view of engaging belligerents: "the kind and degree of force which is permissible against persons not entitled to protection against direct attack must not exceed what is actually necessary to accomplish a legitimate military purpose in the prevailing circumstances."[81]

---

[79] Ibid., para. 18.

[80] This is Hays Park's interpretation of what the Interpretive Guidance does, taking from Jean S. Pictet's theoretical use-of-force continuum articulated during the negotiations of the additional protocols: "Humanity demands capture rather than wounds, and wounds rather than death; that non-combatants shall be spared as much as possible; that wounds shall be inflicted as lightly as circumstances permit, in order that the wounded may be healed as painlessly as possible; and that captivity shall be made as bearable as possible." Parks, *supra* n. 43, 785.

[81] ICRC Guidance, 1040.

Hence, "the object of the state violence is protected from the use of force in excess of that necessary to reduce the threat the individual poses."[82]

In his critique of this position, Parks concludes that this theoretical continuum is not grounded in treaty law, state practice, or domestic or international law. And to rely on the holdings of the Israeli Supreme Court, as the ICRC does, although instructive, is not conclusive because it grapples with "one of the most uncommon situations in the world."[83] But the reality is that the international trend is to extend concepts of human rights law, like the law of humanity and rule of proportionality vis-à-vis the targeted individual, into the law of war. The concept of *lex specialis*— that the specialized law of war trumps the most general law of human rights in the area of armed conflict—is now being challenged.[84] The assault is not a frontal one in which human rights law is being touted as the superior law. Instead, it is an assault around the edges: where the law of war is disputed or unclear, then human rights law is given greater weight. The result is that the principles embedded within the law of war cede ground to human-rights law.[85] Philip Alston, in his UN report on targeted killing, makes this position clear:

> Both [the law of war] and human rights law apply in the context of armed conflict; whether a particular killing is legal is determined by the applicable *lex specialis*. To the extent that [the law of war] does not provide a rule, or the rule is unclear and its meaning cannot be ascertained from the guidance offered by [law of war] principles, it is appropriate to draw guidance from human rights law.[86]

This erosion in the law of war is pursued for the best of intentions: humanity. The erosion is greatest in the area of non-international armed conflict because the law of war is least developed in this area. Under the law-enforcement paradigm, which incorporates human rights law, the use of force is exceptional; under the law of war paradigm, lethal force is authorized by the state but for its political objectives. There are limits to this authorization, but the starting place is the authorization to use force against what the state defines as a military objective. Human rights law centers on the individual; law of war centers on the state.

Professor Corn articulates the tension between these two bodies of law:

> Because th[e human-rights law] presumption is inconsistent with the underlying presumptions related to the use of force against operational opponents that qualify as lawful military objectives, human rights standards for the employment of force

---

[82] Corn and Jenks, *supra* n. 61, 3.

[83] Parks, *supra* n. 43, 829.

[84] This concept, *lex specialis*, "stems from a Roman principle of interpretation, according to which in situations especially regulated by a rule, this rule would displace the more general rule..." C. Droege, "The Interplay Between International Humanitarian Law and International Human Rights Law in Situations of Armed Conflict," 40 *Israel Law Review* 310, 338 (2007). See also Parks, *supra* n. 43, 797–8.

[85] Corn, *supra* n. 29, 78.

[86] Alston UN Report, para. 29.

cannot be relied upon to define what constitutes an arbitrary deprivation of life inflicted upon such opponents.[87]

The problem with the conflation between the law of war and human rights law is that the burden of targeting belligerents is now permanently shifted to the state: the rules on force, as constrained by the law-enforcement paradigm, only apply to the state. The civilian who directly participates in armed conflict can be hostile at one moment and then expect to regain protections as a civilian the next. Such a result stands the law of war framework on its head. The soldier (and the state) can only respond, as in self-defense, to a hostile act or intent and then is restricted to use the minimum force possible. The state is constrained to only responding to the indiscriminate violence perpetuated by the terrorists who are able to go in and out of protection.

This situation is analogous to the game Whack-a-Mole, but with an additional layer of rules. In this game, if the mole (the terrorist) does not pop up its head (take a direct part in hostilities), then the state may not respond. When the mole does pop up, the amount of force the state can use via its mallet is limited to the minimum force required. And instead of whacking the mole with the mallet, if the state can catch the mole, it must. Nice in theory, but with modern-day lethality, and the technology that can be leveraged to orchestrate an attack instantaneously, the mole has been given an enormous advantage. To make matters worse for the state, the mole operates in places where arrest is remote because governance is weak or non-existent. The law-enforcement paradigm assumes some control over the space in which the state is conducting operations. Little to no control over that space exists in places like Yemen.[88] The game can be played under this paradigm, but the winner is assured: the mole.

VIII. Unlawful combatants

In response to this modern-day difficulty of combating terrorism under a law-enforcement paradigm, the governments of the United States and Israel attempted to create a third status: unlawful combatant. This status melds two concepts together: first, "unlawful combatants," like traditional combatants, can be targeted with lethal force as an enemy and there is no proportionality requirement to resort to lesser means; and second, "unlawful combatants," unlike the traditional combatants, are not given combatant immunity if captured, for their previous war-like acts.[89] Terrorist are combatants who are "unlawful" because "they do not

---

[87] Corn, *supra* n. 29, 104.

[88] World Bank ranks Yemen in the bottom quarter of states in the world for degree of governance. See <http://info.worldbank.org/governance/wgi/sc_chart.asp> accessed November 3, 2011.

[89] U.S Department of Defense, Manual for Military Commissions Sec. 6(a)(13)(d)(2009).

differentiate themselves from the civilian population, and since they do not obey the laws of war."[90] Yet when targeting the "unlawful combatant," like a traditional combatant, the state must still adhere to the bedrock principles embedded in the law of war, which are distinction, military necessity ("those measures not prohibited by international law which are indispensable for securing the complete submission of the enemy as soon as possible");[91] and preventing unnecessary suffering ("an attack which may be expected to cause incidental loss of civilian life, injury to civilians...which would be excessive in relation to the concrete and direct military advantage anticipated").[92]

The term "unlawful combatant" first gained currency in the 1942 Supreme Court case of Ex parte *Quirin*.[93] During World War II, President Roosevelt created a military commission to try eight German soldier saboteurs who illegally entered the United States by submarine, shed their military uniforms, and conspired to commit acts of sabotage and espionage and to use explosives on targets within the United States.[94] The U.S. Supreme Court upheld President Roosevelt's actions and a majority of the saboteurs were put to death.[95] In the Court's *per curium* Opinion, the delineation between lawful and unlawful combatants is made clear:

> By universal agreement and practice the law of war draws a distinction between the armed forces and the peaceful populations of belligerent nations and also between those who are lawful and unlawful combatants. Lawful combatants are subject to capture and detention as prisoners of war by opposing military force. Unlawful combatants are subject to capture and detention, but in addition they are subject to trial and punishment by military tribunals for acts which render their belligerency unlawful.[96]

In the aftermath of 9/11, the Bush Administration categorized Al-Qaeda, Taliban, and associated terrorist members as unlawful combatants.[97] This categorization received much criticism, regardless of the U.S. Supreme Court's 1942

---

[90] Targeted Killing Case, para. 27.

[91] U.S. Department of the Army Field Manual, 27–10, The Law of Land Warfare 4 (June 18, 1956) (C6, July 15, 1976).

[92] Protocol I, art. 51(b)(6). This is referred to as proportionality, as well, but the author does not use the term in this chapter because it might confuse the reader. The author, instead, uses the term "unnecessary suffering" because it is the proportionality of force that must be considered vis-à-vis civilians.

[93] Ex parte *Quirin*, 317 U.S. 1 (1942).

[94] Glenn Sulmasy, *The National Security Court System: A Natural Evolution of Justice in an Age of Terror* (Oxford University Press, 2009) 56–8.

[95] Ex parte *Quirin*, 45–6.

[96] Ibid. at 30–1.

[97] Norman G. Printer, J., "The Use of Force Against Non-State Actors under International Law: An Analysis of the U.S. Predator Strike in Yemen," 8 *UCLA Journal of International Law and Foreign Affairs* 331, 363–9 (Fall 2003)(defining unlawful combatant as a "person who takes up arms, without authority, in defiance of the law of war. Because an unlawful combatant uses force without legal justification, he or she may be held liable for the unlawful use of force.").

pronouncements, because a "third" status under international law had not yet developed.[98] Although the United States has moved away from the terminology "unlawful combatant," in lieu of "unprivileged belligerent," the net effect remains the same: it is a third status that is targetable and given fewer protections than the law-enforcement paradigm would provide.[99] For example, the state does not have to capture the belligerent, even if possible.[100]

The State of Israel supported the notion of "unlawful combatant" status in the Targeted Killing Case. The Israeli Supreme Court, however, did not add this status to the other two—combatant and civilian. This "third category"—the term the Court used synonymously with "unlawful combatant"—had not gained currency: "[i]t does not appear to us that we were presented with data sufficient to allow us to say, at the present time, that such a third category has been recognized in customary international law."[101] The Court did not foreclose the prospect that this status would gain acceptance in the international community. The Court acknowledged that Israel's fight against terrorism required a "new reality," and therefore the law "must take on a dynamic interpretation."[102] In the words of Professors Blum and Heymann, the Court "chose [the law of war paradigm] as its point of departure, but then, in consideration of the unique nature of the war on terrorism, added limitations and constraints on the government's war powers..."[103]

Since the law of war governed conflict in the *area*, the Court categorized these terrorists as civilians taking a direct part in hostilities, or in the words of the Court, "civilians who constitute unlawful combatants."[104] The Court acknowledged a new context—the transnational nature and lethality of terrorists—but given the international legal tools at its disposal, it chose the framework, the law of war paradigm, which gave Israel the most protection possible. Yet no matter how robust the law of war paradigm has been *vice* the more restrictive law-enforcement paradigm, the Court's theories regarding targeting of terrorists centers on self-defense; that is, conduct.

The United States has not taken this tack. Instead, certain terrorists are treated as unlawful combatants or unprivileged belligerents who can be targeted based on their status. This approach, however, has been robustly criticized for not giving

---

[98] Antonio Cassese, *International Law*, 2nd edn (Oxford Press University, 2005) 409. There is also the policy argument that the "criminalization of belligerency creates perverse incentives for the unlawful combatants: because their very participation in the hostilities subjects them to criminal prosecution upon capture, they have no incentive to comply with the law of war." Derek Jinks, "The Declining Significance of POW Status," 45 *Harvard International Law Journal* 367, 438 (2004).

[99] U.S Department of Defense, Manual for Military Commissions Sec. 6(a)(13)(d)(2009).

[100] Blum and Heymann, *supra* n. 33, 7.

[101] Targeted Killing Case, para. 28.

[102] Ibid.

[103] Blum and Heymann, *supra* n. 33, 8.

[104] Targeted Killing Case, 28.

terrorists (civilians) more protection. The gap between civilians and combatants seems wide: does another "in-between" status exist? The answer, perhaps ironically, is in the ICRC's Interpretive Guidance on the Direct Participation in Hostilities (hereafter the Guidance), and the answer is yes: the status is being a member of an organized armed group.

IX. The ICRC's interpretive guidance on the direct participation in hostilities

After 9/11, the complexion of warfare changed and a gap developed between what the state of the law is and what it should be. For the first time, the United States, the leading military power in the world, was involved in a novel type of warfare.[105] It was not an armed conflict involving another state, as envisioned by the First Protocol of Geneva on the protection of victims in international armed conflict, nor was it an armed conflict only involving belligerents within the affected state's borders, as envisioned by the Second Protocol of Geneva on the protection of victims in non-international armed conflict. The belligerent actors in this armed conflict were not members of a state's armed force; their motivation was not only to overthrow the internal governance of the state in which they resided but also to perform hostilities against a third state. This armed conflict, as categorized by the U.S. Supreme Court, was a non-international armed conflict.[106] The question of targeting individuals in this unique type of non-international armed conflict was one of the catalysts for the ICRC to convene in 2003. The result was a study written by the ICRC's legal advisor, Nils Melzer. The Guidance, adopted by the ICRC in 2009, attempted to tackle the legal contours of what it means to take a "direct part in hostilities."

The ICRC acknowledged in the Guidance that by treating everyone in a non-international armed conflict as a civilian, the principle of distinction becomes weakened, if not irrelevant. This acknowledgement led the ICRC to posit that "[i]n non-international armed conflict, *organized armed groups* constitute the armed forces of a non-State party to the conflict and consist only of individuals whose continuous function is to take a direct part in hostilities."[107] The ICRC Guidance acknowledges the historic ambiguity of how to treat non-state actors who are a group, organized, and armed:

---

[105] Laura M. Olson, "Guantanamo Habeas Review: Are the D.C. District Court's Decisions Consistent with IHL Internment Standards?," 22 *Case Western Reserve Journal of International Law* 197, 212 (2010). Olson does an excellent job of explaining how the D.C. District Court has interpreted membership in the fighting forces of the enemy.

[106] *Hamdan v. Rumsfeld*, 548 U.S. 557, 628–31 (2006) ("conflict not of an international character").

[107] ICRC Guidance, 1002.

> While it is generally recognized that members of State armed forces in non-international armed conflict do not qualify as civilians, treaty law, State practice, and international jurisprudence have not unequivocally settled whether the same applies to members of organized armed groups (i.e. the armed forces of non-State parties to an armed conflict).[108]

Given this ambiguity, the Guidance does not lump all actors in an armed conflict within the category of civilians even though "it might be tempting to conclude that membership in such groups is simply a continuous form of civilian direct participation in hostilities."[109] This designation would "create parties to non-international armed conflicts whose entire armed forces remain part of the civilian population."[110] Instead, the Guidance boldly concludes that "[a]s the wording and logic of Article 3 G[eneva] C[onventions] I-IV *and* Additional Protocol II reveal, civilians, armed forces, and organized armed groups of the parties to the conflict are mutually exclusive categories also in non-international armed conflict." A status—members of an organized armed group—is crystallized.

The Guidance bifurcates organized armed groups into dissident armed forces and other organized armed groups. The dissident armed forces are former members of the state's armed forces who have turned against their state.[111] The other organized armed groups, which could include non-state terrorist organizations, "recruit their members primarily from the civilian population but develop a sufficient degree of military organization to conduct hostilities on behalf of a party to the conflict, albeit not always with the same means, intensity and level of sophistication as State armed forces."[112] The Guidance narrowly defines what constitutes a member of any organized armed group; the term "refers exclusively to the armed or military wing of a non-State party: its armed forces in a functional sense."[113] This armed wing can be targeted like the armed forces of a state in an armed conflict because the armed wing's purpose is to conduct hostilities.[114] The crux of distinguishing whether an individual is a member of an organized armed group or a civilian, which includes a civilian participating in hostilities, is whether the person performs a continuous combat function.[115]

Therefore, two requirements must be met before an individual can be considered a member of an organized armed group and thereby targeted because of his or her status. First, the individual must be a member of an organized group because the "[c]ontinuous combat function requires lasting integration into an organized

---

108 Ibid.
109 Ibid.
110 Ibid. at 1002–03.
111 Ibid. at 1006.
112 Ibid.
113 Ibid.
114 Corn and Jenks, *supra* n. 61, 8.
115 ICRC Guidance, 1007.

armed group."[116] Second, the organized group must be conducting hostilities. If these two requirements are met, then this translates into a status that means the non-state actor, a belligerent, can be targeted without regard to current or future conduct. Therefore, under this two-part analysis:

> [a]n individual recruited, trained, and equipped by such a group to continuously and directly participate in hostilities on its behalf can be considered to assume a continuous combat function even before he or she first carries out a hostile act.[117]

The Guidance, however, incorporates an additional requirement: the belligerent—regardless of the group—must take a direct part in hostilities. This last hurdle places an additional burden on the state. More perplexing, it eliminates any real difference between the status of being a member of an organized armed group and that of being a civilian who directly participates in hostilities. The example in the Guidance that highlights this additional threshold is an improvised explosive device (IED) maker:

> the assembly and storing of an improvised explosive device (IED) in a workshop, or the purchase or smuggling of its components, may be connected with the resulting harm through an uninterrupted causal chain of events, but, unlike the planting and detonation of that device, do *not* cause that harm directly.[118]

Therefore, according to the Guidance, the IED maker cannot be targeted, even if he is a member of a hostile organized armed group, because the conduct of the individual—*vice* the conduct of the group at large—is not a direct part of the hostilities. And by "direct," the Guidance means "that the harm in question must be brought about in one causal step."[119] The Guidance first establishes a status but then tethers it back to the direct participation in hostilities of the *member* of the organized armed group. It makes direct participation in hostilities the acid test for being a member of an armed organized group: "Individuals who continuously accompany or support an organized armed group, but whose function does not involve direct participation in hostilities, are not members of that group within the meaning of [the law of war]."[120] This additional hurdle "effectively renders all non-state actors civilians who consistently benefit from the presumption of protection from attack."[121]

Under the Guidance's definition, for example, it is questionable whether Mr. al-Awlaki is a member of an organized armed group due to the factual question of whether he has taken a direct part in hostilities. The United States maintains that he plays an operational role in Al Qaeda in the Arabian Peninsula and as such, played

---

[116] Ibid.
[117] Ibid.
[118] Ibid. at 1022.
[119] Ibid. at 1021.
[120] Ibid. at 1008.
[121] Corn and Jenks, *supra* n. 61, 16.

an integral part in planning the destruction of the Northwest flight on Christmas Day.[122] But planning alone might not trigger direct participation. The state must look to the "direct causal link between a specific act and the harm likely to result either from that act, or from a coordinated military operation of which that act constitutes an integral part."[123] But the Commentary to the First Protocol notes, when talking about civilians taking part in hostilities, that "[h]ostile acts should be understood to be acts which by their nature and purpose are intended to cause actual harm to the personnel and equipment of the *armed forces*."[124] The Christmas Day attack was not harm against the armed forces. In addition, if an IED maker does not constitute a civilian taking a direct part in hostilities, then whether someone who instigates another to use violence is such a civilian seems at least questionable.

The ICRC's 2003 response to the criticism that all non-state actors are civilians was eloquently written by Nils Melzer, who focuses on two main approaches. In one approach, Melzer notes that criteria for membership in an organized armed group "can be overextended to include all persons accompanying or supporting that group (i.e., regardless of their function); an excessively wide approach which would completely discard the distinction between 'direct' and 'indirect' participation in hostilities…"[125] The state, under this theory, overextends the pool of individuals against whom it can use force as a measure of first resort. The second approach, which Melzer adopts, is that "the notion of 'organized armed group' can be limited to those persons who represent the functional equivalent of 'combatants' in the regular armed conflict."[126] Hence, if an individual is a member of the state's armed forces, then his function is assumed to involve direct participation in hostilities and he can be targeted. Melzer's approach does not assume that the non-state actor's function involves direct participation of hostilities, but rather requires proof of such a function. If an individual is a member of an organized armed group, then his function within that group must first be established and the required proof is his direct participation in hostilities. For a member of the U.S. armed forces, that function is assumed.

The Guidance is crucial to the debate on non-international armed conflict because it acknowledges that the legal authority to target members of an armed organized group is "based on a fundamentally different presumption than that applicable to civilians directly participating in hostilities."[127] The Guidance has built a structure,

---

[122] Press Release, U.S. Department of State, Listing of Al Qaeda in the Arabian Peninsula (July 20, 2010).

[123] ICRC Guidance, 1019 (defining direct causation).

[124] Commentary to Protocol I, para. 1942 (emphasis added).

[125] Nils Melzer, "Keeping the Balance Between Military Necessity and Humanity: A Response to Four Critiques of the ICRC's Interpretive Guidance on the Notion of Direct Participation in Hostilities," 42 *New York Journal of International Law and Politics*, 831, 850 (Spring 2010).

[126] Ibid.

[127] Corn and Jenks, *supra* n. 61, 16.

much like that in international armed conflict, where there are two different categories of status—civilians and members of an organized armed group. The issue is who should populate each category.

General Kenneth Watkins, the former Judge Advocate General of the Canadian Forces, wrote in critiquing the Guidance, "[t]he decision in 2003 to attempt to define this 25-year-old phrase ["taking a direct part in hostilities"] was undoubtedly influenced by the significant publicity surrounding the use of air power to conduct targeted killing in Yemen, the Occupied Territories, and Iraq."[128] According to Watkins, however, the Guidance "falls short of the mark."[129] It fails to crystallize the law in the much-neglected area of targeting in non-international armed conflict. The ICRC lost an opportunity to provide "workable and practical guidance regarding this longstanding complex problem."[130] On the other hand, the Guidance did provide a roadmap for contending that a status exists in non-international armed conflict that is separate and distinct from both combatants and civilians, as well as the subset of civilians who are taking a direct part in hostilities. The trend to treat everyone in a non-international armed conflict as a civilian— some of whom are uninvolved with the conflict and others who are taking a direct part—is simply rejected by the Guidance.[131]

However, unlike Melzer, General Watkins' test for who is a member of an organized armed group does not begin with an individual's direct participation in hostilities. Instead, he starts with the individual's combat function, which would include "combat, combat support, and combat service support functions, carrying arms openly, exercising command over the armed group, carrying out planning related to the conduct of hostilities, or other activities indicative of membership in an armed group."[132] He highlights that a central factor is whether the organization maintains a command structure; that is, does the organization fight like a group?[133]

Melzer's concern focuses on the individual; if the status is overextended, the civilian who helps the organized armed group on a "spontaneous, sporadic, or unorganized basis"[134] may lose his presumption of protected status. Yet what is missing from Melzer's analysis is the reality that additional facts may lead to a reasonable and compelling conclusion that the individual in question is: (1) a member of an

---

[128] Kenneth Watkins, "Opportunity Lost: Organized Armed Groups and the ICRC Direct Participation in Hostilities Interpretative Guidance," 42 *New York Journal of International Law and Politics* 641, 642 (Spring 2010).

[129] Ibid. at 643.

[130] Ibid. at 645.

[131] Corn and Jenks, *supra* n. 61, 2.

[132] Watkins, *supra* n. 128, 691.

[133] Ibid.

[134] ICRC Guidance, 1007.

organized armed group; (2) performing a combat function within the group; and (3) the group *needs* that member's combat function to perform hostilities.

Melzer's limited focus on the individual and not the organized armed group is flawed. A more precise focus would take account of the organized armed group that is conducting hostilities against the state, and the individuals who fill its ranks. Imagine that an individual, a non-state actor, is an actual member of an armed group whose combat function has inflicted great loss on the state. The state can prove the individual's membership in the organized armed group, but since the individual has not taken direct part in hostilities, the state is obligated not to target that member of the organized armed group. In essence, the threshold to trigger the targetable status of membership in an organized armed group is extremely high and exceedingly narrow. So the IED maker, who is proven to be a member of an organized armed group, and regardless of the destruction his devices cause, continues to hold civilian protections. Conversely, the lone gunman who performs one ambush in combat is targetable. This result is simply not consistent or logical, and it puts U.S. soldiers at grave risk.

A critical shortfall of Melzer's analysis is that he takes the term "direct participation in hostilities"—a term that originates from the status of being a civilian in both the First and Second Protocols—and applies it to a new status of belligerents. Like the armed forces of a state, an organized armed group fights like a group; that is, it has a command structure. The individual civilian, on the other hand, does not. That is the rationale of why the trigger for a civilian to become targetable is the overt act of direct participation in hostilities; it is the danger presented at the time of the direct participation. If the civilian stops directly participating in hostilities, then there is no way to link the individual's acts of violence to an overarching design or plan. The acts of terrorists are not only acts of the individuals who directly do violence, but also the acts of the groups whose planning, command structure, and resources make the acts of violence possible. Melzer's analysis fails to take into account this crucial collective dimension of terrorist violence because he takes a requirement that properly applies only when individual, not collective, violence is in question, namely the "direct participation" requirement, and applies it to a situation in which the collective violence of an organized group is what the law needs to address.

X. A new approach to combat novel warfare

The linkage between the violent designs and acts of an organized armed group, on the one hand, and the acts of its members, on the other, is the crucial consideration which Melzer's analysis fails to adequately address. Like a member of a regular force (a soldier), the member of the armed group is part of a structure whose aim is to inflict violence upon the state. A soldier might never play a direct part in hostilities (many soldiers, in fact, do not), but the soldier holds the status of someone who can be targeted because of his membership in an organization whose function is to perform hostilities. The test for status must be the *threat* posed by the group and the member's course of conduct which allows that threat to persist.

Non-state actors should be targeted only if membership in the organized armed group can be positively established by the state though a pattern of conduct demonstrating a military function.[135] This logic would make it analogous to the soldier: the soldier is a danger and presents one continuously because of his status. Once a state demonstrates membership in an organized armed group, then the members should be presumed to be a continuous danger as well.

If the focus is only on the member's direct hostile acts, then organized armed groups will inevitably compartmentalize their operations. The armed group will section off its base of training and preparation from its fighters—thereby separating the two so as not to trigger the causal step—because the former is protected. Accordingly, one might suggest that the law should anticipate any such strategic response by the group by presuming that anyone who enables the group to plan and execute its violent acts is open to attack.

This suggested approach runs the risk of being overbroad, however. Merely because an individual *supports* an organized armed group, such as a villager who serves as a lookout for the armed group but is not a member of the group, does not mean that the individual loses his status as a civilian. To avoid this risk but still provide the state with the flexibility to combat terrorism, the law of war must evolve and innovate to delineate between the civilian taking direct part in hostilities and the member of the organized armed group.

XI. Redefining "member of an organized armed group"

To retake the initiative in combating terrorism, the law of war must focus on the middle ground, looking at *both* the organized armed group and the *conduct* of the individual within that group to reach a reasoned conclusion that the individual is a member of the group. Therefore, the steps the state should take to reach the conclusion that an individual is targetable based on his status as a member of an organized armed group are threefold. First, the state must determine whether the group that is combating the state is organized and armed. Second, the state must demonstrate that the individual is a member of that group as evidenced by a pattern of conduct which demonstrates a military function. And third, the state must ensure that the protections of the surrounding civilians are honored when the member of the organized armed group, now a belligerent, is targeted.

---

[135] Watkins, *supra* n. 128, 692.

Accordingly, the test of whether a civilian in a non-international armed conflict has lost his protection and is now a targetable belligerent based on status should read:

> For purposes of the principle of distinction in non-international armed conflict, all persons who are not members of State armed forces or organized armed groups of a party to the conflict are civilians and therefore entitled to protection against direct attack unless and for such time as they take a direct part in hostilities. In non-international armed conflict, organized armed groups constitute the armed forces of a non-State party to the conflict and consist only of individuals who are members of the group. Membership is established by a totality of conduct showing that the member is contributing to a military function of the group.

(a) Step one: Is it an armed organized group?[136]

First, in deciding if the group targeting the state is armed, intelligence and self-pronouncements can decipher whether the group uses or intends to use lethal means. Some groups are hostile to the state's interest but use only political means to accomplish their ends.[137] Second, and most important in the global war against transnational terrorism: is the armed group organized? The question asked by General Watkins is central to this determination: is there a command structure? This element must be established by intelligence and the group's practices. The group's coherence does not need to be robust but it must meet the threshold tests of whether (1) there is a level of leadership and (2) that leadership exercises command and control over its members. These tests address whether the organization operates in a military-like capacity; therefore, its primary function is violence or the threat of violence.[138]

(b) Step two: Who fills the ranks of the organized armed group?

If the group is organized and armed, then the state must determine who constitutes its members. In this step, membership is established, and civilian protection is lost, if the individual engages in a military function. This function is established by a pattern of conduct. While General Watkins ties organized armed group status to the *individual*'s direct participation in hostilities ("[a]fter the first involvement, any subsequent act demonstrating direct participation would start to provide that basis to believe that there is the beginning of a pattern of conduct that reflects an intention to regularly engage in the hostilities."),[139] the individual's direct participation in hostilities should be but one indication,

---

[136] For purposes of this chapter, armed conflict with a group like Al Qaeda is presumed between the state and the group.

[137] e.g., the Mothers of the Plaza de Mayo of Argentina protesting the "disappeared" children of the Dirty Wars. John Charles Chasteen, *Born in Blood & Fire: A Concise History of Latin America* (New York: W.W. Norton and Company, 2006) 290.

[138] It is the opinion of the author that all of these are low-threshold issues to meet, given the ease of broadcast (to create the group), the speed of communication (to organize the group); and the lack of expense to acquire weapons (to arm the group). But the analysis must be done by the state.

[139] Watkins, *supra* n. 128, 692.

albeit a significant one, among many to establish the non-state actor's membership in the armed group. In other words, the military functions performed by the actor, when taken as a whole, must establish a reasonable conclusion that the individual is a member of the organized armed group. The military functions include combat (taking a direct part in hostilities), combat support (intelligence, communication, and engineering), and combat service support (logistics). Other indicia would be carrying arms openly, carrying out planning related to the conduct of hostilities,[140] and "whether the individual functions or participates within or under the command structure of the organization—i.e., whether [the individual] receives and executes orders or directions…"[141]

Therefore, membership in the armed group is determined by the totality of the circumstances known to the state at the time the individual is targeted. This requires a case-by-case analysis because the enemy in the war on terrorism does not wear a distinctive uniform or insignia. The covertness makes determining those who are belligerents and civilians difficult, and intelligence will be crucial in distinguishing one from the other. But if a non-state actor is making IEDs that the group then uses to inflict damage upon the state, then a "combat support" function, which is a subset of a military function, is established, which, in turn, supports the state's evidence that he is a belligerent (member of an organized armed group) and therefore can be lawfully targeted because membership is present at the time of the engagement.[142]

(c) Step three: Minimizing civilian casualties

The third step is that when a state determines that a member of an armed group is targetable, it must also establish that the risk of civilian casualties will not exceed the concrete and direct military advantage anticipated.[143] This effort to minimize civilian casualties also drives the state to use munitions that are as precise as possible. These limits will ensure that there will be fewer civilian deaths; when the state ensures that civilian deaths are limited, the support of the civilian population is more likely.[144]

---

[140] Ibid. at 691.

[141] *Hamlily v. Obama*, 616 F. Supp. 2d 63, 75 (D.D.C. May 19, 2009) (citing *Gherebi v. Obama*, 609 F. Supp. 2d 43, 68–9 (D.D.C. April 22, 2009)).

[142] Watkins, "Opportunity Lost," *supra* n. 128, 693. A non-state actor shifts the burden back on the state by showing he is no longer a member of the organized armed group. Although not fully discussed in this chapter, the author believes a starting place of analysis would be analogous to the defense of withdrawal within the law of conspiracy. In order to withdraw from a conspiracy, a person must have taken an affirmative action to disavow the purpose of the conspiracy (ceased his military function) and he must have taken such action before he or any other member of the scheme had committed any overt act (ceased taking part in hostilities). *United States v. Read*, 658 F.2d 1225 (7th Cir. Ill. 1981). The best articulation of this principle is the Israeli Supreme Court's definition of what constitutes "for such time." See *supra* nn. 18–20.

[143] AP I, art. 51(5)(b).

[144] Tactical Directive, Headquarters International Security Assistance Force (July 2, 2009).

The driving force of any law must be to target those who pose a threat—members of the organized armed group—and not to harm those who are truly civilians.

There is a danger that the state's analysis could be overbroad, but to militate against this, the state must begin from the perspective that everyone is a civilian. The burden is on the state to establish membership by a pattern of conduct that the individual is performing a military function. The villager previously mentioned is assumed to be a protected civilian. If the facts reveal, however, that the villager's lookout function is continuous, that intelligence shows he not only holds allegiance to the armed group but also informs the armed group of the location of the state's armed force, and that he receives instructions from the armed group on what to do next, then the state can make the case that he is a member of the organized armed group. Not to allow the state to establish membership in an armed group in such cases as the villager providing integral intelligence to the armed group means the state can never target the person in question absent his direct hostile participation. Instead, the only option for the state is to resort to the law-enforcement paradigm, where the burden is again upon the state to return the situation back to the status quo so the villager can be arrested and potentially tried. This course of action not only affords armed groups protections they have not earned because of their flagrant disregard for the law of war, it also gives them the time and space to redirect their lethality on others within the state. The state is relegated to using law-enforcement norms, which are intended to prioritize the protection afforded an individual, in an armed-conflict setting. In other words, the terrorists' violations accrue to their benefit.

If the civilized world is to retake the upper hand in combating terrorism, it will not be done using law-enforcement norms during an armed conflict, especially in states with weak governance, in which the terrorists take advantage of the situation by intentionally violating the rules while the state must follow them. Terrorists are given an enormous strategic advantage in the present scheme. Instead, the established law of war must evolve to combat this ever-evolving warfare against states.

XII. Mr. al-Awlaki's status?

Al-Awlaki's status would most likely be different under the revised definition of what entails a member of an organized armed group; his pattern of conduct that he is performing a military function would give him the status of being a member of the group. He is now targetable. This pattern would need to be established through facts that show a military function. It is the obligation of the state—in this case, the United States—to establish the facts: al-Awlaki's degree of involvement in the Fort Hood rampage; the degree of support and aid he gave to Abdulutallab in the attempted Christmas Day airliner attack; and his other attempts to use violence against the United States and his function within those efforts. The United States has taken the position that al Awlaki's pattern of conduct justifies his targeting but again, the case-by-case analysis must be done.

XIII. Conclusion

The soldier is trained from day one to know the difference between conduct and status. The difference is profound: one puts the responsibility upon the soldier, the other upon the state. In the current asymmetric warfare environment, everyone, including the terrorist, is assumed to be a protected civilian. This gives terrorists the advantage. But the law of war already gives the state a means to develop criteria to categorize individuals as belligerents; now the law of war must be moved forward to give the state an advantage over the terrorists (or at least to level the playing field). At present, the terrorists wage unrestricted armed conflict against the state, while the state is relegated to using law enforcement against the terrorists. The next evolution of the law of war must make sense in the context of the ongoing armed conflict and not be so onerous that it makes categorizing individuals as belligerents virtually impossible. Tethering a non-state actor's action to how it supports an organized armed group, through a military function evidenced by a pattern of conduct, does that. It protects the individual who is a civilian, because the presumption is that everyone is a civilian, but allows the state to establish belligerency by identifiable criteria and structure. Once this criterion is met, the state can legally and justifiably use force against an actual danger.

In sum, the civilian who eschews taking part in the armed conflict has greater protection than ever before in history because states must use precision to minimize civilian harm. But this protection should extend only to civilians worthy of this status; members of organized armed groups should lose that status. The civilian who participates in armed conflict by performing a combat function for an armed organized group cannot be hostile at one moment and then expect to regain civilian status protections the next. Such a result would undermine the protection of civilians because it stands the law of war framework on its head: states will put less of a premium on precision because distinction is either unrealistic or non-existent. Status is paramount, but the distinction principle should be interpreted so that a non-state actor's pattern of conduct can rebut the presumption that he is a civilian. This understanding of the principle will push members of organized armed groups to recognize that they, like soldiers, will be lawfully targeted and their efforts to hide in the civilian population will not be enabled by the law of war. The conduct of a member of an organized armed group should result in a corresponding status: if he serves a military function, then he should have the status of a belligerent who can be lawfully killed by enemy forces. The U.S. soldier understands the profound significance of status; the time has come for states to follow suit.

2

TARGETING CO-BELLIGERENTS

Jens David Ohlin

I. Introduction

The current debate about targeted killings has revolved around the central divide between *jus ad bellum* and *jus in bello*. Either the launching of a drone strike is considered a defensive use of force to be evaluated under the traditional rules of self-defense under Article 51 of the UN Charter, or the drone strike is to be evaluated under the rules of warfare codified in international humanitarian law.[1] The prohibition against the killing of civilians is of particular concern here. Of course, the two issues are not mutually exclusive. One can coherently claim that drone strikes satisfy the demands of *jus ad bellum* but fail to live up to the requirements of *jus in bello*, and are therefore illegal.[2] The reverse is possible as well. One might conclude that targeted killings do not run afoul of international humanitarian law (IHL) but violate the core *ad bellum* prohibition against the unlawful use of force codified in the UN Charter. These are all logical permutations of the argument.

At a conceptual level, international law is deeply conflicted about how to handle targeted killings; the issue falls between the state-based system of public international law and the individualized system of domestic criminal law. The former contemplates armed conflicts between combatants who open themselves up to the reciprocal risk of killing; the latter contemplates killings in self-defense only when

---

[1] *See*, e.g., Mary Ellen O'Connell, "Unlawful Killing with Combat Drones: A Case Study of Pakistan, 2004–2009" in Simon Bronitt ed., *Shooting to Kill: The Law Governing Lethal Force in Context* (Hart Publishing, forthcoming) (concluding that targeted killings violate both spheres of the law of war); Philip Alston, Special Rapporteur on Extrajudicial, Summary or Arbitrary Executions, *Report of the Special Rapporteur on Extrajudicial, Summary or Arbitrary Execution: Study on Targeted Killings, delivered to the Human Rights Council*, U.N. Doc. A/HRC/14/24/Add.6 (May 28, 2010).

[2] *Cf.* Jordan J. Paust, "Self-Defense Targetings of Non-State Actors and Permissibility of U.S. Use of Drones in Pakistan," 19 *J. Transnational Law and Policy* (2010) 237 (concluding that drone strikes are a valid exercise of self-defense).

the traditional progression of arrest, trial, and punishment is unavailable. Because the terrorist is a non-state actor who falls between these two categories, the current law has had difficulty not only providing a positive rule regarding the legality of targeted killings, but also definitively choosing the correct paradigm. Even the application of traditional rules of IHL to the activity remains contested, since such an application presupposes that one paradigm has been selected over the other.[3] It may even be the case that no positive rule of customary international law has crystallized to govern the practice.[4]

Assuming, *arguendo*, that some form of targeted killing is permissible in some situations, a central and deeply contested question remains: who can be targeted and why? The selection of paradigms again structures our natural intuitions about the answer. Those concerned with national security are inclined to view the question through the lens of the laws of war, where all bona fide combatants are assumed to be targetable with lethal force. Those concerned with civil liberties are inclined to view the question through the lens of the criminal law (or domestic law more generally), where a judge or jury determines outcomes based on a rigorous fact-finding process, and where capture and punishment—not killing—is the default norm. The question of targeting straddles the tension between national security and civil liberties and it is unclear how it can (or should) be resolved.

This chapter investigates the tension between national security and civil liberties through a distinctive conceptual framework: what linking principle can be used to connect the targeted individual with the collective group that represents the security threat? Section II will explain and defend this methodology by demonstrating that no account of targeted killing—whether sounding in *jus in bello* or *jus ad bellum*—can be complete without making explicit reference to a linking principle. Section III will then proceed to catalog five major linking principles—taken from different domains of law including the use of force, international humanitarian law, and criminal law—that could potentially serve that function: direct participation, co-belligerency, membership, control, and complicity/conspiracy. Section IV will then conclude with a comparative evaluation of the linking principles that exposes their strengths and weaknesses.

The resulting conclusion will be counter-intuitive to readers accustomed to the standard positions in the literature. Although one would think that criminal law principles, with their strict adherence to conduct rules and culpability, would result in the greatest maximization of civil liberties, this intuition is not realized once the criminal law principles are divorced from their traditional legal process:

---

[3] See Gabriella Blum and Philip Heymann, "Law and Policy of Targeted Killing," 1 *Harvard National Security Journal* (2010) 145 (comparing two paradigms: war and exceptional peacetime operations).

[4] See *S.S. Lotus (France v. Turkey)*, 1927 P.C.I.J. (ser. A) No. 10, at 18.

the courtroom. The question of who can be targeted (and the individual's relationship to the collective) requires a more nuanced response, one that uses the legal concepts developed for the law of war, but properly reformulated to take into account the realities of asymmetrical warfare with non-state terrorist organizations. The legal concepts developed for use in criminal trials provide false comfort that one is respecting civil liberties, but ironically they offer fewer protections. In the end, reformulated and redefined law of war principles, with their reliance on status concepts and proxies such as membership, do the job better because the concepts are comparatively more public, transparent, and self-administering than their competitors in the criminal law.

II. The problem of linking

Regardless of which paradigm is selected, there is inevitably a deep conceptual puzzle that straddles both sides of the fundamental divide between *jus ad bellum* and *jus in bello*. In both cases, it is unlikely that the single individual who is targeted—in isolation—satisfies the demands of either argument. The individual must be linked to a larger collective—a larger belligerent force—that explains the relevancy of the single individual. This linking requirement is a function of both the *jus ad bellum* and *jus in bello* analyses; for example, one cannot simply avoid the linking issue by switching from *jus ad bellum* to *jus in bello* or vice versa.

Within the context of *jus ad bellum*, the traditional argument for a drone attack relies on the international doctrine of self-defense, recognized in Article 51 of the UN Charter but also certainly recognized in customary law as well as the just war tradition.[5] The United States has argued publicly that its drone attacks in Yemen, Pakistan, and Afghanistan are supported by the doctrine of self-defense.[6] However, under any version of the principle of self-defense—whether expounded by public international lawyers or legal philosophers—the target of the defensive counter-attack must constitute a threat to the United States or its allies.[7] The underlying threat makes the defensive force "necessary"—a universally recognized constraint

---

[5] Compare Legal Consequences of the Construction of a Wall in the Occupied Palestinian Territory, Advisory Opinion, (*Advisory Opinion on the Wall*) 2004 I.C.J. 136, 189, 194 (July 9, 2004) (no international right of self-defense against non-state actors), with Armed Activities on the Territory of the Congo (*Dem. Rep. Congo v. Uganda*), 2005 I.C.J. 168, 222–6 (December 19). *See also* Mary Ellen O'Connell, "The Legal Case Against the Global War on Terror," 36 *Case Western Reserve Journal of International Law* (2004) 349.

[6] See Harold H. Koh, U.S. Department of State, *The Obama Administration and International Law*, Annual Meeting of the American Society of International Law, Washington, DC (March 25, 2010), available at <http://www.state.gov/s/l/releases/remarks/139119.htm> accessed November 4, 2011.

[7] See Ian Brownlie, *Principles of Public International Law*, 7th edn (Oxford University Press, 2008) 732–3.

on the use of force in self-defense under either basic principles of criminal law or international law.[8] The notion that self-defense is a necessary response to a threat is part of the universal structure of self-defense arguments in any legal or moral context.[9]

My point here is not to advocate for any particular version of what constitutes a "threat"—nor what makes a defensive response to it "necessary." These are sticky theoretical questions that form the center of most debates about self-defense. Rather, the issue I want to explore is one level deeper. Regardless of one's assessment of what constitutes a threat to a state's interests—territorial integrity, political independence, etc—it is unlikely that a single individual, by himself or herself, can constitute a threat against a state. It is *theoretically* possible to imagine a hypothetical terrorist who works alone, secretly plotting a devastating attack against a state by procuring weapons and then deploying them without any assistance whatsoever. The Unabomber is one such example, and it is the exception that proves the rule.[10]

The more common situation involves the existence of a terrorist organization or militia that constitutes a threat by plotting and implementing terrorist or military attacks against a particular state. In such cases, the *collective* constitutes the threat against the national interest, thus generating the right of self-defense. Furthermore, the individual stands in a certain relationship with the collective, either by belonging to the terrorist organization, contributing to the collective endeavor, or some other mode of participation in the collective group.[11] For the moment we must postpone consideration of which linking principle is most appropriate. The point here is simply that individuals acting alone almost never constitute a national threat. Within the War on Terror and the asymmetrical use of targeted killings against non-state actors, an even stronger conclusion is warranted: single individuals *never* constitute a threat to the United States. The threat comes from organized groups with political or ideological objectives that they seek to bring about by launching attacks against civilians. This is the raison d'être of global terrorism and jihadism.

Shifting the focus to *jus in bello* does not relieve us of the obligation to find an appropriate linking principle. If terrorists are simply enemy civilians, without any

---

[8] Ibid. at 734 (citing *Caroline* case).

[9] On the structural similarity of the necessity prong in both national and individual self-defense, see G.P Fletcher and J.D. Ohlin, *Defending Humanity: When Force is Justified and Why* (Oxford University Press, 2008) 91–6.

[10] Indeed, for some theorists, the isolated and individualistic nature of the Unabomber's criminal activities precludes applying to him the label of terrorist, a term usually reserved for organizational efforts. *See,* e.g., George P. Fletcher, "The Indefinable Concept of Terrorism," 4 *J. International Criminal Justice* (2006) 894, 907–08 (organization as one element of the family-resemblance concept of terrorism).

[11] For a discussion of participation in collective endeavors, see generally Christopher Kutz, *Complicity: Ethics and Law for a Collective Age* (Cambridge University Press, 2000).

relationship to a larger collective, then no operative principle of IHL permits their summary killing.[12] It is only when their relationship to a larger collective is considered that the use of force against them may be permissible. Under traditional rules of IHL, combatants may be killed to the extent that they belong to an armed fighting force that is engaged in an armed conflict with the United States.[13] Indeed, it is the collective's engaging of the armed conflict with the United States that triggers the operation of the IHL norm allowing combatants to be killed. But it is an open question whether IHL recognizes the existence of an armed conflict with a non-state actor, and whether this is best described as an international armed conflict triggering the Geneva Conventions, a non-international armed conflict triggering Common Article 3 of the same, or neither, thus generating conflict regarding the appropriate default rule in the absence of any governing Geneva Convention regime.[14]

In this context, there are multiple problems associated with linking an individual to the larger terrorist organization that is engaged in an armed conflict with the United States. First, the United States is currently engaged in an armed conflict (international or non-international) with Al Qaeda, but the individuals targeted by US drones may or may not be card-carrying members of Al Qaeda.[15] Indeed, although Al Qaeda may once have been a defined and tightly knit organization controlled by Osama bin Laden, the organization has morphed into an amorphous network of terrorist organizations operating under the common banner of Al Qaeda.[16] In rare instances, various local terrorist organizations operating under the name Al Qaeda may share operational or financial support from their parent organization, and may even respond to hierarchical commands issued by bin Laden himself or his commanders.

In most cases, however, terrorist organizations operating under the banner of Al Qaeda in some form are part of a much looser confederacy of co-sympathetic jihadists who share common inspiration and rhetoric without sharing a common command

---

[12] See Dieter Fleck, *The Handbook of International Humanitarian Law*, 2nd edn (Oxford University Press, 2008) 46 ("The outbreak of an armed conflict between two states will lead to many of the rules of ordinary law of peace being superseded, as between the parties to the conflict, by the rules of humanitarian law.")

[13] Ibid. at 82. *See also* Richard Murphy and Afsheen John Radsan, "Due Process and Targeted Killing of Terrorists," 32 *Cardozo Law Review* (2009) 405, 416.

[14] See, e.g., *Hamdan v. Rumsfeld*, 548 U.S. 557, 630 (2006) (conflict with Al Qaeda is a non-international armed conflict falling under Common Article 3). For a discussion, see D. Glazier, "Full and Fair by What Measure?: Identifying the International Law Regulating Military Commission Procedure," 24 *Boston University International Law Journal* (2006) 55, 60 ("Recognizing that the terrorism conflict does not fit particularly well with traditional classifications of either 'international' or 'non-international' armed conflict, it concludes that this war is instead best defined as 'transnational'.")

[15] See O'Connell, *supra* n. 1, 10–11.

[16] See Manooher Mofidi and Amy E. Eckert, "'Unlawful Combatants' or ''Prisoners of War': The Law and Politics of Labels," 36 *Cornell International Law Journal* (2003) 59, 82.

structure or operational command.[17] They are distinct terrorist organizations linked together by a common cause. It is therefore unclear if the existence of an armed conflict with one Al Qaeda organization can translate into an armed conflict with another sympathetic Al Qaeda organization.[18] In some instances, both organizations may be sufficiently well developed that each, on its own terms, meets the appropriate standard for being engaged in an armed conflict with the United States. In other contexts, however, the over-arching umbrella between the organizations may be crucial for our legal determination of an armed conflict with the United States. This is particularly true in cases where one terrorist organization is well developed and clearly engaged in an armed conflict, but the second organization is a nascent and burgeoning endeavor that has not yet launched significant attacks.

III. Five possible linking principles

The preceding analysis suggests that both the *jus ad bellum* and the *jus in bello* analyses suffer from a deeper confusion about how to relate the individual terrorist with the larger collective. Attacking the problem in this manner will help expose the deeper question of how to integrate the non-state actor—and the individual terrorist—into the inherently collective nature of public international law and the laws of war that arise from it. We should therefore consider all of the possible linking principles and consider which best describes the particular role and function of the individual terrorist. The possible linking principles include: direct participation in an armed conflict, military membership, co-belligerency, control, complicity, and conspiracy.[19] A comparative evaluation of the linking principles will cut across the *jus ad bellum–jus in bello* divide.

(a) Direct participation in an armed conflict

Under a standard *jus in bello* analysis, civilians are generally protected from the reciprocal risk of killing that governs the relations of enemy soldiers.[20] Obviously, though, this protection can be opportunistically exploited by civilians who use their protected status to pursue attacks without subjecting themselves to reciprocal risk.[21] Such a system of perfidy would create a perverse incentive: soldiers would have no incentive to identify themselves as soldiers—the only consequence of their identification would be one of exposure. Consequently, traditional rules of *jus in*

---

[17] See, e.g., *United States v. Mustafa*, 406 Fed. Appx. 526 (2nd Cir. 2011).

[18] For a discussion, see Curtis A. Bradley and Jack L. Goldsmith, "Congressional Authorization and the War on Terrorism," 118 *Harvard Law Review* (2005) 2047, 2112.

[19] The list of linking principles is not meant to be exhaustive, but rather to include a representative cross-section of the relevant types.

[20] See Fleck, *supra* n. 12, 96–7, 237–8.

[21] Ibid. at 80.

bello deny protected status to civilians who directly participate in the armed conflict.[22] The functional justification for this rule is obvious: civilians who engage in combatancy are functionally equivalent to traditional combatants and ought to be treated similarly; that is, ought to be subject to attack. This rule is now codified in Article 51(3) of Additional Protocol 1, which states that "civilians shall enjoy the protection afforded by this section, unless and for such time as they take a direct part in hostilities."[23]

The concept of "direct participation" links the individual to the collective fighting force that is engaged in hostilities. The protection is not lost simply by virtue of holding a gun.[24] If the linking principle merely required the use of weapons, it would have stated that. Rather, the linking principle establishes a quasi-causal relation between the non-protected civilian and the larger armed conflict. Unfortunately, though, nobody really knows what constitutes "direct participation" in an armed conflict. The term is undefined in the Additional Protocol and there is little case law on the subject. The International Committee of the Red Cross (ICRC) notes that it is clear that the "lawfulness of an attack on a civilian depends on what exactly constitutes direct participation in hostilities and, related thereto, when direct participation begins and when it ends . . . [but] the meaning of direct participation in hostilities has not yet been clarified," and concedes that a legal definition of the term does not even exist.[25] The *ICRC Commentary* cites the Inter-American Commission on Human Rights for the proposition that the concept of "direct participation" in hostilities means "acts which, by their nature or purpose, are intended to cause actual harm to enemy personnel and material."[26] Although this interpretation of the concept has some intuitive appeal, it reduces it to a causal criterion—not an inherently objectionable result, although the *type* and *closeness* of causal relation is left similarly undefined.

As any good lawyer knows, the real issue is never whether causation is present or not, but rather what type of causation (but-for, proximate, etc) and whether the causation between the act in question and the desired consequence is close enough to meet the applicable standard. Many genuinely civilian actions that patriotically

---

[22] See International Committee of the Red Cross, *Customary International Humanitarian Law* (Cambridge University Press, 2005) vol. I, 19–24 (hereafter cited as *ICRC Commentary*).

[23] See Protocol Additional to the Geneva Conventions of August 12, 1949, and Relating to the Protection of Victims of International Armed Conflicts (Additional Protocol I), adopted June 8, 1977, art. 51(3), 1125 U.N.T.S. 3.

[24] Even civilians retain the right of individual self-defense, which might be one reason to retain small arms even in a conflict zone. This complicates the ascription of combatancy to individuals carrying weapons—a particular problem during the recent fighting in Libya. See, e.g., Thom Shanker and Charlie Savage, "NATO Warns Libyan Rebels Against Attacking Civilians," *New York Times* (March 31, 2011).

[25] See *ICRC Commentary, supra* n. 22, vol. 1, 21.

[26] Ibid., vol. II, 114.

support a nation's interest would eventually and predictably cause some harm to enemy personnel, but no one would ever suggest that they constitute direct participation in hostilities.[27]

One can imagine a spectrum of participatory acts. At one end of the spectrum are acts that unquestionably represent acts of combatancy, such as firing a weapon at the enemy. No one doubts that this constitutes direct participation. At the other end of the spectrum, one might place activities such as a civilian seamstress who sews uniforms in a civilian factory that will one day be worn by soldiers. Or consider the cook who resides far from the battlefield and makes frozen food, some of which will be sold to the military for inclusion in MREs (Meals Ready to Eat). This clearly does not rise to the level of direct participation. In the middle of the spectrum are the hard cases: the civilian contractor who repairs a tank on the battlefield, or the civilian defense department employee who helps design or deploy a new weapons system. Are these individuals directly participating in hostilities?[28]

One way to get a handle on direct participation is to compare it with indirect participation. The *ICRC Commentary* cites the Inter-American Commission on Human Rights for the proposition that "mere support" of the military effort by civilian personnel—including commercial sales and "expressing sympathy for the cause of one of the parties"—constitutes *indirect* participation.[29] The asserted rationale for this conclusion is that these forms of participation do not involve "acts of violence which pose an immediate threat of actual harm to the adverse party."[30] The concept of immediacy appears to be doing all of the work here, though it is unclear if immediacy is as significant as the Inter-American Commission believes it to be. Similarly, the ICRC notes that a draft statute for the future International Criminal Court defined participating in hostilities to include scouting, spying, and sabotage, but excluded food deliveries and household domestic staff "in an officer's married accommodation."[31]

At Nuremberg, Streicher, Goebels, and others who ran the Nazi propaganda effort were held responsible for aiding the Nazi war machine.[32] Indeed, Streicher was charged with criminal responsibility for his writings, which in today's legal climate would have been described as direct and public incitement to commit genocide, in

---

[27] *Cf.* Michael Walzer, *Just and Unjust Wars*, 3d edn (Basic Books, 2000) 146.
[28] The United States Naval Handbook states that guards, lookouts, and intelligence acts all meet the direct participation standard. See *ICRC Commentary*, *supra* n. 22, vol. 1, 22.
[29] Ibid., vol. II, 114 (citing Third Report on Human Rights in Columbia, Doc. OEA/Ser.L/V/II.102 Doc. 9 rev. 1, February 26, 1999, paras 53–6).
[30] Ibid.
[31] *ICRC Commentary*, *supra* n. 22, vol. II, 116.
[32] Reifenstahl might also be included in that list, though she was never prosecuted for her films.

the words of the Rome Statute.[33] When NATO bombed Serb positions in order to pressure Serbia to withdraw forces from Kosovo, the targets included Serbian state television and other elements of the state's communications regime.[34] Although reasonable persons can disagree over the permissibility of these attacks, I take it that the disagreement stems more from the civilian nature of the employees at the state television station, rather than the indirect nature of their causal contribution to the war effort. In many of these situations, the causal role played by the non-military civilians is quite substantial and might even be described as direct.[35] Perhaps this is the reason that the US Naval Handbook simply concludes that the direct participation standard "must be judged on a case-by-case basis."[36]

The ICRC's latest effort, its *Interpretative Guidance on Direct Participation in Hostilities*, also cashes out the concept in causal terms.[37] Indeed, according to the ICRC, the word "direct" in the legal standard explicitly refers to direct causation as opposed to indirect causation.[38] According to the ICRC's metaphysics, a direct causal result implies that the "harm in question must be brought about in one causal step."[39] In applying this standard, the *ICRC Interpretative Guidance* concludes that building or maintaining the fighting capacity of one party to the conflict is not sufficiently direct because it is a two-step process. Even recruitment of combatants and their military training are excluded because they are two-step processes.[40] Temporal and geographic proximity may imply causal proximity, but they do not wholly determine it, since an action could (in theory) directly cause a particular harm far removed in time and space.[41]

---

[33] *See* Judgment, Streicher, "International Military Tribunal at Nuremberg; D.F. Orentlicher, Criminalizing Hate Speech in the Crucible of Trial: *Prosecutor v. Nahimana*," 21 *American University Int'l L. Rev.* (2006) 557, 582–3.

[34] Final Report to the Prosecutor by the Committee Established to Review the NATO Bombing Campaign Against the Federal Republic of Yugoslavia, 39 I.L.M. 1257 (2000).

[35] *Cf.* Sandoz, Swinarski and Zimmerman, *Commentary on the Additional Protocols* (Martinus Nijhoff Publishers, 1987) 619 (discussing distinction between direct participation in hostilities and the more general participation in the war effort and noting that "even the morale of the population plays a role in this context," but concluding that without a distinction between direct and general participation "international humanitarian law could become meaningless").

[36] *See ICRC Commentary, supra* n. 22, vol. I, 24. However, the US Air Force handbook offers additional examples: civilian ground observers that report the approach of hostile aircraft and rescuers of downed military airmen. *See* ibid., vol. II, 117.

[37] *ICRC Interpretative Guidance* (International Committee of the Red Cross, 2009), 1019 (requiring a "direct causal link between a specific act and the harm likely to result either from that act, or from a coordinated military operation of which that act constitutes an integral part.").

[38] Ibid. at 1021.

[39] Ibid.

[40] Ibid. at 1022 (but concluding that if recruitment and training are for a particular hostile act, these activities are considered "integral" to the hostile act and therefore stand in a one-step causal relation to the harm).

[41] Ibid. at 1023.

The direct participation standard is difficult to apply to terrorists, and there is currently little uniform state practice that would shed light on the content of the alleged customary norm. On the one hand, some nations take a purely causal approach to the notion, whereby any civilian who contributes to the armed conflict loses protected status. For example, India believes that any person who "contributes towards the furtherance of armed conflict" is no longer a protected civilian.[42] On the other hand, some countries conclude that "persons who merely provided support to the enemy…for example those who supplied it with weapons, food or medicine," do not lose their protected status.[43] In between, some nations recognize the inherent ambiguity and lack of clarity in the standard. For example, Israeli practice notes that the carrying of arms is not a sufficient condition for losing protected status, since in many locations (for example, Lebanon), civilians routinely carry firearms even though they have nothing to do with the hostilities, though the Israel report notes that "when returning fire, it is extremely difficult (and probably unwise from a military viewpoint) to differentiate between those individuals actually firing their firearms and those just carrying them."[44]

The ambiguity becomes starker when one considers another linking principle that is often applied to terrorists: providing material support to terrorists. The United States considers this to be a war crime and a violation of both federal and international law.[45] Does providing material support for terrorism constitute direct participation in hostilities? Did Hamdan "directly participate" in the hostilities because he was driving Osama bin Laden?[46] The thing about providing material support is that it rests squarely on the shoulders of a causal contribution to the larger effort. If the individual's actions make a terrorist attack more likely—for example, if he aids or abets the larger effort—then the individual has provided material support to terrorism.[47] Consequently, providing financial support or engaging in advocacy on behalf of a terrorist cause can constitute material support, since terrorist activities require far more than just brute operational support.[48] Many other forms of support are required to bring a terrorist plan to fruition. But providing financial support or ideological advocacy is a far cry from a *direct* participation in hostilities. What is missing is not a causal link, but the *right kind* of causal link.

---

[42] Ibid. at vol. II, 109.

[43] Ibid. at vol. II, 121.

[44] Ibid. at vol. II, 120–1. *See also* Shanker and Savage, *supra* n. 24, 175.

[45] 18 U.S.C. §§ 2339A and 2339B.

[46] *Cf.* George P. Fletcher, "On the Crimes Subject to Prosecution in Military Commissions," 5 *Journal of International Criminal Justice* (2007) 39.

[47] Ibid. ("Virtually any aid or assistance to an organization labeled terrorist would be sufficient to trigger liability. Under these provisions, Bin Laden's driver would clearly be guilty for providing 'transportation.' Anyone who contributes money to terrorist organizations (or one so denominated) is guilty.").

[48] *Holder v. Humanitarian Law Project*, 130 S. Ct. 2705, 2720 (2010).

Although everyone agrees that direct participation requires the right kind of causal link, distinguishing between a direct and indirect causal contribution is far from easy. The "one-step" view espoused by the *ICRC Interpretative Guidance* appears to boil down to the idea that the causal contribution must be operational and on the battlefield, while indirect contributions emanate from beyond the confines of battlefield activity as they have been traditionally defined.[49] But this is not so obvious.[50] Directness appeals to the closeness of the causal route, which may or may not accord with a battlefield movement. It is, for example, possible to envision a close financial connection as well as a remote battlefield connection. Each of these possibilities puts pressure on our intuition that the concept of directness correlates essentially with prototypical battlefield activity.[51] In other words, the *closeness* of the causal connection and the *shape* of the causal route can slip apart. An individual might engage in activity that has only a remote bearing on the hostilities (for example, bearing a weapon when there is no enemy in sight), but the relation between the action and the hostilities can be seen in a straight line. In contrast, an individual might engage in activity that has a strong correlation with the hostilities (for example, transporting a crucial weapon that will change the tide of the battle), but the relation between the action and the hostilities involves a comparatively more circuitous route. At first glance, it is not clear whether the causal element of the direct participation standard ought to be understood with regard to closeness or shape.[52]

(b) Co-belligerency under the law of neutrality

Another solution to the linking problem is to employ the doctrine of co-belligerency from the well-traveled law of neutrality.[53] Under this doctrine, states

---

[49] See *ICRC Interpretative Guidance, supra* n. 37, 1021 (defending one-step causal criterion over allegedly wider alternatives such as "materially facilitating harm").

[50] The one-step view of causation was controversial among the ICRC working group members. Compare, e.g., Michael N. Schmitt, "Deconstructing Direct Participation in Hostilities: The Constitutive Elements", 42 *N.Y.U. Journal of International Law & Policy* (2010) 697, 727, *with* Melzer, "Keeping the Balance," *supra* n. 67, 865–8 (defending one-step causal relation). In particular, Melzer concludes that Schmitt's more permissive definition of causation amounts to an "unlimited causal chain" that would extend as far downstream as the causal relation extends, including individuals who design, manufacture, and store weaponry. Ibid. at 868. Melzer concludes that although this wide causal criterion would be appropriate for ex post determination of *criminal* responsibility, it is inappropriate for an ex ante determination of combatancy under the direct participation standard. Ibid.

[51] The *ICRC Interpretive Guidance, supra* n. 37, 1022, goes part of the way to understanding this issue by noting that the concept of directness must be understood within the context of the collective nature of the hostilities, such that individual actions may produce little causation on their own, but when aggregated together, contribute to the collective hostilities. However, even the notion of collective hostilities does not resolve the tension between directness and shape of the causal route.

[52] The laity's common-sense understanding of the concept of directness arguably includes an ambiguity with regard to closeness vs. shape.

[53] *See* Fleck, *supra* n.12, 576–7.

engaged in an international armed conflict are allowed to consider third-party states as co-belligerents of the enemy and thus subject to attack. However, third-party states must first be given the opportunity to declare their neutrality in the conflict, and only if they refuse to remain neutral can they be declared co-belligerents of the enemy and thereby subject to lawful attack.[54] The application of this doctrine can be quite controversial, in particular whether a state can feign neutrality and yet offer limited assistance to an ally and remain free from attack.[55] This can be referred to as a form of benevolent neutrality, or the idea that a state may "discriminate" against one side of the conflict without necessarily becoming a full co-belligerent in the conflict.[56]

The deeper problem with the doctrine of co-belligerency is whether it can be successfully transplanted from the original state-based system of public international law into the new realm of non-state actors like Al Qaeda. Bradley and Goldsmith have argued that terrorists who are "co-belligerents" of Al Qaeda are by extension engaged in an armed conflict with the United States by virtue of their status as co-belligerents.[57] However, in *Al-Bihani*, a U.S. federal court rejected application of the doctrine to the war against Al Qaeda, concluding that the doctrine was rooted in traditional public international law notions of state sovereignty and that any "attempt to apply the rules of co-belligerency to such a force would be folly, akin to this court ascribing powers of national sovereignty to a local chapter of the Freemasons."[58]

Indeed, the law of neutrality is based on the idea that states have a duty to declare themselves either officially neutral in a conflict or throw their lot in with one side of the conflict over the other—thus sharing the advantages of victory but also sharing the burdens of defeat. In the words of Francis Lieber, they advance and retrograde together.[59] The problem is that irregular fighting forces are not similarly situated with their enemies in an analogous fashion to states within the global Westphalian system.[60] All states in the Westphalian system enjoy the sovereignty associated with the formal equality of nation-states; one expression of this sovereignty is the ability to form strategic alliances, declare war, engage in armed conflict, sign peace treaties, and return to peaceful relations with an enemy

---

[54] Ibid.

[55] W. Heintschel von Heinegg, "'Benevolent' Third States in International Armed Conflict," in M. Schmitt and J. Pejic, *International Law and Armed Conflict: Exploring the Faultlines* (Nijhoff Leiden, 2007) 543–68.

[56] Ibid.

[57] *See* Bradley and Goldsmith, *supra* n. 18, 2112.

[58] *Al-Bihani v. Obama*, 590 F.3d 866, 873 (D.C. Cir. 2010). The issue is also discussed by Kevin Jon Heller, *D.C. Circuit Rejected "Co-Belligerency" in Al-Bihani*, opiniojuris.org (October 17, 2010), available at <http://opiniojuris.org/2010/10/17/dc-circuit-rejects-co-belligerency/> accessed November 4, 2011.

[59] US General Order No. 100, April 24, 1863 (the Lieber Code), art. 20.

[60] *See also* L. Oppenheim, *International Law: A Treatise* (1906) vol. 2, § 74.

state. Non-state actors are neither sovereign entities nor do they enjoy the capacities that flow directly from this sovereignty. Nonetheless, Bradley and Goldsmith have argued that the U.S. president is permitted to target individual terrorists who are co-belligerents of Al Qaeda.[61] The invocation of the concept of co-belligerency allows them to connect the individual terrorist with a fighting force that is currently engaged in an armed conflict with the United States. They invoke this rationale to demonstrate that such targeted killings comply with the congressional authorization that was provided to the president in the Authorization for the Use of Military Force (AUMF) passed after the September 11 attacks.[62]

The concept of co-belligerency is built around the notion that combatants fighting against a common enemy—even if they are not fighting on a unified front—can be linked together simply by virtue of their common enemy. The old adage that the enemy of my enemy is my friend best expresses the principle. Simply by virtue of standing in the common relationship of belligerency against the same enemy, two entities become co-belligerents.

The key thing to remember about the doctrine of co-belligerency, as it exists in the law of neutrality, is that it is built around the notion of publicity. Co-belligerents are not defined simply around their actions on the battlefield. Rather, third-party states must be allowed the opportunity to publicly declare their neutrality in the conflict, and only if they forgo this opportunity may they be labeled co-belligerents and subject to attack. This publicity criterion works well for sovereign entities such as states that are capable of exercising foreign relations. It is less clear how this translates into the domain of individual terrorists who are defined as co-belligerents of Al Qaeda. They are not given the formal opportunity to declare their neutrality, nor are they given a conventional form of notice that they are being declared a co-belligerent of Al Qaeda, except in the generic sense that the United States has publicly declared that *all* militants are subject to attack unless they foreswear allegiance to Al Qaeda or the Taliban. But this certainly does not meet the formal requirements of the law of neutrality, nor does it capture its underlying spirit of publicity.

(c) Military membership

The traditional rules of IHL implicitly rely on a principle of membership in order to link an individual combatant with a larger fighting force. The basic criteria for the fighting force—the wearing of a military uniform, the display of a fixed emblem recognizable at a distance, the carrying of arms openly—defines the collective fighting force as a military organization that deserves the protection of

---

[61] Bradley and Goldsmith, *supra* n. 18, 2113.
[62] Ibid.

IHL.[63] However, the basic criteria also help define the *individuals* who belong to the organization. Determining membership is based on the fact that individuals in the military wear uniforms, display fixed emblems, and carry their arms openly (to the extent that they use weapons); this in turn publicly signals to the world that the individual is part of the fighting force.

Membership is important because it provides a public criterion that is comparatively easy to establish.[64] The link is established simply by virtue of signing up with the military, being drafted, or donning a uniform. No deeper investigation is required. Indeed, it does not even matter if the combatant actually *engages* in combatancy. His status as a combatant is established simply by virtue of his joining the military organization, regardless of whether he actually fires his weapon and kills an enemy soldier.[65] The link is easily administered, public, and clear for *both* sides of a conflict (and even third parties) to identify the relevant individuals. So there is comparatively little ambiguity about membership in a military organization.

Unfortunately, membership in a terrorist organization does not demonstrate any of the hallmarks that IHL typically assigns to membership in a military organization.[66] Terrorists do not wear uniforms or display fixed emblems, nor do they carry arms openly.[67] Perfidy and deception are essential tools that allow the terrorist to complete his deadly craft. It may be the case that membership in a terrorist organization may have other essential attributes, but they are undeniably not the same attributes that IHL assigns to military organizations.[68] The standard IHL categories were specifically designed to link the individual soldier with warring collectives that are the traditional subjects of public international law (that

---

[63] *See,* e.g., Geneva Convention Relative to the Treatment of Prisoners of War of August 12, 1949, opened for signature August 12, 1949, 6 U.S.T. 3316, 75 U.N.T.S. 135.

[64] *See,* e.g., William Bradford, "In the Minds of Men: A Theory of Compliance with the Laws of War," 36 *Ariz. St. L.J.* (2004) 1243, 1269 (identifying transparency as one factor that determines whether states comply with IHL specifically and legal regimes generally).

[65] But see Fleck, *supra* n. 12, 80 (concluding that members of the armed forces who do not take direct part in hostilities are non-combatants); *Prosecutor v. Halilović*, ICTY Trial Chamber, No. IT-01-48-T (November 16, 2005) para. 34.

[66] See, e.g., *Bensayah v. Obama*, 610 F.3d 718, 725 (D.C. Cir. 2010); *Awad v. Obama*, 608 F.3d 1, 11 (D.C. Cir. 2010) (membership in "command structure" is a sufficient but not necessary condition for legal determination that detainee is a member of Al Qaeda). For a discussion, see also John B. Bellinger III and Vijay M. Padmanabhan, "Detention Operations in Contemporary Conflicts: Four Challenges for the Geneva Conventions and Other Existing Law," 105 *AJIL* (2011) 201, 220 (discussing need for workable criteria for detention of unlawful combatants based on their status).

[67] Nils Melzer, "Keeping the Balance Between Military Necessity and Humanity: A Response to the Four Critiques of the ICRC's Interpretive Guidance on the Notion of Direct Participation in Hostilities," 42 *NYU Journal of International Law & Politics* (2010) 831, 843 (distinguishing functional from formal concepts of membership).

[68] See Program on Humanitarian Policy and Conflict Research, Harvard University, "IHL and Civilian Participation in Hostilities in the OPT," Policy Brief, October 2007, 10 ("The end of membership must be objectively communicated, posing the same intelligence problems as the affirmative disengagement approach above, especially given that many groups may not have official rosters of membership, uniforms, or centralized housing.").

is, nation-states), and to provide a first gloss on Lieber's assumption that individual soldiers are linked to the collective such that they advance and retrograde together. With these criteria, however, the terrorist remains in limbo.

(i) Form vs. function   One might solve this problem by moving from a formal concept of membership to a functional concept of membership.[69] Formal membership is built around formal indicia such as membership lists, the wearing of uniforms, and *de jure* requirements of domestic law, while the functional concept of membership can be determined by the individual's role and function within the organization.[70] For the functional definition of membership, it is particularly relevant whether the individual received and carried out orders from the organization's hierarchy.[71] The application of the formal concept of membership, with its emphasis on *de jure* considerations, may not map onto the "the more informal and fluctuating membership structures of irregularly constituted armed forces fighting on behalf of State and non-State belligerents."[72]

In contrast, the functional version of the concept takes that informal structure as given and determines membership based on the individual's place within—and relationship to—that hierarchy, even if that hierarchy is nebulous, irregular, or constantly shifting. The result is a version of the membership concept that can actually be applied to terrorist organizations, even if they are ill-defined and lack the same rigorous structure of state military organizations. Although the functional concept of membership is far less public and transparent than the formal concept of membership, it retains the essential characteristics of a membership criterion insofar as it is nominally based on an individual's status as a member of a terrorist organization.

(d) Control

One might connect an individual terrorist with Al Qaeda—and the armed conflict between Al Qaeda and the United States—with a control test. Under this view, the individual is linked to the collective if Al Qaeda "controls" the actions of the individual. This principle has its genesis in public international law and the standard that the International Court of Justice (ICJ) imposed in the *Nicaragua* case to determine whether the actions of an armed group could be attributed to a state

---

[69] *See Interpretive Guidance, supra* n. 37, 1005 (concluding that membership in military organizations is based on "formal integration into permanent units distinguishable by uniforms, insignia and equipment" but that membership in irregular groups requires functional criteria).

[70] For an example, see *Al Warafi v. Obama*, 704 F. Supp. 2d 32, 38 (D.D.C. 2010) (functional approach requires determination that the individual "functioned or participated within or under the command structure of the Taliban—i.e. whether he received and executed orders or directions"); *Hamlily*, 616, F. Supp. 2d at 75 (same).

[71] *Al Warafi v. Obama*, 704 F. Supp. 2d 32, 38 (but noting that knowledge and intent is required and excluding those who "unwittingly become part of the apparatus").

[72] See Melzer, *supra* n. 67, 845 (defending relevance of functional criteria for membership).

for purposes of assigning state responsibility for the group's actions.[73] The court concluded that state responsibility existed in cases of effective control of the group's actions. In *Nicaragua*, the United States was found not be in control of the contras because, although the US was found to be involved in "planning, direction and support" of the contras' paramilitary activities, there was insufficient evidence that the United States "*directed* or *enforced* the perpetuation of the acts contrary to human rights and humanitarian law alleged by the applicant State."[74]

There are other versions of the control principle. The International Criminal Tribunal for the former Yugoslavia (ICTY) famously rejected the ICJ's effective control test and formulated a different standard based on overall control.[75] Under this new standard, control by the state requires more than mere financing or providing military equipment, but the standard stops short of the strict standard imposed by the ICJ. The overall control standard is met by the planning and supervision of military activities in general, without requiring that the planning or oversight extend down to the level of specific military attacks.[76] A more general level of planning or supervision can constitute overall control of the paramilitary organization even in the absence of specifically directing the organization's military operations.

The problem with borrowing either of these control principles and applying them to the War on Terror is that many of the individuals who are targeted by the Administration are not controlled by Al Qaeda, even under the looser version of the standard articulated by the ICTY. In some cases, to be sure, the individual's activities may indeed be directed by Al Qaeda. In other situations, however, the individual will be affiliated with a regional terrorist organization with very loose ties to the Al Qaeda parent group. Originally, Al Qaeda represented a defined organization with specific individuals committed to a particular political objective. But the organization has now transformed into a looser confederation of like-minded fellow travelers, many of whom are fighting separate armed conflicts in different regions of the globe. These conflicts include different enemies, different objectives, and different techniques, though they might share an overarching ideological commitment to violent jihadism. Consequently, in many situations, the parent organization may provide ideological and rhetorical support but no direct or even general operational control over the local terrorist organization.

One solution to this problem is to redefine the armed conflict as not against Al Qaeda per se but rather the long list of more local organizations that are engaged

---

[73] *Military and Paramilitary Activities In and Against Nicaragua* (*Nicaragua v. United States*), June 27, 1986, ICJ Reports (1986).
[74] Ibid. at 64–5 (emphasis added).
[75] *See Prosecutor v. Tadic*, ICTY Appeals Chamber, Case No. IT-94-1-A, para. 137.
[76] Ibid.

in terrorist activities.[77] This might alleviate the need to use the control principle in the first place, but the strategy can only be imperfectly applied. To the extent that a pre-existing local organization is involved in a bona fide armed conflict with the United States, the strategy works. However, many of these sub-groups might be so localized that they could not be said to be engaged in a declared armed conflict with the United States. Furthermore, some of these local groups might be so loosely organized that even the local group does not "control"— either effectively or overall—the actions of the individual terrorist.

(e) Complicity and conspiracy

Another solution is to import the doctrine of complicity from the domain of criminal law as a way of linking the individual terrorist to a larger group engaged in armed conflict with the United States. The doctrine of complicity implicitly relies on a causal notion, in the sense that complicity liability is generated by an individual's contribution (or attempted contribution) to a criminal endeavor, just as long as the contribution makes the completion of the crime more likely.[78] This broad notion of complicity has increasingly been used as a paradigm to understand an individual's contribution to a national collective endeavor of war-making.[79] The importation of a criminal law notion into the domain of public international law may, at first glance, appear strange, but the concept's intuitive appeal is undeniable. At first glance, the only difference between the classical criminal law situation and the situation of a national armed struggle is the size of the collective endeavor to which the contribution is made.[80] The other side of the equation—the individual, as well as his relationship to the collective—remains the same. Furthermore, the case under consideration here (the individual contributing to the collective terrorist organization) stands in between the classical criminal law paradigm and the state-based paradigm of international conflicts inherent in public international law. This broad notion of complicity in a collective endeavor is also encoded in Article 25(3)(d) of the Rome Statute, which scholars have interpreted as criminalizing a form of residual complicity in a collective criminal endeavor.[81] Although terrorism is not a discrete international crime under the Rome Statute, the mode of liability codified

---

[77] The concept of the "War on Terror" represents an even wider solution, where the enemy is terrorism itself. However, this is just as nonsensical as declaring a War on War or a War on Enemies, with the opponent being defined as anyone who threatens aggressive action. This eviscerates the notion of an armed conflict against a defined enemy.

[78] Compare Sanford H. Kadish, "Complicity, Cause and Blame: A Study in the Interpretation of Doctrine," 73 *California Law Review* (1985) 323, 343 and John Gardner, "Complicity and Causality," 1 *Criminal Law and Philosophy* (2007) 127, with Christopher Kutz, "Causeless Complicity," I *Criminal Law And Philosophy* (2007) 289.

[79] See, e.g., Christopher Kutz, "The Difference Uniforms Make: Collective Violence in Criminal Law and the Law of War," 33 *Philosophy and Public Affairs* (2005) 148.

[80] *Cf.* ibid. at 153.

[81] The provision was interpreted by the ICC in *Lubanga*, ¶ 337.

in Article 25(3)(d) represents a similar invocation of the concept of complicity in group action. The federal crime of providing material support for terrorism is also built around the notion of complicity.[82]

The causal element of criminal complicity picks up quite nicely the causal interpretation of directly participating in hostilities. Under this view, it makes sense to target individual terrorists who are complicit in the larger collective conflict (whether one defines the conflict as a criminal conflict or a war) because complicity represents a form of *participation*. In criminal law, this point is purely definitional; complicity is defined as a form of participation in criminal wrongdoing.[83] A party to an armed conflict has every reason to target an individual whose actions contribute to—or were aimed at contributing to—their eventual defeat.

The question, however, is whether the causal element of criminal complicity is sufficiently *direct* as a linking principle to adequately serve as a gloss on the notion of directly participating in hostilities. Indeed, criminal law scholars often describe aiders and abettors—and other form of accomplices—as having engaged in a form of *indirect* commission of the crime.[84] True, at least some accomplices could be described as direct participants in the endeavor, but the criterion of complicity is notoriously broad and meant to capture a wider scope of participation that plays some causal role in the criminal endeavor, even if that causal role is somewhat attenuated. Even in criminal law, though, the causal role cannot be too attenuated; otherwise criminal liability is usually denied as inappropriate. But even still, the criminal law notion may capture a whole host of individuals whose indirect contributions to the endeavor make them criminally culpable (and hence subject to punishment) but perhaps not subject to the immediate and summary killing implicit in traditional combatancy under the standard rules of IHL.

One might attempt to tighten the complicity link by switching to the concept of conspiracy.[85] Conspiracy as a mode of liability is arguably stricter than complicity, because it requires an underlying agreement between the individual and the associated individuals.[86] As applied to the terrorist, he would be linked to the terrorist organization because he has jointly agreed with other terrorists to pursue an armed struggle against the United States. Individuals who merely contribute to the cause,

---

[82] See Norman Abrams, "The Material Support Terrorism Offenses: Perspectives Derived from the (Early) Model Penal Code," 1 *Journal of National Security Law and Policy* (2005) 5.

[83] *See* George P. Fletcher, "Complicity," 30 *Israel Law Review* (1996) 140.

[84] This is also sometimes described as perpetration-by-means. *See* Rome Statute, art. 25(3)(a). *See also* MPC §2.06. For a discussion, see F. Jessberger, "On the Application of a Theory of Indirect Perpetration in Al Bashir: German Doctrine at The Hague?," 6 *Journal of International Criminal Justice* (2008) 853.

[85] Conspiracy as a mode of liability is sometimes viewed as a separate doctrine from complicity, and occasionally as a subcategory of complicity (with accomplice liability being the other subcategory). This ambiguity is immaterial for our purposes here.

[86] 18 U.S.C. §371.

without an underlying agreement for joint action, would not be linked to the collective under the conspiracy doctrine.[87]

It makes sense to view terrorism through the lens of conspiracy. Terrorists pursue an unlawful objective through conspiratorial means: agreeing to a course of action, collective pursuit of common goals, secret and underground deliberations.[88] Moreover, the entire rationale of the conspiracy doctrine was to create an inchoate offence of preparation for criminality that allows the authorities to intervene quickly in a burgeoning criminal endeavor. Whatever public policy rationale exists for intervening in domestic criminal conspiracies applies with equal or greater force to transnational conspiracies to commit acts of terrorism.

Having sketched out the terrain of possible linking principles, our task is now to evaluate their comparative strengths and weaknesses, both from the perspective of positive law (for example, support in treaty or customary law) and as compliance with the underlying normative principles of international law. That being said, this investigation cannot prejudge the correct paradigm; that is, whether the most appropriate normative principles are those underlying the law enforcement paradigm or the law of war paradigm, or a combination of both. Section IV will pursue this goal by pursuing a comparative evaluation of the linking principles.

IV. A comparative evaluation of the linking principles

When can an individual be linked to a collective group for the purposes of being selected for a targeted killing? A comparative analysis of the linking principles reveals that an individual can be linked either through status alone or by virtue of a more discrete action. So membership in a military organization, by virtue of wearing a uniform or displaying a fixed symbol, confers a status on the individual that links him to the collective fighting force. Similarly, the concept of co-belligerency from the law of neutrality involves a status-like element by virtue of a belligerent's refusal to declare itself neutral in a conflict.

It should come as no surprise that IHL relies on the linking principle of membership in a military organization, given how much is at stake. If individuals are linked for purposes of IHL, they gain the privilege of combatant immunity as well as opening themselves to the risk of reciprocal killing. Individuals who meet these criteria *know* that they meet these criteria, and moreover, their enemies know this as well. In fact, the public nature of the linking principle is internal to the principle itself, because the link is built around the criteria of uniforms, fixed emblems, and weaponry—all of which are designed to publicly convey to one's

---

[87] However, they would be guilty of providing material support.
[88] On this point, see generally J.D. Ohlin, "Group Think: The Law of Conspiracy and Collective Reason," 98 *J. Criminal Law and Criminology* (2007) 147, 201.

enemy that the linking principle is fulfilled. When so much is at stake, it makes sense for the linking principle to be self-publicizing and self-applying.

In contrast, the criminal law notions of conspiracy and complicity are causal criteria that are far less public. The individual's actions that link him to the collective are hardly public at all, because the actions of the terrorist are usually conducted covertly, far from the prying eyes of the enemy. Terrorists are more like spies than traditional combatants. Furthermore, the criteria for conspiracy or complicity are usually complicated and require the testing and fact-finding process that dominates the criminal trial. Allowing criminal law concepts to function as a linking principle cuts against the underlying nature of IHL, which necessarily relies on easy-to-administer criteria in the absence of a judicial system.

In light of this insight, section IV(a) will reconsider the virtues of membership as a linking principle, even though criminal law scholars have given it a bad name. Section IV(b) will then consider an updated version of the membership concept—the continuous combat function—that avoids many of the anxieties that criminal law scholars have about membership principles. Finally, section IV(c) will compare status and conduct principles and demonstrate that membership principles can be modified into a "functional membership" concept that represents a hybrid between status and conduct. The result is a legally defensible and philosophically coherent principle to link suspected terrorists with the non-state organizations that are fighting the United States.

(a) Rethinking membership

We are therefore caught between two types of linking principles. The traditional IHL linking principles are both self-applying and public. The traditional criminal law linking principles are neither self-applying nor public, since they require a comparatively larger degree of fact-finding to determine if their standards are met. At which end of the spectrum should we place targeted killings? Should targeted individuals be linked with the underlying principles of IHL or the criminal law?

Functionally, targeted killings are much closer to the summary killings that are inherent to IHL on the battlefield. Although the criminal law concepts of conspiracy and complicity cast a wide net, this looseness is mitigated by the fact that the criminal law system affords defendants a chance to contest the causal linkage before a neutral decision-maker.[89] No such right exists on the battlefield, which is precisely why the linking principles used by IHL are much narrower.[90] Although many individuals might be causally responsible for helping the war

---

[89] See generally Larry May, *Global Justice and Due Process* (Cambridge University Press, 2011) 117.

[90] *Cf.* Richard Murphy and Afsheen John Radsan, "Due Process and the Targeted Killing of Terrorists," 31 *Cardozo Law Review* (2009) 405, 409; May, *supra* n. 89, 154.

effort, the rules of IHL limit automatic killing to soldiers in uniform (and civilians directly participating in hostilities). Although this classification might be seriously limited, the whole structure of IHL is built around the notion that the reciprocal risk of killing should be underbroad rather than overbroad, precisely because there is no opportunity to contest a determination on the battlefield. The uniformed soldier on the battlefield cannot complain that he was killed before he could contest his status, because he was wearing a uniform.

(i) A functional equivalent

Targeted killings represent the same kind of summary killing that traditional combatants face on the battlefield. While conspiracy and complicity are strict enough for a system with a criminal process, they are not appropriate for summary execution outside of the judicial process. This suggests that however we link individuals to a collective for purposes of targeted killing, it ought to be with a linking principle that is closer to the IHL linking principles rather than criminal law linking principles. The correct linking principle would represent a functional equivalent to the IHL linking principle that governs the targeting of traditional combatants. The difference would be that the functional equivalent ought to be tailored for the specifics of the situation: a non-state group composed of individuals who pursue terrorism without a uniform.

Although it is difficult to sketch out the exact contours of this hypothetical linking principle, it ought to lie somewhere between the doctrine of co-belligerency and membership in a military organization. The doctrine of co-belligerency, as understood by the law of neutrality, has the advantage that it is based on both publicity and self-declared consent; the co-belligerent nation publicly refuses to affirm its neutrality and is therefore declared a co-belligerent. The very same publicity and self-declared consent is performed by the individual soldier who dons a uniform. Both are then subject to summary attack under the laws of war, though one norm flows from *jus ad bellum* and the other flows from *jus in bello*. But the structure of both is remarkably similar.

The functional equivalent in cases of targeted killings would link the individual to the collective terrorist group if the individual is a card-carrying member of a terrorist organization or a self-declared enemy of the United States.[91] Membership might be established in a number of ways, not simply by attending an Al Qaeda training camp.[92] We are therefore left with the following linking principle:

---

[91] In his UN report, Philip Alston denies that membership alone can be sufficient to identify a terrorist as an appropriate target for a killing. *See* U.N. Human Rights Council, *Report of the Special Rapporteur on Extrajudicial, Summary or Arbitrary Executions, Addendum: Study on Targeted Killings*, U.N. Doc. A/HRC/14/24/Add.6 (May 28, 2010) paras 65–6 (criticizing the ICRC standard of "continuous combat function" for its overreliance on membership and other status-based concepts). For a complete discussion of the ICRC notion of the continuous combat function, see *infra* section IV(b).

[92] Although in many cases, prosecution is based precisely on attendance at a training camp. See, e.g., *United States v. Hassoun*, 2007 U.S. Dist. LEXIS 85684 (D. Fla. 2007).

voluntary membership in an organization engaged in an armed conflict with the United States.[93] This linking principle might at first glance sound too narrow, because terrorists might opportunistically avoid declaring their allegiances in order to avoid being targeted—an example of lawfare to be sure. But the anxiety is misplaced. The very concept of terrorism hinges on publicity—publicity for a cause and a political objective, neither of which can be easily disowned without doing damage to the theater of violence implicit in terrorist attacks.[94]

(ii) The transitory requirement

This conclusion is more than just normative-philosophical. It is also a legal conclusion, in the sense that it can be understood as a gloss on the concept of direct participation in hostilities, the original requirement of *jus in bello* that explains when a civilian loses his or her protected status under IHL. On this point, one might object that this understanding—direct participation in hostilities in terms of self-declared membership in an organization engaged in an armed conflict with the United States—conflicts with another aspect of the "direct participation" linking principle. The Additional Protocol withdraws protection from civilians "for such time" as they are directly participating in hostilities.[95] The flexible and temporal work performed by the concept of "for such time" suggests that the associated status (protected civilian vs. unprotected combatant) shifts constantly depending on the actions of the particular individual. He can fall in and out of protection at each moment in time, depending on his conduct—without a reified status that endures throughout the individual's existence. This approach was famously discussed by the Israeli Supreme Court in its Targeted Killings decision.[96]

Is this transitory requirement of the Additional Protocol consistent with membership in an organization engaged in an armed conflict with the United States? Or is the latter far too status-oriented—that is, not sufficiently transitory and flexible—to accord with the "for such time" standard?[97] It strikes me that the notion of self-declared membership is, in fact, consistent with the transitory nature of the "for such time" standard. Individuals join and leave organizations all the time—just as

---

[93] For a discussion, see Program on Humanitarian Policy and Conflict Research, Harvard University, *IHL and Civilian Participation in Hostilities in the OPT*, October 2007, 10 (comparing "membership approach" with "limited membership approach" that restricts targeting to fighting members of armed groups).

[94] Fletcher, *supra* n. 10, 909.

[95] See Additional Protocol I, *supra* n. 23, 174, art. 51(3).

[96] *Public Committee Against Torture v. Israel ("Targeted Killings Case")*, HCJ 769/02 (2005).

[97] The "for such time" requirement is the subject of some controversy. *Compare* Bill Boothby, "'And for such time as': The Time Dimension to Direct Participation in Hostilities," 42 *NYU Journal of International Law & Politics* (2010) 741, 764–5 (questioning the customary status of the norm and suggesting that the "for such time" requirement is limited to treaty signatories of the Additional Protocol), with Melzer, *supra* n. 67, 884–5 (stating that treaty is binding on 169 states and noting that even the Israeli High Court believes that the additional protocol requirement codifies customary law).

they join and leave criminal conspiracies—and such decisions are both legally and morally significant. The individual terrorist is subject to the risk of being killed "for such time" as he is a member of Al Qaeda, though he regains the core protections of IHL if and when he permanently leaves Al Qaeda. At that moment in time he becomes a subject of the criminal process again. This solution avoids some of the most perverse aspects of the revolving door problem that is, the risk that terrorists will launch terrorist attacks but fall back into civilian status to shield themselves from the enemy.[98] If the "for such time" criterion is linked to membership in the organization, such opportunistic shifts are dramatically more difficult.

(b) The continuous combat function standard

This membership principle is arguably what the ICRC was getting at in its *Interpretative Guidance on the Notion of Direct Participation*, which explicitly recognized the significance of engaging in a continuous combat function.[99] According to the *Interpretative Guidance*, membership in an armed group of a non-state party to a non-international armed conflict depends on whether the individual engages in a "continuous combat function."[100] The point of introducing the new continuous combat function criterion is to distinguish between, on the one hand, "members of the organized fighting forces of a non-State party from civilians who directly participate in hostilities on a merely spontaneous, sporadic, or unorganized basis, or who assume exclusively political, administrative or other non-combat functions."[101] The functional consequence of this distinction is to carve out a category under IHL that treats soldiers in a non-state military organization in analogous fashion (for example, according to membership) to soldiers in a more traditional state-party military organization.

How is this distinction to be made? An individual is deemed to be engaged in a continuous combat function, as opposed to the more transitory and fleeting direct participation in hostilities, if their "continuous function involves the preparation, execution, or command of acts or operations amounting to direct participation in hostilities are assuming a continuous combat function. An individual recruited, trained and equipped by such a group to continuously and directly participate in hostilities on its behalf can be considered to assume a continuous combat function even before he or she first carries out a hostile

---

[98] *Targeted Killings Case, supra* n. 96, para. 40 (discussing problem of revolving door and citing 1 Kings 1:50 and Numbers 35:11).

[99] *See Interpretative Guidance, supra* n. 37, 991, 1007–9. The document's principal author was Nils Melzer, ICRC Legal Advisor, and was adopted by the Assembly of the International Committee of the Red Cross on February 26, 2009.

[100] Ibid. 1007 ("membership must depend on whether the continuous function assumed by an individual corresponds to that collectively exercised by the group as a whole, namely the conduct of hostilities on behalf of a non-State party to the conflict").

[101] Ibid.

act."[102] If one applies this standard to Al Qaeda, there is a plausible argument that these terrorists are trained to continuously operate as terrorists with the goal of pursuing attacks against the United States and its allies. Moreover, there is a lasting integration of the individual into the collective, on whose behalf the individual is acting.[103] Although many of these members have not yet finalized an attack, they are engaged in the process of preparing, planning, or training for an attack. Their status as Al Qaeda terrorists therefore makes them subject to military attack.

The ICRC standard of engaging in a continuous combat function was (and remains) highly controversial when it was adopted by the Red Cross working group.[104] Some scholars disapproved of the membership-oriented nature of the concept and believed that the concept of direct participation in hostilities ought to remain transitory and based solely on the actions of the individual at each moment in time.[105] Furthermore, these scholars rejected the rationale that armed groups of a non-state party to an armed conflict ought to have a functional analogue to membership in a state's military organization.[106] On the other hand, other scholars, including some who participated in the ICRC working group that developed the continuous combat function standard, criticized the proposal from the opposite direction; that is, sacrificing the principle of military necessity for the principle of humanity.[107] These criticisms were a natural outgrowth of a pre-existing anxiety about how IHL treats organized armed groups differently depending on whether they are a state party or not. Members of a non-state armed organization receive the added protection of the "for such time" limitation (and are consequently immune from targeting part of the time), while members of a state party's military organization are subject to attack purely on the basis of membership.[108] Why should members of a non-state armed organization receive more protection under the customary rules of IHL, rather than less?

The continuous combat function standard was meant to be a solution to that problem. In fact, the *ICRC Interpretative Guidelines* apply the continuous combat function criterion both to non-international armed conflicts and international

---

[102] Ibid. at 1007–8.

[103] Ibid. at 1007 (discussing lasting integration in an organized armed group as a requirement of the continuous combat function standard).

[104] See Mezler, *supra* n. 67, 831, 834.

[105] Ibid. at 835.

[106] Ibid. ("while Schmitt contends that the Interpretive Guidance's definition of 'direct participation in hostilities' is too restrictive, essentially because it excludes support activities not directly causing harm to the enemy, other experts would criticize the Guidance's definition as too generous because, in certain circumstances, it might allow the targeting of civilians who do not pose an immediate threat to the enemy.").

[107] See, e.g., Kenneth Watkin, "Opportunity Lost: Organized Armed Groups and the ICRC 'Direct Participation in the Hostilities' Interpretive Guidance," 42 *NYU Journal of International Law & Politics* (2010) 641.

[108] Compare Watkin, *supra* n. 107, 644, *with* Melzer, *supra* n. 67, 851.

armed conflicts, such that membership is limited to those individuals who display a continuous combat function as opposed to those who, like reservists, have a combat function that is "spontaneous, sporadic, or temporary" or "assume exclusively political, administrative or other non-combat functions"[109] The problem with the ICRC's particular proposal is that it did not go far enough. According to at least some scholars, the requirement set up a different legal regime that provided an unfair and unwarranted advantage to insurgent groups.[110] Only members of an organized armed group who evidence a continuous combat function could be lawfully targeted; all other members of the group can only be targeted for such time as they are directly participating in hostilities. By contrast, all members of a state's military apparatus are subject to lawfully targeting, even a cook, regardless of whether they are directly participating in hostilities or not.[111] From the point of view of this criticism, the proper remedy is to normalize the standard across all armed groups, whether state actors or non-state actors. In other words, membership in both domains could be limited to those who display a continuous combat function or, in the alternative, membership in both domains could be expanded to all individuals and include the proverbial cook in both the state military *and* the insurgent group, so as to eliminate the unfair advantage conferred on the insurgents.[112] This the Red Cross proposal does not do.

However, even if one sticks with the Red Cross proposal and applies the continuous combat function requirement just to insurgents, it may be the case that some insurgent groups are so entirely focused on planning and perpetrating military attacks that every member of the group is engaged in a continuous combat function.[113]

---

[109] *ICRC Interpretative Guidance, supra* n. 37, 1007.

[110] See, e.g., Michael N. Schmitt, "The Interpretative Guidance on Direct Participation in Hostilities: A Critical Analysis," *Harvard National Security Journal* (2010) 5, 23. See also Adam Roberts, "The Equal Application of the Laws of War: A Principle Under Pressure," 90 *International Review of the Red Cross* (2008) 931.

[111] Schmitt, *supra* n. 110, 23. Melzer contends that the asymmetry is justified because even cooks in a traditional army "are not only entitled, but also trained, armed, and expected to directly participate in hostilities in case of enemy contact and, therefore, also assume a continuous combat function." See Melzer, Halilović *supra* n. 67, 852. The ICTY apparently disagrees. See, e.g., *Prosecutor v. Halilović*, No. IT-01-48-T (November 16, 2005) para. 34 (noting that while "membership of the armed forces can be a strong indication that the victim is directly participating in the hostilities, it is not an indicator which in and of itself is sufficient"). However, the only two counter-examples offered by the ICTY Trial Chamber include non-mobilized reservists and civilian police officers incorporated *de jure* into the armed forces by domestic statute. Ibid., para. 34 n. 78. For a brief discussion, see Ryan Goodman, "The Detention of Civilians in Armed Conflict," 103 *AJIL* (2009) 48, n. 41.

[112] But see Melzer, *supra* n. 67, 851.

[113] For a discussion of the ambiguity in applying this criterion in these situations, *compare* Schmitt, *supra* n. 50, 727 (noting difficulty with defining "capacity-building" activities such as recruitment of suicide bombers, procurement of materials, and assembly and storage of explosives), *with* Melzer, *supra* n. 67, 865–6 ("whether an act constitutes a measure preparatory or otherwise integral to a

The U.S. administration has taken a similar view in habeas corpus proceedings in federal court arising out of Guantanamo Bay detentions.[114] According to the Obama Administration, Al Qaeda is a military organization through-and-through, such that all members of the group are dedicated to planning, supporting, or executing future attacks in some way or another.[115] Unlike other insurgent armed groups that also perform some political or civilian functions (for example, Hamas in Gaza or the Taliban in Afghanistan),[116] Al Qaeda exists solely to plot terrorist attacks against designated targets; it has no positive political program of its own, nor does it aspire to directly control territory through the operation of an Al Qaeda syndicate government. Is it therefore possible that all members of Al Qaeda and similar groups are engaged in a continuous combat function in some way or another?

(c) Status rules vs. conduct rules

Whether one accepts this argument or not, the real point is to emphasize that the entire discussion of the continuous combat function requirement takes place within the general context of membership as a linking principle. As good criminal law scholars, we are supposed to favor conduct rules over outcomes based on status alone. As criminal law professors, we assign our students *Martin v. State* and drive home the proposition that the principle of culpability requires that we punish individuals solely for their blameworthy actions, not their status.[117] This argument is particularly relevant for the War on Terror, where the government arguably uses status to determine who should be declared an unlawful combatant, interned at Guantanamo Bay, tried before a military commission, or even summarily killed by a drone attack.[118] To some critics, this represents an unwarranted infringement on civil liberties in order to protect national security. Under this view, if draconian consequences are required to protect our nation, they should only be visited upon an individual suspect if he has engaged in

---

specific hostile act or operation, or whether it remains limited to general capacity-building, must be determined separately for each case, and it is clear that the same objective criteria must apply to all civilians, regardless of whether they happen to support an unsophisticated insurgency or a technologically advanced State.").

[114] I am indebted to Marty Lederman on this point.

[115] See, e.g., *Al Bihani v. Obama*, 594 F. Supp. 2d 35, 39–40 (concluding that despite petitioner's contention that he was only a cook, he was also carrying a rifle and ammunition and taking orders from an Al Qaeda military commander).

[116] See Schmitt, *supra* n. 110, 23 (noting that Hamas and Hezbollah have political or social wings but also concluding that "while membership in an organized armed group can be uncertain, it may also be irrefutable").

[117] *Martin v. State*, 31 Ala. App. 334, 17 So. 2d 427 (Alabama 1944); *Robinson v. California*, 370 U.S. 660 (1962) (status of being a drug addict). But see *Powell v. Texas*, 392 U.S. 514 (1968) (upholding public intoxication statute).

[118] See, e.g., *Hamlily v. Obama*, 616 F. Supp. 2d 63, (D.D.C. 2009) (status determination of membership is consistent with international laws of war).

proscribed *conduct*. Anything less represents a fundamental betrayal of the civil liberties enshrined in our constitutional structure.

However, the interplay between conduct and status is rich and complex and not so black and white. Status is often a shortcut for a history of repeated conduct, such that the status of being a drug addict or the status of appearing drunk in public are both, with limited exceptions,[119] the product of component actions (consuming alcohol or drugs) that we would naturally classify as conduct. Similarly, the building blocks of IHL demonstrate a complex relationship between conduct and status. Although membership in a military organization is usually described as a status, once one inquires about how this status is determined, one learns that the component requirements are wearing a uniform, the display of a fixed emblem recognizable at a distance, and the carrying of arms openly—all examples of conduct par excellence.[120] It is rare, then, to have a case of status *all the way down*.

(i) Functional membership as a hybrid concept

This is even more true when one considers a functional version of the concept of membership, which looks to the individual's relationship to an organizational hierarchy and whether he receives and carries out orders from that command structure.[121] Unlike a formal version of membership, which relies more heavily on status criteria, the functional concept is halfway along the road to a conduct rule. It relies on the status concept of membership but cashes out that standard by reference to what the individual is actually doing—not necessarily at each discrete moment in time, but rather from the broader perspective of a longer time period: taking orders from commanders, engaging in military operations at the behest of commanders, etc.[122] In fact, one might describe the functional version of membership as a hybrid concept that straddles the distinction between status and conduct—an appropriate

---

[119] There are a few examples of status categories that are not reducible to an individual's own actions, such as an infant drug addict who suffered from fetal intoxication *in utero*. In that case, the individual's status is causally reducible to an individual action, but it is someone else's action—the parent.

[120] Melzer's defense of the *ICRC Interpretative Guidance* appears to be insensitive to this dynamic relationship; e.g., Melzer argues that the asymmetry between state military organizations and non-state armed groups is justified because "members of regular State armed forces are legitimate military targets not because of the 'functions they perform' but because of their formal status as regular combatants." See Melzer, *supra* n. 67, 851. This means that membership can either be based on "formal de jure integration" (for regular armed forces) or on "function de facto performed," i.e. conduct (for irregular forces). Ibid. But at some level, even the formal de jure integration of the armed forces must be based, in part, on their conduct, as he implicitly recognizes when he points out that even cooks in the regular armed forces are always trained in basic combat functions.

[121] See *supra* section III(c)(i) for a complete discussion of formal vs. functional membership.

[122] See, e.g., *Al-Bihani v. Obama*, 590 F.3d 866, 872–3 (functional membership based on "accompanying the brigade on the battlefield, carrying a brigade-issued weapon, cooking for the unit, and retreating and surrendering under brigade orders" even "in the absence of an official membership card").

result for the context of terrorist organizations and other irregular armed groups. The result is hardly Solomonic; rather, it merges the best of both worlds.

That being said, it would be an exaggeration to say that the distinction between conduct and status is wholly illusory. There *is* a fundamental difference between them, albeit one that is often obscured. A status usually represents a proxy for lower-level conduct. Proxies usually get a bad name in both law and philosophy, because it is natural to presume that if the lower-level facts generate the moral or legal significance, one ought to eliminate the higher-level proxy and deal exclusively with the lower-level elements. Under this view, the identification of a proxy suggests eliminativism as the proper course of action. This is a hasty conclusion because one ought to distinguish between crude proxies and successful proxies. Crude proxies take a rough set of intuitions and create a shortcut that obscures the real significance of the underlying elements; what is gained in administrability and convenience is outweighed by the loss of accuracy.[123] By contrast, successful proxies link together a diverse set of lower-level elements, solve evidentiary problems, and help root out inconsistencies.[124] The question is whether the status concept under consideration in this chapter—membership in a terrorist organization engaged in a self-declared armed conflict—is the former or the latter.

There is a plausible argument that the status concept that we have deployed here illuminates more than it obscures. First, it has obvious evidentiary value. Self-declared membership in an organized armed group is public and transparent; those who join a group dedicated to jihad can understand the position of conflict that they have placed themselves in. Second, third parties can monitor compliance with this norm with relative ease. By contrast, limiting targetability based on the conduct of the targeted individual at each cardinal moment in time is comparatively less transparent and very difficult for third parties to monitor. These are precisely the considerations that originally sparked the use of status concepts such as membership in traditional IHL norms.[125]

---

[123] *Cf.* Felix S. Cohen, "Transcendental Nonsense and the Functionalist Approach," 35 *Colum. L. Rev.* (1935) 809 (disparaging the legal utility of metaphysical concepts that have no precise meaning).

[124] Similarly, see Jeremy Waldron, "'Transcendental Nonsense' and System in the Law," 100 *Colum. L. Rev.* (2000) 16 (concluding that metaphysical concepts in the law provide meaningful explanations when their explanatory circle is sufficiently large). *See also* Jens David Ohlin, "Is the Concept of the Person Necessary for Human Rights?," 105 *Colum. L. Rev.* (2005) 209 (invoking Cohen and Waldron and concluding that metaphysical concepts often link together diverse propositions to promote coherence and root out inconsistencies in doctrine).

[125] See Robert Chesney and Jack Goldsmith, "Terrorism and the Convergence of Criminal and Military Detention Models," 60 *Stan. L. Rev.* (2008) 1079, 1084 ("The laws of war traditionally emphasize pure associational status as the primary ground for detention; individual conduct provides only a secondary, alternative predicate.").

(ii) Preserving civil liberties

We are left, then, with a somewhat surprising result. The traditional dichotomy of national security vs. civil liberties turns out to be illusory.[126] When viewed through the lens of domestic criminal law, the use of status concepts appears to threaten the principle of culpability and suggests that the proposed scheme impermissibility infringes civil liberties. But when viewed through the lens of IHL, the use of status concepts reveals itself to be entirely consistent with the conceptual structure of IHL—a structure that is based largely on status concepts, and for good reason. To insist yet again that pure conduct alone should determine targetability is to import criminal law linking principles into a legal terrain—the battlefield—where the preferred linking principles are publicly observable and self-administering status concepts such as membership. Moreover, shifting to a hybrid status-conduct concept such as functional membership goes even further towards ensuring that truly innocent civilians fall outside the scope of legitimate targets.

How could this standard be administered? One might object that it is difficult—if not impossible—to prove that any given individual is truly a member of a terrorist organization engaged in an armed conflict with the United States. After a targeted killing, who is to say that the killing did not live up to this standard? There are two important answers here. Such problems of proof are endemic to all IHL norms governing civilians, and the current problem will be comparatively easier to administer when compared against a more transitory revolving door scheme. Second, the concept of joining and leaving a criminal organization is well worked out in the literature and case law on conspiracies, which in some jurisdictions imposes stringent requirements on individuals seeking to leave a criminal organization and escape the consequences of their membership.[127] These standards sometimes require a public repudiation of the enterprise—either to the leaders of the enterprise or to the relevant authorities.[128] This is a high standard to meet, and appropriately so in the case of domestic criminal law.[129]

Applied to terrorists, the standard would require a public declaration repudiating the armed conflict against the United States before they could regain their protected

---

[126] *Cf.* S. Macdonald, "Why We Should Abandon the Balance Metaphor," 15 *ILSA J. International & Comparative Law* (2008–2009) 95.

[127] *Compare Hyde v. United States*, 225 U.S. 347 (1912) *with United States v. U.S. Gypsum Co.*, 438 U.S. 422, 464–5 (1978) ("Affirmative acts inconsistent with the object of the conspiracy and communicated in a manner reasonably calculated to reach co-conspirators have generally been regarded as sufficient to establish withdrawal or abandonment.").

[128] *See, e.g., Al Ginco v. Obama*, 626 F. Supp. 2d 123, 128 (D.D.C. 2009) ("prior relationship [with] al Qaeda . . . can be sufficiently vitiated by the passage of time, intervening events, or both"). *See also Eldredge v. United States*, 62 F.2d 449, 451 (10th Cir. 1932) (conspiracy).

[129] *See, e.g., ICRC Interpretive Guidance, supra* n. 37, 1008 ("In practice, the principle of distinction must be applied based on information which is practically available and can reasonably be regarded as reliable in the prevailing circumstances.").

status.[130] It is unlikely that any jihadist terrorist would opportunistically exploit this standard in order to falsely gain protected status. Even despite this fact, however, there are strong reasons to defend a modified standard for abandonment. Given that the criteria for membership is our previously identified hybrid concept of functional membership, abandonment or renunciation would be demonstrated by the continued non-existence, for a sustained period of time, of the very factors that led to the finding of functional membership in the first instance. If, for example, the individual no longer receives and carries out orders from the command hierarchy, this would necessarily entail that the individual is no longer a functional member of the terrorist organization. With this caveat, then, the hybrid concept should offer bona fide comfort to civil libertarians committed to conduct rules.

V. Conclusion

This new standard has the virtue that it avoids the "revolving door" problem noted by Justice Barak in the Israeli Supreme Court decision. In fact, the standard is more permanent than the transitory standard offered by Justice Barak, yet it is not so permanent that it runs afoul of the "for such time" requirement of the Additional Protocol. The linking principle is easy to administer, self-applying, and based on semi-public criteria, which makes it a functional equivalent to being a member of a military organization. True, this new linking principle is not as easy to administer as the traditional IHL linking principle of being a member of a military organization, but it is certainly easier to apply than the criminal law notions of conspiracy and complicity that require intensive fact-based determinations by a neutral decision-maker. The linking principle is consistent with the underlying legal principles embedded in the laws of war, as well as the legal instruments that codify them. Although the linking principle may not be as permissive as some governments would wish, it is better to utilize a narrow linking principle that is legally and philosophically justified, rather than a looser linking principle that cannot be justified.

---

130 *Cf.* ibid. ("A continuous combat function may be openly expressed through the carrying of uniforms, distinctive signs, or certain weapons. Yet it may also be identified on the basis of conclusive behaviour, for example, where a person has repeatedly directly participated in hostilities in support of an organized armed group in circumstances indicating that such conduct constitutes a continuous function rather than a spontaneous, sporadic, or temporary role assumed for the duration of a particular operation.")

3

CAN JUST WAR THEORY JUSTIFY TARGETED KILLING? THREE POSSIBLE MODELS

Daniel Statman

I. Introduction

Side by side with conventional methods of warfare practiced openly in the battlefield—whether on the ground, in the air, or on the sea—there were probably always other forms of fighting taking place; leaders were being poisoned, secret agents were dying in questionable car accidents, and developers of new weapons were mysteriously disappearing. While such covert forms of warfare are the mainstay of a whole genre of action movies, by and large, they have escaped the radar of philosophical and legal attention. Things have changed in the past decade from the time such "irregular" killing, now known as targeted killing (hereafter "TK"), became an official tactic in some democratic states, notably Israel and the United States. The question of whether or not such killing is legitimate and towards whom (military activists only or political/religious leaders too) has been extensively discussed over the past decade and is still deeply controversial. Though most of the discussion has been conducted from a legal point of view, for most writers there seems to be no discrepancy between the legal and the moral points of view. Most writers who believe that TK is legally unacceptable also believe that it is morally unacceptable, while those who believe that TK is legally justified tend to think that it is also morally alright. Furthermore, it is often moral arguments that tend to ground the legal conclusions.

In this chapter, however, I say nothing about the legal status of TK, but instead focus on its morality. In section II, against most common wisdom in the field, I suggest that the notion of TK should be released from its association with the war (or wars) against *terror*. In section III, I present three interpretations of just war theory that will serve as the basis for my moral analysis of TK. In section IV, I turn to this analysis and show how each of the three interpretations supports the practice of TK.

II. TK, terrorism and guerilla warfare

I shall take the intentional and indiscriminate killing of civilians to be the salient characteristic of terror. Paradigmatic examples would be the blowing up of a restaurant or of a school bus, or the shooting into a crowd in a shopping mall. Since both Al Qaeda and Hamas are terrorist organizations under this definition, and since many of their members have fallen prey to operations of TK carried out by the United States and Israel respectively, it should come as no surprise to find that most of the literature takes it for granted that the normative status of TK depends on it being a counterterrorism tactic. Blum and Heymann, for instance, start their recent discussion of TK by asking the reader to imagine the following scenario:

> [T]he US intelligence services obtain reliable information that a known individual is plotting a terrorist attack against the United States. The individual is outside the US, in a country where law and order are weak and unreliable. US officials can request that country to arrest the individual, but they fear that by the time the individual is located, arrested, and extradited, the terror plot would be too advanced, or would already have taken place.[1]

Given such circumstances, they ask whether the United States would be allowed to target this suspected terrorist without first capturing, arresting and trying him, and their subsequent discussion is aimed at answering this question. Thus, their entire discussion is conducted under the assumption that TK is a "counterterrorism tactic."

Similarly, in his chapter in this volume, Jeremy Waldron starts his discussion of TK by asking whether we would be comfortable with some norm, N1, concerning TK, being in the hands of our enemies. This is what N1 says: "Named civilians may be targeted with deadly force if either (a) they are guilty of past terrorist atrocities or (b) they are involved in planning *terrorist atrocities* (or are likely to be involved in carrying them out) in the future."[2] Finally, note the title of an influential article by David Kretzmer that poses the central dilemma in the field: "Targeted Killing of Suspected Terrorists: Extra-Judicial Execution or Legitimate Means of Defense?"[3]

---

[1] Gabriella Blum and Philip Heymann, "Law and Policy of Targeted Killing," 1 *Harvard National Security Journal* (2010) 145.

[2] Jeremy Waldron, "Justifying Targeted Killing With a Neutral Principle?," in this Volume, ch. 4.

[3] David Kretzmer, "Targeted Killing of Suspected Terrorists: Extra-Judicial Execution or Legitimate Means of Defence?" 16 *European Journal of International Law* (2005) 171.

This association between TK and counterterrorism is ubiquitous in the moral and legal literature on TK.[4]

To see why the association is misleading, let us slightly change the scenario portrayed by Blum and Heymann. Instead of the potential target plotting a terrorist attack—that is, an indiscriminate attack against civilians—imagine that he is plotting a military attack on some American military facility, in the United States or abroad. Imagine that he plans to launch a very accurate, GPS guided missile against this facility. The other parts of the story remain the same, especially the inability of the United States to rely on law enforcement agents to take care of the threat by arresting this individual. Let's call the original scenario The Terror Scenario (T-Scenario) and the revised one The Military Scenario (M-Scenario). (I realize that nations like the US and Israel often describe any attack against them by non-state groups as a terror attack, regardless of whether the target is military or civilian. However, while their wish to delegitimize their attackers is understandable, calling attacks on military targets "terrorist attacks" is conceptually and normatively misleading.)

Should our judgment regarding the use of TK in the M-Scenario be different than our judgment regarding its use in the T-Scenario? I think not. The moral justification for killing the individual in Blum and Heymann's story—if such a justification exists—must lie in the right to self-defense, and for this right to be activated, a number of conditions must be satisfied: that the plotted attack is unjust; that the only way to stop it is to kill the would-be perpetrator; that such killing is proportionate to the intended evil; and, in the view of some philosophers, that the plotter is morally responsible for the threat posed. Since, *ex hypothesi*, these conditions are satisfied in both scenarios, killing the would-be perpetrator would be permissible in both, which means that the terrorist aspect of the intended attack makes no difference regarding the permissibility of TK.

In response, one might argue that since, by its very nature, the threat in the T-Scenario is much graver than the threat in the M-Scenario, TK would be allowed only in the former but not in the latter. But this response is misguided. First, the fact that an attack is terrorist in the sense used here does not necessarily mean that it is more serious than a non-terrorist attack. The potential harm of terror attacks to human lives and to national security, just like that of military attacks, is a matter of degree. Some terror attacks harm only a few individuals and have only a marginal effect on national security, while some military attacks harm the lives of many and pose a very serious threat to national security. Hence, there is no reason to suppose

---

[4] For other illustrations, see Daniel Statman, "Targeted Killing," 5 *Theoretical Inquiries in Law* (2004) 179; Om M. Jahagirdar, "Targeted Killing, Not Assassination: The Legal Case for the United States to Kill Terrorist Leaders," 10 *Journal of Islamic Law and Culture* (2008) 231; and Richard Murphy and Afsheen John Radsan, "Due Process and Targeted Killing of Terrorists," 32 *Cardozo Law Review* (2009) 405.

a priori that TK would be permitted only against the perpetrators of terror attacks and not against those who attack military targets. Second, even if indiscriminate attacks on civilians were in some sense worse than discriminate attacks on military targets, the latter might still be severe enough to ground a right to self-defense of the potential victims, or of the state acting on their behalf, including the right to use TK if necessary. And, of course, the entire just war tradition is based on the idea that the threat posed to states by attacks on their military facilities and personnel substantiates a right to use lethal force against the attackers. Surely not only full-fledged wars justify such a response, but more limited attacks on military targets as well.[5]

In the past decade, we have become all too accustomed to real-world examples of the T-Scenario. Consequently, we have come to associate TK with counterterrorism, both conceptually, that is, characterizing TK as directed against terrorists, and normatively, that is, regarding its counterterrorist nature as the basis for its moral and legal justification. But one could easily think of examples of M-Scenario too, namely, guerilla organizations that cause serious harm to military facilities and personnel while refraining, as a matter of principle, from attacking civilians. Their members do not wear uniform, they hide among the civilian population, and there is no reliable government to which to turn in order to ask for them to be arrested. If TK is justified against terrorist organizations, it is unclear why it would be unjustified against such guerilla organizations too.[6]

To make the point more concrete, think of the following possibility. Assume that Hamas gets hold of more accurate missiles than those it currently has, and that it decides to fire them only at military targets. This possibility is not altogether imaginary because, in response to the Goldstone Report, Hamas insisted that it had never aimed at civilian targets.[7] This claim is evidently a sham, but nevertheless it might reflect the beginning of an understanding on the part of Hamas that because of the widespread disgust evoked by terror, targeting military objectives might turn out to be more beneficial to their cause than targeting civilians. If Hamas adopts such a

---

[5] The right of nations to launch war to prevent threats to their territory and sovereignty has been challenged by Richard Norman, *Ethics, Killing and War* (Cambridge University Press, 1995) ch. 4, and David Rodin, *War and Self-Defense* (Oxford University Press, 2002). I cannot go into this issue here, so I will just assume that such threats do ground a right to national defense. In the end, even Norman and Rodin accept this, though this move on their part comes somewhat as a surprise. See Norman, ch. 6, Rodin, 196–9, and Daniel Statman, "Moral Tragedies, Supreme Emergencies and National-Defense," 23 *Journal of Applied Philosophy* (2006) 311.

[6] Admittedly, in the real world most guerrilla organizations do not limit their activities to military targets and they resort to terrorism too. But (a) the proportion of civilian and military targets varies, with some organizations (the pre-state Jewish *Haganah*, for instance) adopting quite a restrictive policy regarding the direct attack on civilians, and (b) it is, in any case, surely conceivable that such organizations would adopt such a policy for the reasons mentioned in the text.

[7] See, e.g., the interview with Hamas activist Diya al-Din al-Madhoun at <http://www.terrorism-info.org.il/malam_multimedia/English/eng_n/html/hamas_e096.htm> accessed November 3, 2011.

new tactic and all else remains more or less equal, Israel might still be permitted to use TK against Hamas activists. The same goes for Al Qaeda. Imagine that instead of the World Trade Center, the 9/11 attackers had targeted only military objects: The Pentagon, West Point, The Naval Academy, etc—all of them legitimate targets in war. Would the American response have been less severe? More to the point, would the United States then have been morally prohibited from using TK against bin Laden and his comrades?

It is my contention that terror organizations, such as Hamas or Al Qaeda, manifest all the typical features of guerilla organizations, namely, the conduct of an irregular war against a perceived occupying or colonial entity, the practice of taking shelter within the civilian population, and so on, though their targets are, for the most part, civilian rather than military. The point of this section was to argue that *if* TK can be justified against organizations like Al Qaeda and Hamas, it is by virtue of the guerilla component of these organizations, not by virtue of the terror component. If TK is justified, it is because the members of such organizations do not fight in the open—in the battle*field*—as in regular ("old") wars, but act out of hidden shelters, in a way that often makes TK, especially by drones, the only way to fight against them. The arguments that support TK would be just as convincing, or, at any rate, convincing enough, if these organizations decided to shift their fire from civilian to military targets, if their attacks became discriminate instead of inhumanely indiscriminate.

III. Three explanations of the discrimination principle

Much of the literature on TK concerns the dilemma of whether TK should be analyzed in terms of the rules concerning law enforcement, or in terms of the rules regulating warfare (*jus in bello*).[8] This is indeed a crucial dilemma in this area. However, the impression one gets from some of the literature is that whether or not a situation is defined as war is a bit arbitrary, a matter of formalistic legal definitions whose moral logic is not always clear. What I propose to do in this section is to examine the legitimacy of TK according to three competing interpretations of just war theory (JWT). I hope to show that this examination yields interesting results regarding the legitimacy and scope of TK, as well as regarding the normative definition of war. By examining the way each of these interpretations of JWT would treat TK, I hope to contribute not only to a better understanding of the normative status of TK, but also to a better understanding of JWT itself. (In light of this discussion, the dilemma between the law enforcement model and the war model will turn out to be secondary.)

---

[8] The dilemma comes up in almost all discussions of the topic. See, for instance, Kretzmer, *supra* n. 3; Blum and Heymann, *supra* n. 91.

What is shared by all proponents of JWT is the conviction that wars are not necessarily immoral, and that the conditions for the morality of war are such that they can be and are at times satisfied by the warring parties. But, beyond this shared conviction, there is substantial disagreement about its theoretical basis. In contemporary discussions of JWT, three main models can be identified: the Individualist model ("Individualism"), the Collectivist model ("Collectivism"), and the Contractualist model ("Contractualism"). I present each of them in turn and then try to see what follows with regard to TK.

One further comment before we present these three models. Since TK is a tactic of warfare, its moral status belongs to the domain of *jus in bello*. While traditional JWT, just as international war, regards this domain as independent of questions regarding *jus ad bellum*, this view has been seriously challenged recently, mainly by Jeff McMahan. I suggest we bypass this issue by assuming, for the sake of argument, that in terms of *jus ad bellum*, the countries using TK are justified in their initial decision to go to war, or to use lethal force, as they are responding to unjust threats against them. Everybody agrees that the justness of a cause does not legitimize all means, hence the question we wish to answer: is TK a legitimate means of warfare given that the war of which it is a part is just? Let's see what the various understandings of JWT might offer as answers.

According to Individualism, the permission to kill human beings in war is ultimately the same license we have to kill in individual self-defense. The conditions that must be satisfied for some individual, V, to be permitted to kill another individual, A, in self-defense, are the same conditions that would allow V1 + V2 + V3 to kill A1 + A2 + A3 in self-defense, and the same conditions that would license the use of lethal force by an entire army against another army. In the words of McMahan, the prominent advocate of this model, "the morality of defense in war is continuous with the morality of individual self-defense. Indeed, justified warfare just *is* the collective of individual rights of self- and other-defense in a coordinated manner against a common threat."[9] Individualism might concede that the threats that typically trigger a right to wage war (the threat to territorial integrity or to sovereignty) are almost necessarily posed by collectives, but insist that the moral basis for the killing in war is blind to this collective aspect and recognizes, so to say, only individuals.

If, at the end of the day, the conditions for the permission to kill human beings in war are the same as those required for individual self-defense, then we have to be able to justify ourselves in the world to come, and to do so we have to show that that individual was posing (probably with others) an unjust threat, that he was morally responsible for doing so, that there was no other way of neutralizing the threat other than killing him, and that the killing was not disproportionate to the

---

[9] Jeff McMahan, "The Ethics of Killing in War," 114 *Ethics* (2004) 693, 717.

evil prevented.[10] Since, in McMahan's theory of self-defense, the aggressor's moral responsibility plays a crucial role in making him liable to defensive attack, it is morally better to kill the person who is responsible for *initiating* some unjust threat than to kill the person who, at a given point in time, *poses* the threat, but bears less responsibility for it (acting, for instance, out of excusable ignorance).[11]

The requirement to justify each instance of killing in war on the basis of the same conditions used to justify killing outside the context of war is why I name this position "individualist." As McMahan shows at length, it leads to a refutation of the fundamental tenets of traditional JWT, of which I shall mention only one. Since many civilians, such as politicians, people in the media, or religious authorities bear higher responsibility for the aggression of their country than 18-year-old soldiers thrown into the battlefield, the former might be more liable to attack than the latter, a claim which undermines the most fundamental requirement of *jus in bello*, namely, to maintain a strict distinction in warfare between combatants and noncombatants.

This brief presentation of McMahan's view refers to what he calls "the deep morality of war,"[12] which, I believe, is the morality we should consult if we want to understand the deep morality of TK. In McMahan's view, this deep morality need not shape the actual *laws* of war. We will have to see later whether this dual morality—deep and shallow (so to speak) —is relevant to TK too.

I turn now to Collectivism. On this model, it is metaphysically false to describe wars in purely individualist terms. In war, as Noam Zohar puts it, "it is a collective that defends itself against attack from another collective, rather than simply many individuals protecting their lives in a set of individual confrontations."[13] Wars are irreducibly both collectivist and individualist; they are conflicts between collectives, but they are initiated and fought by individual members of the respective collectives. This dual reality, suggests Zohar, yields a dual morality, one that respects these two aspects of war.

What does this mean in practice? Zohar's basic idea is that some members of a collective can be seen as identifying with it, or as officially (or half-officially) representing it. This is particularly true of soldiers, those individuals selected by the state to represent it, so to say, in the violent encounter with its enemies. When we kill soldiers, we do not kill them qua individuals, but qua agents of the enemy collective. We are under the reign of the collective aspect of war. By contrast, in dealing

---

[10] Elsewhere I show that a consistent application of this requirement leads to pacifism; see Daniel Statman, "Can Wars be Fought Justly? The Necessity Condition Put to the Test," *Journal of Moral Philosophy* (forthcoming, 2011).

[11] In McMahan's jargon, it is better to kill *initiators* than to kill *pursuers*. See McMahan, *supra* n. 9 section VI.

[12] Ibid. at 730.

[13] Noam Zohar, "Collective War and Individualistic Ethics," 21 *Political Theory* 606, 615.

with civilians, we retain the individualist prism, which implies that it would rarely be permissible to target them. While, for McMahan, the key factor for making any individual a legitimate target in war is responsibility, for Zohar "the key factor is participation: combatants are those marked as participating in the collective war effort, whereas the rest of the enemy society retain their exclusive status as individuals."[14] For McMahan, the reason we are usually allowed to attack combatants, but not noncombatants, is that the former tend to be more morally liable than the latter. For Zohar, it is because in attacking the former we are allowed—even obliged—to take the collectivist perspective and ignore questions about individual liability, while in attacking the latter, individualist liability seriously constrains what we might do.

Note that, in Zohar's view, when the relevant morality is not dual, namely, when only the individual perspective applies, what determines liability to defensive attack is moral responsibility. It is because most soldiers are below the threshold of responsibility required to make them liable to attack that we need the collective perspective to explain how killing them might be permissible.

I turn finally to Contractualism, recently developed at length by Yitzhak Benbaji.[15] On this model, the most central aspects of *jus in bello* are based on a tacit agreement between states as to how wars should be conducted. The agreement is made ex ante, and it is binding because it is mutually beneficial and fair. The basic idea is that states have an interest in reducing the horrors of war without thereby preventing themselves from effectively defending themselves against aggression. So they agree in advance that combatants may be attacked with almost no restrictions, while noncombatants may not be (directly) attacked, with almost no exceptions. This involves a tacit agreement on the part of combatants to give up their natural right not to be attacked. By giving up this right, they thereby grant the other side moral license to kill them in warfare, license that is independent of whether the war fought by the other side is just or not. Soldiers marching into battle (to use an image from old wars) are like boxers entering the ring. In both cases, the harm to which they are morally vulnerable has nothing to do with individual desert or liability, and everything to do with a reciprocal forfeiture of rights.

That some aspects of the rules of engagement are a matter of convention is undeniable. For example, while it is forbidden to shoot pilots bailing out of crippled aircraft unless upon landing they refuse to surrender,[16] there is no similar rule restricting

---

[14] Ibid. at 618. Of course, others might participate too in the war effort, but, in Zohar's view, they are not "*marked* as participating in the collective war effort."

[15] Yitzhak Benbaji, "A Defense of the Traditional War Convention," 118 *Ethics* (2008) 464; "The War Convention and the Moral Division of Labour," 59 *Philosophical Quarterly* (2009) 593; "The Moral Power of Soldiers to Undertake the Duty of Obedience: A Contractarian Case for the War Convention," *Ethics* (forthcoming).

[16] See art. 42 of the Protocol Addition to the Geneva Convention:

the shooting of soldiers attempting to escape from burning tanks. And while the use of blinding lasers in battle is not permitted, the use of other weapons which can cause very serious injuries, including blindness, is allowed.[17] If such rules are to be respected, it is only by virtue of their being accepted and followed by all parties to the conflict.[18] The novelty of Contractualism is the idea that such conventions about warfare are not the exception but the rule; that the most basic elements of the *in bello* code are anchored in a tacit contract between the warring parties.

A common response to Contractualism is that if the *in bello* rules are "mere conventions," then they do not carry serious moral weight. But, as emphasized by Waldron, conventions might be in some sense arbitrary, but nevertheless are very serious—*deadly* serious.[19] A good example is the UK convention to drive on the left. This is indeed a "mere" convention, but once it is accepted and followed by the community of drivers, there exists a powerful moral reason to comply with it, even in circumstances in which one can benefit from driving on the right. The same applies with the rules of engagement: although most of them are grounded in a convention, there is a very strong moral reason for nations to stick to them in warfare.

It is important to realize, as will become clear in the next section, that all models accept what I shall call "The Responsibility Condition [RC]" for liability to attack, though they diverge in the way they understand its application. Assume that the other conditions for self-defense are satisfied (unjust threat, success, necessity, and proportionality). According to Individualism, RC would then be both a necessary and a sufficient condition to liability to attack in self-defense. According to Collectivism, it would be a sufficient condition, but not a necessary one (combatants are all liable to attack, although many of them do not satisfy RC). According to Contractualism, in a pre-contract world (a state of nature), RC is both necessary and sufficient for liability while in a post-contract world, it is neither necessary nor sufficient; combatants may all be attacked, although many are below the threshold of moral responsibility, while noncombatants may never be (directly) attacked, though many of them are above the required threshold.

---

1. No person parachuting from an aircraft in distress shall be made the object of attack during his descent.

2. Upon reaching the ground in territory controlled by an adverse party, a person who has parachuted from an aircraft in distress shall be given an opportunity to surrender before being made the object of attack, unless it is apparent that he is engaging in a hostile act.

[17] See Gross, *Moral Dilemmas of Modern War: Torture, Assassination and Blackmail in an Age of Asymmetric Conflict* (Cambridge University Press, 2010) ch. 3 ("Shooting to kill: The paradox of prohibited weapons").

[18] Gross emphasizes that regarding prohibited weapons "the importance of reciprocity is overwhelming" (ibid. at 66).

[19] See Jeremy Waldron, *Torture, Terror, and Trade-Offs* (Oxford University Press, 2010) ch. 4 ("Civilians, Terrorism, and Deadly Serious Conventions").

Table 1 The moral status of combatants and noncombatants

	Individualist morality	Collectivist morality	Contractualist morality
Combatants	Liable for the unjust threat they pose to the just side	Represent the collective	Have forfeited their natural right to life
Noncombatants	Usually not responsible for the unjust threat posed by their countries	Judged as individuals, there is no justification for killing most of them	Protected by the *in bello* contract

Let me then summarize the way these models substantiate the discrimination principle. We should distinguish three groups: innocents, such as young children, who pose no threat at all and are, in any case, below the threshold of moral responsibility; adult noncombatants, some of whom could be thought to culpably contribute to the unjust threat posed by their countries; and combatants. All three models agree that, regarding innocents, the regular presumption against killing human beings is at work, hence they are clearly morally immune to (direct) attack. All three models also accept the traditional distinction between combatants, who may be attacked, and noncombatants, who may not. The reasons they offer for this distinction are presented in Table 1 above.

Finally, how important is it, morally speaking, for each of these models, whether a given situation is defined as *war* or not? According to Individualism, such definition seems to bear no moral significance. Since the moral principles that govern wars are precisely the same as those that govern self-defense in conflicts between individuals, or between groups of individuals, saying that we are "at war" makes no moral difference. I would go further to speculate that for philosophers like McMahan such definitions should always be treated with suspicion, and as attempts to obtain wider moral permissions than those one is entitled to; that is, those entailed by the standard conditions for legitimate self-defense.[20] By contrast, Collectivism seems to assign crucial significance to such definition. Since wars are (violent) conflicts between collectives and since collective morality is activated only in such circumstances, whether or not a conflict is defined as war makes all the difference. If it is war, then a whole category of people—the category of combatants—thereby loses its moral immunity from attack. (Thus, according to Collectivism, whether TK is a domestic, law-enforcing tactic, or an act of warfare against an enemy collective is indeed a central question.) For Contractualism too, defining a conflict as war is morally critical because only in war is the *in bello* contract activated with its

---

[20] McMahan explicitly rejects the view that war is "morally discontinuous with other activities and conditions" ("*The Ethics of Killing in War*," *supra* n. 9, 15).

special permissions (to kill all combatants) and restrictions (not to attack noncombatants). The contract is between *states* and it concerns violent conflicts between them, namely wars. According to both Collectivism and Contractualism, when war breaks out, a whole new moral perspective comes to light, one which has radical implications for what we may or may not do.

IV. TK in light of the three models

What does each of these models entail with regard to the legitimacy of TK? Let's start by reminding ourselves that TK has been used by both Israel and the United States against individuals identified as playing a significant role in initiating and posing perceived unjust threats, some of them against civilians ("terror attacks"), others against military targets ("guerilla attacks"). At least in the case of Israel, even opponents of TK admit that the accuracy of identification has been very good.[21] As emphasized above, these individuals tend to bear full moral responsibility for the attacks that they pose. On the face of it, this would be sufficient to show that the objects of TK cannot enjoy the immunity granted to those in the second row ("noncombatants") of the above table, which implies that they fall within the terms of the first row ("combatants"), hence are morally liable to attack. However, such a move would ignore the fact that, after all, the victims of TK are not soldiers in the usual sense of the word. Moreover, some objects of TK had no direct involvement in military activity, such as Sheikh Ahmad Yassin, the founder and spiritual leader of Hamas, killed by Israel in 2004. Whether or not this fact makes a difference depends, as we shall now see, on which model of JWT is adopted.

According to Individualism, the crucial condition that must be satisfied to justify killing human beings in self-defense is that they are morally responsible for some grave threat whose neutralization is the end in mind.[22] From this point of view, the formal affiliation of such people with some organization, or even some state, plays no intrinsic role in making them lose their moral immunity to being attacked. To be sure, often such affiliation indicates some kind of causal connection to the unjust threat, for instance, in the case of a member of an army or of some other security body. But one could pose an unjust threat to an individual or to a nation even without such membership, and one could be a member of the army—a soldier—and make no contribution, or even, in fact, a *negative* contribution to the

---

[21] See Gross, *Moral Dilemmas in Modern War,* 119 and his reference to the report by the human rights association B'Tselem.

[22] At one point McMahan toys with idea that a person might be liable to attack in order to avert some threat even if he was not responsible for that specific threat but for a similar one in the past or in the present. He even goes on to speculate that one might be liable to self-defensive attack if he is "willing or disposed to create an unjust threat" or if he possesses "a bad moral character" (*supra* n. 9, 722).

threat posed by one's army. (Think of a soldier who spends most of his term in jail because of breaches in discipline, or simply think of a lousy soldier.)

It follows that, on this model, the very fact that activists of Hamas and Al Qaeda are not soldiers in the usual sense of the word makes no difference to their moral status vis-à-vis the potential victims of the threats that they (individually or collectively) pose. Hence, if the only way to block such threats is to kill these activists, there is no reason to see why, according to McMahan and other supporters of Individualism, the use of targeted killing should be impermissible. Moreover, given the voluntary nature of enlisting in these organizations and acting within them, it seems that their members, or activists, are typically *more* liable to defensive attack than conscripted soldiers in regular armies, whose responsibility for their participation in unjust wars is rather weak. Hence, if the latter are legitimate targets for attack, a point on which all non-pacifists agree, the former are certainly so as well.

We can now see how, within the individualist view, TK is not just one permissible tactic among others, but the preferred one (unless it happens to be impractical or ineffective).[23] It does a much better job of distributing the self-defensive harm in accordance with moral responsibility. We must always bear in mind that, in response to a perceived unjust attack, the alternative to targeted killing is not no killing, namely some form of pacifism, but non-*targeted* killing, namely, ordinary military operations which cannot be as sensitive to the differences in moral liability between the activists or combatants on the other side. For McMahan, a targeted killing of 50 initiators and central pursuers of unjust attacks is surely much better, from a moral point of view, than killing the same number of combatants—and probably many more—in a regular military operation.

I mentioned earlier that most of the debate about the legitimacy of TK focuses on the question of whether TK should be understood within the law-enforcement or within the armed conflict model. We can now see that insofar as the deep morality of self-defense is concerned (as interpreted by Individualism), this distinction is quite shallow. What makes a person liable to defensive attack is the fact that he or she satisfies the conditions mentioned above (moral responsibility for an unjust attack, etc), and these conditions are indifferent to whether the threat he or she presents (or is responsible for) is posed on the interstate or the intrastate level; whether it is posed as part of a conflict between two individuals, or between two groups of individuals. *If* it is morally permissible to use TK against the leaders of some military or semi-military organization, it must be because of the gravity of the unjust threat they pose, their moral

---

[23] The effectiveness of TK has been hotly debate in the past decade, see e.g. Gross, *supra* n. 21, 114–21. I cannot go into the matter here. Let me just note my impression that the level of evidence required to establish the effectiveness of TK is much higher than that required to establish the effectiveness of other military measures, in regular wars or in asymmetric conflicts, though the latter measures might be much more destructive.

responsibility for posing it and the inability of the state to neutralize the threat by other means. But surely the same considerations could at times justify the use of TK against some leaders of the mafia too. The current struggle of the Mexican government against the drug industry and against the criminal activity around it might be a case in point.

The conclusion regarding the in-principle legitimacy of using TK even against criminals sounds rather scary, and this is precisely where consequentialist considerations, which, for McMahan, are not part of the "deep morality," kick in. Imagine two similar threats to innocent lives, one posed by an in-state criminal and the other by an out-state terrorist. Suppose that these are circumstances in which it would be permissible to kill the terrorist. It might nevertheless be forbidden to do so in case of the in-state criminal, because of the potentially disastrous ramifications to the rule of law. But would such considerations rule out TK in the context of wars against guerilla or terror organizations too? In arguing that the laws of war need not match the deep morality of war, McMahan seems to open the door to a positive answer to this question. However, the arguments he offers for this mismatch do not seem to apply to the type of conflicts in which TK is being used; that is, conflicts between states like the United States or Israel and organizations such as Al Qaeda and Hamas. In McMahan's view, "it is dangerous to tamper with rules that already command a high degree of allegiance. The stakes are too high to allow for much experimentation with alternatives."[24] This is a fair consideration, but it seems irrelevant to the war against organizations such as Al Qaeda and Hamas, which have already seriously tampered with these rules. When one side stops playing by the rules, it is hard to see the further danger which is created when the other side does so too (except for the danger to the first side, of course). In response, one might argue that the danger McMahan has in mind is not the moral escalation that might accrue as a result of changing the laws of war in the context of some particular conflict between, say, the United States and Al Qaeda, but the escalation that might follow regarding wars in general. That Al Qaeda violates the accepted rules of warfare and directly attacks civilians is one thing. That the United States should do so is entirely different and might seriously destabilize the widely accepted conventions of warfare. I see two difficulties with this response. First, I think that the international community—justifiably or not—sees conflicts with such organizations as different (or "unique") and hence, in practice, is not likely to apply the rules and practices that are used in them to regular wars. Second, even if the danger of such escalation was realistic, I am not sure that it is fair to expect the United States (or any other country) to follow rules that are not mandated by the deep morality of war just in order to minimize the risk of escalation to other countries and to the international community in general.

---

[24] McMahan, *supra* n. 9, 731.

Let us turn now to Collectivism and see what it implies regarding TK. Recall that under this model, even combatants would not be legitimate targets for lethal attack if judged by their personal blame only. If we relied exclusively on the principles of individual morality, pacifism would probably be the only respectable option. However, wars are not only conflicts between individuals—those who actually drop bombs, throw hand-grenades, and fire missiles—but also, essentially, between collectives. When we kill enemy soldiers, we do not kill them qua individuals attacking us, but qua representatives of our enemy, and such killing is permissible only because it expresses the collectivist aspect of war.

Is, then, the American campaign against Al Qaeda a war in the relevant sense, namely a conflict between collectives? To simplify, let us ignore the other allies and assume that it is just the United States versus Al Qaeda. The United States would definitely qualify as a collective in the required sense and, as a result, its soldiers would be legitimate targets in any war situation.[25] But what about Al Qaeda? Though Al Qaeda did attempt to claim that it was acting in the name of all Muslims, the claim was obviously groundless. First, as various polls and surveys demonstrated, an overwhelming majority of Muslims objects to Al Qaeda's tactics.[26] Second, and more importantly, even those who support Al Qaeda cannot be said to constitute a *collective* in the sense of the model we are discussing. Surely a collective in this sense is more than a group of people who happen to share a view about some issue. It must be a group of people with "thick" connections between them, people with some kind of a shared memory, with shared aspirations, people who perceive themselves as members of the same group. The metaphysical claim that the existence of a collective cannot be reduced to that of the individuals comprising it cannot be applied to just any group of people sharing some feature (playing bridge together every Sunday, admiring John Lennon, or hating the United States). There is, therefore, no collective that Al Qaeda can reasonably be said to represent that would make its members or activists liable to lethal attacks in the way proposed by Collectivism.

A possible response to this argument would be to give up the requirement of representation and suggest that the collective assumed by the model at hand is not the nation but its army. Indeed, in his later work, Zohar explicitly takes this line against his initial view.[27] Applying it to the present context would yield the conclusion that

---

[25] Needless to say, not all Americans support the war in Iraq, but, nevertheless, it makes full sense to say that the American forces in Iraq are fighting *on behalf of* the U.S.

[26] See, for instance, <http://articles.cnn.com/2007-12-17/world/saudi.poll_1_qaeda-saudi-arabia-coalition-troops?_s=PM:WORLD and http://www.csmonitor.com/2007/0425/p01s04-wome.html> accessed November 3, 2011.

[27] See Noam Zohar, "Innocence and Complex Threats: Upholding the War Ethic and the Condemnation of Terrorism," 114 *Ethics* (2004) 734, 739–40 and idem., "Should the Naked Soldier be Spared? A Review Essay of Larry May, *War Crimes and Just War*," 34 *Social Theory and Practice* (2008) 623, 633, n. 21 ("Initially I tended to identify the collective entity as 'the nation'; I am now inclined instead to focus on the army as a collective agent.").

Al Qaeda should be regarded as a collective, which would mean that its members may be intentionally killed regardless of their individual responsibility.

I see two difficulties with this revised version of Collectivism. First, if the collective entity is the violent organization that threatens us, then, by the same token, this would apply to intra-state groups too, such as the mafia, or local gangs of criminals, whose actions therefore cannot be reduced to those of their individual members. That would legitimize the use of military measures in general, and TK in particular, against members of such organizations, regardless of their individual responsibility, a conclusion that very few would accept. Second, even if the army we are fighting against should be regarded as a collective, that should not change the obvious fact that—in standard wars—we are also fighting against some *nation* or some *state*. We would then need some account of the relation between the *two* collectives we are fighting against (the nation and its army), and the notion of representation seems to come back as a natural answer.

There is more to say about the merits of these two versions of Collectivism, but this would not be necessary in order to determine the legitimacy of TK against Al Qaeda. If Al Qaeda is a collective in the sense required by Collectivism, then clearly the use of TK against any of its members would be legitimate. But even if not, the same conclusion follows. Recall that the collective perspective in war does not replace the individualist one, but rather supplements it, thus turning what otherwise would be illegitimate killing to legitimate. As mentioned earlier, the reason that such killing would be illegitimate has to do with the reduced responsibility of young conscripted soldiers. But this reason does not apply to Al Qaeda activists, hence individualist morality would be sufficient to justify the use of TK against them, just like in Individualism.

The case of Al Qaeda produces a special challenge to Collectivism because Al Qaeda cannot be reasonably said to stand for an independently defined collective which is in a state of conflict—at *war*—with the United States. But what about Hamas? In the case of Hamas, it does make sense to see its activists as acting on behalf of the Palestinians in their conflict with the Israelis in a way that fits the framework Collectivism has in mind. All the more so if one sees the military activists of Hamas as representing not the Palestinians in general, but those living in the Gaza Strip, over which Hamas has had effective control since 2007. What implications does this state of affairs have with regard to the binding rules of warfare in general, and to the use of TK in particular?

From the point of view of Collectivism, the answer seems to be straightforward. If Israel and the Hamas semi-state in Gaza[28] are at war, then the combatants of one

---

[28] This is still the case in Gaza even after the reconciliation agreement between Hamas and Fatah signed in May 2011.

side—IDF soldiers and Hamas activists, respectively—are permitted to kill the combatants of the other side even if the latter have only diminished responsibility, or even no responsibility at all, for the aggression mounted by their collectives. Just like in conventional wars, this permission is almost unconstrained. Thus, if Hamas is permitted to kill any Israeli soldier, even a conscripted 18-year-old one, it is definitely permitted to use TK against key figures in the Israeli army, officers and commanders, who bear more responsibility for the perceived threat against the Palestinians and play a more central role in its implementation; the permission would also apply to the similar use of TK on the part of Israel.

It seems, then, that the addition of the collectivist perspective makes the use of TK against national organizations such as Hamas[29] even easier to justify than it would have been without this perspective. Since most of Hamas activists are not conscripted,[30] they typically bear enough moral responsibility to make them legitimate targets for lethal attack even if viewed as individuals. That they can—and ought to—be seen also as agents of the Palestinian *collective* makes their killing even more legitimate.

Finally, what would Collectivism say about the targeted killing of political leaders, the paradigmatic case of *assassination*? Zohar clearly wishes to limit the group of those "subsuming under their collective identity,"[31] and who are therefore legitimate targets for lethal attack, to enemy *combatants*, which would rule out the killing of politicians. Yet it seems to me that the logic of his argument could easily be interpreted as including politicians too. After all, there is no person who represents a nation, expresses its identity and acts on its behalf better than its prime minister, president or king. This is why wars are often described as against the leaders of the enemy collective, for example, "the war against Hitler."[32] It would thus make perfect sense to say that when we kill such leaders we are thereby expressing our recognition of the collectivist aspect of the conflict. To be sure, there might be good pragmatic reasons to refrain from such a policy, which Collectivism too could appreciate. But in terms of the deep morality of war, with its individualist and collectivist levels, even targeting politicians would be a legitimate act of war.

Let's turn to the last model I analyzed above, the contractualist one. Although proponents of Contractualism about wars often regard states as the only parties to the contract, there seems to be no reason to limit the parties to the contract in this way. The fundamental logic of Contractualism applies to all groups that realize that one day they might have to defend themselves by force. They all share an interest

---

[29] Hamas started as a religious movement, associated with the Islamic Brotherhood, but since the first Intifada it has undertaken a central role in the Palestinian national movement.

[30] Though last year there were reports that Hamas is considering a draft in Gaza. See <http://www.jpost.com/MiddleEast/Article.aspx?id=182774> accessed November 3, 2011.

[31] Zohar, *supra* n. 13, 618.

[32] Googling this expression yields more than a million results.

in adopting rules that would reduce the horrors of war without making effective defense impossible. In other words, the *in bello* contract is ex ante mutually beneficial and fair not only for states, but also for national liberation movements, and for all groups that fight against oppression and discrimination.

However, such groups might opt out from the contract, or not enter into it, if the behavior of the other side manifests no respect for the accepted conventions. When this is the case, then the *in bello* contract is not activated, so to speak, because no individual will resign his or her fundamental rights, especially the right to life, without a reciprocal resignation by the other relevant parties, and no state has authority to offer such resignation in the name of its citizens. The fact that the *in bello* contract is not activated does not mean that, morally speaking, everything is up for grabs. Even in such grim circumstances, the fundamental rights of people maintain their force; it is still forbidden to rape women, to bomb kindergartens, to torture prisoners.

The first thing we should ask about TK is whether its wrongness, *if* it is wrong, belongs to the category of non-conventional wrongs like rape and torture, or to that of conventional wrongs (that is, actions made wrong merely as a result of a convention) like the prohibition against shooting pilots parachuting from their aircraft, or against directly killing noncombatants. I think it is immediately obvious that TK does not belong to the former. As emphasized throughout the chapter, TK is aimed at people who are actively involved in planning and carrying out perceived unjust threats to other people, hence they are liable to defensive attack against them. Moreover, they seem more liable than plain soldiers in regular wars, the killing of whom is never seriously put in question. Hence, if TK is wrong, it is only conventionally so; wrong because of an accepted convention against it.

This conclusion is sufficient to show that, according to Contractualism, nothing could be wrong with the use of TK against organizations like Al Qaeda which have no respect for the conventions of warfare. Our moral obligations towards Al Qaeda are limited to non-conventional ones and TK is not among them.

But what about military groups that do show at least some respect for the war convention? Does the *in bello* contract—to which they are parties—forbid TK? The way to answer this question within a contractualist framework is to ask whether a rule forbidding TK is one that the parties to the contract would ex ante accept, which is the same as asking whether it is a rule that is mutually beneficial and fair. Imagine, then, that sitting around the table to review proposals for the *in bello* agreement are not only delegates of states but also of various guerilla organizations, mainly those fighting for national liberation. The states unanimously accept the discrimination principle, which grants all sides unrestricted permission to kill combatants while imposing upon them a strong prohibition against killing noncombatants. The natural right to life of combatants is compromised (all of them become legitimate targets regardless of the justness of their cause, their level of responsibility and so on) in order to guarantee the moral immunity of noncombatants (many of whom *would* be legitimate targets otherwise). Since wars are mainly clashes between combatants and not between civilians, this deal does not reduce the parties' ability to achieve effective defense against those attacking them. Would the non-state parties join this deal?

In other words, TK seems perfectly compatible with the fundamental purpose of the *in bello* contract. It enables states to effectively defend themselves from the threats posed against them, without having to opt for full-scale war that, ex hypothesi, *would* be legitimate in the circumstances under discussion. Thus, not only would contractualism license TK, it would recommend it as a preferred tactic. Ex ante, the parties to the contract would find it mutually beneficial to adopt a rule that would lower the chances of a full-scale war by granting permission to all sides to utilize a whole battery of more limited military measures. The use of such measures would be much less destructive and lethal than war, and could provide decent, albeit imperfect, defense. (Remember that wars do not guarantee perfect defense either.)

Furthermore, assuming, as we did, that national liberation movements are sides to the *in bello* contract, we should assume that they must take into consideration not only their current, pre-state situation, but also their (hopefully, in their own eyes) post-state situation. They must envisage a scenario in which one day they themselves (that is, the nation-state they will found) may face threats of guerilla and terror attacks of precisely the same nature that they are at present posing to others. And when they reflect on such a scenario, they will surely see the advantage of a rule permitting the use of measures such as TK in order to avoid full-scale war.[33]

While Contractualism does not ground a prohibition on the use of TK against soldiers in regular armies, or fighters/activists in irregular armies (guerilla/terror organizations), it does ground a prohibition on the use of TK against political leaders. This follows from the basic logic that grounds the *in bello* agreement, namely, the wish to prevent total war. In this vein, each side renounces its natural right to kill those responsible for the unjust threat it faces, in return for a parallel renouncement by the other side. However, as emphasized above, such renouncement must be reciprocal. If one side frees itself from such an agreement,

---

[33] Others might object, arguing that the moral and military advantage of TK might weaken opposition to the use of force. I take the objection to mean that the easy availability of TK would result in an unjustifiable use of it, in circumstances in which refraining from force altogether would be the appropriate behavior. I can see the danger, but the prospects of reducing the chances of a fully-fledged war, or even of a large military operation, seem to me more important. See also Kenneth Anderson, "Efficiency *in Bello* and *ad Bellum* Making the Use of Force Too Easy?", in this Volume, ch. 14.

the other side is no longer bound by it. Political leaders who send their armies to fight unjust wars have no natural right not to be killed by the victims of their aggression.

A common complaint often voiced by terror or guerilla organizations is that of the conventions of warfare work to the advantage of strong parties—that is, the states—and are therefore unfair. To formulate the complaint in reference to the fundamental rationale of Contractualism: if such organizations were bound by these conventions, they would lose their ability to beat their enemies. Our enemy has aircrafts, tanks and drones, they say, while we only have homemade bombs to use against school buses, restaurants, and so on. If we are not allowed these measures, in effect we are prevented from defending our rights.

This complaint is not very convincing. Which constraints do such organizations think should be removed in order to achieve the assumed fairness? To judge by the examples just mentioned, examples which reflect the actual behavior of Al Qaeda and Hamas, these organizations would like to be exempted from the prohibition against intentionally attacking the innocent. But this prohibition is anchored in the *natural* rights of the potential victims, not in any kind of contract, and it is hardly ever overridden by other considerations. Hence, if the difficulties faced by guerilla and terror organizations to advance their goals have to do with constraints of this kind, the object of their complaints is not Contractualism.

They might still insist that the situation is unfair and redirect the complaint to natural morality. But that would amount to a plain rejection of morality. Unfortunately, in the actual world, the wicked often prosper, while the righteous fail. Often, at least in the short run, being loyal to morality—telling the truth, respecting the rights of workers, taking care of sick relatives—is hard, demanding, and not rewarding. Nevertheless, as Kant famously argued, such "subjective restrictions and hindrances" to the notion of duty, "far from concealing it, or rendering it unrecognizable, rather bring it out by contrast *and make it shine forth so much the brighter.*"[34] That following morality puts one at a disadvantage is hardly ever a justification for evading its demands.

I should add that the idea that morality sometimes imposes a price upon us is built into the standard conditions for legitimate self-defense, conditions which quite obviously favor the strong (the aggressor) over the weak (the potential victim). This is most evident with the proportionality condition. Assume that the victim has no other way to defend herself but to do X, but that X would be disproportionate to the harm prevented. The proportionality condition requires

---

[34] Immanuel Kant, *Fundamental Principles of the Metaphysics of Morals* (Prometheus Books, 1988), emphasis added.

that she refrain from X-ing, even though she will be harmed as a result, maybe with no remedy.

The unfairness complaint, then, cannot be taken to apply to the violation of natural rights. So maybe it applies to contractualist rights? Thus understood, the organizations under discussion would be asking for an exemption from the ban against killing noncombatants such as politicians or religious authorities, the killing of whom is ruled out by the *in bello* contract but not by natural morality. "We are too weak and technologically deprived to limit our attacks to military targets," they would say, "hence fairness requires letting us target civilian targets (from the above groups and similar ones) as well." This sounds like a reasonable position. In contractualist terms, it amounts to a refusal to join the contract that is perceived as not mutually beneficial. But, of course, not joining the contract is a double-edged sword; it relieves one of the duties imposed by it, but, at the same time, denies its benefits and protections. If guerilla and terror organizations attack civilians (of the kind that, in the circumstances, do not have a natural right not to be attacked), there is nothing unfair in the other side doing the same to them.[35]

At times, it seems that proponents of the unfairness argument rely on the idea that the very fact that side A loses shows that side B was stronger, which means that the terms of the competition must have been unfair; they enabled the strong side to overcome the weak side. This, of course, is absurd. It would entail the ridiculous conclusion that for the sake of fairness we would have to make sure in all competitions and conflicts that no side prevails.

V. Conclusion

In order to sharpen the question under discussion, I suggested we assume that the relevant circumstances are those in which a semi-military group unjustly attacks the military or civilian targets of some state. In an earlier paper,[36] I argued that since, in such circumstances, almost all non-pacifists would concede that the attacked state has a right to launch a war, or a serious military operation against this group, they are forced to accept the legitimacy of TK which has clear moral advantages over the use of massive military force in the "old" way. In this chapter, I tried to strengthen this conclusion by showing how it follows from the main interpretations of just war theory today. I summarize the results of my discussion

---

[35] One might also say that in such circumstances, these organizations have no *right to complain*, though such claims carry an air of paradox. See Saul Smilansky, "The Paradox of Moral Complaint" in Saul Smilansky, *10 Moral Paradoxes* (Blackwell, 2007), and Talia Shaham, "Is There a Paradox of Moral Complaint?" 33 *Utilitas* (2011) 344.

[36] Statman, *supra* n. 5.

in these tables, Table 2 dealing with TK against militants, and Table 3 with TK against political or religious leaders.

Let me conclude with three final comments:

First, the permissibility referred to in these tables refers to the "deep morality of war," which means, in the present context, *the moral liability of TK victims to being attacked.* Do other considerations, mainly of a consequentialist nature, make a difference to the final moral verdict? As I said earlier, I am somewhat skeptical. McMahan's reason for resisting the consistent implications of the deep morality of war is that he finds it "dangerous to tamper with rules that already command a high degree of allegiance. The stakes are too high to allow for experimentation with alternatives."[39] However, we are currently in a world of "new wars,"[40] and if there is one thing that is obvious about these wars it is that they do *not* have "rules that already command a high degree of allegiance." Rules as well as practices are now in the making. Therefore, the danger

Table 2 Is TK permissible against fighters/military activists and why?

	Terrorist groups	Guerilla groups (limited use or no use of terror)
Individualism	Yes: RC satisfied	Yes: RC satisfied
Collectivism	Yes: RC satisfied and usually *also* the collectivist condition[37]	Yes: RC satisfied and usually *also* the collectivist condition
Contractualism	Yes: RC satisfied (and *no contract*)	Yes: licensed by contract

Table 3 Is TK permissible against political/religious leaders and why?

	Terrorist groups	Guerilla groups that do not use terror
Individualism	Yes: RC satisfied	Yes: RC satisfied
Collectivism	Yes: RC satisfied	Probably no: do not "represent" the collective[38]
Contractualism	Yes: RC satisfied (and *no contract*)	No: breach of the contract

[37] Definitely if the relevant collective is identified with the terrorist organization itself, as in the revised version of Collectivism (*supra* n. 27). The same applies to the next rubric to the right.

[38] I assume that this would be Zohar's view, though, as argued above, in my own understanding of the collectivist model, there are good reasons to see such leaders as "identical" with the collective and hence as legitimate targets under the collective perspective.

[39] McMahan, *supra* n. 9, 731.

[40] See e.g. Mary Kaldor, *New and Old Wars* (Polity Press, 2006).

that bothers McMahan seems less troublesome regarding the rules we construe for fighting these new wars—including those permitting TK.[41]

Second, opponents of TK are shocked by the apparent ease by which countries like the United States or Israel "execute" people with nothing remotely close to due process, and with no need to establish imminent danger or individual responsibility. From the perspective of domestic law-enforcement, this is indeed shocking. But from the perspective of war it is not shocking at all. This is precisely what war is about—killing enemy combatants with no due process and with hardly any constraints whatsoever. This might lead some readers to object to wars in general and opt for pacifism. That is a respectable option. This chapter, however, assumed a *non*-pacifist view and tried to show how the main theories that ground this view and permit the wholesale killing in war, also permit the use of TK. There is nothing about TK that is inconsistent with the main theories of just warfare.

Third, if indeed TK has such military and moral benefits,[42] as I tried to show, and if it is compatible with all current versions of JWT, why do some circles express such strong opposition to it? One suspects that what often underlies this opposition is not a position on the level of *jus in bello*—that is, an objection to TK as a tactic of warfare—but a position at the level of *jus ad bellum*. This is confirmed by the surprisingly positive way TK was regarded in the recent war against Libya. As Anderson rightly remarks, "the speed and timing of this sudden new acceptance of drones in Libya raises questions as to what drove the change of heart."[43] In my view, what drove the change of heart was a change in the way the *cause* of the war was regarded, which helps to see that there was never a real problem with TK on the *jus in bello* level. At any rate, the war in Libya might have transformed the debate about TK. To cite again from Anderson: "Libya might have sanitized drones as a tool of overt, conventional war and might have shifted the debate over their abilities to be discriminating and sparing of civilians."[44]

---

[41] A similar criticism applies to Waldron, who argues that to revise or reformulate norm N0 ("in the conduct of armed operations, only combatants may be targeted deliberately. Civilians may not be targeted deliberately") "involves considerable risk." See J. Waldron, "Justifying Targeted Killing with a Neutral Principle?" this volume, at ch 4. First, it seems to be very forced to group people launching missiles and planting bombs under the morally relevant rubric of "civilians" rather than of "combatants." Second, for the reason mentioned in the text, I see no risk, definitely no considerable one, in using TK against the military activists/fighters of guerilla/terror organizations. I think there is more risk in *not* using TK, and in choosing conventional military operations instead.

[42] Stephen de Wijze suggests that targeted killings "are in essence cases of dirty hands. That is, they are acts that are morally justified, even obligatory, yet also morally wrong." See de Wijze, "Targeted Killing: A 'Dirty Hands' Analysis," 15 *Contemporary Politics* 305, 317. However, in the view presented here, there is nothing morally wrong with TK and, moreover, TK is less dirty than most killing that takes place in conventional warfare.

[43] Kenneth Anderson, "Targeted Killing and Drone Warfare: How We Came to Debate Whether There Is a 'Legal Geography of War'," in Peter Berkowitz (ed.), *Future Challenges in National Security and Law* (Hoover Institution Press, 2011) 17.

[44] Ibid.

4

JUSTIFYING TARGETED KILLING WITH A NEUTRAL PRINCIPLE?

Jeremy Waldron

I. Introduction

Suppose we are convinced by the arguments (moral and pragmatic) in favor of a norm permitting targeted killing of civilians under certain conditions. Should we then be happy with the promulgation of that norm as a norm of national or international law? One of the things that happens when a norm, N, becomes law is that people who argued in favor of it (informally in discussions of policy or in some more formal settings such as a legislature or a convention setting the terms of a treaty) lose control of it. It goes out into the world and becomes the common possession of all, to be used by all comers in ways they think fit. We are not responsible for all uses that may be made of N but, especially if N is to be part of the law of armed conflict, we ought to consider whether we are comfortable with N in the hands of our enemies. So, for instance, if the norm in question is something like

> N_1: Named civilians may be targeted with deadly force if they are presently involved in planning terrorist atrocities or are likely to be involved in carrying them out in the future,

then we should consider whether we are comfortable with N_1 in the hands of Al Qaeda or Hamas or some state that sponsors activities of the kind those organizations engage in.

Our discomfort at this prospect is not, of course, legislatively decisive. But we should reflect on the sources of the discomfort and consider whether it should make any difference to the kind of N we argue for or the kinds of arguments we bring forward in its favor. We should not make the case for such a norm based on the improbable supposition that only fine people like us will be involved in its administration. We should make the case for it (if we can) having in mind both historical and recent experience of how principles like N_1 are actually used in the kinds of situations of war, insurgency, and other destabilizing events that make politicians want to authorize extrajudicial killings, and having in mind too our best guess about how N_1 is likely to be used once it is unleashed in the world in the future. That is the subject of this chapter, and it will be addressed directly in section IV.

This inquiry is important in itself, but it may also be helpful in bringing to the surface any substantive misgivings that we have about the norm in question. Once we see how it is likely to be abused, we may understand better why we are inclined to oppose it. This chapter, then, will explore not only the issue of likely abuses of norms like N_1 but also the way in which those abuses disclose inherent difficulties with the norm. In the last part of the chapter (sections VIII to X), I shall make the case that the liability to abuse of norms like N_1 is not just an instance of the general liability of *any* legal norm to abuse. It is connected also with its content, for N_1 represents a relaxation of one of the most important norms we have—the norm against murder[1]—and the justifications adduced for N_1 or for similar principles represent a significant modification of our usual way of arguing about murder—a modification (I shall argue) in the direction of moral opportunism and unreliable analogy.

II. Herbert Wechsler and Gerald Dworkin

I have chosen to approach these issues using the idea of "neutral principles." Can a norm such as N_1 operate as a neutral principle or does our support for N_1 depend on the assumption that it will not be used by anyone who is very much less scrupulous than we would be in administering its terms? Can it operate as a neutral principle as between people who differ in good faith about how to use and apply the terms it contains? I have in mind the controversial factual judgments involved in the use of "terrorist" in N_1, for example. Or, again, does our support for N_1 depend on its being applied and the appropriate judgments being made by people like us?

The phrase "neutral principles" needs explanation. It was introduced into American constitutional jurisprudence by Herbert Wechsler and into political philosophy by Gerald Dworkin.[2] My use of it is slightly different from theirs, and Wechsler and Dworkin have differences too in their respective uses of the idea. Let me very briefly indicate the concerns they raised under this heading.

---

[1] No apologies for the use of this term. "Homicide" is no doubt calmer. Other terms, besides "targeted killing," might be "extrajudicial killing," "assassination," and "the use of death squads."

[2] Herbert Wechsler, "Toward Neutral Principles of Constitutional Law," *Harvard Law Review*, 7 (1959) 31; Gerald Dworkin, "Non-neutral Principles," *Journal of Philosophy* 71 (1974) 491.

As a constitutional scholar concerned with the rule of law, Wechsler worried in his 1959 Holmes Lectures about the principles that legal scholars and legal activists were using to map the text of the Constitution onto problematic situations like school desegregation. When we say that the 14th Amendment requires the desegregation of schools (even though the Amendment makes no reference to education), we presumably have in mind some mediating principles (for example, principles of interpretation) which explain what "equal protection" means in this (or any) context. No doubt the intermediate principles we invoke will be appealing to us and our supporters. But are they just principles we have tailored to generate the particular outcome that we are looking for? Or are they principles that we think everyone has reason to apply in constitutional cases and that we would be willing to follow even when they lead to less politically palatable outcomes? The demand for neutral principles is a demand for mediating principles that we can commit ourselves to following (or allowing others to follow), once our immediate interest in them—for the bearing they have on this case—has evaporated.[3]

Gerald Dworkin's concern was slightly different. Dworkin was interested in the bearing of something like moral universalization on the practical principles we adopt. We tend to adopt the principles that suit us. But, says Dworkin, "[t]here must be consistency in conduct, a refusal to make special pleas in one's own behalf or to consider oneself an exception to general principles." One way of testing this, he said, is to contemplate a clear case of something that might be regarded (by some) as an application of our principle but which we would certainly not approve of, and to consider—in the face of a possible allegation of inconsistency—what the relevant difference might be between that action and the one we are justifying with our principle. Here is his example:

> [T]hose who defend the civil disobedience of Martin Luther King are asked to specify a relevant difference between his actions and those of George Wallace.... There are obviously a number of ways of defending oneself against such charges of inconsistency.... I want to focus in this essay on one particular way of meeting the accusation of inconsistency.... In the case of civil disobedience the defense is that the laws that King broke were unjust while those Wallace violated were just.[4]

Dworkin says that it is characteristic of this sort of response to the charge of inconsistency that the application of the ancillary principle to particular cases is a matter of controversy for the parties whose conduct they are supposed to regulate. After all, Governor Wallace would not have accepted that the laws he was breaking were just. Dworkin calls a principle "non-neutral" if its application is controversial in this way. Of course, it is not non-neutral in the crude sense that one endorses only

---

[3] Note that Wechsler was not looking, as some have thought, for a neutral version of the 14th Amendment. He was looking for neutral principles to help us apply the 14th Amendment. The amendment itself, of course, conveys certain non-neutral values and commitments.

[4] Dworkin, *supra* n. 2, 491–2.

one's own applications of it (as such) and not those of others. Usually what happens is that one endorses the "*true*" applications of it—which of course one believes, in all humility, one's own applications to be—and condemns false or incorrect applications (by others). One says:

> I did not say that one is justified in breaking the law if one believes it to be unjust. The action is justifiable only if the law *is* unjust. Governor Wallace was quite wrong in thinking the law he was opposing was unjust.[5]

Though he accepted that this was a fair distinction: Dworkin was interested in the circumstances in which this maneuver might be inappropriate or the circumstances in which one is required to test one's principles not just against the prospect of what one judges to be their correct application but also against the prospect of their attempted application in the world that we know by the fallible and quarrelsome beings that we share it with.

Gerald Dworkin's interest is close to mine. He believes that in constructive moral theory (like indirect utilitarianism or Rawlsian contractarianism) one has to consider proposed principles in the light of what will happen when people (as they are) *try* to apply them, not just in the light of their ideal or correct application. So, for example, an excessively complicated principle might have to be rejected if the bad consequences of its incompetent application outweigh the benefits of its correct application. And equally a principle that uses terms like "just" or "unjust" as the condition of an action needs to be considered in light of the consequences of its being applied by people who have the wrong view of justice as well as the consequences of its being applied by people who have the right view.

If this is true of constructive moral principles, it is certainly true of law. When we make something the law, we deliver it into the hands of a large variety of law-appliers, ranging from ordinary people who undertake what jurists call its self-application[6] all the way through to officials and judges whose job it is review other people's applications of the norm. A norm like N_1, which uses terms like "terrorist atrocities," must be evaluated in light of the judgments that are likely to be made about the application of that phrase by all of those to whom N_1 is presented as the law, not just in light of the judgments that are likely to be made by those who apply it correctly.

I have spent this brief time in the company of Gerald Dworkin and Herbert Wechsler mostly to give readers a taste of how the idea of neutral versus non-neutral principles has been used in the past, and to indicate—in a ball-park sort

---

[5] Ibid. at 495. (This is extracted from a dialogue that Dworkin imagines.)

[6] For the idea of self-application, see Henry M. Hart and Albert M Sacks, *The Legal Process: Basic Problems in the Making and Application of Law*, William N. Eskridge and Philip P. Frickey eds, (Foundation Press, 1994) 120.

of way—my misgivings about norms like N₁. Before turning directly to those misgivings, let me say something about another neutrality idea.

III. The neutrality of *jus in bello*

The problem I have identified for this chapter overlaps with an issue that has long been a staple of discussions about the laws of war. As they are organized at present, the laws regarding the actual conduct of war (*jus in bello*) are even-handed as between aggressors and defenders, as between those who went to war unjustly and those who are engaged in a just war. Soldiers of both the unjust aggressive side and the just defending side are legally liable on an equal basis to deadly force at the hands of the other side's combatants; soldiers of either side are entitled to quarter and other protections; forbidden munitions such as poisonous gas are forbidden alike to attackers and defenders; civilians may not be attacked whether they are civilians who belong to an aggressor country or not, and so on. In other words, the application of *jus in bello* works independently of the application of *jus ad bellum*. Being a violator of *jus ad bellum* confers no greater liability to attack than complying with it, nor does it leave combatants with fewer rights. In this sense *jus in bello* is neutral.

This decoupling of *jus in bello* from *jus ad bellum* is controversial.[7] Recently some philosophers—Jeff McMahan, for example—have suggested that it should be adjusted to reflect the moral realities of warfare, so that combatants in an aggressive or other unjust cause should lose the privilege of using deadly force against their opponents and so that civilians responsible for aggressive or other unjust war-making should be liable to attack.[8] This is because he believes that "it is moral responsibility for an unjust threat that is the principal basis of liability to [be the target] of defensive (or preservative) force."[9]

I have my doubts about McMahan's suggestions.[10] A principle that distinguishes among those who are and those who are not liable to deadly force has to be administered among people who almost certainly disagree (or pretend to disagree) about justice and guilt in relation to the armed conflict in question. It may be impossible to administer norms using words like "just" and "guilty" in their traditional moral

---

[7] There is a good discussion in Michael Walzer, *Just and Unjust Wars: A Moral Argument with Historical Illustrations*, 4th edn (Basic Books, 2006) 34 ff.

[8] Jeffrey McMahan, "The Ethics of Killing in War," *Ethics*, 114 (2004) 693.

[9] Ibid. at 722–3.

[10] I have explored these in Jeremy Waldron, "Civilians, Terrorism and Deadly Serious Conventions" in *Torture, Terror and Trade-offs: Philosophy for the White House* (Oxford University Press, 2010) 82–90 and in "Legal Judgment and Moral Reservation" in Agustín José Menéndez and John Erik Fossum (eds), *Law and Democracy in Neil MacCormick's Legal and Political Theory: The Post Sovereign Constellation* (Springer, 2011) 107, 117–24.

senses, or to impose tests about whose application there is likely to be irresolvable disagreement, particularly because most administration of the laws of war is self-application. Laws *in bello* therefore have to use simple categories like the distinction between members of the organized military and civilians even though these categories are certainly over- and under-inclusive by moral standards. This is because the moral standards by which we judge them to be over- and under-inclusive could not possibly themselves be administered effectively in these circumstances of dissensus. McMahan acknowledges this: "[T]he fact that most combatants believe that their cause is just means that the laws of war must be neutral between just combatants and unjust combatants, as the traditional theory insists that the requirements of *jus in bello* are."[11] McMahan suggests that these points are less important for his moral inquiry than they would be if he were making a legal proposal. I will come back to this in section VI.

The difficulty occasioned when the rule that McMahan envisages is entrusted to both sides in a morally controversial war is an instance of the problem of neutral principles. But not all such instances involve connecting *jus in bello* with *jus ad bellum* in this way. One can imagine applications of N_1 that do not depend on controversial judgments about *jus ad bellum*. In a conventional war, people on either side might commit terrorist atrocities and might therefore be liable for deadly force under N_1 whether they were unjustly responsible for initiating the wider war or not.

IV. In whose hands?

When we defend N_1, we imagine its being used against Osama bin Laden or some high operative in Hamas. We think of the worst, most badly behaved civilian leaders of terrorist organizations and we contemplate making arrangements, either through the use of assassins and special forces teams or the use of predator drones or "surgical" air-strikes, to have them killed. It makes most of us feel good to defend principles that might have applications like these.

But what should we make of German claims in 1939–40 that its killing of Polish politicians was a legitimate response to acts of terrorism and aggression that they were fomenting? What should we make of the claim by Osama bin Laden that his organization's killings of Americans are appropriate responses to the "crusaders'" terroristic incursions into sacred Arab lands? Or the preposterous claims made by Bashir Assad that his forces are battling terrorists in the streets of Syria's cities and towns and that people are singled out by his death squads because they are in the vanguard of a terrorist rebellion? That these claims are false goes without saying.

---

[11] McMahan, *supra* n. 8, 730.

That they are made in bad faith goes without saying. But that they might be used in public "justifications" of targeted killings is also beyond doubt, at least in an environment in which all sides are aware that N_1 is the law.

Please do not misunderstand me. People sometimes get very indignant about what they call "moral equivalence" if anyone ever draws any sort of comparison or analogy between the conduct of (say) the British or American governments, on the one hand, and conduct of real bad guys, on the other hand.[12] For the record, I am not claiming "moral equivalence" between Osama bin Laden and those who controlled the operation that killed him. I am just reflecting on the ways—the outrageous ways, no doubt—in which these norms might be used by those we rightly regard as our enemies. I believe that there is a difference between (a) an environment in which it is well known that targeted killing of civilians under any circumstances is impermissible and (b) an environment in which targeted killings are licensed by principles such as N_1. The difference in (b) is not just that the principles are deployed according to their terms and that as a result bad people like bin Laden are killed. The difference is also that N_1 is now there in the world to be abused and we have added another resource to the rhetoric that tyrants, terrorists, and aggressors use to "justify" their murderous behavior.

Of course, no one on our side would accept these "justifications" for a moment, and I shall turn shortly (in section V) to the question of how we might control or regulate the application of norms permitting targeted killing. But first let us consider another range of possible applications which we cannot dismiss so easily.

I have said that if we defend norms like N_1 and N_2 we should consider their use in the hands of others (such as our enemies). In addition—assuming that the "we" in "we should consider" are noble scholars contributing to a volume like this—then we should also think about the use of N_1 in the hands of the people on *our* side who are likely in fact to have authority or power to order actual killings on this basis. I mean people like the Presidents of the United States or France or South Africa, for example, or the Prime Ministers of the United Kingdom or India or Israel. And I mean also the decision-makers under their authority—in the United States, the Secretary of Defense, the leaders of the Central Intelligence Agency, and military commanders in Afghanistan. In the case of the United States and Israel, we should think about the way in which targeted killing, with or without the authorization of national and international law, is being used at the moment. And we should think also about how it is likely to be used in the future.

---

[12] See, e.g., Christopher Hitchens, "Guru of the Left Spouts Ignorance," *Chicago Sun-Times,* May 14, 2011, 17 (complaining that Noam Chomsky "is still arguing loudly for moral equivalence, maintaining that the Abbottabad, Pakistan, strike would justify a contingency whereby 'Iraqi commandos landed at George W. Bush's compound, assassinated him, and dumped his body in the Atlantic'.")

Of course, that involves speculation. More reliable food for thought may be generated by an awareness of the way in which the predecessors of those who occupy these offices have used terms like "terrorism" in the past, and by reflecting on who previous American or South African presidents or previous British Prime Ministers might have wanted to have had killed if only they had had these principles in their legal armory. The history of both successful and inept American conspiracies to assassinate foreign leaders, over the past 50 years, is well known. Less well known are the hundreds or (depending who you believe) thousands of assassinations of communist-inclined village-level officials by American and South Vietnamese forces in the 1960s and '70s under the auspices of "the Phoenix Program."[13] We know the South African government condemned ANC leaders as terrorists and tried to assassinate (and succeeded in assassinating) some of them: in 1988 Albie Sachs, now retired as a justice of the South African constitutional court, lost an arm and an eye in one of these attempted targeted killings. The British experience is particularly sobering. As it clung to the remnants of empire, Britain faced insurgencies in Palestine, Cyprus, Aden, India, Kenya, Malaya, and elsewhere. At one time or another, the British government denounced as terrorists all those who emerged to become leaders of these countries: Kenyatta and Makarios are two well-known examples. The temptation to respond to insurgency by targeting people who could be described (convincingly or, for public relations purposes, plausibly) as terrorists would no doubt be irresistible if it were not for the presence of strong legal norms prohibiting assassination. Or think of the use that might have been made of such principles in the conflict in Northern Ireland. The British government was comfortable framing and imprisoning innocent people in the struggle against terrorism and would no doubt have been comfortable hanging them, had hanging been available. It is impossible to imagine that if a principle like N_1 had been on the books in the 1970s it would not have been used to "take out" IRA and Sinn Fein leaders, including some who are currently Belfast statesmen.

In all or many of these cases, the governments in question were no doubt responding not just to insurgency or terrorism but to something like targeted killing organized by the very people that they would have been tempted to target. That was true, for example, of IRA activity (had been true in fact of Irish insurgency from the days of Michael Collins to the assassination of Earl Mountbatten in 1979), Irgun activity in Palestine in the 1930s and 1940s, Mau-Mau activity in Kenya, and Viet Cong activity in South Vietnam. Terrorist and insurgent organizations have often presented themselves as following some version of these principles (sometimes embodied in their published "rules of engagement"). No doubt such presentations

---

[13] For rival accounts, see Dale Andrade, *Ashes to Ashes: The Phoenix Program and the Vietnam War* (Lexington Books, 1990) and Douglas Valentine, *The Phoenix Program* (William Morrow, 1990). Valentine's figure is 25,000 assassinations; Andrade's view is that the number of assassinations was much, much lower than that.

are often disingenuous. The question for us is whether we would expect the use of such norms to be any less disingenuous in the hands of, say, the British government had the British been willing, in effect, to adopt death squad tactics in their wars against terrorism and insurgency. No doubt the abuses by a government will be somewhat different in character from abuses by terrorists or insurgents. But are they any less worrying and do they afford any less reason for hesitation when we now contemplate making such principles (and at least some of the mentality that inevitably accompanies such principles) into rules of law?

V. Preventing abuses

But isn't every legal principle liable to abuse? Surely—some will say—it is a fallacy to discredit candidate principles like N_1 simply on the ground that our opponents or our predecessors might be inclined disingenuously to claim the benefit of them to cover their crimes or simply on the ground that someone might apply the principles in a mistaken or self-serving fashion. After all, one could say the same about many principles governing the use of force that we recognize without hesitation, such as the elementary principle of self-defense.

Well, let us consider the self-defense principle for a moment. That principle permits a person who faces an immediate deadly threat to use deadly force against the one attacking him. People have certainly claimed the benefit of this principle to "justify" killings that were in fact not justified or to attempt to legitimize their own homicidal activity; or they have used it on the basis of negligent or mistaken assessments of the threats that were in fact facing them. Such abuses are unfortunately part of the life of any legal principle. And surely it would be wrong to say that there should be no such principle of law for decent people to rely on simply because other people might be inclined to abuse it. (Notice, by the way, that this is not just an analogy. Defenses of principles like N_1 are often presented as extensions or extended applications of the principle of self-defense.)

The point about acknowledging the potential for abuse as part of the life of any legal principle is a good one, as far as it goes. Here is where it goes. In the case of the principle of self-defense, we do not simply acknowledge the point and then shrug off any concern about abuse. Instead we make arrangements within our system of law for very careful checks on each and every purported exercise of the principle. In a well-functioning legal system, *every single action using deadly force on this ground* is subject to intense, immediate and sustained investigation by the police, and charges are brought in a great many such cases where there is serious doubt about whether the criteria for self-defense have been properly applied. If there is disagreement, it is settled by a court. It is unthinkable that we would have and recognize and uphold anything like the self-defense principle (let alone its cousin, the license to use deadly force in defense of others) at the level of municipal law without the safeguard of such investigations.

Is any of this envisaged for N_1? It probably depends on which advocate you ask. One thing we do know is that the governments into whose hands the use of these principles would fall in the first instance (governments like ours) are not the kinds of governments that have ever shown themselves to be scrupulous in this regard. In section IV, I suggested that history gives us every indication that if they had such powers these governments would abuse them. And now I am saying that our experience of such governments (again, *our* governments)—and of their activities over the past 50 years or so—also suggests they will do everything in their power to prevent or obstruct retail investigation by the courts and the police of the targeted killings that might be authorized under these principles.[14] They will certainly do so if there is any genuine prospect that real abuses by them or their operatives might be exposed and prosecuted. We have no experience to the contrary on this point.

Of course, there are good reasons for not having in the case of targeted killings the sort of investigations we routinely conduct into domestic cases of self-defense. Intelligence sources might be compromised; the procedures would obstruct military and counter-terrorist activity, and so on. Those are good reasons for not having investigations of this kind (which can be added to the bad reasons of political advantage, secrecy for its own sake, and a desire to cover up the abuses that would undoubtedly flourish in an environment dominated by this principle). The lack of any prospect of investigations analogous to those we conduct in criminal law is therefore understandable. Quite so. In other words, any argument for principles such as N_1 is to be conducted not only on the basis that they are evidently prone to abuse but also on the basis that there will not and cannot be any institutionalized safeguards of this kind to prevent such abuses.

Might there be safeguards of another kind? I have focused mainly on *ex post* investigations analogous to those we use in ordinary cases of self-defense. In the ordinary self-defense situation obviously there is no time for laborious deliberation in advance. But those who defend targeted killings as an extension of the principle of self-defense often do so by jettisoning or modifying the immediacy requirement—at least to the extent that the immediacy of a threat is supposed to preclude anything but the most hasty, immediate and panicked decision-making in response to it. Once one drops that aspect of immediacy—even if the threat referred to N_1 can be called imminent in some other sense—then there might be time and space for ex ante review. A terrorist target is identified and convincing evidence is adduced

---

[14] By retail investigation, I mean investigation case-by-case of every such incident (analogous to what is now routinely done in ordinary cases where someone who has killed another person claims the benefit of self-defense). I do not just mean an occasional (wholesale) investigation of targeted killing as a general policy.

that within a week he will be planting a bomb if he is not stopped in the next few days. Those next few days might give the authorities, both inside and outside the defense and military establishments, an opportunity to review the evidence and the decision to target him that that evidence is supposed to support. I believe that in the past, the IDF has sometimes proceeded on this basis, and maybe it does so still.[15]

However such an ex ante process might still be seen as flawed. The point is that we need to ensure not just that there is some process or other in place, but that it is the sort of process that would be necessary to weed out at least most of the abuses (or most of the worst abuses) to which history has shown such principles are liable, in our hands or in the hands of our predecessors. Think, for example, of other abuses by the authorities to whom it is proposed that these principles be entrusted. There is no particular evidence that, say, the British decision to use torture or inhuman treatment on a very wide scale in Northern Ireland in the 1970s was undertaken hastily, without a process of ministerial review. Similarly the decision to frame, say, the Guildford Four and the Maguire Seven for pub bombings in England was not undertaken without deliberation; their arrest might have been opportunistic but official tampering with the evidence was not. So what we must look for is not just *some* procedure. Given the kind of abuse likely to be endemic to the administration of these principles, we should be looking for a process actually capable of preventing misuses of the principles and prosecuting those who propose abusive exercises. That after all, in the post facto case is what we have for self-defense.

In general I think legal scholars should be much more careful than they have been in offering up the moral basis of the principles that are used in criminal law for principle-building in other environments that differ radically from the integrity of the *administration* of criminal law.[16] Everything we do in criminal law—even when the principles we use and the reasons supporting them seem to be at their most philosophical—is done under the auspices of a well-worked out and fairly reliable system of investigation, procedure and administration. Take that system away, and the principles that remain are naked and precarious. What distinguishes the contribution that legal scholars can make to public debate on an issue like this is not that they can say, along with the denizens of the saloon bar, "Well it's self-defense, isn't it?" Anyone can propose death squads or assassination on that basis. The proper contribution that legal scholars can make is to remind the public how much our acceptance of certain principles in law (including self-defense) is bound up with legal process and how reluctant we should be to deploy principles

---

[15] See Amos Giora, "The Importance of Criteria-based Reasoning in Targeted Killing Conditions," in this Volume at ch. 11. See also the nuanced discussion by the Israel Supreme Court in *Public Committee against Torture in Israel v. Government of Israel* December 14, 2006 (HCJ 769/02) in *Judgments of the Israeli Supreme Court: Fighting Terrorism within the Law*, Vol. 3 (Israeli Ministry of Foreign Affairs, 2009) 85–164.

[16] See, e.g., Russell Christopher, "Imminence in Justified Targeted Killing," in this Volume, ch. 9.

authorizing killing in an environment from which *we know* legal process will be largely banished.

VI. Why not non-neutral principles?

I have proceeded in this chapter on the basis that defenders of norms like N_1 have to contemplate how these norms will be abused if they become public—if, for example, they are promulgated as principles of the laws of war. I have considered them as neutral principles—that is, I have considered how they would work in the hands of those who are inclined to interpret and apply their leading predicates (like "terrorism" and "aggression") in ways different from the ways we think proper. But why should candidate norms be assessed in this way?

One alternative possibility is that N_1 might be proposed, neither as a legal norm nor as a promulgated norm of public policy, but simply as a basis for moral assessment. The idea is that N_1 expresses conditions for the actual justifiability of certain acts of targeted killing. On this account, it is supposed to help us think through the issue of whether all such killings were wrong and it is supposed to help us focus on the factors which, in moral reality, tend to make such killings permissible. Consideration of them is part of what Jeff McMahan has called "the deep morality of war."[17] And it might be part of their status as such that there is an acknowledgment that further reasons and argument will be required before we go anywhere near the prospect of publishing these principles or proposing them as law. The deep morality of war—of which these principles were a part—might have to be, as McMahan puts it, "self-effacing."[18] Still, the delicacy of this relation between deep moral principles and promulgated law does not necessarily discredit the former. For, McMahan would argue, deep moralizing has other uses apart from law reform: "if nothing else, the deep morality of war is a guide to individual conscience" for those who arrive at or happen to stumble upon these principles in their own moral thinking.[19]

So: with this firewall in place (between moral thinking and proposals for law), there is no reason why N_1 should not be considered in the sort of non-neutral spirit that (for example) Gerald Dworkin imagined.[20] For N_1, we would insist that there is a distinction between true imputations of "terrorist atrocity" and false (because mistaken or self-serving or exaggerated) imputations of that kind; and the claim that N_1 sums up the real requirements of deep morality in this area would be a

---

[17] McMahan, *supra* n. 8, 730–3.
[18] Ibid. 732. McMahan gives careful and inconclusive consideration to this prospect; I am not saying he embraces it.
[19] Ibid. 733.
[20] See Dworkin, *supra* n. 4.

claim about a connection (of the appropriate sort) between actual terrorist atrocities (things properly described in those terms) and permissible killings.

Elsewhere in my discussion of McMahan's approach to these matters, I questioned whether there could be any point to the consideration of principles divorced in this way from their possible legal application. McMahan says that even if his moral judgment does not represent a legislative proposal, still it can provide a basis "for the reevaluation of the rules we have inherited," and I responded that that would be an odd sort of "inactive" evaluation.[21]

I now think that is unfair. Just because a norm is not made into law does not mean it has no important practical or political effect. N_1 might be used by scrupulous persons in our security and military apparatus as a basis for establishing, regulating, and limiting the practice of targeted killing, and in particular as a criterion for checking that the right individuals are on the death list; that is, that those targeted for destruction are in fact dangerous in the way the principle describes.[22] Even if it is not policed by a court, N_1 might be politically and militarily effective in this way. And we might trust those to whom its application was assigned to make careful and largely correct determinations of who was engaged in terrorist activity. Our judgment that the use of N_1 was worthwhile in this sense would not be held hostage to any speculation of how it might be abused by our enemies or how similar principles had been abused by less scrupulous officials on our side in the past.

Even so, the neutral principles critique has not yet run its course. I said at the beginning of the chapter that the neutral principles critique of N_1 might be useful not just in itself but also because it might help bring to the surface any substantive misgivings that we have about the norm in question. Our understanding of ways in which the norm is likely to be abused may disclose not just administrative difficulties but substantive objections to a norm of this kind. And those objections will not evaporate just because we take the non-neutral tack.

VII. Assassins, poisoners, and so-called snipers

So what are the substantive objections? One set of difficulties with principles of this kind, was adumbrated by Immanuel Kant in the part of his book *The Metaphysics of Morals* (1797) devoted to the right of nations. Kant wrote:

> A state against which war is being waged is permitted to use any means of defense except those that would make its subjects unfit to be citizens.... Means of defense

---

[21] McMahan, *supra* n. 8, 731 and Waldron, "Legal Judgment and Moral Reservation," *supra* n. 10, 121.

[22] I have in mind here the review processes described in Gregory McNeal, "Are Targeted Killing Unlawful? A Case Study in Empirical Claims Without Empirical Evidence," in this Volume, ch. 12.

that are not permitted include using its own subjects as...assassins or poisoners (among whom so-called snipers, who lie in wait to ambush individuals, might well be classed)...[23]

Some of the reasons Kant adduces for this position have to do with the longer term prospects for peace. In his essay on "Perpetual Peace," written a couple of years earlier, Kant said: "No nation at war with another shall permit such acts of war as shall make mutual trust impossible during some future time of peace," and he cited "the use of Assassins (*percussores*) [and] Poisoners (*venefici*)" as examples.[24] But I think we should take seriously what he says in the version from *The Metaphysics of Morals*. Such stratagems make murderers of our citizens, and whether the philosopher can make sense of it or not—whether with his analytic tool-kit he can plumb the depths of ethos, honor, and tradition that underpin this distinction—being a murderer in this sense is not just a fact about having killed someone (like being a soldier on active service), but something vicious one has become, a dishonorable character one has taken on, that cannot then be sloughed off just as soon as the circumstances that call for targeted killing have passed. And this is not simply a fact about the administration of principles like N_1. It is a consideration—I guess from virtue theory[25]—about the deep morality of targeted killing, and if anything it is exacerbated, not mitigated, by the secrecy with which the deep moral justification (if there is one) of this practice is likely to be shrouded.

This takes us to an important substantive point. Whether we are working in deep morality or law, we must always have an eye to the fact that norms such as N_1 purport to authorize actions that count (or otherwise would count) as murder. They purport to authorize individuals in our armed forces and in our security apparatus to act as murderers. No doubt they do this pursuant to what seem to our leaders to be very good reasons. But it is murder that those reasons are supposed to license and murderers that they are supposed to authorize. That in itself should be enough to stop us in our tracks and to caution us to proceed—if we do proceed with anything like N_1—very, very carefully.

---

23 Immanuel Kant, §57 of "The Doctrine of Right" (6: 347) in *The Metaphysics of Morals* (1797), trans. Mary Gregor (Cambridge University Press, 1991) 154.

24 Immanuel Kant, *Perpetual Peace and Other Essays*, trans. Ted Humphrey (Hackett Publishing, 1983) 109–10. This was what Kant called "The Sixth Preliminary Article for Perpetual Peace among States." More recently it has been argued that a number of the restraints we impose on what may be done *in bello* are oriented to the prospects for peace in the *post bellum* situation. See Jeremy Waldron, "Post Bellum Aspects of the Laws of Armed Conflict," *Loyola of Los Angeles International and Comparative Law Review*, 31 (2009) 31, citing Michael Walzer, *Thinking Politically: Essays in Political Theory* (Yale University Press, 2007) 266 and Oliver O'Donovan, *The Just War Revisited* (Cambridge University Press, 2003) 62.

25 "[L]iberal governments should behave in accordance with the civic virtues that inform the civil society they represent. Assassination seems hardly compatible with political virtue." (Fernando R. Tesón: "Targeted Killing in War and Peace: A Philosophical Analysis" in this Volume, ch. 15.)

Many will say: "Hang on: N_1 does not authorize murder; instead it should be read as defining an exception to the usual understanding of murder—namely an exception based on the desirability of ridding the world of terrorist threats." They may even add, for good measure: "And by the way, the real murderers are those whom these targeted killings aim to eliminate." (On that last point, calling a targeted killer a murderer does not preclude describing his victim as a murderer either.) The point can be conceded to this extent: if it were proposed as law, N_1 would be aiming to refine our understanding of the distinction between justifiable and non-justifiable homicide and thus to refine our sense of which killings count as murder. It is a little more difficult, however, to present it in this light if it is just being used as a policy criterion in the way outlined at the end of section VI.

Either way, N_1 is supposed to do whatever work it does in terrain traditionally patrolled by the prohibition on killing. So any judgment we make about the wisdom or rightfulness of introducing N_1 (whether as law or policy) should be conditioned on our sense of how treacherous this terrain is (the terrain of possible killing), the strength and ubiquity of the temptations that any norm in the area has to contend with, and the way in which norms in this area need to be secured and anchored in order to do their regulative work in an appropriate manner. That background is the basis of the connection in my account between substantive objections to norms like N_1 and the evident and endemic liability of such a norm to being abused and misapplied in its administration. That connection is what I shall outline in the next two sections of the paper.

VIII. The default position and the laws of war

What I have indicated so far is that our default position, the starting point of any serious analysis in this area—what our justificatory considerations of security, strategy and necessity, if they are to succeed, have to move us away from—is the proposition that there is to be no deliberate killing of anyone. None whatever.[26] That is the starting point.

Now, if this is our starting point, then how did we ever end up with laws of war? After all, war involves killings and the laws regulating war authorize some of them. I think the answer goes like this. In order to *regulate* war, rather than simply—and in futility—trying to ban it, our laws (both national and international) and our positive morality (to the extent that we have a positive morality) have taken up a distinction between types of killing: the killing of combatants and the killing of civilians. We use a pretty simple norm like this:

---

[26] See the discussion in Waldron, *supra* n. 10, 106 ff.

N_0: In the conduct of armed operations, only combatants may be targeted deliberately. Civilians may not be targeted deliberately.

We apply N_0 to war rather than the simple default—"Thou shalt not kill"—because we know the default moral principle is not viable. In my view, our laws and our positive morality are not driven to embrace N_0 by the independent array of moral reasons that might support the one kind of killing but not the other. Instead, they have proceeded on the basis of moral sociology, discerning the possibility of a viable norm of restraint in this area. What they have taken up in N_0 is a strand of viable normativity that has emerged from centuries of ghastly conflict: it is a rule that many combatants have shown themselves willing to abide by, which seeks to confine approval of the killing that is endemic to war to the killing of designated and identifiable combatants by other combatants and which continues to condemn as murder the deliberate killing of civilians. To repeat: our laws and our morality have associated themselves with N_0 not because good reasons can be identified for allowing combatants to be killed, though sometimes they can, but largely because it looks as though this is a regulative line that can be defended (just!) in the midst of an activity that is otherwise comprehensively murderous. The line defined by N_0 seems to have proved sustainable—by no means perfectly so, but sort of sustainable—and administrable; and it seems capable of being inculcated as a matter of ethos and professionalism among soldiers. (Again, this is not perfectly so, but it is so to the extent that the inculcation of any viable norm is possible in this area.) We cling to N_0, not because we think the killing of combatants is OK but because we are doubtful of our ability to hold any other line. And even this one comes under a lot of pressure, not just from anger and the heat of battle, but in terms of the advantages that might accrue, in situations where the stakes are as high as they can be imagined, if only we would allow a few violations. Still, pressure or no pressure, it is not entirely unrealistic to think that this line can be held. N_0 has proved capable of anchoring itself in habit, ethos and discipline in the midst of the conduct of war.[27]

Understanding the background just outlined helps us understand the great caution that must be brought to any attempt to change the laws of war, for example by amending N_0 with N_1 as an exception. To change N_0—to revise it or reformulate it—involves considerable risk. Changing or revising the laws of war means letting go of one strand of proven normativity (in an otherwise normative-free zone) in

---

[27] The anchoring of N_0 in military discipline should also lead us to reflect on one other worrying feature of targeted killing, as it is undertaken by American forces. Often the killers and those who supervise them are not military officials at all: they are civilian intelligence operatives, from the CIA. E.g. quite apart from the manifest unlawfulness of this, we should worry about the fact that neither the man operating the joystick that controls the drone that is the instrument of death (perhaps thousands of miles away) nor the persons standing at his shoulder have had the laws-of-war training that many military officers have had.

which over the centuries an awful lot has been invested and seeking to invent or impose another in the hope that the reasons that motivate *us* to propose the change will also be sufficient motivation for men in the heat of battle to adapt their postures, expectations, tactics, training, peer relations, and discipline to the newly formulated version.

Awareness of all this should persuade us of the inadequacy of the usual approach taken by moral philosophers. For many philosophers, the appropriate way to review and criticize the laws of armed conflict is something like the following. First, we try to figure out the reasons that support the content of the existing norm, N_0. And then, second, we consider what analogies those reasons might support or what modified norm might be rigged up to conform more perfectly to the force of those reasons. Or, third, we might eschew N_0 and the reasons underlying it altogether, figuring that it is too confused or too ill-supported, and go back to moral fundamentals (like some sort of enlightened utilitarianism) to come up with our own version of a rule permitting some (but not all) killings in war.[28] In my view, these are all reckless ways to proceed, not just because the wrong people may end up being deliberately killed but because they fail to come to terms with the conditions (set out in the last few paragraphs) under which viable anchored norms are possible for an activity of this sort.

Not only that, but the philosopher's critique of N_0 and its current administration is like shooting fish in a barrel. Of course the existing laws of war are imperfect by moral standards—"A principle that turns on the wearing of uniforms and insignia? Really!"—and of course the reasons adduced to support the killing of combatants could easily be adduced analogically to support the killing of civilians under certain circumstances. I have heard people say, "Well at least we ought to be able to kill the civilians who are effectively in command of a war effort." But does it make a difference that the principle of civilian control of the military is one of the most important constitutional principles we have, so that whenever any constitutional democracy goes to war, you are always going to be able to find a civilian commander to kill, whether it is George Bush or Winston Churchill? By the standards of moral philosophy, this constitutional principle leads to an untidy situation when we interrogate N_0. We say, "A different norm would be tidier, and let's forget the constitutional principle (or pretend we have never heard of it)." But in the context of trying to secure *some* order, *some* normativity in this otherwise murderous situation, an untidy norm is always better than no viable norm at all. If the use of moral analogy forces us to choose between these possibilities, it may be the use of moral analogy that has to be abandoned.

---

[28] One way or another, these are the philosophical tactics deployed in McMahan, *supra* n. 8.

IX. Murder and moral opportunism

I said that the default position is a general norm prohibiting murder, and one of the reasons for not being so free in our use of philosophical analogy is that a norm regarding homicide needs deeper underpinnings than simply acceptance of the balance of reason that supports it. We sometimes say there is a taboo against killing, by which we mean not only that the moral reasons for refraining from killing are very, very serious but also that the kinds of situations where killing might be attractive or otherwise in the offing are situations fraught with such passion and such temptations that something more than mere moral reasoning is required. This is true, as I have said, of the heat of battle: and there we have had to hold a different moral line, represented by N_0, in order to secure anchorage for any effective norm at all. And it may be true for political decision-making also—that is, the kind of decision-making that is likely to be involved in the administration of N_1.

In politics and the pursuit of national security, the stakes sometimes seem to be very high. The viability of national policy may be at stake, or innocent lives, or the survival in office of not-so-innocent politicians. True, we are not talking now about the heat of battle; politicians have opportunities at their leisure that soldiers usually lack to ponder the advantages of various killing strategies. But when lives are at stake (even if it is not the lives of the decision-makers), the temptation to approach the possibility of murder in a calculative spirit is still very strong. For example, politicians have to deal with things like insurgencies. An insurgency, whether it is justified or unjustified, may pose what seems to be a grave threat to values like public order, innocent lives, or the survival in office of not-so-innocent politicians. And it may seem that sometimes it would be better to simply "eliminate" or "take out" (the phrase we use when we are trying to appear hard but still do not want to utter the word "murder") some of those who are leading the insurgency—posing this threat to the life of the nation—than to continue risking the values that the government stands for. Such a tactic may seem less costly and more decisive than what can be achieved through the scrupulous, uncertain and drawn-out procedures of ordinary law-enforcement or less costly and more decisive than what can purchased in the uncertain currency of accommodation, compromise, negotiation, the addressing of grievances, and so on. Assassinating one's enemies (or those who can be designated "enemies of society") is and always has been one of the standing temptations of politics and government. If it has been held at bay in the practice of some advanced democracies over the past 100 years, it has been held at bay only partially and uncertainly, as the incidents alluded to in section IV of this chapter indicate. And that work has been done by legal and moral norms that have had something like the entrenched and anchored character of the norm, N_0, described in section VIII—a norm that is secured (albeit imperfectly) as a taboo by moorings that are only partially a function of the moral reasons that can be articulated in its support.

And now it is proposed that we should unmoor N_0—which inhibits us from killing some of our enemies—and replace it with another norm, with a narrower application, which, it is said, will be more responsive to the balance of underlying reasons regarding justifiable killing. Now it is proposed that we should abandon N_0 and proceed to establish new licenses to kill, along the lines of N_1. We defend this proposal by analogy with reasons we associate with the license already embodied in norm N_0 concerning the killing of combatants, even though we should be bearing in mind that *that* license was established not because reason demanded it but because unless some such concession was made there might be no hope of regulating killing in warfare at all.

With these proposals, what is contemplated in effect is the unraveling of the background taboo against murder or the reduction of it to the balance of reasons that from time to time can be adduced in its favor. Suddenly killing is to be assessed as a matter of the balance of social advantage. I do not want to pretend that the advantages are not real—peace, security, strategic necessity, political stability and the protection of innocent lives. Nor do I deny that those of my colleagues who argue for something like N_1 are arguing for the most part in good faith: they are moved to counsel the pursuit of these advantages through the use of death squads in the circumstances of insecurity that characterize modern politics, because they think of themselves (and all of us) as already being committed to a certain number of killings anyway—and what could be wrong with a few more? It is all done in good faith. But none of us should be surprised to find more comprehensive "abuses" taking place, once politicians are informed by their moral advisors that it is after all not inappropriate to begin thinking in this new way about the whole business of "taking out" one's enemies or those who can be designated as "enemies of society."

That is what I wanted to establish in these last two sections: the liability of a norm like N_1 to be abused is not just an instance of the general liability of *any* legal norm to abuse. It is connected also with its content, for N_1 represents a more general relaxation of one of the most important norms we have—the norm against murder—and the justifications adduced for N_1 represent a significant modification of our usual way of arguing about murder—a modification in the direction of unreliable analogy and moral opportunism.

X. Once more: in whose hands?

I began this chapter by asking readers to imagine norms of targeted killing in the hands of people less scrupulous than ourselves. I went on to remind readers of the actual practice of those who, if they are not "us" exactly, have been in the recent past not our enemies but our representatives; and I asked readers to consider how such people would likely have used the norms of targeted killing that are currently being contemplated. Now I think I have just about circled back to *we*, ourselves, rather than our merciless enemies—"What would bin Laden do with N_1?"—or our unscrupulous representatives—"What would Kissinger do with N_1?" How will this new norm fare in our hands?

I insist that it will depend largely on the attitude towards killing revealed in the reasoning we use. It seems that our first instinct is to search for areas where killing is already "all right"—killing in self-defense or killing of combatants in wartime— and then to see if we can concoct analogies between whatever moral reasons we presently associate with such licenses and the new areas of killing that we want to explore. In my view, that is how a norm against murder unravels. It unravels in our moral repertoire largely because we have forgotten how deeply such a norm needs to be anchored in light of the military and political temptations that it faces and how grudging, cautious, and conservative we need to be—in order to secure that anchorage—with such existing licenses to kill as we have already issued.

In the end, then, the real objection is not that these principles are liable to abuse and cannot be regarded as neutral principles. What is objectionable is the inherently abusive character of the attitude towards killing revealed by reasoning that says: "We are allowed to kill some people by principles we already have; surely, by the same reasoning, in our present circumstances of insecurity, there must be other people we are also allowed to murder."

Part II

NORMATIVE FOUNDATIONS: LAW ENFORCEMENT OR WAR?

5

TARGETED KILLING: MURDER, COMBAT OR LAW ENFORCEMENT?

Jeff McMahan

In announcing that Osama bin Laden had been killed, Barack Obama declared that "justice has been done." In saying this, he was implying, or perhaps even asserting, that the justification for the killing was a matter of retributive justice—that is, of punishment. The announcement was immediately followed by celebrations in the streets throughout the United States. These effusions were not expressions of relief at the passing of a grave danger but exultations over the achievement of vengeance against a hated enemy. This understanding of the justification for the killing was largely unchallenged in popular domestic discourse. About a week after the killing, when I suggested during an interview on Wisconsin Public Radio that the killing ought to have been regarded as an act of defense rather than punishment, the announcer remarked that "you may be the first person I've heard describe this as a defensive action, [to say] that we did this for defense."[1]

There have actually been attempts to defend the moral permissibility of targeted killing on the ground that it offers both vengeance, satisfying the desire of victims for revenge, and retribution, or the infliction of harm according to desert.[2] It is obvious, though, that a policy of targeted killing—by which I mean not political assassination generally but the killing of suspected terrorists by agents of the state— cannot be justified by appeal to vengeance or retribution. Some philosophers argue that no one can deserve to be harmed.[3] Others argue for the more limited claim that no one can deserve to die, or to be killed. But even if some wrongdoers deserve to be killed, the importance of giving them what they deserve is, on its own, insufficient

---

[1] The interview is accessible at <http://wpr.org/wcast/download-mp3-request.cfm?mp3file=dun110509e.mp3&iNoteID=97290> accessed November 3, 2011.

[2] Steven R. David, "Israel's Policy of Targeted Killing," *Ethics and International Affairs* 17 (2003) 111–26.

[3] Derek Parfit, *On What Matters*, vol. 1 (Oxford University Press, 2011) section 39.

to justify the risks that a policy of targeted killing imposes on innocent people—most notably, the risk of misidentifying the intended victim and the risk of harming or killing innocent bystanders as a side effect. This becomes particularly clear when one takes into account that retribution alone cannot justify the preventive killing of a person who will otherwise perpetrate an act of terrorism in the near future but has not yet harmed any innocent person. Retribution can justify the killing only of those who have already engaged in terrorism and, it might be thought, does so even when killing them would do nothing to protect innocent people. If pure retribution were our goal, our means would therefore have to be to capture suspected terrorists and try them in court. Only then might we be justified in punishing those found guilty in accordance with their desert. Pure retribution is insufficiently important to justify other means that involve a higher risk of killing innocent people. Indeed, as opponents of capital punishment have plausibly argued, the importance of retribution alone is insufficient to justify the risks involved in killing people even with the safeguards against mistake provided by a criminal trial.

That targeted killing can be justified, if at all, only on grounds of defense is compatible with its being a legitimate means of law enforcement. One might, indeed, argue that targeted killing can be justified as a form of punishment, on the assumption that the principal function of punishment is not retribution but social defense. While many moral and legal theorists continue to conceive of punishment and defense as entirely distinct, others have recently sought to derive an account of permissible punishment from the principles that govern the permissibility of self- and other-defense.[4] And most people recognize that at least one legitimate function of punishment is to protect innocent people from those who have demonstrated through criminal action that they are potentially dangerous. Yet it would be a mistake to claim that targeted killing could itself constitute a morally or legally permissible form of punishment. That does not, however, exclude its having a legitimate role in law enforcement. I will return to these matters later.

In considering whether targeted killing can be justified, one must separate the question whether it can ever be morally permissible from the question whether it should be permitted in domestic and international law. These questions are interrelated in complex ways, but at least certain dimensions of each can be considered in isolation from the other. I will address the moral question first and then consider what the legal status of targeted killing ought to be.

---

[4] For the view that defense and punishment are distinct, see George P. Fletcher, "Punishment and Self-Defense," *Law and Philosophy* 8 (1989) 201–15, 201; also his "Self-Defense as a Justification for Punishment," *Cardozo Law Review* 12 (1990–1991) 859–66. For accounts that seek to defend punishment by appeal to the permissibility of self- and other-defense, see Thomas Hurka, "Rights and Capital Punishment," *Dialogue* 21 (1982) 647–60; Warren S. Quinn, "The Right to Threaten and the Right to Punish," *Philosophy and Public Affairs* 14 (1985) 327–73; Daniel M. Farrell, "The Justification of Deterrent Violence," *Ethics*, 100 (1990) 301–17; Phillip Montague, *Punishment as Societal Defense* (Rowman & Littlefield, 1995); and Victor Tadros, *The Ends of Harm: The Moral Foundations of Criminal Law* (Oxford University Press, 2011).

I. Morality

There are two basic forms of moral justification that might apply to targeted killing. One appeals to the claim that the potential victim has made himself morally *liable* to be killed by virtue of his moral responsibility for wrongful harm, or a threat of wrongful harm, to others. This claim entails the further claim that he has forfeited his right not to be killed, at least for certain reasons and by certain persons. In this respect, being liable to be killed is like deserving to be killed. The main difference between liability and desert is that the reason given by liability is conditional on the act of killing's being a means or unavoidable side-effect of bringing about some good effect, usually the prevention or correction of a violation of rights. By contrast, the justification for the infliction of deserved harm is not conditional in this way.[5]

The other basic form of moral justification that might apply to targeted killing is a necessity justification, according to which it can be morally justifiable to kill a person who is not liable to be killed if that is necessary to avoid harms to other innocent people that would be significantly worse. Such a person retains his right not to be killed but the right is, in the circumstances, overridden. Necessity justifications are divided between those that are impartial, or agent-neutral, and those that are agent-relative. The impartial form of necessity justification is often called a "lesser evil" justification and is the less controversial of the two. It asserts that the killing of an innocent person or persons can be morally justified when that is necessary to avert harms to other innocent people that would be substantially greater, *impartially considered*. Note that although such a necessity justification is concerned with consequences, it is not a consequentialist justification. It presupposes that there is a constraint against the killing of an innocent person and denies that it can be overridden whenever the overall consequences of doing so would be better. It requires instead that they be *substantially* better. It is usually held, moreover, that in order to justify the *intentional* killing of an innocent person, the harms that one would thereby avert must be even greater than those whose prevention would be necessary to justify the foreseen but unintended killing of the same innocent person.

The agent-relative form of necessity justification does not require the impartial evaluation of consequences, but permits agents to take into account their relations to others. Some philosophers argue that, if one person is related to another in an especially morally significant way—for example, if the one is the parent of the other—there can be a necessity justification for the parent to protect the child by inflicting a harm on another innocent person that is only slightly less than the harm that the child is thereby prevented from suffering. Indeed, some philosophers argue that the parent

---

[5] This claim has recently been forcefully challenged in John Gardner and François Tanguay-Renaud, "Desert and Avoidability in Self-Defense," *Ethics* 122 (2011).

can have a necessity justification for inflicting a harm on an innocent bystander that is *greater* than that which the child would otherwise have suffered. Such views would have to be considered in any comprehensive discussion of targeted killing, as they suggest the possibility that an instance of targeted killing could be justified even if the harm it would prevent the innocent members of one group from suffering would be *less* than the harm it would cause to innocent members of another group as a side-effect. But I will not explore these complications here.

I will, indeed, say little even about the lesser evil form of necessity justification. This is because in those instances in which it is most plausible to suppose that targeted killing is morally justified, such as the killing of bin Laden, the justification seems to be a liability justification. By his own wrongful action, bin Laden had forfeited his right not to be killed if killing him was the best means of preventing innocent people from becoming victims of his terrorist activities. A liability justification is not, however, always decisive. It is possible that there were reasons not to kill bin Laden that made it morally wrong to kill him. But that the killing *wronged* him, or violated his rights, is not among them.

It is perhaps worth mentioning, if only parenthetically, that liability and necessity justifications are in principle combinable. Suppose, for example, that a person, P, has made himself liable to suffer harm up to amount x as a means of preventing an innocent person from suffering a harm for which P would be partly responsible. Yet to prevent this other harm it is necessary to inflict on P a harm greater than x—say, $x + y$. If the harm that the innocent person would otherwise suffer is sufficiently serious, it could be justifiable to inflict a harm in the amount of $x + y$ on P. The harm that P would suffer up to x would be justified as a matter of liability, while the additional harm, y, would be justified on grounds of necessity. Even though P would be liable to be harmed, the infliction of harm beyond that to which he was liable would have to be justified by reference to the demanding standards that govern the intentional harming of innocent people.

There is, however, a feature of targeted killing that would appear to make it difficult to justify on grounds of liability. This is that targeted killing is *preventive*—that is, it is done not when the victim is engaged in terrorist activity but at a time when he is not attacking, nor actively posing a threat. This is a defining rather than contingent feature of targeted killing. The killing of a terrorist while he is attempting to carry out a terrorist attack is not an instance of targeted killing but a straightforward instance of third party defense of innocent people and as such raises no special issues. Only an absolute pacifist might object to the killing of a terrorist as a necessary and proportionate means of thwarting a terrorist attack that is in progress. But how can a person be liable to be killed as a matter of defense at a time when he is not actively posing a threat?

The answer is that a person can make himself liable to be killed if he acts in a way that increases the objective probability that he will wrongly kill an innocent person. For example, a person who plans and prepares for the murder of an innocent person thereby increases the potential victim's risk of being murdered. If the *only* opportunity to prevent the murder occurs in advance of the time that the potential murderer plans to commit the murder, he can be liable to be killed at that time. For even at that time he has made it the case through his own wrongful action that either he must be killed or his intended victim must remain at high risk of being murdered by him.[6] It is, of course, not certain at the time that, if he is not preventively killed, the potential murderer will later kill his intended victim. Perhaps he will change his mind. But unless the objective probability that he will kill his intended victim is so low that killing him defensively would be disproportionate, it would be unjust for his wholly innocent potential victim to have to bear a risk of being murdered by him in order that he should be spared.[7]

The targeted killing of a person who is in fact a terrorist is morally—though not legally—quite similar to the killing of an "unjust combatant" (that is, a combatant fighting in a war that lacks a just cause) while he is asleep, which most people regard as permissible. A sleeping unjust combatant in a time of war has committed his will to the killing of opposing "just combatants" (who fight in a just war). He intends, or intends conditionally on receipt of an order, to kill them. The broad contours of his life are shaped and guided by this commitment: he has trained and planned and prepared for this. He is where he is, doing what he does day after day, in order to contribute to his state's unjust war. Much the same is true of the terrorist: he is committed to and guided by the aim of killing innocent people. Both he and the unjust combatant have acted in ways that have raised the objective probability that people who are not liable to be killed (which in my view includes just combatants who fight by permissible means) will be wrongly killed. The main difference between a terrorist who is preparing for his mission or awaiting orders and a sleeping unjust combatant is that the latter keeps about him the visible indicators of his commitment to attack his adversaries, such as his uniform and weapons, while the terrorist seeks to conceal his intentions, preparations, weapons, and identity as a terrorist.

It does not matter to the sleeping unjust combatant's liability to defensive killing whether he has killed in the past. The newly arrived soldier who has not yet participated in combat is no less liable than the veteran of many campaigns sleeping next to him. The liability of each to defensive action is based on the threat he will

---

[6] For a hypothetical example and further discussion, see Jeff McMahan, "Preventive War and the Killing of the Innocent" in David Rodin and Richard Sorabji (eds), *The Ethics of War: Shared Problems in Different Traditions* (Ashgate Publishing, 2005) 169–90.

[7] For further discussion, in which I suggest that even mental acts such as the formation of an intention or even mere deliberation could in principle be a basis of liability to defensive harm, see Jeff McMahan, "The Conditions of Liability to Preventive Attack" in Deen K. Chatterjee (ed.), *Gathering Threats: The Ethics of Preventive War* (Cambridge University Press, 2012).

pose when he wakes—or, in an extended sense, the threat he poses now—not on what he has done in the past. The same is true of the terrorist. Two people who are together planning and preparing to carry out a terrorist attack may be equally liable to be preventively killed, even if one has conducted such attacks in the past while the other has not. Their liability to defensive action is based on their responsibility for the threat that the defensive action would be intended to prevent, not on their responsibility for unrelated threats from the past.

Whether a person has engaged in terrorism in the past is not, however, irrelevant to the justification for a particular instance of targeted killing. Its primary significance is evidential. If a person is known to have engaged in terrorist activity in the past, that provides some reinforcement for whatever other evidence there is that he is preparing to do so again. There is in general, therefore, less moral risk involved in the targeted killing of a person who has a confirmed history of terrorist activity.

That a person has engaged in terrorism in the past is also relevant to the weight that it is reasonable to attribute to the possibility of mistake. Compare two targeted killings, each of which is based on a mistake. In the first case, there was no reason to believe that the person killed had engaged in terrorism in the past and in fact he had not. He was believed, however, to be preparing to engage in terrorism. But that belief was false: he was not and would never have been involved with terrorism in any way. In the second case, the person killed was correctly believed to have conducted terrorist attacks in the past. It was also believed that he was preparing for another attack, but in fact his career as a terrorist had ended. By the time he was killed he had become entirely harmless.

Neither of these people was liable to defensive killing, as neither posed a threat. Yet the wrong done to the second person, who had been guilty of terrorist action in the past, is less. Because of his history of terrorist action, he is morally responsible for *appearing* to pose a threat of wrongful harm to innocent people. If he had not killed people in the past, or had surrendered himself earlier, other people would not now be forced to choose between killing him and allowing him to live when they reasonably believe that the latter alternative would allow innocent people to remain at risk of being murdered by him. Through his past action, he has forfeited any claim to the benefit of the doubt. He has also, it seems, forfeited his right to kill in self-defense, despite the fact that he no longer poses a threat. He is, one might say, liable to be killed on the basis of a mistake that he is responsible for making it reasonable for others to make, even though he is not liable to be killed for defensive reasons. This is similar to the claim, which I also accept, that a person can be liable to be killed as a side-effect of defensive action even when he is not liable to be killed intentionally as a means of defense.[8]

---

[8] For further discussion of the relevance of responsibility for appearances, see Jeff McMahan, "Who is Morally Liable to be Killed in War," *Analysis* 71 (2011) 544–59. On liability to unintended harm, see Jeff McMahan, *Killing in War* (Clarendon Press, 2009) 218–21.

Another possible reason why the erstwhile terrorist has been wronged to a lesser degree than the person who was innocent of any involvement with terrorism is that he may have deserved to suffer some degree of harm because of his past action. As I noted earlier, it may be doubtful that he deserved to be killed. But if he deserved to be harmed to *some* extent for the harms he inflicted on innocent people in the past, it seems that the *undeserved* harm he suffered in being killed must be less than that of the wholly innocent person. (There is disagreement about whether a person who deserves to be harmed gets what he deserves when he is harmed by natural causes or for reasons unrelated to his desert. Those who think he does not will join those who do not believe in desert in rejecting this second possible reason for thinking that the former terrorist suffers a lesser wrong in being killed than the innocent person does.)

In summary, although targeted killing is necessarily preventive, that does not exclude the possibility of there being a liability justification for it, since people can make themselves liable to be preventively killed. The conditions in which there might be a liability justification for the targeted killing of a terrorist are that, by intending, planning, or preparing to commit or contribute to an act of terrorism, this person is morally responsible for an increase in the objective probability that innocent people will be murdered; that killing him is the best means of averting the threat he poses (both because of the probability of success and because of the expected effects that other options would have on innocent people, including innocent bystanders and anti-terrorist agents); and that killing him is proportionate in the sense that the expected saving of the lives of innocent people substantially outweighs any expected harms that the killing might cause to innocent bystanders as a side-effect.

II. Law

That targeted killing can in some cases be morally justified on grounds of liability does not entail that it ought to be legally permitted in those cases. Legal permissions and prohibitions cannot simply restate moral permissions and prohibitions. Although perfect congruence between criminal law and morality is perhaps the ideal, laws must be evaluated on the basis of their likely effects. This may be particularly true of laws governing the action of states, since the abuse of legal permissions by states can have unusually bad consequences. One question, therefore, is whether at least some instances of targeted killing ought to be legal under international law.

But a different and more urgent question is how targeted killing ought to be regarded in relation to the law as it is now. Targeted killing might be thought to come within the scope of either of two legal paradigms. One of these is the set of legal norms governing law enforcement, or police action. The other is the set of legal norms governing the conduct of war. If terrorists are criminals, or criminal suspects, their treatment ought to be governed by the norms of law enforcement. If they are combatants, their treatment ought to be governed by the laws of war. It cannot be the case that terrorists—that is, actual terrorists and not merely suspected terrorists—are neither criminals nor combatants; for if they are not combatants, they are definitely criminals. Yet there may be no determinate, objective truth about which they are as a matter of law. There is certainly no agreement, no consensus, on this matter. There is, it seems, some legitimate scope for choice. The relevant question may not be whether terrorists *are* criminals or combatants but whether it is *better* to classify them as criminals or as combatants.

Whether terrorists are best treated as criminals or combatants, and thus whether anti-terrorist activity is best understood as law enforcement or war, is highly relevant to the status of targeted killing in the law. In the law enforcement paradigm, those who are in fact criminals must be treated as criminal suspects prior to conviction. Their treatment is governed by a requirement of arrest: they must be arrested and tried in a court of law. They may not be hunted and killed, for that would constitute "extrajudicial execution"—a charge often made against targeted killing. If, therefore, terrorists are best regarded as criminals, targeted killing is in most cases illegal. There are exceptions, as I will indicate later, but targeted killing must be ruled out as a *policy* that substitutes for efforts to capture terrorists and place them on trial.

If, by contrast, terrorists are combatants, they may, like other combatants, be permissibly killed at any time during a state of war. The state of war is, of course, essential for the activation of the laws of war. There is no legal permission for soldiers in one state to kill soldiers in another if the two states are not at war. This is one reason why it was important to members of the Bush Administration to have a "*war* on terror." They wanted to kill terrorists as well as to capture them for interrogation; hence they sought to bring their anti-terrorist activities within the scope of the norms governing the practice of war by declaring terrorists to be enemy combatants at war with the United States.

Terrorists often conceive of themselves as combatants and wish to be regarded as such. This may have been part of the reason for Osama bin Laden's fatuous attempt at a declaration of war against the United States, an act that was merely an attempt because a private person does not have the legal power to declare war. Combatant status has at least two sources of appeal. One is that it confers a specious aura of legitimacy that terrorists sometimes covet. The other is that it might seem to entitle terrorists to the legal rights of prisoners of war when they are captured—rights that, however unrealistically, they sometimes demand. Yet it may actually be against their interests to be recognized as combatants. For that recognition provides their adversaries with a public justification for killing rather than capturing them. The Bush Administration's violations of rights of *habeas corpus* and its repellent torturing of detainees, along with the Obama Administration's pusillanimous unwillingness to conduct civilian trials of terrorist suspects, have made the practice of capturing and imprisoning suspected terrorists politically unpopular in the United States. The Obama Administration greatly prefers to kill such people rather than capture them—as in the case of bin Laden himself.

One might argue that if terrorists are combatants, that gives them, among their other rights, a right of surrender, which they can use to compel their adversaries to capture rather than kill them. But this ignores two obvious points. First, the targeted killing of suspected terrorists is increasingly done with remotely controlled weapons, such as Predator drones. This denies the victims any option of surrender, which many members of the Obama Administration no doubt regard as an advantage. Second, even when there are opportunities to capture terrorists rather than kill them, there may be little incentive for anti-terrorist agents or their leaders to avail themselves of those opportunities. It may well be that the right of surrender is, unlike some of the rights of prisoners of war, more than merely conventional. But the motivation to respect it often comes from an expectation of reciprocity. That is, persons on one side of a conflict will be willing to accept the burdens involved in holding prisoners only if they can expect that they and others on their side will, if the opportunity arises, be taken prisoner rather than killed. But terrorists are not in the business of taking prisoners. They "fight" against civilians, not anti-terrorist agents. They take only hostages, not prisoners. There is therefore no basis for an expectation of reciprocity, and thus little reason to expect that terrorist suspects will be offered an opportunity to surrender as long as killing them is politically more expedient.

Although the Bush Administration claimed that terrorists are combatants, it was unwilling to accord them any of the rights that go with combatant status. It therefore declared them to be "unlawful combatants," a category whose members supposedly have all the liabilities of combatant status, such as being liable to be killed at any time, but none of the corresponding rights or immunities, nor even any of the rights of criminal suspects. The notion of an unlawful combatant is, however, of disputed application. It was originally invoked in the *Quirin* case during the Second World War to justify the execution of a group of German military personnel who had entered the United States clandestinely and were impersonating civilians in an effort to sabotage war-making facilities on American soil. They were official agents of an enemy state who, disguised as civilians, were carrying out military functions in a legally recognized war against the United States. They were not terrorists attempting to kill civilians.

Just as it is unclear what the criteria are for being an unlawful combatant, so it is unclear what rights and liabilities unlawful combatants would have if they could be reliably identified. Certainly their legal status is not what the Bush Administration in practice took it to be—that is, people who may be either hunted and killed or captured and imprisoned indefinitely with no right to legal representation, no right to trial, no right against torture, indeed no rights at all.

The idea that terrorists who are not members of any regular, legally recognized military organization can have some form of combatant status is doubtfully coherent.[9] Combatant status is a legal artifact. The role of the combatant is defined by reference to legal rights and duties and has been designed so that conferral of combatant status will serve certain purposes—primarily the reduction of violence and harm in war through the insulation of ordinary civilian life from the destructive and disruptive effects of war. The granting of combatant status involves a tacit bargain. Those to whom it is granted are thereby guaranteed immunity from legal prosecution for acts, such as killing and maiming, that would ordinarily be criminal, even if the war in which they fight is unjust and illegal. And they are also granted legal rights to humane treatment and release at the end of the war if they are captured. In exchange for these rights and immunities, they acquire certain duties: they must visually identify themselves as combatants and carry their weapons openly. More importantly, combatants have a legal duty not to conduct intentional attacks against civilians. Combatant status is conditional on reciprocity: one is entitled to the benefits only if one fulfills the duties. Combatants who intentionally kill civilians forfeit some of the privileges and immunities conferred by combatant status—though they do not forfeit combatant status altogether, since even war criminals retain the legal right to kill enemy combatants until they cease to be combatants, either when war ends or they are rendered *hors de combat*. (It is one of the many implausible elements of the law of war and the traditional theory of the just war that they permit all combatants, including those fighting for unjust ends, to kill enemy combatants even when the latter are trying to stop them from committing an atrocity.)

While combatant status is thus awarded in part to draw a sharp moral and legal line between those who have it and those who do not, terrorism seeks to erase that line. It is a defining characteristic of terrorism that its instrumental purpose is precisely to expose ordinary civilian life to the violence characteristic of war. Terrorists also subvert the purpose of distinguishing between combatants and noncombatants by concealing themselves among ordinary people and carrying out their attacks without identifying themselves as threateners, thereby limiting the ability of their opponents to distinguish between those who threaten them and those who do not. It is thus the essence of terrorism that terrorists do exactly what the legal category of the combatant has been designed to prevent people from doing. Combatant status

---

[9] For related discussion, see Jeff McMahan, "War, Terrorism, and the 'War on Terror'" in Christopher Miller (ed.), *"War on Terror": The Oxford Amnesty Lectures 2006* (Manchester University Press, 2009) 166–70.

is, in effect, a reward offered as an incentive not to do precisely what terrorists do. It would therefore be pointless to grant the rewards for refraining from engaging in terrorism to terrorists themselves.

Despite this argument, many people will remain convinced that terrorists must count as combatants because the dangers they pose often require a military response, as in the case of bin Laden, who had to be killed by a team of elite military commandos. But these people would do well to consider what this idea implies. It implies, for example, that if, on September 11, 2001, members of Al Qaeda had had a jet of their own that was not intended to resemble a civilian jetliner, and if there had been no one on board other than themselves, their flying it into the Pentagon would have been a legitimate act of war. For the Pentagon is a military headquarters and is thus a legitimate target for enemy combatants during a state of war. One might object that there was no state of war between Al Qaeda and the United States at that time, but the attack itself would have initiated such a state if the Al Qaeda operatives had been combatants.

I should clarify that I do not deny that some terrorists can be combatants. But this is not because terrorists generally are combatants but because a combatant can become a terrorist by using terrorist means rather than legitimate military means in an effort to achieve his ends. During the Second World War, for example, political leaders, military commanders, and flight crews collaborated in the bombing of cities with the intention of killing their civilian inhabitants as a means of breaking the morale of their enemies and coercing the enemy government to surrender. These people were engaged in terrorism, which can be deployed in service of just as well as unjust ends. We do not, however, usually refer to such people as terrorists, partly for patriotic reasons if they were on our side, but also because we have another label for regular combatants who commit acts of terrorism: war criminals. Robert McNamara, who was involved in planning the bombings of Japanese cities, made the following observation during an interview conducted late in his life: "Was there a rule that said you shouldn't bomb, kill, shouldn't burn to death 100,000 civilians in a night? [General Curtis] LeMay said that if we'd lost the war, we'd all have been prosecuted as war criminals. And I think he's right. He, and I'd say I, were behaving as war criminals."[10] He could with equal justice have confessed that they were acting as terrorists. I will not, however, discuss combatants who become war criminals by engaging in terrorism; rather, in what follows, I will use "terrorist" to refer only to those who engage in terrorism outside of any legally recognized role within a regular military organization. (Some writers tendentiously define "terrorism" so that it can be perpetrated only by "non-state actors." That is not my suggestion. I am simply limiting the scope of this discussion.)

---

[10] The interview is in a film called "The Fog of War," directed by Errol Morris, which can be accessed at <http://video.google.com/videoplay?docid=-8653788864462752804#> accessed November 3, 2011. The relevant comment occurs about 42 minutes into the documentary. I am grateful to Robert Van Gulick for the reference.

As I noted earlier, if terrorists are not combatants, they must be criminals. They are civilians who are engaged in an egregious form of criminal activity. Anti-terrorist action is therefore a form of law enforcement, and thus comes within the scope of the norms governing police action. If this is right, terrorists may not be hunted and killed but must instead be arrested and brought to trial.

Critics of this view sometimes object that if anti-terrorism is a form of law enforcement, its aim must be punishment, for the aim of law enforcement is criminal justice—that is, the punishment of the guilty. But anti-terrorism does not aim at punishment; it is, as I claimed earlier, a form of *defense*.

These critics are right that it can be important to keep defense and punishment distinct, even though they are closely related. Although some of the classical just war theorists held that the sole just cause for war is the punishment of the guilty, almost no one holds that view now. Until quite recently, many just war theorists have held instead that the only just cause for war is national defense, either self-defense or third party defense of another state. Retribution, they have held, has no role in the justification of war. According to this view, the reason it is permissible to kill combatants is not that they are guilty and deserve punishment but because killing them is necessary to defend other people from the threat they pose. But if this is right, the idea that it was permissible to kill bin Laden because he was a combatant in the "war on terror" is doubtfully compatible with the idea that his having been killed meant that justice had been done, as Obama proclaimed. To claim both that he could be killed because he was a combatant and that killing him was just punishment is to conflate defense and retribution.

That said, it is important to note both that punishment is only one aim of law enforcement and that one of the functions of punishment is societal defense—that is, the removal of dangerous criminals from society for a period in part to protect the other members of the society from them. But law enforcement also has the protection of innocent people as an aim that is independent of punishment. It can be a legitimate police function to kill a violently dangerous person if he cannot be otherwise subdued for arrest, even if this person is known not to be responsible for his action and thus not someone who deserves to be punished as a matter of retribution.

Defense is an aim of law enforcement in both these ways. When the law aims at defense through punishment, the immediate danger from the criminal has usually passed. A crime has been committed. There is often a threat of further criminal action by the same person, but the need for defensive action may not be urgent. And in most cases of domestic criminal activity, it is normally just as effective and no riskier to law enforcement agents to seek to arrest the suspect than to kill him. Once he has been arrested and no longer poses an immediate threat, it is necessary to try him in court in order to ensure, to the greatest degree possible, not only that no harm is inflicted on an innocent person but also that any harm that is inflicted will be *effectively* defensive—which it will not be if an innocent person is punished by mistake, for in that case the real culprit is left free to cause further harm. The requirement of arrest is thus both a safeguard against mistake and an important element in the process of ensuring that defensive action is effective.

The second way in which law enforcement can be defensive is quite different. When a criminal suspect evades arrest and poses a clear danger to innocent people, the urgency of defensive action is considerable. Continued efforts to arrest him may leave innocent people—further intended victims, innocent bystanders, and police officers—exposed to a level of risk so high that the requirement of arrest must be suspended. The conditions in which the requirement is suspended resemble those in which private individuals are permitted to kill in self- or other-defense. In such conditions, police officers may then permissibly kill the suspect. Granting law enforcement agents this permission involves significant risks: they may kill the wrong person, they may fail to see that there is an effective alternative to killing, their action may pose a threat to innocent bystanders that is at least as great as that posed by the suspect, and so on. But sometimes these risks are outweighed by the risks involved in failing to eliminate the threat posed by the suspect.

Because anti-terrorist action is generally preventive in character, there is normally less urgency than there is when a violent individual is on a rampage, and the risk of misidentification is significantly greater. In these conditions, it may be reasonable to subject defensive action to safeguards that are not possible, or would be unduly risky, in the case of more immediate threats posed by readily identifiable threateners. In general, therefore, anti-terrorist action should be constrained in the ways characteristic of law enforcement and the administration of criminal justice; that is, there should be a requirement of arrest, a presumption of innocence, an insistence on proof of guilt beyond reasonable doubt, and so on. Observance of these restrictions may even yield an important benefit as side-effect: namely, the divulging of information by the terrorist that facilitates the prevention of terrorist acts by others.

Yet there are various other features that characterize much anti-terrorist action that may make it morally necessary on certain occasions to suspend these requirements. Among these features are that terrorists often live, conspire, and train in a state other than the one that is the target of their terrorist action, and that they are often protected by the government of that state and sheltered by local supporters. When anti-terrorist agents can thus expect to be denied permission to make an arrest and to face resistance if they try, the probability of a successful arrest may be low while the risks involved in the attempt may be high. When an unusually dangerous terrorist is inaccessible to arrest at a reasonable level of risk for these or other reasons, conditions may be analogous to those that justify the suspension of the requirement of arrest in cases of domestic law enforcement. In these conditions, targeted killing may be justified for reasons similar to those that can justify the police in killing a rampaging gunman who resists arrest.

Many of these conditions obtained in the case of Osama bin Laden. He had proven himself to be a highly dangerous terrorist. There was no risk that, in killing him, anti-terrorist agents would be killing an innocent or unthreatening person. And there can be little doubt that he was being sheltered by certain individuals in the Pakistani government or military, or both. Any effort to secure the cooperation of the Pakistani government or military in arresting him would therefore almost certainly have resulted in his being alerted and allowed to escape. Finally, there was good reason to believe that he was heavily protected by armed guards. Yet in spite of all this, it turned out to have been possible to capture him alive at little or no more risk than was involved in killing him. The initial reports revealed that, *before* they shot bin Laden himself, the SEALs incapacitated a woman who charged them as they entered bin Laden's room by shooting her in the leg. That immediately raised the question why they could not have done the same with him. The Obama Administration soon conceded that he was unarmed and, despite the Administration's assertion that the SEALs were "prepared" to capture him if possible, *The New Yorker* has quoted "a special-operations officer who is deeply familiar with the bin Laden raid" as saying that "there was never any question of detaining or capturing him—it wasn't a split-second decision. No one wanted detainees."[11]

It seems, then, that according to the view for which I have been arguing, it was wrong to kill bin Laden rather than capture him. The reason has nothing to do with the fact that he was defenseless. That is a distraction, a sentimental relic of medieval codes of chivalry. If killing bin Laden had been necessary to eliminate a significant threat for which he was responsible, even if he did not *pose* that threat at the time, it would have been unambiguously *good* that he was defenseless when the killing had to be done, so that no harm might be done to those acting justifiably to eliminate the threat. The reason is instead that killing him does not seem to have been necessary to avert any threat for which he was responsible.

Yet that might not be true. There are at least two reasons that may have motivated members of the Obama Administration to order that he be killed rather than captured, either of which might provide a justification for the killing, despite the many reasons why it would have been desirable to capture him and place him on trial. One is that the Administration may have decided in advance that it was not worth the loss of even one more American life to enable bin Laden to live to face trial rather than be killed. So the SEALs may have been instructed simply to take no chances. The other is that the Administration may have reasonably feared that if he had been taken captive, his followers would then have taken American

---

[11] Nicholas Schmidle, "Getting Bin Laden," *The New Yorker* (August 8, 2011) 43.

hostages and begun killing them one by one in an effort, however futile, to coerce the United States to release him. It is not unreasonable to suppose that the reasons favoring capture rather than killing may have been outweighed by that risk. (I would not include among those reasons that he had a right not to be killed. If killing him was necessary to avoid a significant risk that innocent people would be killed by his followers, then he was liable to be killed, as he would have borne some responsibility for the acts of his followers. This is the kind of case to which I referred in the previous paragraph.) The risk that hostages might be taken in an effort to secure his release could, however, have been minimized if the Obama Administration had postponed the announcement of his capture long enough to have placed him in the custody of an international body, such the International Criminal Court in the Hague. But this option was, of course, politically impossible in the United States, where the outrage and jeers of Republican politicians at the Administration's placing the United States' greatest enemy under international jurisdiction would have converted the capture from a triumph to a humiliation. As recent experience demonstrates, Republican politicians can be counted on to obstruct the best solution to any problem.

There are various reasons why capture followed by trial is generally preferable to killing. Apart from the fact that a dead terrorist can provide no information about other terrorists or planned terrorist operations, most of the disadvantages of targeted killing have to do with the risks it involves that can be mitigated through the safeguards provided by the alternative of capture and trial. Perhaps the most obvious risk is that the victim may be misidentified. In one of the earliest instances of targeted killing, agents of Mossad, the Israeli intelligence and counterterrorism agency, killed an innocent Moroccan waiter in Norway in 1973 in the mistaken belief that he was the leader of the Palestinian "Black September" group that had massacred Israeli athletes at the 1972 Munich Olympics. This case provoked an international scandal, but in general the incentives to exercise reasonable care in identifying and attacking foreign terrorists are weaker than those for exercising care in domestic police work. Governments naturally take greater precautions to avoid killing their own citizens by mistake. Another instance of misidentification occurred in London when British police killed a Brazilian man whom they mistook for a terrorist shortly after the terrorist bombings there in 2005.

In addition to the mistake of misidentification, there is also the possibility that killing someone known to have engaged in terrorist action in the past will serve no defensive purpose, perhaps because the person has altogether ceased to be involved in terrorist activity. As I noted earlier, however, the wrong done to the victim in this kind of case is significantly less than it would be if he had not been a terrorist and thus bore no responsibility for the reasonable belief of others that he continued to pose a threat of wrongful harm. For much the same reason, a lesser wrong is also done when a member of a terrorist organization is killed when his contribution to the organization's action was, while sufficient for liability to a lesser form of harm, insufficiently significant to make him liable to be killed.

Another risk of targeted killing that might be lessened by pursuing the alternative of capture and trial is the harming of innocent people as a side-effect. Because terrorists tend to live and move freely among ordinary people, it is difficult to attack them without killing or injuring innocent bystanders as well. This is particularly true when targeted killing is attempted using remotely controlled weapons. This problem is not, however, unique to targeted killing; it arises as well for defensive action taken in response to an actual terrorist attack and even for efforts to capture or arrest a terrorist suspect who can be expected to engage in violent resistance. In some cases, indeed, targeted killing can be carried out with almost no danger to innocent bystanders. The classic example is the killing of Hamas's bomb maker, Yahya Ayyash, by agents of the Israeli security service, Shin Bet, who managed to transfer to him a cell phone rigged with explosives, which they then detonated when they confirmed that he was using it. More recently, the targeted killing of Osama bin Laden was accomplished without harm to any innocent bystanders.

In addition to the risks of mistake, there are also risks of abuse. Even in the case of a government that is scrupulous in limiting its use of targeted killing to cases of confirmed terrorists, subtle forms of abuse are likely to develop, such as carelessness about side-effects if those involved believe that they can get away with it without adverse publicity. But the most serious form of abuse by a government that kills only confirmed terrorists is one that, as I mentioned earlier, characterizes the Obama Administration's policy of targeted killing. This is the use of targeted killing as a tactic of first rather than last resort, as a replacement for other forms of anti-terrorist action, such as capture and trial, that incorporate stronger safeguards against the inadvertent killing of innocent people.

The greatest danger from any legal recognition of the permissibility of targeted killing is, however, that unscrupulous regimes will exploit that legal permission in offering public justifications for the killing of political opponents who are not terrorists at all but will be said to be by their killers. There is ample precedent for this—for example, the killing in 1982 of the anti-Apartheid activist Ruth First with a parcel bomb sent by agents of the South African government. That government had declared the African National Congress to be a terrorist organization; hence anyone associated with it could conveniently be branded a terrorist. A similar targeted killing was even carried out in Washington, DC, in 1976, when agents of the Pinochet dictatorship in Chile detonated a bomb under the car of Orlando Letelier, a former minister of the government that Pinochet had overthrown and an opponent of the new regime. In this case the killers were working for a regime that had seized power with U.S. assistance and maintained close ties to the Ford Administration, so protests were muted. But the United States may have to reconsider the precedent it is setting with its targeted killings when regimes with leaders similar to Saddam Hussein, Muammar Qaddafi, or Kim Jung Il acquire small, remotely controlled drones that can be used to kill their opponents on U.S. soil.[12]

The careful development and elaboration of this objection to targeted killing is the main aim of Jeremy Waldron's contribution to this volume and I will not attempt to improve on his superb exposition. It is worth remarking, however, that the objection is compatible with the recognition that targeted killing may in some instances be morally permissible, or even morally required. One might, therefore, accept the same view about targeted killing that some, myself included, have argued is the right view of torture: namely, that while it can on some occasions be morally permissible, it ought to be categorically prohibited by law. According to this view,

> if we grant any legal permission to use torture, particularly one that attempts to capture the complex conditions of moral justification, it will be exploited by those whose aims are unjust and [will be] either abused or interpreted overly generously even by those whose aims are just. Throughout human history, torture has been very extensively employed, but the proportion of cases in which the use appears to have been morally justified seems almost negligible....Any legal permission to use torture, however restricted, would make it easier for governments to use torture, and would therefore have terrible effects overall, including more extensive violations of fundamental human rights. The legal prohibition of torture must therefore be absolute....We cannot proceed with torture the way we have with nuclear weapons—that is, by permitting it to ourselves while denying it to others by means of security guarantees, economic rewards, and other measures designed to make abstention in the interests of all. If we permit ourselves to use torture, we thereby forfeit any ability we might otherwise have to prevent its use by others....Our only hope of being able to impose legal and other constraints on the use of torture in the service of unjust ends by vicious and cruel regimes is to deny the option to ourselves as well, even in cases in which we believe it would be permissible.[13]

It may be tempting to argue that, whatever may be true about the law, a state's adversaries cannot make it impermissible for that state to engage in otherwise permissible acts of targeted killing simply because that action would encourage *them* to act impermissibly, or provide a rationale for their doing so. One might say that if a state's otherwise justified use of targeted killing would prompt unjust regimes to

---

[12] As I was making final revisions to this essay, the Obama Administration accused Iran of plotting to kill the Saudi ambassador to the United States. The Justice Department's accusation can be found at <http://www.justice.gov/opa/pr/2011/October/11-ag-1339.html> accessed November 3, 2011, This is not the first time that the theocratic regime in Iran has engaged in targeted killing. See Roya Hakakian, *Assassins of the Turquoise Palace* (Grove Press, 2011).

[13] Jeff McMahan, "Torture in Principle and in Practice," *Public Affairs Quarterly* 22 (2008) 124–6.

engage in the unjustified use of targeted killing, their unjustified use is not attributable to that state's action and thus cannot make that action disproportionate or otherwise impermissible.

Even if this were true as a matter of morality, however, it would not address the claim that legal arrangements that would permit the targeted killing of, for example, Osama bin Laden by the United States would on balance be worse for everyone, including the United States, because these arrangements would eventually be exploited by all states, not just those that subject the practice of targeted killing to stringent procedural constraints and have the ability to conduct these killings in a reasonably discriminating way. But even as a matter of morality, the view that the permissibility of one agent's action cannot be affected by what it might prompt other agents to do is untenable. To the extent that one can predict what unjust agents would do in response to one's action, one may have to regard their responsive action the way one would regard a natural event that one's action would trigger. If one's action would precipitate an avalanche that would kill a certain number of people, that weighs against the action's being proportionate. Similarly, if one's action would provoke a despot to kill an equal number of innocent people, either intentionally or as a side-effect of responsive action, that too may render one's action disproportionate. Even if one's action would otherwise be permissible, the fact that the despot would bear full *responsibility* for the killings is insufficient to render one's action *permissible*.[14]

Consider a simplified example. Suppose there are two equally important military targets but we can attack only one of them. If we attack one, the explosion will precipitate an avalanche that will kill 50 innocent bystanders. If we attack the other, our adversaries will kill 51 innocent bystanders they would otherwise not kill. Suppose that either attack would be proportionate. In neither case would we directly kill the innocent bystanders. But in both, our action would precipitate and be a necessary condition of the event that would be the proximate cause of their deaths. If we think that killings done by others cannot affect the proportionality of our action, or that effects mediated through the agency of others must be discounted in the determination of proportionality, then we ought to attack the second target, so that 51 innocent bystanders will be killed. People will disagree about this, but my view is that we ought in these circumstances to do what will cause the fewest deaths of innocent bystanders, other things being equal.

A more significant objection to the claim that any legal recognition of the permissibility of targeted killing will be abused by vicious regimes is that the same is true of the alternative means of anti-terrorism consisting of arrest, trial, and punishment.

---

[14] For further discussion, see Jeff McMahan, "Responsibility, Permissibility, and Vicarious Agency," *Philosophy and Phenomenological Research* 80 (2010) 673–80.

It has always been possible for repressive, nondemocratic regimes to seize their political opponents, subject them to a sham or rigged trial, and then execute them, claiming that justice has been done. This problem is exacerbated for the United States by its embrace of capital punishment. Although the United States has not recently legally executed a foreign terrorist, it did execute a domestic one—Timothy McVeigh—and may eventually execute one or more terrorists captured in the "war on terror" and tried by a military court. The practice of judicial execution in the United States sets a dangerous precedent, just as the practice of targeted killing does. Yet even the abolition of capital punishment in the United States would only weaken rather than dispel this concern about the precedent-based objection to targeted killing. For repressive, nondemocratic regimes can also exploit the legal mechanisms of trial and imprisonment to silence their political opponents indefinitely, and to deter other potential opponents from engaging in political action.

One could respond to this problem by insisting that norms of anti-terrorist action requiring arrest and trial must specify standards of fairness and openness for trials and sentencing. There would, for example, have to be transparency and public disclosure of the evidence against the suspect. This would prohibit the United States' use of secret military tribunals or trials that grant fewer rights to defendants than it would demand that its adversaries grant to U.S. citizens in trials they might conduct.

But if one claims that there can be a neutral norm of arrest and trial provided that certain constraints are imposed on what counts as acceptable forms of arrest, trial, and punishment, then a parallel claim might be made on behalf of a neutral norm of targeted killing. Perhaps there could be a neutral norm that permits targeted killing provided that it set high standards of *post facto* justification, with requirements for the disclosure of evidence, a demonstration that killing was both necessary and proportionate, and so on. There could then be legal provisions for international sanctions against states that failed to satisfy the demand for *post facto* justification.

Perhaps, therefore, targeted killing has more in common with ordinary killing in self-defense than we have thought. For there is ample scope for abuse of the legal permission to kill in self-defense in domestic criminal law. If, for example, a woman has a husband with a known record of physical violence, she may be able to provoke him to hit her, then murder him in their home, and afterwards make a successful plea of self-defense at trial. Yet we do not respond to this risk by denying that there can be a neutral rule permitting killing in individual self-defense. We recognize that a trade-off has to be made between the need to permit self-defense in a great range of cases and the need to deter the exploitation of that permission by would-be murderers. But we resolve that problem by imposing a variety of legal constraints on the right of self-defense, rather than by denying a legal right of self-defense altogether. Admittedly, these legal constraints can be reasonably effective in domestic criminal law because there are institutions that can enforce them, whereas there are no even remotely comparable enforcement mechanisms in international law. But the difficulty of enforcement is as much a problem for the legal prohibition of targeted killing as it is for the imposition of constraints on a limited legal permission to engage in targeted killing.

The trade-off between the wrongful harms that might be prevented by legally permitting some instances of targeted killing and those that might be facilitated by the exploitation of that permission should be negotiated differently from the trade-off between the wrongful harms that might be prevented by legally permitting some instances of torture and those that might be facilitated by the abuse of that permission. This is mainly because targeted killing may often be both necessary and effective in preventing or limiting terrorist action, whereas torture can rarely be effective as a means of defense. Thus, if there were a limited legal permission to engage in targeted killing, the ratio of justified to unjustified targeted killings would likely be much higher than the ratio of justified to unjustified instances of torture if there were a limited legal permission to engage in torture. It seems, therefore, that the argument cited earlier against even a limited legal permission to practise torture cannot be extrapolated to the case of targeted killing, or not without significant qualification.

Waldron articulates another concern, which is that acceptance of targeted killing will erode the distinction between combatants and noncombatants as it functions in the war convention. The convention of noncombatant immunity has evolved over a long period of time, has a variety of supporting rationales (it limits the violence of war, protects the rights of the innocent, and so on), and is generally believed, though perhaps mistakenly, to have deep foundations in basic, nonconventional morality, so that many people believe that to violate it is to be guilty of murder. It is hard to deny that this convention is of great practical importance.[15] Would the legal acceptance of targeted killing undermine it?

It is at least worth considering whether there could be an effective firewall between the targeted killing of terrorists in peacetime and the killing of civilians in war. Note that not all killings of civilians are legally prohibited in war. It can be legally permissible foreseeably to kill innocent civilians as an unavoidable and proportionate side-effect of an attack on a military target. And it can be permissible to kill a civilian if he is armed and threatens the life of a combatant. What is prohibited by the principle of noncombatant immunity is the *intentional, nondefensive* killing of civilians as a means of coercing others, usually their political leaders. What this prohibited form of killing and targeted killing have in common is that they both

---

[15] See Jeremy Waldron, "Civilians, Terrorism, and Deadly Serious Conventions" in his *Torture, Terror, and Trade-Offs: Philosophy for the White House* (Oxford University Press, 2010).

involve the intentional killing of civilians. But the difference between them is salient and of obvious moral significance: namely, that what is prohibited in war is the intentional killing of people who do not threaten to harm or kill anyone, whereas the victims of morally justified targeted killing are terrorists who will otherwise harm or kill innocent people. Although terrorists may be civilians, they are civilians who have made themselves morally liable to defensive killing. So what the principle of noncombatant immunity prohibits is terrorism, or the use of terrorist tactics in war, while targeted killing aims to prevent acts of terrorism through the killing of terrorists. Rather than subverting noncombatant immunity, therefore, morally justified instances of targeted killing protect innocent, unthreatening people from terrorist attacks. They enforce the principle of noncombatant immunity.

This difference between the killing of civilians for terrorist reasons and the targeted killing of terrorists themselves is sufficiently clear that people everywhere can understand it. Anyone can see the difference between the killing of Ruth First and the killing of Osama bin Laden. There are thus clear criteria by which it could be shown that a legal permission to engage in targeted killing was being abused.

Ideally what is needed is cooperation both among national law enforcement agencies and between national and international law enforcement agencies, so that terrorists can be dealt with efficiently solely by means of traditional methods of law enforcement. But this cannot happen while law enforcement agencies in states that harbor terrorists are controlled by governments that support the terrorists. In these conditions, what is needed is a new body of anti-terrorist law based on the recognition that terrorists are neither combatants in the legal sense nor ordinary criminals, but instead have an intermediate status that combines elements of criminality with elements of combatancy. Although they have some of the defining features of both criminals and combatants, terrorists lack some of the defining characteristics of combatants and are considerably more dangerous than ordinary criminals. It is for these reasons that anti-terrorist action cannot be well governed within either the law-enforcement paradigm or the war convention. A new body of law designed specifically to regulate anti-terrorist action is therefore urgently needed. It is possible that a tightly circumscribed and constrained permission for targeted killing could be a part of that law. But it would have to be formulated to take account of the grave risks to which Waldron calls attention. And given those risks, its acceptance might be explicitly provisional. There is no reason why certain elements of a new law might not be adopted on a trial basis, to be repealed if, once they have been implemented, their costs appear to outweigh their benefits. But what the precise elements of a new body of law designed to govern anti-terrorist action ought to be is obviously a matter that should be addressed by people better qualified than I.

6

TARGETED KILLING AS PREEMPTIVE ACTION

Claire Finkelstein

I. Introduction

The policy of the Bush Administration with regard to terror suspects focused on detention and interrogation: detention as a temporary immobilization of potential terrorists, and interrogation to gather information needed to fight the war on terror. With emerging public awareness of the inhumane conditions of detention and the harshness of our so-called "enhanced interrogation" techniques, our practices in the war on terror had become a stain on America's conscience and a source of international embarrassment.[1]

No one was surprised, then, when the new Obama Administration wanted to distance itself from the tactics of the former Bush Administration. It sought ways of addressing the threat of terrorism that avoided the brutality in interrogations,

---

[1] President Obama issued an executive order authorizing the continuation of a system of permanent detention for terror suspects detained in the course of fighting the war on terror. Periodic Review of Individuals Detained at Guantanamo Bay Naval Station Pursuant to the Authorization for Use of Military Force, Exec. Order No. 13567 (March 7, 2011). Criticism of this Order was immediate and unambiguous. The Center for Constitutional Rights (CCR) said: "Today's executive order ... codif[ies the lawless] status quo. The creation of a review process that will take up to a year is a tacit acknowledgment that the Obama administration intends to leave Guantanamo as a scheme for unlawful detention without charge and trial for future presidents to clean up." Press Release, Center for Constitutional Rights, "CCR Condemns President Obama's Lifting of Stay in Military Tribunals" (March 7, 2011), available at <http://ccrjustice.org/newsroom/press-releases/ccr-condemns-president-obama%E2%80%99s-lifting-of-stay-military-tribunals>. Executive Director of the ACLU, Anthony Romero, issued the following statement: "providing more process to Guantánamo detainees is just window dressing for the reality that today's executive order institutionalizes indefinite detention, which is unlawful, unwise and un-American." Press Release, ACLU, "President Obama Issues Executive Order Institutionalizing Indefinite Detention" (March 7, 2011), available at <http://www.aclu.org/national-security/president-obama-issues-executive-order-institutionalizing-indefinite-detention> accessed November 4, 2011.

indefinite detentions, and the moral and legal thicket of conducting legal proceedings against terror suspects, whose situations were dramatically different from ordinary criminal defendants. It is perhaps no accident, then, that targeted killing emerged as the central strategy for fighting the war on terror. The new policy involved a dramatic shift in operations.[2] To look only at the statistics for targeted killing operations undertaken by drone, for example, between the years 2004 to 2008, the Bush Administration authorized 42 targeted killings, by comparison with the Obama Administration's count of 180 authorized drone strikes as of February 11, 2011.[3] Between February and the time of this writing (November, 2011), the number of drone strikes has further increased significantly.[4-5]

While there has been a steady increase in reliance on targeted killing as a technique of war, the willingness on the part of the Obama Administration to subject the new policy to the legal and moral examination it appears to warrant has not kept pace. There are signs that the Administration has embarked on a campaign of targeted killing with the same unreflective enthusiasm that the Bush Administration displayed with regard to the use of torture to aid interrogations. To be sure, it is not difficult to understand the attractions of the practice: it allows the more unsavory aspects of the war on terror to be sanitized and removed from public view. But perhaps more legitimately, it allows the United States to avoid the problems associated with amassing large numbers of detainees whose captivity is difficult to manage or justify under principles of international law, and who cannot easily be brought into any court of law for trial. As law professor Ken Anderson has suggested: "Since the U.S. political and legal situation has made aggressive interrogation a questionable activity anyway, there is less reason to seek to capture rather than kill . . . . And if one intends to kill, the incentive is to do so from a standoff position because it removes potentially messy questions

---

[2] See Harold Koh, Legal Adviser to Dept. of State, Address at American Society of International Law, "International Law and the Obama Administration" (March 25, 2010), available at <http://www.state.gov/s/l/releases/remarks/139119.htm> accessed November 4, 2011 (defending the use of targeted killing as part of armed conflict with enemies in the war on terror).

[3] Tara Mckelvey, "Inside the Killing Machine," Newsweek, February 13, 2011.

[4-5] There were 1,172 reported kill or capture raids completed between March 2011 and September; see Alex Strick van Linschoten and Felix Kuehn, "A Knock on the Door: 22 Months of ISAF Press Releases" p. 12, available at (https://www.afghanistan-analysts.net/uploads/AAN_2011_ISAFPressReleases.pdf).

of surrender."[6] Anderson's point seems hard to deny: if our interrogation and detention policies were typically conducted at the edge of, or beyond the bounds, of what is legally and ethically permissible, does it worsen our moral position to kill without attempting to capture? Might not targeted killing be thought the lesser of two evils?

Yet the turn away from interrogation and detention towards that of targeted killing has not succeeded in removing the war on terror from political controversy in the way the Obama Administration may have hoped.[7] On the contrary, it now appears that killing terror suspects in lieu of detaining them does not eliminate the myriad difficulties the world witnessed with capture and detention. The problem has just been moved to a different spot under the rug. The operations involved in combating terrorist activity do not fit squarely within the principles of justification required by just war theory, and this has created legal and moral dilemmas in many domains simultaneously. We have sometimes attempted to solve those difficulties by relabeling the key distinctions on which just war theory depends, but this has not resolved the deeper legal challenges posed by the war on terror.[8]

The most serious of the conceptual difficulties the new style of warfare faces is the fact that in a war waged against terrorists and civilian militants, it is not clear who, if anyone, should count as a "combatant." This fundamental indeterminacy renders obscure who can be legitimately targeted, who can be detained, as well as the justification for targeting or detaining, the extent of the duty to seek capture before killing, and, more generally, whether detainees in the war on terror should fall under the protections traditionally extended to prisoners of war. The lack of theoretical clarity in this area allowed Bush Administration lawyers to interpret any applicable legal constraints "loosely," namely in a way that was designed to enhance

---

[6] Kenneth Anderson, *Targeted Killing in U.S. Counterterrorism Strategy and Law* 7 (Series on Counterterrorism and American Statutory Law, Working Paper, May 11, 2009), <http://papers.ssrn.com/sol3/Delivery.cfm/SSRN_ID1415070_code235051.pdf?abstractid=1415070&mirid=1> accessed November 4, 2011.

[7] *See* U.N. Gen. Assem. [GAOR], Hum. Rts Council, *Report of the Special Rapporteur on Extrajudicial, Summary or Arbitrary Executions* (May, 2010) (prepared by Philip Alston) (criticizing use of targeted killing in areas beyond zone of hostilities); Mary Ellen O'Connell, *Unlawful Killing with Combat Drones: A Case Study of Pakistan, 2004–2009* (Notre Dame Law Sch. Legal Stud., Research Paper No. 09-43, 2010), <http://papers.ssrn.com/sol3/Delivery.cfm/SSRN_ID1654055_code1212987.pdf?abstractid=1501144&mirid=1> accessed November 4, 2011.

[8] See Scott Wilson and Al Kamen, "'Global War on Terror' Is Given New Name," The Washington Post, March 25, 2011, available at <http://www.washingtonpost.com/wp-dyn/content/article/2009/03/24/AR2009032402818.html> last accessed November 2, 2011. In a memo purportedly at the direction of the Office of Management and Budget, the Defense Department's office of security review noted that "this administration prefers to avoid using the term 'Long War' or 'Global War on Terror' [GWOT.] Please use 'Overseas Contingency Operation.'"

the legitimacy of the Administration's interrogation practices without excessive focus on the traditions and laws of war, as well as with international humanitarian law.[9] In particular, an enduring legacy of these efforts was the adoption of a third legal category, one intended to identify the central figures in the war on terror as targetable, like combatants, but exempt from the protections afforded co-belligerents under Article IV of the fourth Geneva Convention and under traditional just war theory.[10] These were the so-called "unlawful" combatants. In this way, the Administration was able to avoid the constraints of the Geneva Conventions' protections for prisoners of war, but also the Federal Torture statute,[11] the Convention on Torture (CAT),[12] and other national and international rules governing the trial and detention procedures for captured enemy combatants in dealing with members of Al Qaeda. The idea of treating members of Al Qaeda as non-enemy combatants was of course the central legal rationale for the former Administration's interrogation policies. Without this convenient middle tier, our treatment of terror suspects would likely have been legally indefensible.

These same aims have induced the Obama Administration to retain the Bush legal structure with regard to suspected terrorists. The in-between category has been as significant for justifying the policy on targeted killing as it was for the proffered justification of enhanced interrogation techniques. The legal and moral obstacles to legitimizing enhanced interrogation of non-enemy combatants now arises with respect to the legitimacy of targeting individuals who are arguably civilians, but whose contribution to the terrorist objectives of Al Qaeda have increased the reach and danger of the primary actors in the war on terror. The recent killing of Anwar al-Awlaki provides a clear example. Given that al-Awlaki's activities in support of Al Qaeda were propagandistic rather than actively belligerent,[13] it is not clear he should have been regarded as a "combatant" under principles of traditional just war theory, and for purposes of the Geneva Conventions, and hence the legitimacy of killing rather than capturing him is subject to doubt. Similar concerns arise with regard to whether the constraints that operate on military interrogators also apply to members of the executive branch, such as the CIA, and whether it is legitimate

---

[9] J.S. Bybee, "Memorandum for John Rizzo: Acting General Counsel of the Central Intelligence Agency" memo, US Deparment of Justice, August 1, 2002.

[10] See, e.g., Convention (IV) relative to the Protection of Civilian Persons in Time of War. Geneva, 12 August 1949.

[11] 18 U.S.C. § 2340A.

[12] "Convention against Torture and Other Cruel, Inhuman or Degrading Treatment or Punishment," General Assembly resolution 39/46 of 10 December 1984.

[13] *See Al-Aulaqi v. Obama*, No. 10–1469 (JDB) (D.D.C. December 7, 2010). For more information on the lawfulness of operations against propagandists, see Lawrence Preuss, "International Responsibility for Hostile Propaganda against Foreign States," *The American Journal of International Law*, Vol. 28, No. 4 (Oct., 1934), 649–68; and Frits Kalshoven, *Reflections on the Law of War: Collected Essays* (Leiden, Martinus Nijhoff Publishers, 2007), 493.

for non-uniformed executive officials to engage in targeted killing.[14] The dilemmas are the same; only their expression has changed.

In both of these morally and legally fraught areas of policy we essentially find ourselves caught between two paradigms of justification: the basic paradigm of killing in war, which depends crucially on the distinction between combatants and civilians, on the one hand, and a more generic framework for justifying the use of violence, such as grounds the entitlement to use force in a law-enforcement context. The first paradigm is a specialized one: the available justifications for killing in war are domain-specific, meaning that they apply to war and to no other domain. The distinction between the *jus ad bellum* and the *jus in bello* captures this idea. While the former domain is open to all of morality, the latter brackets general moral concerns, in favor of arguments and rationales that apply narrowly to the context of aggression between co-belligerents. The second paradigm is open to general arguments of morality and is not domain-limited. Its logic pervades general moral practice, as well as the basic approach to the concepts of justification and excuse in the criminal law. The latter domain is highly reflective of moral practice, and thus studying the structure of the criminal law will provide us with something like a template for the demands of ordinary morality regarding judgments of responsibility.[15] While it is not clear that either will ultimately succeed in rationalizing the use of enhanced interrogation techniques or the targeting of noncombatants, these two sources of possible justification exhaust the moral resources we have at our disposal to address the ethics of these marginal practices in war.

The practice of targeted killing is conducted by military personnel or executive branch officials according to a policy of tracking down and killing individuals whose names appear on a classified kill or capture list known as the Joint Prioritized Effects List (JPEL). An individual's appearance on the list is based on his importance to the noncombatant enemy force, as well as on the degree to which he threatens domestic interests. Suitability for the list, however, is not exclusively a product of the imminent danger the "target" is taken to pose, as would be the case were the justification for killing limited to self-defense, defense of others, or law-enforcement. According to a former U.S. Foreign Service officer, "the list included bomb makers, commanders, financiers, people who coordinate the weapons transport

---

[14] Gary Solis also makes the point that this potentially makes these officials legitimate targets themselves. *See* "CIA Drone Attacks Produce America's Own Unlawful Combatants," *Wash. Post*, March 12, 2010 ("It makes no difference that CIA civilians are employed by, or in the service of, the U.S. government or its armed forces. They are civilians; they wear no distinguishing uniform or sign, and if they input target data or pilot armed drones in the combat zone, they directly participate in hostilities—which means they may be lawfully targeted.").

[15] For an argument against this position, see Richard V. Meyer, "The Privilege of Belligerency and Formal Declarations of War," in this Volume, ch. 7. Responding to Claire Finkelstein, "Responsibility for Acts of War" (2011) (unpublished manuscript, on file with author).

and even [public relations] people." The list has been described as part of "an almost industrial-scale counterterrorism killing machine."[16]

What is the justification for the practice of targeted killing, as described above? Let us ask the question of justification from the standpoint of what Michael Walzer calls "the war convention," namely the combined set of moral principles and background set of legitimating norms that make up what has traditionally been called "just war theory."[17] Justifications for the practice must belong to one of two categories: either the practice is justified killing of co-belligerents, as set out by the traditions and laws of war, or it is a form of law-enforcement, whose norms are established by the parameters of the general principles of morality relating to the justifications and excuses of everyday morality. If the practice of targeted killing cannot be justified under one or the other of these categories, it cannot be justified at all. As Michael Gross writes:

> Either soldiers are criminals or they are not. If they are not outlaws, then there is no cause to declare them criminals or kill them covertly. If they are criminals, however, then they should be charged, arrested, tried and sentenced, not shot on sight. Killing criminals without the benefit of trial smacks of extrajudicial execution.[18]

Our current approach to targeted killing is betwixt and between. We treat targeted individuals as belligerents insofar as we regard them as legitimate targets by virtue of status, rather than action. But we treat them as subjects of law enforcement in that we resist according them the privileges that go along with the status of combatants, such as affording them the rights of P.O.W.s and recognizing their equal right to kill in combat.

As is the case with all intentional killing, in the absence of an affirmative justification, targeted killing is morally impermissible. If an actor kills intentionally and lacks a reason that could justify his actions, he must be called to account. He may turn out to be exempt from responsibility by a personal defense, such as insanity, infancy, involuntary intoxication, duress, or for other status-based reasons. He may even in some cases be able to name the fact that he was following orders as an *excuse,* rather than a justification, in cases in which he made a reasonable mistake about the legitimacy of the orders.[19] This chapter will consider the prospects for

---

[16] Remarks presented in the Frontline program Kill/Capture by John Nagl, a former counterinsurgency adviser to the former commander of forces in Afghanistan, and General Petraeus, current Director of the CIA. Discussed in Kevin Govern, "Operation Neptune Spear: Was Killing Bin Laden a Legitimate Military objective?," in this Volume, ch. 13.

[17] Walzer, *Just and Unjust Wars,* 4th edn (Basic Books, 2006).

[18] Michael L. Gross, *Moral Dilemmas of Modern War: Torture, Assassination, and Blackmail in an Age of Asymmetric Conflict* (Cambridge University Press, 2010) 102. Note that Richard Meyer strongly agrees with this assertion about justifying acts of war. See Meyer, "The Privilege of Belligerency," in this Volume, ch. 7.

[19] The Model Penal Code, § 2.10 provides: "It is an affirmative defense that the actor, in engaging in the conduct charged to constitute an offense, does no more than execute an order of his superior in the armed services that he does not know to be unlawful."

justifying targeted killing according to the foregoing paradigms, and will ultimately suggest a justification for the practice that falls, roughly speaking, within the law-enforcement model, according to a somewhat attenuated version of that basis for legitimizing the use of force.

I shall begin by arguing that the justification that applies to the practice of killing in war, in its traditional form, cannot properly be extended to the practice of targeting previously identified individuals in a way that abstracts from the proximity of their connection to active hostilities. The practice of targeted killing, as currently fashioned, is for this reason not easily justifiable under the traditional laws of war. I shall suggest however, that there are yet other rationales for killing those who pose a danger to national security that do not rely on either traditional just war theory or on the domestic law of personal justifications. One such alternative can be found in an extension of the privilege to *prevent* the commission of rights violations against one's person or the person of another whom one is entitled to defend. Although as applied to the practice of targeted killing, the justification will not turn out to be a traditional preventive rationale, I shall advance an argument for an expansive approach to prevention I call "preemptive killing." Preemption, unlike prevention, extends the preventive privilege to a number of cases in which the anticipated harm is non-imminent. Preemptive killing, however, is also more limited than either preventive killing or killing in accordance with just war theory, and thus its scope needs to be carefully identified and its application sharply circumscribed in accordance with its background justification.[20] The practice that emerges as justified on this account is somewhat different from the use of targeted killing as currently practiced. Normative theory as applied to national security practices in the war on terror thus suggest a re-examination of current policy. I shall then address the pragmatic implications of the theory of justification I present.

II. Targeted killing and the realities of modern warfare

Even more than the legal and moral soul-searching raised by the practice of detaining so-called "non-enemy" or "unlawful" combatants, the practice of targeted killing, and its perceived role in judgments of military necessity, casts in relief the complicated realities of modern warfare. This is in significant part a reflection of the degree to which the practice of targeted killing departs from the traditional battlefield form of combat, and hence from the core justifications for killing in war. There are four distinct ethical concerns that targeted killing, as currently

---

[20] I develop the category of preemptive practices in response to threats of violence in "Threats and Preemptive Practices," 5 *Leg. Theory* 311 (1999).

practiced, raises. I shall identify them briefly here, and then proceed to a more detailed discussion of these concerns in what follows.

First is the fact that individuals "targeted" according to a policy of targeted killing are *named* in advance of the attempt on their lives. The authorization to kill or capture them does not hinge, once they are on the list, on any particular behavior on their part. The relevant list is the JPEL and this is amended weekly and drawn up with intelligence input from the National Directorate of Security and the U.S. Central Intelligence Agency.[21] The authors of the list then assign serial numbers and code names to the identified suspects, who become the objects of intensive research in order to determine their patterns of behavior and to maximize the chances of killing (or in theory capturing) them in a planned operation. Those on the JPEL eventually become the targets of a Predator drone attack, a strike by F-15E strike aircraft or, in the last resort, a night-time assault by a TF 373 mission dispatched from a local military base.[22]

That the killing is "targeted" is not the issue. On the contrary, that killing is directed towards a target rather than randomly fired would appear to be a *sine qua non* for justifying it. The alternative, namely random killing, is hardly a practice worth seeking to defend. The problem is that the list involves the advance naming of individuals for targeting, a practice that presents justificatory problems. Commentators have mostly overlooked this aspect of the practice, and their criticisms have focused not on the individual identification of those targeted, but on the mere fact that individuals are targeted at all. It is important to notice, however, that there is a significant moral difference between *targeting anyone who satisfies certain generic criteria,* and *targeting a particular person* on the basis of the fact that he meets those criteria.

Second, a quite independent concern from advance naming is the relative expansiveness of the criteria for inclusion on the list of named suspects. Unlike where killing in war is concerned, the practice of naming and targeting terror suspects extends beyond those who are engaged in active combat.[23] The question then arises whether it is legitimate to target individuals involved in the "war on terror" who lack the status of active combatants, and what the outer reaches of the criteria for inclusion on the list of those who can be targeted should be. Without a clear theory of the justification that lies behind targeted killing operations, we cannot begin to identify the legitimate scope of the practice. This is a significant lacuna in the

---

[21] *See* Michael L. Gross, "Assassination and Targeted Killing: Law Enforcement, Execution or Self-Defense?" 23 *J. Applied Phil.* 323, 324 (2006).

[22] See, e.g., Nigel West, "International Special Operations Forces 2010 Year in Review," June 15, 2011, available at <http://www.defensemedianetwork.com/stories/international-special-operations-forces-2010-year-in-review/> last accessed November 2, 2011. See also Philip Alston, "The CIA and Targeted Killings Beyond Borders," September 2011, at 43–4, available at <http://ssrn.com/abstract=1928963> last accessed November 2, 2011.

[23] *See,* e.g., *Al-Aulaqi v. Obama, supra* n. 13.

jurisprudence of the war on terror, because the relationship between the standard act of killing in war and the targeted killing of quasi-combatants, "non-enemy combatants," or engaged and active bystanders has not as of yet been adequately theorized.

Third, if we allow that targeting at least certain individuals who are instrumental to the war on terror is legitimate, the further question arises of who may engage in the killing. If targeting those with a more attenuated relationship to active combat does not strictly speaking constitute an act of war, does that have implications for who may legitimately engage in targeting? Does relaxing the rules on the identity of the target imply a similar relaxation of the rules on the identity of the killer? The difficulty is that allowing CIA officials to conduct targeted killing, while a natural extension of many of its past practices, seems tantamount to hiring civilians to engage in acts of war, albeit executive branch officials. As Gary Solis has argued, allowing CIA officials to operate unmanned aerial vehicles makes them "civilians directly engaged in hostilities," an act for which they could themselves be branded "unlawful combatants" and subject to prosecution.[24] He writes:

> CIA civilian personnel who repeatedly and directly participate in hostilities may have what recent guidance from the International Committee of the Red Cross terms "a continuous combat function." That status, the ICRC guidance says, makes them legitimate targets whenever and wherever they may be found...While the guidance speaks in terms of non-state actors, there is no reason why the same is not true of civilian agents of state actors such as the United States.[25]

As for the arguments in defense of the practice that CIA officials can constitute belligerents assisting the military, the practice arguably flies in the face of a time-honored constraint on the right to kill in war: that belligerents identify themselves with visible insignia.[26] When combined with the second point, namely that it is not always active combatants that are placed on the "kill list," we potentially have an official governmental policy of hiring civilians to target other civilians—a far cry from the traditional reciprocity conditions and the principle of distinction that have been central to the maintenance of ethical standards in war. Thus although

---

[24] McKelvey, *supra* n. 3.

[25] Solis, *supra* n. 14.

[26] *See* Hague Convention (IV) Respecting the Laws and Customs of War on Land, Annex art. 23 (b) (1907) (defining qualifications of "belligerents" as requiring "a fixed distinctive emblem recognizable at a distance"). See also Protocol Additional to the Geneva Conventions of August 12, 1949 and Relating to the Protection of Victims of International Armed Conflicts (Protocol I), June 8, 1977, 1125 U.N.T.S. 3, art. 37 (1)(c) ("It is prohibited to kill, injure or capture an adversary by resort to perfidy [including].... the feigning of civilian, non-combatant status."). For a criticism of this view that uniforms matter, see Christopher Kutz, "The Difference Uniforms Make: Collective Violence in Criminal Law and War," 33 *Phil. & Public Aff.* 148, 180 (2005). For more information on recent developments in this view, see Kevin H. Govern, "The Hunt for Bin Laden—Task Force Dagger—On the Ground with the Special Forces in Afganistan: Reviewed by Lieutenant Colonel Kevin H. Govern," 179 *Mil. L. Rev.* 210, 217–18.

the practice of targeted killing is derived from a model based on combatant killing in war, the practice is a *significantly* attenuated version of that model, and hence merits careful legal and moral scrutiny. Ultimately what would be needed to justify the practice in its current form is a reconceptualization of the relevant portion of just war theory to take account of the "asymmetrical" nature of modern warfare. Whether such a reconceptualization is possible within the constraints of the justificatory constraints that typically apply to intentional killing is a serious question, one whose answer should not be taken for granted.

Fourth, the practice of targeted killing has become associated with the use of drones in order to effectuate the assassination of individuals on the named list. As Ken Anderson rightly points out, this is at least in part because drone killing minimizes the risk that the target will attempt to surrender and convert himself into a detainee.[27] The question that arises, however, is whether the justification for targeted killing, once identified, should be understood as placing any restrictions on the method or form such killing takes. While commentators often express ambivalence about the use of drone technology,[28] whether it is ultimately justified depends on several crucial factors. Does the "target" have a right under the laws of war to surrender if affording him this opportunity is militarily feasible?[29] If he has the right, does the use of drones make it significantly more difficult for him to exercise that right? From the standpoint of the duty to minimize casualties, there may be an obligation to treat drone killing as a last resort, given that it unduly escalates killing, and thus draws international conflict further and further away from a model of lawful, symmetrical killing in war.[30] Because these fundamental questions in just war theory have not been answered, we do not know how to assess the moral status of using drone technology in targeted killing. The reverse is also true: the failure to resolve issues connected with problems at the margins of just war theory, such as the use of drone technology, has a reverse inferential effect on the more standard cases of killing in war. If the justification for using drones or for killing without affording an opportunity to surrender is not clearly established, the practice calls the most fundamental premises of just war theory into question. The moral and legal ambiguities of modern "targeted killing" are thus a reflection of the profound ambiguities of modern warfare, which press at the boundaries of the traditional ways in which war has been conceived, and with the moral justification for intentional killing that has historically been offered as accompanying the reciprocal approach to war. For this reason, the traditional paradigm, represented in just war theory as a conflict between enemy soldiers

[27] Anderson *supra* n. 6.

[28] See O'Connell, *supra* n. 7.

[29] For one response to this question, see Kevin Govern, "Operation Neptune Spear: Was Killing Bin Laden a Legitimate Military Objective?" in this Volume, ch. 13.

[30] For one response to this question, see Kenneth Anderson, "Efficiency *in Bello* and *ad Bellum*: Making the Use of Force Too Easy," in this Volume ch. 14.

attacking and counter-attacking in a clearly defined physical space of combat, has only a tenuous application to the moral problem of justifying lethal acts in the War on Terror.

In what follows, I shall restrict my focus to the first and the final aspects of the current practice of targeted killing. While I will make reference to the other two problems, it is the first and the fourth problems that most clearly distinguish targeted killing as it is currently practiced from other practices in war, and they are also the aspects of that practice that most cast distinctive doubt on its legitimacy. If we are able to justify the practice of targeted killing in the face of these two significant challenges to its legitimacy, we will have addressed the central objections to the use of targeted killing, and in this way substantially answered the concerns recent leveled against the practice.

III. The legitimacy of naming targets

Let us begin by focusing on the concerns I raised in the previous section about the practice of naming subjects to be targeted. What difference does it make whether subjects are identified by name on a "kill or capture list", or whether the decision to identify someone as a target is based on actual threatening behavior? There are two reasons to object to the advance naming practice from an ethical standpoint, and these differences with the standard form of killing in war suggests significantly increased difficulties finding a justification for the practice in its current form. The two problems are, as I shall call them, first, *the bootstrapping problem,* and second, *the problem of statistical versus identified targets*. First, the bootstrapping problem.

The question has recently arisen whether it would have been permissible for the United States to target Colonel Muammar Qaddafi, who as it happens met his demise at the hands of Libyan National Transition Council (NTC) forces after fleeing his convoy which had been attacked by NATO warplanes and a U.S. drone.[31] On the one hand, he was, by his own admission, responsible for terrorist attacks against the United States, in particular the bombing of Pan Am Flight 103 over Lockerbie, Scotland in 1988.[32] He continued to support terrorism, and he was a sworn enemy of the United States and of his own civilian population. Surely the world is a better place without him, almost no matter what

---

[31] Kevin Govern, *"Expedited Justice: Gaddafi's Death and the Rise of Targeted Killings,"* JURIST— Forum, Oct. 25, 2011, available at <http://jurist.org/forum/2011/10/expedited-justice-the-trend-to-kill-over-capture.php> accessed November 2, 2011.

[32] On This Day: 1988: "Jumbo jet crashes onto Lockerbie," *BBC News,* December 21, 1988, <http://news.bbc.co.uk/onthisday/hi/dates/stories/december/21/newsid_2539000/2539447.stm> accessed November 2, 2011.

arises in Libya to fill the void he has left. On the other hand, it is not clear under the laws of war whether the foregoing considerations are relevant. Whatever his crimes, Qaddafi was a sitting head of state, recognized by various groups as a legitimate ruler, and as such possesses certain rights of sovereignty that cannot be ignored with respect to any foreign leader.[33] There is little justification under the laws of war for assassinating a head of state on the ground that he is guilty of a crime against the United States, for which he could potentially be tried in the International Criminal Court, or because we see him as a tyrant to his own people and may be guilty of crimes against humanity on multiple occasions. The only legitimate basis for targeting him in the absence of an existing state of war between the United States and Libya would have been that we had reason to fear his instigation of imminent attacks against the United States through terrorism or otherwise that could not be prevented by lesser means.

Matters would have been different, of course, if we had been war with Libya, as was the case with Saddam Hussein. Qaddafi was the commander of the armed forces and therefore by definition a part of Libya's combat forces in times of war.[34] That enemy forces would be entitled to kill him under these circumstances is a non-controversial byproduct of the theory of war, at least to the extent that killing him can be deemed militarily necessary. It is, of course, a further question whether they are entitled to give up an opportunity to *capture* him in order to kill him instead, if they are in a position of being able to do either (and either would serve the purposes of military necessity). One would have thought the moral principle *outside* the context of war that dictates using the least amount of force necessary to satisfy the demands of military necessity would govern this case, but that added dimension of the debate about targeted killing is one I will leave to one side for the moment.[35]

There is, however, a rather more controversial aspect of the hypothetical targeted killing of Qaddafi we are considering. Had we attacked Qaddafi we would have been at war with Libya, and that would appear to justify treating him as a combatant and targeting him, given his position as head of the armed forces. But presumably in that case, we ought not to regard a war with Libya as a neutral fact, something that just happened all by itself. We are the ones in this scenario, after all, who would have initiated acts of war against Libya. To treat such acts as justifying targeting Qaddafi as a combatant seems like a piece of morally specious bootstrapping. It is, indeed, reminiscent of the doctrine of the *Actio Libera in*

---

[33] For instance, as the leader of Libya, Qaddafi became Chairperson of the African Union on February 9, 2009. Press Release, African Union, Leader Muammar Gaddafi Visits AU Headquarters (Feb. 5, 2009).

[34] See Kristin Eichensehr, "On the Offensive: Assassination Policy under International Law" 25(3) *Harvard Law Review.*

[35] For more on this issue, see Kevin Govern "Operation Neptune Spear: Was Killing Bin Laden a Legitimate Military Objective?," in this Volume, ch. 13.

Causa, otherwise known as *creating the conditions of one's own defense*.[36] Consider the following case.

If I want to kill my enemy, but do not want to be guilty of murder, one thing I could do is to induce him to attack me with the advance plan of killing him in supposed *self-defense*. Most criminal codes will, however, deny a defendant a self-defense claim if "the actor, with the purpose of causing death or serious bodily injury, provoked the use of force against himself in the same encounter."[37] Similarly, the defense of duress is generally unavailable "if the actor recklessly placed himself in a situation in which it was probable that he would be subjected to duress."[38]

Intuition speaks strongly against allowing the defense in such situations, though the point remains controversial. Would Qaddafi's status as a "belligerent" have been a product of our own attacks o Libya, and if so, would this be a basis for denying the traditional justification for killing co-belligerents in war?[39] The concern about the application of the reasoning of the *Actio Libera in Causa* in this context makes clear that there are at least some situations in which the justification for targeting a given individual may depend in a crucial way on *why* he bears the status of *belligerent* with respect to the United States, thus effacing to some degree the line between the *jus ad bellum* and the *jus in bello*.[40] At the very least, a total severance of *ad bellum* reasoning and *in bello* reasoning would allow for the following sort of abuse.

Imagine we would like to target a head of state of a humane democracy. We know placing such an individual, who is a nonbelligerent, on the list of targets is impermissible under the laws of war. According to the above logic, we have only to declare war on that country in order to convert the relationship into one between belligerents, and although such a declaration would be impermissible from an *ad bellum* standpoint, it would entitle us to target the now-enemy head of state without subjecting ourselves to liability for war crimes. As long as the *in bello* criterion for the legitimacy of killing enemy combatants does not depend on the justice of

---

[36] On this doctrine see Claire Finkelstein and Leo Katz, "Contrived Defenses and Deterrent Threats: Two Facets of One Problem," 5 *Ohio. J. Crim. L.* 479 (2008); Paul Robinson, "Causing the Conditions of One's Own Defense: A Study of the Limits of Theory in Criminal Law Doctrine," 71 *Va. L. Rev.* 1 (1985); also see Leo Katz, "Targeted Killing and the Strategic Use of Self-Defense," in this Volume, ch. 17.

[37] Model Penal Code § 3.04(2)(b)(i).

[38] MPC § 2.09(2).

[39] The point remains controversial in domestic criminal law as well, as some commentators take the view that creating the conditions of our own defense does not eliminate the entitlement to claim it, since from the standpoint of the aims of the criminal law, the self-defender has done "nothing wrong," even if his own impermissible scheming placed him in a position in which he was able to claim the defense.

[40] I discuss the general point below in commenting on Jeff McMahan's view of the relation between these two concepts. *See infra* section III.

our cause in declaring war in the first place, we can kill with impunity as long as we have committed the quite different wrongful act of engaging in a wrongful declaration or act of war. The final step in this hypothetical is to notice that wars are rarely "declared" these days, and we do not generally consider the onset of war to be a violation of *ad bellum* constraints just because it was not declared. If this is correct, then it seems we need only perform an act of combat in order to turn ourselves, and our opponents, into combatants. And *this* requirement is satisfied by an attempt to assassinate the sitting head of state of the other country! So it seems we can bootstrap our way up into establishing the legitimacy of our own wrongful acts of targeting by engaging in illegal-targeting-turned-legal by its own existence. The constraints formerly posed by the law of war here do no work towards establishing normative constraints on the act of killing in war.

The bootstrapping scenario is of concern in its own right. But it is of particular relevance here, because it makes clear the potential moral risks in *status* rather than *conduct*, based killing. Naming a target in advance, and then killing him based on his status, requires that he fall into the category of combatant if such actions are to be permissible under principles of just war theory. But many targets we currently name, perhaps most of them, cannot be justifiably identified as status-based targets without relying on a distortion of the category of "combatant." Such distortions, in effect, stem from a failure to adequately distinguish *jus ad bellum* from *jus in bello* norms. Lack of clarity about what constitutes a legitimate ground for war then translates into a weakening of the traditional conduct requirements for justly prosecuting a war. The bootstrapping phenomenon thus arises out of the same decision to ignore the age-old principle of distinction between combatants and civilians. The principle of distinction must be significantly attenuated before we can seek to justify killing members of a non-governmental terrorist organization as combatants: unlawful combatants in the War on Terror are treated like combatants for the purpose of claiming the legitimacy of using status-based justified killing against them, but we treat them like civilians with regard to their own combatant and detainee privileges. The second questionable aspect about naming nonbelligerents (or self-created belligerents) in advance of an actual attack based on their current conduct has to do with the difference between statistical and previously named victims, a moral phenomenon of much more general applicability that nevertheless appears to play a role in this context. Consider the following example.

Suppose a real estate developer is trying to decide whether to proceed with the building of a large skyscraper in the middle of a busy downtown area. Imagine two possible scenarios. Scenario One: the developer knows to a very high degree of likelihood that at least one person will die in the construction of this building.[41]

---

[41] *See* Guido Calabresi, *The Cost of Accidents: A Legal and Economic Analysis* (Yale University Press, 1970).

He will of course take all precautions against the materialization of this risk, but he must consider the "cost" of going ahead with the project as containing some forecast of either wrongful death compensation or of payment for injury and/or disability. In general, we accept the permissibility of welfare-enhancing projects that bear negative externalities, as long as those projects remain socially productive once externalities are internalized. A foreseeable risk of social loss does not leave a moral stain on high-risk construction, any more than foreseeable risk of a certain level of road fatalities leaves a moral stain on driving.

Consider, however, Scenario Two. The developer this time is aware not only that there is a high degree of certainty that *someone* will die or become severely injured in the building of the sky scraper, but that Fred, one of his workers, will be the one to succumb to this loss. Is it permissible for the developer to proceed with the construction project in the face of the *known* or *anticipated* loss of an identifiable member of his work team? Philosophers and legal scholars generally treat risks that fall in the first category, which they call "statistical risks", as acceptable to run, but regard risks to identifiable individuals, which we might call "named risks", as wholly different in character. Why is not clear, but the intuition tends to be strongly felt. It is particularly odd, given that statistical risks can be run over a group of individuals all of whom are known to the risk taker, and yet the sense is that statistical risks are acceptable under certain conditions, but that named risks never are.

It seems reasonable to suppose that the discomfort one might feel with the fact that targeted killing involves the prior identification of *named* targets may be comparable to the different reactions we tend to have to statistical versus named risk. Now it is true that the imaginary example of building a skyscraper knowing exactly *who* is likely to be killed when we undertake the work is different in important ways from the scenario of targeted killing we are attempting to assess. Most importantly, the skyscraper scenario involves exposing human beings to a *foreseen,* rather than an intentional risk of death. Death, in both the statistical and the non-statistical version of the skyscraper example, is a side-effect of an otherwise productive activity. But notice which way this argument cuts. If one cleaves to the moral significance of intention, then targeted killing should be *more* difficult to justify than building skyscrapers, even knowing that a particular person, Joe, is highly likely to be killed in the procedure. Since intentional harm is thought by many to be more difficult to justify than incidental or foreseeable harm, then *a fortiori* if we would not proceed in the skyscraper case having identified the victim, we ought not to proceed in the targeted killing case, where the victim is comparably identified. The intuition that it is impermissible to build the skyscraper in the named case, then, does have implications for the targeted killing practice insofar as the latter involves advance naming, rather than mere statistical identification.

To better understand the intuition at work here, consider the constitutional prohibition on *bills of attainder,* in which individuals were previously identified as meriting judicial exile, and their status as legal persons was systematically eliminated, both through criminal punishment and through escheat of their possessions to the state.[42] While I do not have an explanation for why prior identification is so objectionable, whether in the case of a "kill list" or in that of bills of attainder, it seems reasonable to think the practice inconsistent with just war theory. Killing in war is a statistical process: each soldier places himself at risk for the sake of advances of the collective. He retains, however, a chance of being among those to survive, and thus the process of waging war doesnot require his overt sacrifice, but rather a personal exposure based on the place occupied by an individual in the context of a collective. A targeted individual, however, does not share in the possibility of survival granted to members of the collective. He is singled out, not for exposure to greater risks than comparably situated others, but for elimination. His risks relative to others fighting on his side are *not* statistical risks, and do not carry the upside of membership in the war-making collective. He is a criminal awaiting execution rather than a belligerent fighting for a cause or for his own defense.

A subsidiary problem is the criteria for identifying someone by name on a "kill" list, in this case the JPEL. As we touched on in the preceding discussion of the bootstrapping problem, it is not clear it is legitimate to place people on the target list we do not regard as full-blown belligerents in all respects. To elaborate on this point, the issue was raised in a prominent way in the case of *Al-Aulaqi v. Obama, Gates and Panetta.*[43] Al-Awlaki was threatening to U.S. National Security by being a member of a terrorist organization that has hostile intentions towards the United States, and by his acts of propaganda supporting the operation and expansion of that terrorist organization.[44] With group membership as the primary criterion for his inclusion in the government "kill list," we have no assurance that al-Awlaki's inclusion on the list was based on either his status as a belligerent in the traditional sense, or that it was based on a personal self-defense claim, that would also suffice to bring it within the permissible grounds for fighting in war. The threat he posed might not have risen to the level of full-blown belligerency, and it might also have failed as providing a basis for the exercise of self-defense against him by U.S. agents, due to lack of imminence. In this case al-Awlaki's representation on the targeted list arguably should not have been justified in terms of the privilege to kill in war, and his status as a combatant depends on an attenuation of the laws and principles of reciprocal war. Without belligerency on the one hand, or an imminent threat on the other, that might justify killing him

---

[42] See, e.g., Ryan P. Alford, "The Rule of Law at the Crossroads: Consequences of Targeted Killing of Citizens," *Utah Law Review* (forthcoming).

[43] See *Al-Aulaqi v. Obama, supra* n. 13.

[44] For more on the circumstances under which he was targeted, see Govern, *supra* n. 31.

in the name of national self-defense, the targeting of al-Awlaki was not defensible from traditional theory of fair combat.

IV. Using drones to kill

A distinctive, though by no means necessary, feature of targeted killing is that it often takes place by drone technology.[45] Are there any morally relevant differences between killing with a remotely controlled drone and killing in hand-to-hand combat? As mentioned above, one important difference between "manual" killing by visually sited gunfire and electro-optically sited "distance" killing is that the "target" is more likely to be deprived of the opportunity to surrender. One should, however, be more precise: where drones are used, the target is likely to be deprived of the opportunity to surrender *at the point at which surrenders typically occur in traditional combat*, namely death. This also has implications for the duty to capture rather than kill: assuming the targeting takes place at a distance, and the missile is fired in an autonomous "fire and forget" mode,[46] the target could not, even in theory, effectuate a surrender, since one cannot surrender to a drone. This in turn substantially enhances the difficulty for the killer of fulfilling his obligation to capture rather than kill. In this regard, the use of drone technology locks the aggressor into a killing scenario, where the initiation of the plan of action starting with the placing of an individual's name on a 'Kill list,' and committing to effectuate that killing with a technology that enables killing at a distance.

One is tempted here to draw a parallel to the domestic criminal law cases involving spring guns, in which the firing device is automatically triggered by the presence of an intruder on the protected property. Courts have found the use of automatic firing devices of this sort to be impermissible, on the ground that they constitute a commitment to a course of action that is both irreversible once initiated and highly subject to error.[47-48] The use of the spring gun is thus reminiscent of the rational choice strategy of *binding oneself to the mast*, or precommitment. Such *automatic plan execution devices* require an agent to weigh the costs and benefits of an entire course of conduct up front, in an ex ante position of choice. The difficulties courts have found with spring guns point out the general objections to

---

[45] See Kenneth Anderson, "Targeted Killing and Drone Warfare: How We Came to Debate Whether There Is a 'Legal Geography of War'" in Peter Berkowitz (ed.), *Future Challenges in National Security and Law* (Hoover Institution, Stanford University, forthcoming).

[46] On the importance of the firing mode, see Henry S. Kenyon, "Multipurpose Missile Program Accelerates," *Signal Online*, June 2009, available at <http://www.afcea.org/signal/articles/templates/Signal_Article_Template.asp?articleid=1962&zoneid=263> accessed November 2, 2011.

[47-48] *Katko v. Briney*, 183 N.W.2d 257 (Iowa 1971) (holding a home owner liable for injuries to a trespasser caused by the owner's use of a spring gun to protect the property). The Supreme Court of Iowa had found the use of a spring gun to protect a home from intruders impermissible, on the ground that the automatic firing of the device made adjustment to unusual emergency situations impossible.

any kind of automatic plan execution: while the automaticity allows the planner to execute a course of action that might otherwise have been rationally or morally foreclosed to him, the benefits from automatic plan execution are often quickly outweighed by the inability to reassess costs.

In drone killings, however, the killing itself is not "automatic" in the sense identified in the spring gun cases. The drone is manually operated from a remote location, and missiles launched can be under continuous guidance and observation of the target. Still, even in the face of continuous guidance, the likelihood of deflecting the killing into a non-lethal course of action is greatly reduced as compared with manual, person-to-person killing. As the court said in *Katko v. Briney*,

> A possessor of land cannot do indirectly and by a mechanical device that which, were he present, he could not do immediately and in person. Therefore, he cannot gain a privilege to install, for the purpose of protecting his land from intrusions harmless to the lives and limbs of the occupiers or users of it, a mechanical device whose only purpose is to inflict death or serious harm upon such as may intrude, by giving notice of his intention to inflict, by mechanical means and indirectly, harm which he could not, even after request, inflict directly were he present.[49]

The court's thought here is that because there is no privilege to protect one's home with deadly force against a non-violent trespasser, the same cannot be accomplished by means of an indiscriminate mechanical device that "automatically" targets anyone who enters the property, whether malevolent or excused, justified or merely misguided. The same point can be made about drones: the element of human judgment is eliminated when distant technologies are used to implement decisions about life and death, and this plays an essential role in *justifying* the decision to kill. Though technically reversible, decisions to target subjects with remote technology obviate the role of human judgment that would most readily allow for reversal or adjustment based on the target's demeanor or activity. As such it operates like a mandatory death sentence that leaves no room for individual mitigating evidence.[50]

Finally, even if one were to regard being "locked in" to a killing rather than capturing as desirable, and hence justified from the standpoint of military necessity, there is a question whether it is morally acceptable to conduct killings of suspected, low-level terrorists at a great remove, given that the distance between attacker and victim also minimizes the opportunity for human intuition and appropriate empathy to play a role.[51] Consider the heart-wrenching scene in *The Mascot*, a memoir written by a son of the tragic tale of his survivor father, who fled the small village of Koidanov, Belarus at the age of five after witnessing his mother and two

---

[49] *Ibid*. at 260.

[50] Such have been held to be unconstitutional. *See Woodson v. N.C.*, 428 U.S. 280, 303 (1976) (holding that mandatory death penalty statute was unconstitutional because it failed "to allow the particularized consideration of relevant aspects of the character and record of each convicted defendant before the imposition upon him of a sentence of death").

[51] For more on this issue, see Anderson, "Efficiency *in Bello* and *ad Bellum*: Make the Use of Force Too Easy?," *supra* n. 30.

siblings, along with several hundred other Jews from their village, murdered and thrown into a pit by a Belarussian Einsatzgruppen.[52] After wandering through the forest for a period of months, he was caught by a Latvian SS unit in the process of executing group of Jewish prisoners who were at that moment lined up against a Church wall waiting to be shot. For some reason, the boy at that moment asked the Commander, who was about the pull the trigger, if he could have a piece of bread. As the author explains, the simple humanity of the request, the reminder that the executioner and victim were both embodied and creatures of appetite, led the Latvian SS officer to remove the boy from the line-up.[53] The shared humanity of the moment of rescue depended upon the physical proximity of attacker and victim—the interlocking gazes and the officer's consequent ability to see a piece of himself in the desperate, ill-fated child. The more distance, the less interaction; the less interaction, the weaker the tug of humanity, that can, on occasion, lead to spontaneous acts of mercy.

For all of the above reasons, I conclude that the traditional justification for targeted killing in war fails with respect to the attenuated cases of modern warfare. Failing the just war hypothesis about why such killings might be justified, there is a second possibility that merits consideration, namely that an alternative reason for killing in war is that there is an imminent threat to the personal security of combatants. While the just war hypothesis is about why such killings might be justified, there is a second possibility that merits consideration, namely that an alternate reason for killing in war is that there is an imminent threat to the personal security of combatants. While the just war and the personal defense rationales for killing in war operate substantially differently, both are valid in traditional combat, and both provide a justification for targeted killing in the context of traditional battlefield warfare. If the status-centered approach of traditional just war theory fails to justify a practice of advance identification of quasi-combatants, could the realm of agent-relative, personal justifications fare any better?

V. Belligerency, law-enforcement and self-defense

Thus far I have argued that there are at least two reasons why traditional just war theory does not readily accommodate the practice of targeted killing. Although we have not explored the traditional justification for killing in war in any depth, the relevant normative framework is that provided by the concept of *belligerency*. It is

---

[52] *See* Mark Kurzem, *The Mascot: Unraveling the Mystery of My Jewish Father's Nazi Boyhood*, (Penguin Publishers, 2002).

[53] After verifying his Jewish identify, and instructing the boy never to let anyone "pull down his pants," the officer adopted and protected the child, fitting him with a child-size Latvian SS uniform of his own, and allowing him to live as the "mascot" of the SS unit of which he was a part until near the end of the war.

the notion of belligerency that makes it permissible for one soldier to kill another in war, and for him to kill not just *defensively*, namely because he is attacked, but *offensively* as well, namely in pursuit of victory for his side in the battle, regardless of the danger posed by the enemy soldier. The concept of belligerency is also what makes it permissible for one soldier to kill an enemy soldier regardless of the moral status of their country's claim to justice in the cause of war. The status of a solider as combatant in war carries with it the justification to kill and be killed, because the relationship among enemy combatants reflects a "moral equality" in which each combatant, regardless of the moral status of his country's cause, possesses an equal entitlement to kill soldiers of the other side in virtue of his own adherence to a set of neutral rules governing the waging of war.[54] These are the *jus in bello* rules for conduct war: those that govern *how* war is waged, rather than the *jus ad bellum,* namely *why* it was waged in the first place. The "moral equality of soldiers," as Walzer puts it, is a function of adherence to the *jus in bello*, rather than the *jus ad bellum*, or the justness of an enemy's cause in war,[55] and belligerency is a concept that operates in the *jus in bello*, rather than in the *jus ad bellum.* The right to kill the enemy soldier at all times, then, is a *status-dependent justification* for killing, rather than an act-or character-dependent criterion.

Jeff McMahan, by contrast, rejects the traditional thesis of the moral equality of soldiers, but he nevertheless subscribes to the thought that there is a justification for killing in war that stands apart from the justification for killing in other situations. For McMahan, it is the combatant whose cause reflects the true *jus ad bellum*, meaning that his fight reflects the just cause of his country in going to war. The individual combatant inherits his country's right to wage war on the side of justice, just as the individual soldier fighting an unjust war is deprived of any such right, and the fact that his conduct adheres to the *jus in bello* does not immunize him from moral criticism based on his inherited reason for fighting.[56]

On either account—Walzer's or McMahan's—the justification for killing in war remains particular to the domain of war, despite the imperfect parallels that both authors attempt to make between warfare and the concept of self-defense in domestic criminal law. The distinctiveness of just war theory is particularly clear in Walzer's account. The *moral equality* thesis would appear to be unique to war, and the attempt to find parallels in the personal morality of life-and-death situations seems to elude the Walzerian theorist.[57] McMahan, by contrast, is explicit both in rejecting the moral equality thesis, and in claiming that the moral significance of the *jus ad bellum* over the

---

[54] According to Michael Walzer, this is the central concept in the theory of war. Michael Walzer, *Just and Unjust Wars, supra* n. 17 ch. 1.

[55] Ibid. at 34–41.

[56] Jeff McMahan, *Killing in War* (Oxford University Press, 2009).

[57] But see my argument in *Responsibility for Acts of War* (2011) (unpublished manuscript) to the effect that the moral equality thesis exists in domestic criminal law doctrine as well.

jus in bello finds a parallel in the domestic rules regarding justification, in particular with regard to the law of self-defense. The rules of combat are, by McMahan's lights, mirrored in the normative relationship of agents aggressive against one another in ordinary morality, and outside the context of war. There too, McMahan suggests that the strength of an agent's right to kill another person depends significantly on the moral justifiability of the aggressor's cause as compared with that of the self-defender.[58]

Yet, by McMahan's own admission, various domains of domestic law, largely those areas that we think of as highly reflective of ordinary morality, would require significant revision if we attempted to maintain the parallels between the *ad bellum/in bello* split of traditional just war theory in the context of ordinary morality. McMahan believes that although the law of self-defense, and its corresponding principles in ordinary morality, provide a fairly compelling match for just war theory, the law of self-defense would require considerable revision to fully capture the moral logic that undergirds it. To cite just one example, McMahan thinks that an individual attacked who is lacking in an overall justification for killing based on the superior morality of his cause, and who is confronted with a morally adequate basis for killing *him* on the part of his adversary, should, strictly speaking, just stand there and allow himself to be killed.[59] This is because he has no moral ground for attacking the adversary who is fighting a just war, as the fact that he is being attacked is not strictly speaking relevant to answering the question whether he has a justification for killing a belligerent attacker. But since it is not reasonable to expect a person attacked by an aggressor, even a justified aggressor, to remain still and allow himself to be attacked without counter-response, McMahan is willing to say that the non-justified victim of an attack, although not justified, is nevertheless *excused* if he exercises self-defense in the face of a justified attack.[60] Thus although the law of war and the domestic law of self-defense may on the deepest normative level display the same logic of moral justification, the law of self-defense as currently structured fails to reflect the law of war, and hence in practice, though perhaps not in theory, the law of war and the domestic law of violence come apart. On either account, the right to kill in war is conceived of as isolated from the rest of the law on the use of force in our personal morality and in our domestic legal provisions.

Perhaps the most significant divergence between ordinary morality and just war theory is that the right to kill in the latter context relies on a *status* justification— that of belligerency—in a way that is never the case in domestic criminal law.

---

[58] McMahan, *supra* n. 56, at 15–32.

[59] Ibid. at 174.

[60] Ibid. at 162. While I would agree with McMahan, that the domestic criminal law echoes just war theory, I see both as committed to the moral equality of combatants, whereas he argues against the thesis in both contexts. As I have pointed out above, however, maintaining the correspondence of justification in war and justification in domestic defenses is acknowledged by McMahan to be at least a somewhat revisionary project on the criminal law side. If we are engaged in normative reconstruction of actual practices, then, it seems it may be more defensible to side with the theory that better captures the norms of current justificatory practice in the criminal law.

The aggressor in a case of self-defense is the fitting object of violence only if, and to the extent that, he is aggressing against the defendant. Once his aggression is discontinued, the legitimacy of attacking him also ceases, and he regains his right not to be killed. The same is true in law enforcement: a person who poses a danger to others can be targeted and killed by police, but only insofar as he continues to pose a danger, and as long as he could not be apprehended by non-violent means. The same holds true of defense of others: one is privileged to defend third parties with force in certain instances, but only when, and to the extent, that the first party would have the right to defend himself under the circumstances. What is noteworthy about standard criminal law justifications in this context is that although the right to kill in just war theory is considerably broader than the right to self-defense and other standard criminal law justifications, the latter set of reasons to kill provides in another respect a more *expansive* entitlement than just war theory.

For example, the right to kill in war is limited to combatants, even if on standard accounts at least, it is an "expansive" right in the sense that even combatants whose cause is lacking in moral justice can avail themselves of the entitlement. For this reason, it is a violation of the laws and morality of war to kill an enemy combatant if the soldier is aware of a substantial risk he will kill a non-combatant civilian in the process. But, for example, on the theory of self-defense this concern is less pressing. If a terrorist threatens to throw a bomb at you, and the terrorist is standing next to his wife, who is unaware of his aggressive plot to deprive you of your life, you are entitled to throw a bomb preemptively at him in order to save your life, despite the fact that you will almost certainly kill the innocent wife in the process. Killing in war, therefore, may not be as constrained with respect to the lives of bystanders as it is under the parameters of just war theory.

This is a curious result for the right to kill in war. It is perhaps for this reason that commentators on the laws of war see the private right to self-defense of soldiers as absorbed into the rights of enemy combatants.[61] To allow such defenses to exist side-by-side appears to threaten the coherence of the laws of war, since as "combatant" the soldier may not target enemy combatants where to do so would threaten the life of a bystander. If the justification for killing *were* based on an individual's private right to self-defense, or on the privilege to protect third parties, the application of the theory

---

[61] See Hugo Grotius, *De Iure Belli ac Pacis*, G.L. Williams (trans.), (Clarendon Press, 1950), 2:10–11, "first, that It shall be permissible to defend [one's own] life and to shun that which threatens to prove injurious; secondly, that It shall be permissible to acquire for oneself, and to retain, those things which are useful for life. The latter precept, indeed, we shall interpret with Cicero as an admission that each individual may, without violating the precepts of nature, prefer to see acquired for himself rather than for another, that which is important for the conduct of life. Moreover, no member of any sect of philosophers, when embarking upon a discussion of the ends [of good and evil], has ever failed to lay down these two laws first of all as indisputable axioms. For on this point the Stoics, the Epicureans, and the Peripatetics are in complete agreement, and apparently even the Academics [i.e., the Skeptics] have entertained no doubt."

would be substantially broader. If the right to engage in targeted killing were somehow predicated on one of the criminal law justifications, this would substantially reduce the need for the combatant to concern himself with collateral damage.

If an individual satisfies the criteria for belligerency, he is no longer treated as an attenuated threat to National Security; he is viewed as an immediate threat, and he is then a legitimate target by virtue of his status, provided that the killing is done in a way that respects other independent boundaries, such as the restriction on causing disproportionate collateral damage implicit in the notion of military necessity. Self-defense or other-defense, by contrast, knows no limitations based on the identity of the person threatened, and therefore it does not matter whether the use of force is initiated by military personnel, CIA agents, or others. But, I shall argue, when an individual poses a threat to National Security interests, but that threat is non-imminent,[62] or it is not immediately necessary to respond with force, and when the person of the responder is not personally threatened with an imminent use of force (or that it is immediately necessary to use force by way of response), the permission to use targeted killing fails.

In the previous section we saw that killing in war according to the belligerency rationale may fail to justify the practice of targeted killing, and this is for several reasons. First, the practice pre-names individuals to be assassinated, a practice that goes significantly beyond the military practice of killing in battle and the level of "targeting" it involves. Second, as actually practiced, targeted killing does not restrict the "kill list" to those who would traditionally be considered belligerents. Finally, I raised concerns about the usual way in which targeted killing is conducted, namely with drone technology. While this does not go directly to the justification for the practice, insofar as one can engage in targeted killing without drones, it does raise some doubts about the current form the practice typically takes, as well as raising some basis for reflecting back on the basic rationale for targeted killing in traditional just war theory. On the other hand, the criminal law justifications are highly likely to fail with respect to those on a named kill list, because the threat they pose is clearly going to be regarded as non-imminent. If just war theory and self-defense both fail to explain the legitimacy of killing according to a named target list, is there any other justification for the practice that *would* help to justify it?

VI. Preemptive killing in war

In this section, I shall argue that there is a justification for the use of force that falls into a middle-tier category between the status-dependent law of war and what would

---

[62] For more on the imminence requirement, see Russell Christopher, "Imminence in Justified Targeted Killing," in this Volume, ch. 9.

amount to an extrapolation of personal defense in criminal law, as applied to a targeted killing situation. The kind of justification I have in mind is most clearly demonstrated by certain domestic law enforcement circumstances. I shall refer to such cases as instances of "preemptive" force. In these cases, I argue, despite the fact that neither of the standard justifications of *killing the enemy combatant under the laws of war,* or *self-defense against an imminent or immediate threat of serious bodily injury or death* is applicable, I shall claim that the use of targeted killing as an instance of preemptive force renders the practice justifiable, subject to certain more restrictive conditions having to do with the apprehension of suspects and avoidance of collateral damage. Thus the concept of "preemptive force" may explain why it is sometimes permissible to kill nonbelligerents who are not posing an imminent threat to one's own or another's security. At the same time, however, it is crucial to understand that the entitlement to kill that falls under this rationale will be of a more limited sort than the justifications that stem from the entitlements that flank it—the killing of belligerents in an armed conflict, justified under traditional laws of war, on the one hand, and the killing of those posing an imminent threat to one's person or the person of another, justified by the traditional self-defense defense, on the other.

I shall approach the topic of preemptive force in war by focusing at first on a closely related topic, the topic of *preventive* force. Preventive force is primarily force exercised in self-defense or defense of others. It will be helpful to approach the topic from this direction, since there has been a great deal of confusion in recent years about the limits of preventive force. Since that concept is very often equated with self-defense (a mistake), it will be important to explain the privilege to kill in prevention, and to distinguish it from the more specific and slightly different concept of self-defense. We will then return to the laws of war to compare the right to preemptive force with the offensive entitlement to kill fellow belligerents in an appropriately identified armed conflict.

It is sometimes permissible to use more force to prevent harm than it is to punish instances of that same harm. In many cases, for example, the victim of an assault may use deadly force to defend herself against a harm that could not be permissibly punished with death. It is even permissible in many jurisdictions to use deadly force in defense of habitation, but no jurisdiction has ever authorized the death penalty for intrusions into one's home alone. Finally, the police may use lethal force to pursue a fleeing suspect who is resisting arrest, as long as they suspect him of having committed a felony, believe he poses a risk of future felonious activity, and have warned him of their intent to use force if he does not submit to custody.[63] In most such cases, however, the felony for which the use of lethal force is authorized is not murder, and hence would not merit the death penalty as punishment. These examples permit a generalization about the relation between preventive and

---

[63] *Tennessee v. Garner,* 471 U.S. 1, 722 (1985).

retributive force, namely that *the extent of permissible preventive force is broader than the extent of permissible retributive force.* Thus if targeted killing is conceived as a form of punishment for prior terroristic activities, or as a method of deterring other terrorists (one of the standard functions of punishment), its scope will be narrower than if it is conceived as a method of preventive law enforcement.

While the foregoing states an oft-made point, scholars of domestic criminal law tend neither to opine about the source of this curious dichotomy, nor to trace its implications for other aspects of the criminal law. Discovering the philosophical foundation of a doctrine will often shed light on the scope of its implications. While I cannot undertake a full analysis of preventive force and its relation to retributive force in the current context, I do wish to focus on one particularly helpful aspect of this dichotomy. Suppose one subscribes to a deterrence theory of punishment, according to which one seeks both to explain the current structure of criminal sanctions and prescribe modifications in that structure according to a theory of adequate general deterrence, then the preventive privilege cannot be explained in deterrence terms as well. The reason should be clear: if the amount of punishment generally prescribed by way of retribution is thought roughly adequate for deterring rational prospective criminals, relative to a desired base-line reduction in the societal levels of crime, then the amount of force author-ized by way of *prevention* would represent *overdeterrence* relative to that same baseline. In short, if it is not necessary to use the death penalty to deter assault, then the preventive permission to kill in order to avoid being assaulted cannot be required for deterrence purposes, and must be explained according to some non-deterrence-based logic.

What sort of logic would that be? The authorization to use preventive force in self or other defense, or even to prevent the commission of a variety of offenses that are not against the person, must be explained according to one of the available alternatives to deterrence theory. Preventive force may be permissible because it involves the exercise of a *right*, meaning that it stems from some set of deontological norms, or it may be permissible because it represents the expression in some sense of our non-negotiable rational agency. Such would be the case on a social contract picture of preventive rights. The implications of the comparably more expansive authority to use preventive force, as compared with retributive punishment, would then point in either of two directions: instances of social prevention would either be explicable as an expression of a set of societal deontological rights, or as an implicit global covenant for self-protection based on mutual advantage. I tend to the latter view. That view is both sensitive to the interest all have in deterring violent activities and the need to respect basic autonomy conditions in the face of the right to kill in war. The traditional laws of war contain, at their core, a set of rational restrictions on the offensive right to kill. In the framework I am advancing, these limitations can best be understood as premised on mutual advantage. When countries observe the restrictions on aggression contained in the laws of war, they fare better than those countries that do not. This assertion, however, only holds as long as the forbearance from unbridled aggression in a conflict with the enemy is mutually observed. Where it is not mutually observed, war degenerates into "total war," a Hobbesian state of nature in which "every man is enemy to every man."[64] Because Al Qaeda, and groups with terroristic aims, can be expected to violate these conditions of mutuality, it is not possible to apply the rules of reciprocal engagement to collectivities of this sort. It is this insight that provides the most support for the thought that we must treat those who would plunge us in to "asymmetrical" warfare as agents in a self-produced condition of "total war." But there may as yet be obligations to bring such individuals into the fold of reciprocity, by continuing to respect, albeit unilaterally, the basic conditions of civilized, humanitarian discourse.

In keeping with the foregoing observations from domestic criminal law, I shall elaborate a distinction between two kinds of preventive killing. The first I shall call simply "preventive" killing, and the second I shall refer to as "preemptive" killing. Preventive killing, when justified, is dependent on the need to physically put a stop to the use of force on the part of another. Preemptive killing, by contrast, bears a more attenuated relation to the harm it is designed to forestall; its permissibility follows from the use of rational techniques legitimately employed to dissuade a potential aggressor from following through with his course of action. In particular, it often depends on the fact that it is sometimes permissible to threaten to inflict a harm in order to deter another from the use of violence. In such a case, when deterrence fails and when the threat constituted a legitimate response to the fear of force on the part of another, it may be permissible to follow through on a threat it was morally permissible to issue, despite the fact that the threatened action would not have been permissible as straightforward preventive action. Such is arguably true of law-enforcement action, despite the fact that law enforcement is thought to preclude military enforcement, and that these two types of enforcement are fundamentally at odds with one another. The concept of *preemptive killing* provides a sound model of the crossover between law enforcement and military. It also provides a useful example of targeted killing, or at least a model that situates the practice correctly relative to its own ambitions, and allows it to be normatively justified as well.

My suggestion is that targeted killing is permissible when it falls squarely into the category of justified preemptive killing. It is rarely, if ever, justified as a form of preventive action. This places certain constraints on the legitimate reach of targeted killing that would not apply if the action must be considered purely preventive. But these restrictions do not seem overly stringent when articulated in the context of the practice of targeted killing. They imply, for example, that targeting must be preceded by a threat to use force, along with an attempt to apprehend the source of the threat. This squares

---

[64] Hobbes, *Leviathan,* Part I, Chapter XIII, para. 9.

with the duty to capture rather than kill that applies to attacks on non-combatants, along with the requirement that applies to everyone, namely that individuals have a right to surrender. Respecting these deep sources of respect and reciprocity in war, despite the fact that one's enemy does not, may be a moral duty, just as the obligation of the police to extend and protect certain rights of suspects cannot be derogated from on the grounds that the suspects themselves do not observe the same conditions with respect to us. Considering targeted killing a form of preemptive killing also has ramifications for the crucial questions of who may be targeted, the extent to which bystanders may be endangered, and other policy aspects of the current debate over targeted killing. It is beyond the scope of this chapter to trace all the implications of adopting a preemptive, rather than a preventive, framework for analyzing targeted killing. The rough outlines of those implications can be easily identified, however: While a preventive framework uses force to *impede* infringements of self or societal security in a given case, a preemptive framework accomplishes its objective by implicitly or explicitly threatening the use of force to *deter* such infringements in a given case. Preemption is thus like prevention in that it is particular to a given case, but it partakes in the indirect logic of rational deterrence to induce compliance. Unlike prevention, it appeals to the *reason* of the agent on whom is operates. It alters behavior by changing the payoffs for (roughly speaking) rational agents, and thus appeals to their ability to project their reasons for acting into the future.

By linking the logic of targeted killing to preemption, I am suggesting that the legitimacy of this technique lies not in the relabeling of the target as a kind of "combatant," such that it becomes legitimate to target him without the implicit duty of capture. Instead, I am arguing that the permission to target between non-co-belligerents is linked to the legitimacy of issuing a threat to use force if the other does not surrender. The threat is important, because it is an enactment of the duty to capture, in recognition of the fact that one is operating in a non-traditional combatant situation. When the threat is ignored, and the duty to capture cannot be met in other ways, it is then permissible in some cases to follow through on the threat. This places the legitimacy of targeted killing outside the traditional co-belligerency setting, firmly within the purview of practices like nuclear deterrence: it is permissible in some cases to *threaten* to use force that it would not be, by itself, permissible to use to deter wrongful action. And when the threat is ignored, it becomes permissible to carry through on the action threatened because the demand implicit in the threat was legitimate and the target had the opportunity to conform his behavior to his best reasons for acting by presenting himself for surrender. If this is correct, we can say that the central difficulty with the practice of targeted killing is that it ignores the importance of the public warning or threat. The target is entitled to the opportunity to surrender, and the targeting is legitimate only if the target has been fully afforded the possibility of conformity to the terms of his obligations as expressed in the demand for surrender.

7

THE PRIVILEGE OF BELLIGERENCY AND FORMAL DECLARATIONS OF WAR

Richard V. Meyer

On May 2, 2011, United States military forces entered the town of Abbottabad in the Waziristan region of Pakistan under cover of darkness.[1] They entered a compound and killed a civilian and his son and shot his wife. In the process they also killed two other men and injured at least one other woman.[2] The target, Osama bin Laden, was not a member of a nation's military, was not sentenced to death by any tribunal, and there is no evidence that at the time of the attack he was an imminent threat to another human.[3] He was gunned down at night, in his home, by trained killers from a distant state acting without the permission of the host nation.[4]

At face value under domestic criminal law, these killers are criminals. They committed acts with the intent to kill bin Laden and these acts resulted in his death and the deaths of others. These acts are qatl-e-amd, or culpable homicide under sections 300 and 301 of the Penal Code of Pakistan and are punishable with death.[5]

---

[1] "Bin Laden Killing Caps Decade Long Manhunt," CNN, May 3, 2011, at <http://edition.cnn.com/2011/WORLD/asiapcf/05/02/bin.laden.dead/index.html?eref=edition> accessed November 3, 2011.

[2] Ibid.

[3] Ibid.

[4] Karin Bruilliard and Karen DeYoung, "Failure to Discover Bin Laden's Refuge Stirs Suspicion Over Pakistan's Role", *The Washington Post*, May 2, 2011. The article includes the quotation that "U.S. officials insisted that Pakistan was not told about the operation until U.S. forces had left Pakistani airspace."

[5] Pakistan Penal Code (Act XLV of 1860) §300: "Whoever, with the intention of causing death or with the intention of causing bodily injury to a person, by doing an act which in the ordinary course of nature is likely to cause death, or with the knowledge that his act is so imminently dangerous that it must in all probability cause death, causes the death of such person, is said to commit qatl-e-amd." §301: "Where a person, by doing anything which he intends or knows to be likely to cause death, causes death of any person whose death he neither intends nor knows himself to be likely to cause, such an act committed by the offender shall be liable for qatl-i-amd."

Had these been common thugs, Pakistan would have demanded their extradition from the United States under a bilateral extradition treaty that has been in place since 1942, and that a Pakistani Court adjudicate their guilt or innocence.[6] These were not common thugs, however. They were uniformed members of the U.S. military acting under the orders of the President.[7] This is not a legal ground to refuse extradition, however. Only if the United States were able to find that the acts of the killers were either not violations of either U.S. or Pakistani law or the killers acted under the protection of a valid legal defense such as a justification or an excuse could the United States refuse extradition under the treaty,[8] and obedience to orders is not a affirmative defense to intentional homicide.[9] The United States might argue self-defense or defense of others based upon bin Laden's prior acts of violence and predilection towards similar future acts as their valid defense,[10] but this would require an extremely elongated view of these legal concepts and should not succeed.[11] Thus, if we limit the discussion to a criminal law paradigm, these individuals who have been hailed as heroes by both the U.S. government and the general populace would be returning to Pakistan to face trial.[12] There is potentially a second legal paradigm at play here, however, that of international humanitarian law (IHL).[13]

For the killing of bin Laden to be a lawful act within IHL, four tests must be met: an armed conflict must exist,[14] the killers must be privileged belligerents,[15] bin

---

[6] This treaty was originally between the U.S. and the U.K. (who possessed Pakistan at that time), but by Article 14 of the treaty it is also binding between the U.S. and Pakistan.

[7] See *supra* n. 1.

[8] 18 United States Code §3184 and *Peroff v. Hylton*, 563 Federal Reporter 2d (F. 2d) 1099 (1977). The extradition could also be refused for humanitarian reasons, but that is not germane to this discussion.

[9] Unless these orders are the result of a judicial finding of guilt and sentence to death under §78 of the Penal Code of Pakistan.

[10] This presumes that the intent of the raid was to kill rather than apprehend bin Laden.

[11] Generally, defense of others requires that the other person be entitled to use self-defense. Self-defense requires that the threat be imminent. See 22A American Jurisprudence (AmJur) 2d. §134: An imminent threat must be immediate. See "danger" under *Black's Law Dictionary* 9th edn (2009).

[12] This assumes Pakistan would be able to identify the specific individuals and present the necessary evidence in order to request their extradition.

[13] IHL is also referred to as the laws of armed conflict (LOAC) and the laws of war (LOW). The primary sources of this body of law are the Hague Conventions of 1907, the Geneva Conventions of 1949 and the Additional Protocols to the Geneva Conventions. [Author's note: The Hague Conventions of 1907 will be cited as Hague III, Hague IV, and Hague V; the Geneva Conventions of 1949 will be cited as Geneva I, Geneva II, Geneva III and Geneva IV; the Additional Protocols to the Geneva Conventions will be cited as AP1 and AP2.]

[14] Common Article 2 to the Geneva Conventions; Article 1 of AP1.

[15] Article 1, Hague IV Annex; Article 4, Geneva III; Article 43, AP1. Hague IV cites the qualifications to be a "belligerent," Geneva III cites the qualifications to be a "prisoner of war" and AP1 cites the qualifications to be a "combatant." All three statuses refer to the ability to be immune from punishment by the enemy for your lawful acts of combat which this chapter refers to as privileged belligerency.

Laden must be a lawful target,[16] and the method of engagement must be lawful.[17] Two of these tests appear to be met; the killers are members of a state's uniformed military[18] so they can qualify as privileged belligerents, and the method of engagement was direct fire small arms which is ordinarily lawful.[19] The other two factors are the subject of debate.

Bin Laden did not fall under any of the typical categories of lawful targets. He was not a uniformed member of a state's armed forces, nor was he a civilian currently engaged in conducting hostilities.[20] The armed conflict is not between states, is not officially declared, and is not confined to any geographic or even temporal region[21] so it is also atypical to traditional IHL scenarios. There are multiple arguments for and against the existence of this armed conflict and bin Laden's targetability by other scholars within this volume,[22] as well as countless other sources. This chapter is not an analysis of their merit, but rather a complaint against their necessity. For both legal and moral reasons, the existence or absence of war should not be so nebulous as to be the subject of scholarly debate and the law should have provided a process to determine the targetability of an individual as notorious as Osama bin Laden years in advance of the night of May 2.

To illustrate these points, consider the night-time raid of May 2 from the point of view of the Abbottabad police force. These individuals are charged with keeping the peace in this town and protecting its residents from criminal acts. When they saw armed foreigners drop from helicopters and attack a home and its residents, should they have tried to intervene? Legally, if this is an armed conflict under IHL and they are captured by the U.S. forces after engaging in hostilities, they could be convicted of their hostile acts by a U.S. military tribunal.[23] Morally, they have no responsibility to protect foreign combatants like bin Laden. Alternatively, if this is not an armed conflict, they have the legal right and legal and moral responsibility to act to repel the attack and could be subject to adverse action and public shame if they fail to act. Note that, unlike the plethora of legal scholars debating targeted

---

[16] Article 48, AP1.

[17] Article 35, AP1.

[18] See *supra* n. 1. The attack was reportedly conducted by U.S. Navy Special Operations Forces known as the Navy SEALs.

[19] Certain ammunition, such as dumdum bullets that flip in flight to cause additional damage upon impact would have been illegal if used.

[20] Article 51(3) of AP1: Civilians shall enjoy the protection afforded by this section, unless and for such time as they take a direct part in hostilities.

[21] One of the most difficult aspects of asymmetric warfare is determining the start and end time for the conflict.

[22] See, in this Volume, chs 1, 2, 3, 8, 13.

[23] Since there does not appear to be evidence that they would qualify for privileged belligerency, their conduct would be evaluated under domestic criminal law. In this case, they could theoretically be charged under the Military Commissions Act of 2006.

killings, they do not share the luxury of an advanced legal education and time for research and reflection. They must decide instantly and suffer the significant risks of the wrong determination.

In the above scenario, the law, as well as the political and legal communities, has failed the Abbottabad police force. As embodied in the tenets of *nullem crimen sine lege* and *nulla poena sine lege* as well as the writings of luminaries such as H.L.A. Hart,[24] Joseph Raz,[25] Oliver Wendell Holmes[26] and many others, the law has a legal and moral responsibility to provide its subjects sufficient advance information for them to make a knowledgeable choice. Some might argue that the lack of fair warning is an unavoidable byproduct of the continued evolution and growing overlap and conflation of criminal law and IHL. I disagree with both the premise and conclusion. The blurring of the lines between domestic law and morality on the one side and the law and morality of war on the other is artificial and based upon a fundamental misunderstanding of the realm of combat. War, which I favor as a much more definitive term than armed conflict, if it is to continue to exist in the human experience, must operate largely outside the realm of domestic criminal law and ordinary morality. Any blurring of the lines should be actively opposed in order to protect both combatants and noncombatants from being placed in the untenable situation of the Abbottabad police.

To accomplish this goal of increased legal clarity, this chapter proposes the following changes to international law:

1. With minor exceptions, privileged belligerency will be limited to the uniformed military, militias and populace (in the event of a *levée en masse*) of a state that has declared war publicly and officially.

2. States may declare war against other states, non-state organizations, or individuals, provided these declarations comply with Articles 2(4) and 51 of the United Nations Charter.

3. The International Court of Justice has the power to nullify declarations of war.

To prove the need for these revisions, this chapter will first explore the fundamental moral and legal differences between the ordinary human experience and armed combat (section I). Next it will briefly examine the confusing and problematic status quo versus the intended regime of war (section II), and finally it will discuss the specifics of the above proposal, its merits and challenges (section III).

---

[24] H.L.A. Hart, *The Concept of Law* (Oxford University Press, 1961).

[25] Joseph Raz, *The Authority of Law, Essay IV: The Rule of Law and Its Virtue* (Oxford University Press, 2009).

[26] Oliver Wendell Holmes, Jr, "The Path of the Law," 10 *Harvard Law Review* 457 (1897).

I. The moral blurring of the delineation of war: a combatant's perspective

Consider a world where political disputes between states are no longer resolved by war, but a contest of champions. If State A and State B disputed ownership over a tract of land, two champions would meet and fight, and the state with the prevailing champion would win the dispute. These bouts would use the rules of the "Ultimate Fighting Championship" as it began in the early 1990s: no biting, no eye-gouging, no weapons.[27] Other then these simple rules, all other methods of weaponless combat are allowed. The bout is resolved when either party is knocked unconscious or surrenders by tapping three times. Serious and/or permanent injuries are not infrequent during these bouts.

What of the morality of these bouts? In theory, only one of the states is just in the dispute, and yet both champions are inflicting harms upon the other. If State A has the just cause, is the champion of State B justified in permanently injuring the champion from State A only to win the bout? Does it change if this same State B champion personally believes that his state is unjust in the dispute? Does Champion B have the natural moral right and/or obligation to refuse to fight?

Jeff McMahan argues that the acts of combatants in furtherance of an unjust cause can never be justified[28] and that such combatants have a moral obligation to refuse to fight in an unjust war.[29] He steadfastly disputes the moral equality of combatants in war and argues that the morality of combatant acts (*jus in bello*) is inextricably linked to the morality of the overall conflict (*jus ad bellum*).[30] While he is careful to segregate killing from the other harms committed during war in his pre-preface,[31] the arguments within the text itself are not dependent upon this distinction. Therefore, in the above example, Champion B's acts of harm to Champion A in furtherance of an unjust cause would not be justified and Champion B has a moral obligation to refuse to participate in the contest. I believe this hypothetical clarifies this moral issue facing a soldier in the United States. According to McMahan, this soldier has the moral responsibility to supplant the decision of the collective with his own political views. Although he has been the beneficiary of extensive training and resources, he must refuse to serve as a champion when the match begins, thereby forcing another less qualified individual to face the danger, increasing the probability that his state and people will lose the dispute.

---

[27] *The Ultimate Fighting Championship, Rules and History*, available at <http://www.mmawild.com/ufc/> accessed September 4, 2011.

[28] Jeff McMahan, *Killing in War* (Oxford University Press, 2009) 6.

[29] Ibid.

[30] Ibid.

[31] Ibid. at i.

McMahan's intent is to develop a political environment where governments face greater resistance to initiating and conducting unjust wars.[32] To accomplish this, he applies moral intuitions derived from criminal law to acts of combat in order to defeat the "moral equality of combatants" theory. By defeating this theory, McMahan hopes to convince military members that their violent acts in further-ance of an unjust cause are not justified, and therefore these same soldiers should refuse to participate in unjust wars.[33] His goal is laudable, but his method unethi-cally places the moral burden of a collective decision on a minority that has the fewest legal and social protections if they resist that decision.[34] Further, he under-cuts a critical facet of a successful democracy: civilian control of the military.[35] McMahan's goal of preventing unjust wars is better accomplished by reinforcing rather than weakening the delineation between peace and war. Furthermore, his argument from criminal law (moral) intuitions to acts of combat is flawed; war necessarily has its own moral code that is fundamentally dissimilar.

(a) The unique nature of war

I see the enemy soldier in the distance. He is busy polishing his boots, probably for an upcoming inspection. His weapon is nowhere to be seen. He is not aware of my presence or even of my individual existence. I could easily leave the area and he would be no real threat to me. Instead, I slowly take aim with my rifle and fire, ending his life.

I knew nothing about the man as an individual. Assume he was an accomplished violinist, devoted husband and loving father of two beautiful young girls, who was forced to set his violin aside and join a military and cause that he personally opposed. Further, he would have immediately surrendered had I given him the opportunity. In ordinary life this man would be protected and revered. In war he was a member of the enemy military so I executed him as quickly as possible.[36] This was a status-based death authorized by both the laws and morality of armed conflict.[37]

---

[32] Ibid. at vii–viii.

[33] Ibid.

[34] Soldiers do not share the same freedom of speech rights as civilians. See generally *Parker v. Levy*, 417 U.S. 733 (1974).

[35] Louis Henkin has labeled civilian control of the military one of the elements required for constitutionalism. See Louis Henkin, "Constitutions and the Elements of Constitutionalism," Occasional Paper Series, November 1992, Center for the Study of Human Rights, Columbia University.

[36] Of course, the laws of war would also prevent me from killing him if he was *hors de combat*, had surrendered or possessed a protected status (e.g. a doctor wearing a red cross). See Article 3, Geneva IV.

[37] See Article 43, AP1 and also Geoff Corn and Michael Schmidt, "To Be or Not to Be, That is the Question: Contemporary Military Operations and the Status of Captured Personnel," 1999 *Army Lawyer* 1 (1999) n. 124."The GPW does not specifically mention combatant immunity. As discussed in the above listed articles, it is considered to be customary international law. Moreover,

In any other legal or moral paradigm, this act would be punishable and/or morally abhorrent.[38] Any justification to kill another must normally be rooted in the guilt and/or imminent threat posed by that individual.[39] In war, this victim's innocence and the imminence of the threat he posed were irrelevant. In war this act is not only acceptable, but publicly honored and rewarded (even when the overall cause may be unjust). Simply put, the rules and mores of war are dramatically different to those restricting ordinary life. Even if these differences result in philosophical quandaries, they are necessary to protect both combatants and noncombatants from injustice and even greater barbarity.

One such philosophical quandary is the normative evaluation of combatants in relation to their overall cause. Michael Walzer, in *Just and Unjust Wars*, affirmed the long-held belief that the justice of the cause of a state party to a conflict, or lack thereof, did not affect the morality of the actions of individual combatants employed by that state.[40] In other words, the *jus ad bellum* determination did not affect the morality of *jus in bello* actions. As noted above, McMahan attacked this long-held belief, concluding that the combatant activities of a belligerent in an unjust cause could not be considered morally justified or permissible. He shied away from finding these soldiers necessarily culpable, however, and instead found their actions possibly to be a form of excused self-defense.[41]

Claire Finkelstein has rebutted McMahan's attack on the moral equality of soldiers, showing the difficulties in applying his one side justified/one side excused paradigm of combatant morality.[42] However, Finkelstein shares with McMahan the premise that the same moral principles that apply to actions in a peacetime domestic setting apply to the conduct of soldiers in wartime. Walzer also appears to share McMahan's belief that the morality of ordinary life is continuous with the morality of combat. Accordingly, Walzer seeks to explain the liability of combatants to deliberate attack in terms of the concepts of express consent (which he labels

---

it can be inferred from the cumulative affect of protections within the GPW. For example, Article 13 requires that prisoners not be killed, and Article 118 requires their immediate repatriation after the cessation of hostilities. Although Article 85 does indicate that there are times when a prisoner of war may be prosecuted for precapture violations of the laws of the detaining power, the Official Commentary accompanying Article 85 limits this jurisdiction to only two types of crimes. A prisoner may be prosecuted only for: (1) war crimes, and (2) crimes that have no connection to the state of war."

[38] . . . absent additional facts, of course.

[39] American Jurisprudence 2d, § 134.

[40] Michael Walzer, *Just and Unjust Wars: A Moral Argument with Historical Illustrations*, 3rd edn (Basic Books, 2000).

[41] See McMahan, *supra* n. 28, ch. 3.

[42] Claire Finkelstein, *Responsibility for Acts of War* (draft unpublished manuscript, hereafter *Finkelstein*). Professor Finkelstein was kind enough to share and present a draft of this work at the Telford Taylor Conference. It has played such a pivotal role in my analysis of this topic that I felt the need to cite it heavily, despite its unpublished status.

the Boxing Match Model)[43] and coerced consent (labeled the Gladiator Model).[44] By attempting to extrapolate ideas about consent to cover combat, Walzer joins forces with McMahan in finding a continuity between the moral principles that govern ordinary life and those that govern combat.

However, an insightful comment by Luis Chiesa has led me to doubt the continuity thesis.[45] Chiesa, using the German tripartite approach to criminal liability, argued that belligerent acts are neither justified nor excused, but in fact, fail to meet the substantive elements of the offense. At first blush this view does not appear to have any merit. A battlefield "targeted" death seems to meet the elements of homicide: the intentional killing of another human.[46] Yet, this appearance proves to be misleading, because the legal and moral norms of criminal law, the very basis for the elements of the offense, do not turn out to apply to acts of combat. I now elaborate and defend this crucial point.

(i) The development of criminal law

Finkelstein began her rebuttal of McMahan by stating, "It is tempting to suppose that the moral rules that govern responsibility for acts of war and those that govern ordinary wrongdoing are radically different."[47] I have fallen for this "temptation" and fully support the supposition. The moral and regulatory paradigms for "ordinary wrongdoing" as evidenced by criminal law and those concerning acts of war are so dissimilar in origin and historical practice that it is improper and even immoral to cross-apply the terms and lessons of the former into the latter when evaluating the criminal and moral responsibility of individual combatants.

One fundamental precept of criminal law systems is the sovereign's monopoly on the use of violence/force to achieve its ends.[48] In most situations, the individual must rely upon the state to exercise the necessary force or threat of force to protect her body and her property. It is the state and only the state that has the power to arrest, try and punish the criminal.[49] It is the state that can use violence or the threat thereof to tax income

---

[43] In the Boxing Match Model, by wearing a uniform and entering combat, soldiers consent to any resultant attacks on themselves just as a boxer consents to be hit by his opponent by entering the ring. McMahan, *supra* n. 28, 51–7.

[44] Ibid. at 58. In the Gladiator Model, the combatants are coerced into fighting each other.

[45] This comment was made at the third session of the Telford Taylor Conference for the Journal of International Justice at Columbia Law School, September 17, 2010.

[46] This point was raised by Professor Thomas Weigend at the same session.

[47] Finkelstein, *supra* n. 42, 1.

[48] I mean, of course, violence and the use of force between humans rather than the use of violence to say, chop down one's own trees. See Viet D. Dinh, "Dunwoody Distinguished Lecture in Law: Nationalism in the Age of Terror," 56 *Florida Law Review* 867 (2004) 872.

[49] Lynne Henderson, "Revisiting Victim's Rights," 1999 *Utah Law Review* 393 (1999) 392: "But the constitutional concern for negative liberties stems in large part from the government's monopoly on the use of force and its ability to use the criminal law to control and punish the population. Whether one grounds the argument for the social contract embodied in the Constitution on Hobbes, Locke, Nozick, Rawls, or other political philosophers, the theory is that we cede our right

or possessions for the public good, seize personal property through models like eminent domain, quarantine individuals for public safety, and even conscript individuals into military service. Even possessing the most benevolent of motives focusing on the public good, the individual is prohibited from using force in a similar manner.[50]

The paradigm for criminal law is that all non-state use of violence or threat of violence against another human or the possessions of another human is prohibited.[51] Criminal law grants back to the individual certain narrow exceptions to this blanket prohibition that are incorporated within the concepts of justification and excuse.[52] These concepts include self-defense, necessity and duress.

Under criminal law, self-defense is rooted in the idea of allowing the individual to react to an imminent or ongoing attack in a manner timely enough to prevent the threatened harm.[53] Said another way, when time constraints preclude the force of the state from preventing a serious harm, an individual may exercise the necessary (and proportional) force to prevent that harm.[54] If the attack is not imminent to the point where state action is precluded, even self-defensive force may not be authorized. If a neighbor attacks you with a knife evincing an unlawful intent to kill or seriously harm, because the ordinary power of the state cannot react quickly enough to eliminate this threat to your person, the imminence of the situation authorizes force normally exercised by the state.[55] If, however, the neighbor's threatened attack is days away, the state will maintain its monopoly and require you to notify its agents (law enforcement) to eliminate the threat. Similarly, necessity may authorize the individual to use force normally reserved to the state in situations where the state is incapable of reacting quickly enough to an amoral danger.[56] For example, normally only the state has the authority to take property and

---

to exact revenge or restitution to the State and to the law in return for the State's protection and enforcement of the law. Accordingly, the state and federal governments of this country hold a formal constitutional monopoly on the use of force. The criminal law, enacted by legislatures, is part of that monopoly. Crimes are legally defined as offenses against the State and the community, even if those offenses involve individual victims."

[50] Erika Cudworth, John McGovern and Tomthy Hall, *The Modern State, Theories and Ideologies* (Edinburgh University Press, 2007) 95.

[51] Model Penal Code (MPC) sections 210, 211, 212, 213, 220, and 222.

[52] George P. Fletcher, *Basic Concepts of Criminal Law* (New York: Oxford University Press, 1998) ch. 8.

[53] MPC, section 3.04.

[54] *People v. Shields*, 298 Illinois Appellate 3d 943,947: "A defendant may assert the affirmative defense of defense of person when unlawful force was threatened against him or the person he was defending, defendant was not the aggressor, defendant believed that danger of harm was imminent, the use of force was necessary to avert the danger, and the amount of force used was appropriate."

[55] An alternate view is that the state is not ceding back the ability to use self-defensive force, but rather the state is precluded from pulling self-defensive force from the individual, i.e. self-defense is a natural right.

[56] See *supra* n. 52. Fletcher uses the German tripartite approach to explaining the stages of proving a criminal offense. The first stage is the proof of the elements of the offense, the second stage is to prove that the offense was not justified/unlawful, and in the third and final stage the prosecution

use it for the general welfare under concepts such as eminent domain. Necessity, however, may authorize an individual to seize another's abandoned vehicle and use it to escape an oncoming tsunami. Note that, in both of these situations, the individual is granted temporary authority, either by the state or by individual right, to use the force normally reserved to the state.

Dissimilar to self-defense and necessity, duress does not authorize the temporary use of force normally reserved to the state, but rather allows the individual to avoid culpability for her actions in situations where no force, state or otherwise, would be authorized under the law.[57] The quintessential example to show the differences between justified conduct such as self-defense and excused conduct such as duress is Kant's North Sea Plank. There are two men in the ocean and a wooden plank that is sufficient to keep only one of them from drowning.[58] The individual who originally possesses the plank is justified in using force to fend off the other, who is attempting to co-opt the plank for his own survival. Meanwhile, the drowning man, who is plankless, is not justified in stealing the other's life-sustaining plank to save his own life. If he does use force towards those ends, however, his homicidal act may be excused under the law. The general term of excuse applies to those acts that, although legally prohibited and blameworthy, do not justify criminal punishment.[59] The drowning man's violent acts to seize the plank are visceral and could not be deterred. Subsequent punishment by the state accomplishes nothing.

In sum, I believe the criminal law paradigm concerning the use of violence is one of comprehensive prohibition with limited exceptions[60] and I do not believe McMahan or Finkelstein would disagree with this general characterization. Their next assertion is that the common intuitions of substantive criminal law are an appropriate proxy for general morality.[61] I do not believe they mean to limit general morality to those common intuitions of criminal law, but rather to use criminal law intuitions to reveal or clarify specific aspects of common morality.[62] In other words, unjustified homicide would be a moral wrong irrespective of its prohibition within criminal codes;

---

must show the absence of excuse/culpability. Note that necessity may sometimes provide a justification (like self-defense) and other times serve merely as an excuse (like duress).

[57] American Jurisprudence 2d (AmJur 2d) Criminal Law § 142. "The defense of duress is available when the defendant is coerced to engage in unlawful conduct by the threat or use of unlawful physical force of such degree that a person of reasonable firmness could not resist. To establish a defense of duress or coercion, a defendant must show that he or she was under an unlawful threat of such nature as to induce a well-grounded apprehension of death or serious bodily injury."

[58] See, e.g., Immanuel Kant, *Lectures on Ethics* (Cambridge University Press, 1997) 346–7.

[59] Fletcher, *supra* n. 52. "A duress defense has three elements: (1) an immediate threat of death or serious bodily injury; (2) a well-grounded fear that the threat will be carried out; and (3) no reasonable opportunity to escape the threatened harm."

[60] Even the state's law enforcement agents are authorized to use force only by matter of exception. MPC, section 3.07.

[61] Finkelstein, *supra* n. 42, 2; McMahan, *supra* n. 28, chs 3 and 4.

[62] Ibid.

however, identifying which acts committed under what conditions would constitute an unjustified homicide can be informed by the common intuitions embodied in those codes and in criminal jurisprudence. I agree only so far as this proxy is limited to the general morality of peacetime existence. However, both try to draw a connection between this general morality and the morality of acts of combat.[63]

I want to further delineate the specific area of our disagreement. Like Finkelstein and McMahan, I agree that the common intuitions of criminal law can and should be used to determine the justice of a war/*jus ad bellum*.[64,65] But I reject the premise that criminal law intuitions can be transposed willy-nilly into the paradigm of *jus in bello*.

Finkelstein comments that "...many scholars have noted the commonality of intuitions concerning justice across a broad array of peoples and cultures," and that "there is a common moral sentiment consistently expressed across different approaches in reaction to the central elements of substantive criminal law."[66] I agree that most or all human cultures share certain moral views revealed in their criminal codes, and that those shared views constitute a general morality that can be applied to human conduct. However, I do not limit the search for shared moral principles to an examination of criminal law, as Finkelstein and McMahan have done. I believe that the *jus in bello* of IHL, which has more global commonality than criminal law,[67] is also evidence of and a proxy for general morality.

If the common intuitions of criminal law and IHL are both proxies for general morality, one must either strive to find a congruence between the two, as Finkelstein

---

[63] See McMahan, *supra* n. 28 and Finkelstein, *supra* n. 42.

[64] See Richard V. Meyer and Mark David "Max" Maxwell, "The Natural Right to Intervene: The Evolution of the Concepts of Justification and Excuse for Both State and Individual," 7 *Journal of International Criminal Justice* 555 (2009).

[65] One can draw a parallel between this historical development of criminal law's restriction on the use of force and the relatively modern concept of *jus ad bellum*. It might be helpful to view the world community of states as a group of individuals forced to cohabit on the proverbial island. Initially there is violence between the individuals as they fight for control of the limited resources. Eventually a sort of social contract evolves between the members as they come to realize some semblance of order is preferable. Consequently, a sovereign is created to maintain that order, and this sovereign is given the exclusive right to use force to preserve the order on the island. So too, the international community, operating as independent states, initially quarreled over limited resources until the sheer cost of the violence (e.g., the Second World War) brought about the sovereign-like entity that is the United Nations (U.N.). Further, this sovereign claims the exclusive right to use violence to maintain international peace and security. To complete the analogy, both the U.N. Charter and criminal jurisprudence return certain limited powers to use violence to the "individuals." Given this parallel historical and philosophical development, it makes rational sense that the voluminous body of criminal jurisprudence be used to help provide meaning to similar concepts in international law as George Fletcher and Jens Ohlin have argued. George P. Fletcher and Jens David Ohlin, *Defending Humanity* (Oxford University Press, 2008).

[66] Finkelstein, *supra* n. 42, 2–3.

[67] *Jus in bello* is largely a product of customary international law and, as such, has been identified as the legal practice (and opinion) of states.

and McMahan have attempted to do, or concede that the general morality that humanity has developed for combat is intrinsically different and divergent from the general morality they have developed for ordinary life. I believe this divergence exists and I will attempt to prove its existence historically and legally.

(ii) The historical development of the laws of war

A fundamental principle of the laws of war is that of military necessity: the principle whereby a belligerent has the right to apply any measures which are required to bring about the successful conclusion of a military operation and which are not forbidden by the laws of war.[68] Said another way, a belligerent has the right to do anything and everything to win the war except violate the laws of war.[69] Note that no other systems of law are included in this narrow limitation within this blanket authorization. Thus, under the laws of war, a privileged belligerent can potentially violate each and every one of the domestic laws of the enemy state in its sovereign territory in order to achieve victory and yet retain immunity from prosecution (provided that it does not violate the laws of war as well). Not only is this conduct authorized, but it is mandated by the controlling sovereign.[70] Unlike other professions, a soldier can be prosecuted for negligently failing to perform his duties, in this case the duty to wage war effectively.[71]

The blanket authorization/mandate for violence was originally without any form of meaningful legal limitation.[72] Long after states had developed criminal prohibitions against murder, rape, theft and pillage, combatants were allowed to engage in all four with impunity.[73] What restrictions states did put on their combatants were often limited to amoral issues such as shares of pillaged wealth.[74] Originally war approached Clausewitz's theory of " . . . absolute and unlimited brutality."[75]

Into this moral vacuum, a code of arms/chivalry emerged.[76] Although clothed in romantic notions, the essence was an ethical code of conduct for combatants.[77] Genteel belligerents had grown to abhor the unrestricted violence of war. Through

---

[68] See General Order 100 (The Lieber Code) Article 14.

[69] See Gary D. Solis, *The Law of Armed Conflict* (Cambridge University Press, 2010) 259, citing *United States v. Wilhelm List et al.* (1948) "Military necessity permits a belligerent, subject to the laws of war, to apply any amount and kind of force to compel the complete submission of the enemy with the least possible expenditure of time, life, and money."

[70] See Article I section 8 and Article II, sections 2–3 of the US Constitution.

[71] Article 92, Uniform Code of Military Justice (UCMJ).

[72] Solis, *supra*, n. 69, 3 citing Cicero "*inter armes leges silent,*"—in time of war the laws are silent.

[73] Ibid.

[74] Theodor Meron, "Medieval and Renaissance Ordinances of War: Codifying Discipline and Humanity," in *War Crimes Law Comes of Age* (Oxford University Press, 2006) 1–10.

[75] Carl von Clausewitz, *On War* (Penguin Books, 1968).

[76] Solis, *supra* n. 69, 3–6.

[77] Ibid. and Chris af Jochnick and Roger Normand, "The Legitimization of Violence," 35 *Harvard International Law Journal* 1 (1994).

custom/practice they created restrictions on wartime violence and applied them exclusively to combatants.[78]

Unlike the criminal law's presumption that violence is prohibited unless specifically authorized, the laws of war take the reverse approach: all violence is authorized (and potentially mandated) unless specifically prohibited.[79] Modern principles of the laws of war that prohibit violence include: the responsibility to discriminate between military and civilian targets;[80] the responsibility to limit collateral (non-military) damage in an attack to less than the military advantage gained;[81] and to refrain from causing unnecessary physical suffering (for example, using glass fragmentation to inhibit lifesaving procedures).[82] Note that every one of these starts with the concept that violence is authorized *unless* it violates these prohibitions.[83]

The effect of this reversed approach to violence can best be explored by examining the concept of proportionality. McMahan presents a detailed analysis of proportionality under the laws of war. In it, he discusses the concept of "narrow" proportionality, which primarily concerns harms intentionally done to enemy combatants, and "wide" proportionality, which primarily concerns harms unintentionally done to noncombatants. He then correctly states that the laws of war focus exclusively on the "wide" view of proportionality. However, he follows this with an argument for the application of the narrow view to certain acts of war.[84] He proposes an example where 500 conscripted military guards are killed to free 10 innocent civilians and argues that this would be a disproportionate death.[85] In this, he completely ignores the precepts of *jus in bello*. The principle of proportionality under IHL can only be violated by excessive damage to civilians and civilian property.[86] Remember that under the laws of war, the default is that violence is permitted unless restricted. Since IHL does not prohibit killing any number of enemy combatants as long as those deaths further the war effort,[87] extreme numeric disproportions could result. A lawful combatant could kill 10,000 enemy combatants just to protect a single civilian or soldier or merely to recapture the unit flag if this furthered the war effort. McMahan could counter that these acts violate the concept of military necessity, and at face value, he would be correct. A literal reading

---

[78] Solis, *supra* n. 69, 7.

[79] Ibid. at fn. 67.

[80] The Principle of Distinction requires belligerents to direct attacks and operations only against combatants and military objectives. It forbids targeting noncombatants or indiscriminate attacks. The Judge Advocate General's Legal Center and School, *Operational Law Handbook*, (OPLAW) (2009) 11.

[81] Ibid.,12. This is the IHL principle of proportionality.

[82] Ibid. The IHL principle of unnecessary suffering.

[83] As mandated by the principle of military necessity.

[84] McMahan, *supra* n. 28, 23.

[85] Ibid.

[86] AP1, Article 51.5b.

[87] Solis, *supra* n. 69.

of Lieber's definition of military necessity would require that only acts of violence that are "indispensable" to ultimate victory are authorized.[88] Such an interpretation would create an unobtainable standard of proof for almost any act of violence in war. One could never prove that the death of a single given soldier was indispensable to victory. However, Lieber clarified his definition by stating that "Military necessity admits of all direct destruction of life or limb of armed enemies."[89] The concept of military necessity has been legally interpreted to authorize any acts of violence that are not unlawful provided they achieve or further a war aim or provide some military advantage.[90]

McMahan's error on proportionality stems from his desire to apply the general morality gleaned from criminal law to *jus in bello*. Both individuals and the state itself are limited to proportional responses to wrongs and threats of wrong. When an individual is a wrongdoer fleeing from justice, even the state, by and through its police officer, is limited to a proportional use of force against that individual.[91] Under criminal law, unless that individual presents a current serious threat that is, "armed and dangerous"—deadly force is prohibited even if he is a proven wrongdoer.[92] In contrast, a lawful combatant can shoot the innocent but uniformed violinist while he is polishing his boots and has no weapon in sight.

In addition to necessity and proportionality, substantive criminal law concepts like self-defense and duress also have significantly different meanings and application in the realm of combat and military law. Consider that soldiers can have their individual right of self-defense pulled from them, for the purposes of unit self-defense, by the order of a superior even if they are facing imminent death from an unjust aggressor.[93] (Not even duress is a valid defense to a charge of violating a lawful order to withhold fire.) This concept is entirely outside of any aspect of criminal jurisprudence that I am aware of, and would appear to violate human rights law[94] if it was not.

The focus of this argument has been on legality rather than the morality of combatant acts, but as in criminal law, the former can be viewed as exemplary of the latter. The common "general intuitions" that are the moral basis of criminal law are a product of interpersonal relations in civilized society.[95] They are fundamentally

---

[88] Lieber, *supra* n. 68.

[89] Ibid.

[90] Solis, *supra* n. 69 citing *U.S. v. Wilhelm List et al. (The Hostage Case)* (1948).

[91] *Tennessee v. Garner*, 47 U.S. 1 (1985) Police were found to have improperly used deadly force when shooting a burglar fleeing arrest.

[92] Ibid.

[93] I have written in opposition to this, however. See *supra* n. 64.

[94] Claire Finkelstein, "On the Obligation of the State to Extend the Right to Self-Defense to its Citizens," 147 *University of Pennsylvania Law Review* 1361 (1999).

[95] Richard B. Brandt, "The Utilitarian Theory of Criminal Punishment," in Arthur and Shaw, *Readings in the Philosophy of Law*, 5th edn (Prentice Hall Press, 2010) 262–6.

based on the human desire for stability.[96] Every civilized society can intuitively see the benefit of having a near total restriction on the use of violence within that community. These same common intuitions give rise to substantive crimes such as homicide and defenses such as justifications and excuses.[97] They are part and parcel of any and every civilization going back millennia.[98] The existence of shared principles among the vast array of civilian criminal systems has been used to validate some level of objective general morality across humanity.[99] If this is an appropriate method and conclusion, the same test applied to the shared principles within the laws of war is evidence of the existence of a separate, and incongruent, moral code for acts of combat.

The principles of the laws of war arose from customary practice on the battlefield. The existence of customary international law (CIL) is shown by the general practice of states and the opinion that these practices are required by legal obligation.[100] This "legal obligation" however, does not stem from a positive source but is historically the product of natural law... or morality.[101] In other words, the laws of war are the products of the commonly held moral beliefs of combatants. (Note that the genesis of the laws of war was in the minds of combatants, not sovereigns. Even the famous Lieber Code was the product of a committee consisting of a combat veteran (Lieber) and active duty general officers). CIL remains a viable progenitor of new legal, and arguably moral, obligations for *jus in bello* under current international law.[102] Further, just as IHL was primarily a creation by those linked to combat rather than traditional statute-making entities, the most recent comprehensive compilation by the International Committee of the Red Cross (ICRC) continues to use a vast array of military sources to identify current CIL.[103]

---

[96] The UCMJ espouses the goal of "good order and discipline in the armed forces."

[97] See Paul Robinson, Robert Kurzban and Owen Jones, "The Origins of Shared Intuitions of Justice," 60 *Vanderbilt Law Review* 1633 (2007) 1633.

[98] The Sumerians have been credited with the first written code from the era of 2100–2050 B.C.E. Kramer, Samuel Noah, *The Sumerians: Their History, Culture, and Character* (University of Chicago Press, 1971).

[99] Brandt, *supra* n. 95.

[100] See John R. Crook, "Contemporary Practice Of The United States Relating To International Law: General International And U.S. Foreign Relations Law: United States Responds To ICRC Study On Customary International Law," 10 *American Journal of International Law* 639, which was written in response to the comprehensive text, Jean-Marie Henckaerts and Louise Doswald-Beck, *Customary International Humanitarian Law* (International Committee of the Red Cross and Cambridge University Press, 2005).

[101] See Emer de Vattel, *The Law of Nations, Or, Principles of the Law of Nature, Applied to the Conduct and Affairs of Nations and Sovereigns, with Three Early Essays on the Origin and Nature of Natural Law and on Luxury,* edited and with an introduction by Béla Kapossy and Richard Whitmore (Liberty Fund, 2008) 76.

[102] The International Court of Justice used CIL to determine the legality of nuclear weapons. See "Legality of the Threat or Use of Nuclear Weapons," July 8, 1996.

[103] Jean-Marie Henckaerts and Louise Doswald-Beck, *Customary International Humanitarian Law* (International Committee of the Red Cross and Cambridge University Press, 2005).

There are two possible reactions from moral philosophers like McMahan and Finkelstein, given this dissonance and incongruence between the common intuitions embodied in criminal law and those reflected in *jus in bello*. Such philosophers can either accept parallel yet incongruent codes of morality due to diametrically opposed historical developments, or they can seek to reinterpret moral and legal concepts developed over centuries to eliminate the incongruence. McMahan has adapted the latter approach, hence his erroneous reinterpretation on proportionality under *jus in bello,* discussed above. Rather than pursue this path, I will take up McMahan's challenge and justify the existence of an alternate incongruent moral code through the concept of privileged belligerency.

(iii) The essence of combat morality

Under CIL and IHL, a lawful combatant cannot be punished for any acts of combat committed in accordance with the laws of war.[104] This means that if a lawful military combatant should kill the poor innocent violinist father/enemy soldier, be immediately captured by the dead man's friends, family and countrymen, and confess to the killing, the combatant remains immune from any type of punishment. Certainly, the combatant could be held as a prisoner of war and treated humanely,[105] but he must be released immediately upon the cessation of hostilities[106] ... even if that is the following day. The reverse is, of course, also true. Should the violinist have killed a U.S. soldier and been captured by U.S. forces, he could brag about the act for the rest of his life with absolute impunity.

Unlike any theory of consent, the current source of privileged immunity does not stem from an individual soldier, group of soldiers, or even any given state. As black letter CIL and IHL, privileged belligerency is the gift of the entire world. Humanity, acting en masse, has created, recognized and enforced a rule that makes the killing of one lawful combatant by another lawful combatant a legally protected act. Unlike the death row inmate, there is no higher authority to which the combatant can appeal this sentence. Should a uniformed member of the military refuse to serve or immediately surrender for fear of death, she is labeled craven and subject to punishment by the state for which she was tasked to fight.[107] Simply put, her life is no longer protected. In the sense similar to that of a criminal from the middle ages, she is declared outside the protections of the law, or "outlaw"[108] ... a

---

[104] See *supra* n. 15 and Geoff Corn and Michael Schmidt, *supra* n. 37, fn. 124.

[105] See generally Geneva III.

[106] Ibid. at Article 118.

[107] See UCMJ Articles 85 and 92. Also, the public has little respect for those who refuse to fight. A simple search for Ehren Watada will return countless instances where he, an officer who refused to serve in Iraq, has been labeled a coward.

[108] See William Ian Miller, "Symposium: One Hundred Years Of Uniform State Laws: Of Outlaws, Christians, Horsemeat, And Writing: Uniform Laws And Saga Iceland," 89 *Michigan Law Review* 2081 (1991). The term "outlaw" indicated someone who had been expelled from the

lawful target for any enemy soldier that may happen upon her, whether she is sleeping or engaged in battle and regardless of her absolute moral and legal innocence or guilt. It is in this narrow paradigm, totally unique in the human experience, that the incongruent morality of combat exists.

In lawful combat, due to privileged belligerence, a state's domestic laws do not protect its soldiers. This absence of protection makes any application of criminal law intuitions difficult if not impossible, since all depend on the continuing presence and power of some type of sovereign. Reconsider self-defense under criminal law. If an individual is attacked by an unlawful aggressor, he can respond if and only if the attack is imminent, his response is necessary to prevent the harm and the level of his response is appropriate to the threatened harm.[109] As noted above, a finding of each of these three elements is necessarily linked to the continuing power of the law to intercede and eliminate the threat. In lawful combat, since the world has eliminated the ability of the law to protect the combatant, it also eliminates the need for him to limit the force he uses against enemy combatants; hence the absence of imminence, "narrow" proportionality, or even necessity[110] as precursors and limitations to the use of deadly force. The wealth of criminal jurisprudence developing the concept of self-defense is rooted in these elements;[111] if you eliminate the elements' applicability to combat, you also eliminate the application of the corresponding "intuitions" upon which McMahan's arguments depend. In the above case, the law has declared the violin player and his attacking enemy as equals. Note that this privilege is silent as to the justice of their respective causes. Lawful combatants from both the just and unjust sides of a conflict share equal access to the benefits of privileged belligerency.

The unique morality of combat and war goes beyond the protections of privileged belligerency. For example, if we apply the common intuitions of criminal law to a murder committed abroad, the morality of the act is not altered. Let's assume an American travels to Germany where he witnesses a violent crime. The German police seize him and refuse to allow him to go free, holding him indefinitely as a material witness. He does not want to miss a sporting event scheduled the following week, so he kills his prison guard and successfully escapes back to the United States and attends the event. Even though the act occurred outside the jurisdiction of the United States, Americans would share the common intuitions of criminal law with the Germans and believe his act to be reprehensible and properly subject to punishment. Compare that to the following example:

---

community and who as an outlaw was shorn of all jural status and all jural rights: he or she was supposed to be killed by anyone hearty enough to undertake the task.

[109] See *supra* n. 53.

[110] As noted above, in all but the most academic of scenarios, killing an enemy combatant furthers the war effort and thus satisfies the *jus in bello* principle of military necessity.

[111] See generally *supra* n. 91.

Private Smith is a combatant for State A, which does not have a just cause in the conflict. Private Smith engages in combat and kills soldiers from State B in the sovereign territory of State B. When Private Smith is subsequently captured by State B, the concept of privileged belligerency prevents his prosecution for murder, even though he engaged in the intentional killing of a citizen soldier of State B on that state's sovereign territory. Next, Private Smith, while a prisoner of war, kills his military prison guard and escapes back to the forces of State A. Since Smith was a prisoner, he was legally *hors de combat* and *not eligible* for privileged belligerency.[112] Thus, legally, he committed the punishable crime of homicide in State B without justification or excuse.

Theoretically, if the general morality applicable to criminal law applied equally to times of conflict, once peace is restored State A would extradite Private Smith to State B for prosecution just as the American sports fan from above would be extradited back to Germany. However, this is neither required by IHL nor the common practice of states. Instead, Private Smith has historically been not only protected from punishment, but even rewarded for his "heroic" escape. If the common morality of criminal law applies to this situation, the entire world would abhor this immoral act of murder, rather than ignore and/or reward it. A different general intuition is at play here that goes beyond the mere legal realm of privileged belligerency.

(b) Duty: the essence of soldiering

In his criticisms of the doctrine of the moral equality of combatants,[113] McMahan fails to appreciate adequately the unique role and status of the active duty military. As noted above, the world has declared combatants outside the protections of criminal law when targeted by an enemy lawful combatant. This is not the only stick the law has pulled from the soldier's bundle of human rights, however. Soldiers have knowingly surrendered many more as part of their enlistment contract and oath. Among other things, they lose: the Constitutional right to trial by jury;[114] the right to quit their job for the duration of the contract or beyond;[115] the right to collectively bargain in labor negotiations or strike; the right to publicly criticize superiors;[116] and the right to disobey any lawful command from their superiors,[117] even if they believe that command to be illogical, unreasonable, or even unjust.[118] Said a different way, by taking the oath of enlistment, they agree to subordinate

---

[112] Article 3 and Article 82, Geneva III.

[113] McMahan, *supra* n. 28, 60–5.

[114] Amendment V, "…except in those cases arising in the armed forces."

[115] Article 85, UCMJ.

[116] Article 88, UCMJ.

[117] Article 92, UCMJ.

[118] Ibid. An order is lawful unless contrary to the Constitution, the laws of the U.S., or lawful superior orders.

their personal judgment to that of the collective, as expressed by the orders of those appointed over them, for the duration of their service.

This obedience to orders has been labeled the "cardinal virtue" and the "backbone"[119] of the profession of arms and its importance cannot be overstated. Under modern military leadership philosophy, the strength of a military unit is dependent upon its ability to place accomplishment of the mission over any self-interest, both individually and collectively. Soldiers are trained to operate at a level of interdependence, trust and teamwork that is the envy of every other occupation. At the core root of this interdependence, trust and teamwork is each soldier's dedication to performance of duty.

Just as there is a polar opposition in the approach to violence found in criminal law and *jus in bello*, soldiers and civilians have virtually opposite approaches to duty. Paraphrasing many a civilian, "The only things I must do are die and pay taxes." For the civilian, duty is ordinarily correlated with benefit; that is, if I want benefit X, I must be willing to assume duty Y. Inversely, if a civilian does not want or gain benefit X, he can avoid duty Y. Even when a civilian decides to enlist, the act of enlistment is an assumption of duty in exchange for a perceived benefit. From his enlistment, the soldier gains valuable training, benefits, pay, and possibly the respect of the general populace.[120] The state and its constituents gain an individual who agrees to subordinate much of his judgment and will to the collective. (This soldier is not a Nazi robot, however, and the presence of orders does not exonerate him from the moral or legal responsibility for his acts. *Jus in bello* and military law holds soldiers accountable for any acts that are "manifestly unlawful," even if pursuant to orders. Both *jus in bello* and military law not only provide the soldier the ability to refuse such an order with impunity, but often require him to do so.)[121]

Once the civilian becomes a soldier, however, duty is no longer a cost—benefit analysis, but a *raison d'etre*…an end in and of itself. Performance of duty, as defined by the orders of superiors, is the default and only in rare circumstance (manifestly unlawful) can it legally or morally be refused or avoided.[122] Unlike a civilian, a soldier is expected to continue performing his duty even after there is no longer any personal benefit.[123] Inversely, a civilian who stops receiving the benefit of performing a duty is expected to stop performing it. Civilians have the luxury

---

[119] Mark J. Osiel, *Obeying Orders: Atrocity, Military Discipline & the Law of War* (Transaction Publishers, 1999) 1, quoting Field Marshal Wilhelm Keitel and Sir Charles Napier.

[120] See <http://www.goarmy.com> accessed November 3, 2011 for all the proposed benefits of enlisting.

[121] *U.S. v. Kinder*, 14 Court of Military Review 742 (Air Force Board of Review, 1954) 776.

[122] Ibid.

[123] See generally *Parker v. Levy*, 417 U.S. 733 (1974).

and right to question nearly all authority in their lives, where soldiers have only a radically circumscribed right to question.

The duty of the soldier is analogous to that of keeping the proverbial finger in the dyke holding back the destructive flood from destroying the community.[124] McMahan argues that a soldier's subordination of individual judgment to the collective should only occur if the soldier believes that there are sufficient safeguards within the collective decision-making process as to justify the reliance on the result.[125] I agree. However, the time to verify those safeguards is prior to agreeing to be the one with your finger in the dyke. As the only individuals capable of protecting the community from armed attack, soldiers necessarily waive the right to refuse the will of the collective on decisions of *jus ad bellum*. The duty of a soldier is itself a moral obligation that preempts McMahan's duty to refuse the collective will of the democratic state when the state makes a decision to resort to war. At its core, the duty of the soldier protects the continued existence of the state,[126] and it is the soldier's moral belief in the overall justice of the state that morally permits him to subordinate his will to its collective decisions.[127] The morality of the soldier, both in and out of combat, is inextricably linked to the performance of duty. This duty requires a combatant soldier to serve as both righteous avenger and tangible representation of the might of the state, as well as the community's designated target for the might of the enemy hordes. The over-simplified corollary to the flippant civilians' saying about death and taxes is the equally flippant soldiers' axiom of "Ours is not to question why, ours is but to do and die."

In sum, the state demands, morally and legally, the complete loyalty and (nearly) unquestioning obedience of its soldiers, all the while waiving its right to legally (and morally) protect their lives. These soldiers are forced into the realm of combat where violence is not only authorized and accepted, but mandated. In that realm, the desire for stability and order that drives a civilized community to create a criminal law that embodies the moral norms of peaceful life has little relevance. Combat is entirely unique in the human experience and it possesses its own moral code, incongruent with the general intuitions of ordinary morality.

---

[124] The U.S. has enjoyed relative immunity from the effects of war thanks to its beneficial geographic location. I do not believe, however, this immunity is a necessary constant. War has shown itself to be such a powerful and unpredictable agent of change that any of its iterations could predictably threaten the continued existence of any of the participant states.

[125] McMahan, *supra* n. 28, 63.

[126] A byproduct of this primary duty of state preservation is the duty the solider owes to each other individual designated to share that task and the designation as "outlaw."

[127] Even the smallest of acts on the battlefield could turn out to be pivotal to the result. Thus the soldier immediately obeys all orders without question, with the narrow exception of those that are manifestly unlawful. Theoretically I suppose this manifestly unlawful standard could also be applied to *jus ad bellum* questions, but from my 26 years of experience as a soldier in the U.S. Army, I cannot envision a realistic scenario where this standard could be met.

(c) The unacceptable nature of the status quo

In a boxing match, competitors are permitted to do violent acts to another human. This permission is based, both morally and legally, upon the concept that the participants have consented to the violence.[128] It is tempting to compare this boxing match to combat, as Walzer and McMahan have done.[129] Physiologically they may be similar events, but normatively and legally they do not correlate. In the boxing match, the entire event operates under the brooding omnipresence of the sovereign. It is the sovereign that often determines the extent of the violence of the fight rather than the limit of the fighters' consent.[130] It is the power of the sovereign that allows the spectators to observe this compartmentalized violence without fear of it extending beyond the ring. Further, both competitors and spectators know that every act in the ring still falls under legal supervision. This universality, or the concept that every act is either permitted or forbidden by law, is an essential characteristic of any state's legal system.[131] As Joseph H. Beale notes, "A hiatus or vacuum in the law would mean anarchy."[132] This "hiatus or vacuum" is the status quo in the realm of targeted killing.

The current realm of targeted killing is analogous to a boxing match where there is no set time, ring, or referee and only one of the competitors is dressed for the competition. A man wearing boxing shorts and gloves walks into a home or restaurant where a man known to be an auto mechanic is sitting down to dinner with friends or family. The boxer walks up and pummels the man to death in front of everyone. When the police arrive and capture this boxer, he claims that it is part of the match and so he is not subject to punishment for his acts. The police release him and he blithely walks away and starts looking for another "competitor" to pummel. Friends, family, and observers of the victim may be given no evidence that the deceased was a boxer, or that there was ever going to be a boxing match at all. They are left with the impression that the attacking boxer can bring about arbitrary death with impunity.

U.S. military forces engaging in targeted killings are the equivalent of this boxer. Although they wear a uniform, they do not limit their attacks to a combat zone

---

[128] Peter Westen, *The Logic of Consent* (Ashgate Publishing, 2004).

[129] McMahan, *supra* n. 28, 51–7.

[130] E.g., even if the fighters would consent to bare-knuckle boxing, the power of the sovereign limits the violence by making this type of fight illegal.

[131] Joseph H. Beale, *A Treatise on the Conflict of Laws* (Baker Voorhis & Co., 1935) § 4.12: "Another characteristic of law is universality. It is unthinkable in a civilized country that any act should fall outside of the domain of law. If law be regarded as a command, then every act done must either be permitted or forbidden. If law be regarded as a right-producing principle, then every act must in accordance with the law change or not change existing rights."

[132] Ibid.

where the significance of this uniform is understood.[133] They select targets based on information that may never be shared. They attack without warning and sometimes in traditional areas of privacy and safety, such as homes.[134] If captured by civilian law enforcement, they could claim immunity thanks to privileged belligerency. Theoretically, the same crowd could see the same soldiers one month later, this time killing their neighbor who they believe was a simple barber, and again walking away without trial or punishment by the government empowered to protect its populace.

U.S. soldiers are not subject to the jurisdiction of the International Criminal Court (ICC),[135] and because of the status of the United States as a permanent member of the Security Council with veto power,[136] they need not fear an ad hoc tribunal.[137] As a member of the U.S. military, I see how we enjoy extensive flexibility in combating an elusive enemy that does not follow the rules. As a lawyer and world citizen, I see the same thing as friends of the auto mechanic and Professor Beale: anarchy.

The other side of the argument is that the U.S. military is forced into this role by criminal non-state actors who wish to enjoy any and all benefits they might receive under domestic or international law without subjecting their own actions to its limitations. The United States would see the appropriate boxing analogy as one in which the other competitor refuses to enter the ring or even submit his name as a competitor. He hides in the middle of a residential neighborhood and avoids any and all personal confrontations with the U.S. boxer. Instead, he recruits adolescent males, women and children to conduct suicidal attacks against the boxer (or even the boxer's friends and family) with weapons and methods prohibited by the rules of the match. These criminals act with an even greater level of impunity because the host state has the power and moral imperative to capture and prosecute them but elects to look the other way for political or ideological reasons.[138]

Both the populace and governments of the locales where the strikes occur and the military personnel who conduct the strikes[139] have legitimate complaints about the status quo. So too do the U.S. voters disenfranchised by the absence of a public debate before starting a war and the marginalized international community of states held impotent by the U.S. veto power. Not only is the status quo

---

[133] CNN, *supra*, n. 1.

[134] Ibid.

[135] The U.S. has signed but not ratified the Rome Statute creating the ICC.

[136] U.N. Charter (Charter), Articles 23 and 27.

[137] Ad hoc tribunals are created by Security Council resolutions.

[138] Pakistan was alleged to have been aware of bin Laden's location. See *supra* n. 4.

[139] Author's note: There are reports that civilian CIA employees also conduct targeted strikes through the use of drones; I do not believe there is a credible argument to support the legality of targeted non-military strikes in a foreign country so these are not germane to this discussion.

unacceptable from all of these perspectives, it is an extreme deviation from the intended moral and legal paradigm of war detailed by IHL.

II. The characteristics of a "proper" war

IHL is neither a "gentlemen's code"[140] nor a malleable political instrument; rather, it is a legal code intended to have a relatively narrow application.[141] It is the culmination of over 150 years of work by military professionals, legal scholars and national leaders.[142] Its tenets are not meant to be selectively applied, but to serve as a moral and legal guide to states, combatants, and noncombatants concerning the initiation and conduct of organized hostilities.[143] Importantly, while it may operate contemporaneously with domestic and international criminal law systems, it is not intended to work as a subset but as a standalone comprehensive legal system with subject matter jurisdiction over the legal "gap" created by armed conflict.[144] This *lex specialis*[145] identifies the specific characteristics of a "proper" war.

(a) Wars should be declared

The Third Hague Convention of 1907 (Hague III) states:

> The Contracting Powers recognize that hostilities between themselves must not commence without previous and explicit warning, in the form either of a reasoned declaration of war or of an ultimatum with conditional declaration of war.[146]

This is not merely a positive requirement provided for by Hague III, but a necessary axiom to the philosophy behind one of the fundamental principles of IHL: distinction. Distinction requires states to distinguish between the civilian and military populations of the enemy and to provide a means (for example, the wearing of military uniforms) for an enemy to distinguish between its own military and civilians.[147] When viewed in conjunction with the IHL principle of proportionality, which requires combatants to limit collateral damage to civilians and

---

[140] McMahan infers this.

[141] Common Article 2 of the Geneva Conventions.

[142] The Lieber Code is commonly recognized as the first written code of the modern laws of war.

[143] Hague IV; Preamble, AP1.

[144] Solis, *supra* n. 69, 3.

[145] *Lex specialis* is a law specific to a given situation and takes precedence when in conflict with a more general law.

[146] Article 1, Hague III.

[147] Article 48, AP1: "In order to ensure respect for and protection of the civilian population and civilian objects, the Parties to the conflict shall at all times distinguish between the civilian population and combatants and between civilian objects and military objectives and accordingly shall direct their operations only against military objectives."

civilian property,[148] the underlying philosophy is revealed to be that the violence of war should be contained to the military combatants of the warring parties. This is further supported by the IHL proscriptions against the military use of certain property and locations[149] and the responsibility to safeguard noncombatants in a combat zone, including captured enemy soldiers.[150] Returning to the boxing analogy, the overarching philosophy of IHL is to limit violence (as much as possible) to the designated boxers. Fighting should be kept in the ring (away from the civilian onlookers) and the methods of engagement should limit the risk of injury to members of the crowd. As noted in section I above, to protect the majority of its populace, the state has selected the fighters to serve as the designated targets of any enemy strikes and in order to support this discriminatory practice, it grants immunity to enemy combatants who comply. Thus, privileged belligerency is also a critical cog in the paradigm of distinction.

If the goal is to contain the violence of war to the military combatants of the warring states, it rationally follows that these same warring parties must be clearly identified. The millennia-old manner in which this identification has occurred is by a declaration of war. This declaration provides warning not just to the civilians and military of the warring parties, but to the citizens and military of all neutral states and parties. A declaration of war provides humanity legal notice that a state is invoking the rules and morals of IHL. It notifies observers that *lex specialis* now governs the conduct of its military, rather than the rules and mores of domestic criminal law. It is the bell announcing that the boxing match has begun.

(b) Wars should be authorized by the United Nations or in self-defense

Whether the result of the Kellogg-Briand Pact[151] or the U.N. Charter,[152] after the armed conflicts at the beginning of the twentieth century the community of states officially decided that wars must be avoided. No longer could states seek to advance their political, financial or ideological goals through the use of mass violence or

---

[148] Article 51, AP1: "An attack which may be expected to cause incidental loss of civilian life, injury to civilians, damage to civilian objects,...which would be excessive in relation to the concrete military advantage anticipated" violates the concept of proportionality.

[149] Convention for the Protection of Cultural Property in the Event of Armed Conflict, The Hague, May 14, 1954, (Hague 1954) Article 4: "The High Contracting Parties undertake to respect cultural property situated within their own territory as well as within the territory of other High Contracting Parties by refraining from any use of the property and its immediate surroundings or of the appliances in use for its protection for purposes which are likely to expose it to destruction or damage in the event of armed convict; and by refraining from any act of hostility directed against such property."

[150] Geneva III and Article 27, Geneva IV: "Protected persons...shall be protected especially against all acts of violence."

[151] The charge of Aggression at Nuremburg was rooted in the Kellogg-Briand Pact of 1928, also known as the World Peace Act.

[152] Article 2.4, Charter.

threat thereof. The Charter contains the current legal prohibition in Article 2.4.[153] There are only two exceptions to this blanket prohibition against war. The first is action by the U.N, itself. For example, Article 42 of the Charter authorizes the Security Council to "take such action by air, sea, or land forces as may be necessary to maintain or restore international peace and security."[154] U.N. Resolution 678, which authorized the use of force in the First Gulf War, is the quintessential example of the Security Council "declaring" war to restore international peace and security.[155] The second exception to the Article 2.4 prohibition against war is Article 51, which recognizes the "inherent right of individual and collective self-defense"[156] in response to an "armed attack."[157]

The only entity authorized to enforce violations of Article 2.4 is the Security Council, which contains five members with veto power.[158] The obvious objection to this arrangement is that one of these five members could be the aggressing state, such as is alleged in the U.S. targeted killing activities.

(c) Wars should be geographically contained

Simultaneously issued with the Third Hague Convention requiring wars to be declared[159] and the Fourth Hague Convention detailing the law and customs of land warfare,[160] the international community issued detailed wartime responsibilities regarding neutral states in the Fifth Hague Convention. It prevents warring states from using neutral territory to move troops or munitions or to recruit.[161] It requires neutral states to enforce these provisions and to intern any combatants who enter their territory for the duration of the conflict.[162]

This treaty evinces a clear intent to contain the violence of war and makes this the responsibility of not just the warring parties and their combatants, but also the entire world community.

---

[153] Ibid.

[154] Article 42, Charter.

[155] Passed on November 29, 1990, the resolution authorized member states to "…use all necessary means to uphold and implement resolution 660 (1990) and all subsequent relevant resolutions and to restore international peace and security in the area." U.N. Security Council Resolution 678 (1990).

[156] Article 51, Charter.

[157] Ibid.

[158] Articles 23–27, Charter.

[159] Article 1, Hague III.

[160] Hague IV.

[161] Article 2, Hague V: "Belligerents are forbidden to move troops or convoys of either munitions of war or supplies across the territory of a neutral Power"; Article 4: "Corps of combatants cannot be formed nor recruiting agencies opened on the territory of a neutral Power to assist the belligerents."

[162] Article 5, Hague V: "A neutral Power must not allow any of the acts referred to in Articles 2 to 4 to occur on its territory."

(d) Wars should distinguish between combatants and noncombatants

In addition to identifying the warring parties by declaration, IHL requires that all combatants distinguish themselves from noncombatants.[163] This provides three types of legal notice: (1) it notifies the opposing party of whom the government has designated to serve as a target; (2) it notifies neutral parties and noncombatants which individuals or locations may be the subject of a violent attack so these noncombatants can segregate themselves for safety; and (3) it notifies civilian law enforcement of which individual's violent acts they are not required (or possibly not allowed) to prevent. One dilemma in this area of distinction is that, unlike other prohibited activities under IHL, failure to properly distinguish oneself is not a punishable violation of IHL (unless perfidious).[164] Instead, IHL simply pulls back the immunity a combatant would have received from privileged belligerency.[165] Therefore, if a person engages in combat without properly identifying herself as a combatant (for example, by wearing a uniform), the enemy state regains the authority to prosecute her for any acts of violence she committed against their military.[166] This is a critical legal wrinkle in the IHL analysis of modern asymmetric warfare. Al Qaeda members who attack U.S. soldiers violate the laws of the host state and the laws of the United States, not IHL, which leads to the final characteristic of a proper war.

(e) Wars should incidentally contain criminal prosecutions, not the reverse

In a prescient editorial in the *Washington Post* on October 6, 2001, George Fletcher opined that the United States needed to decide whether it was pursuing a war or criminal prosecutions following the attacks or 9/11.[167] Fletcher segregated war from justice by stating that justice is "…about restoring moral order," whereas war is "…about securing survival."[168] Justice is concerned with the punishment of individual culprits; in war, the individual is merely an incidental cog of a whole. Fletcher makes the point that war is potentially more merciful than justice, since

---

[163] Article 1, Hague IV; Article 44, AP1: "In order to promote the protection of the civilian population from the effects of hostilities, combatants are obliged to distinguish themselves from the civilian population while they are engaged in an attack or in a military operation preparatory to an attack."

[164] Article 37, AP1: "It is prohibited to kill, injure or capture an adversary by resort to perfidy. Acts inviting the confidence of an adversary to lead him to believe that he is entitled to, or is obliged to accord, protection under the rules of international law applicable in armed conflict, with intent to betray that confidence, shall constitute perfidy."

[165] Article 44, AP1: "A combatant who falls into the power of an adverse Party while failing to meet the requirements set forth in the second sentence of paragraph 3 shall forfeit his right to be a prisoner of war."

[166] As noted earlier, prisoner of war status is another manner to identify individuals who possess privileged belligerency.

[167] George P. Fletcher, "We Must Choose: Justice Or War?," *The Washington Post*, October 6, 2001.

[168] Ibid.

actions against enemy combatants cease with the hostilities, whereas justice would still scream for a reckoning.[169]

As noted above, the axioms of criminal law are useful in determining the merits of a state's *jus ad bellum* decision even though they have no role in *jus in bello* determinations. In deciding Fletcher's quandary of war or justice, the state acts and is evaluated as a single entity composed of many organs. Under the U.N. Charter, the sole authorization for state-initiated war is an armed attack against an organ of that state.[170] If that state has a reasonable belief that it must use force to prevent or eliminate this external threat of violence, then it is morally and legally authorized to use that violence, even if that reasonable belief is incorrect or if the actual intent of the "attacker" is benevolent.[171] In self-defense, the enemy presenting the threat is also treated as a single entity, allowing the state to use force against organs of the enemy that had no role in the attack.[172] (Perhaps a helpful illustration would be when an attacker swings a fist at someone; he could kick at his leg in a defensive response. Likewise if 20 Al Qaeda combatants are attacking the U.S. Capitol Building, the self-defensive response could be a U.S. airstrike against a base in Afghanistan where they were trained.) The standard of proof is low (reasonable belief) because the threatened harm to the entity or its organs is immediate and severe. The force is being used to prevent further harm to self (or others), not to exact punishment or vengeance on the attacker.[173]

In contrast, when pursuing justice, the enemy as a whole is irrelevant. The state is focused on the conduct of the individual. The goal is not the elimination of a threat, but rather to make a definitive moral statement about a single individual's conduct.[174] Any use of force is incidental to this purpose and limited. The state has the much higher standard of actually proving an individual's wrongful conduct beyond a reasonable doubt.[175] It must also provide the defendant with the appropriate levels of due process while doing so,[176] since, in pursuing justice, the state has the liberty of time and the absence of a physical imperative.

The due process gauntlet of justice makes the flexibility and instant gratification of a violent war an attractive alternative. However, this sacrifices much of the moral

---

[169] Ibid.

[170] Article 51, Charter.

[171] These conclusions are based on the application of criminal law jurisprudence of self-defense to the *jus ad bellum* scenario.

[172] All members of the enemy military (excepting those *hors de combat* or medical and religious personnel) are lawful targets during an armed conflict.

[173] Again, this is based on the jurisprudence of criminal law self-defense.

[174] Fletcher, *supra* n. 167.

[175] This is the standard of proof in adversarial systems and in the ad hoc tribunals.

[176] For the U.S., the due process requirements come from the fifth and fourteenth Amendments to the Constitution.

high ground that is part and parcel of obtaining a criminal conviction. As Fletcher points out, war is not a righteous pursuit, but merely an admission about the failure of politics.[177] A "proper" war is focused on victory, the elimination of the threat, and the resumption of peace ... not the public humiliation of the individual enemy. In fact, as we have learned from the conflicts in Africa, victory in war sometimes requires that justice be sacrificed.[178]

A quick review of the status quo will show that arguably none of the characteristics of a "proper" war are present in the targeted killing paradigm. No war has been declared, it is debatable if many of the killings retain a viable self-defense justification, the conflict is not geographically contained, the combatants do not distinguish themselves from noncombatants, and the prolonged imprisonment and continuing prosecutions seem to imply that moral justice, rather than simple victory, is the goal. The challenge is to craft a solution that will transform the status quo into a "proper" war.

III. A simple, legal solution to a complex political and moral problem

There is some level of convergence between McMahan's stated desire to create a moral disincentive to participation in unjust wars[179] and the legal community's struggle with the idiosyncrasies of asymmetric warfare. Both struggle because they attempt to find commonality between ordinary morality and criminal justice on the one hand and the unique morality and laws of combat on the other. They differ, however, in method. McMahan seeks a new type of clarity, whereas legal commentators seem to accept obfuscation.[180] McMahan, in extrapolating the moral intuitions of civilian life to the battlefield, is trying to create a clear moral benchmark, even if it may only be entirely viewed in hindsight. Legal scholars, in an attempt to prevent politicians from applying the moral permissiveness of war to situations calling for the more tempered civilian criminal justice, appear to revel in the valley of uncertainty that exists between two different legal paradigms. On that part of the debate, I side with McMahan. Clarity is required ... but not the new reinterpreted clarity McMahan proposes, which unjustly places the moral and legal responsibility of a collective decision on a minority with reduced rights to challenge the sovereign, but the original clarity proposed and designed by the laws of war.

---

[177] *Supra*, n. 68.

[178] In post-conflict Africa, vehicles such as Truth and Reconciliation Commissions are used, rather than criminal prosecutions.

[179] McMahan, *supra*, n. 28, vii–viii.

[180] See, in this volume, chs 2, 8, 11, and 13.

> The Proposal Clause 1: With minor exceptions, privileged belligerency will be limited to the uniformed military, militias and populace (in the event of a levée en masse) of a State that has declared war publicly and officially.

Article 43 of Additional Protocol I to the Geneva Conventions states that combatants, or members of a "Party's"[181] armed forces or similar organization, have the " ... right to participate in hostilities."[182] The right is unique in that it only exists in relation to the power of a foreign government.[183] If a combatant is captured by the enemy, it is this right, linked to the combatant's "prisoner of war" status, which prevents that enemy from punishing the combatant for his prior hostile acts. This is the concept this chapter has referred to as privileged belligerency. Under current interpretation, privileged belligerency applies to prior acts of combat if: there is a declared war or international armed conflict,[184] the individual qualifies for combatant status;[185] and the individual's acts were within the constraints of the laws of war.[186]

(a) The existence of an armed conflict

Pictet's commentary to the Geneva Conventions notes that the inclusion of the undefined nebulous term of "armed conflict" was intended to ensure that states could not avoid their responsibilities under the Conventions by simply labeling the conflict something other than war.[187] Although this purpose of broadening the application of states' affirmative responsibilities is laudable, its method is regrettable in the era of asymmetric warfare. The current conundrum of targeted killing is the byproduct of this flaw. In a modern world where the restriction of Article 2.4 of the U.N. Charter is intended to eliminate a state's aggressive acts, this "armed conflict" ambiguity allows a state to selectively claim the right to engage in hostilities in a foreign territory without meaningful legal challenge. Pictet viewed a world where states wanted to avoid the application of the Conventions because of the plethora of obligations they entail; however, when the state can commit its hostilities without any forces on the ground, many of these obligations are irrelevant. The United States does not have to concern itself with the wounded and sick,[188] prisoners of war,[189] or affirmative responsibilities to protect civilian populations[190]

---

181 The term "Party" refers to the Contracting Parties to the Convention.
182 Article 43, AP1.
183 Only captured enemy need to invoke privileged belligerency.
184 Common Article 2 to the Geneva Conventions.
185 Article 43, AP1.
186 Solis, *supra*, n. 69, 91–7.
187 J.S. Pictet (ed.), *I Commentary on the Geneva Conventions of August 12, 1949* (Geneva: ICRC, 1960) 32.
188 Article 12, Geneva I.
189 Geneva III.
190 Geneva IV.

and cultural property[191] when its only presence is a drone thousands of feet in the air, or a raid that has all military personnel out of the region in a matter of minutes.[192] In the modern world, the United States has only incentives to invoke IHL. Specifically, IHL allows combatants to kill without warning[193] and to detain enemy combatants indefinitely.[194]

In keeping with the purpose of broad application of the humanitarian protections within the Conventions, the application of all state responsibilities should continue to apply in any "armed conflict." The rights, however, should be treated differently. Specifically the right to engage in hostilities or, as Colonel Maxwell has effectively explained elsewhere in this volume,[195] the right to engage in status-based killing, destruction or detention should require definitive legal notice to the entire world. It should require a declaration of war.

The consequences of when to allow individuals to engage in status-based killing and destruction with impunity are too severe to rely on the vagaries of a factual determination. In granting privileged belligerency to a foreign combatant, a state is sacrificing a sovereign right to use the power of the law to protect the people and property within its jurisdiction. Since privileged belligerency is recognized as customary international law,[196] states may even be forced to surrender these sovereign rights involuntarily.[197] The international community, writ large, which mandates this sacrifice, has the responsibility to clearly define when it occurs. The various opinions on the meaning of "armed conflict" within this volume[198] show that the community has utterly failed in this responsibility. Worse yet, these determinations may occur post hoc. The famous International Criminal Tribunal for the Former Yugoslavia (ICTY) *Tadic* case included the phrase "protracted armed violence"[199] in its definition of armed conflict. This would mean that the initial hostilities could not be determined to be an "armed conflict" until after one is able to verify that they have continued long enough to be "protracted." Consider the soldier who, under orders, kills an enemy soldier in the opening hostilities and is then captured. He must hope for subsequent fighting. If the violence becomes

---

[191] Hague 1954.

[192] The drones or forces on a quick raid never control or occupy a territory in a manner to cause the affirmative responsibilities to spring into effect.

[193] Article 43, AP1.

[194] Article 118, Geneva III: "Prisoners of war shall be released...after the cessation of hostilities."

[195] See Colonel Mark Maxwell, "Rebutting the Civilian Presumption: Playing Whack-A-Mole Without a Mallet?", this Volume, at ch. 1.

[196] Michael Matheson, "A Workshop on Customary International Law and the 1977 Protocols," 2 *American University Journal of Law & Policy* 419 (1987).

[197] CILis binding on all states unless they have made a persistent objection to its application.

[198] See, in this Volume, Colonel Mark Maxwell, "Rebutting the Civilian Presumption: Playing Whack-A-Mole Without a Mallet," ch. 1; Jens Davidoblin, "Targeting Co-belligerents," David ch 2; Statman, "Can Just War Theory Justify Targeted Killing," ch. 3;

[199] *Tadic Case*: The Judgment of the Appeals Chamber, The Hague, July 15, 1999.

"protracted," he receives immunity for the original killing. If it does not, he can be charged with murder. This is both legally and morally abhorrent.

A legal declaration, publicly filed before an international body in accordance with some agreed upon process, provides definitive notice that a state is claiming the right to engage in hostilities. Now the soldier, above, knows that his hostile acts are legally authorized and he is protected from subsequent prosecution by the enemy.[200] Civilians are on notice that any further association with military targets places them at risk of being collateral damage to a lawful attack. Neutral countries are on notice of their responsibilities to prevent the belligerents from operating within their borders.[201] Conversely, under this requirement, the absence of a declaration provides the Abbottabad police force legal certainty that a foreign attack against any of the town's residents is under their jurisdiction and probably criminal behavior. This also supports an informed democracy since, if a state's military forces engage in hostilities without a declaration, the citizens of that state know that these acts are not protected or authorized by international law. There must be an emergency exception that would cover events like an unexpected invasion, but this exception would last only long enough to give the defending state a reasonable time to declare war.[202] Also, any actions in accordance with a U.N. Security Council Resolution authorizing force would not require the supporting states to file a declaration since the resolution itself provides the necessary notice.

(b) The individual qualifies for combatant status

One aspect of the first prong of this proposal is that only a state can declare war and thus only a state's forces can ever obtain privileged belligerency. This appears to contradict Article 6 of Additional Protocol 2, which calls for the authorities in power to grant amnesty to persons who participated in the conflict.[203] This granting of amnesty to insurgents or former government forces, however, is not the equivalent of combatant immunity. Under amnesty, the state elects to waive its right to prosecute for the general social welfare;[204] under privileged belligerency, the state is legally precluded from prosecuting the lawful combatant. Further, a

---

[200] Unless those acts violated the laws of war.

[201] Article 5, Hague V.

[202] Author's note: I am undecided if the specific details of this exception require further definition beyond "a reasonable time."

[203] Article 6, AP2: "At the end of hostilities, the authorities in power shall endeavor to grant the broadest possible amnesty to persons who have participated in the armed conflict, or those deprived of their liberty for reasons related to the armed conflict, whether they are interned or detained."

[204] *Black's Law Dictionary*, 9th edn (2009) Amnesty is defined as: "A pardon extended by the government to a group or class of persons, usu. for a political offense; the act of a sovereign power officially forgiving certain classes of persons who are subject to trial but have not yet been convicted. Unlike an ordinary pardon, amnesty is usually addressed to crimes against state sovereignty—that is, to political offenses with respect to which forgiveness is deemed more expedient for the public welfare than prosecution and punishment."

grant of amnesty would provide immunity for all criminal offenses, including a loyalty offense like treason.[205] Privileged immunity covers only the hostile acts committed as part of an armed conflict. A U.S. citizen who joined the Nazi forces in the Second World War may have obtained privileged belligerency, but he could still be tried for treason if captured.

Both the Fourth Hague Convention and Third Geneva Convention identify combatants by their relation to a given state, country, or territory.[206] They do not include the modern "non-state actor" such as Al Qaeda, even if Al Qaeda were to comply with the requirements: chain of command, distinctive uniforms, carrying arms openly, and conducting operations in accordance with the laws of war.[207] Thus, the forces of Al Qaeda could never obtain the belligerent rights possessed by their state-sponsored opponents unless they also obtained overt state sponsorship.[208] Though overtly "unfair," forcing a state, rather than a group of non-state actors, to make the public decision to declare war allows the international community greater ability to exert pressure to prevent this decision. Note that this has no effect on Al Qaeda members' right to humane treatment under

---

[205] Ibid.

[206] Article 1, Hague IV; Article 4, Geneva III: "A. Prisoners of war, in the sense of the present Convention, are persons belonging to one of the following categories, who have fallen into the power of the enemy:

(1) Members of the armed forces of a Party to the conflict, as well as members of militias or volunteer corps forming part of such armed forces.

(2) Members of other militias and members of other volunteer corps, including those of organized resistance movements, belonging to a Party to the conflict and operating in or outside their own territory, even if this territory is occupied, provided that such militias or volunteer corps, including such organized resistance movements, fulfill the following conditions:
(a) that of being commanded by a person responsible for his subordinates;
(b) that of having a fixed distinctive sign recognizable at a distance;
(c) that of carrying arms openly;
(d) that of conducting their operations in accordance with the laws and customs of war.

(3) Members of regular armed forces who profess allegiance to a government or an authority not recognized by the Detaining Power.

(4) Persons who accompany the armed forces without actually being members thereof, such as civilian members of military aircraft crews, war correspondents, supply contractors, members of labour units or of services responsible for the welfare of the armed forces, provided that they have received authorization, from the armed forces which they accompany, who shall provide them for that purpose with an identity card similar to the annexed model.

(5) Members of crews, including masters, pilots and apprentices, of the merchant marine and the crews of civil aircraft of the Parties to the conflict, who do not benefit by more favourable treatment under any other provisions of international law.

(6) Inhabitants of a non-occupied territory, who on the approach of the enemy spontaneously take up arms to resist the invading forces, without having had time to form themselves into regular armed units, provided they carry arms openly and respect the laws and customs of war."

[207] Ibid.

[208] Theoretically, a state could decide that they support the Al Qaeda cause. They could declare war against the U.S. and incorporate Al Qaeda into their armed forces. Al Qaeda members could then obtain privileged belligerency.

human rights law or IHL,[209] but only restricts their ability to gain legal protection for hostile acts.

(c) The individual's acts comply with the laws of war

Privileged belligerent status does not provide protection for acts that violate the laws of war.[210] The prohibitions and obligations of privileged belligerents under the laws of war include: limiting attacks to lawful targets,[211] avoiding causing unnecessary suffering,[212] ensuring that any collateral damage is proportional to the military advantage gained,[213] and providing protection and humane treatment to civilians and noncombatants under their control.[214] If a combatant violates the laws of war, he is subject to prosecution by the enemy, his own state and even neutral states.[215] In the asymmetric war paradigm, attacking civilian/unlawful targets is problematic.

In asymmetric war, the non-state actor, having no possibility of obtaining privileged belligerency, has no incentive to distinguish himself from the civilian population even if and when he engages in hostilities. This largely defeats the entire IHL concept of distinction, or keeping the combatants and the combat away from civilians. In reaction to this reality, the international community needs to change its concept of a war declaration.

> The Proposal Clause 2: States may declare war against other states, non-state organizations, or individuals provided these declarations comply with Article 2(4) and Article 51 of the United Nations Charter.

Declarations of war have traditionally been limited to one state against another.[216] If we are going to require states to declare war publicly before obtaining belligerency rights for their militaries, this concept will need to be expanded. The United States, for example, should be permitted to declare war against the non-state actor, Al Qaeda. An organization like Al Qaeda fighting an asymmetric conflict with a world superpower, understands the strategic and tactical necessity that it not be

---

[209] Geneva IV.

[210] *Supra*, n. 186.

[211] Article 48, AP1.

[212] Article 35, AP1: "It is prohibited to employ weapons, projectiles and material and methods of warfare of a nature to cause superfluous injury or unnecessary suffering."

[213] Article 51, AP1; Article 57, AP1: Combatants should: "... refrain from deciding to launch any attack which may be expected to cause incidental loss of civilian life, injury to civilians, damage to civilian objects, or a combination thereof, which would be excessive in relation to the concrete and direct military advantage anticipated."

[214] *Supra*, n. 210 and *supra* n. 187.

[215] Article 129, Geneva VI: "Each High Contracting Party shall be under the obligation to search for persons alleged to have committed, or to have ordered to be committed, such grave breaches, and shall bring such persons, regardless of their nationality, before its own courts."

[216] Even though one state may not recognize the other as a state. War on terror or war on drugs are not declarations of war.

linked to a given state or geographic region. By globally decentralizing its organization and forces, it marginalizes most of the combat capability of the U.S. military. Tanks, howitzers and ships simply cannot be moved around the world quickly enough to counter small Al Qaeda strike forces.[217] Given that Al Qaeda will not link itself to a state or region, the United States will need to declare war against the group itself. If we limited declarations of war to only identifiable groups, however, the non-state actor group would simply avoid giving itself a name, or, as it does now, attempt to operate without a traceable organization. For this instance, a state needs the capability to declare war against specific individuals.

It is this last instance, a declaration of war against an individual, that will cause significant discomfort to the legal community. Critics will argue that a state will surreptitiously use a declaration of war to kill an individual for political benefit or to avoid providing that individual with the due process rights within the criminal process. How is this different from a state simply ordering executions and assassinations extrajudicially and arbitrarily?

> The Proposal Clause 3: The International Court of Justice has the power to nullify declarations of war.

Perhaps the greatest threat to international peace, security and stability over time is not the actions of non-state actors like Al Qaeda, but a loss of confidence in the U.N. This organization was formed to prevent all war,[218] not to prevent all but five nations using war to achieve their political goals. By refusing to join the International Criminal Court, withdrawing from the compulsory jurisdiction of the International Court of Justice,[219] and retaining its veto power in the Security Council, the United States has protected an enforcement gap that permits its military to act with near impunity. Even if we assume the 2003 invasion of Iraq and every targeted killing to be both morally and legally justified, the absence of forum to challenge these conclusions creates a dangerous perception of arbitrary power.[220] Also, it creates a dangerous precedent. China could conduct targeted killings of Taiwanese or Tibetans using legal arguments very similar to U.S. justifications for targeted killings. Currently there is no venue empowered to effectively challenge the actions of the permanent members, and so they appear to operate above the law.

Compare the 1990 Iraqi invasion of Kuwait to the 2008 South Ossetia war. One day after Saddam Hussein sent forces into Kuwait claiming that the state did not possess independent sovereignty, the Security Council condemned the invasion,[221] and it subsequently authorized the First Gulf War. Three years after the 2008

---

[217] The Desert Shield operation lasted seven months, in part to give the allied forces time to get sufficient troops to the region.

[218] Preamble to the Charter.

[219] Secretary of State George P. Shultz's letter to the Secretary General, dated October 7, 1985.

[220] Joseph Raz characterizes arbitrary power as possibly the greatest evil. Raz, *supra* n. 25.

[221] Security Council Resolution 660, August 2, 1990.

conflict between Russia and Georgia, the Security Council has yet to issue any statement or take action on the issue. When the United States attempted to complain about Russia recognizing the independence of the two Georgian republics that gave rise to the conflict, the Russian delegate alleged that the U.S. was unjustified in its 2003 invasion of Iraq.[222] The Security Council does not appear to serve as even a moral check on the use of military power by its permanent members.

Giving the International Court of Justice power to nullify declarations of war would provide a needed legal and moral venue to evaluate a state's claims of self-defense, even if it has no direct authority or capability to end a conflict. Currently the Court has the power to rule on disputes between the states, but it must depend on the Security Council to enforce its rulings.[223] Under this proposal, the Court will not need Security Council support, since it is the states, themselves, that will enforce its rulings by prosecuting captured combatants no longer entitled to privileged belligerency. The nullification will need to be prospective rather than retroactive, lest it create an ex post facto criminal violation. Once the Court nullifies the declaration, the declaring state should be given a reasonable time to notify its forces and withdraw from the zone of conflict and any combatants that engage in hostilities after that time will not have privileged belligerency. The tangible effect of this power will be minimal, since it will only concern the criminal prosecutions of military personnel who engaged in combat and were captured after the ruling. The moral effect, however, would be more significant.

Declarations of war against groups or individuals could be challenged by states where any of those individuals is located, since it is their sovereignty that is sacrificed under privileged belligerency. Declarations of war against an individual would have the twofold purpose of identifying that individual as a continuing threat against the declaring state and that the individual is a lawful target. The declaration should be treated as a rebuttable presumption that both are true. If the individual wants to contest her status as either a threat to the declaring state or her status as a lawful target, she can simply turn herself in to any neutral state. That state can intern her pursuant to its responsibilities as a neutral party under the Fifth Hague Convention. The state can then challenge the declaration of war before the International Court of Justice. If the declaration is set aside, the individual could be released. Some might complain that this forces individuals accused of criminal offenses to surrender to authorities to prevent their summary execution. This should be viewed as a benefit, rather than an injustice. The proper adjudication of allegations is the goal of any legal system and I know of no right, moral or legal, to remain a fugitive.

---

[222] United Nations Security Council, meeting 5969, at p 16 of the report.

[223] The Statute of the International Court of Justice has no clause that contemplates a failure to comply with its ruling. Article 94 of the Charter requires member states to comply with the Court's rulings, but only the Security Council has the power to exert the force of the U.N. in the event of noncompliance.

IV. May 2, 2011 Redux—Anwar al-Awlaki under this proposal[224]

The Obama Administration authorized the targeted killing of an American citizen, Muslim cleric Anwar al-Awlaki in 2010.[225] It has done the de facto equivalent of declaring war against this individual under this proposal, but importantly, not the legal equivalent. Al-Awlaki's father attempted to challenge this determination in the U.S. court system, but his suit was dismissed for lack of standing and political question.[226] (Al-Awlaki is allegedly currently being hidden among his familial tribe in Yemen.) However, he may be living in an urban residence in a different country, as bin Laden was when most reports had him living in the wilds of either Afghanistan or Pakistan. Assume that al-Awlaki is located in a large home in the small town of Caracas, Venezuela, possibly with the awareness and tacit protection of anti-American Venezuelan President Hugo Chavez. Under the status quo, his life and the lives of many of those around him, including innocent police officers in Caracas, may soon be ended in a raid similar to that on bin Laden.

If the United States, under this proposal, filed a public declaration of war against al-Awlaki, multiple facets would change from the status quo. First, the U.S. Constitution has a clear delineation of power as to who can "declare war."[227] The wording of this proposal intentionally mirrors the Constitutional language so that there can be no ambiguity in the eyes of Congress or the American public as to what is being decided.[228] The Administration would have to present the evidence justifying the declaration as an action in self-defense to an armed attack under Article 51 of the U.N. Charter.[229] This type of public declaration would receive world-wide coverage, so individuals living near al-Awlaki, including the local police, would have a greater opportunity to avoid being collateral damage. Venezuela would have the legal responsibility to seize al-Awlaki as a belligerent on its territory and intern him. The Venezuelan government would have the legal capability to challenge the declaration of war before the International Court of Justice. If the Court nullified

---

[224] Anwar al-Awlaki was reported killed after this article was drafted, but his situation as of August 2011 still serves as an excellent example for this discussion.

[225] Scott Shane, "U.S. Approves Targeted Killing of American Cleric,"*The New York Times*, April 6, 2010.

[226] Evan Perez, "Judge Dismisses Targeted-Killing Suit," *The Wall Street Journal*, December 8, 2010.

[227] Article 1, section 8 of the U.S. Constitution: "Congress shall have the power to…declare war."

[228] Consider the cases of *Doe v. Bush*, 323 Federal Reporter 3rd 133 (First Circuit Court of Appeals, 2003) and *Massachusetts v. Laird*, 451 Federal Reporter 2d 26 (First Circuit Court of Appeals, 1971). In both cases the court found that acts of Congress other than declarations of war had authorized the military force sufficient to satisfy the constraints of the Constitution.

[229] Congress is not actually constitutionally limited by the Charter as to its declarations of war, but they would be aware of the review power of the ICJ and would not want to be embarrassed by a nullification.

the declaration, al-Awlaki could be released, and any further U.S. attack on him would subject those attackers to prosecution under Venezuelan law. If the Court upheld the declaration, Awlaki would remain interned until he elected to end the war by surrendering or agreeing to whatever terms he negotiated with the United States. A "proper" war has the goal of survival, not justice or vengeance, so if al-Awlaki is neutralized as a physical threat to the United States, this is a victory.

V. Conclusion

War is a horrible event, possibly the worst, in the human experience. All humans should work toward making it obsolete and extinct. Until that time, however, it remains subject to a unique moral paradigm that is incongruent with all other aspects of civilized life. Rather than attempting to morally or legally blur the distinction between war, on the one hand, and criminal justice on the other, we should try to reinforce the separation. A system that requires a formal declaration of war to invoke the legal and moral concept of privileged belligerency is a simple way to accomplish this. This declaration will support the IHL goal of distinction between combatants and noncombatants for belligerents. It will also safeguard innocent bystanders by allowing them increased opportunity to avoid association with civilians who are engaging in hostilities and are thus lawful targets. It will clarify the role and responsibilities of states where civilian belligerents reside. Belligerent states are given the moral and legal authority to publicly require other states to defend their neutrality by seizing all combatants in their territory or those other states legally invite violations of their sovereignty. For the citizens of liberal democracies, the decision to go to war will regain the seriousness it deserves. Making this declaration challengeable before the International Court of Justice will provide a necessary check on the power of the five permanent members of the Security Council, and weaker states are given a real power to voice their objections and regain the moral and legal authority to prosecute violations of their sovereignty. War becomes clearly severed from civilized life; by forcing a war to be a "proper" war, a concept for which humanity has evolved a strong distaste, perhaps it will occur less often.

PART III

TARGETED KILLING AND SELF-DEFENSE

8

GOING MEDIEVAL: TARGETED KILLING, SELF-DEFENSE AND THE *JUS AD BELLUM* REGIME

Craig Martin

In the aftermath of the 9/11 attacks, the United States began using drone-mounted missile strikes for the targeted killing[1] of terrorists and militants considered to be a threat to the United States. While largely associated with efforts against Al Qaeda, and operations against the Afghan insurgency, the American use of drones to kill targeted individuals has extended to at least six countries so far.[2] Targeted killing is not entirely new in the annals of American national security policy,[3] but this targeted killing program has been controversial. There are several characteristics of the current policy that distinguish it from past practice, and raise significant legal issues relating to the international law regime that governs the use of force (the *jus ad bellum* regime), international humanitarian law (IHL—the legal regime that

---

[1] The term "targeted killing" here refers to the deliberate killing of specifically identified individuals who are not clearly combatants in an armed conflict under international law. This definition is itself contentious. Who, and according to what criteria, is to be defined as a combatant? How do we decide whether such persons are operating in the context of an armed conflict? These issues are themselves controversial, and so determining whether a particular killing constitutes a targeted killing is not without debate. Some in the U.S. argue that those targeted under this policy are combatants in an armed conflict—but then the killing of those persons would not be distinguishable from other killing in war, and so would not be subject to particular study as "targeted killing." See Nils Meltzer, *Targeted Killing in International Law* (Oxford University Press, 2008) 3–5; David Kretzmer, "Targeted Killing of Suspected Terrorists: Extra-Judicial Executions or Legitimate Means of Defense?," 16 *The European Journal of International Law* (2005) 171, 174–6; Gary Solis, "Targeted Killing and the Law of Armed Conflict," 60 *Naval War College Review* (2007) 127, 127–30; and Philip Alston, "Report of the Special Rapporteur on Extrajudicial, Summary or Arbitrary Executions," May 28, 2010, U.N. Doc. A/HRC/14/24/Add.6, 3.

[2] The six confirmed countries are Afghanistan, Iraq, Pakistan, Yemen, Somalia and Libya.

[3] The Phoenix program included the extensive use of targeted killing to "neutralize" high-ranking members of the Viet Cong. *Vietnam: Policy and Prospects, 1970: Hearings Before the Committee on Foreign Relations, on Civil Operations and Rural Development Support Program*, United States Senate, (U.S. Government Printing Office, 1970).

governs the conduct of forces in armed conflict), international human rights law (IHRL), and even domestic criminal and constitutional law. The features of the targeted killing program that trigger the application of *jus ad bellum* principles in particular, are the use of drone-mounted missile strikes to prosecute the targets, which likely constitute a use of force within the meaning of Article 2(4) of the United Nations Charter,[4] together with the American reliance upon the right of self-defense as a justification for such strikes.

In this chapter I analyze the U.S. claims that the targeted killing policy is justified under the *jus ad bellum* doctrine of self-defense, and argue that this very broad and general claim, as a basis for strikes against targets in countries that are not sufficiently responsible for the actions of the terrorists, and in which the United States is not clearly a belligerent in an armed conflict, is not consistent with current international law principles. Arguments that the targeted killing policy is unlawful are not of course new or novel—others have already made this point quite persuasively.[5] But the *jus ad bellum* issues raised by the policy have not received as much attention in the literature as the IHL and IHRL aspects.[6] Moreover, in addition to assessing the policy from a *jus ad bellum* perspective, this chapter considers the impact that the policy may have on the legal regime itself. The manner in which the targeted killing program is being prosecuted, together with its justifications and rationales, may lead to changes to the *jus ad bellum* regime, and to the nature of the relationship between it and the IHL regime, and my analysis here explores how such changes could have harmful unintended consequences for the entire system of constraints on the use of force and armed conflict. The implications and rationales of the U.S. policy tend to resurrect old principles, some dating back to the medieval period, which are not consistent with the theoretical premises underlying the modern U.N. system. In its efforts to address an admittedly real and present danger of transnational terrorism, the United States may undermine the

---

[4] Art. 2(4) of the U.N. Charter provides that states "shall refrain in their international relations from the threat or use of force against the territorial integrity or political independence of any state, or in any other manner inconsistent with the Purposes of the United Nations."

[5] Mary Ellen O'Connell, "Unlawful Killing with Combat Drones: A Case Study of Pakistan, 2004–2009" in Simon Bronitt (ed.), *Shooting to Kill: The Law Governing Lethal Force in Context* (Hart Publishing, forthcoming); cites here are to the unpublished draft available online at <http://papers.ssrn.com/sol3/papers.cfm?abstract_id=1501144> accessed November 4, 2011; Melzer, *supra* n.1.

[6] Some studies that have examined the *jus ad bellum* aspects include; O'Connell, *supra* n.5; Norman G. Printer Jr, "The Use of Force Against Non-State Actors Under International Law: An Analysis of the U.S. Predator Strike in Yemen," 8 *UCLA Journal of International Law and Foreign Affairs* (2003) 332; Jordan J. Paust, "Self-Defense Targetings of Non-State Actors and Permissibility of U.S. Use of Drones in Pakistan," *Journal of Transnational Law & Policy* (2010) 237; Chris Jenks, "Law from Above: Unmanned Ariel Systems, the Use of Force, and Armed Conflict," 85 *North Dakota Law Review* 649 (2009); and more broadly, Naom Lubell, *Extraterritorial Use of Force Against Non-State Actors* (Oxford University Press, 2010); Michael N. Schmitt, "Responding to Transnational Terrorism Under the *Jus ad Bellum*: A Normative Framework," 56 *Naval Law Review* 1 (2008).

system that was developed to prevent war among states and thereby increase the risk of international armed conflict, which in the long run is a far graver danger to international society than the threat posed by terrorists.

I. The policy and its justifications

The targeted killing policy is said to be aimed at members of Al Qaeda, the Taliban, and associated forces.[7] While primarily explained as being responsive to the planning and perpetration of terrorist attacks, it also clearly includes the targeting of those thought to be involved in the insurgency in Afghanistan, and may include persons involved in the "material support" of terrorism.[8] There are features of the policy that are significant for the purposes of the *jus ad bellum* analysis. The use of methods that would constitute a use of force against the state in which the targets is attacked are important—the use of drone-mounted missile strikes in particular, though the military strike into Pakistan to kill bin Laden raised similar issues. As well, the fact that strikes are being made in countries such as Yemen, Somalia, and Pakistan, which were not sufficiently responsible for the operations of the targeted terrorists, and in which the United States is not clearly a belligerent in an armed conflict. These features of the policy trigger the application of the *jus ad bellum* regime, but in addition the targeted killing strikes have been justified by the United States on the basis of the *jus ad bellum* doctrine of self-defense.

While the government policy of targeted killing remains technically a covert operation, Harold Koh, then the legal counsel to the Department of State, provided two justifications for the government's policy of targeted killing in a short official statement in 2010.[9] The first was that the United States is engaged in an international armed conflict with Al Qaeda and other forces associated with it, and thus the members of such groups are combatants and legitimate targets under IHL. The second justification offered was that the United States is entitled to use lethal force against such groups as an exercise of the right of self-defense. While Koh did not say so explicitly, this is interpreted to mean that the targeting of members of these

---

[7] Harold Koh, speaking to the American Society of International Law, Washington, D.C., March 25, 2010 (transcript available online at <http://www.state.gov/s/l/releases/remarks/139119.htm> accessed November 4, 2011).

[8] As several other chapters in this Volume describe in greater detail, there is little non-classified information on the criteria for targeting, the standards of proof required, or any other details of the process of selecting targets, final decision-making on issues of necessity and proportionality, and ex post review of the decision-making. For the extent to which the policy may come to extend to killing individuals for their "material support" of terrorists, see Section 7 of the draft legislation that was before the Armed Services Committee as this chapter was going to press: *The Detainee Security Act of 2011*, H.R. 968 I.H. (112th Congress 2011–12), available online at <http://thomas.loc.gov/cgi-bin/query/z?c112:H.R.968:> accessed November 4, 2011.

[9] Koh, *supra* n. 7.

groups constitutes a use of force justified by the *jus ad bellum* right of self-defense provided for in Article 51 of the U.N. Charter. Such targeting is a use of force against the states in which the members of these groups are being targeted, and Koh indicated that among the considerations for each such use of force, were the sovereignty of the state involved, and "the willingness and ability of those states to suppress the threat the target poses." This was an echo of President George W. Bush's assertion that "we will make no distinction between the terrorists who committed these acts and those who harbor them."[10]

Koh's speech was explicitly not a detailed legal opinion, but both his speech and the manner in which the policy has been executed suggest that these two justifications are understood as independent arguments—that is, the United States could use force to kill Al Qaeda members in other countries on the justification that it was engaged in an armed conflict with Al Qaeda, and as a separate justification, it could do so under the right of self-defense.[11] In the analysis that follows, I will examine the second justification in particular, though I will also suggest that to the extent these are indeed independent rationales (a question we will return to), the first would also operate to undermine the *jus ad bellum* regime.

II. The *jus ad bellum* regime

The conduct of targeted killing implicates three distinct regimes in international law, namely: *jus ad bellum*; IHL; and IHRL. In examining the legitimacy of the targeted killing policy under the principles of the *jus ad bellum* regime and the policy's possible impact on that regime, we need to lay out the relevant principles and their underlying rationale. Moreover, to understand the full scope of that potential impact, it is important to explore how the policy might affect the relationship between the *jus ad bellum* and IHL regimes. I begin, therefore, with a brief examination of the historical development of the regime and the relationship between it and IHL. While some areas of these legal regimes remain deeply contested, this brief overview provides a mainstream perspective on the relevant principles.[12]

---

[10] Speech of President George W. Bush, September 11, 2001, cited in Steven R. Ratner, "*Jus ad Bellum* and *Jus in Bello* After September 11," 96 *American Journal of International Law* 905 (2002) 906.

[11] See text associated with *infra* nn. 103–05.

[12] I will below discuss some of the recent objections to the position taken here on those principles most central to the issue of targeted killing. This section begins with a sketch of the conventional understanding, as reflected in many leading works on the use of force and the decisions of the ICJ, as a baseline for discussion.

The *jus ad bellum* regime is traceable to Classical Greece, but its primary origins are in medieval just war theory.[13] Just war theory entrenched the very idea that a legal justification is required for the use of armed force. It also articulated the idea that just war could only be waged by a sovereign authority, thus developing the state monopoly on the legitimate use of armed force.[14] With Grotius and the emergence of the law of nations came the further development of war as a legal concept—rather than being merely a description for the conduct of hostilities, war was understood as a state of relations among states that triggered specific laws that displaced the operation of other legal regimes.[15] Finally, there emerged during the Grotian period the notion of defensive war, which contemplated the use of force to prevent the development of future threats, and even to punish past attacks. This expansive doctrine was in stark contrast to the narrow right of self-defense under natural law, which was limited to responding with force to an immediate threat for the purposes of self-protection.[16] Moreover, Grotius posited that the enforcement of certain natural law principles could also constitute just cause for the use of force.[17]

By the beginning of the nineteenth century, just war theory and the Grotian school on the laws of war had lost virtually all influence on the practice of nations.[18] There was essentially no international law limitation on the resort to war, though there were principles governing the scope of certain measures short of war.[19] It was only at the end of the nineteenth century that a new movement developed to reintroduce legal limits on the recourse to war, with first the Hague treaties of 1899 and 1907, followed by the Covenant of the League of Nations in 1919, and the Kellogg-Briand Pact in 1928. These developments reflected an effort to increasingly strengthen the legal limitations on the use of force, culminating with the establishment of the U.N. system after the Second World War.[20] The U.N. system

---

[13] G.I.A.D. Draper, "Grotius' Place in the Development of Legal Ideas About War" in Hedley Bull et al. (eds) *Hugo Grotius and International Relations* (Oxford University Press, 1990) 177–9; G.I.A.D. Draper, "The Origins of the Just War Tradition," 46 *New Blackfriars* (2007) 82, 82–3; Stephen Neff, *War and the Law of Nations: A General History* (Cambridge University Press, 2005) chs 1 and 2.

[14] Neff, *supra* n. 13, 49–53 Draper, *supra* n. 13, 180–3.

[15] Neff, *supra* n. 13, 57–8, 102, and 176–8.

[16] Ibid. at 59–61 and 126–9; also, on the writing of Gentili and Grotius on preventative and punitive war, see Richard Tuck, *The Rights of War and Peace* (Oxford University Press, 1999) 18–31 and 79–94; but see Larry May, *Aggression and Crimes Against Peace* (Cambridge University Press, 2008) 75–84.

[17] Neff, *supra* n. 13, 97–102; and Tuck, *supra* n. 16, 102–06.

[18] Neff, *supra* n. 13, 161–5, and ch 5. See also, generally, Tuck, *supra* n. 13; and Philip Bobbitt, *The Shield of Achilles* (Anchor Books, 2007) chs 8 and 21–3; and Yoram Dinstein, *War, Aggression and Self-Defense*, 4th edn (Cambridge University Press, 2005) ch. 3.

[19] Dinstein, *supra* n. 18, 75–8 and 184–5; Neff, *supra* n. 13, ch. 6.

[20] For a history of these developments, see Neff, *supra* n. 13, chs 8–9; Brownlie, *International Law and the Use of Force by States* (Oxford University Press, 1963) chs 4–6; Dinstein, *supra* n. 18, ch. 4. For my own summary of these development of legal constraints on the use of force, see

prohibits the threat or use of force against the political independence or territorial integrity of other states, or in any other way inconsistent with the principles enshrined in the Charter.[21] The Charter provides for two general exceptions to the prohibition, being the right of individual and collective self-defense, and the use of force in collective security operations authorized by the U.N. Security Council.[22]

A number of features of this development should be emphasized. First, the modern *jus ad bellum* regime under the U.N. system reflected an effort to create a stronger system of constraints on the use of force, in order to reduce the incidence of armed conflict among states. For that purpose a number of earlier ideas were rejected. In contrast to the early twentieth-century attempts to limit the recourse to "war," the U.N. system prohibits all "use of force." This move addressed the distinctions that had been made between "war" as a legal state of relations, and various "measures short of war." Which states had attempted to exploit this distinction by characterizing their impugned use of force as permissible measures short of war, which was viewed as having contributed to the onset of the Second World War.[23]

Second, the individual and collective rights of self-defense articulated in Article 51 of the Charter are much closer to the narrow natural law right than they are to the late medieval notions of defensive war. The provision permits the use of force only in response to an "armed attack," or at most, in anticipation of an imminent armed attack—so-called "anticipatory self-defense." The modern doctrine of self-defense does not permit the use of force to prevent the development of potential future threats, or to punish past attacks.[24] Even in the event of attack, the threshold for justified use of force is high, in that the use of force constituting an "armed attack" sufficient to trigger this right of self-defense is substantially greater than the use of force that is itself subject to the general prohibition.[25]

Craig Martin, "Taking War Seriously: A Model for Constitutional Constraints on the Use of Force in Compliance with International Law," 76 *Brooklyn Law Review* 611 (2011) 633–61.

[21] Art. 2(4) of the U.N. Charter.

[22] U.N. Charter, arts 51 and 39–43, respectively. For an analysis of the modern *jus ad bellum* system, see e.g., Brownlie, *supra* n. 20, and Brownlie, "International Law and the Use of Force by States Revisited," 21 *Australian Year Book of International Law* (2001); Dinstein, *supra* n. 18; Christine Gray, *International Law and the Use of Force* (Oxford University Press, 2008); Thomas M. Franck, *Recourse to Force: State Action Against Threats and Armed Attacks* (Cambridge University Press, 2002); Lindsey Moir, *Reappraising the Resort to Force: International Law,* Jus ad Bellum *and the War on Terror* (Hart Publishing, 2010); and Christopher Greenwood, *Essays on War in International Law* (Cameron May, 2006).

[23] Neff, *supra* n. 13, 279–80, 285–6, and 296–313. The Japanese invasion of Manchuria, characterized as an "incident," and the Italian intervention in Ethiopia, were two of the primary examples of this failure of the League system.

[24] This issue will be examined in detail below: see *infra* nn. 80–87, and associated text.

[25] The mining of a naval vessel, and the firing of a silkworm missile at an ocean-going oil-tanker, for instance, were held not to constitute armed attacks for the purposes of triggering the right of self-defense. See in particular *Oil Platforms (Iran v. U.S.),* 42 I.L.M. 1334 (November 6, 2003), paras 51 and 64; see also *Military and Paramilitary Activities in and Against Nicaragua*

Finally, the traditional position has been that the regime governs states alone among the possible subjects of international law. Thus, the justification of self-defense is available for the use of force against states that are responsible for the armed attacks of non-state actors (NSAs), but not against NSAs *as such*—by which is meant NSAs independent of the state in which they are operating. In other words, it is the state to which the operations of the NSA can be imputed for purposes of legal responsibility that is the sole legal object of the state use of force. And such use of force can only be justified if indeed the actions of the NSA can be imputed to the state against which the force is being employed. A state cannot use force against another state on the grounds that it is targeting an NSA within that state's territory, unless that state bears sufficient responsibility for the armed attacks mounted by the NSA. If it is so justified, the defending state may also target the members of the NSA in the course of the operations, so long as the relevant conditions of IHL are satisfied; but the defending state cannot assert a right to use force against an NSA in the abstract, and strike its members in other countries that have no responsibility for the NAS's attacks.[26] However, this and several of the other propositions outlined above have become deeply contested after 9/11. I will return to these issues in more detail below in examining self-defense in the targeted killing context.

Rounding out the discussion of the basic principles of the doctrine, the use of self-defense is strictly governed by the principles of necessity and proportionality. This means that the use of force must be the only practical way to prevent the continuation of the armed attacks being defended against, and the force used and injury thus caused must be proportionate to the harm that would likely result if further aggression is not prevented.[27] While the principles of necessity and proportionality date back to the medieval period and natural law, the parameters of these principles as they are now understood are consistent with the narrowed scope of the right of self-defense, as compared to principles of the defensive war in the Grotian school.[28] We will return to this issue below when we examine claims of preventative self-defense.

In sum, the *jus ad bellum* regime of the U.N. system completed the development of rules designed to significantly constrain the state use of force and reduce the incidence of armed conflict. It did so in ways that reflected the continued operation of some principles from just war theory and the early law of nations, such as the basic notion that a legal justification is required to use force, that the legitimate use of force is reserved to sovereign states, and that the use of force gives rise to a legal

---

(Nicaragua v. U.S.A.), (Merits Judgment), 1986 I.C.J. Reports 14, paras 191, 210–11, and 230–2.

[26] For further analysis and sources, see *infra* nn. 50–71 and associated text.

[27] Dinstein, *supra* n. 18, 237–42; Gray, *supra* n. 22, 148–55.

[28] Neff, *supra* n. 13, 326–34 (though tracing how states have tried to expand the concept since adoption of the U.N. Charter).

state of armed conflict, and thereby triggers the operation of special legal regimes and displaces to some extent peacetime laws. But in developing the modern system, there were also quite deliberate decisions to reject and abandon several earlier ideas such as the medieval concept of broad defensive war, the nineteenth-century tolerance of war as a legitimate tool of state policy, and the later efforts to introduce different categories of armed force up to and including "war," each with different levels of constraint.

Turning to the relationship between IHL and *jus ad bellum*, it was only in the nineteenth century that IHL became a fully developed system largely, but not entirely, separate from the *jus ad bellum* regime.[29] Governing the conduct of armed forces within armed conflict, IHL is based on two core ideas that co-existed in constant tension—namely, that there must be constraints placed on how military forces fight, and in particular who they can target on the one hand; and on the other, the notion that there is legal authority for the use of deadly force by legitimate armed forces of a state in the pursuit of valid military objectives in war.[30] These twin ideas are reflected within the principle of distinction, which requires that belligerents maintain a clear distinction between civilian and military targets, and between combatants and civilians.[31]

The IHL regime only operates, however, in the context of armed conflict. And the IHL regime itself provides the criteria for determining the existence of an armed conflict. The Geneva Conventions and their Additional Protocols contemplate two different kinds of armed conflict, being "international armed conflict" and "non-international armed conflict." International armed conflict is an armed conflict among states.[32] Non-international armed conflict is more difficult to define and is subject to a more limited set of IHL principles. "Armed conflict not of an international character," refers to hostilities occurring within the territory of a state.[33] Subsequent jurispru-

---

[29] Neff, *supra* n. 13, 111–14 and 186–9.

[30] On the IHL regime, see e.g. Yoram Dinstein, *The Conduct of Hostilities Under the Law of International Armed Conflict* (Cambridge University Press, 2004); Gary D. Solis, *The Law of Armed Conflict: International Humanitarian Law in War* (Cambridge University Press, 2010); Lindsay Moir, *The Law of Internal Armed Conflict* (Cambridge University Press, 2002); Anthony Cullen, *The Concept of Non-International Armed Conflict in International Humanitarian Law* (Cambridge University Press, 2010).

[31] Jean-Marie Henckaerts and Louise Doswald-Beck (eds), *Customary International Humanitarian Law*, Vol. 2, (Cambridge: Cambridge University of Press, 2005) chs 1 and 2; Dinstein, *supra* n. 30, 27–8, 82–7; Solis, *supra* n. 30, 251–3;

[32] *Geneva Convention Relative to the Treatment of Prisoners of War*, August 12, 1949, 75 UNTS (1950) 135, Art. 2, and *Protocol Additional to the Geneva Conventions of August 12, 1949, and Relating to the Protection of Victims of International Armed Conflicts, (Protocol I)*, 1125 UNTS (1979) 3, Art. 1(3) and (4); See also *Prosecutor v. Duško Tadiać*, IT-94-1-A, July 15, 1999, (Appeals Chamber), para 84.

[33] *Geneva Conventions*, Common Art. 3; *Protocol Additional to the Geneva Conventions of August 12, 1949, and Relating to the Protection of Victims of Non-International Armed Conflicts, (Protocol II)*, 1342 UNTS (1983) 137, Art. 1(1) (though note that the narrower definition in the Additional Protocol is not understood to constitute the minimum requirements for the existence of non-international

dence has further defined non-international armed conflict as being characterized by armed violence of sufficiently significant intensity and duration between governmental authorities and organized armed groups, or among such groups, within the state.[34] There continues to be debate over the exact parameters of non-international armed conflict, which are relevant to the controversy over the validity of the claim that the United States is, as a matter of law, engaged in a "transnational armed conflict" with Al Qaeda and others.[35] That issue is significant for questions regarding the policy's legality under IHL, which is not our focus here. But I do want to explore the relationship between the *jus ad bellum* regime and IHL, in order to understand how the policy's impact on the IHL regime could also significantly affect the *jus ad bellum* regime, and ultimately the overall system comprised of both.

While the two regimes were once closely related, they are now in many important respects independent and distinct. This separation is crucial to the principle of equality inherent in IHL, meaning that the rights and obligations under IHL apply equally to the armed forces of all belligerents regardless of which side ultimately had legal authority to use force under the rules of *jus ad bellum*. That principle of equality, and the underlying independence from *jus ad bellum*, is considered essential to achieving the ultimate objective of maximizing adherence to the rules of IHL for the purpose of reducing the amount of suffering in armed conflict.[36] Having said that the two regimes are largely independent, however, it is important to note that there continues to be a connection between them, and that the relationship is significant.[37] To put it another way, the two regimes operate independently, but as part of a single overall system of international law that governs the use of force and armed conflict—what I would call the laws of war in the broadest sense.[38]

---

armed conflict—see Melzer, *supra* n. 1, 256). Convention on Prohibitions or Restrictions on the Use of Certain Conventional Weapons Which May be Deemed to be Excessively Injurious or to Have Indiscriminate Effects, Protocol II is 1125 U.N.T.S. 609.

[34] See in particular *Prosecutor v. Tadic*, (Decision on the Defence Motion for Interlocutory Appeal on Jurisdiction) October 2, 1995 (Jurisdiction Motion Appeal), paras 66–70; *Prosecutor v. Tadic*, Appeal Judgment, paras 83–96. See also Moir, *supra* n. 30, 489 *et seq*; and Melzer, *supra* n. 1, 252–61.

[35] Melzer, *supra* n. 1, 257–61; Marko Milanovic, "What Exactly Internationalizes an Internal Armed Conflict?," *EJIL Talk!*, May 7, 2010, available online at <http://www.ejiltalk.org/what-exactly-internationalizes-an-internal-armed-conflict/> accessed November 4, 2011.

[36] Dinstein, *supra* n. 18, 156–68; Neff, *supra* n. 13, 340–6, 366–9; see also generally, Robert D. Sloane, "The Cost of Conflation: Preserving the Dualism of *Jus ad Bellum* and *Jus in Bello* in the Contemporary Law of War," 34 *Yale Journal of International Law* 47 (2009); Alexander Orakhelashvili, "Overlap and Convergence: *Jus ad Bellum* and *Jus in Bello*," 12 *Journal of Conflict & Security Law* 157 (2007); and Eyal Benvenisti, "Rethinking the Divide between *Jus ad Bellum* and *Jus in Bello* in Warfare Against Non-State Actors," 34 *Yale Journal of International Law* 541 (2009).

[37] In fact, Sloane suggests that the independence of the regimes in the Charter era is actually exaggerated: Sloane, *supra* n. 36, 67–9.

[38] The "laws of war" is a term that is typically employed to describe the IHL regime alone, but I use it here to capture the overall system comprised of the two regimes.

In particular, when a state uses armed force against or within the territory of another state, in the sense captured by Article 2(4) of the U.N. Charter, such that the rules of *jus ad bellum* would apply and a *jus ad bellum* justification is required to legitimize the action, then that action constitutes either the initiation of an international armed conflict, or is an act within an ongoing international armed conflict (or in some circumstances, a non-international armed conflict), to which the rules of IHL will apply.[39] And when force is used by a state, both *jus ad bellum* and IHL will have to be considered for the purposes of determining the legality of the different aspects of the action.[40] Looking back to the historical development of the two regimes, this connection between them reflects the evolution of war as a legal concept during the Grotian era. "War" went from being a term merely describing violent conflict, to constituting a legal state that triggered the operation of a number of special legal regimes. The modern concepts of the "use of force" and "armed conflict," and the legal regimes that govern them, have their origins in the legal institution of war. As I will return to in the last section of this chapter, there remains a fundamental relationship between the two regimes that is crucially important to the integrity and coherence of the overall system. The two regimes underwent considerable development after the Second World War, with adjustments to several of the core concepts in each and an accentuation of their mutual independence, but we should not lose sight of their common origin and the inherent relationship that continues to connect them. Together, they comprise an overall system within which the targeted killing policy is operating, and which stands in danger of being harmed by that policy.

III. Targeted killing and the self-defense justification

The second pillar of the administration's justification for the targeted killing policy is that it is legitimate as an exercise of the right of self-defense. To the extent that this is grounded in an international law principle,[41] this is a claim based on the application of the principles of *jus ad bellum*—that is, the right of the state to use armed force in response to an armed attack, as codified in Article 51 of the U.N. Charter. As such, in order to determine whether the justification is valid, we have to assess whether the use of force employed in the course of the targeted killings satisfies the requirements of the self-defense doctrine just reviewed. In the process of

---

[39] Dinstein, *supra* n. 18, 156–62 (also tracing how the evolution of *jus ad bellum* led to arguments in favor of re-integration of the regimes); Dinstein, *supra* n. 30, 14–16; Kretzmer, *supra* n. 1, 188; Melzer, *supra* n. 1, 247–51 and 394–5.

[40] *Legality of the Threat or Use of Nuclear Weapons*, ICJ Reports 1996, paras 75–87, and 95.

[41] Ken Anderson has suggested that the self-defense claim can be grounded in domestic law arguments: Kenneth Anderson, "Targeted Killing in U.S. Counterterrorism Strategy and Law" in Benjamin Wittes (ed.), *Legislating the War on Terror: An Agenda for Reform* (Brookings Institution, 2009) 346, 347–8, 366–70.

doing so, we will explore in more detail the contentious elements of that doctrine, and how they relate to the targeted killing policy.

What makes the analysis of the self-defense justification particularly complicated in the circumstances of the U.S. targeted killing program is that force is being used against a number of different groups, and in a number of different countries, but there has been no clear explanation to identify the armed attacks against which the use of force is responsive. In order to invoke this principle the U.S. government has to provide clear answers to two questions. First, against precisely what entities is the use of force being directed? And second, in response to exactly which armed attacks is the use of force being employed? Quite obviously, these two questions are related. It would seem self-evident that the entity against which the use of force is directed has to be connected to the attacks against which the state is defending itself. But the U.S. government has provided no detailed account to explain how the use of force against various organizations and states is tied to specific attacks, which makes it impossible to explain how such use of force is necessary and proportionate in each of the different circumstances. The government has only provided a vague suggestion that the targeted killing program in general is in response to the 9/11 attacks, and is directed at Al Qaeda, the Taliban, and "associated forces." There is the further implication that it is directed at states that are unwilling or unable to suppress the threat the targets pose.[42] As will be discussed below, these very general assertions are not sufficient to ground a claim of self-defense justifying the use of force directed against such states as Yemen, Somalia, and Pakistan.

We should pause to address a preliminary issue, before launching into the analysis of precisely what entities are subject to this use of force. That is the issue of consent. It may be objected that Pakistan, Yemen, and Somalia have consented to the use of force, and thus the use of force against and within their territory cannot be an unlawful use of force against those states. How exactly does state consent to the use of force affect the analysis? Where there is true consent, the strikes would not constitute a use of force against the state in the *jus ad bellum* sense. If Pakistan, for instance, consents to such strikes against insurgent forces that are waging a non-international armed conflict within Pakistan, the U.S. attacks would be viewed as assisting another government in responding to an internal conflict. Similarly, if Pakistan consents to the strikes as a form of cooperation with coalition forces in the non-international armed conflict in Afghanistan, then again it is not a use of

---

[42] Harold Koh stated that "the United States is in an armed conflict with Al Qaeda, as well as the Taliban and associated forces, in response to the horrific 9/11 attacks, and may use force consistent with its right to self-defense under international law." This may be interpreted as two independent justifications, and the 9/11 attacks are linked specifically to the existence of an armed conflict, not the exercise of self-defense. See *supra* n. 9.

force against Pakistan. Where there is such consent, a self-defense justification is not required, at least for the use of force against Pakistan itself.

Moreover, if the state within which the use of force is being deployed consents to the operations, there is no requirement for *jus ad bellum* justifications for military action against an NSA that is operating from within that state.[43] As will be discussed further below, this is because *jus ad bellum* does not contemplate the use of force against NSAs as such, but only against states.[44] The use of force against an NSA within Pakistan, with Pakistan's consent, is not a use of force against Pakistan, but is an action taken on behalf of the government of Pakistan, and is indeed limited to such authority that the government of Pakistan itself would have to take such action, pursuant to whatever laws govern in the circumstance— whether it is IHL in the context of a non-international armed conflict, or domestic criminal law and IHRL limiting a law enforcement operation.[45] The *jus ad bellum* regime is not implicated (beyond the *jus ad bellum* principle that permits precisely such assistance against an insurgency), any more than Pakistan's use of force internally against an insurgent force triggers *jus ad bellum* issues. If a state consents to another state's using military force to kill members of an NSA within its territory, there may be serious questions regarding the legality of the killing if the host state's government did not itself have the legal authority to engage in such killing, but such issues would relate to IHL, IHRL and the consenting state's domestic law, not *jus ad bellum*.

That does not mean, however, that the *jus ad bellum* regime does not apply to the targeted killing policy, or that analysis here is unwarranted. Aside from the factual matter that all three of these countries have at various times indicated a lack of consent to the targeted killing strikes,[46] not least of which Pakistan after the

---

[43] But see Printer, *supra* n. 6, 352–8 (analyzing how self-defense is justified under *jus ad bellum* in a strike within Yemen, facilitated by the Yemeni government).

[44] O'Connell, *supra* n. 5, 16. And see *infra* nn. 51–71 and associated text.

[45] Ibid. at 16; Michael N. Schmitt, "Drone Attack Under the *Jus ad Bellum* and *Jus in Bello*: Clearing the 'Fog of War'," in *Yearbook of International Humanitarian Law 2011* (Cambridge University Press, forthcoming) (cites to unpublished draft available online at <http://papers.ssrn.com/sol3/papers.cfm?abstract_id=1801179> 4-5, accessed November 4, 2011.

[46] There has been considerable ambiguity over the extent to which the government of Pakistan has consented to or acquiesced in the targeted killing, which has also varied over the years. There can be little doubt that the Pakistani military, if not the government, has at various times consented to some of these strikes. At other times, such as following the killing of bin Laden, the government has quite clearly objected to them. See, e.g. O'Connell, *supra* n. 5, 16–18; David Sanger and Eric Schmitt, "As Rift Deepens, Kerry has Warning for Pakistan," *The New York Times*, May 15, 2011, A16; and Greg Bruno, "U.S. Drone Activities in Pakistan," *Council on Foreign Relations Backgrounder*, available online at <http://www.cfr.org/pakistan/us-drone-activities-pakistan/p22659#p6> accessed November 4, 2011. Similarly, there are questions regarding Yemen's consent to strikes: Mark Mazzetti, "U.S. Intensifying a Secret Campaign of Yemen Airstrikes," *The New York Times*, June 8, 2011; on occasion this has been explicitly with the cooperation of the Yemeni government: see Walter Pincus, "Missile Strike Carried Out with Yemeni Cooperation," *Washington Post*, November 6, 2002, A10. Strikes in

killing of Osama bin Laden himself, the point is that the United States has itself advanced the doctrine of self-defense as a justification for this use of force. That is an invocation of the *jus ad bellum* regime. To the extent that this is meant to justify the use of force against the states in which the strikes are implemented, the necessary implication is that at least in some circumstances force is being used in the absence of consent, and a justification is understood to be required. It may be objected that the claim to self-defense is being asserted to justify the use of force against the NSAs as such, notwithstanding the argument just made—but as will be examined below, not all aspects of the targeted killing policy can be explained by that premise. Thus, for the purposes of our analysis here, the assumption is that at least in some circumstances the policy is undertaken without consent of the target state, and that these strikes therefore constitute a use of force in *Jus ad bellum* terms giving rise to aspects of international armed conflict.[47]

(a) Use of force against what entities?

Returning then to the question of which entities, precisely, are the subject of the use of force in the targeting program, Harold Koh suggested that the primary targets are Al Qaeda, the Taliban, and associated forces. That is, NSAs, or more specifically, the members of NSAs. It has been suggested by many scholars that this means both a use of force against, and an armed conflict with NSAs, independent from the states in which they happen to be located. We must therefore fully examine this proposition against the traditional principle outlined earlier, that *jus ad bellum* only contemplates the use of force against states. A preliminary distinction has to be made between the question of whether strikes by terrorists can constitute "armed attacks" for the purposes of Article 51 of the Charter, and the separate question of whether the victim state, in exercising its right of self-defense, can direct its use of force against the terrorist organization as such, as opposed to a state that may be responsible in law for facilitating the attacks. On the first of these issues, there is widespread acceptance that strikes by terrorists can rise to the level of "armed attack," in the *jus ad bellum* sense. It is generally acknowledged that the 9/11 attacks in particular did rise to that level, and did constitute an armed attack.[48] Moreover, each single attack need not constitute an "armed attack," but

---

Somalia have occurred when there has been arguably insufficient central authority to provide consent. See Mark Mazzetti and Eric Schmitt, "U.S. Expands its Drone War Into Somalia," *The New York Times*, July 2, 2011, A1.

[47] Consistent with this are the reports that the U.S. team that entered Pakistan for the purposes of killing bin Laden was prepared to use force against Pakistani forces if necessary; and reports that Pakistani authorities subsequently warned that it would use force against any such further violation of its sovereignty. See Eric Schmitt, et al. "U.S. Was Braced for Fight With Pakistanis in bin Laden Raid," *The New York Times*, May 10, 2011, A1.

[48] See, e.g., Sean Murphy, "Terrorism and the Concept of 'Armed Attack' in Article 51 of the U.N. Charter," 43 *Harvard International Law Journal* 41 (2002) 41–51; Dinstein, 207 *supra* n. 18;

a series of attacks of sufficient gravity may be taken cumulatively to constitute an armed attack for the purposes of triggering the right of self-defense.[49] So this is not the basis for any objection to a use of force against NSAs as such.

Accepting that attacks by terrorists can constitute an "armed attack" in *jus ad bellum* terms, however, does not mean that states may use force in self-defense against the terrorist organization as such, in whatever state to which it may have re-located following the attacks, and quite separate and apart from considerations of whether the "host" states bear legal responsibility for the attacks.[50] At the outset, it should be recalled that the right to use armed force in self-defense is an exception to a general prohibition on states against the threat or use of force against the territorial integrity or political independence of other states, or in any other manner inconsistent with the purposes of the U.N. Charter.[51] The very purpose of the U.N. system is to narrow the legitimate grounds for the use of force and reduce the incidence of armed conflict among *states*. The *jus ad bellum* system simply does not contemplate the use of force against NSAs as such. On the other hand, military operations against transnational terrorist groups is necessarily going to occur within the territory of another sovereign state, unless they happen to be on the high seas. Thus, absent the consent of that state, the use of force against the NSA could never actually be just against the NSA in the abstract, but will also constitute a use of force against another state. As we will review, the *jus ad bellum* system requires a significant degree of involvement by a state in the operations of the NSAs within its territory before the use of force against that state can be justified. That is of course consistent with the purpose of reducing the incidence of war among states.

Some scholars have tried to reach back to the famous *Caroline* incident and other nineteenth-century episodes in order to demonstrate that there is some broader customary international law right to use force against NSAs as such.[52] Such

---

Lubell, *supra* n. 6, 33–4. For an extensive list of authorities supporting the proposition, see Paust, *supra* n. 7.

[49] Dinstein, *supra* n. 18, 202, citing Y.Z. Blum, "State Response to Acts of Terrorism," 19 *German Yearbook of International Law* 223 (1976) 233; Tom Ruys, *"Armed Attack" and Article 51 of the UN Charter: Evolutions in Customary Low and Practice* (Cambridge: Cambridge University Press, 2010) 168–75; Gray, *supra* n. 22, 148; and Cassese, "The International Community's 'Legal' Response to Terrorism," 38 *International and Comparative Law Quarterly* (1989) 589, 596.

[50] See e.g., Gray, *supra* n. 22, 198–202; Dinstein, *supra* n. 18, 206–08; and Alston, *supra* n. 1, paras 40–1. Of course, there are many in the U.S. who reject this view. See, e.g. Paust, *supra* n. 6.

[51] Art. 2(4) of the United Nations Charter.

[52] See, e.g., Paust, *supra* n. 6. The *Caroline* incident involved a British attack in 1837 on a vessel being used by American sympathizers to supply a rebel force that had taken up arms against the British in Upper Canada. While Secretary of State Webster's formulation of the right to self-defense in correspondence relating to the incident has come to comprise the seminal articulation of the principle, as Dinstein points out the incident took place at a time when there was no prohibition on the use of force, and was in essence about preventing a measure short of war leading to the outbreak of full-blown hostilities. See Dinstein, *supra* n. 18, 274–5.

arguments are not persuasive. They constitute cherry-picking from a period when there were simply no effective legal constraints on the use of force in any event. The arguments ignore the customary principles actually in place at the time the Charter was concluded, in favor of principles from a far earlier period. Moreover, the suggestion that the Charter was intended to leave in operation customary rules permitting broader justifications for the use of force than those included in the treaty, flies in the face of the very purpose of the Charter system. Nor are such claims consistent with the drafting history of Article 51.[53] That the right of self-defense exists as a principle of customary international law, and that it does not exactly coincide with Article 51, is generally recognized.[54] But, as will be discussed below, custom does not permit the use of force against states that are not substantially involved in the armed attacks by NSAs. State attempts to justify the use of force against other states on the grounds that it is directed at NSAs, in the absence of evidence of the state's material support for the terrorist operations, were widely rejected and condemned prior to 9/11, and state practice remains mixed in the last decade.[55] While some scholars have more recently begun to posit that there may be a distinction between the concept of using force *against* a state and that of using force *within* a state,[56] that is not a distinction that is yet recognized in international law.

States may, of course, use force against a state to which it can attribute the armed attacks of an NSA. The key issue is identifying the criteria to be used in fixing a state with responsibility for the armed attacks of the NSA. In the U.N. General Assembly Resolution on the "Definition of Aggression," the attacks on a state by armed bands or irregular forces that were either sent "by or on behalf of" another state, or in which that state had a "substantial involvement," are defined as constituting acts of aggression by the supporting state.[57] In *Nicaragua v. U.S.A.*, the ICJ held this provision to constitute a principle of customary international law, but it also placed the bar rather high, holding that mere provision of arms and supplies by a state to an armed group that then launches armed attacks against a neighboring state does not itself constitute an armed attack triggering rights of self-defense

---

[53] Brownlie, *supra* n. 20, ch. 13, and Brownlie, "Legal Regulation of the Use of Force," 8 *International and Comparative Law Quarterly* (1959) 717–20. See also Dinstein, *supra* n. 18, 182–7. On the drafting history and interpretation of Art. 51, in addition to Brownlie, see e.g. Ruys, *supra* n. 49, 55–68; and Franck, *supra* n. 22, 45–50 (Kindle edition); also Nicholas Tsagourias, "Non-State Actors and the Use of Force" in J. d'Aspremont (ed.), *Participants in the International Legal System: Multiple Perspectives on Non-State Actors in International Law* (Routledge, 2011) 326, 328–9.

[54] On the overlap between art. 51 and customary international law, see *Nicaragua v. U.S.A.*, *supra* n. 28, paras 172–82 and 187–201.

[55] See Gray, *supra* n. 22, 195; Lubell, *supra* n. 6, 29–31; and Ruys, *supra* n. 49, 369–485.

[56] See, e.g. Dinstein, *supra* n. 18, 245–51 (making a claim for such use of force as a form of extra-territorial law enforcement), and Lubell, *supra* n. 6, 36–7. The classic example cited is the use of force by Israel in Lebanon, against the PLO in 1982, and against Hezobllah in 2006.

[57] U.N. General Assembly Resolution 3314, (XXIX) (1974), Annex, art. 3(g).

against that supplying state.[58] "Substantial involvement" required more than mere supply.[59]

In *Congo v. Uganda* the ICJ again took up the issue, examining whether Uganda's use of force against the DRC could be justified as self-defense in response to attacks by the ADF, an irregular guerrilla force alleged to be supported and supplied by the DRC. The Court held that while the ADF had indeed been responsible for armed attacks against Uganda,[60] there was insufficient evidence to establish that the ADF was acting on behalf of the DRC, or that the DRC was sufficiently involved in the operations, for the attacks to be attributed to the DRC. Thus, the justification of self-defense was not available to Uganda, and its use of force against the DRC was a violation of the prohibition on the use of force.[61]

The precise contours of the concept of "substantial involvement" in the operations of an NSA that has mounted armed attacks against another state remains somewhat unclear. It is nonetheless well established that there must be some significant nexus between the state and the NSA's actions in order to attribute those actions to the state for the purposes of justifying the use of force in self-defense. It is certainly more than a mere failure by the state to prevent the attacks or terminate the operations of the non-state entity.[62] And it is important in this context not to confuse responsibility in the sense meant in the law of state responsibility, with the narrower issue of liability for armed attacks sufficient to trigger the right of self-defense in *jus ad bellum*. It is a long-established principle under the law of state responsibility that a state has an obligation "not to allow knowingly its territory to be used for acts contrary to the rights of other states."[63] As Dinstein puts it, "it is irrefutable that the toleration by a State of activities by terrorists or armed bandits, directed against another country is

---

[58] *Nicaragua v. U.S.A.*, *supra* n. 25, paras 103; and 195. The dissenting judgments, particularly that of Judge Schwebel, disagreed strongly on the facts as to whether Nicaragua had been "substantially involved" in the operations of insurgents within El Salvador, and differed on where to draw the line between mere support and substantial involvement, but did not disagree with the principle. See opinion of Schwebel J., paras 154–71.

[59] Many scholars here discuss the court's articulation of an "effective control" test, and contrast it to the ICTY "overall control" test in Tädic, but it is submitted that the effective control test was applied for the purposes of determining responsibility for violations of IHL, and not the use of force. See *Nicaragua v. U.S.A.*, *supra* n. 25, paras 115 and 227.

[60] *Case Concerning Armed Activities of the Territories of the Congo (Democratic Republic of the Congo v. Uganda)* 2005 ICJ Reports *116*, paras 132–3.

[61] Ibid. paras 146–7. Though, in a cryptic paragraph ending this analysis, the court stated that it did not need to address the question of "whether and under what conditions contemporary international law provides for a right of self-defense against large-scale attacks by irregular forces." Ibid. para 147.

[62] For further discussion of factors that might be considered, see Lubell, *supra* n. 6, 36–8.

[63] *Corfu Channel (United Kingdom v. Albania)* (Merits), ICJ Reports (1949), 18–23.

unlawful."[64] But that such inability or unwillingness on the part of Utopia to prevent the operations of terrorists within its territory is unlawful, and that it may thus be legally responsible to those states injured by the terrorist activity, does not establish a justification for the use of force against Utopia. The criteria under the law of state responsibility are different, constituting a lower threshold for liability, than the conditions justifying the use of force in self-defense against another state for the actions of NSAs operating from within its territory.

It has been suggested by some that the gap between these two doctrines has narrowed since 9/11, particularly given the actions of the United States and others in using force against Afghanistan in response to those attacks.[65] But many of these arguments over-reach. For instance, the Security Council resolutions immediately following 9/11, which acknowledged the right of self-defense in response to such attacks, did not thereby create, or reflect the emergence of, a right to use force against NSAs as such.[66] The Security Council's resolutions can be interpreted as recognizing that the 9/11 attacks constituted armed attacks against the United States, justifying the exercise of the right of self-defense against the state deemed to be responsible for them, consistent with established principles of *jus ad bellum*.[67] The letters to the Security Council from both the United States and the United Kingdom, reporting on the use of force against Afghanistan as an exercise of self-defense in accordance with Article 51 of the Charter, specifically emphasized the close relationship between Al Qaeda and the Taliban regime, the level of support provided to Al Qaeda by the Taliban, and the regime's refusal to turn over Al Qaeda leadership for prosecution.[68] Taken together, the letters and the resolutions can be interpreted as grounding an exercise of self-defense against a state that was "substantially involved" in the operations that led to the 9/11 attacks.

---

[64] Dinstein, *supra* n. 18, 206.

[65] See, e.g. Dinstein, *supra* n. 18, 207; Christian J. Tams, "The Use of Force Against Terrorists," 20 *European Journal of International Law* (2009) 359.

[66] U.N. Security Council Resolutions 1368, September 12, 2001, U.N. Doc. S/RES/1368 (2001); and Resolution 1373, September 28, 2001, U.N. Doc. S/RES/1373 (2001).

[67] The preambles of both resolutions recognize "the inherent right of individual or collective self-defence in accordance with the Charter," while Res. 1368 condemned the terrorist attacks of 9/11 as a threat to peace and security; and Res. 1373 reaffirmed the duty of states to refrain from assisting or participating in terrorist acts against another state, and in its operable paragraphs also "decided" that states shall refrain from providing any such support. In short, the resolutions do not tie the acknowledgement of the right of self-defense to a use of force against terrorist groups *per se*, and they can indeed be interpreted as acknowledging the right of self-defense against states that are sufficiently responsible for supporting the terrorist activities leading to such attack. The ICJ interpreted these resolutions in this restrictive fashion in *Advisory Opinion on the Security Wall in the Palestine Occupied Territories*, para 139. See also, Gray, *supra* n. 22, 193–4, and 199; but see Dinstein, *supra* n. 18, 207; and Lubell, *supra* n. 6, 35.

[68] Gray, *supra* n. 22, 200.

Having said that, the events following 9/11 have made the situation somewhat more ambiguous.[69] There is unquestionably disagreement over the extent to which the invasion of Afghanistan itself can be explained by the traditional "substantial involvement" framework, or whether it represents state practice that has lowered the bar for use of force against states harboring terrorist groups. It may in any event constitute a *sui generis* case.[70] But while there may be some increased ambiguity, and possibly some shifting in the principles of attribution, there nonetheless continues to be a requirement to establish some significant level of involvement or support of the NSAs' operations in order to attribute their actions to the state for the purposes of justifying the use of force against that state in self-defense. And that necessary level of state involvement has not yet been reduced to a mere inability, or even unwillingness, to suppress the operations of the non-state entity.[71]

Aside from this central problem with the proposition that states can use force against NSAs as such (which is more accurately characterized as a problem of asserting a right to use force against states that are not sufficiently responsible for the actions of NSAs), there are other grounds for objecting to the proposition. These relate to the difficulties associated with determining the scope of any such principle. Precisely what kinds of NSA could be the subject of state use of force? What objective criteria could be used for defining the nature of the entity against which force is to be used? States, as legal entities, have relatively clear parameters in international law, and indeed traditionally were the only entities to have legal personality as subjects of international law. There are relatively clear criteria defining whether and when a state exists.[72] As such, to say that only states are subject to the *jus ad bellum* regime, and that the only use of force that can be justified under the doctrine of self-defense is that directed against states, is to provide some certainty and clear limits as to when force may be used. The use of force, as the modern successor to the nineteenth-century institution of war, is a *legal* concept, constituting a *legal* process between entities with *legal* personality. Terrorist organizations, like other criminal enterprises (or indeed non-criminal entities such as churches or not-for-profit organizations), are not international organizations that have any such certain legal identity. It is not possible to make them the subject of this legal process.[73] In the end the argument that states can use force against NSAs as such,

---

[69] See Ruys, *Article 51 of the UN Charter, supra* n. 53, 486–7, on the nature of ambiguity.

[70] See ibid. at 199.

[71] Ruys, *Article 51 of the UN Charter, supra* n. 53, 485–9. As Ratner puts it, "harboring" as articulated by the Bush administration at least means toleration, and that while the Bush doctrine on harboring may have been vague at the margins, it did not endorse the view that states "despite *bona fide* law enforcement, are unable to prevent or punish [terrorist actions], are harboring terrorists." Ratner, *supra* n. 10, 907–08, and fn. 15. But see Tsagourias, *supra* n. 53, 328–9, and Schmitt, *supra* n. 46, 5.

[72] Montevideo Convention on the Rights and Duties of States, 165 L.N.T.S. 19, signed December 26, 1933, art. 1.

[73] For a useful analysis of the structure of terrorist organizations and the extent to which they might be subject to the laws of war, see Matthew C. Waxman, "The Structure of Terrorism Threats

suggests that we are looking to the wrong legal regime for assistance in governing the activity in question, which has traditionally been dealt with as a criminal law matter.

It may be said in response that IHL has evolved such that states may, as a matter of law, become involved in armed conflict with armed groups that are not representatives of states—that is, in non-international armed conflict. And so, it will be said, in the context of the IHL regime, force is not limited to states or entities with formal legal personality. If IHL could adapt in this way, why not *jus ad bellum*? But one of the primary criteria for establishing that there is in fact a non-international armed conflict to which the IHL regime applies, is the requirement that the opposing force is an entity that is of sufficient organization and cohesion to constitute an armed group that can be identified by objectively verifiable criteria.[74] In other words, there are limits built into the system for determining the kinds of NSA that may become a participant in hostilities. If *jus ad bellum* were to similarly adapt, there would nonetheless have to be serious consideration of the criteria that would be applied in determining the kinds of NSAs that might be subject to the regime. The question of whether states can use force against non-state entities as such, as a matter of *jus ad bellum*, is both analogous to and relates in some fundamental ways to the question of whether transnational military operations against terrorist organizations can qualify as an armed conflict for the purposes of IHL—an issue that is no less controversial in the debate over targeted killing. The problem with suggestions that international law should develop in order that a state could use force against an ill-defined collection of amorphous terrorist organizations, and that the state would thereby be in a global armed conflict with such organizations under IHL, is that such developments would undermine the objective criteria for defining both the limits on the use of armed force, and the parameters of armed conflict.

In sum, the proposition that states can use force against NSAs as such, and thereby against states with little responsibility for the NSAs actions, is not consistent with the current *jus ad bellum* system, and moreover there are good reasons why this is so. It will be objected that this tends to create something of an asymmetry, as well as to give rise to something of a paradox—for while under the current law a terrorist attack may constitute an armed attack in *jus ad bellum* terms, a response to the attack is not permissible if there was not sufficient state complicity in the NSAs operation. Thus, so the objection would go, the *jus ad*

---

and the Laws of War," 20 *Duke Journal of Comparative & International Law* (2010) 429; on the nature of legal personality in international law, the seminal case is *Reparation for Injuries Suffered in the Service of the United Nations*, 1949 I.C.J. Reports 174.

[74] Cullen, *supra* n. 30, ch. 4; Melzer, *supra* n. 1, 254. Moir, *supra* n. 30, 489 (Kindle edition). *Additional Protocol II to the Geneva Conventions*, Art. 1(2).

bellum regime recognizes that NSAs can mount armed attacks, but then it insulates them from the responding use of force in self-defense.[75] There is thereby a recognition of a wrong, but the denial of a remedy. Of course, in response to this it must be pointed out that the current law exists precisely because the remedy sought would be inflicted on states that are not themselves guilty of the kind of wrong that legitimates the use of force against them. But even to this the detractors would argue that from a philosophical and moral perspective it might be entirely defensible to inflict a remedy on a not entirely blameless state. As between Utopia, the innocent victim of terrorist attacks, and Oceania, which while not sufficiently responsible for the attacks to justify a response in self-defense is not blameless, surely we should permit harm to the latter.[76] However, in response to this entire line of argument it has be emphasized that the modern *jus ad bellum* regime is not primarily grounded in such moral balancing, or even in a sense of justice, but rather is founded on the profound need to *prevent war* among states. Permitting the use of force against states that have not assisted terrorists acting from within their territory would create a different and far more serious asymmetry, which would distort and undermine the integrity of the *jus ad bellum* regime, and increase the risk of armed conflict among nations.

Such risk is not mere idle speculation. In Columbian raids against NSAs in Ecuador in 2006, and Turkish attacks on Kurds in Iraq in 2007–08, there was a serious risk of escalation. Consider the ramifications if India had characterized the Mumbai attack of 2008 as an "armed attack" justifying the use of force in self-defense against Lashkar-e-Taiba, quite independent of whether there was sufficient evidence to establish that its operations could be attributed to Pakistan. The use of force against the group within the territory of Pakistan would have nonetheless been viewed as an act of war by Pakistan, and there would have been a real risk of a full-blown armed conflict between nuclear powers.[77]

---

[75] My thanks to Jens Ohlin for bringing this paradox into stark relief.

[76] This is akin to the analysis of the rights of self-defense, of both the potential victim and a bystander, against the "psychotic aggressor"—i.e., an aggressor who is morally blameless, but who is nonetheless intent on attacking the victim. See, George P. Fletcher and Jens David Ohlin, *Defending Humanity: When Force is Justified and Why* (Oxford University Press, 2008) 107–09. However, states are not, of course, monolithic entities, and so in some contexts the analogies to domestic criminal law can break down. Here we are not really talking about the choice of harm to one of two moral entities, but missile strikes that most often result in the killing of innocent civilians on the one hand, versus the possible future deaths of undetermined civilians in the defending state if the strike is not undertaken. The German Constitutional Court considered such a dilemma in a challenge to aerial security law authorizing the military to shoot down an airliner to prevent it being employed as a weapon. The court held that the law was unconstitutional, a violation of the right to life and guarantee of human dignity. Federal Constitutional Court, *"Luftsicherheitsgesetz" Case*, January 11, 2005, BVerfG, 1BvR 357/05; and see discussion of the case in Melzer, *supra* n. 1, 16–18.

[77] Ruys, *Article 51 of the Charter, supra* n. 53, 488–9.

(b) Use of force in response to what attacks?

We turn next to the second question identified at the outset of this section, namely: in response to which armed attacks are the targeted killings being conducted? First, one has to establish whether the self-defense claimed is in respect of each individual strike, for the policy of strikes as a whole, or separately for the collective strikes against each of the various states. The proposition that each launch of hellfire missiles to implement a kill constitutes a separate act of self-defense is untenable.[78] Notwithstanding the lack of evidence from the U.S. government, there is little basis for believing that each act of terrorism that was being contemplated by all the persons so far targeted would by themselves have risen to the level of constituting an armed attack against the United States, had they been launched.[79] While the 9/11 attacks clearly reached the level of "armed attack," most of the other publicly disclosed plots that have been uncovered subsequently would not. Moreover, the killings have apparently taken place before the planned attacks had reached anything close to being imminent. Each use of force would thus have to be characterized as a preventative strike in response to a speculative future threat.

This brings us back to an aspect of self-defense doctrine that, as mentioned earlier, has become controversial in the post 9/11 era, namely the anticipatory and preventative use of force. It has been argued that the killings can be justified on the basis of a "preemptive" or "preventative" conception of self-defense,[80] a principle formalized in the so-called "Bush Doctrine."[81] This argument is used both in the context of the theory that each strike constitutes a separate act of self-defense, and arguments that all the targeted killings are part of a response to terrorist attacks generally, so it bears analysis. The claims to a right of "preventative" self-defense are, like the arguments that self-defense is not limited to the use of force against states, grounded in arguments that there are broader customary international law principles that co-exist with Article 51 of the U.N. Charter. These underlying arguments were addressed above.[82] In addition, however, these assertions as they relate to preventative use of force are also not consistent with state practice.[83] Preventative

---

[78] For an example of an individual strike approach, see e.g., Jenks, "Law from Above," 85 *North Dakota Law Review* (2010) 659–60.

[79] For one thing, many of those targeted have been low-level operatives. Eric Schmitt, "New C.I.A. Drone Attack Draws Rebuke from Pakistan," *The New York Times*, April 14, 2011, A10.

[80] Jenks, "Law from Above," *supra* n. 78, 656–60. It should be noted that there is no well-established usage of these terms—some commentators distinguish between "anticipatory" and "preemptive," others between "preemptive" (in a sense similar to "anticipatory," or in response to imminent attack) and "preventative." As Greenwood notes, therefore, some caution is necessary in interpreting the positions adopted by commentators: Greenwood, *supra* n. 22, 668. For a fuller analysis of this issue, see chapter 6 of this Volume, Claire Finkelstein, "Targeted Killing as Preemptive Action." In this Volume, ch. 6.

[81] The so-called Bush Doctrine, justifying the use of force to prevent the development of future threats, was formalized in the *National Security Strategy for the United States, 2002*.

[82] See text associated with *supra* nn. 52–57.

[83] Gray, *supra* n. 22, 118 and 160; Ruys, *Article 51 of the Charter*, *supra* n. 53, ch. 5.

self-defense as a concept was roundly rejected by the international community when it was floated as a justification for the invasion of Iraq in 2003, and it is not part of established customary international law.[84] The claims are inconsistent with the judgments of the ICJ.[85] The principle of preventative self-defense goes well beyond an anticipatory use of force against an imminent armed attack, and cannot satisfy the principle of necessity that is one of the foundations of the doctrine of self-defense.[86] And while these arguments in support of a preventive use of force have increased in the post 9/11 era, they do not represent the mainstream of scholarly opinion.[87] This might lead some to argue that the *jus ad bellum* regime is an anachronism that must adapt to the new realities of transnational terrorism if it is not to become irrelevant. But as will be argued below, that would be to increase the risk of war simply to address the threat of terrorism.

Returning to the issue of identifying the armed attacks, and the better argument that the targeted killing strikes collectively constitute a response to an armed attack or series of such attacks, the drone strikes might be characterized as an ongoing use of force in response to the armed attacks of 9/11. This was indeed the implication in Harold Koh's speech. The U.S. invasion of Afghanistan in November 2001 was a legitimate use of force in self-defense in response to those attacks, against the state from which the attacks had been launched, and which supported the terrorist entity that had planned and executed the attacks.[88] Within the context of the resulting international armed conflict, and even the non-international armed conflict that developed within Afghanistan in late 2002, military operations could

---

[84] Gray, *supra* n. 22, 160–6; Greenwood, *Essays on War, supra* n. 22, 675–6.

[85] The ICJ has continued to insist that an armed attack is a necessary pre-condition to the use of force in self-defense (though in *Nicaragua* it expressed "no view" on the validity of anticipating self-defense). See, e.g. Nicaragua v. U.S.A., *supra* n. 25, paras 194–95; *Oil platforms, supra* n. 25, paras 61–64: *Congo v. Uganda, supra* n.60, paras 143–47.

[86] Dinstein, *supra* n. 18, 185–91; Greenwood, *supra* n. 22, 672–5; Gray, *supra* n. 22, 117–19 and 160–6; and Lubell, *supra* n. 6, 55–7; see also, Peter Goldsmith, Attorney Gen., Testimony Before the U.K. Iraq Inquiry (January 27, 2010), available at <http://www.iraqinquiry.org.uk/transcripts/oralevidence-bydate/100127.aspx> accessed November 4, 2011.

[87] Caution has to be observed in distinguishing between arguments supporting "anticipatory self-defense," and the much broader "preventative" use of force inherent to the Bush Doctrine. But rejecting the broad customary international law view, see, e.g., Brownlie, *supra* n. 22, 24–5; Dinstein, *supra* n. 18, 175–87 and 247–9; Gray, *supra* n. 22, 117–19 and 160–6; Franck, *supra* n. 22, ch. 7 ("defending a narrow conception of anticipatory self-defense"); Ruys, *Article 51 of the charter, supra* n. 53, 255–305 and 318–42; Greenwood, *supra* n. 22, 672–7 and 699; Printer, *supra* n. 6, 337–44. *Contra*, see e.g. Paust, *supra* n. 6, 238–49; and more broadly, William C. Bradford, "The Duty to Defend Them: A Natural Law Justification for the Bush Doctrine of Preventative War," 79 *Notre Dame L. Rev.* 1365 (2004); Sean Murphy, "The Doctrine of Preemptive Self-Defense," 50 *Villanova Law Review* (2005) 699. There are more philosophical normative works that explore why the right of self-defense *ought* to be broader than that allowed by art. 51: see e.g. Michael Walzer, *Just and Unjust War,* 3rd edn (Basic Books, 2000), and more recently, Fletcher and Ohlin, *supra* n. 76.

[88] Dinstein, *supra* n. 18, 236–7; Gray, *supra* n. 22, 193–4 (though acknowledging broader claims); Greenwood, *supra* n. 22, 424–5.

be legitimately taken against members of Al Qaeda, so long as the conditions of IHL were satisfied. But aside from operations in Afghanistan, the theory that the ongoing policy of targeted killing against not only members of Al Qaeda and the Taliban, but also other terrorist or militant groups, operating in various countries other than Afghanistan, becomes increasingly difficult to justify as a response to the 9/11 attacks.[89] The arguments run into problems raised by issues we have already addressed regarding the entities against which the use of force is being directed. Many of the groups now being targeted had nothing to do with 9/11, and force is being used against countries that bear no responsibility for the 9/11 attacks.

For instance, the targeted killing policy is directed against a wide range of groups in Pakistan, including not only foreign "affiliates" of Al Qaeda such as the Harakat-ul Jihad Islami, but also various indigenous groups within the umbrella term "Pakistani Taliban," and yet other independent groups involved in Afghan operations such as the Haqanni Network.[90] In Yemen the attacks conducted by the military (soon to be augmented by a larger CIA drone campaign),[91] have included not only Al Qaeda in the Arabian Peninsula (which while sharing a name, and said to be "affiliated' with Al Qaeda, was initially quite independent from Al Qaeda, and its exact relationship remains the subject of debate),[92] but also other militant groups such a Islamic Jihad in Yemen, which are said to have "links" to Al Qaeda. In Somalia, the United States has targeted and killed members of al-Shabaab, a nationalist group that has little in common with Al Qaeda (though also said to have "links" to it).[93] While there is evidence of varying degrees of involvement by these groups in attacks on the United States, or U.S. forces in Afghanistan, there is no publicly disclosed evidence that any of these groups are directly connected to the attacks of 9/11, or integrated into Al Qaeda's attempts to continue such attacks. The drone strikes against them cannot, therefore, be justified as being an exercise of the right of self-defense in response to those attacks. Loose assertions of "affiliation" and "links" to Al Qaeda simply do not provide the basis for analogies

---

[89] Anderson, a strong advocate for the policy, recognizes this very problem in his argument that the U.S. needs to ground its justification in non-IHL principles: Anderson, *supra* n. 41, 357–8.

[90] For more on the nature of the various groups operating in the tribal areas of Western Pakistan, see Jayshree Bajoria, "Pakistan's New Generation of Terrorists," *Council for Foreign Relations*, available at <http://www.cfr.org/pakistan/pakistans-new-generation-terrorists/p15422#p1.> accessed November 4, 2011. John Rollins, "Al Qaeda and Affiliates: Historical Perspective, Global Presence, and Implications for U.S. Policy," *Congressional Research Service*, January 25, 2011; and also, the FATA Research Center reports on drone attacks, available at <http://www.frc.com.pk/linkc/otherContent/6#4>.

[91] Ken Dilanian, "CIA Plans Drone Campaign in Yemen," *Los Angeles Times*, June 14, 2011.

[92] See Jane Novak, "Arabian Peninsula al Qaeda Groups Merge," The Long War Journal, January 26, 2009, available at: <http://www.longwarjournal.org/archives/2009/01/arabian_peninsula_al.php> accessed November 4, 2011; and Alistair Harris, "Exploiting Grievances: Al Qaeda in the Arabian Peninsula," *A Carnegie Paper Series*, No. 111, May 2010.

[93] Greg Jaffe and Karen de Young, "U.S. Drone Targets Two Leaders of Somali Group Allied With Al Qaeda, Official Says," *The Washington Post*, June 29, 2011.

to alliances among states in common cause against an enemy in an international armed conflict.

Similarly problematic is the extent to which the strikes against members of these various groups constitute uses of force against the countries in which they are targeted, as already discussed. The 9/11 attacks were not launched from Yemen, Somalia, or Pakistan, nor did any of those countries have anything to do with those attacks. They have not been "substantially involved" in, or otherwise supported, subsequent attacks planned or launched by Al Qaeda (as distinct from other groups).[94] These states may now be the launching pad for other threats against the United States, but those subsequent threats posed by different groups cannot be simply rolled into the 9/11 justification for the use of armed force against these states. Thus, the use of force beyond the theatre of Afghanistan, against persons with only tenuous links to the perpetrators of 9/11, ten years after the fact, begins to look increasingly dubious under the justification of self-defense in response to 9/11 and the possible continuation of such attacks by Al Qaeda.

An alternative theory would be that the drone strikes in Pakistan are not acts of self-defense in response to 9/11, but rather are in response to the ongoing attacks against coalition forces engaged in the counter insurgency within Afghanistan by militant forces operating from within Pakistan. Indeed, the strikes launched against groups like the Haqqani network can only be credibly explained this way. But whether or not the United States can use force against Pakistan in an effort to prevent such cross-border attacks depends on factual determinations of whether the scale of such attacks rise to the level of being armed attacks against Afghanistan, thus justifying the use of force as an exercise of collective self-defense, and the extent to which Pakistan is sufficiently involved in supporting such attacks by the Haqqani network for purposes of attribution.

The analysis with respect to the killings in Yemen, however, would again be entirely different. The targeted killing of members of Al Qaeda in the Arabian Peninsula (AQAP) has nothing to do with the non-international armed conflict in Afghanistan, but is based on the assertion that the AQAP is engaging in a campaign of terrorist strikes against the United States. But to what theory of armed attack do the strikes against AQAP, and against Yemen, relate? Presumably such attempted attacks as that of the Christmas day bomber, and the printer cartridge bomb attempts.[95] The question then remains whether the terrorist strikes that were preempted rose to the level of constituting armed attacks giving rise to an independent right of self-defense; and whether their actions can be imputed to the state of Yemen for the purposes of justifying the use of force against that state. And a similar analysis would be required

---

[94] Yet many scholars tend to characterize the strikes in Yemen as being a response to 9/11. See, e.g., Printer, *supra* n. 6, 352–5.

[95] Harris, *supra* n. 92, 4.

for the strikes against al-Shabaab members in Somalia, where there has been even less evidence of imminent threats of armed attack against the United States.

Without going through the analysis for each of these scenarios in detail, we can nonetheless conclude that while it may be possible to justify the use of force against these states on the basis of self-defense, the crucial point is that the justificatory analysis is case-dependent. When the United States engages in strikes that constitute the use of force against each of these states, the claim of the right of self-defense must make specific reference to the armed attacks that justify it, how the group that is the object of the use of force is responsible for the attacks, and how the state in which the group is being targeted can itself be held legally responsible for the operations of that group so as to justify the use of force against the state. The problem with the current U.S. claim of self-defense is that it does none of this, but rather asserts a general right to use force against Al Qaeda, the Taliban, and any other groups associated with them; and against any country in which the members of such groups are located, not based on the state's actual involvement in the group's attacks, but merely on it being insufficiently willing or able to suppress the group's operations.[96]

It almost goes without saying that the principles of necessity and proportionality cannot be satisfied under such sweeping and general claims of self-defense. It is not possible to demonstrate that the use of force was strictly necessary when there has been no identification of the armed attacks in question, or explanation of how the specific groups being targeted pose the threat of imminent armed attacks, that can only be stopped through the use of force. Similarly, there can be no proportionality analysis without the identification of the harm that would be caused by specific attacks, against which one can compare the harm being inflicted by the defensive use of force.[97] Thus, in order to satisfy the necessity and proportionality principles that are at the core of the doctrine, the United States must provide the information required for such analysis.

In sum, the U.S. government's reliance upon self-defense as a justification for the targeted killing policy in countries such as Yemen, Somalia, and Pakistan, at least in the very general terms with which it has been asserted, is not consistent with the principles of self-defense under the *jus ad bellum* regime. This finding would suggest that, unless and until the administration offers more particularized support for this justification, the ongoing use of missile strikes for the purposes of killing suspected "terrorists," "militants" and "insurgents" in countries like Somalia, Yemen, and Pakistan, is a violation of the prohibition on the use of armed force.

---

[96] Moreover, the intention is to extend this general right of self-defense to any group that the U.S. determines to be "hostile." See *supra* n. 8.

[97] The ICJ has held, for instance, that the U.S. destruction of Iranian oil platforms in response to the mining of an American frigate was neither necessary nor proportionate, and thus not a justifiable use of force under the self-defense exception. *Oil Platforms Case*, para. 77.

Such a conclusion is troubling enough. But even more important in the long run is the potential harm this continued practice could cause to the *jus ad bellum* regime, and to the relationship between the *jus ad bellum* and IHL regimes, to which we turn next.

IV. The potential impact of the targeted killing policy on international law

The United States has been engaging in this practice of using drone-mounted missile systems to kill targeted individuals since at least 2002.[98] An increasing number of countries are developing drone capabilities, and other countries have employed different methods of targeted killing that constitute a use of force under *jus ad bellum*.[99] The evidence suggests that the United States intends to continue and indeed expand the program, and there is a growing body of scholarly literature that either defends the policy's legality, or advocates adjustment in international law to permit such action. There is, therefore, a real prospect that the practice could become more widespread, and that customary international law could begin to shift to reflect the principles implicit in the U.S. justification and in accordance with the rationales developed to support it.

Some of the implications of such an adjustment in the *jus ad bellum* regime are obvious from the foregoing analysis. As discussed, there would be a rejection of the narrow principle of self-defense in favor of something much closer to the Grotian concept of defensive war, encompassing punitive measures in response to past attacks and preventative uses of force to halt the development of future threats. The current conditions for a legitimate use of force in self-defense, namely the occurrence or imminence of an armed attack, necessity, and proportionality, would be significantly diluted or abandoned. Not only the doctrine of self-defense, but other aspects of the collective security system would be relaxed as well. Harkening back to Grotian notions of law enforcement constituting a just cause for war, the adjusted *jus ad bellum* regime would potentially permit the unilateral use of force against and within states for the purpose of attacking NSAs as such, in effect to enforce international law in jurisdictions that were incapable of doing so themselves.[100] This would not only further undermine the concept of self-defense, but would undermine the exclusive jurisdiction that the U.N. Security Council currently has to authorize the use of force for purposes of "law enforcement" under Chapter VII

---

[98] Walter Pincus, "Missile Strike Carried Out with Yemeni Cooperation," *Washington Post*, November 6, 2002, A10.

[99] Melzer, *supra* n. 1, ch. 2. An increasing number of countries are reported to be developing military drone capabilities: see Jenks, "Law from Above," *supra* n. 78, 654.

[100] See Dinstein for this argument in support of limited use of force against terrorists operating within the territory of another state: Dinstein, *supra* n. 18, 244–7.

of the Charter. Thus, both of the exceptions to the Article 2(4) prohibition on the use of force would be expanded.

In addition, however, the targeted killing policy threatens to create other holes in the *jus ad bellum* regime. This less obvious injury would arise from changes that would be similarly required of the IHL regime, and the resulting modifications to the fundamental relationship between the two regimes. These changes could lead to a complete severance of the remaining connection between the two regimes. Indeed, Ken Anderson, a scholar who has testified more than once on this subject before the U.S. Congress,[101] has advocated just such a position, suggesting that the United States should assert that its use of force against other states in the process of targeted killings, while justified by the right to self-defense, does not rise to such a level that it would trigger the existence of an international armed conflict or the operation of IHL principles.[102] If customary international law evolved along such lines, reverting to gradations in the types of use of force the change would destroy the unity of the system comprised of the *jus ad bellum* and IHL regimes, and there would be legal "black holes" in which states could use force without being subject to the limitations and conditions imposed by the IHL regime.

The structure of Harold Koh's two-pronged justification similarly implies a severance of this relationship between *jus ad bellum* and IHL, albeit in a different and even more troubling way. His policy justification consists of two apparently independent and alternative arguments—that the United States is in an armed conflict with Al Qaeda and associated groups; and that the actions are justified as an exercise of self-defense. The suggestion seems to be that the United States is entitled on *either basis* to use armed force not just against the individuals targeted, but also against states in which the terrorist members are located. In other words, the first prong of the argument is that the use of force against another sovereign state, for the purposes of targeting Al Qaeda members, is justified by the existence of an armed conflict with Al Qaeda. If this is indeed what is intended by the policy justification, it represents an extraordinary move, not just because it purports to create a new category of armed conflict (that is, a "transnational" armed conflict without geographic limitation),[103] but because it also suggests that there need be no *jus ad bellum* justification at all for a use of force against another state. Rather, the implication of Koh's rationale is that the existence of an armed conflict under IHL can by itself provide grounds for exemption from the prohibition against the threat or use of force under the *jus ad bellum* regime.

---

[101] See Kenneth Anderson, Written Testimony to U.S. House of Representatives Committee on Oversight and Government Reform, Subcommittee on National Security and Foreign Policy, Subcommittee Hearing "Drones II," April 26, 2010; and Subcommittee Hearing "Rise of the Drones: Unmanned Systems and the Future of War," March 18, 2010.

[102] Anderson, *supra* n. 41, 347–8 and 356–7.

[103] See *supra* n. 35.

This interpretation of the justifications cannot be pressed too far on the basis of the language of Mr. Koh's speech alone, which he hastened to explain at the time was not a legal opinion.[104] The two justifications could be explained as being supplementary rather than independent and alternative in nature. But the conduct of the United States in the prosecution of the policy would appear to confirm that it is based on these two independent justifications.[105] The strikes against groups and states unrelated to the 9/11 attacks could be explained in part by the novel idea that force can be used against NSAs as such, wherever they may be situated. But even assuming some sort of strict liability for states in which guilty NSAs are found, that explanation still does not entirely account for the failure to tie the use of force against the different groups to specific armed attacks launched by each such group. This suggests that the United States is also relying quite independently on the argument that it is engaged in an armed conflict with all of these groups, and that the existence of such an armed conflict provides an independent justification for the use of force against the states in which the groups may be operating.

While the initial use of force in *jus ad bellum* terms is currently understood to bring into existence an international armed conflict and trigger the operation of IHL, the changes suggested by the policy would turn this on its head, by permitting the alleged existence of a "transnational" armed conflict to justify the initial use of force against third states. Whereas the two regimes currently operate as two components of an overall legal system relating to war, with one regime governing the use of force and the other the conduct of hostilities in the resulting armed conflict, the move attempted by the U.S. policy would terminate these independent but inter-related roles within a single system, and expand the role and scope of IHL to essentially replace aspects of the *jus ad bellum* regime. This would not only radically erode the *jus ad bellum* regime's control over the state use of force, but it could potentially undermine the core idea that war, or in more modern terms the use of force and armed conflict, constitutes a legal state that triggers the operation of special laws that govern the various aspects of the phenomenon. There is a risk of return to a pre-Grotian perspective in which "war" was simply a term used to describe certain kinds of organized violence, rather than constituting a legal

---

[104] As this Volume was going to press, evidence emerged that there continues to be a debate within the government on the relationship between the two justifications: Charlie Savage, "At White House, Weighing the Limits of Terror Fight," *The New York Times*, September 16, 2011, A1; and Marty Lederman, "John Brennan Speech on Obama Administration Antiterrorism Policies and Practices," *Opinio Juris*, September 16, 2011, available at <http://opiniojuris.org/2011/09/16/john-brennan-speech-on-obama-administration-antiterrorism-policies-and-practices/> accessed November 4, 2011. To his credit, Ken Anderson has, in his testimony before Congress and his scholarship, argued that the U.S. government ought to develop and clearly articulate a much more detailed legal justification for its policy in this area. See *supra* nn. 100–101.

[105] Anderson also interprets U.S. policy as being based on alternative arguments. Anderson, *supra* n. 41, 365–6; as does the Pentagon: Charlie Savage, "At White House, Weighing the Limits of Terror Fight," *The New York Times*, September 16, 2011, A1.

institution characterized by a coherent system of laws designed to govern and constrain all aspects of its operation.

There is a tendency in the U.S. approach to the so-called "global war on terror" to cherry-pick principles of the laws of war and to apply them in ways and in circumstances that are inconsistent with the very criteria within that legal system that determine when and how it is to operate. This reflects a certain disdain for the idea that the laws of war constitute an internally coherent system of law.[106] In short, the advocated changes to the *jus ad bellum* regime and to the relationship between it and the IHL regime, and thus to the laws of war system as a whole,[107] would constitute marked departures from the trajectory the system has been on during its development over the past century, and would be a repudiation of deliberate decisions that were made in creating the U.N. system after the Second World War.[108]

The premise of my argument is not that any return to past principles is inherently regressive. A rejection of recent innovations in favor of certain past practices might be attractive to some in the face of new transnational threats. The argument here is not even to deny the idea that the international law system may have to adapt to respond to the transnational terrorist threat. The point, rather, is that the kind of changes to the international law system that are implicit in the targeted killing policy, and which are advocated by its supporters, would serve to radically reduce the limitations and constraints on the use of force by states against states. The modern principles that are being abandoned were created for the purpose of limiting the use of force and thus reducing the incidence of armed conflict among nations. The rejection of those ideas and a return to older concepts relating to the law of war would restore aspects of a system in which war was a legitimate tool of statecraft, and international armed conflict was thus far more frequent and widespread.[109]

The entire debate on targeted killing is so narrowly focused on the particular problems posed by transnational terrorist threats, and how to manipulate the legal limitations that tend to frustrate some of the desired policy choices, that there is insufficient reflection on the broader context, and the consequences that proposed changes to the legal constraints would have on the wider legal system of which they are a part. It may serve the immediate requirements of the American government, in order to legitimize the killing of AQAP members in Yemen, to expand the concept of self-defense, and to suggest that states can use force on the basis of a putative "transnational" armed conflict with NSAs. The problem is that the *jus ad bellum*

---

[106] This propensity is similarly seen in the detention and military commission policies.

[107] See *supra* n. 38.

[108] On the debate leading to these "decisions," see Neff, *supra* n. 13, 335–40.

[109] See the Correlates of War Project—J. David Singer and Melvin Small, *Resort to Arms: International and Civil Wars*, 1816–1980, 2nd edn (Sage, 1982).

regime applies to all state use of force, and it is not being adjusted in some tailored way to deal with terrorism alone. If the doctrine of self-defense is expanded to include preventative and punitive elements, it will be so expanded for all *jus ad bellum* purposes. The expanded doctrine of self-defense will not only justify the use of force to kill individual terrorists alleged to be plotting future attacks, but to strike the military facilities of states suspected of preparing for future aggression. If the threshold for use of force against states "harboring" NSAs is significantly reduced, the gap between state responsibility and the criteria for use of force will be reduced for all purposes. If the relationship between *jus ad bellum* and IHL is severed or altered, so as to create justifications for the use of force that are entirely independent of the *jus ad bellum* regime, then states will be entitled to use force against other states under the pretext of self-proclaimed armed conflict with NSAs generally.

We may think about each of these innovations as being related specifically to operations against terrorist groups that have been responsible for heinous attacks, and applied to states that have proven uniquely unwilling or unable to take the actions necessary to deal with the terrorists operating within their territory. But no clear criteria or qualifications are in fact tied to the modifications that are being advanced by the targeted killing policy. Relaxing the current legal constraints on the use of force and introducing new but poorly defined standards, will open up opportunities for states to use force against other states for reasons that have nothing to do with anti-terrorist objectives. Along the lines that Jeremy Waldron argues in chapter 4 in this volume,[110] more careful thought ought to be given to the general norms that we are at risk of developing in the interest of justifying the very specific targeted killing policy. Ultimately, war between nations is a far greater threat, and is a potential source of so much more human suffering than the danger posed by transnational terrorism. This is not to trivialize the risks that terrorism represents, particularly in an age when Al Qaeda and others have sought nuclear weapons. But we must be careful not to undermine the system designed to constrain the use of force and reduce the incidence of international armed conflict, in order to address a threat that is much less serious in the grand scheme of things.

---

[110] Jeremy Waldron, "In Justifying Targeted Killing with a Neutral Principle?," in this Volume, ch. 4.

9

IMMINENCE IN JUSTIFIED TARGETED KILLING

Russell Christopher

I. Introduction

Targeted killing is not new. Construed most broadly, the practice constitutes the killing of an individual previously identified as a suitable candidate for killing. But surely most killings are targeted killings as such. Construed somewhat more narrowly, the killing follows the identification of the target by an appreciable period of time. But this construction is still too broad—it is nothing more than a premeditated or deliberated killing. Consider the following examples. An Allied forces military sniper killing General Rommel (pursuant to a specific order) during the Second World War,[1] a state executing a prisoner on death row, a police officer shooting a bank robber who has taken hostages and threatened to kill them after negotiations fail, the killing of an outlaw in the old Wild West after a territory posts the proclamation, "Wanted: Dead or Alive," or a twice-victimized homeowner killing a robber after initially threatening, "Next time you break into my house I will kill you." These too would be targeted killings. But these types of killings, whether justified or unjustified, easily fit within existing paradigms. They may be readily analyzed as justified or unjustified within the paradigms of war, law enforcement or self-defense.[2] They do not pose the special, new problems of a certain type of targeted killing—the killing by a state of a suspected terrorist physically located

---

[1] For another example, see P. Montague, "Defending Defensive Targeted Killings" in this Volume, ch. 10. On April 18th, American fighter planes located and shot down the plane in which Yamamoto was flying.

[2] *See*, e.g., J.P. Paust, "Self-Defense Targetings of Non-state Actors and Permissibility of U.S. Use of Drones in Pakistan," 19 *Journal of Transnational Law & Policy* (2010) 237, 279–80 (distinguishing between the three paradigms in their application to targeted killings).

outside that state.[3] The moral and legal justification for such killings is unclear and the subject of much debate.

Compounding the difficulty in justifying such killings are the following features present in some, but not all, targeted killings: (i) the state perpetrating the killing and the state where the killing occurs are not formally at war; (ii) the actor perpetrating the killing on behalf of a state may neither be wearing a military uniform nor be a member of the military,[4] nor even be an employee of the state;[5] (iii) the targeted victim may neither be a member of another state's military nor wearing a military uniform; (iv) the terrorist group in which the targeted victim is a member, and which may supply the rationale for the individual to be targeted for killing, is not a sovereign state; (v) neither the state in which the victim is killed nor the state in which the victim is a citizen explicitly consents to the killing; (vi) the killing occurs without the authorization of some internationally recognized legal body like the United Nations or the International Criminal Court; (vii) the killing is effected by means involving sophisticated technology such as Predator drones[6] or other unmanned aircraft and/or the killer is at a significant physical and psychological distance from the victim at the time of the killing;[7] (viii) perhaps due to the means of killing in (vii), the victim is killed without any opportunity to surrender and be subject to due process of law,[8] or perhaps, despite having surrendered; (ix) perhaps due to the means of killing in (vii), the risk of mistaken targeted killings of innocents[9] as well as innocent bystanders is unacceptably high;[10] and (x) the victim is neither presently engaging nor even about to engage in the very sort of conduct that has identified him

---

[3] *See*, e.g., F.R. Teson, "Targeted Killing in War and Peace: A Philosophical Analysis," in the Volume, ch. 15, 403. (defining targeted killing as a type of assassination that is sanctioned by the state; defining assassination as "the extrajudicial intentional killing of a named person for a public purpose").

[4] *See*, e.g., C. Finkelstein, "Targeted Killing as Preemptive Action," in this Volume ch. 1.

[5] *See* K.H. Govern, "Operation Neptune Spear: Was Killing Bin Laden a Legitimate Military Objective?," in this Volume, ch. 13.

[6] J. Jaffer, "Op-Ed," *Los Angeles Times*, April 6, 2011 (noting that John Rizzo, a lawyer for the CIA responsible for approving persons to be placed on the targeted killing list, states that "[t]he Predator is the weapon of choice").

[7] *See*, e.g., M.E. O'Connell, "Unlawful Killing with Combat Drones: A Case Study of Pakistan, 2004–2009," available at <http://papers.ssrn.com/abstract=1501144>, 8–9.

[8] *See*, e.g., Finkelstein, *supra* n. 4; M.L. Gross, "Assassination and Targeted Killing: Law Enforcement, Execution or Self-Defence?," 23 *Journal of Applied Philosophy* (2006) 323, 324–35.

[9] *See*, e.g., J. McMahan, "Targeted Killing: Murder, Combat or Law Enforcement?," in this Volume, at ch. 5.

[10] G.S. McNeal, Are Targeted Killings Unlawful? A Case Study in Empirical Claims Without Empirical Evidence, in this Volume ch. 12; D. Kilcullen and A.M. Exum, "Death From Above, Outrage Down Below," *New York Times*, March 17, 2009 (claiming that the ratio of unintended killings to intended killings was 50:1 involving Predator drone targeted killings of suspected terrorists).

as a suitable candidate for a targeted killing.[11] The presence of all of these features is not necessary for the justification of targeted killing to be unclear. Neither is the presence of any specific individual feature. But the presence of one or more of these features is sufficient.

The presence of some of these features makes targeted killing resist easy classification within existing possible approaches. Features (i)–(vii) and possibly (ix) raise problems for fitting the targeted killings of terrorists easily within a justification under the laws of war. At least some of those features problematic under a law of war approach, however, would not be problematic under a law enforcement model. But features (viii)–(ix) and possibly (vi) do raise difficulties under a law enforcement model. In turn, at least some of the features rendering such targeted killings problematic under either a laws of war or law enforcement approach would not be problematic under a self-defense approach. But feature (x)—that the victim is neither presently involved in terrorist activities nor even about to be involved in terrorist activities at the time of the killing—does make the self-defense approach problematic.

As a result, targeted killings of terrorists do not fit easily within any of these paradigms. Terrorists are neither legally recognized combatants nor mere civilians, nor domestic criminals, nor ordinary aggressors.[12] If such targeted killings are to be justified, either they must be demonstrated to somehow fit within the existing paradigms or a new, more appropriate, paradigm must be developed.[13] This chapter focuses on how a principal requirement of the self-defense paradigm, that bars targeted killing of terrorists, should be rejected. With this requirement removed, targeted killings of terrorists possibly may fit within the self-defense approach.

Under the self-defense approach, the individual targeted for killing is claimed to be an aggressor against the state perpetrating the killing and that the killing is in self-defense of the state. A fundamental condition for justified self-defense is that the aggressor poses an unlawful imminent threat.[14] This is known as the imminence

---

[11] C. Martin, "Going Medieval: Targeted Killing, Self-Defense and the *Jus ad Bellum* Regime" in this Volume ch. 8 (arguing that many, if not all, instances of targeted killing have "not been in response to or in anticipation of an imminent act [of aggression]").

[12] E.g., J.D. Ohlin, "Targeting Co-belligerents," in this Volume, ch. 2 (noting that "the terrorist is a non-state actor who falls between these two categories [of lawful combatant and domestic criminal]"); McMahan, "Targeted Killing: Murder, Combat or Law Enforcement?," in this volume, ch. 5 155 ("Because terrorists are thus intermediate between combatants and ordinary criminals, neither the conventional norms of war nor the norms of police action are well suited to the governance of anti-terrorist action.").

[13] McMahan, "Targeted Killing: Murder, Combat or Law Enforcement?," in this volume, ch. 5.

[14] G. P. Fletcher and J. D. Ohlin, *Defending Humanity: When Force is Justified and Why* (Oxford University Press, 2008) 90–1 (identifying the imminence of the threatened aggression as one of the six fundamental requirements for justified self-defense); D. Rodin, *War & Self-Defense* (Oxford University Press, 2002) 41 (characterizing imminence as one of the three principal limitations on

requirement. The target of justified self-defense force must be either presently aggressing or temporally about to aggress. In addition to this temporal component of the imminence requirement, some formulations of self-defense also require that the claimed aggressor manifest the future aggression by some action or conduct. This might be termed the action component.

Perhaps the principal difficulty with justifying targeted killings of terrorists under a self-defense approach is the imminence requirement. Typically, the victim of the targeted killing is neither presently aggressing nor is temporally about to aggress, nor is manifesting any sign of being about to aggress. For example, a suspected terrorist targeted for a Predator drone strike might be killed while asleep or eating dinner or otherwise not posing an imminent threat of unlawful aggression at the time of the strike. As a result, critics of targeted killings argue that because the imminence requirement is not satisfied, targeted killings cannot be understood, as permissible or justified self-defense. If targeted killings are to be understood as permissible or justified self-defense, either targeted killings must be shown to somehow satisfy the imminence requirement or the validity of the imminence requirement must be placed in doubt. Demonstrating the invalidity of the imminence requirement sets the stage for consideration of alternative standards, other than imminence, that targeted killings might satisfy.

Some argue that targeted killings of terrorists do satisfy the imminence requirement. The strategy is to claim that the terrorists represent continuous and ongoing threats of unlawful aggression. Despite their failure to be either presently aggressing or temporally about to aggress, their very *status* as terrorists qualifies as the *conduct* of posing an imminent threat.[15] As Jeff McMahan argues, even while terrorists are sleeping or eating dinner or doing some other innocuous activity, they do not lose their status as terrorists and thus are continuously and invariably constituting imminent threats.[16] The argument finds support in the analogy to the killing of soldiers during war. Soldiers are subject to being permissibly killed whether in the heat of battle or while they are sleeping. So also, the argument contends, are terrorists. But the obvious difference between terrorists and soldiers, which McMahan addresses, is that the killing of soldiers during a war easily fits within the laws of war model. But the killing of terrorists does not.[17]

---

the right of self-defense); M. Walzer, *Just and Unjust Wars*, 3rd edn (Basic Books, 1977) 74 ("Both individuals and states can rightfully defend themselves against violence that is imminent but not actual; they can fire the first shots if they know themselves about to be attacked.").

  [15] For a discussion of the fundamental distinction between status and conduct, see M. Maxwell, "Rebutting the Civilian Presumption: Playing Whack-A-Mole Without a Mallet?" in this Volume, ch. 1.

  [16] McMahan, "Targeted Killing: Murder, Combat or Law Enforcement?," in this Volume, ch. 5.

  [17] Ibid.

This chapter takes the other tack. The targeted killing of terrorists fails to satisfy the imminence requirement of self-defense. But this chapter argues that the imminence requirement itself is problematic and should be abandoned. If this argument is successful, the principal obstacle to justifying targeted killings under the self-defense approach might be circumvented. But whether targeted killings are ultimately permissible or justifiable under the self-defense model or some other model is beyond the scope of this chapter. This chapter only argues against the principal impediment to justifying targeted killings under self-defense—the imminence requirement.

Demonstrating the invalidity of the imminence requirement lays the foundation for consideration of alternative standards. Perhaps the principal alternative standard is whether defensive force is necessary to prevent the aggression;[18] that is, rather than focusing on the imminence of the aggression, the standard focuses on the necessity of the defensive response to the (imminent or non-imminent) aggression. In addition to necessity, there is another alternative discussed in this volume. Phillip Montague defends an account of self-defense based on the inevitability of aggression, whether imminent or non-imminent.[19] Under his account, targeted killing of a terrorist or one who aids a terrorist may be permissible to prevent inevitable terrorist acts. One possible difficulty with this account is the epistemic hurdle of determining whether a terrorist act is truly inevitable.

While a number of commentators have criticized the imminence requirement, these criticisms have not been sufficient to alter the traditional and consensus view of the importance of the imminence requirement. This chapter will attempt to advance some new arguments against, and rebut some existing arguments in favor of, the imminence requirement. The principal focus is to show why the imminence requirement is problematic, rather than to advance a preferable standard.

II. A parable of imminence

It is often said that our law of self-defense reflects and is guided by the use of force and violence in the western frontier. Imagine the archetypal scenario of self-defense that has been endlessly portrayed in television and film Westerns. The bad guy Gunslinger, who enjoys the reputation of being the fastest gun in the territory, is walking down a dusty street. He sees the good guy humble homesteading

---

[18] *See infra* n. 26 and accompanying text; *see also,* e.g., P. Robinson, *Criminal Law Defenses* (St Paul, Minnesota: West, 1984) Vol. II, 78 ("If a threatened harm is such that it cannot be avoided if the intended victim waits until the last moment, the principle of self-defense must permit him to act earlier—as early as is required to defend himself effectively."); L. Alexander, "A Unified Excuse of Preemptive Self-Protection," 74 *Notre Dame Law Review* (1999) 1475, 1494 ("It shall be a defense to any crime that the defendant committed it to avoid a harm to himself or others, and a 'person of reasonable firmness' in the defendant's situation would have committed the crime.").

[19] Montague, *supra* n. 1.

Sheepherder (or peace-loving sheriff) and calls him out. Sheepherder says, "I don't want any trouble." Gunslinger replies, "Well, you just might get some." Each have their hands at their sides poised above each holstered gun. Invariably, Sheepherder never makes the first move for his guns. He waits for Gunslinger to make the first move. Viewers of this archetypal scenario need not be criminal law scholars to realize that the good guy must never draw first; it is the bad guy that always draws first. In order to be the good guy, one must wait for the other to make the first move, the first sign of aggression. Only after the bad guy makes a move for his guns may the good guy reach for, draw, and fire his guns.

Our current law of self-defense incorporates the implicit messages of this Hollywood staple of the climactic scene in a Western. In order to be justified in self-defense against the wrongful force of an unlawful aggressor, one must wait until the unlawful aggression is imminent. And imminence, in this scenario, is signaled by reaching for and drawing one's gun. Were the good guy to reach for, draw, and fire his gun first, he would not be the good guy. He would be the unlawful aggressor whose force would not be justified in self-defense. And this is true despite the good guy (and all the townspeople lining the street) knowing that the bad guy has the wrongful intent to kill him and will eventually draw and fire his gun, thereby killing him. These are the immutable conventions of the scenario as well as our law of self-defense. So Sheepherder waits. Finally, after some cat-and-mouse dialogue in which Gunslinger taunts and toys with Sheepherder, Gunslinger reaches for his gun. The camera cuts to Sheepherder subsequently reaching for his gun. Gunslinger now has his gun in his hand, drawing it out of his holster, and raising it. Subsequently, we see Sheepherder do the same. Gunslinger starts to level the gun at Sheepherder. Next, Sheepherder begins to level his gun at Gunslinger.

At this point, the suspense is excruciating. Surely, Sheepherder will be killed. Gunslinger is always one step ahead. By the time that Sheepherder reaches for his gun, Gunslinger already has his in his hand; by the time that Sheepherder has his gun in hand, Gunslinger is already raising it to shoot, etc. How will Sheepherder ever catch up and be able to shoot his gun first and kill Gunslinger and save the day?

The scenario calls to mind Zeno's paradox of the tortoise and the hare.[20] Zeno challenged us to explain how the much faster hare could ever catch up with the much slower tortoise if the tortoise had a head start in a race. By the time the hare reaches the starting place of the tortoise, the tortoise has moved ahead, say five feet. And by the time the hare travels the five feet to reach the tortoise's previous position, the tortoise has again moved on ahead. Though the hare gets closer and closer, Zeno claimed that, paradoxically, the faster hare could never overtake the slower tortoise.

---

[20] For an account of the paradox, see R.M. Sainsbury, *Paradoxes* (Cambridge University Press, 1993) 21–2.

But through the magic of the Hollywood ending, somehow Sheepherder does overcome Gunslinger's head start and Sheepherder fires his gun first and Gunslinger falls into a heap on the street. Not only does good triumph over evil, but good does so in a way that does not undermine, but only confirms, our prior view as to who is the good guy and who is the bad guy. Good not only triumphs over evil, but emerges from the confrontation with clean hands, untainted by the brush with evil.

The magical Hollywood ending supplies a twist on Zeno's paradox. Here the magical Hollywood ending depicts how the good tortoise (Sheepherder) gives the bad hare (Gunslinger) a head start and still beats the bad hare in the race. The magical Hollywood ending goes Zeno's paradox one better: how can the tortoise give the hare a head start and still beat the hare in the race?

The imminence requirement of our current law of self-defense shares much with the conventions of the magical Hollywood ending. The good guy must give the bad guy a head start. In order to prevail against a bad guy tortoise, the good guy must be a hare. In order to prevail against a bad guy hare, the good guy must be an even faster hare.

And the imminence requirement of our current law of self-defense is just as unrealistic as the magical Hollywood ending. Not all victims of aggression will be hares in tortoise clothing or faster hares in ordinary hare clothing. Not all humble, peaceful sheepherding homesteaders will be faster than the professional gunslinger. That is, not all victims of aggression will be able to employ force faster than their aggressor. Not all such victims will be able to overcome the head start that the law of imminence provides to the aggressor. Not all such victims will be able to overcome the handicap that the law of imminence imposes on the self-defender.

Consider the effect of the imminence requirement in either allowing or precluding effective self-defense force as a function of the comparative speed in the employment of force by the aggressor and self-defender:

(i) self-defender is substantially slower than aggressor
—NO RIGHT OF EFFECTIVE SELF-DEFENSE

(ii) self-defender is slightly slower than aggressor
—NO RIGHT OF EFFECTIVE SELF-DEFENSE

(iii) self-defender is the same as aggressor
—NO RIGHT OF EFFECTIVE SELF-DEFENSE

(iv) self-defender is slightly faster than aggressor
—NO RIGHT OF EFFECTIVE SELF-DEFENSE[21]

---

[21] This assumes that despite the slight comparative advantage of speed in the employment of force that the self-defender enjoys, it is still not sufficient to overcome the head start that the imminence requirement provides to the slightly slower aggressor. As a result, there is no effective right of self-defense. But if the slight comparative advantage of speed did suffice to overcome the head start that the imminence requirement provides to the aggressor, then there would be an effective right of

(v) self-defender is substantially faster than aggressor[22]
   —RIGHT OF EFFECTIVE SELF-DEFENSE.

As we can see from the above categories, the imminence requirement only allows an effective right of self-defense when the self-defender is substantially faster than the aggressor and sufficiently so that the self-defender's speed can overcome the head start or advantage that the imminence requirement provides to the aggressor. But in all the other possible categories, four out of the five above, the self-defender lacks an effective right of self-defense. The imminence requirement bars an effective right of self-defense.

Moreover, even an effective right of self-defense in only one of the above five categories perhaps overstates the scope of an effective right of self-defense. Realistically, category (v) will represent significantly less than 20 per cent of the cases. There are perhaps few aggressors who engage in unlawful aggression against victims who can employ force appreciably faster than their aggressor. Most aggressors will avoid such victims and instead select the comparatively more vulnerable victims depicted in categories (i)–(iv).

While the imminence requirement does not provide an effective right of self-defense to many victims of aggression, it should. While the imminence requirement seems to favor only the quick and the agile, it should not. The law of self-defense should protect not only those who may employ force faster than their aggressor, but less physically adept victims as well. The right of effective self-defense should not be a function of one's physical advantages. The fast as well as the slow should equally enjoy a right of effective self-defense. One's right to effective self-defense should not be a function of one's physical attributes. The law of self-defense should not be only for the hare but for the tortoise as well.

If anything, the law of self-defense, incorporating an imminence requirement, has it backwards. It favors the fleet afoot over the slow and cumbersome. Rather than enhancing the advantages already enjoyed by the physically blessed, the law of self-defense should be seeking to neutralize those advantages. Any bias in the law of self-defense should favor the less physically advantaged, not the more physically advantaged. But even if the law of self-defense fails to neutralize the physical advantages of the fleet over the slow, it should not further handicap the already less physically advantaged. And this applies regardless of the source of the aggression— gunslingers, strangers in dark alleys, countries pointing missiles at one another, or nimble, elusive terrorists.

---

self-defense. The upshot is that where the self-defender's speed advantage is only slight, there would not clearly be an effective right of self-defense.

[22] That is, a self-defender who employs force substantially faster than the aggressor and that is sufficiently faster to overcome the head start or advantage that the imminence requirement grants to the unlawful aggressor.

III. Preliminary considerations

What is the point of a law of self-defense granting a right of self-defense when that right only attaches after it is too late to effectively employ? And what is the point of requiring a self-defender to wait until the aggressor physically manifests or signals her imminent aggression by some action if such aggressor's force is temporally imminent, inevitable, and defensive force is necessary now?

Defenders of the imminence requirement answer these questions by making two central claims. First, the right to self-defense is not a right to effective self-defense, and second, imminence has important independent substantive and conceptual significance. Before we examine more closely the specific arguments on behalf of the imminence requirement, let us preliminarily test our commitment to these claims.

(a) Right of self-defense v. right of effective self-defense

To test our commitment to the first claim, suppose that the imminence requirement forced self-defenders to wait so long before using defensive force that it was *always* ineffective. By the time that self-defenders were permitted to prepare to employ force against their aggressors, the self-defenders were already battered or dead. As a result, aggressors *always* triumphed over their victims. The victims, of course, had a right of self-defense, but one that was *never* effective. Would we not reconsider the imminence requirement? If yes, then the right to self-defense at least somewhat entails a right to effective self-defense. If no, what then is the purpose of a right of self-defense? The purpose would have to be something other than to protect victims from unlawful aggression.

This suggests that the law of self-defense attempts to strike a balance between protecting the rights of victims of possible aggression and protecting possible aggressors from unnecessary defensive force. Thus, a law of self-defense that overly protected aggressors at the expense of self-defenders would be just as wrong as a law of self-defense that overly protected self-defenders at the expense of aggressors. As a result, considerations of the effectiveness of the right of self-defense are relevant considerations in setting the parameters and contours of the law of self-defense. The law of self-defense does entail a right to at least somewhat effective self-defense.

That the right of self-defense includes a right to effective self-defense also finds support by considering why the law of self-defense does not require the more stringent trigger of present aggression. Rather than allowing self-defense force when aggression is merely imminent, we might require aggression to be actually present. Presumably we reject this standard because it would not allow self-defense force until it was too late to be effective. As a result, the right to effective self-defense is implicitly part of the very rationale for the imminence requirement. If affording an opportunity for effective self-defense was an irrelevant consideration in determining the standards and principles of justified self-defense, as some defenders of the imminence requirement maintain, then the very rationale for the imminence requirement is undermined.

This also suggests that our law of self-defense is not written in stone and may evolve as the times and technologies change. Over time, the tactics and weapons employed by aggressors has evolved from sticks and stones, and knives and guns, that are employed at close range and have a limited capacity to kill in great numbers, to nuclear missiles and weapons of mass destruction that may be employed from a great distance and have the capacity to kill millions. In addition, we now face the prospect of nimble, elusive non-state actors gaining access to the sort of advanced weapons which once only state actors could have employed and which these non-state actors can employ with greater surprise and camouflage. As a result, it is not surprising that the law of self-defense that was appropriate for aggression with guns and knives may not be appropriate for aggression with radiological dirty bombs.

(b) Imminence requirement having independent substantive significance v. imminence as evidentiary requirement or proxy

To test our commitment to the second claim, suppose an actor believes that another poses a temporally imminent unlawful threat of aggression but there is no action by the aggressor signaling imminent aggression. The actor employs self-defense force anyway. Under an imminence requirement with such an action component, the defensive force would be unjustified. But suppose that the aggressor subsequently confesses that the self-defender was correct: the aggressor was about to aggress after all. Would we still treat the defender's force as unjustified? If no, then what precisely is the independent substantive significance of the action component of the imminence requirement? If yes, why would we privilege the absence of an imperfect evidentiary signal over the ontological truth that the aggressor was about to aggress?[23]

---

[23] Perhaps some might quibble that the aggressor's confession of aggression is not quite the same as ontological truth of aggression. Even so, the point can be made another way. Imagine we are watching footage of a security camera depicting an alternative scenario to the actual *Norman Case North Carolina v. Norman*, 378 S.E.2d 8 (N.C. 1989). *See infra* text accompanying n. 30 for a discussion of *Norman*. All the facts are the same except that at the precise time that the real Judy Norman did shoot her sleeping husband, the alternative Judy Norman decides not to shoot her sleeping husband because of the imminence requirement. One second later, her husband wakes up and shoots her with a gun he hid under his pillow. In this alternative scenario did her husband pose an imminent threat to alternative Judy Norman at precisely the time she decided not to shoot her husband? If yes, then it is possible for the actual husband to have posed an imminent threat to the actual Judy Norman at precisely the time she shot him. It is merely that she lacked evidence that he posed an imminent threat while he was sleeping. If the answer is no to the above question, then exactly when did the husband pose an imminent threat? Is it possible that he killed her without ever posing an imminent threat?

262

This suggests that the action component of the imminence requirement may not have independent substantive significance but may merely be a proxy or evidentiary signal of something else. In most cases it may correspond well to the underlying principle or provide dispositive evidence, but it will not in all cases. It may well be the most important factor to consider, but it is still but one factor among many to assess. In the unusual cases where the proxy conflicts with the principle or its evidentiary value conflicts with other evidence, the imminence requirement should not be dispositive.

If we answer these questions as I believe we should, then much of the defense of the imminence requirement is questionable. If we analyze the two above situations as I believe we should, then there is ample reason to either reconsider, or modify, or even reject the imminence requirement. Keeping our preliminary views on these two considerations in mind, let us examine more closely the specific defenses of the imminence requirement offered by defenders of the imminence requirement.

IV. Defenses of the imminence requirement

Much of the defense of the imminence requirement focuses on rebutting its primary criticism. The primary criticism is that imminence serves as a proxy or evidentiary requirement for the underlying principle that defensive force be necessary. Richard Rosen, in arguing against the traditionally narrow imminence requirement, maintains that a standard of necessity is the underlying principle and that imminence is only the proxy for that principle.[24] Self-defense that is employed when necessary, but not clearly against an imminent threat, should be understood as justified. The proxy should not be elevated over the principle. While imminence is convenient shorthand for when force is necessary and will translate the principle well in most cases, occasionally they will conflict. In such cases of conflict, satisfaction of the principle should control over non-satisfaction of the proxy. That is, in a situation where force is necessary, though not evidently employed against an imminent threat, the force should be eligible for justification. The criticism is

---

[24] R.A. Rosen, "On Self-Defense, Imminence, and Women Who Kill Their Batterers," 71 *North Carolina Law Review* (1993) 371. David Rodin might also agree that the imminence requirement is a proxy or evidentiary device:

> In legal discussions imminence is often treated as an independent requirement for self-defense; however, it would appear on reflection that imminence is conceptually derivative from necessity.... The requirement not to act before the infliction of harm becomes imminent... is simply the application of the necessity requirement subject to epistemic limitations. The point is that we cannot know with the required degree of certainty that a defensive act is necessary until the infliction of harm is imminent. If, *per impossibile*, we could know that a certain defensive act was necessary to prevent some harm long before the harm was to be inflicted, would we still have to wait until the harm became imminent before acting? It does not seem to me that we would: necessity is enough.
> Rodin, *supra* n. 14, 41.

not merely that the imminence requirement is a proxy or evidentiary requirement and, as such, is a sufficient basis to reject the imminence requirement. Rather, the criticism is that, as a proxy or evidentiary signal, the imminence requirement sometimes imperfectly translates the underlying principle. Thus, the imminence requirement should be rejected because it is an unsuccessful proxy or evidentiary signal.[25]

Different defenders of the imminence requirement address this criticism differently. Joshua Dressler seems to accept the premise of the criticism—that the imminence requirement is a proxy or evidentiary device—but argues that it is a successful one. He maintains that utilization of the proxy or evidentiary device has greater efficacy in furthering the principle than direct application of the principle itself. Jens David Ohlin, George Fletcher, and Kim Ferzan resist the premise of the criticism and argue that the imminence requirement has independent substantive significance. Fletcher and Ohlin shelter the imminence requirement under a protective mantle of furthering important goals of political theory, while Ferzan grounds the imminence requirement in the principles of criminal law theory. But despite the window-dressing, both arguments seem to devolve into arguments on behalf of the imminence requirement as an evidentiary device. Or so I will argue.

(a) Imminence requirement more efficacious than underlying principle

Joshua Dressler views the imminence requirement as imposing a temporal limitation on the right of self-defense.[26] While acknowledging the necessity, certainty or inevitability of aggression as the moral principle underlying the imminence requirement, Dressler rejects an "inevitability" of future aggression standard because it is too speculative and involves too great a chance of error.[27] There is too great a chance that future aggression which seems inevitable will not actually occur. While predictions of inevitable aggression in the distant future are too speculative, "when an attack is underway or imminent, the risk of factual error is reduced to virtually nil."[28] Apparently, the prospect of the imminence requirement being underinclusive—precluding genuine instances of self-defense—does not outweigh the harms of overinclusiveness incurred by the more generous standard of when force is necessary.

---

[25] I am indebted to Jens Ohlin for pointing out the distinction between successful proxies or evidentiary devices and unsuccessful ones. Rodin, *supra* n. 14, and Joshua Dressler, see *infra* text accompanying n. 26, might find the imminence requirement a successful proxy or evidentiary device.

[26] J. Dressler, "Battered Women Who Kill Their Sleeping Tormentors: Reflections on Maintaining Respect for Human Life while Killing Moral Monsters," in S. Shute and A.P. Simester (eds), *Criminal Law Theory: Doctrines of the General Part* (Oxford University Press, 2002) 259, 260, 274.

[27] Ibid. at 274–5.

[28] See also ibid. at 274 ("Once the temporal limitations are gone—once we move past imminent or "immediately necessary...on the present occasion" threats—how well can one predict what human conduct is inevitable?").

But the imminence requirement does not, as Dressler maintains, assure that defensive force is necessary. Though most critics of the imminence requirement focus on its underinclusiveness, the imminence requirement is also overinclusive. Suppose an aggressor unlawfully puts a gun to my head and starts to pull the trigger. If any example satisfies the imminence requirement, surely this does. One would be hard-pressed to imagine a more imminent threat. But defensive force may be unnecessary against even this most imminent of threats. For example, after the aggressor begins to pull the trigger, but before the aggressor pulls it sufficiently far to fire the gun, the aggressor has a change of heart and abandons his plan of killing me.[29] The aggressor's threat is imminent, yet it is not necessary for me to use defensive force against the aggressor.

However, Dressler's point is not necessarily that the imminence requirement guarantees that defensive force will be necessary, but that it is merely the best means to assure that defensive force is necessary. But even this limited claim is questionable. As compared to the imminence requirement, would not a standard of actual, present aggression be preferable? If the goal, as Dressler claims, is to reduce instances of unnecessary defensive force, then a standard of requiring the defender to wait until not merely when action manifesting aggression is imminent but, rather, when aggression is actual and present would be that much better. It would avoid the overinclusiveness of the imminence requirement. As a result, the stated rationale does not support the imminence requirement. Instead, it proves too much and supports a standard of actual, present force.

Would Dressler wish to support a standard of actual, present force? No, presumably not. It would be underinclusive; it would bar genuine instances of self-defense. It would bar situations where defensive force was necessary even in the absence of the actual presence of the aggressor's force. But if that is a sufficient reason to reject the actual presence of force standard, then the underinclusiveness of the imminence standard is a sufficient reason to reject the imminence requirement. But if under-inclusiveness is not a sufficient reason to reject the imminence standard, then it is also not a sufficient reason to reject the actual presence of force standard. And if underinclusiveness is insufficient to reject either standard, then what basis supports the imminence standard?

Once we deviate from a standard of actual presence of force and allow self-defense force to be employed at an earlier point, how do we establish how long prior to actual force defensive force may be employed? The law's answer of imminence leaves unanswered the question of why not near imminence, almost imminence, or pre-imminence? And if a rationale is still lacking, then why not substantially pre-imminent? And so on and so on. Once we deviate from a requirement of actual

---

[29] For a similar example, see K. Kessler Ferzan, "Defending Imminence: From Battered Women to Iraq," 46 *Arizona Law Review* (2004) 213, 256 fn. 227.

presence of force, there seems little principled reason to support one temporal time period rather than another as *the* time the right of self-defense attaches.

Dressler applies his understanding of the imminence requirement to the *Norman* case[30]—one of the more infamous cases rejecting a claim of self-defense because imminence was lacking. After twenty years of horrific and nightmarish physical abuse by her husband, Judy Norman shot and killed her husband while he was sleeping. Dressler and other defenders of the imminence requirement hold up this case as a paradigmatic example of force used against a non-imminent threat. As Dressler puts it, "[t]here is simply no basis for suggesting that J.T. Norman, as he slept in bed, *in reality* represented an imminent threat to Judy Norman."[31] Though it was not highly probable that he would have imminently killed her, it was possible. Apart from Judy killing him, there was nothing to prevent the husband from waking up and killing her. If it is possible that he would have killed her, and hardly wildly implausible given his twenty-year history of horrific physical abuse, it is not irrational to claim that he did pose an imminent threat at the very time that she killed him. For the very reason that she did kill him, we will never know whether he would have imminently killed her and whether he posed an imminent threat. So, if it is possible and not implausible and not irrational, could it not be reasonable to suppose that he did pose an imminent threat?

(b) Imminence as a right to respond to aggression

Kim Ferzan rejects the criticism that imminence is merely a proxy for the more fundamental and underlying principle of necessity. And she rejects the claim that the focus of self-defense should be on what is necessary or immediately necessary for the self-defender. Such a focus, Ferzan argues, collapses the distinction between the defenses of self-defense and necessity. And it improperly treats all self-preferential force as self-defensive force. While "[a]ll self-defense cases are instances of self-preference ... not all self-preferential actions constitute self-defense."[32] The difficulty with the focus on when defensive force is necessary is that it "operates independently of the intentions, capabilities, or actions of a putative aggressor."[33] Disregarding those aspects and focusing exclusively on the necessity of defensive force conflates self-defense with the general defense of necessity. But unlike necessity, self-defense limits the class of persons against whom force may be employed to unlawful aggressors. And unlike necessity, "self-defense is an action against a threat."[34] Under Ferzan's account, "[t]he critical question is not *when* the defender needs to act but *what* kind of threat triggers the right to self-defense."[35]

---

[30] *North Carolina v. Norman*, 378 S.E.2d 8 (N.C. 1989).
[31] J Dressler, *supra* n. 26, 267.
[32] Ferzan, *supra* n. 29, 248.
[33] Ibid. at 250.
[34] Ibid. at 252 (emphasis omitted).
[35] Ibid. at 255.

According to Ferzan, the independent substantive significance of the imminence requirement is that it specifies the type of threat or aggression that triggers a right of self-defense. And the type of threat or aggression that triggers a right of self-defense involves action. "The imminence requirement is best understood as the *actus reus* of aggression."[36] Ferzan arrives at this view by comparing the imminence requirement with the *actus reus* of attempt. Under the common law of attempt, the *actus reus* assures that the defendant's conduct is sufficiently proximate to completing the crime; the defendant has crossed the line from lawful preparation to unlawful attempt. Similarly, "the aggressor's action signifies the breach of the community rules"; "the aggressor's action 'starts it.' "[37] In international law terms, the action component of the imminence requirement serves as the aggressor's " 'unmistakable signal that he has crossed the line from diplomacy to force.' "[38] Ferzan concludes that "the right to self-defense is not the right to act as early as is necessary to defend oneself effectively. The right to self-defense is the right to respond to aggression."[39]

But the attempt analogy that Ferzan relies on to bolster the independent substantive significance of the action component of the imminence requirement also cuts the other way. Under some views of attempts, the *actus reus* has no independent substantive significance.[40] It only plays an evidentiary role in establishing the defendant's *mens rea*. In corroborating the defendant's *mens rea*, it serves as a proxy for the defendant's *mens rea*. As an evidentiary device or proxy, it has no independent substantive significance.

(c) Imminence as a requirement of political theory

George Fletcher and Jens David Ohlin view the imminence requirement as a matter of political theory, rather than moral theory.[41] It is only when aggression is imminent that the state cannot intervene and secure the safety of the victim. According to Fletcher, only "when the danger...is imminent and unavoidable" may a private citizen exercise defensive force against aggression.[42] And "[p]recisely because the issue is political rather than moral, the [imminence] requirement must

---

[36] Ibid. at 257–8.

[37] Ibid. at 259.

[38] Ibid. at 257 (quoting D. J. Luban, "Preventive War," available at <http://papers.ssrn.com/abstract=469862> 21, accessed November 4, 2011).

[39] Ferzan, *supra* n. 29, 262.

[40] *See*, e.g., G. Williams, *Criminal Law: The General Part*, 2nd edn (Sweet & Maxwell Ltd, 1961) 631 ("[John L.] Austin put forward the interesting view that in attempt the party is really punished for his intention, the act being required as evidence of a *firm* intention. There is much to be said for this.").

[41] G. P. Fletcher, "Domination in the Theory of Justification and Excuse," 57 *University of Pittsburgh Law Review* (1996) 553, 570–1; see also Fletcher and Ohlin, *supra* n. 14, 155–76.

[42] Fletcher, *supra* n. 41, 570.

be both objective and public. There must be a signal to the community...."[43] Fletcher further explains that the "'imminent attack' must actually occur in the real world. The attack signals to the community that the defensive response is not a form of aggression but a legitimate response in the name of self-protection."[44] In the sphere of international relations, Fletcher and Ohlin similarly argue that "the use of defensive force should be based on public evidence—evidence that the world can see."[45] The imminent attack "must be based on publicly observable facts;" it must be "manifested in publicly observable facts."[46] Fletcher and Ohlin conclude that "[t]he appeal of imminence is precisely that it provides a nearly fool-proof standard for distinguishing between the aggressor and the defender."[47]

(d) Ferzan, Fletcher and Ohlin's evidentiary view of the imminence requirement

Ferzan, Fletcher and Ohlin argue for the independent substantive significance of the imminence requirement. It is neither merely a proxy for the underlying principle of necessary force, nor is it merely an evidentiary requirement. But their arguments seem to collapse into arguments for imminence as an evidentiary requirement. This is particularly true with respect to each scholar's argument for an action component, a physical manifestation of aggression.

What Fletcher and Ohlin cleverly couch as a requirement of political theory might be better understood as an evidentiary requirement. They maintain that the imminence of the attack must be objective, public and provide a signal to the community. Imminence is thus not a moral requirement or substantive principle of justified self-defense, but rather an evidentiary rule or requirement. Imminence of attack is serving as an objective manifestation of aggression. It suggests that there may well be genuine instances of justified self-defense for which there are not sufficient publicly observable facts that manifest the justifiability of the self-defense (just as there are factually guilty offenders for whom there is insufficient legal evidence to sustain a conviction). Utilizing imminence as an evidentiary requirement allows a determination of which party in a conflict is the aggressor and which is the victim/self-defender.

Similarly, Ferzan's argument for the action component of the imminence require-ment seems to serve only an evidentiary function in establishing that the recipient of the defensive force is an aggressor posing a threat that makes defensive force neces-sary. As Ferzan herself puts it, the action component is a "signal,"[48] "signif[ying]"[49]

---

43 Ibid.
44 Ibid. at 571.
45 Fletcher and Ohlin, *supra* n. 14, 161.
46 Ibid. at 167.
47 Ibid. at 169.
48 Ferzan, *supra* n. 29, 257.
49 Ibid. at 259.

future aggression. It "signals the end of peaceful resolution and an initiation of an assault on sovereignty."[50] And what is the purpose of this signaling? It allows us to "distinguish self-defensive conduct from aggressive conduct."[51]

(e) Why imminence as merely an evidentiary requirement is problematic

Critics of the imminence requirement have argued that it is merely a proxy for or evidence establishing a deeper principle—the necessity of defensive force. And if imminence is merely a proxy or an evidentiary requirement, in a case of defensive force that fails to satisfy the proxy but does satisfy the principle, these critics argue that self-defense should be justified. The underlying substantive principle should trump the evidentiary requirement when the two conflict. Ferzan explicitly acknowledges the premise of this criticism—that substantive principle should trump mere proxy or evidentiary requirement. (But she disagrees that the imminence requirement is a mere proxy. To avoid the critics of the imminence requirement, she attempts to independently ground the imminence requirement as a substantive principle.)

Unlike Ferzan, Fletcher and Ohlin do not expressly acknowledge that imminence as a mere proxy or evidentiary requirement is problematic. But they implicitly acknowledge this by attempting to ground the importance of the imminence requirement in political theory. Outside the context of the imminence requirement, Fletcher has warned of the dangers of conflating substantive principles and evidentiary requirements. Fletcher distinguishes substantive rules from procedural and evidentiary rules as follows: "the rules of procedure [and evidence] do not bear on the morality of acting."[52] As an example, "[w]hether evidence of prior spousal abuse is admissible against O.J. Simpson has nothing to do with the morality of killing his wife." Similarly, whether a victim of future aggression uses force under conditions where there is an objective manifestation of an imminent aggression has nothing to do with the morality of whether the self-defender employed force when necessary to do so.

Other scholars also warn of the inherent problems in mixing evidentiary requirements and substantive principles. Consider Doug Husak's admonition to keep substantive principles free from the infection of evidentiary issues:

> [Because of concern for social protection and utilitarian reasoning], conclusions about what justice demands in a particular case are often infected with practical problems of obtaining reliable evidence. . . . If theorists are to be taken seriously in construing these principles as requirements of justice, it is crucial that questions about evidence be placed to one side, at least temporarily. . . . Theorists who specify the scope and application of the fundamental principles of criminal liability should . . . resist the

---

[50] Ibid. at 261.
[51] Ibid. at 259.
[52] G. P. Fletcher, *Basic Concepts of Criminal Law* (Oxford University Press, 1998) 13.

tendency to compromise their answers by practical difficulties of obtaining reliable evidence. . . . The scope and application of the fundamental principles of liability will differ if criminal theory is not infected by evidentiary questions. It is hardly surprising that the just outcome of a case may conflict with what is most efficient or practical. . . . Intellectual clarity is best served by divorcing questions of justice and evidence altogether. . . . [Conflating principle and evidence] should be recognized for what it is—an unfortunate and regrettable *retreat* from what criminal theory demands as a matter of justice. Worries about evidence should not be reflected in the content of the fundamental principles of criminal liability, as long as they are to be construed as requirements of justice.[53]

Replacing what should be substantive principles with evidentiary rules obscures the underlying moral principles. Failure to satisfy the evidentiary requirement will tend to be confused with failing to satisfy the underlying substantive principle.

(f) Imminence as evidentiary requirement analogous to the widely condemned resistance requirement in rape law

A comparison with the effort to abolish the resistance requirement in rape law might be helpful. Traditionally, in order to secure a conviction for rape, the victim had to prove that s/he resisted. Though not a formal element of the offense of rape, resistance on the part of the victim was considered as the preferred means to prove the formal elements of force and non-consent. Resistance was considered an objective manifestation of, and more reliable evidence of, the victim's non-consent. But recent efforts in rape reform have persuaded many jurisdictions to abolish this evidentiary requirement because it endangered victims' lives. Rape victims should not be forced to subject themselves to additional risk of harm to improve the criminal law's ability to sort out which cases of intercourse are consensual and which are not. While the presence of resistance may dispositively establish non-consent, the absence of resistance does not dispositively establish consent.

Similarly, victims facing aggression should not have to wait until the aggression is imminent, if doing so would endanger them, in order to aid the criminal law's sorting mechanism differentiating aggressors from self-defenders. And similarly, while the presence of objective manifestations of imminence may dispositively establish imminence, the absence of such objective manifestations should not be dispositive in barring justified self-defense.

(g) Arbitrariness of the action component

Regardless of whether the imminence requirement is merely a proxy/evidentiary requirement or has independent substantive significance, Ferzan, Fletcher and Ohlin fail to explain why only action manifesting aggression can serve the function of supplying the requisite signal to the relevant community so as to easily

---

[53] D. N. Husak, *Philosophy of Criminal Law* (Rowman & Littlefield, 1987) 58–60.

determine who is aggressor and who is defender. Could not stated intentions of unlawful aggression also supply this signal? Or evidence obtained after the defensive force demonstrating the aggressor's planned aggression? Or perhaps even the aggressor's confession that but for the self-defender's force the aggression would have commenced? That action is only one of many different possible means to supply this signal suggests that it has no independent substantive importance but is merely an evidentiary device.

True, the action component of the imminence requirement works well in providing a clear signal in most cases. But that which provides a bright-line rule is not necessarily the best rule. What should we do when the cleanest rule to distinguish self-defender from aggressor in most cases unduly limits a self-defender's right to self-defense in some cases? When the factual contexts are too varied and too ambiguous and reality is too messy to be neatly compartmentalized, the better rule may be the duller, more ambiguous rule.

V. Problem with a purely temporal imminence requirement

Defenders of the imminence requirement maintain that "[t]he appeal of imminence is precisely that it provides a nearly foolproof standard for distinguishing between the aggressor and the defender."[54] But this is far from clear. And it is not even clear what precisely the imminence requirement requires. While some formulations refer to imminence in purely temporal terms, others additionally or alternatively add an action component, a physical manifestation of aggression.

If understood as a purely temporal relation between the time when possibly aggressive force will actually be applied and the time when force may first be used in self-defense against that possibly aggressive force, the imminence requirement fails to work properly.[55] Consider the following example. Suppose that A poses a threat of force to SD and will use force at a time, T_{10}, against SD unless SD employs defensive force that neutralizes A's threat. Let us further say that the period of imminence is five units of time. (By not specifying precisely how long or short the units of time, five units of time is consistent with anyone's conception of how long or short the period of time expressed by the concept of imminence.) As a result, A poses an imminent threat to SD at T_5 and any force employed by SD against A from T_5 to T_{10} would satisfy the imminence requirement. Suppose that SD employs force against A at T_6. SD would thereby seemingly satisfy the imminence requirement. The hypothetical might be more easily understood in the following form:

---

54 Fletcher and Ohlin, *supra* n. 14, 169.

55 Some parts of the argument presented here are a further elaboration of an argument first presented in R. Christopher, "Self-Defense and Objectivity: A Reply to Judith Jarvis Thomson," 1 *Buffalo Criminal Law Review* (1998) 537.

T_5 A poses a temporally imminent threat

T_6 SD applies force

T_{10} A will aggress (if not neutralized).

But at what point in time did SD pose an imminent threat to A? In general, imminence is understood as the period of time prior to the employment of possibly aggressive force that one may use defensive force against that aggressive force and still be eligible for a self-defense justification. Specifically, we have arbitrarily defined that period of time to be five units of time. As a result, if SD employs force against A at T_6, then it was imminent that SD would use force against A at T_1 (just as A posed an imminent threat to SD at T_5 because he would have used force against SD at T_{10} unless stopped by SD). Between A and SD, the party who first posed an imminent threat was SD—SD posing an imminent threat at T_1 occurs prior to A posing an imminent threat at T_5. In any such confrontation between two parties, the first party that actually uses force will necessarily be the first party that imminently would use force. Because some self-defenders will be the first party to actually apply force, some self-defenders will be the first party to pose an imminent threat and thus paradoxically will be understood as the aggressor.

Rather than neatly sorting aggressor and defender, the imminence requirement seems to get it backward. Because the party we intuitively find to be the self-defender (SD) is the first party (between A and SD) to actually use force, the self-defender is the first party to pose an imminent threat and is thus the aggressor after all. Starting at T_1, SD poses an imminent threat to A; A does not pose an imminent threat to SD until T_5.

By treating the first party to actually use force as the aggressor, this purely temporal understanding of the imminence requirement defeats the very purpose of an imminence standard. As opposed to an actual force standard, a standard of imminence is designed to afford a self-defender an opportunity to actually use force first and prevent the use of aggressive force. If the purely temporal version treats the first party to actually apply force as the aggressor, what is the point of an imminence standard? It produces the same results as an actual force standard.

Although the imminence requirement is most simply understood as a temporal relation, formulations of the imminence requirement commonly include an additional component—some action or some physical manifestation of the impending attack or aggression. How this possible additional component is understood is not entirely clear. And the legitimacy of this additional component is also unclear. But it would avoid the problem above.[56]

---

[56] Suppose that A commences some action in furtherance of the impending attack or physically manifests his attack at T_5 and will carry out the attack at T_{10}. Only after T_5 does SD physically manifest his use of force that he will carry out at T_9. So rather than the first party that actually uses force being the first party that poses an imminent threat and is thus the aggressor, imminence

VI. Problems with an imminence requirement with temporal and action components

An imminence requirement containing both temporal and action components presumably requires the satisfaction of both components. In order for a possible aggressor to be understood as posing an imminent threat, the possible aggressor's aggression would have to be both temporally imminent and physically manifested by some action or conduct. In order for a self-defender to be eligible to use justified self-defense force against an aggressor, the aggressor must have satisfied both components. If either component is not satisfied, the possible aggressor is not an imminent aggressor and self-defense force is not eligible for justification. Self-defense force would be eligible for justification in neither of the following two examples. First, suppose *A* manifests future aggression but the future aggression is not yet temporally imminent. *A* does not yet pose a fully imminent threat and force by *SD* would not satisfy the imminence requirement. Second, suppose *A*'s future aggression is temporally imminent but *A* has not yet manifested this future aggression by some act or conduct. In neither case does *A* pose a fully imminent threat and in neither case would force by *SD* satisfy the imminence requirement.

As a result, under an imminence requirement containing both temporal and action components, the first party whose force is both temporally imminent and manifested by some action is the aggressor. The imminence requirement thus differentiates between aggressor and self-defender by determining which is the first party to satisfy both components. The first party to satisfy both components is the aggressor.

But this understanding of the imminence requirement, with both temporal and action components, also incurs difficulties.

(a) Arbitrariness

A conception of the imminence requirement as composed of both temporal and action components leads to arbitrary results. Consider two variations on a situation involving two actors who each have reason to use force against the other.

(i) *A* and *SD* are walking toward each other across a large field. Each is wary that the other might pose an unlawful threat of aggression. Because *A* has an old gun that takes longer to operate and sometimes jams, *A* decides that he had better get

---

is measured by the physical manifestation of the attack. Whoever is the first party to both pose a temporally imminent threat and manifest that threat by some act is the first to pose an imminent threat and is thus the aggressor. Under this construction of the imminence requirement, *A* would be the aggressor and *SD* the self-defender. As a result, this alternative understanding of the imminence requirement avoids the problem above and does properly sort, in this case, which party should be the aggressor and which party should be the self-defender.

the jump on *SD* and be the first to use force. At T_0, *A* takes out his gun and begins to raise it toward *SD*. If not neutralized, *A* will shoot at *SD* at T_5. (Again, let us assume that temporal imminence is five units of time.) Thus, *A* poses an imminent threat—both temporally and physically—to *SD* at T_0. At T_1, *SD* takes out his gun and, at T_4, shoots *A*. *SD* is the self-defender and *A* is the aggressor because *A* was the first to pose a fully imminent threat (both temporally and physically) and *SD* shot at *A* during the period of imminence.

(ii) *A* gets a new gun that is lightning quick to operate and never jams. *A* and *SD* are again walking toward each other across a large field. *A* now realizes that *A* need not make the first move. At T_1, *SD* takes out his gun and raises it to shoot at *A*. If not neutralized, *SD* will shoot at *A* at T_4. At T_2, *A* takes out his gun and, at T_3, shoots at *SD*. Because *SD* would shoot at *A* at T_4 if not neutralized and *SD* manifested that aggression at T_1, *SD* posed an imminent threat to *A* starting at T_1. *A* did not pose an imminent threat to *SD* until T_2. Thus, *SD* was the first between the two parties to pose an imminent threat. As a result, *A* would be the self-defender and *SD* the aggressor.

In comparing cases (i) and (ii), *A* is the aggressor in (i) and the defender in (ii); *SD* the defender in (i) and the aggressor in (ii). *A* is the aggressor in (i) because he was the first to manifest aggression; *A* was the defender in (ii) because he was not the first to manifest aggression. But *SD*'s conduct was the same in both cases. How can we explain why *SD* varies as defender and aggressor for the very same conduct? Because which party is identified as aggressor or defender depends exclusively on which party has the faster gun. In (i), when *SD* has the faster gun he can afford to wait longer before manifesting aggression, thereby inducing *A* to become the first to pose an imminent threat. But in (ii), when *A* has the faster gun, he can afford to wait longer before manifesting aggression thereby inducing *SD* to become the first to pose an imminent threat.

But which party has the faster gun or weapon or which party can employ force more quickly is hardly a principled basis for determining which party should be the unlawful aggressor and which party should be the lawful self-defender. While the inclusion of the action component in the imminence requirement avoids the problem above besetting an exclusively temporal construction of the imminence requirement, inclusion of an action component produces arbitrary results.

(b) Overinclusiveness

In addition to arbitrariness, the addition of the action component is both over-inclusive and underinclusive. To see that it is overinclusive, consider the following hypothetical. At T_0, *A* physically manifests a threat to kill *SD* at T_5. As a result, *SD*'s use of force from T_0 to T_5 would satisfy the imminence requirement. *SD* uses force against *A* at T_3. But had *SD* not used force against *A* at T_3, *A* would have changed his mind and not used force after all. As compared to a standard of waiting until A actually uses force against SD, the imminence requirement is overinclusive in allowing SD's force to be eligible to be justified as self-defense, despite it not being necessary.

(c) Underinclusiveness

Inclusion of an action component is also underinclusive. Suppose that A will kill SD at T_5. And, at T_0, SD knows this. Under a purely temporal understanding of the imminence requirement, A poses an imminent threat at T_0. Force used by SD from T_0 to T_5 would satisfy this temporal understanding of the imminence requirement. But A does not physically manifest his aggression until T_4. As a result, under the action component of the imminence requirement A does not become an imminent threat until T_4. Although SD knows that A will kill SD at T_5 unless stopped and that, temporally speaking, A poses an imminent threat at T_0, SD must wait to employ defensive force until A physically manifests this aggression at T_4. With both the temporal and physical components of the imminence requirement satisfied, SD's force can now satisfy the imminence requirement. But after all the time SD has waited until the imminence requirement is satisfied, SD now lacks sufficient time to employ force against A. SD starts to employ his defensive force but it is too late. It is now T_5 and A has killed SD. The action component of the imminence requirement is underinclusive. Our intuitions suggest that the law of self-defense should allow SD's right to use both effective and justified self-defense. But what the imminence requirement grants is only one or the other—effective but non-justified self-defense (earlier than T_4) or ineffective but justified self-defense (from T_4 to T_5).

(d) Action component distorts the balance of interests between aggressor and self-defender

In some situations, the action component shortens the time period under which the temporal component of the imminence requirement alone would allow self-defense. But if the temporal component of the imminence requirement is meant to strike a balance between the interests of defender and (potential) aggressor, then the action component distorts this balance. The purpose of the imminence requirement is to give the defender sufficient time to mount a defense against aggression while not allowing defensive force at so early a point in time that it is not truly necessary. If required to wait until the actual presence of aggression, self-defense force would be too late. If allowed to use defensive force prior to imminence, the defensive force might be unnecessary. The imminence requirement is thereby claimed to reflect a careful balance between the defender's interest in protection from aggression and the potential aggressor's interest in not being the victim of unnecessary defensive force. But the action component upsets this balance by restricting the defender's ability to employ effective force despite the presence of temporal imminence of aggression. As merely an evidentiary device to aid the state (or international community) in determining who is the defender and who is the aggressor, it restricts and distorts the scope of the right to self-defense.

And not only does it distort the right of self-defense, it does so asymmetrically. It only distorts the right of self-defense in favor of the (potential) aggressor. It does not expand the right of self-defense; it only restricts it.

And this asymmetrical distortion of the right of self-defense is entirely within the control and whim of the aggressor. By manifesting her aggression at or prior to the temporal imminence period, the self-defender enjoys a temporally maximal right of self-defense. But by opting to manifest her aggression subsequent to the temporal imminence period, the aggressor shrinks the self-defender's right down to a temporally minimal right of self-defense. And by opting to wait to manifest her aggression until just prior to the actual aggression, the aggressor can further shrink the right to self-defense, thereby virtually eliminating a self-defender's right to effective self-defense. Why should the law of self-defense allow the aggressor to determine whether the self-defender enjoys a temporally maximal or minimal right of self-defense?

And why should the self-defender bear the brunt of the law's difficulty in determining which party is aggressor and which party is self-defender? Why are not the aggressor's interests diminished in the name of divining which party is aggressor and which is defender? Should not the burden at least be borne equally?

The action component only furthers the handicap already imposed on the self-defender by the temporal component. A self-defender is only allowed to employ effective justified self-defense if the self-defender can employ force appreciably faster than the aggressor. The head start supplied to the aggressor and the handicap imposed on the self-defender is only exacerbated by the action component. It affords the aggressor an even bigger head start and imposes on the self-defender an even greater handicap. Not only must a self-defender wait until an aggressor poses a temporally imminent threat, but also the self-defender must further wait until the aggressor's temporally imminent threat manifests itself in some physical action.

This section demonstrated the problem where an aggressor first satisfies the temporal component and then subsequently satisfies the action component, especially when the action component is satisfied just before the aggressor would actually use force. In the next three sections, problems arise when the aggressor does the converse—when the aggressor first satisfies the action component and then subsequently satisfies the temporal component.

(e) A minor paradox: imminence v. post-imminence

In addition to being arbitrary, overinclusive, and underinclusive, and restricting and distorting the right of self-defense, an imminence requirement including an action component incurs a minor paradox. Consider the following example. A will aggress against SD at T_{10} unless neutralized. Thus, at T_5 A's threat is temporally imminent. A physically manifests his threat by some action at T_0. Thus A's threat becomes fully imminent at the point when both components are satisfied—at T_5. The unchallenged assumption is that SD may employ defensive force when the aggressor poses a fully (temporally and physically) imminent threat; specifically, at T_5. At the point when an aggressor's threat is imminent, the self-defender is eligible to use justified force. But this assumption is false.

Paradoxically, if the self-defender uses force at the time when the aggressor poses an imminent threat, the self-defender will become the first to pose an imminent threat and thus will become the aggressor. For example, if SD applies force at T_5—the time when the aggressor's force became imminent—SD would necessarily have had to physically manifest such force prior to T_5, say at T_4. Presumably, one cannot apply force without first manifesting that force by some physical act. For example, if SD was to shoot A at T_5, SD would necessarily have to take preparatory steps prior to T_5, say at T_4—raising the gun, pointing the gun, pulling the trigger, etc. The hypothetical may be more readily understood in the following form:

T_0	A's action manifests future aggression
T_0	SD poses a temporally imminent threat
T_4	D's action manifests future aggression
T_5	A poses a temporally imminent threat
T_5	SD applies force
T_{10}	A will aggress (if not neutralized).

As a result, if SD actually did what the imminence requirement seemingly allows, SD would become the first party to physically manifest aggression and the first to pose a fully imminent threat. Thus, SD would become the aggressor and A the defender. Despite A posing an imminent threat at T_5, curiously SD must wait until *after* T_5 to apply force. Despite A posing an imminent threat at T_5, SD must not actually apply force at T_5.

Inherent in the concept of the imminence requirement seems to be a waiting period after the point of imminence. But what do we say of the time period between when aggression is imminent, and when a self-defender may actually apply defensive force? It would seem that a defender has the right to apply force in the abstract at the point of imminence, but if this right is exercised it cancels or negates the right. The use of defensive force, at the precise point in which aggression is imminent, converts justified self-defense into unlawful aggression. The self-defender becomes the aggressor. But as long as the self-defender does not exercise this right, the self-defender may be said to have the right to use force when aggression is imminent. Is the imminence requirement really a "nearly foolproof method" for distinguishing aggressor from defender?

As a technical matter, the paradox may easily be solved. Rather than stating that defensive force is eligible for justification when used against an aggressor's fully imminent threat, the rule may be changed to subsequent to imminence. That is, defensive force is not permissible at the point of imminence but, rather, subsequent to imminence. Thus, applying this new rule to the above hypothetical situation, *A* becomes an imminent threat at T_5 and *SD* may permissibly apply force subsequent to the point of imminence—T_6 and thereafter.

But even if altering the standard from imminence to *post*-imminence easily resolves the problem, it is unclear what moral reason explains why defensive force may not be used when an aggressor poses an imminent threat. The solution is ad hoc and lacks a satisfactory moral rationale. Moreover, a standard of post-imminence does not necessarily resolve the problem, as the next section will demonstrate.

(f) Indeterminacy of which party is aggressor and self-defender

The solution of a standard of post-imminence as to when defensive force is permissible is also problematic. Suppose similar facts obtain as in the above hypothetical, except that *SD* applies force at T_6. Because *A* became a fully imminent threat at T_5, *SD*'s use of force at T_6 would seemingly satisfy the new requisite standard of post-imminence. But, as noted above, if *SD* applies force at T_6, *SD* must necessarily prepare to use force prior to T_6. Suppose that *SD* prepares to use force at T_5 such that *SD*'s preparations would satisfy the action component. The hypothetical may be more readily understood in the following form:

T_0 *A*'s action manifests future aggression
T_1 *SD* poses a temporally imminent threat
T_5 *A* poses a temporally imminent threat
T_5 *SD*'s action manifests future aggression
T_6 *SD* applies force
T_{10} *A* will aggress (if not neutralized).

By satisfying the action component at T_5 (and satisfying the temporal component at T_1), *SD* poses a fully imminent threat to *A* at T_5. But *A*, by satisfying the action component at T_0 and the temporal component at T_5, also poses a fully imminent threat to *SD* at T_5. If each becomes a fully imminent threat to the other at the same time—T_5—which party is the aggressor and which party is the self-defender?

The imminence requirement with an action component purports to supply a nearly foolproof means of distinguishing between aggressor and self-defender. The test is which party is the first to pose a fully imminent threat. The first party to do so is the aggressor. But here, which party is the aggressor and which party is the self-defender is indeterminate. Each becomes a fully imminent threat at the same time. And each does so despite each party using force at different times (*SD* at T_6, and *A* at T_{10}), each party manifesting their force at different times (SD at T_5 and A at T_0), and each party's force being temporally imminent at different times (SD at T_1 and A at T_5). The imminence requirement, containing both temporal and action components, fails to determine which party is the aggressor and which party is the self-defender.

(g) A further puzzle: why a defender may neither use nor even prepare to use force until post-imminence

The problems raised in the two previous sections can easily be technically resolved. The problem raised by a defender applying force at the point when an aggressor's force is imminent can be resolved by a standard of *post*-imminence. A defender may not apply force until subsequent to the point of the aggressor's threat being imminent. And the problem of a defender physically manifesting his force at the point of imminence could similarly be easily resolved by a standard of *post post*-imminence. Not only may a defender not apply force at the point of the aggressor posing an imminent threat, but also a defender may not even prepare to apply force until after the aggressor has become a fully imminent threat. Thus in the example above, despite A posing a fully imminent threat at T_5, SD may not apply force at T_5. SD must wait until after T_5. And SD must not even use force at T_6 and prepare to use force at T_5. SD must wait until after the point of imminence to even prepare to use force. SD must wait until T_6 to prepare to use force and then may only apply force starting at T_7, despite that A poses a fully imminent threat at T_5. Only in this way may SD avoid being determined to be the aggressor and be eligible to use justified defensive force.

While such an extended waiting period after the point of imminence technically resolves the problems, left unexplained is why? Why must a defender wait until after the point of imminence to even prepare to use force? What moral reason explains why a self-defender must wait for so long past the point of imminence?

Consider the following hypothetical. Suppose that at T_1, A readies his gun to shoot at and kill SD at T_{10}. SD sees A do this and realizes that he must be prepared to use force against A. At T_3, SD readies his gun to shoot at and neutralize SD. Because A will kill SD at T_{10} unless stopped and A has already satisfied the action component at T_1, A becomes a temporally and fully imminent threat to aggress against SD at T_5. Thus after T_5, SD should be eligible to use force against A. If SD is to prevent A's aggression and save his own life, SD must shoot at and neutralize A prior to T_{10}. Thus, in order for SD's force to be both justified and effective it must be employed after T_5 and prior to T_{10}. SD waits as long as he can and finally shoots A at T_9, thereby neutralizing him. This is just in time because otherwise A would have killed SD at T_{10}. The hypothetical may be more readily understood in the following form:

T_1 A's action manifests future aggression
T_3 SD's action manifests future aggression
T_4 SD poses a temporally imminent threat

T_5 *A* poses a temporally imminent threat

T_9 *SD* applies force

T_{10} *A* will aggress (if not neutralized).

Intuitively, *SD*'s force should be eligible to be justified in self-defense. *A* manifested his aggression first. *A* became an imminent threat at T_5 and *SD* did not shoot at *A* until after T_5. Moreover, he even waited until the last moment and shot at *A* at T_9.

But surprisingly, under the imminence requirement, *SD* is the aggressor and *A* is the self-defender. According to the imminence requirement, the first party to satisfy both the action and temporal components is the first to pose an imminent threat. By shooting at *A* at T_9, *SD* became a temporally imminent threat at T_4. And because *SD* satisfied the action component at T_3, *SD* posed a fully imminent threat at T_4. *A* did not pose a fully imminent threat to *SD* until T_5. Because *SD* posed an imminent threat to *A* at T_4 which is prior to *A* posing a fully imminent threat to *SD* until T_5, *SD* is the aggressor and *A* the self-defender.

How can we explain *why SD* is the aggressor? True, as a technical matter, *SD* is the aggressor because *SD* was the first to pose a fully imminent threat. But intuitively it seems that *A* should be the aggressor because (i) *A* was the first to manifest force; (ii) *SD* waited to use force until after *A*'s force was fully imminent; and (iii) *SD* waited even longer until it was just prior to *A*'s use of force.

To understand this, it might be helpful to see how *SD* could have avoided becoming the aggressor. Consider a variation on the above hypothetical, involving *A* and *SD2*. All the facts are the same except that *SD2* does not manifest his force at T_3. Instead, *SD2* manifests his force at T_6. Thus *SD2* did not pose a fully imminent threat until T_6, which was after *A*'s fully imminent threat at T_5. The hypothetical may be more readily understood in the following form:

T_1 *A*'s action manifests future aggression

T_4 *SD2* poses a temporally imminent threat

T_5 *A* poses a temporally imminent threat

T_6 *SD2*'s action manifests future aggression

T_9 *SD2* applies force

T_{10} *A* will aggress (if not neutralized).

Because *A* at T_5 was the first to pose a fully imminent threat, *A* is the aggressor and *SD2* is the self-defender.

Is there a morally relevant difference between *SD* who the imminence requirement determines is an aggressor and *SD2*, who the imminence requirement determines is a self-defender? In each case, *A* is still the first to manifest force and in each case *SD/SD2* does not employ force until after *A* poses a fully imminent threat. Intuitively, we might think that *SD/SD2* should be the self-defender and *A* the aggressor in both cases. Why is it impermissible for *SD* to make preparations outside the imminence period as to force that will only be actually employed inside the imminence period?

While it is understandable for the imminence requirement to obligate *SD* to wait until *A*'s threat becomes fully imminent before using force, why must *SD* also wait to *prepare* to use force until after *A*'s threat becomes fully imminent? Moreover, why must *SD* so wait to even prepare to use force when *A* has already manifested force first?

When an aggressor has already manifested aggression and a self-defender waits to actually apply defensive force until after the aggressor's threat is fully imminent, why would the imminence requirement bar a self-defender from preparing to use that defensive force? Requiring a self-defender to wait to use force until an aggressor poses a fully imminent threat would seem to provide adequate protection to the aggressor. What purpose of the imminence requirement is advanced by also requiring a self-defender to wait before even preparing to use force? While not providing any further protection to the aggressor from unnecessary defensive force, it does restrict a self-defender's ability to employ effective self-defense. By requiring a self-defender to wait to even prepare to use force, the self-defender may not have sufficient time to effectively employ defensive force. And again, regardless of the significance of the paradox or puzzle, the effect is to shorten the period in which *SD* can employ effective self-defense. By further handicapping the self-defender without further protecting the aggressor, the imminence requirement is irrational.

(h) An attempted resolution

One might argue that these paradoxes and puzzles can be easily resolved in a way that does not render the imminence requirement problematic. The paradoxes and puzzles arise only because an additional, independent criterion of self-defense—the aggressor's imminent attack is unlawful, unjustified or wrongful—has been improperly omitted from the analysis.[57] By properly considering the relevance of the wrongfulness requirement, the puzzles and paradoxes dissolve. And with the dissolution of the paradoxes and puzzles regarding the imminence requirement, the case against the imminence requirement is weakened.

Consider again the hypothetical in section VI(e) above:

T_0 *A*'s action manifests future aggression

T_0 *SD* poses a temporally imminent threat

T_4 *SD*'s action manifests future aggression

T_5 *A* poses a temporally imminent threat

T_5 *SD* applies force

T_{10} *A* will aggress (if not neutralized)

---

[57] I am indebted to Jens Ohlin for suggesting this possible resolution.

Because A's action manifesting future aggression at T_0 occurs prior to SD's action manifesting future aggression at T_4, A's action is wrongful. SD's action is not wrongful because it is only a response to A's previous wrongful conduct. And A is the wrongful party despite that SD is the first to pose a fully imminent threat (SD poses a fully imminent threat at T_4, whereas A poses a fully imminent threat at T_5). Because SD applies force against A at T_5, when A poses a wrongful and imminent threat, SD is unproblematically justified in self-defense. The paradoxes and puzzles, one might argue, dissolve.

But even under the proposed resolution, problems remain. First, defenders of the imminence requirement touted the imminence requirement, and not the wrongfulness requirement, as that which determines which party is the aggressor and which is the self-defender. As Fletcher and Ohlin contend, "the appeal of imminence is precisely that it provides a nearly foolproof standard for distinguishing between aggressor and the defender."[58] But under the proposed resolution, it is the wrongfulness requirement that is doing this work.

Second, defenders of the imminence requirement maintain that it must include an action component. But if the action component is what determines whether the independent wrongfulness requirement is satisfied or not, why must the imminence requirement also contain it? It would seem redundant for the action component to be contained in both independent requirements. So, is the action component part of the independent imminence requirement or part of the independent wrongfulness requirement? The difficulty in answering this question suggests that the above resolution's reliance on the wrongfulness requirement renders an account of the wrongfulness and imminence requirements incoherent.

Third, the resolution still fails to adequately distinguish between aggressors and self-defenders. Consider the following hypothetical:

T_5 A poses a temporally imminent threat
T_9 A's action manifests future aggression
T_{10} A will aggress (if not neutralized).

When may SD justifiably apply force against A? The imminence requirement allows self-defense force to be applied prior to the aggressor's use of force at T_{10}. Thus, assuming other requirements are met SD should be able to employ force at T_9. The imminence requirement also requires that self-defense not be employed prior to the aggressor being a fully imminent threat. A does not pose a fully imminent threat until T_9. Based on what the imminence requirement both allows and requires, SD may use force at T_9, but no earlier than T_9. Thus, based on the imminence requirement SD's force at T_9 is permissible.

---

[58] Fletcher and Ohlin, *supra* n. 14, 169.

But if *SD* applies force at T_9, *SD* will necessarily manifest the use of this force prior to T_9, say at T_8. (*SD* cannot instantaneously apply force without prior preparations, and these preparations would constitute a manifestation of that force.) The resulting hypothetical is as follows:

T_4 *SD* poses a temporally imminent threat

T_5 *A* poses a temporally imminent threat

T_8 *SD*'s action manifests future aggression

T_9 *SD* applies force

T_9 *A*'s action manifests future aggression

T_{10} *A* will aggress (if not neutralized).

By manifesting force at T_8, *SD* manifests force prior to *A*. By manifesting force prior to *A*, *SD* now becomes the wrongful party as per the resolution above. *SD* also poses a fully imminent threat prior to *A*. So it seems that *SD* is the aggressor as per both the imminence and wrongfulness requirements if *SD* applies force at T_9.

So, when will it be permissible for *SD* to apply force against *A*? Must *SD* wait until T_{10} when *A* will be applying force against *SD*? No, even then it will be impermissible. If *SD* applies force at T_{10}, *SD* must necessarily have manifested that use of force at an earlier point in time, say at T_9. The resulting hypothetical is as follows:

T_5 *SD* poses a temporally imminent threat

T_5 *A* poses a temporally imminent threat

T_9 *SD*'s action manifests future aggression

T_9 *A*'s action manifests future aggression

T_{10} *A* does aggress

T_{10} *SD* applies force.

SD manifesting the use of force at T_9, the same time as *A*, makes it indeterminate as to which party is wrongful and which party is the first to pose an imminent threat. Because *A* is neither the first party to act wrongfully nor the first to pose an imminent threat, *SD* would still not be justified in using force against *A* at T_{10}.

SD must wait to use force against *A* until T_{11} in order that A will be the first to pose a wrongful and imminent threat. But requiring a self-defender to wait until *after* the aggressor uses force defeats the very purpose of the imminence requirement— allowing a self-defender to use force prior to the aggressor's force so that the aggressor's force may be prevented. This point may be even more dramatically illustrated if we suppose that *A* uses lethal force against *SD* at T_{10}. By the time the imminence and wrongfulness requirements allow *SD* to use justifiable self-defense at T_{11}, *SD* is already dead. As a result, the proposed resolution of incorporating the wrongfulness requirement into the analysis fails to adequately resolve the problems incurred by the imminence requirement.

VII. Conclusion

The imminence requirement for justified self-defense is problematic and should be abandoned. As a proxy or evidentiary requirement, it unduly distorts and restricts an actor's moral right to effective self-defense when necessary. Though defended as crucial for differentiating between unlawful aggressors and lawful defenders, the imminence requirement fails to properly distinguish them. Understood in purely temporal terms, the imminence requirement reverses our intuitions and classifies aggressors as defenders and defenders as aggressors. Understood as containing both temporal and action components, the imminence requirement is arbitrary, overinclusive, underinclusive, and distorts the balance of interests—between aggressor and defender—that it is designed to maintain. Close analysis of the interrelation between the temporal and action components reveals a number of puzzles. In some situations, despite facing an imminent threat, a defender either using force or even merely preparing to use force at the point of imminence would be paradoxically deemed the aggressor by the imminence requirement. While these puzzles may be technically resolved by adopting a post-imminence standard, a moral rationale for such an extended waiting period subsequent to the point of imminence is still lacking.

Demonstrating that the imminence requirement is seriously problematic has significant implications for the permissibility of targeted killing. The principal obstacle to targeted killings being justified as a form of national self-defense is the imminence requirement. The imminence requirement is not typically satisfied because the targeted victim is neither presently aggressing nor temporally about to aggress, nor physically manifesting future aggression at the time of the killing. The targeted victim might well be asleep or engaged in some other innocuous conduct. But if the imminence requirement itself is problematic, the failure of targeted killings to satisfy the imminence requirement may no longer bar targeted killings from being justified in self-defense. Of course, in order for targeted killings to be justified in self-defense, the other requirements of self-defense must be satisfied. And targeted killings would also have to satisfy whatever standard is selected to replace imminence—for example, that the targeted killing be necessary. Whether targeted killing would satisfy an alternative standard is unclear. But demonstrating the invalidity of the imminence requirement lays the foundation for consideration of alternative standards that targeted killing would possibly satisfy. The rejection of the imminence requirement and the adoption of an alternative standard alter the answer to the question "Is targeted killing justifiable in self-defense?" from "No" to "Maybe".

10

DEFENDING DEFENSIVE TARGETED KILLINGS

Phillip Montague

Targeted killings of the controversial sort that will be focused on here are exemplified by the following hypothetical case:

> Al is a special-forces sniper whose team is assigned the mission of killing a certain terrorist. This particular terrorist is responsible for fabricating devices that are used by suicide bombers who detonate their explosives in places frequented by large numbers of civilians. Al's team is provided with reliable information regarding the terrorist's plan to travel by car to his bomb factory. Al and his team are flown by helicopter to a suitable location along the terrorist's route, where they wait for him to arrive. When the terrorist does come within range, Al shoots and kills him.

Al's action is seriously problematic from a legal standpoint. First of all, his killing the terrorist possesses none of the features that would render it permissible according to the criminal law. Al is certainly not acting self-defensively, for example. Moreover, the status of his action within the laws of war is at best unclear. These laws do permit members of opposing forces in wars to kill each other, even if doing so is not self-defensive, or is not otherwise necessary to avert imminent threats of serious harm. But the laws of war have traditionally been interpreted as applying only to conflicts between the military forces of political communities, or at least to groups whose members overtly distinguish themselves from civilian noncombatants.[1] On this view, the laws of war are inapplicable to a political community's conflict with terrorist organizations, and hence can provide no basis for concluding that Al's action is legally permissible.

The moral status of targeted killings is problematic for analogous reasons. Ordinary moral principles permit homicide only when necessary to prevent the loss of life or comparably serious harms. This restriction does seem to be relaxed in various ways

---

[1] On this point, see especially Michael Walzer's discussion of guerilla warfare in Michael Walzer, *Just and Unjust Wars* (Basic Books, 1977) 179–206.

for killings within wars. In particular, combatants on opposing sides can be morally permitted to kill each other even when, in doing so, they are not responding to imminent threats of serious harm. However, this relaxation of ordinary morality's prohibition against homicide would seem to require the existence of a special set of moral norms that—like the laws of war—apply only to wars strictly so-called; that is, these moral norms of war would apply only to conflicts between the military forces of political communities. Accordingly, a "morality of war" would not apply to the targeted killing of terrorists, and would provide no better basis than ordinary morality for establishing the permissibility of these killings.

I will argue here, however, that this explanation of the moral status of targeted killing is mistaken because of what it assumes about the implications of ordinary morality. I will argue more specifically that targeted killings can be morally permissible according to ordinary moral principles of self-defense.[2] Central to my argument is the idea that individuals, like the terrorist in our example, perform actions that are connected in morally significant ways with the actions of others (of suicide bombers, for example). More specifically, the idea is that, while the terrorist is not himself acting aggressively, his actions can be components of an action that has multiple agents, and that is *jointly* aggressive. As will be explained in the course of the discussion that follows, ordinary moral principles of self-defense whose applicability is commonly restricted to individually aggressive actions, can also be applied to actions that are jointly aggressive.

---

[2] It seems to me that there is no good reason for believing in a special morality of war unless ordinary morality yields mistaken results when applied to actions performed within wars. If my arguments for the permissibility of targeted killings succeed, however, then they also suggest that ordinary morality provides a much better basis for appraising actions in wars than is commonly thought. The arguments would therefore cast doubt on the need for a special morality of war. I will return to this point at the end of this discussion.

Richard Meyer offers a very different reason for believing in a special morality of war. He states that:

> The common "general intuitions" that are the moral basis of criminal law are a product of interpersonal relations in civilized society. They are fundamentally based on the human desire for stability. Every civilized society can intuitively see the benefit of having a near total restriction on the use of violence within that community. These same common intuitions give rise to substantive crimes such as homicide and defenses such as justifications and excuses. They are part and parcel to any and every civilization going back millennia. The existence of commonality of intuitions within the vast array of civilian criminal systems has been used to prove the existence of some level of objective morality. (See Lon Fuller) If this is an appropriate method and conclusion, the same test applied to common intuitions within the laws of war is evidence of the existence of a separate moral code for acts of combat. ("The Privilege of Belligerency and Formal Declarations of War," in this Volume, at ch. 7.)

Meyer's last claim has matters reversed, however. That is, facts about the development of law provide no basis for drawing conclusions about the content of morality, although the existence of "a separate moral code for acts of combat" would provide reasons for creating or maintaining a separate set of laws for such actions.

Actions can be jointly defensive as well as jointly aggressive. This move in the direction of collectivizing defensive and aggressive actions might seem to imply that, in the final analysis, targeted killings must be viewed as acts of *national* self-defense that are responses to aggressive actions on the part of terrorist organizations. I will, however, provide reasons for regarding appeals to national self-defense as, at best, unhelpful in the present context.

I.

As a useful first step towards explaining how principles of self-defense apply to targeted killings, let us examine these principles in a somewhat broader context.

Given how theories of self-defense are invariably formulated, their primary applications are to defensive actions performed by individuals in response to aggressive actions performed by other individuals. Judith Thomson depicts a hypothetical situation of this sort in her classic paper "Self-Defense and Rights":

> Suppose Aggressor has got hold of a tank. He has told Victim that if he gets a tank, he's going to get in it and run Victim down. Victim sees Aggressor get in his tank and start towards Victim. It is open country, and Victim can see that there is no place to hide, and nothing he can put between himself and Aggressor which Aggressor cannot circle round. Fortunately, Victim happens to have an anti-tank gun with him, and it is in good working order, so he can use it to blow up the tank, thereby saving his life, but of course thereby also killing Aggressor.[3]

Assuming that, when Aggressor launches his attack, Victim's actions are morally innocuous, and assuming too that no one else is involved in this situation, Victim's action is a paradigm instance of morally permissible self-defensive homicide.

Of course, our example of Al and the terrorist is very different from Thomson's. The terrorist is not acting aggressively, and Al's action is not self-defensive, so the question of whether Al is permitted to kill the terrorist in self-defense does not even arise. Theories of self-defense almost invariably apply as well to other-defense, however. For example, a key component of Thomson's account of self-defense is her claim that a person has no right to life if killing him is the only way in which to prevent him from performing an action that would violate another's right to life (and other things are equal).[4] Nothing in this account implies that it is restricted to *self*-defensive homicide. A person who does lack a right to life in virtue of satisfying the condition stipulated by Thomson can be permissibly killed by anyone in a position to do so.[5]

---

[3] Judith Jarvis Thomson, "Self-Defense and Rights," *The Lindley Lecture* (University of Kansas Press, 1977) 3.

[4] Thomson presents her account of self-defense in "Self-Defense," 20 *Philosophy and Public Affairs* (1991) 283–310.

[5] A similar result follows from Suzanne Uniacke's account of self-defense. According to Uniacke, "as individuals we possess . . . [the right to life] only so far as we are not an unjust immediate threat

We must therefore consider whether targeted killings like the one carried out by Al could be morally permissible in virtue of being appropriately other-defensive. Taken in context, the following remarks by Andrew Altman and Christopher Heath Wellman suggest that they might answer this last question affirmatively:

> Surely, it would have been permissible for someone to have assassinated Stalin in the 1930s. It seems, then, that political assassination is, in principle at least, a morally permissible means of stopping or halting human-rights abuses.[6]

These remarks raise an important question regarding the conditions that govern morally permissible defensive homicide. This question concerns what might be called the "inevitability condition," according to which killing x in self- or other-defense is morally permissible only if x's killing an innocent person would otherwise be inevitable.[7]

It might be thought that "highly probable" should replace "inevitable" in the aforementioned condition. But suppose that x is attacking y at time t, and that—at t—x's killing y is highly probable if y does not kill x first. Suppose too that, as a matter of fact, x's attack will fail regardless of what y does.[8] Is y nevertheless permitted to kill x at t? I would argue that she is not. Probability considerations can, of course, play an epistemic role in the contexts we are examining. However, whether a defensive homicide is permissible depends on whether it is in fact the only way in which to avoid an innocent's death—not on whether anyone reasonably believes that it is. Such epistemic considerations are (indirectly) relevant to moral culpability or blameworthiness after the fact, but they are irrelevant to moral permissibility before the fact.[9]

The underlying distinction here is between negative moral appraisals of actions and negative moral appraisals of their agents. My primary focus is on the former appraisals—not because they are more important than the latter—but because they are more basic in this respect: a person is morally blameworthy or culpable *for performing a certain action* only if the action is morally impermissible. Blameworthiness and culpability for acting also depend on what the agent could

---

to another person's life or proportionate interest." Suzanne Uniacke, *Permissible Killing* (Cambridge University Press, 1994) 196. Hence, someone who is an "unjust immediate threat" to another's life has no right to life, and can be permissibly killed in either self- or other-defense.

[6] Andrew Altman and Christopher Heath Wellman, "From Humanitarian Intervention to Assassination: Human Rights and Political Violence," 118 *Ethics* (2008) 253.

[7] This condition is sometimes stated in terms of necessity: killing x in self- or other-defense is morally permissible only if doing so is necessary to prevent x from killing an innocent person. I have avoided this terminology because the concept of necessity has other uses in both law and philosophy.

[8] The implication here is that, at a certain time t, the occurrence of an event e at a later time t, can be highly probable relative to the evidence available at t, even though e does not actually occur at t.

[9] I argue for some closely related positions in Phillip Montague, "Blameworthiness, Vice, and the Objectivity of Morals," 85 *Pacific Philosophical Quarterly* (2004) 68–84.

reasonably have been expected to believe about the nature of the action and its consequences; and here is where probability considerations enter into the picture.

The preceding remarks lead to a second point that needs to be made before proceeding—namely, that inevitability is distinct from imminence. That inevitability does not imply imminence becomes clear on considering the following variant of Thomson's example:

> Some Third Party (rather than Victim) has the anti-tank gun. Aggressor isn't yet aware of Victim's presence, but, when he does see Victim, he will launch his attack. Third Party can prevent Aggressor from killing Victim only if he fires his weapon before Aggressor begins his attack.

Third Party's killing Aggressor in these circumstances would be *preemptive* other-defense, and would satisfy the inevitability condition referred to above, even though the threat posed by Aggressor is not imminent.[10] Killing Aggressor would also be morally permissible according to some familiar theories of self-defense (including Thomson's own theory).[11]

As it stands, however, our example of Al and the terrorist is not about preemptive other-defense, since nothing in the example suggests that the terrorist will inevitably attack and kill innocent people if he is not killed.[12] But the example does seem relevantly similar to this variation on Thomson's theme:

> Prior to launching his attack on Victim, Aggressor must refuel his tank, and Accessory's truck is the only available source of additional fuel. Accessory is happy to help, since she also wants Victim killed. The only way in which Third Party can prevent Aggressor from eventually attacking Victim and running him down with his tank is by destroying Accessory's truck and Accessory along with it.

Third Party can save Victim's life by—and only by—killing Accessory. Doing so would not be individually other-defensive, however (at least not obviously so), since Accessory is not attacking Victim. It is therefore difficult to see how theories that are aimed at determining the moral dimensions of individually defensive homicide can have anything to say about this case—or our example of Al and the terrorist.

Thomson's theory is a case in point. Its central thesis (components of which were stated above) can be put as follows: killing x is morally permissible if x lacks a right to life; and x lacks a right to life if killing him is necessary to prevent him from

---

[10] For an extended discussion of the concept of imminence, see Russell Christopher, "Imminence in Justified Targeted Killing", in this Volume, ch. 10.

[11] Thomson's view implies that x is permitted to kill y if y would otherwise violate someone's right to life. Since, in the preceding example, Aggressor will violate Victim's right to life if Third Party does not kill Aggressor, Third Party is permitted to kill Aggressor.

[12] Although these brief remarks on the nature of preemption suffice for my purposes, much broader purposes are served by the more complete account that is provided by Claire Finkelstein in "Targeted Killing as Preemptive Action," in this Volume, ch. 6.

violating another's right to life (and other things are equal). Since it does not appear that killing Accessory is necessary to prevent *him* from violating Victim's right to life, Thomson's theory does not seem to imply that Third Party is permitted to kill Accessory. And, given the relevant similarity of this case to that of Al and the terrorist, Thomson's theory does not appear to imply that Al's targeted killing is permissible.[13]

Of course, self- and other-defense situations are not the only ones in which people are permitted to prevent the deaths of innocents by killing non-innocents. There are also what might be called "self-preservation" and "other-preservation" situations, the latter of which might be thought to include Third Party's killing Accessory and Al's killing the terrorist. By itself, however, this change of direction would be incapable of solving the problem at hand. This is because the permissibility of killing individuals in circumstances like those surrounding Accessory and the terrorist depends on connections between their actions and the actions of others.

---

[13] Thomson's interpretation of what it takes to violate rights is extremely broad, however, as is evident from her claim that "agency is...[not] required for violating a right." Thomson, *supra* n. 4, 302. Arguably, Thomson's account implies that killing *x* counts as permissible defensive homicide if killing *x* is the only way to disrupt a causal sequence that would otherwise result in an innocent's death, even if *x*'s role in that sequence is purely passive. Perhaps, then, Thomson would regard her theory as encompassing Accessory's action. After all, Accessory plays an active role in a causal sequence that will result in Victim's death if Accessory is not himself killed. And similar remarks might apply to the terrorist in our example, and his potential role in the deaths of innocents.

The matter is, if anything, even less clear when examined in the light of Uniacke's theory. She maintains that defensive force is morally permissible only if used against someone who is "presently" a threat, because "the positive right of self-defense is grounded in the fact that force directly blocks the infliction of unjust harm." (Uniacke, *supra* n. 5, 185–6) These remarks certainly seem to preclude the possibility of using Uniacke's account as a basis for establishing the permissibility of killing either Accessory or the terrorist in our example. But Uniacke also maintains that the use of force against "contingent threats" can be defensive and permissible, and that contingent threats include those who facilitate or assist immediate threats (ibid. at 169).

According to Jeff McMahan, if a person is "morally liable to defensive harm," then killing the person does not wrong him. He explains the former expression as follows:

> the criterion of liability to defensive killing is moral responsibility, through action that lacks objective justification, for a threat of unjust harm to others, where a harm is unjust if it is one to which the victim is not liable and to which she has not consented. Jeff McMahan, "The Basis of Moral Liability to Defensive Killing," 15 *Philosophical Issues* (2005) 394.

McMahan's position might accommodate the idea that both killing Accessory and killing the terrorist in our example are permissible, but determining whether it does would require an explanation of the concept of responsibility for a threat of harm.

What has been said here about the implications of these theories for the "Accessory" example, also applies to cases involving accomplices. Here is such a case: Aggressor will shoot and kill Victim using the gun on a tank driven by Accomplice; Aggressor is hidden, but Third Party has a clear shot at Accomplice; if Third Party shoots and kills Accomplice, Victim will have time to escape—and this is the only way that Victim's life can be saved.

Let me hasten to add that my own account of self-defense is no clearer on these issues.

Hence, an explanation of the permissibility of Third Party's killing Accessory would need to incorporate an account of how Accessory's and Aggressor's actions combine to create a lethal threat for Victim. In a parallel fashion, the permissibility of Al's killing the terrorist could not be explained without locating the terrorist's actions within a nexus that includes the actions of others associated with his terrorist group—suicide bombers in particular. It is worth bearing in mind, by the way, that Al's action was part of a joint effort that included contributions by many individuals serving in various capacities, some of whom (planners, for example) were not directly involved in the shooting.

These remarks shift the focus of this inquiry from actions that are individually defensive or aggressive to actions that are in some sense collectively defensive or aggressive. This shift in focus leads quite naturally to the idea that targeted killings are matters of national self-defense—that their permissibility follows from the role they play in defensive actions by political communities in response to aggression by terrorist organizations.

II.

Certain targeted killings are morally problematic because neither ordinary morality nor (assuming there is such a thing) the morality of war seems to provide a basis for establishing their permissibility. Ordinary morality seemingly will not do because the targeted killings in question do not avert imminent threats of death or comparably serious harm to anyone. And since a morality of war would apply only to conflicts between political communities, it would be inapplicable to the killing of terrorists. However, if targeted killings were matters of national self-defense, then—contrary to much of what has been said to this point—principles of self-defense, understood as components of ordinary morality, might indeed be relevant to the morality of targeted killings.

It is important to recognize that the appeal to national self-defense that we are considering is meant to establish that *individual* targeted killings (for example, Al's killing the terrorist) are morally permissible.[14] For this to work, there must be valid arguments whose central premises are exemplified by "The United States has a right of self-defense," and whose conclusions are exemplified by "Al is morally

---

[14] The proposition that individual targeted killings can be morally permissible as matters of national self-defense might cross the *jus ad bellum/jus in bello* divide, and therefore contradict a basic tenet of just war theory. However, the fact that a proposition is incompatible with just war theory is not in itself a reason for regarding the proposition as unworthy of serious consideration.

permitted to kill the terrorist."[15] But how do we proceed logically from the central premises of such arguments to their conclusions?

A natural first step would be to infer that, because political communities have a right of self-defense, they have a right to establish policies that are aimed at defending themselves against aggression. Then, assuming that targeted-killing policies have this aim, the next step would be to infer that political communities have a right to establish such policies. However, even if the argument were valid to this point, there would be no logical way in which to derive conclusions about the moral permissibility of particular targeted killings. For example, there would be no valid way to infer that, because the United States has a right of self-defense, Al is permitted to kill the terrorist. Hence, even if a political community is fighting a defensive war against terrorists, this has no logical bearing on whether any specific targeted killings are morally permissible.

The logical problems associated with appeals to national self-defense become especially clear on attempting actually to employ theories of self-defense to show that particular targeted killings can count as morally permissible defensive homicides.

Consider Thomson's theory, for example, according to which x is permitted to kill y in self-defense if and only if y would otherwise violate x's right to life (and other things are equal). Applying this theory to our example of Al and the terrorist, we have "The United States is permitted to kill the terrorist if and only if the terrorist would otherwise violate the United States' right to life (and other things are equal)." Even if sense could be made of the idea that the United States has a right to life, this proposition is obviously incapable of being used as a basis for inferring that Al's killing the terrorist is morally permissible. Moreover, a similar result would be equally obvious if other theories of self-defense (Uniacke's or McMahan's, for example) were appealed to.

While our example of Al and the terrorist might be locatable within the broad context of a conflict between the United States and the organization to which the terrorist belongs, explaining its defensive character requires a much narrower context. As was suggested in the preceding section, this narrower context cannot be restricted to Al and the terrorist, but must also include members of broader groups with whom Al and the terrorist are respectively connected in certain ways. For convenience, Al's group will be referred to as an assassination team (consisting of

---

[15] This sort of argument seems at least implicit in remarks made by Attorney General Eric Holder during an interview following the killing of Osama bin Laden. In that interview, Holder characterized bin Laden as "a commander in the field," and he also claimed that the killing was justified as a matter of "national self-defense." (Note, however, that if the appeal to self-defense here is appropriate and is *moral* in nature, then there is no need to claim that killing bin Laden was permissible in virtue of his status as commander of a military force.)

members of the U.S. military and perhaps the CIA), and the opposing group will be referred to as a terrorist cell.[16]

It seems reasonable to say that the assassination team is responding to aggressive actions on the part of the terrorist cell. The fact remains that *the assassination team* does not kill *the terrorist cell*; rather, Al kills the terrorist. And it is the moral permissibility of Al's action that is in question. Answering this question requires examining certain of the ways in which the actions of members of a group are related to actions of the group as a whole.

Note first of all that statements of the truth-conditions for propositions that do attribute actions to groups always contain references to appropriate actions on the part of members of those groups. For example, if it is true that Green Bay played in the 2011 Super Bowl, then this is because individuals who were members of the Green Bay Packers on February 6, 2011 performed actions of certain sorts on that date. And if it is true that the Royal Shakespeare Company performed *Romeo and Juliet* during March of 2010, then this is because of certain of the things done by members of the Company during that period.

Football games and dramatic performances are not simply collections of individual actions, however. More specifically, the truth-conditions for the proposition that the Royal Shakespeare Company performed *Romeo and Juliet* would not be equivalent to anything like this: x_1 performed a_1 at t_1 and x_2 performed a_2 at t_2 and.... In addition to such references to actions performed individually, a statement of the truth-conditions for the proposition in question would also include references to actions that are performed *in concert* or *jointly* with others—references that presuppose the concept of joint agency. Note too that, although the proposition on which we are focusing concerns a dramatic performance, not all of the actions to which it refers are individual dramatic performances. Some of these references are to actions on the part of individuals who manipulate scenery or control lighting, for example.

In a parallel fashion, if the assassination team is responding to aggressive actions on the part of the terrorist cell, then this is because members of the respective groups act jointly in certain ways. Moreover, just as the individual actions that compose a dramatic performance need not themselves be dramatic performances, so the members of the terrorist cell can be engaged in joint aggression even though not all of the actions composing their joint action are individually aggressive. Similarly, actions of the assassination team can be jointly defensive without all of their actions being individually defensive.

---

[16] Since the assassination team is not defending itself against aggression on the part of the terrorist cell, if the case is to count as morally permissible defensive homicide, then it must somehow be construed as permissible *other*-defense. I will return to this point later in the discussion.

In order to elucidate the implications of these considerations for the permissibility of targeted killings, an account of joint action—and its companion concept of joint agency—is required. With this account in hand, it will be possible to explain how familiar theories of self-defense imply that targeted killings like the one in our example can count as morally permissible defensive homicide.

III.

Joint actions differ from individual actions in that, while the latter are performed by single agents, the former are performed by multiple agents and have individual actions as components. Here is a homely example that illustrates this distinction:

> Dale's car has a dead battery. Roy offers to help with her problem by connecting her battery to his by means of jumper cables, and Dale accepts his offer. When Roy completes the connection, he signals Dale who is at the controls. She engages the starter and the car starts.

The car is started by Dale and Roy. However, while the proposition that Dale and Roy started the car is true, the proposition that Dale started the car and Roy started the car is false. We might interpret this proposition as implying that a pair of people started Dale's car; that is, a group containing Dale and Roy as members. However, a more perspicuous interpretation would refer to the truth-conditions for the initial proposition.

A statement of these truth-conditions would refer to certain individual actions performed by Dale and Roy respectively, and to ways in which these actions are connected with each other. It is in virtue of the nature of the individual actions that are respectively performed by Dale and Roy, and of how these actions are connected with each other, that it is true that *they* started the car. That is, over and above the individual actions respectively performed by Dale and Roy, there is a joint action that consists in the starting of Dale's car, and whose agents are both Dale and Roy.

In order for Dale and Roy to be acting jointly in the relevant sense, they must be exercising joint agency. And this latter concept can be explained in light of the following, more detailed version of the example:

> Dale wants her car to be started. She believes that, if she engages the starter and Roy does his part, then the car will start. Roy wants Dale's car to be started. He believes that, if he connects her battery to his and Dale does her part, then the car will start. Dale's desires and beliefs lead her to engage the starter (call this action A). Roy's desires and beliefs lead him to connect the two batteries (call this action B). Assuming that the car is otherwise in working order and the cables are properly connected, Dale's performing A initiates a sequence of events that merges with the sequence of events initiated by Roy's performing B, forming a sequence of events that results in the starting of Dale's car.

While it is not true that Dale started her car, and it is not true that Roy started her car, each of them performs an action (A and B, respectively) that is a component of the joint action that consists in starting Dale's car. They exercise joint agency in doing so, in virtue of the common contents of the beliefs and desires that lead them to perform the individual components of their joint action. Although Dale and Roy's joint action and joint agency are distinct from their individual actions and exercises of agency, the former are explicable in terms of the latter. As a result, the only agents involved in the example are concrete individuals.

What has been said here about the Dale/Roy example can be generalized as follows:

> x and y act jointly in bringing about state of affairs S if and only if (a) x and y desire that S obtains, and each believes that there is another person who also desires that S obtains; (b) x and y each believes that, if she acts on these beliefs and desires, and if the other person does so as well, then S will obtain; (c) x's beliefs and desires lead her to perform action v, and y's beliefs and desires lead him to perform w; (d) x's performing v and y's performing w initiate causal sequences that merge to form a sequence that results in S's obtaining.

The joint agency exercised by x and y consists in the common contents of the beliefs and desires that initiate the merging causal sequences that produce S.[17]

This account of joint action and agency can straightforwardly be extended to situations containing more than just two agents.[18] Moreover, joint actions can be composed not only of individual actions, but also of other joint actions. If, in our example, some friend of Roy's helps him connect the cables and does so with appropriate beliefs and desires, then their joint action is a component of a larger joint action performed by Dale, Roy, and the friend.

Because joint actions admit of this sort of structuring, they can be quite complex, and involve large numbers of agents. As was pointed out above, plays and games provide contexts within which complex joint actions are commonly performed. So do construction projects, sessions of legislative bodies, and battles. Regardless of the composition of a joint action, however, its agents are always concrete individuals exercising joint agency.

---

[17] Joint agency is actually a bit more complex than these remarks suggest because a person's actions can be initiated by more than one pair of the person's beliefs and desires. E.g., Roy's connecting the battery cables might be caused not only by his desire to start Dale's car and his belief that his connecting the cables will help cause this to happen, but also by his desire, say, to check on his memory of how correctly to connect battery cables, together with the corresponding belief.

[18] My explanation of joint actions resembles in certain respects Michael Bratman's account of "shared cooperative activities." "Shared Cooperative Activity," 101 *Philosophical Review* (1992) 327–42. Bratman's account is more restrictive than the explanation of joint actions presented here; e.g., the actions of soldiers on one side in a battle could be a joint action in my sense without being a shared cooperative activity in Bratman's sense. (Bratman actually uses the expression "joint action" in his account of shared cooperative activities, although without explaining what joint actions are.)

Now recall our "Accessory" example, in which Aggressor and Accessory both want Aggressor to kill Victim, and in which he will do so if and only if Accessory is not prevented from refueling Aggressor's tank. If Third Party were to refrain from acting, then the proposed account of joint action and agency would imply that Victim's death would result from a joint action performed by Accessory and Aggressor. Theirs would be a joint action in virtue of the merging causal sequences resulting from their individual actions, and in virtue of the common contents of the beliefs and desires with which these actions would respectively be performed.

If Third Party were to destroy Accessory's truck before he could refuel Aggressor's tank, then Third Party's action would be preemptively other-defensive. While killing Accessory would not preempt an aggressive action on his part, it would preempt a jointly aggressive action on the part of Accessory and Aggressor.

We can now return to our original example of Al and the terrorist. Let us assume that, if nothing is done to stop him, the terrorist will provide explosive devices to suicide bombers who cannot be prevented from detonating their devices and thereby killing many innocent people. This case is similar in obvious and significant respects to our "Accessory" example. That is, the terrorist bomb-maker and the suicide bombers (and perhaps others as well) are performing a jointly aggressive action that will result in the deaths of innocents unless something is done to prevent this joint action from being performed.

And there is only one way in which to prevent its performance: Al must kill the terrorist. If Al does so, then his targeted killing is an act of preemptive other-defense against joint aggression. And in virtue of the ways in which Al's action is connected with individual actions performed by other members of the assassination team, together they perform an action that is jointly defensive.

Having explained how targeted killings can count as defensive homicides, we can now consider whether there are conditions under which they are morally permissible. Doing so will require examining the moral properties of joint actions.

Like individual actions, joint actions can be morally permissible, impermissible, or required. They can also be actions that their agents have a right to perform, or actions that violate the rights of others. Moreover, joint actions possess moral properties in virtue of possessing the same non-moral properties that determine the possession of moral properties by individual actions. If, for example, a joint action would result in the deaths of innocent people, then it violates the rights to life of those people, and is therefore morally impermissible (other things being equal).[19]

Additionally, the agents of joint actions can possess moral properties in virtue of the nature of their agency. In particular, they can be morally blameworthy or

---

[19] The moral properties of a joint action are related to the moral properties of its individual components in complex ways that—fortunately—can be ignored here.

praiseworthy for contributing to the performance of joint actions which themselves have relevant moral properties. If, say, a joint action is morally impermissible, and if its agents perform their individual actions with appropriately bad intentions and lack excuses for what they do, then they are blameworthy for their contributions to the joint action.

Now, in the realm of individual actions, theories of self-defense typically imply that defensive homicides are permissible only as responses to actions that possess certain sorts of moral defects. According to Thomson, for example, an action possesses the relevant sort of moral defect if it will violate someone's right to life if its agent is not killed. And according to Susan Uniacke and Jeff McMahan, the relevant defect consists in an action's posing a certain kind of threat to others.[20] The moral defects in individual actions to which these theories refer can also be present in joint actions. Specifically, killing one or more agents of a joint action might be necessary and sufficient to prevent the action from violating someone's right to life. Or a joint action might pose the sorts of threats to which Uniacke's and McMahan's theories refer.

Hence, the theories to which I have alluded could naturally and plausibly be extended from individual defense to joint defense. Rather than attempting to develop any of these possibilities for theories proposed by others, however, I will do so for one that I have defended on a number of occasions.[21]

This theory focuses on situations in which individuals face "closed choices" in the distribution of harm.[22] In a closed-choice situation, an individual x cannot prevent harm from befalling some members of a group G (that might include x), although x can determine which members of G are harmed. The theory implies that, if some member of G culpably created the closed choice situation, then, other things being equal, x is morally permitted (as a matter of justice) to distribute the harm to that individual.[23]

---

[20] McMahan's theory also refers to moral responsibility for creating threats, where moral responsibility is clearly a property of agents rather than of actions. Whether it is a *moral* property, however, is unclear. McMahan emphasizes that moral responsibility is not culpability or blameworthiness, and so he might simply be identifying a kind of responsibility that differs from mere causal responsibility. If so, then being morally responsible for posing a threat might be equivalent to posing it freely, or voluntarily, or intentionally—implying that moral responsibility is not a moral property.

[21] This theory is developed at length in "Self-Defense and Choosing Among Lives," 40 *Philosophical Studies* (1981) 207–19 and in *Punishment as Societal Defense* (Rowman and Littlefield, 1995).

[22] I originally referred to these as "forced choices," but this terminology led to misinterpretations of my position.

[23] The *ceteris paribus* conditions referred to here pertain to proportionality, to doing the minimum harm necessary to accomplish the permitted distributions, and to "side effects" such as harm to innocent bystanders.

Although I have formulated the theory in terms of reference to moral permissibility, a more precise formulation would refer to moral rights and moral requirements. ie, in culpably created closed-choice situations, people have moral rights to favor themselves, and are morally required to favor other innocents. In virtue of its reference to culpability, this theory implies that defensive

Closed-choice situations can clearly be created by multiple agents acting jointly, and these agents can be culpable for doing so. Justice permits the harm to be distributed to as many of these agents as is necessary to prevent it from being inflicted on innocent potential victims. Suppose, for example, that three individuals jointly and culpably create a situation in which x can prevent the death of an innocent person by—and only by—causing the death of one or more of the individuals who created the situation. Then x is permitted to cause the deaths of as many of these individuals as is necessary to defend their intended victim. This same line of reasoning is applicable to our "Accessory" example. It also applies to our original case of Al and the terrorist. It implies that Al is morally permitted to kill the terrorist, and that the killing is defensive in nature.

This result can be generalized, and applied to any targeted killing that is relevantly similar to Al's killing of the terrorist in the circumstances that we are currently envisioning. These are killings that satisfy the following condition: a number of individuals are culpable for jointly creating a closed-choice situation in which killing some number of them is necessary and sufficient to prevent the loss of innocent lives. This condition is satisfied, as many of the individuals who created the closed-choice situation can be permissibly targeted and killed as is necessary to prevent the loss of innocent lives. Such killings would count as morally permissible defensive homicide even if those who are killed are not themselves performing actions that are individually aggressive.

Although my specific concern here is with the question of whether targeted killings can be morally permissible, the approach to answering this question that I have proposed has broader implications for the morality of killings that occur within wars.

As was pointed out much earlier in the discussion, belief in the need for a special morality of war is based largely on the proposition that certain homicides in wars that seem clearly to be permissible, turn out to be impermissible according to the principles of ordinary morality. For example, shelling trucks that are carrying reinforcements to the front lines can be morally permissible. Yet, assuming that those reinforcements pose no imminent threats to anyone, shelling them would appear to be prohibited by ordinary morality.

In order for the proposition that there exists a special morality of war to be even minimally plausible, however, the kinds of conflicts to which it applies must be narrowly restricted. Traditionally, the morality of war has been restricted to conflicts

---

homicide—understood as a moral right or a moral requirement—is a response not only to morally defective actions, but also to morally defective agency. In closed-choice situations that are impermissibly but not culpably created, defensive homicide is merely permissible. (This position is defended in Phillip Montague, "Self-defense and Innocence: Aggressors and Active Threats," 12 *Utilitas* (2000) 62–78.)

between political communities. But tradition is no substitute for an argument and, in fact, the idea of a special morality of war cannot withstand close scrutiny. Its weakness has become especially clear in recent years, with increases in the occurrence of "asymmetrical" wars.

The problem here has a number of sources, but one that seems to me to be especially important, has received almost no attention. I refer to the assumption that wars must be understood as waged either by political communities per se, or by members of those communities acting individually. This assumption is a barrier not only to providing an adequate basis for morally appraising acts of war, but even for accurately describing the events that occur within actual wars.

In addition to references to actions on the part of political communities and on the part of combatants acting individually, references to joint actions are necessary for both moral appraisals and descriptions of acts of war. Indeed, wars should be thought of as being composed of joint actions whose agents are members of the opposing sides. Some of these joint actions are extremely complex, while others are not. Compare, for example, the D-Day invasion with an attack by an American patrol on a German pillbox that occurred during that invasion.

Now, neither the invasion nor the patrol's attack appears to be defensive. But both occur within the context of a response by the forces of a number of political communities to aggression by the forces of other political communities. As was pointed out earlier, a complex joint action can be defensive (aggressive) even if not all of its components are defensive (aggressive). And the aggressive component of a defensive joint action can be morally permissible according to ordinary morality because the defensive joint action is morally permissible. In this way, principles of ordinary morality can be extended to actions that are commonly regarded as open to moral appraisal only within a special morality of war. These ordinary moral principles apply not only to actions that are responses to culpable aggression, but also to those (alluded to in n. 23) that are responses to nonculpable but impermissible aggression.

PART IV

EXERCISING JUDGMENT IN TARGETED KILLING DECISIONS

11

THE IMPORTANCE OF CRITERIA-BASED REASONING IN TARGETED KILLING DECISIONS

Amos N. Guiora

The Obama Administration is clearly committed to a policy of using remotely piloted drones to commit targeted killings. In fact, it has significantly increased the number of drone attacks in comparison to the Bush Administration.[1] Scholars have addressed both targeted killing[2] and the drone policy;[3] the latter has been

---

[1] Alex Strick van Linschoten and Felix Kuehn, "A Knock on the Door: 22 Months of ISAF Press Releases," available at <https://www.afghanistan-analysts.net/uploads/AAN_2011_ISAFPressReleases.pdf> accessed November 4, 2011.

[2] See David Kretzmer, "Targeted Killing of Suspected Terrorists: Extra Judicial Executions or Legitimate Means of Defence?," 2.16 *Eur. J. Int'l. L.* 171 (2005) 171–212; Steve R. David, "Fatal Choices: Israel's Policy of Targeted Killings," *The Begin-Sadat Center For Strategic Studies Bar-Ilan University Mideast Security and Policy Studies No. 51*; Orna Ben-Naftali and Keren Michaeli, "Justice-Ability: A Critique of the Non-Justiciability of The Israeli Policy of Targeted Killing," 1(2) *Journal of International Criminal Justice* 368–405 (2003); Niles Meltzer, *Targeted Killing in International Law* (Oxford University Press, 2008); Edward Kaplan and Daniel Jacobson, "Suicide Bombings and Targeted Killings in (Counter) Terror Games," 51q *Journal of Conflict Resolution* 5, 772–92 (2007).

[3] Jordan Paust, "Self-Defense Targetings of Non-State Actors and Permissibility of U.S. Use of Drones in Pakistan," 19 *Journal of Transnational Law & Policy* 2, 237, (2010); Mary Ellen O'Connell, *Unlawful Killing with Combat Drones: A Case Study of Pakistan 2004–2009*, Notre Dame Legal Studies Paper No. 09-43, available at <http://ssrn.com/abstract=1501144> accessed November 3, 2011; Simon Bronitt (ed.), *Shooting To Kill: The Law Governing Lethal Force In Context* (forthcoming); Afsheen John Radsan and Richard Murphy, "Due Process and Targeted Killing of Terrorists," 31 *Cardozo Law Rev* 405, (2009); Kenneth Anderson, *Targeted Killing in US Counterterrorism Strategy and Law*, available at <http://papers.ssrn.com/sol3/papers.cfm?abstract_id=1415070&rec=1&srcabs=1349357> accessed December 12, 2010; Kenneth Anderson, "Predators Over Pakistan," 15 *The Weekly Standard* 24, 26–34, (2010); Jane Mayer, "The Predator War," *The New Yorker*, October 19, 2009, available at <http://www.newyorker.com/reporting/2009/10/26/091026fa_fact_mayer> accessed November 3, 2011; Geoffrey S. Corn, *Targeting, Command Judgment, and a Proposed Quantum of Proof Component: A Fourth Amendment Lesson in Contextual Reasonableness*, available at <http://papers.ssrn.com/sol3/papers.cfm?abstract_id=1762894> accessed November 3, 2011.

the subject of Congressional hearings,[4] public debates, academic conferences, a major public address by the State Department Legal Advisor,[5] and innumerable newspaper articles.[6] Needless to say, the drone attack policy is not controversy-free. Those engaged in the public debate must focus on proposing both a legal framework and appropriate operational guidelines to enhance effectiveness and efficacy.

Targeted killing and drone attacks are philosophically similar and premised on comparable legal analysis, even though operational differences clearly exist. Both Israel and the United States have concluded that preemptive self-defense justifies killing a target that the intelligence community has determined is involved in planning or executing a future terrorist attack. From the perspective of international law, an expansive reading of the inherent right of self-defense in Article 51 of the U.N. Charter is at the policy's core.[7]

Given the inherent moral, legal and operational complexity of this subject, it is important to articulate and define terms that will hopefully facilitate a reasoned, nuanced and sophisticated conversation. Unfortunately, much of the public debate regarding drones and targeted killing has been distinguished by a lack of understanding regarding the policy—articulation and implementation alike—and the attendant cost–benefit analysis essential to a rational discussion. The discussion here will elaborate on the constituent aspects of a targeted killing, including terms such as legitimate target, threat and imminence, in order to demonstrate the need for a criteria-based process that analyzes such concepts sufficiently.

Targeted killing can be implemented with unmanned aerial vehicles, operated by remote control thousands of miles removed from the "kill site," like the U.S. drone program. Israel's targeted killing policy, in contrast, is largely implemented by manned helicopters. In addition, it is important to note that targeted killing can also be the responsibility of ground forces.[8] For example, the specific scenario presented later in this chapter refers to a targeted killing

---

[4] "'Drones II'—Kenneth Anderson Testimony Submitted to U.S. House of Representatives Committee on Oversight and Government Reform, Subcommittee on National Security and Foreign Affairs, Second Hearing on Drone Warfare," April 28, 2010, available at <http://papers.ssrn.com/sol3/papers.cfm?abstract_id=1619819&rec=1&srcabs=1561229> accessed December 12, 2010.

[5] Harold Koh, "The Obama Administration and International Law," Annual Meeting of the American Society of International Law Washington, DC, March 25, 2010, available at <http://www.state.gov/s/l/releases/remarks/139119.htm> accessed December 12, 2010.

[6] Available at <http://www.washingtonpost.com/wp-dyn/content/article/2011/02/20/AR2011022002975.html?hpid=topnews> accessed February 20, 2011.

[7] Charter of the United Nations, art. 51 (1945), available at <http://www.un.org/en/documents/charter/index.shtml> accessed November 3, 2011.

[8] See the killing of Osama bin Laden.

dilemma involving Israeli Defense Forces (IDF) ground forces in which I was directly involved.[9]

The question that drives this chapter is the following: what are the criteria necessary for a targeted killing decision? The working premise is that targeted killing—as a policy—is both lawful and effective. In that sense, this chapter brackets off many of the normative legal and philosophical questions that determine, in the abstract, the lawfulness or moral permissibility of targeted killing. These questions include, inter alia, the proper scope of Article 51 self-defense, the question of imminence and preemptive self-defense, the role of non-state actors, and the status of terrorists as either civilians or combatants subject to the reciprocal risk of killing. Instead, this chapter cuts across the legal terrain in a wholly different manner: assuming that targeted killing is legally and morally justified in the abstract, how can individual targeted killing decisions be made such that they comply with the basic principles of both law and morality? Do law and morality place additional restrictions on the practice that restrict how a particular country can—and should—implement a targeted killing policy? Ironically, this reverse methodology will then provide some insight into the general legal and moral principles underlying targeted killing.

In other words, assuming the overall legality of targeted killing in the abstract does not mean that every targeted killing is both lawful and effective. Indeed, how the policy is implemented in a particular situation is relevant for determining its legality; that is, the theoretical architecture of the targeted killing policy in both the United States and Israel is just the first step in analyzing the legality of a particular strike. While the theory at the core of the policy emphasizes self-defense, an equally important question is how the policy is implemented in fact. That is the distinctive question addressed in this chapter.

Furthermore, the legal framework is only one facet of an effective paradigm. In the absence of a process—one based on criteria and operational realities—effective decision-making is fundamentally limited. In the arena of targeted killing, the decision is, in many ways, the most important aspect of the operation; the process by which the decision is made is truly central to the lawfulness of the action. Therefore, this chapter argues that a criteria-based approach to the decision-making process simultaneously facilitates operational success and minimizes harm to innocent civilians. The first section presents two components of the theoretical underpinnings for the more practical, operational discussion to follow. First, the need for criterial decision-making by a legal advisor, rather than intuitionism at the discretion of a military commander, is fundamental in counterterrorism in general and targeted killing in particular. Second, the legal and moral principles at the heart of targeted killing drive the criteria-based

---

[9] Because my "hands on" professional experience is limited to targeted killing (as compared to the U.S. drone policy), I will refer to the policy as "targeted killing," although the reader can view the terms as interchangeable, subject to the distinctions explained above.

process and govern the relevant issues and determinations. The second section of the chapter presents a scenario that highlights the need for a criteria-based process and the dangers of an intuition-based approach, and then introduces the key issues and components of such a process. Finally, the third section builds the criteria-based process, focusing on the central elements of threat, source and target and how to identify and apply the relevant criteria to ensure lawful and effective counterterrorism.

The proposal that targeted killing be subject to legal criteria is not a given. Some might suggest that imposing criteria on the decision-maker arguably impedes aggressive operational counterterrorism. A powerful argument can be made that its implementation significantly hampers command discretion. In this view, the military commander should make an all-things-considered judgment about how to proceed—a judgment that relies more on his military and command experience than it does on specific criteria determined in advance by experts in the laws of war and then applied in practice by military lawyers. The rationale for this unfettered discretion- and intuition-based approach would be that "excessive" involvement by lawyers hampers the ability of commanders to make quick and aggressive decisions to hit targets of opportunity. This is a legitimate concern that cannot be easily dismissed and warrants serious discussion. It is, frankly, a discussion that must be had for a number of reasons, most notably because President Obama has significantly increased the implementation of the drone policy in comparison to President Bush. The chart below depicts the dramatic increase in the use of drones under President Obama; all signs clearly indicate this policy will continue to be implemented for years to come.

The core requirement to minimize collateral damage is one of the fundamental motivations for criteria-based decision-making in targeted killing. In the absence of criteria

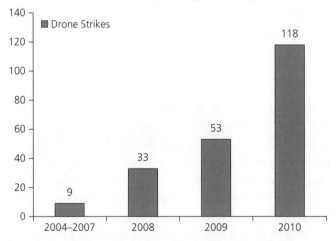

U.S Drone strikes in Pakistan: 2004–2010

Source: O'Connell, Mary Ellen, "Unlawful Killing with Combat Drones: A Case Study of Pakistan, 2004–2009. Shooting to Kill: The Law Governing Lethal Force in Context," Simon Bonitt (ed.), Notre Dame Legal Studies Paper No. 09–43 forthcoming. Available at: <http://ssrn.com/atract/501144>.

for decision-making, at best targeted killing will pay mere lip service to this key international law requirement. In that vein, the recent CIA claim that not one noncombatant has been killed in drone attacks in 2011 is,[10] at the least, an eyebrow raiser.[11]

The world of operational counterterrorism decision-making is extraordinarily complex; it is also high-risk and fraught with danger. The burdens imposed on the decision-maker are extraordinary because of the overwhelming responsibility to ensure the safety of soldiers under his command and also to protect innocent civilians. Although the rules of engagement that codify when an "open fire" order may be given are carefully written and subject to thorough examination by a wide range of experienced professionals, the ultimate decision is made in the field by a commander exercising discretion subject to an infinite set of circumstances.

Precisely because those circumstances impact the commander's judgment, the criteria-based model is an essential mechanism for increasing the effectiveness of the targeted killing policy. To that end, I define effectiveness as the correct identification and targeting of a legitimate target (based on imminent threat and necessity) subject to stringent collateral damage restrictions. Implementing this policy in accordance with this two-part test demands a criteria-based approach.

This chapter is based on my twin perspectives of having served as a legal advisor in the IDF and now as a professor of law with numerous opportunities to reflect on decisions in which I was involved.[12] My concentration on "process" stems from my belief that a criteria-based model of decision-making is essential to minimizing collateral damage and enhancing the effectiveness of existing policies. Simply put, beyond the legal, moral and theoretical underpinnings, lawful targeted killing must be based on criteria-based decision-making, which increases the probability of correctly identifying and attacking the legitimate target. A state's decision to kill a human being during a counterterrorism operation must be predicated on an

---

[10] Available at <http://www.guardian.co.uk/commentisfree/cifamerica/2011/aug/11/civilian-victims-cia-drones> accessed August 14, 2011.

[11] Available at <http://www.nytimes.com/2011/08/14/opinion/sunday/the-cia-and-drone-strikes.html?nl=todaysheadlines&emc=tha211> accessed August 14, 2011. For more information on the military's attempts to limit noncombatant death, see Gregory McNeal, "Are Targeted Killings Unlawful? A Case Study in Empirical Claims Without Empirical Evidence" in this Volume, ch. 12.

[12] As legal advisor, my legal advice was requested on a 24/7 basis. My advice was based on interpretation of international law, Israeli statutes, Israeli Supreme Court precedent and an assessment whether the Supreme Court, sitting as the High Court of Justice, would, based on robust and rigorous judicial review, intervene in the commander's decision. The Supreme Court sitting as the High Court of Justice (HCJ) is empowered to issue temporary restraining orders and to hear petitions filed on behalf of individuals—including Palestinian residents of the West Bank and Gaza Strip—claiming that an executive branch decision will infringe on or take away their rights. The advice, rooted in the rule of law, required a balancing of legitimate individual rights with equally legitimate national security considerations. On the role of robust judicial review, see Aharon Barak, "A Judge on Judging: The Role of a Supreme Court in a Democracy," 116 *Harv. L. Rev.* 16 (2002); Amos N. Guiora and Erin M. Page, "Going Toe to Toe: President Barak's and Chief Justice Rehnquist's Theories of Judicial Activism," 29 *Hastings Int'l & Comp. L. Rev.* 51 (2005).

objective determination that the "target" is, indeed, a legitimate target. Otherwise, the state's action is illegal, immoral and ultimately ineffective. Subjective decisions based on fear or perception alone pose grave danger to both the suspected terrorist and innocent civilians.

It goes without saying that many object to the killing of a human being when less lethal alternatives are available to neutralize the "target." Others will suggest—not incorrectly—that targeted killing is nothing but a manifestation of the state acting as "judge, jury and executioner." On the other hand, the state has a responsibility to develop and implement measures protecting innocent civilians from enemies who kill and maim innocent civilians. The need for an objective determination that the person in the crosshairs is a legitimate target requires a method to enhance the decision-making process in the face of extreme pressure.

I. The normative framework

(a) The need for criterial decision-making

(i) *Process vs. intuition-based responses*

Effective counterterrorism requires the nation-state to apply self-imposed restraints; otherwise violations of both international law and morality in armed conflict are all but inevitable. Aharon Barak, the former President (Chief Justice) of the Israeli Supreme Court addressed the issue of self-imposed restraint in his seminal article, "A Judge on Judging."[13] According to Barak, the nation-state is subject to legal and moral restrictions with the understanding that limits on state power are the essence of the rule of law. In order to implement Barak's theory on a practical basis, the nation-state must develop clear criteria with respect to operational decision-making.[14] This is in direct contrast to intuitive decision-making, which, dependent on the notion that a person simply knows what is right, is devoid of articulated standards and guidelines.

As background, the theater of war, regardless of whether it is traditional warfare between nation-states or state/non-state conflicts, requires articulated standard operating procedures addressing a wide range of issues including (but not restricted

---

[13] Aharon Barak, "A Judge on Judging: The Role of a Supreme Court in a Democracy," *supra* n. 12.

[14] The term "criteria" is used in the common-sense understanding of the term. Criteria help guide decisions by providing a test that captures the relevant reasons for an outcome. In that sense, criteria are neither standards nor rules as those terms are understood in the field of jurisprudence. However, criteria are closer to standards than they are to rules, which are specific and easy to apply without exercising significant discretion. In the classic example, a 65-mph speed limit is a rule, whereas a standard might require the motorist to not drive dangerously or to drive at a prudent speed. The criteria discussed in this chapter provide a specific test, but they cannot be mechanically applied like a numerical speed limit.

to): open-fire orders, treatment of captives, prohibitions on particular weapons, limits on use of force with respect to collateral damage and application of the rules of proportionality. Indeed, the law of armed conflict—that is, the law governing the conduct of hostilities—mandates such clear-cut parameters. A standard-less theater of war in which these ground rules are neither agreed upon by international convention nor self-imposed will result in unconscionable harm to innocent civilians, ill-treatment of captives and unlimited use of force.

For commanders, who are responsible for both the conduct and the welfare of their soldiers, a theater of war not subject to restrictions and criteria would both subject their soldiers to extraordinary harm (through unlawful means and methods of attack or upon capture) and give them the freedom to act immorally, devoid of standards of decency and humanism. A standard-free military paradigm where soldiers' conduct is not subject to limits or restrictions would be a disturbing reversion to a Hobbesian State of Nature.

As a general methodology for moral theory, intuitionism has many adherents.[15] But intuitive decision-making, rather than criteria-based decision-making, is particularly problematic if it is imported into the realm of operational counterterrorism. As Professor Sauter writes:

> This intuitive thought process is vastly different from the analytical approach. Analytic thought involves defining the problem, deciding on exact solution methodologies, conducting an orderly search for information, increasingly refining the analysis, aiming for predictability and a minimum of uncertainty. Intuitive thought, on the other hand, avoids commitment to a particular strategy. The problem-solver acts without specifying premises or procedures, experiments with unknowns to get a feel for what is required.... [Intuitive decision-making] has its faults, most obvious of which is the absence of data based theories and the use of methodology that cannot be duplicated.[16]

The instinctual response is arguably appropriate when an individual is confronted with a stark life-and-death dilemma where a failure to respond quickly and aggressively will, in near certainty, result in death. For example, if a homeowner were to walk into his home and catch an intruder by surprise, the principle of self-defense would justify—depending on the circumstances—a violent reaction.

Moreover, an intuition-based approach leaves little in the way of parameters for post-operation analysis. If there is no process for the decision, it will be difficult

---

[15] Vicki L. Sauter, "Intuitive Decision Making," Communications of the ACM, June 1999, Vol. 42, No. 6; Eric Chaffee, "Always Do the Right Thing," available at <http://lawreview.wustl.edu/commentaries/always-do-the-right-thing-ethical-intuitionism-and-legal-compliance/> accessed August 1, 2011, referencing G.E. Moore, the "father of ethical intuitionism"; Kurt Matzler, Franz Bailom and Todd Mooradian, "Intuitive Decision Making," *MIT Sloan Management Review*, Vol. 49, No. 1, Fall 2007.

[16] Vicki L. Sauter, "Intuitive Decision Making," *supra* n. 15.

to judge when the decision was right or wrong. Such a lack of parameters seems to fly in the face of the basic goals of a legal regime, especially one regulating life-and-death issues. The essence of targeted killing is proactive—not reactive—self-defense based on sophisticated intelligence gathering and analysis, and careful consideration of the international law principles of collateral damage, proportionality and military necessity.[17] The criteria-based approach facilitates careful identification of a legitimate target and ex post evaluation of this decision, thus enhancing both short- and long-term effectiveness.

(ii) Criteria: essential to lawful counterterrorism

In the context of counterterrorism, however, intuitionism is profoundly dangerous due to its lack of process and criteria. Without these, operational decision-making loses its legal and ethical moorings. The decision-maker will be acting primarily on what he believes he sees without taking into consideration all relevant information. A decision based exclusively on the action-reaction of one individual, divorced from broader considerations, poses extraordinary dangers.

Targeted killing operations involve more than a simple analysis of "threat or no threat," where a combination of process and instinct may be an appropriate fit. In reality, in counterterrorism—and targeted killing in particular—individuals are making decisions almost entirely based on information received second- or even third-hand, and in an environment that blends extraordinary intensity with multiple competing and complex factors. Simply having a process alone—such as the requirement that a military lawyer approve the operation—is not sufficient. Criteria, guidelines and standards that define the parameters—and even the paradigm—for the decision are key tools for ensuring lawfulness and effectiveness in a targeted killing policy.

A decision to authorize a targeted killing requires a confluence between the imminence of the threat and the necessity of responding with deadly force. As Section III below explains in greater detail, such determinations depend on a careful and sophisticated analysis of the intelligence, the parameters of the operation, the situation on the ground, including the presence of innocent civilians, and above all, the nature of the threat posed. Several factors play a central role here: the degree of danger; the strength of the intelligence; the reliability and credibility of the source; and timeliness, both of the intelligence and the attack.

Appropriate consideration of these factors is the only mechanism for implementing a targeted killing in accordance with the international law requirements set forth below. In essence, a successful targeted killing is not simply one that hits

---

[17] *See* Amos N. Guiora, "Targeted Killing As Active Self-Defense," 36 *Case W. Res. J. Int'l L.* 319 (2004); Amos N. Guiora, "Determining a Legitimate Target: The Dilemma of the Decision Maker," 47 *Tex. Int'l L. J.* (forthcoming, 2011).

the designated target. Rather, a successful targeted killing is one that hits the target while ensuring protection of innocent civilians and upholding the rule of law. Creating a structured system and process based on criteria and standards will facilitate state action within these parameters; the absence of criteria will, unfortunately, enable a restraint-less paradigm and lead to unwarranted and unjustified collateral damage.

For example, more than one type of potential terrorist attack can pose a threat, but not all trigger the justifiable use of targeted killing. There are relevant differences between a plot to plant a bomb in a coffee house somewhere in Jerusalem next week, a plan to throw Molotov cocktails at a protest, and a suicide bombing operation at a designated pizza parlor. Degree of harm, concreteness of plan and information, number of similar attacks or attackers, operational feasibility of detention instead of targeted killing—these are just a few factors which can change continually as the operational landscape and intelligence information shift and fill out. Which factors should be included? How should they be weighed? Whose information can be trusted? Whose information carries more or less weight? Only a criteria-based process can manage a decision-making paradigm of this complexity and intensity with full regard for the operational and legal obligations.

Furthermore, criteria-based decision-making contributes greatly to reliability and consistency: similar situations beget similar responses and results. This notion of "repeatability" is essential for operators, civilians, judges and policy makers, and depends on rational criteria. Not only might the same decision-maker respond differently to what should be similar situations (or similarly to what should be different situations), but targeted killing inherently involves multiple, and often different, decision-makers. Intuition and unrestrained discretion pose far too significant a risk of subjective responses and cannot ground lawful and moral decision-making in such a scenario.

Emphasizing a criteria-based approach rather than an intuition-based approach minimizes risk and thus enhances protection of the otherwise unprotected civilian population and the state's own citizens. By imposing limits and criteria on both the decision-maker and the actor, the decision-making process creates a structure for determining when an open fire order can be given. The process rejects spontaneity and minimal infrastructure. In that sense, intuitive decision-making, as defined by Professor Sauter, arguably contributes to a "Lord of the Flies" approach to operational counterterrorism. As President Barak convincingly argues, nothing could be more dangerous to a democracy engaged in aggressive operational counterterrorism.

(b) The legal framework: self-defense and morality in armed conflict

I argue that the principal tenet of a sound targeted killing policy is that the need to prevent a specific, planned attack justifies killing the individuals involved in the attack. The framework relies on a combination of robust self-defense under international law and key principles of the law of armed conflict. The legal framework is complex and well developed, thus firmly supporting the push for a criteria-based approach over intuitionism. As the following discussion shows, these principles would face disregard or emasculation in the absence of a coherent and rational process for decision-making.

(i) Self-defense against terrorists

The principle of self-defense is a fundamental principle of customary and conventional international law and its modern foundations date back to the *Caroline* Incident. The *Caroline* was a U.S. steamboat attempting to transport supplies to Canadian insurgents. A British force interrupted the *Caroline's* voyage, fired on it, set it on fire and let it wash over Niagara Falls. Webster said that Britain's act did not qualify as self-defense because self-defense is only justified "if the necessity of that self-defense is instant, overwhelming, and leaving no choice of means, and no moment for deliberation."[18] According to Webster, Britain could have addressed the *Caroline's* threat in a more diplomatic manner. He thus limited the right to self-defense to situations where there is a real threat, the response is essential and proportionate and all peaceful means of resolving the dispute have been exhausted. Article 51 of the U.N. Charter reaffirms this inherent right of self-defense. Although the Charter provision specifically speaks of self-defense in the event of an "armed attack," states have traditionally recognized a right to anticipatory self-defense in response to an imminent attack, as set forth in the *Caroline* framework.

Targeted killing is the manifestation of self-defense at its most basic: the nation-state is defending its citizens from violent attack. It does, however, demand careful analysis of the nature of self-defense under international law. International law was originally intended to apply to war and peace between recognized states; the concept of non-state actors was not contemplated. In addition, a thorough review of international law demonstrates that terrorism as a subject of international law has only been considered in the past few decades. Clearly, the tragic events of 9/11 significantly contributed to this development. Thus, in studying responses to terrorism under international law, one of the issues that must be examined is the relevance and applicability of international law to this new form of warfare.

The question that must be addressed in the face of these developments is: does the right to self-defense allow states to effectively combat both state-sponsored and non-state-sponsored terrorism? Because the fight against terrorism takes place against an unseen enemy, the state, in order to defend itself adequately, must be able to take the fight to the terrorist before the terrorist takes the fight to it. In other words, the state must be able to act preemptively in order to deter terrorists

---

[18] Letter from Daniel Webster, U.S. Secretary of State, to Lord Ashburton, Special British Minister (August 6, 1842) reprinted in 2 *J. Moore, Digest of Int'l Law* § 217, 409 (1906).

or prevent them from completing their terrorist plot. By now, we have learned the price society pays if it is unable to prevent terrorist acts. The question that must be answered—both from a legal and policy perspective—is what tools should be given to the state to combat terrorism? Rather than wait for the actual armed attack to occur, the state must be able to act anticipatorily (as in the *Caroline* incident) against the non-state actor (a factor not considered in *Caroline*).

(ii) Key principles of international law

Beyond the legal justification for the use of force (self-defense against a non-state actor), the conduct of the operation must be consistent with existing principles and obligations under the law of armed conflict. First, the fundamental principle of distinction requires that any attack distinguish between combatants and innocent civilians. An individual can be a legitimate target of attack based on his status as a member of the enemy forces, whether a soldier in the regular armed forces of an opposing state in the conflict or a fighter in a non-state armed group engaged in the conflict. Alternatively, the determination that an individual is a legitimate target can be based on his or her conduct. Thus, civilians who "directly participate in hostilities" lose their immunity from attack and become legitimate targets during the time they are participating in hostilities.

Second, international law requires that targeted killing operations meet a four-part test: (1) it must be proportionate to the threat posed by the individual; (2) collateral damage must be minimal; (3) alternatives have been weighed, considered and deemed operationally unfeasible; and (4) military necessity justifies the action. Even though the individual targeted is a legitimate target, if the attack fails to satisfy these obligations, it will not be lawful. Thus, the Special Investigatory Commission examining the targeted killing of Saleh Shehadah recently concluded that although the targeting of Shehadeh—head of Hamas' Operational Branch and the driving force behind many terrorist attacks—was legitimate, the extensive collateral damage caused by the attack was disproportionate.[19] As will be shown in greater detail below, the absence of a criteria-based decision-making process can severely compromise adherence to, and implementation of, these key obligations.

The uncertainty inherent in contemporary conflict has significantly compli-cated wartime conduct. However, that ambiguity cannot—must not—be used to facilitate departures from these key principles or to justify the commission of war crimes. The self-imposed restraint doctrine articulated by Justice Barak is the philosophical and jurisprudential essence of lawful operational counterter-rorism.[20] It imposes on commanders the obligation—in accordance with Barak's

---

[19] Available at <http://www.pmo.gov.il/PMOEng/Communication/Spokesman/2011/02/spokeshchade270211.htm> accessed March 8, 2011.

[20] Aharon Barak, "The Role of the Judge in a Democracy," *Justice In The World Magazine No. 3*, available at <http://justiceintheworld.org/n14/cover.shtml> accessed Novermber 3, 2011.

legal architecture—to develop strategies that facilitate aggressive counterterrorism while imposing restraint on soldiers facing a foe dressed exactly the same as the innocent civilian standing next to him. Specifically, Barak noted:

> The examination of the "targeted killing" —and in our terms, the preventative strike causing the deaths of terrorists, and at times also of innocent civilians—has shown that the question of the legality of the preventative strike according to customary international law is complex. The result of that examination is not that such strikes are always permissible or that they are always forbidden. The approach of customary international law applying to armed conflicts of an international nature is that civilians are protected from attacks by the army. However, that protection does not exist regarding those civilians "for such time as they take a direct part in hostilities." Harming such civilians, even if the result is death, is permitted, on the condition that there is no other less harmful means, and on the condition that innocent civilians nearby are not harmed. Harm to the latter must be proportionate. That proportionality is determined according to a values based test, intended to balance between the military advantage and the civilian damage. As we have seen, we cannot determine that a preventative strike is always legal, just as we cannot determine that it is always illegal. All depends upon the question whether the standards of customary international law regarding international armed conflict allow that preventative strike or not.[21]

International law requires distinguishing between the terrorists and innocent civilians, but even beyond that, Barak's thesis imposes a heavy burden on commanders. According to Barak, the state *must* impose limits on itself; otherwise, illegality and immorality are all but certain in counterterrorism operations. How that plays out is essential for our discussion because it accentuates the requirement of command discretion. The following vignette offers a useful example:

> An IDF battalion commander (Lt. Col.) was given an order to detain three suspected terrorists believed to be in the West Bank city of Nablus (Shekem). At the city outskirts, he received an intelligence report at 10:00 am that hundreds of school children were milling about the village square. According to the commander, three options were operationally viable: (1) continue and ignore any consequences; (2) retreat; or (3) play a game of cat and mouse. It became clear to the commander that the reason why the school children were milling about (and not in school) was that the school principal had been ordered to close the school when the IDF force was spotted. This was a classic human shielding by the terrorists, a clear violation of international law; nevertheless, the risks to the innocent civilian population (the school children)—willingly and deliberately endangered by terrorists—led the commander to abort the mission.[22]

The vignette shows that the two concepts—self-defense and the four fundamental principles listed above—are not in conflict. Instead, they must be considered in formulating international law's response to modem warfare, which is clearly a very

---

[21] *The Public Committee against Torture in Israel vs. The Government of Israel* (HCJ 769/02).

[22] When we spoke regarding his decision-making process—in the face of clear and lawful operational orders—I was struck by how the commander had internalized Barak's philosophy (although he did not phrase it in those words) and how it directly impacted his operational decision-making.

different kind of war than all previous ones. Self-defense (in the form of targeted killing), if properly executed, not only enables the state to protect itself more effectively within a legal context but also leads to minimizing the danger to innocent civilians caught between the terrorists (who regularly violate international law by directly targeting civilians and by using innocents as human shields) and the state. As David explains, "in time of war or armed conflict innocents always become casualties. It is precisely because targeted killing, when carried out correctly, minimizes such casualties that it is a preferable option to bombing or large-scale military sweeps that do far more harm to genuine noncombatants."[23]

Preemptive self-defense aimed at the terrorist contains an element of pinpointing: the state will only attack those terrorists who are directly threatening society. The fundamental advantage of preemptive self-defense subject to recognized restraints of fundamental international law principles is that the state will be authorized to act against terrorists who present a real threat *prior* to a plot's consummation (based on sound, reliable and corroborated intelligence information or sufficient criminal evidence), rather than reacting to an attack that has already occurred in the past.

The only difference between the *Caroline* doctrine and the version of preemptive self-defense espoused here is the extension of *Caroline* to non-state actors involved in terrorism. If properly executed, this policy would reflect the appropriate response by international law in adjusting itself to the new dangers facing society today. In essence, it recognizes the state's right to act preemptively against terrorists planning an attack. Although there is much disagreement among legal scholars as to the exact threshold that constitutes "planning," targeted killing as preemptive self-defense enables the state to undertake all operational measures required to protect itself. As states increasingly engage in conflicts against non-state actors, international lawyers will have to address the precise contours of this right. However, the goal of this chapter is not to provide a complete account of preemptive self-defense, but rather to explain how a theory of preemptive self-defense should be operationalized into a particular policy for conducting targeted killings.

II. Criteria in practice

The scenario below reflects operational and legal dilemmas at the core of the targeted killing decision-making process: that is, whether the information provided by the intelligence community to the commander is sufficient to engage an individual. In accordance with standard operating procedure, the commander

---

[23] Stephen R. David, "Reply to Yael Stein: If Not Combatants, Certainly Not Civilians," 17 *Ethics & Int'l Aff.* 138, 139 (2003).

communicates with the legal advisor; the latter's assessment is based on the law and morality of armed conflict and policy effectiveness.

(a) Scenario: decision-making in action

Consider the following situation. An individual receives a phone call at 3:00 am: "We need to talk; the window of opportunity to neutralize the target is only a few minutes." The commander is calling his legal advisor with the following question: based on the following facts, is the proposed targeted killing legal?

The intelligence community supplied the commander with information received from a case officer,[24] who met with a source, who heard from someone that so and so said such and such, which then led the case officer to issue a request for a targeted killing. Based on this flimsy piece of information, the commander had stationed 10 soldiers at the target's supposed location.

The conversation is tense, compounded by the steady flow of reports the commander receives in his earpiece about the target's movements and the inherent tension of the operation—does he give the "shoot to kill" order? The legal advisor understands the commander's imperatives: the mission and the safety of his troops. Both focus on two key issues: (1) engaging an individual identified as a threat to state security is precisely what they signed up for; and (2) they have a responsibility to ensure that an order to "engage" is given only when it is fully justified by the circumstances and in accordance with standing orders regarding rules of engagement.

The commander hears increasingly agitated information from the spotter; the situation grows more dangerous with each passing minute because the target is closer, the unit spends more time in the field, and it is close to sunrise. The legal advisor hears this and faces the tension of assessing the information from the commander and making a decision in light of the legal and moral principles guiding state action.

From an operational perspective, the commander was ready to give the "open fire" order. In response to the legal advisor's questions, he was convinced that he had taken all necessary measures to minimize collateral damage. He had also made clear that his soldiers were ready for an "open fire" order; the ambush was properly organized, the soldiers were ready and the target was in the crosshairs. By daybreak, the target, reported to be wearing a blue shirt and blue jeans and holding a bag in his left hand, would either be dead or safely on his way.

This type of situation—making a decision at 3:00 am, in a time-sensitive environment, fraught with anxiety and high risk, based on imperfect intelligence

---

[24] The case officer is a civilian in the intelligence community who is the link between the commander and the source.

information provided by someone who neither the commander nor the legal advisor would ever meet or know—highlights the extraordinary nature of decision-making in this situation. What should be the guiding force: intuition and a gut reaction based on unfettered discretion? Or a process based on rigorous criteria?

(b) Evaluation

The discussion in Section I above demonstrates the shortcomings of intuitionism and unfettered discretion in this situation, shortcomings that can have drastic and fatal consequences. Instead, the decision-making process depends on information and analysis, on an objective process that can identify, isolate and target the key pieces of information. The following questions are essential to that process and are now summarized as follows:

Who is the target?

How do you know that he is the correct target? For example, do his clothes and his appearance match what the source told the case officer?

Who is the source? Commanders rarely—if ever—have direct contact with sources and are totally dependent on analysis and reports from case officers.

What are the alternatives—without unduly endangering the lives of the soldiers—to neutralizing the target? Can the target be detained instead?

What are the risks of collateral damage and have you endeavored to minimize collateral damage?

What is the quality and training of your soldiers?

Has your unit suffered from disciplinary issues? An ill-disciplined unit is, in all probability, not combat ready because the commander has expended too much time and energy on discipline rather than training.

What weapons do your soldiers have at their disposal and when was the last time they participated in a night-time mission? How good is the soldiers' night-time vision?

Are you (the commander) with your soldiers? If yes, will you be the "trigger man"? If not, who is the officer in command and where are you?

What is your previous experience with the case officer and when was the last time the case officer spoke with the source? Did he assure you that the source met the four-part test regarding the source's reliability?
Are you and the case officer convinced that the source, with whom the commander has not spoken, does not have an ulterior motive or a grudge against the target?[25]

This checklist approach forms the nascent beginnings of a criteria-based methodology for operational decision-making. The circumstances are less than ideal: imperfect

---

25 These are the questions I asked in the scenario above—a real situation.

intelligence information, time-limited decision-making framework, high risk with respect to possible loss of life (soldiers, identified target and innocent civilians alike) and foreseeable danger to national security. Without a process based on criteria and objective considerations, codified in a military-ready checklist, those factors will play a much more substantial—and problematic—role in any decision-making process.

In the face of the extraordinary time pressure, any legal advisor would have great difficulty being systematic with questions and might fumble from issue to issue in a haphazard way. Without a checklist, there is no clear road map to guide decision-makers through the information that they need to collect. Even if they asked many of the right questions, the absence of a checklist might produce mistakes under time pressure. For example, in the scenario above, the legal advisor would likely have given greater weight to the case officer's report and insufficient weight to what the commander was actually seeing at the time.[26] These considerations form the central impetus for the proposal for a criteria-based decision-making process.

III. Operational decision-making: putting criteria into practice

(a) Decision-making in counterterrorism

Criteria-based decision-making is intended to foster objective decisions. The proposed model is based on the nation-state's obligation to respect international legal principles and norms. That commitment—based on customary international law, international conventions and treaties—imposes restrictions and burdens that inherently limit counterterrorism operations. It is also what distinguishes the nation-state from a non-state actor that is held accountable neither to international law nor international public opinion.

The criteria-based decision-making process seeks to enhance understanding of the process and to provide tools to the decision-maker in a situation where uncertainties

---

[26] In the scenario above (the facts are necessarily fudged), my advice to the commander was that the facts—as presented—did not justify a targeted killing. I was not convinced that information regarding the person in the crosshairs sufficiently matched the description provided to the commander. The information about the individual unequivocally indicated that the danger posed to national security was palpable. Although I was convinced that detention was unfeasible, I was not convinced—ultimately because of insufficient information—that the individual in the commander's scope was the same one referenced by the case officer. I had no reason then—and have no reason 15 years later—to doubt that the commander provided me with the information conveyed to him by the case agent. Based on my professional experience with the commander, I was—and am—convinced that he was an honest conveyer of the information presented to him. The circumstances—3:00 am, extraordinary tension and responsibility inherent to the decision that had to be made—unquestionably impacted our conversation, which was fast, direct, devoid of any unnecessary commentary, and business-like. Though my questions (perhaps endless from his perspective) impacted the decision-making process, I felt the answers accurately reflected the commander's situation and the realities of the operation.

far outweigh certainties, where the unknown largely outnumbers the known.[27] Thus, the goal is not to hinder decisions and implementation, but to minimize mistakes. In these circumstances, a mistake is primarily the targeting of an otherwise innocent individual because of faulty intelligence information, incorrect assessment of received intelligence, or incorrect calibration of coordinates when opening fire. Although the incidental death of an innocent bystander during a targeted killing is doubtlessly unfortunate, international law accepts collateral damage provided it is not excessive, although this term is rarely quantified with any great precision.

The proposal is not—under any circumstance—intended to facilitate or justify criminal conduct of soldiers; a soldier or commander who violates standing orders and unlawfully causes the loss of innocent life must be either brought before a disciplinary hearing or court-martialed; the same is true for a soldier who follows a blatantly unlawful order.[28] Rather, the proposal's goal is to facilitate implementation of effective counterterrorism measures within the framework of respect for individual rights and the protection of civilians.

(b) Defining threats and understanding imminence: the essence of counterterrorism

The first step in creating an effective counterterrorism measure is analyzing the threat, including its nature, its origin, and when it is likely to materialize. This latter factor—imminence—will have a significant legal impact on the operational choices made in response. Taken together, these considerations directly impact the international law obligation of distinction and the notion of direct participation in hostilities. A person who is a legitimate target because of his status as a combatant is considered to be a threat at all times by virtue of that very status. In contrast, a civilian who is a legitimate target based on his conduct is—under the same framework—a threat when he is "directly participating in hostilities" as that concept is understood within international humanitarian law.

---

[27] For additional material regarding check-lists please see Atul Gawande, *The Checklist Manifesto* (Metropolitan Books, 2009); Daniel Kahneman, Paul Slovic and Amos Tversky (eds), *Judgment under Uncertainty: Heuristics and Biases* (Cambridge Uuniversity Press, 1982).

[28] In this regard, the legal and moral standard for lawful military action is the guilty verdict issued by an Israeli military court in 1957 against members of the Border Police who carried out an order enforcing a curfew against field hands returning to their village when they did not have notice of the curfew. As a result, the Border Police killed 47 innocent Arab-Israelis. The court held the order was blatantly illegal and that a "black flag" should have been raised regarding both its inherent unlawfulness and the absolute requirement to disregard it; See <http://meretzusa.blog-spot.com/2006/11/tom-segev-on-atrocity-at-kafr-kasem.html> accessed February 16, 2011; also <http://www.haaretz.co.il/hasite/spages/1026968.html> accessed February 16, 2011, Hebrew version—English unavailable. According to the court, the black flag standard imposed on soldiers the obligation to disregard a blatantly illegal order, even if issued by their commander.

In a nutshell, the jurisprudential underpinning of targeted killing is that it is necessary to protect the civilian population in the face of an imminent threat. Simply put, self-defense is at the core of the policy. This includes a determination that a particular individual poses an imminent threat and that no viable alternative exists to mitigate the threat posed by that individual. The two critical questions, then, in both the theoretical and practical discussion, are whether a viable threat exists and whether that threat is imminent. The imminence requirement is one of the most analyzed yet controversial aspects in the use of force literature. To suggest that targeted killing is only lawful when used against an individual minutes away from detonating himself inside a packed coffee shop is to misunderstand the range of imminence. But drawing a more exact line is difficult and requires further analysis.

Specifically, the imminence requirement as traditionally understood can sometimes lead to problematic results.[29] For example, suppose that the intelligence community determines that an individual is involved in planning a future terrorist attack and that his role is essential to the plan's success. Furthermore, suppose that intelligence indicates that the terrorist attack is being planned for next week, but the intelligence community has determined that the window of opportunity to target the terrorist is limited to now. If the target's location has been identified and arrest is not feasible, then the targeted killing ought to be justified, notwithstanding the fact that the terrorist attack is still a week away from being consummated. In other words, any analysis regarding the lawfulness of targeted killing ought to include the question of whether he or she can be targeted effectively. Some scholars have solved this problem by arguing for a switch from imminence to a new requirement of immediate necessity, a position adopted by the U.S. Model Penal Code in the context of individual self-defense under domestic criminal law, and also supported by some international lawyers. This theoretical move could be justified on the grounds that imminence appears to be a proxy for necessity anyway; what relevance does imminence have other than its implication that the use of defensive force is necessary at that moment in time when it is actually exercised?

Other scholars have solved the same problem with a far less ambitious proposal: develop a nuanced theory of imminence that recognizes that imminent threats can extend further back in time than previously acknowledged. For self-defense to be effective, imminence should not be limited to the suicide bomber minutes away from detonation; it should also extend to the individual who is planning the attack. Although the planning of the attack may happen days before the bomb is actually detonated, the planning may still be imminent enough to justify the use of defensive force so long as one's theory of imminence is sufficiently elastic. There is no a priori reason that imminence has to be defined in seconds or minutes.

---

[29] For more on the imminence requirement and its problems, see Russell Christopher, "Imminence in Justified Targeted Killing" in this Volume, ch. 9.

There are good reasons to support each proposal. For the moment, ultimate resolution of this theoretical dilemma need not be resolved here. In that sense, the general issue can be understood from two distinct perspectives: the imminent threat posed by a terrorist attack, including the bomber, planner and financier, or the immediate necessity of engaging a particular target with defensive force at a discrete moment in time. The first perspective focuses on the temporality of the threat, while the second perspective focuses on the temporality of the defensive response. A targeted killing/drone policy can be justified under either model. What matters is the conclusion that defensive force can be justified against more than a suicide bomber engaged in the physical act of detonating his explosives.

However, limits must be imposed on the implementation of self-defense so that targeted killings will be applied in accordance with the rule of law. Not all threats are imminent and not all uses of defensive force are immediately necessary. Some threats might be uncertain or merely hypothetical, while the supposed closing of a window of opportunity to exercise defensive force might be illusory. Each issue will affect how decision-makers view the balancing of individual rights and national security in various ways. In addition, these different types of threats will have different impacts on key interests and principles, such as collateral damage, the rule of law, and the preservation of civil liberties. In order to grant these interests sufficient weight, targeted killing will—or certainly should—be used only in response to threats that are imminent rather than distant, or only when the response is immediately necessary. Finally, the imminence of the threat and the immediacy of the response are not the end of the process—the threat must also pose a sufficiently grave danger of the loss of innocent life. Here, the distinction raised above between a suicide bombing at a pizza parlor and the throwing of Molotov cocktails is instructive: the latter does not pose the same danger of harm to the same number of individuals.

The essence of the decision to authorize a targeted killing depends on a process that allows for a careful analysis of both the nature of the threat, the identity of the threat, the imminence of the threat, and the immediate necessity of the response— all factors that invoke the full range of considerations elucidated in this chapter. The following operational considerations also play a role: whether the individual is detainable, or whether it is possible to postpone detention until the plan reaches later stages of fruition in order to apprehend additional perpetrators. Trying to undertake that analysis in the absence of clear criteria and guidelines for decision-making can lead to decision paralysis or an incomplete consideration of critical issues. Therefore, the following section summarizes the proposed model for determining the nature of the threat, its imminence and the consequences of particular responses in particular legal and policy areas. The proposed model also addresses the relationship between counterterrorism measures available and the measure actually chosen and provides a matrix to evaluate whether the decision was appropriate.

(c) Source analysis

Threat analysis refers to the nature of the target and his or her planned activities and attacks. Assessing where the information about the target and the planned attack comes from is an equally vital aspect of the decision-making process. Thus, source analysis must be a major component of the criteria-based approach. The intelligence community receives information from three different intelligence sources: human sources (that is, individuals who live in the community about which they are providing information to a case officer who serves in the intelligence community); signal intelligence (that is, intercepted phone and email conversations); and open sources (that is, internet and newspapers). The responsibility of the intelligence community is to analyze the gathered information in an effort to develop an accurate picture. Targeted killing is largely dependent on the intelligence information received from a source; the recipient of the information is the case officer who is tasked with identifying a potential source and then cultivating that individual over a period of time. The following chart explains the sequence:

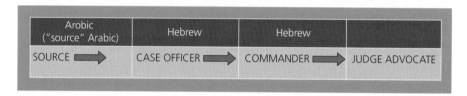

One of the most important questions in putting together an operation is whether the received information is actionable; that is, does the information received from the source warrant an operational response? That question is central to criteria-based decision-making or at least to decision-making that requires objective standards for making decisions based on imperfect information. In other words, the goal is to enhance objectivity and minimize subjectivity in the decision-making process. However, it is essential that the information, including its source, be subjected to rigorous analysis. To that end, the following definitions of reliability, viability, relevancy, and corroboration (created to explain detention decisions) articulate the guidelines for determining whether the intelligence is sufficiently actionable.

First, is the intelligence reliable? In other words, do past experiences show the source to be a dependable provider of correct information? This requires that the case officer discern whether the information is useful and accurate and whether the source has a personal agenda or grudge against the identified target. Second, is the intelligence viable? In particular, is it possible that an attack could occur in accordance with the source's information? Does the information provided by the source indicate that a feasible terrorist attack could be mounted? Third, is the intelligence relevant? To determine relevancy, the legal advisor must consider both the timeliness of the information and whether it is time-sensitive and requires an immediate counterterrorism measure. Fourth, can the intelligence be corroborated; that is, can another source (who meets the reliability test above) confirm the information in whole or in part?

With these criteria in mind, the advisor needs to consider both the source and the target and make more specific determinations. Consider the source first:

What is the source's background and how does that affect the information provided?

Does the source have a grudge or personal score to settle based on a personal or family relationship with the target?

What are the risks to the source if the target is killed? Source protection is essential to continued and effective intelligence gathering. Protecting the source is essential both with respect to that source and additional—present or future—sources.

What are the risks to the source if the intelligence is made public? This factor is relevant for selecting the proper forum for trying suspected terrorists because a civilian trial may require public disclosure of the evidence.

Now consider the target:

Who is the target of the source's information? What is the person's role in the terrorist organization? How would his or her detention affect that organization, short-term and long-term alike? What insight can the source provide regarding impact? For example, in the suicide-bombing infrastructure there are four distinct actors: the bomber, the logistician, the planner and the financier. Determining the legitimacy of the target (for a targeted killing) requires that one ascertain the potential target's specific role in the infrastructure. Subject to the two four–part tests above, the following four actors are prima facie legitimate targets. First, the planner is a legitimate target 24 hours a day, seven days a week, precisely because the planner is the mastermind who sits atop the chain of command and directs the entire operation. Second, the bomber is a legitimate target, but arguably only when engaged in the operation. The bomber engages in terrorist activity occasionally but might very well return to civilian life at other points in time, at which point he could regain protected status. Third, the logistician is a legitimate target when involved in all aspects of implementing a suicide bombing but, unlike the planner, is not a legitimate target when not involved in a specific, future attack. The warrant for this conclusion is that the logistician is not the mastermind of the operation and, in fact, is much closer to the bomber than the planner. The essential difference between the logistician and the bomber is that the logistician's support of the operation does not involve carrying the bomb; both are, in a sense, providing operational support. Fourth, the financier is a legitimate target when involved in wiring money or laundering money, both of which are essential for terrorist attacks. However, there remains significant room for debate and discussion regarding the nature and significance of the financier's contribution to the terrorist plot. To that extent, the question is whether the financier is more akin to the bomber and the logistician on the one hand, or the planner on the other hand. Arguably, given the centrality of the financier's role, the correct placing is *between* the logistician and planner. The financier's contribution is usually more significant and essential than the mere logistician, in the sense that nothing in the operation happens without funding. That places the financier one step below the mastermind who has ultimate control over the operation.

What are the costs and benefits if the targeted killing is delayed? How time-relevant is the source's information? Does it justify immediate action? Or, is the information insufficient to justify a targeted killing but significant enough to justify other measures, including detention?

What is the nature of the suspicious activity? Does the information suggest involvement in significant acts of terrorism justifying immediate counterterrorism measures? Or is the information more suggestive than concrete? In addition, if the information is indicative of minor (not harmful) possible action, effective counterterrorism might suggest additional information-gathering—from the same or additional source— before authorization of targeted killing.

What information could the target provide if he was detained and interrogated rather than killed? Does the individual possess information—to varying degrees of specificity—relevant to future acts of terrorism?

IV. Developing and implementing criteria-based decision-making

In a targeted killing decision, three aspects of the decision stand out: (1) can the target be identified accurately and reliably?; (2) does the threat the target poses justify an attack at that moment or are there other alternatives?; and (3) what is the extent of the anticipated collateral damage? A criteria-based decision-making process must therefore amass, assess and analyze the information necessary to make these determinations effectively.

The larger questions force us to consider the legality and morality of the policy and of its application in specific cases. In examining both legality and morality, decision-makers must avoid falling into the pitfall of decision by routine. There is, perhaps, nothing more dangerous than decision-makers who fail to inquire into considerations that extend beyond mere operational factors. That is not to minimize the complicated reality of operational decision-making, but simply to emphasize that *additional* questions must be asked in the context of criteria-based operational counter terrorism.

In that vein, my decision in the situation memorialized above—whether right or wrong—regarding the information the source provided to the case agent, the case agent gave to the commander, and the commander conveyed to me, was based on four characteristics. First, I was influenced by the commander's interpretation of that information and his framing of the information, both how he initially framed the dilemma and his responses to my questions based on the checklist above. Second, my decision was affected by interpretation and classification of the answers into three distinct categories: legal, moral and operational. Third, my pre-existing personal and professional skills, as well as my previous experiences in these operations, all had an influence in the outcome. And finally, my understanding of the targeted killing policy and my frame of reference as a senior officer in the IDF, including my involvement in the implementation of the Oslo Peace Process, inevitably played a role in the decision. These personal factors are necessarily in the background of any decision-making process. To suggest otherwise is to profoundly overestimate the capacity of individuals to form all-things-considered judgments from a third-person point of view. In the absence of rigorous criteria for decision-making, these factors can degenerate into wholly subjective and irrational decisions. But with a rigorous and detailed criteria-based decision-making process, the inherent subjectivity of individual decision-making can be transformed from a source of error to a potential benefit. In other words, the legal advisor can use his or her extensive experience to augment the decision by framing that experience through the explicit criteria that have been determined in advance. The goal of this chapter has been to offer a prolegomenon to codifying that process.

Criteria-based decision-making enables decision-makers to operationalize counterterrorism policy within a framework of legal and moral principles, both of which are essential to effective and legal counterterrorism. While self-defense is a recognized principle in international law, it is not unlimited. Moreover, the grave risks of terrorism threaten to overrun any decision-making process relying on intuition and unconstrained discretion: everything and everyone will appear to be a severe and imminent threat in the heat of the moment. Rather, operational counterterrorism conducted in accordance with the rule of law requires the nation-state to engage in self-imposed limits when it conducts defensive operations. The criteria-based rational decision-making model proposed in this chapter significantly enhances operational counterterrorism that achieves two critical goals: engaging the legitimate target and minimizing collateral damage. Adoption of a checklist approach greatly facilitates the conduct of drone policy/targeted killing in accordance with the principles of international law. By developing a sophisticated mechanism to weigh and measure the reliability of intelligence, the decision-maker will be able to determine whether an individual is truly a legitimate target and whether circumstances justify engaging the identified individual. This facilitates lawful and effective targeted killing; at its core, the policy will be based on a *process* predicated on criteria, thereby significantly enhancing lawful aggressive self-defense.

12

ARE TARGETED KILLINGS UNLAWFUL? A CASE STUDY IN EMPIRICAL CLAIMS WITHOUT EMPIRICAL EVIDENCE

Gregory S. McNeal

Critics of the U.S. policy of targeted killing by unmanned aerial vehicles (UAVs or drones) generally lack credible information to justify their critiques. In fact, in many instances their claims are easily refuted, calling into question the reliability of their criticism. This chapter highlights some of the most striking examples of inaccurate claims raised by critics of the U.S. policy of drone-based targeted killing. Specifically, this chapter offers a much-needed corrective to clarify the public record or offer empirical nuance where targeted killing critics offer only unsubstantiated and conclusory statements of fact and law.

Section I of this chapter discusses the decision protocol used by the U.S. military before launching a drone strike, a process that goes to extraordinary lengths to minimize civilian casualties. Although this decision protocol was once secret, recent litigation in federal court has resulted in the release of extensive information regarding U.S. targeting practices. An analysis of this information indicates that the U.S. military engages in an unparalleled and rigorous procedure to minimize, if not eliminate entirely, civilian casualties. Although independent empirical evidence regarding civilian casualties is hard to come by, it is certainly the case that statistics proffered by some critics cannot be empirically verified; their skepticism of U.S. government statements is not backed up by anything more substantial than generic suspicion.

Section II of this chapter addresses the critics' unsubstantiated claims about the legal, diplomatic and strategic results of drone strikes. Although the counter-observations raised in this chapter do not, by themselves, demonstrate that targeted killings are morally or legally justified, they do suggest that some of the moral or legal objections to targeted killings are based on empirical claims that are either dubious, impossible to verify or just plain false.

I. Claims about the process of targeted killing

The central claim raised by critics of the U.S. policy is that drone attacks are indiscriminate and result in a high number of civilian casualties. The claims are dramatic. For example, David Kilcullen and Andrew Exum argued in the *New York Times* that "drone strikes have killed about 14 terrorist leaders. However, according to Pakistani sources, drones also have killed some 700 civilians. This is 50 civilians for every militant killed, a hit rate of 2 per cent—hardly 'precision'."[1] In a more moderate estimate, the non-profit *Bureau of Investigative Journalism* claims that since August 2010, "45 or more civilians *appear* to have died" in CIA drone attacks.[2] Before citing contrary claims, it is important to note the lack of precision in the Bureau's own numbers. They are not certain if 45 civilians—or some higher number—were killed, and, rather than cite an actual death toll, they simply claim that some civilians "appear" to have died. Similarly, the claims made by David Kilcullen and Andrew Exum that drone strikes have a two per cent hit rate have little, if any, evidentiary support. In regard to these figures, Foreign Policy's Christine Fair concludes, "It would be a damning argument—if the data weren't simply bogus."[3] She points out to readers that "The only publicly available civilian casualty figures for drone strikes in Pakistan come from their targets: the Pakistani Taliban, which report the alleged numbers to the Pakistani press, which dutifully publishes the fiction."[4]

Contrast this with the definitive claims made by the U.S. government in response to the Bureau's report. The first comes from a senior U.S. counterterrorism official who stated:

> There haven't been any noncombatant casualties for about a year, and assertions to the contrary are wrong. The most accurate information on counter-terror operations resides with the United States, and this list is wildly inaccurate. Those operations are designed to protect America and our allies, including Pakistan, from terrorists who continue to seek to kill innocents around the world.[5]

The second statement comes from John Brennan, Assistant to the President for Homeland Security and Counterterrorism, who said, "In fact I can say that the types of operations...that the US has been involved in, in the counter-terrorism

---

[1] See David Kilcullen and Andrew Exum, "Death from Above, Outrage Down Below," *New York Times*, May 16, 2009.

[2] Emphasis added, Chris Woods, "U.S. Claims of 'No Civilian Deaths' are Untrue," *The Bureau of Investigative Journalism*, July 18, 2011, Covert Drone War; available at <http://www.thebureauinvestigates.com/2011/07/18/washingtons-untrue-claims-no-civilian-deaths-in-pakistan-drone-strikes/> accessed November 4, 2011.

[3] C. Christine Fair, "Drone Wars," *Foreign Policy*, May 28, 2010; available at <http://www.foreignpolicy.com/articles/2010/05/28/drone_wars> accessed November 4, 2011.

[4] Ibid.

[5] Woods, *supra* n. 2.

realm, that nearly for the past year there hasn't been a single collateral death because of the exceptional proficiency, precision of the capabilities that we've been able to develop."[6]

Further undermining the claims of the Bureau, another U.S. counterterrorism official stated that:

> [o]ne of the loudest voices claiming all these civilian casualties is a Pakistani lawyer who's pushing a lawsuit to stop operations against some of the most dangerous terrorists on the planet...His evidence, if you can call it that, comes from a press release. His publicity is designed to put targets on the backs of Americans serving in Pakistan and Afghanistan. His agenda is crystal clear.[7]

Although drone critics are not required to take government denials at face value, these statements by U.S. officials demonstrate that the empirical claims made by critics are highly contested by those who operate or oversee these programs. If critics wish to discredit these official statements, the critics should marshal supportable evidence for their statistics.

(a) The administrative process of collateral damage estimation and mitigation

In my own field of research I have reported on the administrative process the U.S. military follows to prevent civilian casualties in combat.[8] Many critics of the U.S. policy of targeted killing fail to address the scientifically grounded mitigation steps followed by U.S. armed forces. Those mitigation steps are designed to ensure that the probability of collateral damage from a pre-planned operation is below 10 per cent. In practice, the mitigation steps have resulted in a collateral damage rate of less than one per cent. Specifically, in pre-planned operations the U.S. military follows a rigorous collateral damage estimation process based on a progressively refined analysis of intelligence, weapon effects, and other variables.

To gather the evidence to support the information summarized above and explained in greater detail below, I followed proven case study research techniques[9] designed to ensure construct validity, external validity and reliability. Construct validity was ensured by using varied sources of evidence, including publicly available government documents, multiple open-ended interviews, and scholarly and press accounts of the collateral damage estimation and mitigation

---

[6] Ibid.

[7] Pam Benson and Elise Labott, "U.S. Denies Report Alleging Drone Strikes Kill 160 Kids in Pakistan," *CNN World*, August 12, 2011, available at <http://articles.cnn.com/2011-08-12/world/pakistan.us.drone.strikes_1_drone-strikes-drone-campaign-drone-program/3?_s=PM:WORLD> accessed November 4, 2011.

[8] Gregory S. McNeal, "Collateral Damage and Accountability," Pepperdine University School of Law Working Paper (April 22, 2011), available at <http://papers.ssrn.com/sol3/papers.cfm?abstract_id=1819583> accessed November 4, 2011 (hereafter Collateral Damage and Accountability).

[9] Joe R. Feagin et al., *A Case for the Case Study* (University of North Carolina Press, 1991); Robert K. Yin, *Case Study Research: Design and Methods 2*, 2nd edn (Sage, 1994).

process. I began by collecting and reviewing sources in the public record such as court documents and government declarations and then summarized my initial tentative observations. Then I tested these observations using triangulation techniques and multiple data sources to confirm or falsify my observations and test my research methods. Triangulation is the process by which a case study researcher provides confidence that findings are meaningful and reflect scientific truth.[10] External validity was achieved by limiting the generalizability of the findings to the U.S. practice of collateral damage estimation and mitigation during pre-planned military operations.

During any military operation, armed forces are required by the laws of war to minimize collateral damage.[11] Following international humanitarian law (IHL) concepts of distinction, proportionality and precautions generally satisfies this requirement. In pre-planned operations, or when time and combat circumstances permit, the U.S. military implements its IHL obligations by employing a multi-step process known as the "collateral damage methodology" (CDM).[12] This methodology is grounded in scientific evidence derived from research, experiments, history, and battlefield intelligence, and is designed to adapt to time-critical events.[13] The CDM takes into account every conventional weapon in the U.S. air to surface and indirect fire inventory and is a tool that assists commanders in mitigating unintended or incidental damage or injury to civilians, property, and the environment.[14] The methodology assists commanders in assessing proportionality and in weighing risks to the collateral objects.[15] The CDM is based on empirical data, probability, historical observations from the battlefield, and physics-based computerized models for collateral damage estimates.[16]

If in the targeting process a commander or their subordinates realize that there is a possibility of collateral damage resulting from an operation, they will employ a series of mitigation techniques intended to ensure, with a high degree of certainty, that there will not be an unacceptable probability of damage or injury to collateral concerns. This mitigation process involves a series of steps based on a progressively refined analysis of available intelligence, weapon type and effect, the physical environment, target characteristics and delivery scenarios keyed to risk thresholds established by the Secretary of Defense and the President of the United States.[17]

Perhaps the simplest way to understand the mitigation process undertaken by U.S. forces is to think of it as a series of tests based on risk to collateral concerns. These

---

[10] Yin, *supra* n. 9, 91–3.
[11] Laurie Blank and Amos Guiora, "Teaching an Old Dog New Tricks: Operationalizing the Law of Armed Conflict in New Warfare," 1 *Harv. Nat'l Sec. J.* 45, 56 (2010).
[12] Hereafter CDM, the methodology or methodology.
[13] McNeal, *supra* n. 8, 4.
[14] Ibid.
[15] Ibid. at 12.
[16] Ibid.
[17] Ibid.

tests are implemented in five levels (known as CDE levels); at each level, if a commander determines that collateral concerns are not within the collateral hazard area for a given weapon system, an operation can be commenced. However, if collateral concerns are within the collateral hazard area the operation cannot be undertaken without employing the available mitigation techniques at the next higher level of analysis. At the highest level (CDE Level 5) no mitigation technique will prevent civilian casualties and a senior commander, the Secretary of Defense or the President of the United States must make a judgment about proportionality.[18]

A few examples can illustrate these concepts. In Iraq, as of 2003, high collateral damage targets were defined as those that "if struck, have a ten percent probability of causing collateral damage through blast debris and fragmentation and are estimated to result in significant collateral effects on non-combatant persons or structures, including: (A) Non-combatant casualties estimated at 30 or greater…[including those]…in close proximity to human shields."[19] Thus, if after mitigation a commander in Iraq expected a pre-planned operation would result in more than 30 noncombatant casualties, the strike would have to be briefed through the chain of command and authorized by the Secretary of Defense. If the collateral damage estimate was less than 30, the target was defined as a low collateral damage target, and, in most circumstances,[20] required approval by either the Commander of Multinational Forces Iraq[21] or a Division Commander.[22]

Notably, Iraq in 2003 was not a counterinsurgency operation, whereas current (2011) operations in Afghanistan, relying on counterinsurgency doctrine, employ a noncombatant casualty value (NCV) of 1 for pre-planned operations.[23] This

---

[18] Ibid., citing Declaration of Jonathan Manes, *The Joint Targeting Definitions and Process*; see also *Nasser Al-Aulaqi vs. Obama*, 727 F. Supp. 2d 1, 46–7, 51–2 (D.D.C. 2010) (the person responsible for making this decision is prescribed by the Rules of Engagement).

[19] McNeal, *supra* n. 8, 19, citing "The Dissident Voice," *U.S. Iraq Rules of Engagement Leaked*, available at <http:// dissidentvoice.org/2008/02/us-iraq-rules-of-engagement-leaked-raises-question-about-rumsfeld-authorizing-war-crimes/> (linking to MNFI Rules of Engagement published by WikiLeaks and quoting the relevant sections of the ROE regarding High Collateral Damage targets).

[20] McNeal, *supra* n. 8, 18. (The Rules of Engagement in Iraq made complex and significant distinctions between types of targets and approval authority. These distinctions ranged from facilities with significant cultural or political value, to individuals such as former regime members to members of specified terrorist groups.)

[21] Ibid. at 19, noting this will usually be an officer holding the rank of General (4-star).

[22] Ibid. at 19, noting this will usually be an officer holding the rank of Major General (2-star). The Rules of Engagement may allow for delegation of this authority, depending on the weapons used and circumstances.

[23] Ibid. at 19. See also, Pamela Constable, "NATO Hopes to Undercut Taliban With Surge of Projects," *Washington Post*, September 27, 2008, A12 (quoting Brig. Gen. Richard Blanchette, chief spokesman for NATO forces stating "—[i]f there is the likelihood of even one civilian casualty, [NATO] will not strike, not even if we think Osama bin Laden is down there." This quote may be an overstatement; it is reasonable to conclude that a more accurate statement is that NATO will not strike *until* proportionality balancing and a decision is made by the President or the Secretary of Defense).

NCV of 1 reflects the strategic importance of minimizing collateral damage in counterinsurgency operations. Thus in pre-planned operations (for example, circumstances when troops are not in contact, or a target is not time-sensitive) in Afghanistan, if an operation is expected to result in even one civilian casualty, the strike must be approved by the National Command Authority.[24]

(b) The results of the administrative process

When followed, this administrative process dramatically reduces the collateral damage in U.S. military operations and also ensures high levels of political accountability. According to my research, less than one percent of pre-planned operations that followed the collateral damage estimation process resulted in collateral damage. When collateral damage has occurred, 70 per cent of the time it was due to failed "positive identification" of a target. Twenty-two per cent of the time it was attributable to weapons malfunction, and a mere eight per cent of the time it was attributable to proportionality balancing; that is, a conscious decision that anticipated military advantage outweighed collateral damage. Furthermore, according to public statements made by U.S. government officials as described above, the President or the Secretary of Defense (also known as the National Command Authority) must approve any pre-planned ISAF strike where one civilian casualty or greater is expected, thus ensuring high levels of political accountability.

This is an important point for the debate over CIA targeted killing operations. The military, operating in Afghanistan, follows a rigorous process of collateral damage estimation and mitigation. If, at the end of that process, mitigation is impossible and the estimated number of civilian casualties exceeds pre-determined limits,[25] commanders must complete a sensitive target approval and review (STAR) process. This process is for targets whose engagement presents: the potential for damage and/or injury to noncombatant property and persons; potential political consequences; or other significant effects estimated to exceed predetermined criteria, thus presenting an unacceptable strategic risk.[26] The National Command Authority must approve STAR targets.[27] As discussed above, in Iraq in 2003 the President determined any operation in which 30 or greater civilian casualties were expected represented a significant strategic level event with geopolitical ramifications necessitating approval at the highest levels of government.[28] Thus, if after mitigation a commander in Iraq expected a pre-planned operation would result in more than 30 noncombatant casualties, the strike would have to be briefed to—and

---

[24] McNeal, *supra* n. 8, 19. (Notably this authority may be delegated. Depending on the ROE.)

[25] Ibid. (This acceptability threshold is established by the President of the United States or the Secretary of Defense.)

[26] Ibid.; Declaration of Jonathan Manes, *supra* n. 18, 38.

[27] Ibid.

[28] See McNeal, *supra* n. 8. See also, "The Dissident Voice", *supra* n. 19.

authorized by—the Secretary of Defense. If the collateral damage estimate was less than 30, the target was defined as a low collateral damage target and, in most circumstances,[29] still required high-level approval, although that approval would occur within the military chain of command, usually with approval by either the Commander of Multinational Forces Iraq,[30] or a Division Commander.[31] Notably, the difference in strategy between Iraq in 2003 (major combat operations) versus Afghanistan in 2011 (counterinsurgency operations) was a driving factor in the different NCV (with the Afghanistan NCV being set at 1), meaning high levels of approval and therefore care prior to any air strike.[32] This is a critically important point, as this very low NCV reflects the strategic importance of minimizing collateral damage in counterinsurgency operations.

These points regarding the care exercised by the U.S. military in targeted killing operations, and the recognition by the President of the political consequences that flow from civilian casualties, raise questions about the logic behind the arguments made by targeted killing critics. If an operation in Afghanistan is expected to result in *even one* civilian casualty, the strike must be approved by the National Command Authority.[33] In light of this fact, it seems questionable that the CIA would exercise less care in its targeted killing operations just over the border. This is especially curious when one considers that the CENTCOM commander supervises U.S. forces in Afghanistan and has responsibility for operations in Pakistan. That commander personally approves nearly all strikes that are expected to result in one or more civilian casualties in Afghanistan, yet if the critics are to be believed this same commander is sidelined (and apparently silent) when it comes to CIA strikes in Pakistan. Are we to believe that the CENTCOM commander, who reports directly to the President, has no input into the fact that the CIA is allegedly inflicting 50 civilian casualties for every militant killed? Why would the CENTCOM commander be directed by the President to minimize civilian casualties for strategic and political reasons on the Afghanistan side of the border, yet the Director of the CIA, who also reports to the President, would have a free hand to inflict massive civilian casualties on the Pakistani side of the border? Perhaps the more likely conclusion is that the critics lack reliable information.

---

[29] See McNeal, "Collateral Damage and Accountability," *supra* n. 8. The Rules of Engagement in Iraq made complex and significant distinctions between types of targets and approval authority. These distinctions ranged from facilities with significant cultural or political value to individuals such as former regime members to members of specified terrorist groups.

[30] Usually an officer holding the rank of General (4-star).

[31] Usually an officer holding the rank of Major General (2-star). The Rules of Engagement may allow for delegation of this authority, depending on the weapons used and circumstances.

[32] See n. 23. For a lengthier discussion of these concepts, see Gregory S. McNeal, *Collateral Damage and Accountability.*

[33] See Declaration of Jonathan Manes, *supra* n. 18. Reports indicate that this authority has been delegated to the commander of US and ISAF forces (previously General Petraeus, currently General Allen), delegation confirmed in Interview 1 and Interview 3.

In fact, these issues call into question the claims made by critics, in particular the logic behind their claims. While it is true that the CIA operates covertly and therefore has more leeway in its operations, and it is also true that the campaign in the tribal areas of Pakistan is a counterterrorism rather than a counterinsurgency operation,[34] in order to believe the critics, one would nonetheless have to believe in grand inconsistencies in care and outcomes for agencies that both directly report to the President. As I have detailed in my research, the military follows a rigorous targeting process designed for use in most combat operations. That process has been highly successful in minimizing the number of civilian casualties from military airstrikes. Yet the numbers cited by critics, such as the ratio of 50 civilians killed for every strike is beyond even the 30 civilian NCV in Iraq at the height of major combat operations (not counterinsurgency operations). If we are to believe that the CIA substantially departs from the military's collateral damage estimation and mitigation processes, the onus should be on the critics to demonstrate this fact, which they plainly have failed to do. Moreover, the statements of the government with its own access to real-time information about operations must be weighed against those of journalists who cannot travel to remote regions of Pakistan,[35] and civilians who are paid "blood money" if they claim to be collateral victims.[36] Finally, even if the critics are correct and the CIA operates with fewer targeting restrictions, this would not demonstrate the illegality of targeted killing per se but would only support the prudential conclusion that drone operations should be handled by the U.S. military exclusively or the CIA should adopt the military targeting process.

Not only should the claims of critics be viewed skeptically because they are illogical, they should also be viewed skeptically because they are inconsistent. For example, one of the most prominent critics of U.S. targeted killing policy is law professor Mary Ellen O'Connell. In her essay "Unlawful Killing with Combat Drones: A Case Study of Pakistan 2004–2009," she criticizes the U.S. policy by frequently relying on media reports (or others who summarize media reports) to bolster her claim that air strikes are causing high numbers of civilian

---

[34] Adam Entous, "Special Report: How the White House Learned to Love the Drone," May 18, 2010, Thomson Reuters, available at <http://www.reuters.com/article/2010/05/18/us-pakistan-drones-idUSTRE64H5SL20100518> accessed November 4, 2011.

[35] See Brian Glyn Williams, "Accuracy of U.S. Drone Campaign: The Views of a Pakistani General," *CTC Sentinel*, March 2011, Vol. 4, Issue 3, 9.

[36] See Matt J. Martin and Charles W. Sasser, *Predator: The Remote-Control Air War Over Iraq and Afghanistan: A Pilot's Story* (Zenith Press, 2010) 136. (Martin, a Predator pilot, noted that U.S. Army lawyers would arrive in post-strike areas "with suitcases full of cash to award people with damage claims." He further states, "Most of the people who collected were righteous bystanders. Others who showed up to collect cash were undoubtedly the same people we were trying to kill.") See also, "Drone Attacks: Altaf Demands Blood Money For Victims," *The Express Tribune*, March 18, 2011, available at <http://tribune.com.pk/story/134294/drone-attacks-altaf-demands-blood-money-for-victims/> accessed November 4, 2011.

deaths.[37] However, when General McChrystal ordered restrictions on air strikes and media sources noted a decline in the number of unintended victims, she suddenly began to question the reliability of the media. In her words, "[w]hether the numbers have actually declined is difficult to confirm because the U.S. and Pakistan have succeeded in keeping journalists out of the border region."[38] This passage reveals an inconsistency in O'Connell's claims. If media reports are not to be believed when they report a reduction in civilian casualties, why should they be believed when they report consistent or increasing civilian casualties? O'Connell offers no explanation for her inconsistent analytical techniques.

A similar inconsistency is displayed in O'Connell's criticism of U.S. claims of no or few civilian casualties. She writes that "the U.S. has little reliable on-the-ground information to confirm or discredit computer data,"[39] and that "[i]n Afghanistan and Pakistan, the local informants, who also serve as confirming witnesses for the air strikes are notoriously unreliable."[40] If these people are unreliable as informants in support of strikes, why are they reliable as witnesses to collateral damage? How can any critic of targeted killing claim to be better at the task of sorting out reliable from unreliable informants than the CIA and other government officials on the ground in Afghanistan and Pakistan? Writer Jane Mayer, in her frequently cited *New Yorker* article, makes similar claims without much evidence, short of CIA officers who noted that sometimes informants were unreliable.[41] O'Connell favorably cites Mayer, stating that "[i]n Pakistan, the U.S. has had little on-the-ground

---

[37] Simon Bronitt (ed.), *Shooting To Kill: The Law Governing Lethal Force In Context*, forthcoming, available at <http://papers.ssrn.com/sol3/papers.cfm?abstract_id=1501144>; David Kilcullen and Andrew Exum, "Death from Above, Outrage Down Below," *New York Times*, May 16, 2009 (O'Connell principally relies on this source to assert that "the U.S. was killing 50 unintended targets for each intended target"); Hearing of the House Armed Services Committee, Effective Counterinsurgency: the Future of the U.S. Pakistan Military Partnership, April 23, 2009; available at (Testimony of David Kilcullen) (claiming that "Since 2006, [the U.S.] has killed 14 senior Al Qaeda leaders using drone strikes. In the same time period [the U.S.] has killed 700 Pakistani civilians in the same area"); Peter Bergen and Katherine Tiedemann, "Revenge of the Drones," *New America Foundation,* October 19, 2009, available at <http://newamerica.net/publications/policy/revenge_of_the_drones> (claiming that this article supports the ratios provided by Kilcullen and Exum, noting that Bergen and Tiedemann state, "Since 2006, our analysis indicates 82 U.S. drone attacks in Pakistan have killed between 750 and 1000 people. Among them were about 20 leaders of Al Qaeda, the Taliban, and allied groups, all of whom have been killed since January 2008." O'Connell claims that this article supports the figures provided by Kilcullen and Exum; however, she downplays the fact that Bergen and Tiedemann only distinguish Al Qaeda and Taliban *leaders* from the remaining number of people that have been killed by drones. In fact, Bergen and Tiedemann even criticize Kilcullen and Exum's figures, stating, "in [Kilcullen and Exum's] analysis, 98 percent of those killed in drone attacks were civilians... Our analysis suggests quite different conclusions than those of...Kilcullen and Exum.").

[38] O'Connell, *supra* n. 37, 10.

[39] O'Connell, *supra* n. 37, 6. (Curiously, she does not explain what "computer data" means.)

[40] Ibid. at 7.

[41] Jane Mayer, "The Predator War, What are the Risks of the C.I.A.'s Covert Drone Program?," *The New Yorker*, October 26, 2009, 36, 37, available at <http://www.newyorker.com/reporting/2009/10/26/091026fa_fact_mayer> accessed November 4, 2011.

information, and what it has had has not been very reliable."[42] Yet Mayer does *not* claim that the United States has little on-the-ground information, and even if she did make such a claim, one would want to know how a journalist had enough information about covert CIA assets to render such a conclusion.

This is especially the case when one considers Mayer's claim that one of President Obama's first drone strikes, on January 23, 2009, "targeted the wrong house, hitting the residence of a pro-government tribal leader six miles outside the town of Wana, in South Waziristan. The blast killed the leader's entire family, including three children, one of them five years old."[43] There is no evidence that this information was verified independently in Mayer's article or in O'Connell's favorable citation of it. In fact, both Mayer and O'Connell cite a New America Foundation database that claims the Wana strike killed no Al Qaeda or Taliban leaders but did kill eight other individuals. However, both the New America Foundation and Mayer failed to note a conflicting report in the *Times* of London. That report stated that "[s]even more died when hours later two missiles hit a house in Wana, in South Waziristan. Local officials said the target in Wana was a guest house *owned by a pro-Taleban tribesman*. One said that as well as three children, the tribesman's relatives were killed in the blast."[44] Based on these reports, there is a conflict over whether this house was the right house, specifically whether it was the home of a "pro-government tribal leader" or a "pro-Taleban tribesman." Despite conflicting information from different sources, both authors only cite the evidence that supports their conclusion.

Critics also make bold and unsubstantiated claims about the accuracy of drones. For example, O'Connell writes that

> one thing is clear, the use of drones in Pakistan has resulted in a large number of persons being killed along with the intended targets. Several factors suggest why this has been the case. One problem is structural. The remote pilot of a drone is relying on cameras and sensors to transmit the information he or she needs to decide on an attack. The technology is improving, but it is still difficult to be certain about targets.[45]

However, O'Connell fails to clarify how the reliance on cameras and sensors by drone operators is any different from the reliance on cameras and sensors by a helicopter or F-16 pilot (who will have far less time loitering over the target area compared to a drone). As Predator pilot Lt Colonel Matt J. Martin has noted:

> We followed the same rules of engagement and used the same procedures as all other aircraft, manned or unmanned, that employed weapons in support of the fight on the ground. To us the Predator is a longer-duration, lightly armed (and much less

---

42 O'Connell, *supra* n. 37, 7.
43 Mayer, *supra* n. 41.
44 Ibid. (emphasis added)
45 O'Connell, *supra* n. 37, 7.

survivable) version of an F-16—with the benefits of persistence, global distribution of video and data, the ability to leverage the entire intelligence apparatus through ground communications links, and the ability to think clearly at zero knots and one G.[46]

If anything, the technology employed by drones is an argument in favor of their usage. As a recent article in the *Economist* points out:

> Drones such as the Predator and the Reaper can loiter, maintaining what one former CIA director described as an 'unblinking stare'...Thanks to the drone's ability to watch and wait, its 'pilot,' often thousands of miles away, can patiently choose the best moment to fire its missiles, both increasing the chances of success and minimizing the harm to civilians.[47]

Moreover, even Mayer conceded the point that drones are probably more accurate than conventional aircraft when she wrote "Predator drones, with their superior surveillance abilities, have a better track record for accuracy than fighter jets, according to intelligence officials."[48] Despite this fact, O'Connell further claims that "[t]he operators never see with their own eyes the persons they have killed."[49] If by this she means that the operators are not standing above the bodies of their targets, looking with the naked eye, her claim is correct. However, this is also true of nearly every air campaign since the Second World War, every naval campaign that used cannons or naval guns aided by a telescope, and every shot fired by a rifle using a scope. As the *Economist* notes, "There are still plenty of human beings in the operational loop—it takes a team of about 180 to run and service a Predator—and it is clear that the responsibility for the decision to fire a missile rests as much with the pilot in a distant command centre as with a pilot in any cockpit."[50] O'Connell continues, "[i]n the trailer in Nevada, the pilot knows she will not be attacked. She will go home to her family at the end of the day, coach a soccer game, make dinner, and help with homework." But these same facts could be used as an argument in favor of targeted killings as such a person will be more apt to exercise care.

In fact, it seems more likely that a person who is not dodging anti-aircraft fire and is not exposed to danger will be calm, careful, and deliberative. As Randall Hansen noted in his book about the Allied bombing of Germany in the Second World War, bomb aimers struggled to do their jobs when faced with the mortal fear of anti-aircraft flak;[51] the use of remotely piloted aircraft removes that fear. Retired Lieutenant General David Deptula, who oversaw the U.S. Air Force's drone

---

[46] Martin and Sasser, *supra* n. 36, 104.

[47] "Drones and the man: Although It Raises Difficult Questions, The Use of Drones Does Not Contravene the Rules of War," *The Economist Online*, July 30, 2011, available at <http://www.economist.com/node/21524876> accessed November 4, 2011.

[48] Mayer, *supra* n. 41.

[49] O'Connell, *supra* n. 37, 8.

[50] "Drones and the Man," *supra* n. 47.

[51] Randall Hansen, *Fire and Fury: The Allied Bombing of Germany 1942–1945* (Random House, 2008) 114.

program from 2006 to 2010, questions O'Connell's logic, asking, "Are these people arguing that... we should only fight if you are exposed to threats and putting your life at risk?"[52] Deptula concludes, "That's silly, and I think it's ill-founded."[53] Edward Barrett, director of strategy and research at the U.S. Naval Academy's Stockdale Center for Ethical Leadership expands on this critique. Barrett points out, "A soldier in the situation is scared and possibly hasty in deciding what to do and acting—and possibly even angry, whereas an operator who's not threatened can use tighter rules of engagement and is not going to be fearful and therefore is going have a much cooler head."[54] These factors are especially relevant given the measures taken to enhance accountability in target acquisition, as well as in actually engaging the target. Furthermore, as O'Connell herself notes, "a—1000 people see the video [from the drone]—from—pilots in their trailers in Nevada and New Mexico, to intelligence analysts at Central Command (CENTCOM) headquarters in Florida, to persons in—Japan, to—POTUS (the President of the United States)."[55] A pilot subject to that level of scrutiny certainly will be more careful and discriminating than a traditional pilot faced with imminent danger whose gun camera footage will only be reviewed after the fact.

Critics also frequently make arguments that display an utter lack of familiarity with the U.S. military's targeting and strike practices. For example, a recent *Nation* article defined "bug splat" as "the splotch of blood, bones, and viscera that marks the site of a successful drone strike. To those manning the consoles in Nevada, it signifies 'suspected militants' who have just been 'neutralized'; to those on the ground, in most cases, it represents a family that has been shattered, a home destroyed."[56] In fact, the term "bug splat" does not refer to people, blood, or bones at all; rather, it refers to the predicted blast pattern made by explosives (based on simulations). Contrary to popular conception, bombs do not explode in a perfect circle but are flattened on one side, similar to the shape of a bug that hits a windshield. A "bug splat" refers to the shape of the planning tool used as an overlay to predict a collateral effects radius. This sounds highly technical, but one need not complete military training to know this fact; one only needs to Google the words "bug splat" and "drone" to find a *Washington Post* article explaining the term.[57]

---

[52] "The Ethics of Drones," August 26, 2011, PBS, *Religion & Ethics Newsweekly*, available at <http://www.pbs.org/wnet/religionandethics/episodes/august-26–2011/ethics-of-drones/9350/> accessed November 4, 2011.

[53] Ibid.

[54] Ibid.

[55] O'Connell, *supra* n. 37, 6.

[56] Muhammad Idrees Ahmad, "Fighting Back Against the CIA Drone War," *The Nation*, July 31, 2011, available at <http://www.nation.com.pk/pakistan-news-newspaper-daily-english-on-line/International/31-Jul-2011/Fighting-back-against-the-CIA-drone-war> accessed November 4, 2011.

[57] Walter Pincus, "Are Drones a Technological Tipping Point?" *Washington Post*, April 24, 2011, available at <http://www.washingtonpost.com/world/are-predator-drones-a-technological-tipping-point-in-warfare/2011/04/19/AFmC6PdE_story.html> accessed November 4, 2011.

The criticisms reveal other problems. O'Connell claims, for example, that "[s]uspected militant leaders wear civilian clothes. Even the sophisticated cameras of a drone cannot reveal with certainty that a suspect being targeted is not a civilian." This straw man argument displays a lack of familiarity with the targeting cycle followed by the U.S. military.[58] The cycle includes a minimum of 24 hours of "cycle of life surveillance" prior to an attack, and according to Mayer "the recent Senate Foreign Relations Committee report [notes that] the U.S. military places no name on its targeting list until there are 'two verifiable human sources' and 'substantial additional evidence' that the person is an enemy."[59] Of course, if the *only* information about a suspected militant in civilian clothes came from the camera of an attacking drone, that would be insufficient evidence for a strike. But that hypothetical does not reflect actual U.S. practice. In actual practice, U.S. forces must positively identify that the person they are targeting is who they believe they are. Moreover, since at least June 2008, no ISAF pilot (drone or otherwise) could fire a weapon at their own discretion, because there is no Fire Support Coordination Line (FSCL). What this means is that air power has no battlespace where they can engage targets without clearance from the battlespace owner (the ground commander).[60] Thus all strikes in Afghanistan post-June 2008 must be either pre-planned or contemporaneously authorized by the ground commander and directed by a Joint Terminal Attack Controller (JTAC) (a trained officer on the ground directing aircraft fires); this practice is reflected in U.S. military doctrine[61] and reflects the fact that in close air support missions the ultimate responsibility for engagements rests with the ground commander. Thus, the only discretion the pilot has in most circumstances is to *not* fire their weapon (for example, when they see something that the commander does not, such as the presence of civilians or other collateral concerns). This is the reality of air ground operations in Afghanistan, not the fanciful camera-driven, push-button, videogame-style warfare story that is told by O'Connell and Mayer.

Furthermore, it is inexplicable why critics would believe that the image from a drone camera is the only piece of information on which the military or CIA relies. Why would the United States ignore signals and human intelligence ranging from cell phone intercepts to on-the-ground informants? Just because O'Connell's hypothetical supports her conclusion does not mean it is grounded in reality, especially when the U.S. government has released detailed information about its targeting

---

[58] Steven A. Emerson, "In Defense of Drones," *The Invesitgative Project on Terrorism*, October 17, 2010, available at <http://www.investigativeproject.org/2249/in-defense-of-drones> accessed November 4, 2011.

[59] Mayer, *supra* n. 41.

[60] Sarah Sewall and Larry Lewis, "Reducing and Mitigating Civilian Casualties: Afghanistan and Beyond: Joint Civilian Casualty Final Report," 31 August 2010, 51 fn.110 (hereafter CIVCAS Report).

[61] Joint Publication 3-09.3, Close Air Support, June 2009.

cycle.[62] She further errs when she writes that "[l]ittle information is available as to whether the U.S. takes *any* precautions when carrying out drone strikes." In fact, prior to the publication of her draft chapter the U.S. released information about the precautions taken during drone strikes; for example on March 5, 2003 at 11:55 a.m. CENTCOM publicized a series of briefing slides entitled "Targeting and Collateral Damage." These slides were presented at a Department of Defense News Briefing where military officials detailed a simplified version of the CDE process I explained in the beginning of this chapter. Moreover, since the publication of her draft chapter, the U.S. released substantial information in the *al-Awlaki* litigation—a case in which O'Connell herself filed an expert affidavit. In that case, the United States revealed extensive details about its collateral damage estimation and mitigation techniques.[63] Although there might be an empirical debate about the true number of casualties caused by any particular drone strike, the targeting process used by the U.S. military is now a matter of public record.

Another questionable claim by O'Connell is that "the U.S. military is no longer training its members in the law of war as it once did."[64] Citing a "former drone commander," O'Connell noted that he claims "he had never had a single day of training in the law of armed conflict (LOAC) in his 17 years of active duty." On its face this claim should strike any reader familiar with the U.S. military as questionable. First, Air Force Instruction 51–401 mandates that:

> All Air Force military and civilian personnel will comply with the LOAC in the conduct of military operations and related activities in armed conflict, regardless of how such conflicts are characterized. In support of this policy, the Air Force will conduct specialized training programs for military and civilian personnel designed to prevent LOAC violations.[65]

Furthermore, the Air Force's Air Education Training Command is required to "[d]evelop training plans, and procedures to instruct and train Air Force personnel at the start of their service on the content and requirements of the LOAC. The amount and content of any specialized training and instruction shall be commensurate with each individual's projected duties and responsibilities."[66] Thus, any "drone commander" who had responsibility for targeting operations would have to comply with Air Force doctrine on targeting;[67] that doctrine spells out in an appendix the basic principles of the Law of Armed Conflict as it relates to

---

[62] Ibid.

[63] See Declaration of Jonathan Manes, *supra* n. 18.

[64] O'Connell, *supra* n. 37, 7.

[65] U.S. Air Force, available at <http://www.af.mil/shared/media/epubs/AFI51-401.pdf> accessed November 4, 2011.

[66] Ibid.

[67] Specifically Air Force Doctrine Document 2-1.9 *Targeting* and Joint Publication 3-60 *Joint Doctrine for Targeting*.

targeting.[68] Moreover, other sources make clear that, "[a]t the most basic level, the Department of Defense (DoD) has institutionalized law of war training in the services through DoD Directive Number 5100.77 DoD Law of War Program."[69] Additional training protocols exist for the Air Force to ensure familiarity with law of armed conflict rules, including relevant Hague and Geneva conventions.[70]

Perhaps the anonymous "former commander" interviewed by O'Connell never received the training mandated by the Secretary of the Air Force, but in that unlikely case it is not a result of a policy of neglect on the part of the U.S. government, or as she claims a decision to "no longer train its members in the law of war as it once did." Rather, there are clear requirements for continued officer training that mandate the very training that the critics claim is absent.

Furthermore, even if the "drone commander's" claim were true, it simply does not have the significance that critics assign to it. A "drone commander" is not in the operational chain of command for UAV operations and does not exercise control

---

[68] Excerpts from the 2-1.9 include passages such as "Targeting must adhere to the LOAC and all applicable ROE. It is the policy of the DOD that the Armed Forces of the United States will comply with the law of war during all armed conflicts, however such conflicts are characterized, and, unless otherwise directed by competent authorities, the US Armed Forces will comply with the principles and spirit of the law of war during all other operations. The 'law of war' is a term encompassing all international law for the conduct of hostilities binding on the United States including treaties and international agreements to which the United States is a party, and applicable customary international law. The 'law of war' is also commonly referred to as the LOAC." (88) and "LOAC rests on four fundamental principles that are inherent to all targeting decisions: military necessity, unnecessary suffering, proportionality, and distinction (discrimination)." (88).

[69] Major Jerry Swift, "The Teaching of Morality in Warfighting in Today's Officer Corps," 8, April 10, 2001, available at <http://www.au.af.mil/au/awc/awcgate/acsc/01-208.pdf> accessed November 4, 2011. ("Each service implements DoD 5100.77 through compliance with their individual service instructions on law of armed conflict. Air Force guidance is provided in Air Force Policy Directive (AFPD) 51–4, *Compliance with the Law of Armed Conflict*, and Instruction (AFI) 51–401, *Training and Reporting to Ensure Compliance with the Law of Armed Conflict*. Army guidance is through Field Manual (FM) 27–10, *The Law of Land Warfare*. Marine Corps implement MRCP 5-12.1A, *The Law of Land Warfare*. Navy guidance is provided through OPNAVINST 3300.52, Law of Armed Conflict (Law of War) Program to Ensure Compliance by the U.S. Navy and Naval Reserve and through Naval Warfare Publication (NWP) 1-14M, *The Commander's Handbook on the Law of Naval Operations*. Implementation is accomplished by assigning functional compliance, formalizing instruction and training, and institutionalizing reporting and investigations of violations of LOAC." Focusing strictly on training, each Secretary of the Military Departments must ensure that "the principles and rules of the law of war will be known to members of their respective Departments, the extent of such knowledge to be commensurate with each individual's duties and responsibilities.").

[70] Ibid. ("AFPD 51-4 ensures that 'once each year, all commanders make sure their people are trained in the principles and rules of LOAC needed to carry out their duties and responsibilities.' (AFPD 51-4, pg. 1.) It states that as a minimum, instruction is to include 'training required by the 1949 Geneva Conventions for the Protection of War Victims and the Hague Convention IV of 1907, including annexes.' (AFPD 51-4, pg. 1.) Furthermore, AFI 51–401 assigns Air University the additional responsibility to 'include instruction on LOAC in Air War College, Air Command and Staff College, Squadron Officer School, Reserve Officer Training Corps, and Senior Noncommissioned Officer Academy curricula to ensure adequate knowledge of the subject commensurate with the nature of each enrollee's duties and responsibilities.' (AFI 51–401, pg. 4.")

over targeting decisions. Air assets are attached to the *combatant* commander, who is most certainly well versed in the law of war.[71] For example, in Afghanistan, UAV pilots operate under the direction of CENTCOM, ISAF and subordinate commands; the commanders of those units are graduates of the U.S. Army's Command and General Staff College. Training for those graduates includes:

> The 27 credit hour course, *Case Studies in the Law of War*, focuses on the application of the law of war during high-intensity conflict. The focus is on in-depth examination of the application of international human law through case studies. Specific topics include the principles of the law of war, targeting decisions, projected persons and places on the battlefield, prisoners of war, war crimes prosecution, genocide, the legality of weapons, and training on the law of war. In addition to the readings and case studies, a student briefing on the course subject matter is required. The other 27 credit hour course, *Legal Issues in Contingency Operations*, covers legal issues commanders and staff officers are likely to face in future contingency operations. A portion of the course specifically deals with cooperation with war crimes tribunals.[72]

O'Connell's claims about a lack of law of war training is false and her conclusion that this has somehow impacted targeted killing operations by drones is simply wrong.

In the same passage, O'Connell further notes, without citation, that an unnamed "currently serving Army lawyer reported he had had only three days of international law training during his specialized course at the Army Judge Advocate General (JAG) School in Charlottesville, Virginia in 2005." I looked at the curriculum for the Army JAG School and, contrary to O'Connell's claims, I was able to confirm that the Basic Course requires eight days of instruction in Operational Law.[73] Moreover, a JAG officer advising on operational law would likely not come straight from the Basic Course, but would instead have years of experience and education that would also include a supplemental advanced two-week course in

---

[71] Martin and Sasser, *supra* n. 36, 92 (describing how "Ops officers, pilots, the MCC, and the sensor operators engaged in a spirited discussion over the best method for striking to destroy [a target]. Of course, the final decision over what action to take wasn't ours to make. The ground commander had the last word.").

[72] Ibid. at 13.

[73] See Maj Sean Condron (ed.), *Operational Law Handbook (2011),* International and Operational Law Department: The Judge Advocate General's Legal Center & School, U.S. Army. (The handbook summarizes the law of war "provisions for military personnel and commanders in the conduct of operations in both international and non-international armed conflicts"; citing DoDD 2311.01E, para. 3.1, the law of war is defined as "that part of international law that regulates the conduct of armed hostilities." Section IV defines the purposes for the law of war as both "humanitarian and functional in nature." Humanitarian purposes include: (1) protecting both combatants and noncombatants from unnecessary suffering; (2) safeguarding persons who fall into the hands of the enemy; and (3) facilitating the restoration of peace. Functional purposes include: (1) ensuring good order and discipline; (2) fighting in a disciplined manner consistent with national values; and (3) maintaining domestic and international public support. Section VI (A) states the Law of War "applies to all cases of declared war or any other armed conflicts that arise between the United States and other nations, even if the state of war is not recognized by one of them.")

Operational Law. In addition to this training, all JAGs undergo training with their unit and pre-deployment training to further enhance their skills. Finally, one JAG officer would not be operating alone, especially if he or she were inexperienced; they would instead have an entire technical chain of more experienced JAGs to whom they could turn for guidance and verification of judgments.[74] The claims of this unnamed "currently serving Army lawyer" are not a reflection of U.S. military practice, and even if they are, they are not as significant as O'Connell suggests. Finally, O'Connell also states in passing—and again without citation—that the "Naval War College may be trimming its law of armed conflict program."[75] This statement suggests that the Naval War College has lost interest in law of armed conflict training, a surprising point given that in the past two years the Naval War College sponsored major international law conferences focused on the law of armed conflict.[76]

Taken together, O'Connell uses a series of unsubstantiated suggestions to support her conclusion that "inadequate training may account for the high rate of unintended deaths" by drones.[77] This conclusion rests on two false premises: first, that there is a high rate of unintended deaths, a controversial point at best; and second, that there is inadequate training, a point that lacks substantial foundation as the preceding discussion illustrates. The fact that O'Connell fails to substantiate her claims with adequate citations and fails to consider that those claims could be easily refuted, undermines the force of her provocative argument that the United States is engaged in "unlawful killing by Predator drone."

II. Claims about drones and the targeted killing policy itself

Beyond claims about the process of targeted killing itself, critics also make unsupportable geo-political claims. For example, O'Connell writes (without a supporting citation) that "the U.S. needs Afghanistan's consent to carry out [drone] raids from Afghan territory. Afghanistan has not, apparently, given this consent." How can she know whether Afghanistan has given its consent? In fact, O'Connell's

---

[74] All of these claims are substantied by the DoD Law Of War Program policy memo cited above. Moreover, The U.S. Institute of Peace in their study of Law of War Training (<http://www.usip.org/files/resources/LawofWartext-final.pdf>), accessed November 4, 2011, notes that such training is an annual requirement for all U.S. military personnel, and is required before deployment. See also the ICRC's report on U.S. compliance with Law of War training at <http://www.icrc.org/customary-ihl/eng/docs/v2_cou_us_rule142> accessed November 4, 2011.

[75] O'Connell, *supra* n. 37, 8.

[76] See, eg, specifically "Non International Armed Conflict," *International Law Conference*, 2011, available at <http://www.usnwc.edu/Events/International-Law-Conference-2011.aspx> accessed November 4, 2011; "International Law and the Changing Character of Law" in 2010, available at <http://www.usnwc.edu/Events/International-Law-Conference-2010.aspx> accessed November 4, 2011.

[77] O'Connnell, *supra* n. 37, 8.

conclusions run counter to that of Amrullah Saleh, head of Afghan intelligence from 2004 to 2010, a position under the direct control of President Karzai. In a Frontline documentary, "Fighting for bin Laden," Saleh admits to supplying the CIA with on-the-ground intelligence to carry out drone strikes.[78] Further, O'Connell maintains that the United States and Pakistan disagree as a matter of policy as to what steps Pakistan should take, and because Pakistan has not given consent to the United States to use drones in Pakistani territory she writes that "The U.S. may not disregard (Pakistani) sovereignty to carry out its own police actions."[79] She also writes that "Pakistan has not expressly invited the United States to assist it in using force,"[80] and that "Pakistan has neither requested U.S. assistance in the form of drone attacks nor expressly consented to them."[81] Is she privy to private diplomatic communications between the United States and Pakistan? If such strident claims about Pakistani sovereignty are to be believed, critics ought to provide evidence that Pakistan has not consented to U.S. operations.

In fact, the body of evidence available to the public runs contrary to the notion that the United States is violating Pakistani sovereignty. It has been widely documented that there has always been at least tacit Pakistani approval for the drone program. A Reuters article provides an American diplomat's account of a meeting in Pakistan, which illustrates such approval.[82] The diplomat describes a meeting in which Pakistani parliamentarians repeatedly condemned the drone program. "Then, in the middle of the session... one of the parliamentarians slipped the American guest, who specializes in the region, a handwritten note." The note read, "The people in the tribal areas support the drones. They cause very little collateral damage. But we cannot say so publicly for reasons you understand." The Reuters article also cites several tribal elders from the regions most frequently targeted by the drones.[83] One tribal elder commented, "[civilians] want to get rid of the Taliban and if the (Pakistani) army cannot do it now, then it (drone attacks) is fine with them."[84]

It is also widely understood that Pakistani military and intelligence services provide essential assistance to the drone program. The same Reuters article also quotes Ikram Sehgal, a Pakistani security expert. Sehgal agrees that, "the intelligence underpinning the drone strikes has improved precisely because of increased Pakistani cooperation."[85] Likewise, terrorism expert Peter Bergen notes how U.S. and Pakistani strategic interests are now more aligned than they were at the outset of operations in Pakistan and that proof of this can be seen in the fact that the

---

[78] Frontline, "Fighting for bin Laden" (2011), WGBH/Frontline.
[79] O'Connell, *supra* n. 37, 21, fn. 88.
[80] Ibid. at 25.
[81] Ibid. at 21.
[82] Entous, *supra* n. 34.
[83] Ibid.
[84] Ibid.
[85] Ibid.

"United States is [operating] the drones with Pakistani government permission and also Pakistani government intelligence."[86] In fact, easily verifiable facts, such as the existence of U.S. air bases in Pakistan since 2006, undercut O'Connell's claims. For example, *The Times* reported in February 2009 that "[t]he US was secretly flying unmanned drones from the Shamsi airbase in Pakistan's southwestern province of Baluchistan as early as 2006, according to an image of the base from Google Earth."[87] The article further noted that "Major-General Athar Abbas, Pakistan's chief military spokesman...admitted on Tuesday that US forces were using Shamsi, but only for logistics. He also said that the Americans were using another air base in the city of Jacobabad for logistics and military operations."[88] Beyond this article, there are other sources that undermine O'Connell's sovereignty claim, albeit after the date of her most recently updated draft. For example, diplomatic cables published by Wikileaks reveal that:

> At the same time the Pakistani public was decrying the CIA's use of drone strikes in their country, Pakistan's top army general was asking a top U.S. official in behind-the-scenes meetings for more drones to help during military operations... Referring to the situation in Waziristan, [Pakistani General Ashfaq] Kayani asked if [U.S. Admiral William] Fallon could assist in providing continuous Predator coverage of the conflict area. Fallon regretted that he did not have the assets to support this request.[89]

Furthermore, as Islamic History Professor Brian Glyn Williams has noted, members of the Pakistani military have made statements lending support to the notion that the United States and Pakistan are working closely on drone strikes. Specifically, "the Pakistani general in command of forces in the embattled North Waziristan tribal agency told reporters that 'a majority of those eliminated [in drone strikes] are terrorists, including foreign terrorist elements.' Until this statement, the Pakistani military and government had not confronted the perception created by Pakistani media and anti-U.S. politicians that U.S. drones target, almost exclusively, civilians."[90] Williams concludes that:

> There is, however, little precedent for a general of Mehmood's rank speaking out on such a sensitive topic without the approval of his superiors. To do so would be a grave breach of military decorum, if not a breaking of direct orders, and would certainly lead to the end of an offending officer's career. The fact that no one in the Pakistani military or government has rejected Mehmood's statements is indicative. Clearly, there are voices in the Pakistani military who support the drone strikes against an

---

[86] National Geographic Channel, "CIA Confidential: Inside the Drone War" (2011).

[87] Jeremy Page, "Google Earth Reveals Secret History of US Base in Pakistan," *The Times*, February 19, 2009.

[88] Ibid.

[89] Jim Sciutto, "Wikileaks: Pakistan Asked for More, Not Fewer Drones," *ABC News*, May 20, 2011, available at <http://abcnews.go.com/Blotter/wikileaks-cable-pakistan-asked-fewer-drones/story?id=13647893> accessed November 4, 2011.

[90] Human Security Report Project, "Accuracy of the U.S. Drone Campaign: The Views of a Pakistani General," *CTC Sentinel*, March 2011, Vol. 4, Issue 3, 9.

enemy that many in Pakistan's military establishment have come to see as the greatest threat to the Pakistani state...Those making public statements on the drones, both in Pakistan and in the West, must now take General Mehmood's on-the-ground perspective about the effectiveness of the drone's targeting into consideration.[91]

Beyond law, O'Connell also questions the strategy of targeted killing. She notes that Baitullah Mehsud, who was killed in a drone strike, was quickly replaced by other leaders. To bolster her criticism she cites David Kilcullen, who believes that "going after leaders with drones is proving counterproductive of peace and stability in Pakistan."[92] However, such a claim fails to recognize that other counterterrorism experts believe that a policy of targeted killing, even if it results in leaders being replaced, still imposes costs on enemies. For example, Boaz Ganor, writing about the effectiveness of targeted killing, notes that:

> ...when the goal is to deter an organization from terrorist activity and to obstruct its actions, it would appear that this goal can be achieved by hurting a senior terrorist in that organization, which will then embark on a 'power struggle' among those eager to fulfill his role. The difficulty in finding another leader with professional skills, charisma or other positive characteristics to fill the position left by the dead activist could interfere with the organization's activities. Disrupting the organization's routine is liable to have ongoing consequences, rather than merely a short-term effect. The organization might then have to invest considerable resources—financial resources, manpower, and time—in defense and ongoing protection for its senior officials. In certain cases, the organization's senior activists take preventive steps and long-term security measures, and may even adopt new behavior because of their fear of personal attack.[93]

This imposition of costs—including the fear of attack—was proven recently when it was revealed that Osama bin Laden had to rely on couriers to supervise Al Qaeda operations and situated himself far from a personal leadership role out of fear that he might be targeted by U.S. air power.[94] Many officials believe this phenomenon also extends to significant Taliban leaders captured in large urban centers, such as Mullah Abdul Ghani Baradar.[95] When the infamous Taliban commander, best known for rapidly increasing the use of improvised explosive devices (IEDs) in Afghanistan, was captured by Pakistani intelligence officers in Karachi, Baradar became yet another example of top Taliban and Al Qaeda leaders fleeing the battlefield for a more densely populated city center out of fear of being targeted by a drone strike. Michael Scheuer, the former head of the CIA's bin Laden unit, summarized

---

[91] Ibid. at 11.

[92] O'Connell, *supra* n. 37, 11.

[93] Boaz Ganor, *The Counter-Terrorism Puzzle: A Guide for Decision Makers* (New Brunswick, N.J.: Transaction, 2005) 128.

[94] See Gregory S. McNeal, "The bin Laden Aftermath: Why Obama Chose SEALS Not Drones," *Foreign Policy*, May 5, 2011.

[95] Entous, "Special Report," *supra*, n. 34.

Baradar's capture, stating, "The more violence you inflict, the more intelligence you get because people who are being shot at make mistakes."[96]

Taken together, the claims of critics regarding the wisdom, efficacy and legality of targeted killing operations that have been surveyed here simply cannot be believed because they are riddled with inaccuracies or amount to nothing more than easily refuted empirical claims. In fact, in many instances critics reveal a fundamental lack of familiarity with basic aspects of military operations, doctrine, or training. Moreover, their geopolitical claims fail to take account of a wealth of contrary information contained in the public record. Such errors render their criticism unreliable at best.

III. Conclusion

This chapter has highlighted the lack of empirical foundation for many of the most common criticisms raised by targeted killing opponents. This chapter demonstrated how many claims made by critics are easily refuted, which calls into question the reliability of their criticism. Evidence in the public record and research I conducted indicates that the U.S. military follows a rigorous collateral damage estimation and mitigation process designed to minimize civilian casualties. The U.S. military takes unparalleled steps to eliminate civilian casualties. While evidence of civilian casualties is hard to come by, it is certainly the case that statistics proffered by some critics cannot be empirically verified; their skepticism of U.S. government statements is not backed up by anything more substantial than generic suspicion. Moreover, critics of targeted killing also lack proof for their claims about the legal, diplomatic and strategic results of drone strikes. Although the counter-observations raised in this chapter do not, by themselves, demonstrate that targeted killings are morally or legally justified, they do suggest that some of the moral or legal objections to targeted killings are based on empirical claims that are either dubious, impossible to verify or just plain false. This chapter provides a necessary corrective to some of the most strident claims raised by critics.

---

[96] Ibid.

13

OPERATION NEPTUNE SPEAR: WAS KILLING BIN LADEN A LEGITIMATE MILITARY OBJECTIVE?

Kevin H. Govern

Under U.S. domestic law, as well as foreign domestic and international law, targeted killings may be conducted by governmental elements under fairly specific circumstances. Forces conducting such targeted killing operations tend to encounter unique moral and legal dilemmas that do not admit of resolution according to the traditional principles of war. Nevertheless, targeted killing, as currently practised, can be conducted in ways that are consistent with time-tested and customarily accepted norms of legality, morality, and the general constraints of just war theory.

In this chapter I take the killing of Osama bin Laden as a test case for considering the moral and legal status of intentionally killing individuals deemed a threat to national security, under conditions in which the object of the targeted attack is offered little or no opportunity to surrender to attacking forces. The target in such operations, in short, is treated as though he were a belligerent: a person placed on a kill list may be targeted in a way that would be legitimate if he were an enemy combatant. In such cases, we think of him as having no personal right to self-defense and we attempt to use the element of surprise to avoid affording him an opportunity to surrender or evade capture. But where we are targeting non-uniformed civilians, who do not possess all the trappings of an enemy combatant, is it legitimate to target them in the same open-ended way that we target co-belligerents? In particular, is it legitimate to target them in a way that deprives them of a right of surrender?

My assertion in this chapter is that bin Laden was a legitimate military target, and that the decision-makers involved in his killing had thoroughly considered the range of options available to stop bin Laden from further terroristic acts, and were warranted in the decision to lean towards targeted killing in lieu of a capture operation. I thus conclude that those who carried out the killing were within their scope of authority and responsibility for killing rather than for capturing bin Laden. The structure of the operation, then, and the set of moral prohibitions operating on any such plan, should in theory *not* require new rules or new law of war prescripts. This holds true, despite the short- and long-term implications of this use of force. What is critical is an abiding and firm moral force underlying this and every other form of warfare, regardless of any minor or significant changes to the legal or operational framework in which it may be undertaken.

Section I will examine the political and military necessity considerations that gave rise to the Neptune Spear "capture or kill" decision-making process at the very highest echelons of the Executive Branch, with the evolution of political will, expressed into military directive, reflecting a careful analysis of authority and opportunity to end bin Laden's reign of terror. This will afford us an opportunity to distinguish between those who can be the permissible subject of "targeted killing" and those who cannot. Section II considers the operational and legal foundation for undertaking a war against one person via targeted killing. As to the targeted killing of bin Laden, this section will show the operation to be on a continuum of legitimate, operational options, from pursuit and capture under warrant-based targeting. Section III examines the moral foundations of foregoing war in favor of more isolated military operations, such as is involved in targeted killing. Section IV concludes with an examination of how the polarizing paradigm of Neptune Spear affects not only current contexts of counterterrorism operations but how it will shape U.S. and international political will to accept targeted killing over capture and prosecution, not just out of political pragmatism and military necessity, but as an emergent norm of customary international law.

I. The politics and military necessity behind Operation Neptune Spear

In order to understand why bin Laden became America's "Public Enemy Number One,"[1] and the subject of what may prove to be the most (in)famous "targeted killing" to date, we must understand the history, activities and implications of Al Qaeda (AQ) (Arabic for "the base"), and the evolution of a plan, ultimately executed, to conduct what resulted in a licit targeted killing of bin Laden. As an organization, AQ's origins lay in what the Congressional Research Service (CRS) described as "a

---

[1] Associated Press, "Bin Laden's Path To Public Enemy Number One," *Washington Post National Online* (Washington, D.C., May 2, 2011), available at <http://www.washingtonpost.com/national/bin-ladens-path-to-public-enemy-number-one/2011/05/02/AFt0RGYF_video.html> accessed October 28, 2011.

core cadre of veterans of the Afghan insurgency against the Soviet Union, with a centralized leadership structure;"[2] Co-founders Abdullah al Azzam, a key figure in the Jordanian Muslim Brotherhood,[3] and bin Laden, seventeenth of 20 sons of a Saudi construction magnate, struggled over the structure of so-called *mujahedin*[4] factions that had successfully fought and helped expel Soviet forces from Afghanistan.[5]

Following Azzam's death,[6] bin Laden gained control of the organizational mechanisms, but continued to adhere to the shared principle of global *jihad* that he and Azzam had devised.[7] After Azzam, bin Laden's key advisors became anti-Soviet *jihad* leader Umar Abd al Rahman (also known as "the blind *shaykh*" or elder leader), the spiritual leader of radical Egyptian Islamist group *Al Jihad*,[8] and Ayman al-Zawahiri operational leader of Al Jihad in Egypt, who was acquitted of the October 1981 assassination of Egyptian President Anwar Sadat and arrived from Egypt in the Afghanistan theater in 1986.[9] Abd al Rahman came to the United States in 1990 from Sudan and was convicted in October 1995 for terrorist plots related to the February 1993 bombing of the World Trade Center.[10] Zawahiri stayed with bin Laden and became bin Laden's main strategist until six weeks after bin Laden's targeted killing, whereupon he assumed leadership of AQ.[11] Bin Laden and Zawahiri vowed to take the loose coalition of radical Islamic cells and associates in over 70 countries to create a global threat to U.S. national security, with at least nine separate attacks against the United States or U.S.-supported regimes[12] prior to the culminating event of the September 11, 2001 attacks on U.S. soil.[13]

---

[2] John Rollins, "Al Qaeda and Affiliates: Historical Perspective, Global Presence, and Implications for U.S. Policy," Congressional Research Service (CRS) Report R41070, January 25, 2011, available at <http://www.fas.org/sgp/crs/terror/R41070.pdf> accessed October 28, 2011.

[3] As noted by Rollins, ibid. at 5, the Muslim Brotherhood was "founded in 1928 in Egypt, and it has since spawned numerous Islamist movements throughout the region, some as branches of the Brotherhood, others with new names."

[4] The term "mujahadeen," also sometimes spelled "mujahideen," "mujahedeen," "mujahedin," "mujahidin," and "mujaheddin," refers to a military force of Muslim guerrilla fighters engaged in a "holy war" or "jihad," available at <http://www.thefreedictionary.com/mujahedeen> accessed October 28, 2011.

[5] Rollins, *supra* n. 2, 5.

[6] Asaf Maliach, "Abdullah Azzam, Al-Qaeda, And Hamas," *Military and Strategic Affairs* Vol. 2, No. 2 October 2010, at 83, available at <http://www.inss.org.il/upload/(FILE)1298359986.pdf> accessed October 28, 2011.

[7] Ibid. at 83.

[8] See, e.g., Omar Abdel Rahman, *NY Times.com,* available at <http://topics.nytimes.com/top/reference/timestopics/people/a/omar_abdel_rahman/index.html> accessed October 28, 2011.

[9] Rollins, *supra* n. 2, 6.

[10] Ibid.

[11] See, eg, Ayman Al-Zawahri, *NY Times.com* <http://topics.nytimes.com/top/reference/timestopics/people/z/ayman_al_zawahri/index.html?scp=1-spot&sq=Zawahiri&st=cse> accessed October 28, 2011.

[12] Ibid. at 3–4 for a listing of those attacks between 1993 and 2000.

[13] Ibid.

In the wake of the September 2001 terrorist attacks on the United States, President George W. Bush launched major military operations in South and Southwest Asia as part of the global U.S.-led counterterrorism effort. Operation Enduring Freedom (OEF) in Afghanistan has seen substantive success with the assistance of neighboring Pakistan, but not without some U.S. criticism of Pakistani incompetence, if not complicity, with respect to AQ presence on its soil. This included allegations by the U.S. Ambassador to Islamabad that the Pakistani government had ties to a terror network causing attacks in Afghanistan, and the U.S. Chairman of the Joint Chiefs of Staff supporting that claim and directly naming Pakistani Inter-Service Intelligence (ISI) as supporting terrorist activities.[14] While successes mounted against Taliban, and certain elements of AQ that it supported, top AQ leadership largely eluded U.S. forces in Afghanistan and other efforts in Pakistan.[15] This was part of a U.S. move towards "anticipatory self-defense" acts that would eventually involve killing or capturing terrorist suspects worldwide, to include coercive interrogations that, in the absence of classified confirmatory data, produced unknown quantities of actionable intelligence to prevent future attacks or prosecute past perpetrators.[16]

In October 2001, on the first night of the Congressionally authorized campaign against AQ and the Taliban, a Predator drone deployed over southern Afghanistan identified Taliban leader Mullah Mohammed Omar in a convoy of cars fleeing Kabul. Following its agreement with military commanders, the Central Intelligence Agency (CIA) operators sought approval from the United States Central Command (USCENTCOM) in Tampa, Florida to launch a Hellfire missile at Mullah Omar, who by then had sought cover in a building with an estimated 100 guards. General Tommy Franks reportedly declined to give approval, based upon on-the-spot advice

---

[14] Omar Waraich, "US Ambassador Stokes Anger in Pakistan Over Embassy Attack Claims," *The Independent,* September 19, 2011, available at <http://www.independent.co.uk/news/world/asia/us-ambassador-stokes-anger-in-pakistan-over-embassy-attack-claims-2356871.html> accessed October 28, 2011, and see Elisabeth Bumiller and Jane Perlez, "Mullen Asserts Pakistani Role in Attack on U.S. Embassy," *New York Times,* September 22, 2011, available at <http://www.nytimes.com/2011/09/23/world/asia/mullen-asserts-pakistani-role-in-attack-on-us-embassy.html> accessed October 28, 2011.

[15] See, e.g., Greg Bruno and Eben Kaplan, *The Taliban in Afghanistan,* Council on Foreign Relations Backgrounder, available at <http://www.cfr.org/afghanistan/taliban-afghanistan/p10551> accessed October 28, 2011. See also CRS conversations with journalists and experts in Washington, D.C. December 2004–January 2005; James Risen and David Rohde, "A Hostile Land Foils the Quest for Bin Laden," *New York Times,* December 13, 2004.

[16] For an in-depth analysis of U.S. foreign policy under the Bush Administration, see Betty Glad and Chris J. Dolan, *Striking First* (New York: Palgrave Macmillan, 2004), cited with authority in Thomas Byron Hunter, "Targeted Killing: Self-Defense, Preemption, and the War on Terrorism," *Journal of Strategic Security* (2009) 18. For the perspective of the co-author of the so-called "torture memos," issued by the Department of Justice, regarding coercive/enhanced interrogation techniques, see John Yoo, "The Cost of Killing bin Laden," Reuters, September 7, 2011, available at <http://blogs.reuters.com/great-debate/2011/09/07/the-cost-of-killing-osama-bin-laden/> accessed October 28, 2011.

of his military lawyer.[17] Since that time, Predator drones have reportedly been used "at least hundreds of times to fire on targets in Afghanistan, Pakistan, Yemen, Iraq, and elsewhere."[18] Apart from Osama bin Laden, a number of senior Taliban and AQ operatives have been killed in these attacks, including AQ's reputed chief of military operations, Mohammed Atef,[19] as well as the unintended "collateral damage (incidental to the intended strike)" deaths of an untold number of civilians.[20]

Focusing on bin Laden, from December 2001 onward, in the course of the post-September 11 major combat effort, U.S. Special Operations Forces (SOF) and CIA operatives reportedly narrowed their combined US-Afghan-Coalitional unconventional warfare pursuit of bin Laden to the Tora Bora mountains in Nangarhar Province (near the city of Khost and 30 miles west of the Khyber Pass),[21] but in the ensuing years between 2001 and 2011, bin Laden was not found, captured or killed.

In a foreshadowing of their future stances on targeted killing as a component of a national security strategy, and the politics of targeted killing, then Senator Barack Obama faced off to debate Senator McCain in a debate at Belmont University,

---

[17] See, e.g., Institute for National Security and Counterterrorism (INSCT), Syracuse University, "Case Study: Targeted Killing by the United States After 9/11," insct.org, available at <http://insct. org/commentary-analysis/2011/05/04/case-study-targeted-killing-by-the-united-states-after-911/> accessed October 28, 2011.

[18] Ibid. The NSC made a decision that all potentially sensitive targets were to be cleared by Secretary Rumsfeld himself. The authority for these decisions was eventually delegated to Gen. Tommy Franks, the CENTCOM Commander and Joint Forces Commander (JFC). See Michael W. Kometer, *Command in Air War: Centralized vs. Decentralized Control of Combat Airpower*, Doctoral Dissertation in Partial Fulfillment of Doctor of Philosophy in Technology, Management, and Policy, Massachusetts Institute of Technology, May 2005, 104, citing with authority William M. Arkin, "The Rules of Engagement," *Los Angeles Times*, April 21, 2002. See also Bob Woodward, *Bush at War* (New York: Simon & Schuster, 2002) 166. The exception was "if CIA had bin Laden or al Qaeda leadership in its crosshairs," according to Woodward.

[19] For a glimpse into the U.S. targeted killing program and use of drones by the CIA, see, e.g., Nils Melzer, *Targeted Killing In International Law* (Oxford University Press, 2008), 41–2; A. John Radsan, "An Overt Turn On Covert Action," 53 *St Louis U. L.J.* 485, 488–9, 539–42 (2009); Mohammed Khan and Douglas Jehl, "The Reach of War: Anti-Terrorism: Attack Kills a Top Leader of Al Qaeda, Pakistan Says," *N.Y. Times*, December 4, 2005, 24; Josh Meyer, "CIA Expands Use of Drones in Terror War," *L.A. Times*, January 29, 2006, A1; James Risen and Mark Mazzetti, "C.I.A. Said to Use Outsiders to Put Bombs on Drones," *N.Y.Times*, August 21, 2009, A1; and Jordan J. Paust, "Self-Defense Targetings of Non-State Actors and Permissibility of U.S. Use of Drones in Pakistan" (December 8, 2009), *Journal of Transnational Law & Policy*, Vol. 19, No. 2, 237, 2010.

[20] Glen W. Johnson "Mortus Discriminatus: Procedures in Targeted Killing" (M.S. thesis, Naval Postgraduate School 2007) 22. Johnson notes that "[a]ll targeted killing guidelines should include directives on capture, collateral damage, mission approval, timing, and areas of operation." Ibid. at 43.

[21] Rollins, *supra* n. 2, 8. See U.S. Joint Publication (JP) 1-02, Department of Defense (DoD) *Dictionary of Military and Associated Terms*, April 12, 2001, as amended through July 31, 2010, 375, available at <http://www.dtic.mil/doctrine/jel/new_pubs/jp1_02.pdf> accessed October 28, 2011, for a definition of Unconventional Warfare: "Activities conducted to enable a resistance movement or insurgency to coerce, disrupt, or overthrow a government or occupying power by operating through or with an underground, auxiliary, and guerrilla force in a denied area. Also called UW."

in Nashville, Tennessee.[22] Fielding a question from the audience as to whether he would pursue AQ leaders inside Pakistan, even if that meant invading an ally nation, candidate Obama replied with a statement of prospective policy consistent with customary international law, wherein sovereignty of the state is not absolute under international law or impervious to the reach of another nation in its exercise of self defense. He said:

> If we have Osama bin Laden in our sights and the Pakistani government is unable, or unwilling, to take them out, then I think that we have to act and we will take them out. We will kill bin Laden. We will crush Al Qaeda. That has to be our biggest national-security priority.[23]

Up to that point, Obama castigated McCain's foreign policy stances as laden with "hysterical diatribe"[24] or being "naïve and irresponsible;"[25] of Obama's vow to kill bin Laden, McCain characterized the promise as foolish, saying, "I'm not going to telegraph my punches."[26]

From the time of his inauguration in 2009, U.S. President Obama bolstered the U.S. military presence in Afghanistan with a central goal of neutralizing the AQ threat emanating from the region,[27] yet neighboring Pakistan would come to be identified as the "epicenter of terrorism"[28] from which threats to the U.S. and other western countries had come, and from which they would continue to emanate. The U.S. government uncovered evidence suggesting that the 9/11 hijackers were themselves based in western Pakistan in early 2001 and, by one account, AQ and its Pakistani affiliates provided operational direction in 38 per cent of the serious terrorist plots against Western countries since 2004.[29]

It is within this context that we next consider the so-called "hunt for bin Laden" as the target came into clearer view, and targeted killing "crosshairs" were being aimed from the 2009–2011 timeframe. Four months after the start of the Obama Administration, CIA Director Leon Panetta briefed Obama on the agency's latest

---

[22] Transcript of Second McCain, Obama Debate, CNN Politics, cnn.com (October 8, 2008), available at <http://articles.cnn.com/2008-10-07/politics/presidential.debate.transcript_1_commission-on-presidential-debates-obama-debate-town-hall-format?_s=PM:POLITICS> accessed November 3, 2011.

[23] Ibid.

[24] See comment by John McCain on Barack Obama's foreign policy in Mike Glover, 'Obama Criticizes McCain for "Naïve" Foreign Policy," *USA Today* (May 17, 2008), available at <http://www.usatoday.com/news/politics/2008-05-16-2967008008_x.htm> accessed October 28, 2011.

[25] See comment by Barack Obama on John McCain's foreign policy, ibid.

[26] Transcript, *supra* n. 22.

[27] Ibid. at 13.

[28] "PTI, Pakistan 'Epicenter' of Terrorism, Says Mullen," *Times of India*, January 13, 2011, available at <http://articles.timesofindia.indiatimes.com/2011-01-13/pakistan/28371105_1_safe-havens-kayani-ways-that-two-years> accessed October 28, 2011.

[29] "In Military Campaign, Pakistan Finds Hint of 9/11," *New York Times*, October 30, 2009; Paul Cruickshank, "The Militant Pipeline," New American Foundation Counterterrorism Strategy Initiative Policy Paper, February 2010, cited with authority in Rollins, *supra* n. 2, at 13.

programs and initiatives for tracking bin Laden.[30] Obama in turn drafted a memo to Panetta in June, 2009 directing the CIA to create a "detailed operation plan" for finding the AQ leader and to "ensure that we have expended every effort" to track bin Laden down, as well as to intensify the CIA's classified drone program. In the execution of this plan, more missile attacks were carried out during the first year of the Obama Administration than the eight years of the preceding Bush Administration; since bin Laden's death, the United States has been "doubling down" on its strategy of covert targeted missile strikes in Pakistan, believing that Al Qaeda is susceptible to a decisive blow via targeted killings.[31]

After nearly a decade of hunting Osama bin Laden, a breakthrough came in August of 2010 when bin Laden's most trusted courier was located and identified, and the large, secure compound where deliveries were made became a High Value Target (HVT).[32] The CIA began to brief President Obama on assessments[33] that led them to believe that bin Laden may have been located at the million-dollar compound in Abbottabad, Pakistan, some 800 yards away from the Kakul Military Academy.[34] In late 2010, Obama ordered CIA Director Panetta to begin exploring options for a military strike on the compound;[35] Panetta then reportedly contacted the commander of U.S. Special Operations Command's (USSOCOM's)[36] Joint Special Operations Command (JSOC)[37] to begin planning a kill-or-capture mission.[38]

---

[30] Nicholas Schmidle, "Getting Bin Laden," *The New Yorker* August 8, 2011, available at <http://www.newyorker.com/reporting/2011/08/08/110808fa_fact_schmidle?currentPage=all> accessed October 28, 2011.

[31] Ibid. See "9/11 and Al Qaeda: The Price of Victory," *LA Times* August 29, 2011, available at <http://opinion.latimes.com/opinionla/2011/08/911-al-qaeda-homeland-security-spending-war-dead.html> accessed October 28, 2011.

[32] "How Osama Bin Laden Was Located and Killed," *New York Times,* May 8, 2011, available at <http://www.nytimes.com/interactive/2011/05/02/world/asia/abbottabad-map-of-where-osama-bin-laden-was-killed.html> accessed October 28, 2011.

[33] Ibid.

[34] "Osama Was Just 800 yards from the Pakistan Military Academy," World News NDTV, ndtv.com, May 2, 2011, available at <http://www.ndtv.com/article/world/osama-was-just-800-yards-from-the-pakistan-military-academy-102890> accessed October 28, 2011.

[35] Schmidle, *supra* n. 30.

[36] At the time of this chapter's writing there were 10 Unified Combatant Commands (UCCs) within the U.S. Department of Defense; four were organized as functional commands with specific capabilities like Special Operations, as in the case of USSOCOM, and six geographical commands with regional responsibilities like U.S. Africa Command (USAFRICOM). See U.S. Joint Publication JP 1–02, *supra* n. 21, at 487.

[37] Created in 1980 after the disastrous hostage-rescue mission in Iran, JSOC is part of the U.S. Special Operations Command. Over the past 10 years, JSOC units, which include Army, Navy, and Air Force elements operating jointly with each other and in interagency operations with other government agencies, have been essential to U.S. military efforts in Afghanistan and Iraq. Purportedly, in annexes to several presidential directives not available for public viewing, JSOC is designated as the official executive agent for counterterrorism worldwide. See, e.g., Marc Ambinder, "Then Came 'Geronimo'," *The National Journal* (May 5, 2011), available at <http://www.nationaljournal.com/magazine/practicing-with-the-pirates-these-navy-seals-were-ready-for-bin-laden-mission-20110505> accessed October 28, 2011.

[38] Schmidle, *supra* n. 30.

The kill-or-capture campaign that JSOC would be conducting involved targeting enemies on a classified list called a JPEL (Joint Prioritized Effects List).[39] According to Matthew Hoh, a former U.S. Foreign Service officer, "the list included bomb makers, commanders, financiers, people who coordinate the weapons transport and even [public relations] people."[40] John Nagl, a former counterinsurgency adviser to the former commander of forces in Afghanistan and current Director of the CIA, General Petraeus, described JSOC's kill-or-capture campaign to PBS Frontline as part of "an almost industrial-scale counterterrorism killing machine."[41] Nagl went on to say of the JPEL process in 2011 that "[w]hat's happened over the past five years is we've gotten far, far better at correlating human intelligence and signals intelligence to paint a very tight, coherent picture of who the enemy is and where the enemy hangs his hat," and in his estimation "we've gotten better at using precision firepower to give those people very, very bad days."[42]

In January 2011, JSOC was said to have developed and presented a raid plan—an in-progress version of what would become code-named Neptune Spear[43]—to USSOCOM. Interagency CIA-USSOCOM planning continued through March 2011 to develop for the President and National Security Council various options for capturing or killing bin Laden,[44] to include a raid or airstrike, with or without Pakistani cooperation or even prior knowledge of the mission.[45] Sources indicate Obama decided against informing or working with Pakistan, consistent with a confidential Presidential advisor's assessment that there was "a real lack of confidence that the Pakistanis could keep this secret for more than a nanosecond."[46]

---

[39] Nick Davies, "Afghanistan war logs: Task Force 373—Special Forces Hunting Top Taliban," *The Guardian* July 25 2010, available at <http://www.guardian.co.uk/world/2010/jul/25/task-force-373-secret-afghanistan-taliban> accessed October 28, 2011.

[40] Gretchen Gavett, "What is the Secretive U.S. 'Kill/Capture' Campaign?," PBS Frontline, June 17, 2011, available at <http://www.pbs.org/wgbh/pages/frontline/afghanistan-pakistan/kill-capture/what-is-the-secretive-us-killca/> accessed October 28, 2011. See also Kevin Govern, "Resigned to Failure or Committed to a Just Cause of Justice? The Matthew Hoh Resignation, Our Current Politico-Military Strategy in Afghanistan, and Lessons Learned from the Panama Intervention of Twenty Years Ago," *Oregon Review of International Law*, Spring 2011, Vol. 13, No. 1, 161–77. As an aside, Hoh resigned in 2009 because he felt U.S. tactics were only fueling the insurgency in Afghanistan.

[41] Gavett, ibid.

[42] Ibid.

[43] Note: operational code words are intended to not relate in any way to the action, and so they are quickly and easily identified and communicated. For a good article on the history of these code words, see Ed O'Keefe, "Why Is It Called 'Operation Odyssey Dawn'?" *Washington Post,* March 22, 2011, available at <http://www.washingtonpost.com/blogs/federal-eye/post/why-is-it-called-operation-odyssey-dawn/2011/03/22/ABLaaFDB_blog.html> accessed October 28, 2011.

[44] See, e.g., Philip Sherwell, "Osama bin Laden Killed: Behind the Scenes of the Deadly Raid," *The Daily Telegraph,* May 7, 2011, available at <http://www.telegraph.co.uk/news/worldnews/al-qaeda/8500431/Osama-bin-Laden-killed-Behind-the-scenes-of-the-deadly-raid.html> accessed October 28, 2011.

[45] "How Osama Bin Laden was Located and Killed," *supra* n. 32.

[46] Schmidle, *supra* n. 30.

The order to execute the mission against bin Laden came on April 29, 2011,[47] and shortly after eleven o'clock on the night of May 1st, the assault team of 23 SEAL[48] operators and additional support members lifted off from Jalalabad Air Field, in eastern Afghanistan. They embarked on what the media has questionably called a "covert"[49] mission into Pakistan to capture or kill bin Laden.[50] The assault team entered the compound, and what happened next is subject to conjecture, shaped by unclassified press releases as well as confidential leaks. With regards to senior administration oversight, former CIA Director Panetta said "I can tell you that there was a time period of almost twenty to twenty-five minutes where we really didn't know just exactly what was going on."[51] This meant during the critical decision-making period of confronting bin Laden, and opting to capture or kill him, that the assault team would not have had real-time input from, or feedback to, the National Command Authority.[52] This was despite the fact that the operation had been monitored by dozens of defense, intelligence, and Administration officials watching the drone's video feed.[53]

The *New Yorker* journalist Nicholas Schmidle's compilation of reports indicates next that:

> Three SEALs shuttled past [bin Laden's 23-year-old son] Khalid's body and blew open another metal cage, which obstructed the staircase leading to the third floor.

[47] See, e.g., Matt Apuzzo, "Inside The Raid That Killed Bin Laden," *The Seattle Times, seattletimes.nwsource.com*, May 02, 2011, available at <http://seattletimes.nwsource.com/html/nationworld/2014933984_apusbinladentheraid.html> accessed October 28, 2011.

[48] SEAL stands for "Sea, Air, Land," and is a common acronym used to describe those specially trained Special Operations Force (SOF) "operators" who are part of USSOCOM's Naval Special Warfare Command. See, e.g., Naval Special Operations Command (NSW), available at <http://www.public.navy.mil/nsw/Pages/welcome.aspx> accessed October 28, 2011. See also Sherwell, *supra* n. 44.

[49] U.S. Joint Publication JP 1–02, *supra* n. 21, defines "covert" as "[a]n operation that is so planned and executed as to conceal the identity of or permit plausible denial by the sponsor," ibid. at 87. Contrast this with the definition of "clandestine," which is an "operation sponsored or conducted by governmental departments or agencies in such a way as to assure secrecy or concealment. A clandestine operation differs from a covert operation in that emphasis is placed on concealment of the operation rather than on concealment of the identity of the sponsor. In special operations, an activity may be both covert and clandestine and may focus equally on operational considerations and intelligence-related activities." Ibid. at 55.

[50] Schmidle, *supra* n. 30.

[51] Steven Swinford, "Osama Bin Laden Dead: Blackout During Raid on Bin Laden Compound," *The Telegraph*, May 4, 2011, available at < http://www.telegraph.co.uk/news/worldnews/al-qaeda/8493391/Osama-bin-Laden-dead-Blackout-during-raid-on-bin-Laden-compound.html> accessed October 28, 2011.

[52] The "National Command Authority" (NCA) is comprised of the President and Secretary of Defense together or their duly deputized alternates or successors. The term NCA is used to signify constitutional authority to direct the Armed Forces in their execution of military action. Both the movement of troops and execution of military action must be directed by the NCA; by law, no one else in the chain of command has the authority to take such action. See e.g., Naval Doctrine Publication (NDP) 1, Naval Warfare March 28, 1994, 9, available at <http://www.dtic.mil/doctrine/jel/service_pubs/ndp1.pdf> accessed October 28, 2011.

[53] Swinford, *supra* n. 51.

Bounding up the unlit stairs, they scanned the railed landing. On the top stair, the lead SEAL swiveled right; with his night-vision goggles, he discerned that a tall, rangy man with a fist-length beard was peeking out from behind a bedroom door, ten feet away…Crankshaft [code word for bin Laden himself]…The Americans hurried toward the bedroom door. The first SEAL pushed it open. Two of bin Laden's wives had placed themselves in front of him. Amal al-Fatah, bin Laden's fifth wife, was screaming in Arabic. She motioned as if she were going to charge; the SEAL lowered his sights and shot her once, in the calf. Fearing that one or both women were wearing suicide jackets, he stepped forward, wrapped them in a bear hug, and drove them aside…A second SEAL stepped into the room and trained the infrared laser of his M4 on bin Laden's chest. The Al Qaeda chief, who was wearing a tan *shalwar kameez* [tunic and trousers] and a prayer cap on his head, froze; he was unarmed. "There was never any question of detaining or capturing him—it wasn't a split-second decision. No one wanted detainees," the special-operations officer told me…The first round, a 5.56-mm. bullet, struck bin Laden in the chest. As he fell backward, the SEAL fired a second round into his head, just above his left eye. On his radio, he reported, "For God and country—Geronimo, Geronimo, Geronimo." After a pause, he added, "Geronimo E.K.I.A."—"enemy killed in action."[54]

Aside from bin Laden, and his son Khalid having been killed, assaulting commandos killed the brother of the courier known as Kuwaiti—Tareq Khan—both reported to have been unarmed, and a fourth person, a woman, believed to be the wife of one of the compound residents.[55] Accounts indicate next that the assault team "swept through the buildings, collecting a 'mother lode' of intelligence material—computers, cell phones, thumb drives and written documents," then went back into the compound to demolish to the extent possible sensitive equipment in a downed helicopter.[56]

The body of bin Laden was photographed, and biometric measurements taken, with confirmation of bin Laden's demise relayed back to the White House Situation Room.[57] Within 38 minutes of the raid's initiation, another helicopter joined the operation to ferry out the uninjured raid team and the body of bin Laden to Bagram, Afghanistan for further identification and disposition, departing before the Pakistani military ever had forces on site to investigate what had happened.[58] Then, bin Laden's body was transported to the U.S.S. Carl Vinson, a U.S. aircraft carrier off the Pakistani cost in the Arabian sea.[59] His body was then prepared for burial under Islamic tradition, and as a lawful military target during a time of armed conflict, bin Laden's remains were interred by burial at sea.[60]

---

[54] Schmidle, *supra* n. 30.
[55] Sherwell, *supra* n. 44.
[56] Ibid.
[57] Schmidle, *supra* n 30.
[58] Ibid.
[59] Ibid.
[60] David Crane, "Burial at Sea: The End of Osama bin Laden," *JURIST*—Forum, May 4, 2011, available at <http://jurist.org/forum/2011/05/burial-at-sea-the-end-of-osama-bin-laden.php> accessed September 22, 2011.

II. Legal and moral foundations of a law of war against terrorists

Since September 11, 2001, the US has categorized its fight against AQ as an armed conflict, a framework upheld by all three branches of the US government.[61] Having recounted the circumstances leading up to bin Laden's death, a number of normative questions arise, not the least of which is consideration of whether there are distinctions with a meaningful difference between assassinations and targeted killings.

Due to the complexity of conducting surprise attacks for political reasons, targeted killings cannot occur without significant legal ramifications. Our ability to make sense of such operations from the standpoint of justification is further complicated by the classified nature of sensitive activities such as these.[62] Concurrently, no widely established standard or published set of unclassified guidelines or planning considerations exist for operational planners to conduct targeted killing operations.[63] This begs the question: what exactly constitutes a permissible targeted killing, as compared with a morally permissible assassination? The answer to this question is far from settled, largely because there is profound disagreement about which body of law should be used to authorize targeted killing operations. By contrast, the category of assassinations refers to killings of a similar nature, but these are illegal per se given the absence of legal necessity and/or authority to kill.[64]

Targeted killings, whether conducted by Israel, the United States, Great Britain, or other nations, are "more frequently the result of action undertaken not by conventional military forces, but rather by specialized troops, such as SOF, police, and intelligence agents."[65] Alternately, some nations have turned increasingly to specialized equipment, such as unmanned aerial vehicles (UAVs), commonly known as drones, in order to track their enemies. These specialized troops and equipment have

---

[61] Laurie Blank, "Finding the Paradigm: Investigating bin Laden's Demise," *JURIST*—Forum, May 8, 2011, available at <http://jurist.law.pitt.edu/forum/2011/05/laurie-blank-finding-the-paradigm.php>; http://jurist.org/forum/2011/05/laurie-blank-findingthe-paradigm.php> accessed October 28, 2011.

[62] See, e.g., Army Regulation (AR) 380–1, Special Access Programs (SAPs) and Sensitive Activities, April 21, 2004, available at <http://www.fas.org/irp/doddir/army/ar380-381.pdf> accessed October 28, 2011. AR 380–1 defines sensitive activities as "Programs that restrict personnel access, such as [Alternative Compensatory Control, or] ACC measures; sensitive support to other Federal agencies; clandestine or covert operational or intelligence activities; sensitive research, development, acquisition, or contracting activities; special activities; and other activities excluded from normal staff review and oversight because of restrictions on access to information." Ibid. at 84.

[63] Johnson, *supra* n. 20, v. Having said this, we must not discount the likelihood that classified guidelines and/or planning considerations have existed for U.S. targeted killing operations.

[64] For a detailed yet accessible review of this subject, see Elizabeth B. Bazan, Assassination Ban and E.O. 12333: A Brief Summary, Congressional Research Service (CRS) Report RS21037, 2004, available at <http://www.fas.org/irp/crs/RS21037.pdf > accessed October 28, 2011.

[65] See, e.g., David Tucker, "Counterterrorism and the Perils of Preemption Problems and Command and Control" in Betty Glad and Chris Dolan (eds), *Striking First: The Preventative War Doctrine and the Reshaping of U.S. Foreign Policy* (New York: Palgrave McMillan, 2004) 75–89, cited with authority in Hunter, *supra* n. 16, 3.

proven to be an essential component of targeted killing, due primarily to the elusive and clandestine nature of terrorists themselves.

Law of war expert Professor Gary Solis terms "targeted killing" "the targeting and killing, by a government or its agents, of a civilian or 'unlawful combatant' taking a direct part in hostilities in the context of an armed conflict who is not in that government's custody and cannot be reasonably apprehended."[66] Former Special Ambassador for Counterterrorism Dell Dailey, has said "targeted killing, as understood by select members of Special Operations Forces ('Operators'), is the employment of a weapons platform designed for both sensing and destroying an identified enemy target with the maximum use of current technology while retaining a human in the decision making process."[67] Taking exception to the notion that targeted killings can be permissible, U.N. Special Rapporteur on extrajudicial, summary or arbitrary executions Philip Alston has said "a targeted killing is the intentional, premeditated and deliberate use of lethal force, by States or their agents acting under color of law, or by an organized armed group in armed conflict, against a specific individual who is not in the physical custody of the perpetrator."[68]

Perhaps most indicative of what is or is not a permissible targeted killing comes from the Naval operational history scholar Glenn Johnson, who examined successful and unsuccessful targeted killings operations in the twentieth and twenty-first centuries: Operation Anthropoid in October 28, 1941 and the ultimately successful targeted killing of *Obergruppenführer* ("Senior Group Leader") Reinhard Heydrich, who chaired the 1942 Wannsee Conference that discussed plans for the deportation and extermination of all Jews in German-occupied territory;[69]

---

[66] Gary D. Solis, *The Law of Armed Conflict: International Humanitarian Law in War* (Cambridge: Cambridge University Press, 2010) 542.

[67] Keynote Address from Ambassador (Retired) Dell L. Dailey at Conference "Using Targeted Killing to Fight the War on Terror: Philosophical, Moral and Legal Challenges" University of Pennsylvania Law School (April 15, 2011). Among his many military and diplomatic assignments, Dailey commanded JSOC, and directed the new Center for Special Operations, the military hub for all counterterrorism, before retiring to control of the State Department's counterterrorism office, from which he "promoted interagency collaboration and built closer partnerships between military personnel and the members of other U.S. Government departments and agencies involved in global counterterrorism activities." "Biography—Dell L. Dailey" U.S. Dep't of State Website, available at <http://www.state.gov/outofdate/bios/87639.htm> accessed October 28, 2011.

[68] Philip Alston, *The Project on Extrajudicial Executions*, U.N. General Assembly Special Report 5/2010, available at <http://www.extrajudicialexecutions.org/application/media/14%20 HRC%20Targeted%20Killings%20Report%20%28A.HRC.14.24.Add6%29.pdf> accessed October 28, 2011.

[69] Glen W. Johnson, *supra* n. 20, v. Johnson's Abstract noted that as of 2007, at least in the unclassified realm, a consequentialist viewpoint that "[d]ue to the political complexity intertwined with targeted killing these types of operations rarely occur without repercussion. Operational planners need to understand that targeted killing operations cannot exist solely at the operational level because their consequences have strategic and political ramifications. By utilizing a case study analysis, this thesis will identify the operational planning considerations that need to be addressed to successfully conduct a targeted killing mission."

the successful targeted killing of Admiral Isoroku Yamamoto, Japanese Naval Marshal General and the commander-in-chief of the Combined Fleet during the Second World War, on April 18, 1943;[70] the successful targeted killing of the Palestinian terrorists in Israel's 1972 Operation Wrath Of God—also known as Operation Bayonet—who were involved in the 1972 massacre of Israeli Olympians at Munich, Germany;[71] Israel's unsuccessful efforts of targeted killing aimed at A. Ahmed Jibril, the founder and leader of the Popular Front for the Liberation of Palestine, from the 1980s through present;[72] the operations against Pablo Escobar, Colombian drug lord, with combined U.S.–Colombian targeted killing ultimately successful on July 2, 1994;[73] and, the targeted killing of Hamas terrorists on various dates in the mid-2000s with varying success by Israel.[74]

This chapter does not consider, for instance, the prescriptions and proscriptions on targeted killing in other nations, or the ways in which other nations have addressed legal aspects related to targeted killing. For instance, Israel's Supreme Court ruled in 2006 that the Israeli government's targeted killing policy was legal, within certain specified constraints.[75] While other nations have prescribed or proscribed various forms of targeted killings in contemporary times, U.S. presidents have been delegated by inferred rather than explicit authority, the power to order and authorize targeted killing operations under the U.S. Constitution. On December 4, 1981, President Ronald Reagan signed into law Executive Order 12333, "United States Intelligence Activities," which came about from a long line of Congressional concerns expressed regarding alleged abuses by the U.S. intelligence community in the 1970s.[76] Section 2.11 of the order provides the following brief but powerful proscription: "Prohibition on Assassination. No person employed by or acting on behalf of the United States Government shall engage in, or conspire to engage in, assassination."[77] Unfortunately, while this Executive Order prohibits assassination, it does not define what constitutes assassination, nor does any other U.S. statute or law define that term!

---

[70] Ibid. at 34–36.

[71] Ibid. at 39–41.

[72] Ibid. at 30–33.

[73] Ibid. at 25–29.

[74] Ibid. at 39–42.

[75] Note: See HCJ 760/02, *The Public Committee Against Torture in Israel v. The Government of Israel*, Decision of the Israeli Supreme Court, issued on December 14, 2006, available at < http:// www.jewishvirtuallibrary.org/jsource/Politics/sctterror.html> accessed October 28, 2011. For more on Israeli targeted killing, superbly written about by one of the world's foremost counterterrorism experts, see Amos N. Guiora, "Targeted Killing as *Active Self-Defense,*" *Case Western Research Journal Int'l Law*, Vol. 36, 319, 2004.

[76] Office of the President of the United States, *United States Intelligence Activities* (E.O. 12333, 1981), available at <http://www.au.af.mil/au/awc/awcgate/whitehouse/eo12333.htm> accessed October 28, 2011.

[77] Executive Order 12333 was the last of three executive orders banning assassination. For a detailed yet accessible review of this subject, see Elizabeth B. Bazan, "Assassination Ban and E.O. 12333: A Brief Summary," Congressional Research Service (CRS) Report RS21037, 2004, available at <http://www.fas.org/irp/crs/RS21037.pdf > accessed October 30, 2011.

Section 2.12 of Executive Order 12333 forbids indirect participation in activities prohibited by the order, stating: "Indirect participation. No agency of the Intelligence Community shall participate in or request any person to undertake activities forbidden by this Order."[78] While Executive Order 12333 is still in force, post September 11, 2001 legislation has "opened the door" to a very significant reinterpretation of the assassination ban, if not repealing it entirely. On Friday, September 14, 2001, both the House and the Senate passed joint resolutions, S.J. Resolution 23 and H.J. Resolution 64, authorizing the President to:

> Use all necessary and appropriate force against those nations, organizations, or persons he determines planned, authorized, committed, or aided the terrorist attacks that occurred on September 11, 2001, or harbored such organizations or persons, in order to prevent any future acts of international terrorism against the United States by such nations, organizations or persons.[79]

Published reports in popular media[80] as well as governmental sources[81] have suggested that in the wake of the 9/11 terrorist attacks, the Pentagon has expanded its counterterrorism intelligence activities, and targeted killing as a subset of the latter, while Congress has maintained legal authority for oversight of such activities. Sections 601–604 of the 1991 Joint Explanatory Statement of the Committee of Conference, H.R. 1455, set forth significant provisions regarding such congressional oversight of intelligence activities, including requirements relating to the authorization of covert actions by the President and the reporting of covert actions to Congress. If we are to assume that bin Laden's targeted killing was part of a covert operation, either in intelligence collection, dissemination, or the conduct of the operation, then those aspects which were covert would have included a written "finding" and be subject to Congressional notification and oversight in order to comply with U.S. Federal law on covert operations.[82]

---

[78] Ibid. at n. 3.

[79] Note: The Senate passed S.J.Res. 23, before 11:00 a.m. on Friday, September 14, 2001. The House passed it late Friday evening, September 14, 2001. The President signed it into law on Tuesday, September 18, 2001 as P.L. 107–40, 115 Stat. 224 (2001). For a detailed discussion of authorizations of the use of U.S. military force see Jennifer K. Elsea and Richard F. Grimmett, *Congressional Research Service Report* (RL31133, 2007), *Declarations of War and Authorizations of Use of Military Force: Historical Background and Legal Implications* (2007), available at <http://www.fas.org/sgp/crs/natsec/RS22357.pdf> accessed October 28, 2011.

[80] Siobhan Gorman, "CIA Had Secret Al Qaeda Plan," *The Wall Street Journal*, July 13, 2009, available at <http://online.wsj.com/article/SB124736381913627661.html#mod=djemalert NEWS> accessed October 28, 2011, and see Marc Ambinder, "What Was That Secret CIA Operation? Targeted Assassinations?," *The Atlantic*, (Boston, July 31, 2009), available at <http://www.theatlantic.com/politics/archive/2009/07/what-was-that-secret-cia-operation-targeted-assassinations/21144/> accessed October 28, 2011.

[81] Alfred Cumming, *Covert Action: Legislative Background and Possible Policy Questions*, (CRS Report RL33715, 2009), available at <http://www.fas.org/sgp/crs/intel/RL33715.pdf> accessed October 28, 2011.

[82] Ibid. citing Sec. 503 of the National Security Act of 1947 [50 U.S.C. 413b], and see U.S. Joint Publication JP 1–02, *supra* n. 21, regarding the differentiation between "clandestine" and "covert."

One might suppose that bin Laden was an obviously permissible target. He was the head of AQ, a non-state-actor that had declared war on the United States,[83] and that his compound in Abbottabad had served as the headquarters for running the AQ operations since 2005.[84]

Though it is not our central concern in the present chapter, in addition to other concerns about the legitimacy of the operation, some may contest as illegal the use of force against the territorial integrity and political independence of a foreign state, Pakistan.[85] Recently leaked revelations rebut this assertion, with claims by serving and retired Pakistani and U.S. officials that the then-U.S. President George Bush and Pakistan's then military leader Pervez Musharraf "struck a secret deal almost a decade ago permitting a US operation against Osama bin Laden on Pakistani soil, after Bin Laden escaped US forces in the mountains of Tora Bora in late 2001."[86] The reported terms were that "Pakistan would allow US forces to conduct a unilateral raid inside Pakistan in search of Bin Laden, his deputy, Ayman al-Zawahiri, and the al-Qaida No 3 [and a]fterwards, both sides agreed, Pakistan would vociferously protest the incursion."[87] Such an agreement would have been consistent with Pakistan's unspoken policy towards CIA drone strikes in the tribal belt, which was revealed by the publicly revealed WikiLeaks U.S. embassy cables of November 2010,[88] which contained amongst other messages an account that current Pakistani Prime Minister Syed Yousaf Raza Gillani told a US official: "I don't care if they do it, as long as they get the right people. We'll protest in the National Assembly and then ignore it."[89]

Regardless of preserved or violated sovereignty, and national consent or lack thereof to such operations, the question of moral justification circumscribed in law, not politics, remains a profound challenge. Regarding this question, there are two major

---

[83] According to Paust, *supra* n. 19, 262, "[t]he targeted killing of certain persons is clearly lawful under the laws of war, during war the selective killing of persons who are taking a direct part in armed hostilities, including enemy combatants, unprivileged combatants, and their civilian leaders (and, thus, excluding captured persons of any status), would not be impermissible 'assassination'." See also Benjamin Davis, "Post-Osama: The Way Forward for the United States," *JURIST*—Forum, May 2, 2011, available at <http://jurist.org/forum/2011/05/benjamin-davis-post-osama.php> accessed October 28, 2011. See also David Crane, "Legal Arithmetic: Adding Up the Legality of Operation Geronimo," *JURIST*—Forum, May 14, 2011, available at <http://jurist.org/forum/2011/05/david-crane-legal-arithmetic.php> accessed October 28, 2011.

[84] Ibid.

[85] See, e.g., Curtis Doebbler, "The Illegal Killing of Osama Bin Laden," *JURIST*—Forum, May 5, 2011, available at <http://jurist.org/forum/2011/05/curtis-doebbler-illegal-killing-obl.php> accessed October 28, 2011.

[86] Declan Walsh, "Osama bin Laden Mission Agreed in Secret 10 Years Ago by US and Pakistan," *The Guardian*, May 9, 2011, available at <http://www.guardian.co.uk/world/2011/may/09/osama-bin-laden-us-pakistan-deal> accessed October 28, 2011.

[87] Ibid.

[88] See, e.g., "The US Embassy Cables," *The Guardian*, September 22, 2011, available at <http://www.guardian.co.uk/world/the-us-embassy-cables> accessed October 28, 2011.

[89] Walsh, *supra* n. 86.

camps that have emerged with competing views about choice of law that should have governed the prescriptions and proscriptions regarding bin Laden's targeted killing, as well as other targeted killings in the international arena. First, there is international human rights law (IHRL), which argues a more restricted view of targeted killings.[90] Second, there is international humanitarian law (IHL), also known as the law of war or the law of armed conflict, which argues for a broader view of targeted killings.[91] Generally speaking, IHL is a set of rules that seek, for humanitarian reasons, to limit the effects of armed conflict. It protects persons who are not or are no longer participating in the hostilities and restricts the means and methods of warfare.[92]

Targeted killings are largely viewed as illegal from the framework of IHRL because this view gives a presumption of innocence that would be violated by a targeted killing from, say, a predator drone-launched missile attack. Instead, the objects of targeted killings, under such a theory, "should be arrested, detained,[93] and interrogated with due process of law;" and force should be employed only if necessary. Under such a theory, there must be no other measures available, and lethal force should not be used if a lesser degree of force can be effective."[94] Thus, for bin Laden's targeted killing to be permissible, lethal force would have to have been not the only option or course of action given in military directive to the SEAL team conducting the raid, and their responsibility among all their tactical and operational considerations must have necessarily included exhausting all nonlethal means available.

It is nevertheless crucial to clarify the important nature of the difficulty here: critics often confuse the IHL prohibition against declaring that no quarter will be given (which is also a war crime under the Rome Statute) with an affirmative obligation to capture rather than kill. But these two points are conceptually and legally distinct. The prohibition against declaring no quarter establishes that no party to the conflict may simply kill soldiers who have clearly surrendered. The underlying rationale

---

[90] W. Jason Fisher, "Targeted Killing, Norms, and International Law," (2007) 45 *Colum. J. Transnat'l L.* 711, 719.

[91] Ibid. at 719. See also Office of the High Commissioner for Human Rights, "International Human Rights Law" (*United Nations Human Rights*, June 23, 2011), available at <http://www.ohchr.org/en/professionalinterest/Pages/InternationalLaw.aspx> accessed October 28, 2011, noting that "International human rights law lays down obligations which States are bound to respect."

[92] For what comprises IHL, see "What is International Humanitarian Law?," Advisory Service On International Humanitarian Law, 07/2004, available at < http://www.icrc.org/eng/what-we-do/building-respect-ihl/advisory-service/index.jsp> accessed October 28, 2011. This is also consistent with the United Nations Global Counter-Terrorism Strategy, adopted by Member States on September 8, 2006, available at <http://www.un.org/terrorism/strategy-counter-terrorism.shtml#poa2> accessed October 28, 2011.

[93] See John Embry Parkerson, Jr, "United States Compliance with Humanitarian Law Respecting Civilians During Operation Just Cause," 133 *Mil. L. Rev.* 31, 41–2 (1991) and Kevin H. Govern, "Sorting the Wolves from the Sheep," 19 *Military Police* 1, 1–5 (2004); see also Major Geoffrey S. Corn and Major Michael Smidt, "To Be or Not to Be, That is the Question: Contemporary Military Operations and the Status of Captured Personnel," *Army Law*, June 1999, 1.

[94] Fisher, *supra* n. 90, 719.

behind this legal norm is the classic distinction between civilians and combatants, and the notion that surrendering soldiers are "hors de combat" and have therefore regained the same protections that civilians have under the laws of war. They are no longer combatants because they have laid down their arms and firmly indicated their surrender. Their status calls them out as deserving of protection.

This is not, however, the same thing as requiring a party to the conflict to give enemy targets the opportunity to surrender before killing them. If the targets communicate their surrender, that surrender must be respected, but there is no affirmative requirement to give them an opportunity to surrender before killing them. If there were such an obligation, aerial bombardment per se would be illegal under the laws of armed conflict, which it clearly is not. This would require a wholesale revision in the practice of modern warfare, something that is clearly not supported by the state practice by any state that has military aircraft. This demonstrates the *reductio ad absurdum* of this argument. Of course, some critics assert that the obligation to capture versus kill comes from IHRL. While this may be a plausible reading of IHRL, it simply assumes precisely what is denied here; that is, that the appropriate law governing the armed conflict with Al Qaeda is IHL and the law of armed conflict. Therefore, the obligation to capture versus kill is only legally sustainable if the critic can muster a convincing argument that IHL does not apply here at all. This, arguably, they cannot do.

The administration has consistently maintained that the operatives engaged in the bin Laden raid were counseled regarding their IHL obligations. Both John Brennan and Harold Koh have explained that bin Laden was to be captured if he clearly surrendered. Even if we speculate that U.S. commandos did not give him an opportunity to surrender, they were not required to do so under IHL. To suggest that they were under such an obligation is to presuppose that the raid was governed by the law enforcement paradigm with its typical "police-freeze!" predicate that begins a domestic arrest situation. As a final point, there is absolutely no evidence on the record that the Navy SEALs violated the IHL norm and in fact executed a surrendering bin Laden. Such an explosive allegation ought to be accompanied by some proffer of proof, which is currently lacking. Alleged comments that commanders indicated a preference for killing bin Laden do not qualify. As explained above, denying bin Laden the opportunity to surrender is far different from issuing an order that no quarter would be given to him during the raid, even if he affirmatively surrendered. That would indeed have made the raid illegal, but there is no evidence that this happened.

III. Resolving moral doubts about targeted killing

The choice of legal analysis framework for combating terrorism, and specifically the targeted killing of bin Laden, is integrally tied into the so-called just war tradition that is coupled with a concurrent moral condemnation of terrorism.[95] Professor of Religion Edmund Santurri, who directs The Great Conversation program at St Olaf College, has surveyed what he calls "a rough consensus among contemporary proponents of that [just war] tradition—moralists, philosophers, theologians and international legal theorists" with respect to terrorism.[96] In so doing, he finds the spectrum of just war thinkers who argue that while a group might resort to political violation under certain moral conditions (for example, to protect the innocent), this use of political violence—even when the cause is just—must still be governed by certain moral constraints prohibiting terrorist acts *inter alia*.[97] Santurri counters the notion that "Islamic radicals like bin Laden are [or were] right in their assessments of the state of affairs, that Islam is, indeed, threatened decisively by American actions, or that figures like bin Laden have morally legitimate authority to issue such judgments, to call for belligerent response."[98] For Santurri, "terrorism is a moral wrong but that the distribution of responsibility for particular terrorist acts is an enormously complex matter—when the cause of the terrorist is just,"[99] something which Santurri stops short of saying existed as the basis for bin Laden's directing, leading, and taking part in terrorism.

Did the U.S. government ever consider any moral obligation, if any, to capture bin Laden and bring him to justice, versus ending his leadership through targeted killing? Can and should operational expediency ever trump legal and moral propriety with regards to the choice between kill and capture? We have no unclassified documentary proof, or definitive policy statement, which indicates that the Bush or Obama Administrations ever considered these matters as factors with regards to the targeted killing program in general, or the operation against bin Laden in particular. What is evident in inferred motive from change of policy is that expediency became a significant factor in bringing swift, decisive action against AQ in the Spring of 2011.

In April 2011, the Obama Administration ended the CIA's role in capturing and interrogating terror suspects overseas, with the exception of the battlefields of Iraq and Afghanistan.[100] With bin Laden's location being pinpointed to Pakistan, was there a political, if not legal or moral reason not to capture bin Laden from that point onward? International humanitarian law expert Laurie Blank has opined that "[w]hen the law of armed conflict mandates the use of deadly force as a first resort

---

[95] Edmund N. Santurri, "Philosophical Ambiguities in Ostensibly Unambiguous Times: The Moral Evaluation of Terrorism," *Journal of Peace & Justice Studies* 12:2 (2002) 137.

[96] Ibid. at 138.

[97] Ibid.

[98] Ibid. at 153.

[99] Ibid. at 155.

[100] Ken Dilanian, "CIA has Slashed its Terrorism Interrogation Role," *LA Times* April 10, 2011, available at <http://articles.latimes.com/2011/apr/10/world/la-fg-cia-interrogation-20110411> accessed October 28, 2011.

and human rights law prohibits the use of deadly force except as a last resort, we can see that the two paradigms will often be irreconcilable when applied to the same incident," yet both regimes "have the protection of persons as a core value."[101] John Brennan, the Obama Administration's top counterterrorism official, told reporters after the successful operation that if "we had the opportunity to take him alive, we would have done that."[102] A senior intelligence official echoed that sentiment in an interview on the Tuesday following bin Laden's death, telling *National Journal* that if bin Laden "had indicated surrender, he would have been captured."[103] While the JPEL remains classified,[104] and the kill-or-capture order remains unknown to the general public, we have strong indications as to the mindset of the then-CIA director Panetta on the operation and of bin Laden's opportunity to surrender and be captured or resist and be killed: "To be frank, I don't think he had a lot of time to say anything."[105] In Panetta's estimation, "[i]t was a firefight going up that compound. By the time they got to the third floor and found bin Laden, I think this was all split-second action on the part of the SEALs."[106] If these accounts by some of the United States' top national security advisors happen to be true, it would be appropriate then to not "second-guess" the SEAL operatives in their making a professional judgment call that was within the range of what would have been briefed as legal and appropriate options within their "Rules of Engagement," or "ROE,"[107] which rules would have necessarily been crafted to cover any instance of bin Laden being *hors de combat* (out of combat by injury or surrendering).[108] Once bin Laden was killed, assaulting

---

[101] Blank, *supra* n. 61.

[102] UPI, "Officer: Raid Was Always to Kill bin Laden," UPI.com, August 2, 2011, available at <http://www.upi.com/Top_News/US/2011/08/02/Officer-Raid-was-always-to-kill-bin-Laden/UPI-92811312270200/#ixzz1X12GywZF> accessed October 28, 2011.

[103] Yochi J. Dreazen, Aamer Madhani and Marc Ambinder, "For Obama, Killing—Not Capturing—bin Laden Was Goal," *National Journal,* May 4, 2011, available at <http://www.nationaljournal.com/for-obama-killing-not-capturing-nobr-bin-laden-nobr-was-goal-20110503> accessed October 28, 2011.

[104] Davies, *supra* n. 39.

[105] Gavett, *supra* n. 40, cited with authority in Dreazen, *supra* n. 103.

[106] Ibid.

[107] ROE are directives issued by competent superior authority that delineate the circumstances and limitations under which military forces will initiate and continue engagement with other forces. ROE are drafted in consideration of the law of war, national policy, public opinion, and military operational constraints. ROE are often more restrictive than the law of war would allow. ROE will normally determine the legally justified uses of force during international military operations. See, e.g., U.S. Joint Publication JP 1–02, *supra* n. 21, 309.

[108] The ROE for Neptune Spear would have necessarily been drafted to be in accord with the so-called Common Article 3 protections of the Geneva Conventions. See, e.g., *Convention (III) Relative to the Treatment of Prisoners of War. Geneva,* August 12, 1949, available at <http://www.icrc.org/ihl.nsf/FULL/375?OpenDocument> accessed October 28, 2011. This Convention and its Commentaries fail to address the rights and responsibilities of terrorists other than noting in the Commentaries that "it was not possible to talk of 'terrorism,' 'anarchy' or 'disorder' in the case of rebels who complied with humanitarian principles," which has never been persuasively alleged that bin Laden or AQ ever did. See *Commentaries to Convention (III) Relative to the Treatment of Prisoners of War. Geneva,* August 12, 1949, available at <http://www.icrc.org/ihl.nsf/COM/375–590006?OpenDocument> accessed October 28, 2011.

forces would also have been obligated under their ROE, to handle his remains in accordance with IHL and concurrently with respect for Islamic law.[109]

IV. Conclusion: the polarizing paradigm of Neptune Spear

The targeted killing of bin Laden has already been thought to have a strong influence on U.S. and international responses to terrorism. Significantly, on May 16, 2011, the United Kingdom Parliament indicated that the bin Laden killing portends not only a trend within the United States defense strategy, but also an emergent international political and operational orientation towards intractable terrorist regimes and individuals. In a report, prepared by the House of Commons Library as charting future politico-military and legal approaches to terrorism, bin Laden's "targeted killing" had "significant implications" for how the United States and other countries deal with terrorist suspects.[110] Such methods could be seen to be "accepted politically," it argues, with a trend in customary international law emerging with "[a] wider implication is that the killing may be seen as a precedent for targeted killings of individuals by any state, across international boundaries, at least where terrorism is involved. The more states act in this way, the more likely it is to become accepted, at least politically if not as a matter of international law."[111]

As customary national security policy if not customary international law, President Obama has authorized nearly four times the number of drone strikes for targeted killing in Pakistan in his first two years in office as President Bush did in his eight years. According to unclassified media accounts of attacks, some 225 strikes have taken place since 2009, resulting in the targeted killing of between 1,100 and 1,800 militants at the time of writing.[112] This, of course, does not account for casualties not involving deaths; under this escalation of targeted killing force, some 1,100 militants and noncombatant civilian deaths may have occurred in Pakistan alone.[113] This trend in targeted killing is not just a distantly removed drone-fired

---

[109] Crane, *supra* nn. 60 and 83.

[110] Arabella, Thorp, "Killing Osama bin Laden: Has Justice Been Done?," *House of Commons Library Standard Report* SN/IA/5967, May 16, 2011, available at <http://www.parliament.uk/briefing-papers/SN05967> accessed October 28, 2011.

[111] Ibid. at 9.

[112] "The Year of the Drone: An Analysis of U.S. Drone Strikes in Pakistan, 2004–2011", *New America Foundation*, 11 September 2011, available at <http://counterterrorism.newamerica.net/drones> accessed October 28, 2011. The New America Foundation claimed to rely upon open-source (unclassified) reports as available from including the *New York Times*, *Washington Post*, and *Wall Street Journal*, accounts by major news services and networks—the Associated Press, Reuters, Agence France-Presse, CNN, and the BBC—and reports in the leading English-language newspapers in Pakistan—the *Daily Times*, *Dawn*, the *Express Tribune*, and the *News*—as well as those from Geo TV, the largest independent Pakistani television network.

[113] Chris Woods, "Covert Drone War—'You Cannot Call Me Lucky'—Drones Injure Over 1,100", *The Bureau of Investigative Journalism*, 10 August 2011, available at <http://www.thebureauinvestigates.com/category/projects/drones/> accessed October 28, 2011.

missile tactic; the use of special operations raids (to capture or conduct targeted killing) have increased from 675 covert raids in 2009 to 1,879 so far in 2011, with Pentagon reports assessing that approximately 84 to 86 per cent of these night raids end without violence;[114] NATO reports further clarify those ambiguous statistics, stating that in such raids, the target is successfully killed or captured 50 to 60 per cent of the time.[115] As conventional U.S. forces begin to draw down and redeploy to their home stations, "the role of counterterrorism operations, and in particular these kinds of special missions, will become prominent," says International Security Assistance Force (ISAF) commander General John Allen.[116]

This trend towards killing instead of capturing following the death of bin Laden has continued, with notable examples being the September 30, 2011 targeted killings by drone-launched missile attack on the radical U.S.-born Islamic cleric in Yemen, Anwar al-Awlaki, along with Samir Khan, U.S.-born editor of AQ's online jihadist magazine.[117] As with the attack on bin Laden, evidently this strike on AQ militants was planned and authorized long in advance. Nine months before that strike, the U.S. Director of National Intelligence, Dennis C. Blair, told a House of Representatives hearing in February 2011 that such a step was possible, even if not naming al-Awlaki specifically: "We take direct actions against terrorists in the intelligence community…If we think that direct action will involve killing an American, we get specific permission to do that."[118] Then, open-source media identified six months before the strike that the Obama administration had "taken the extraordinary step of authorizing the targeted killing of an American citizen."[119] In that same reportage, Obama administration officials claimed "it is extremely rare, if not unprecedented, for an American to be approved for targeted killing," while a former senior legal official in the Administration of George W. Bush said "he did

---

[114] Sean Naylor, "Chinook Crash Highlights Rise in Spec Ops Raids", *Army Times*, 21 August 2011, available at <http://www.armytimes.com/news/2011/08/army-chinook-crash-highlights-rise-in-spec-ops-raids-082111w/> accessed October 28, 2011.

[115] Joshua Partlow, "Karzai Wants U.S. to Reduce Military Operations in Afghanistan, *Washington Post*, November 14, 2010, available at <http://www.washingtonpost.com/wp-dyn/content/article/2010/11/13/AR2010111304001.html> last accessed October 28, 2011.

[116] Naylor, *supra* n. 114, cited with authority in Jonathan Masters, "Backgrounder—Targeted Killing, Council on Foreign Relations," 29 August 2011, available at <http://www.cfr.org/intelligence/targeted-killings/p9627> accessed October 28, 2011. Readers are reminded that counterterrorism operations are ordinarily, but not exclusively, conducted by highly trained SOF and/or national intelligence assets.

[117] See, e.g., Martin Chulov and Paul Harris, "Anwar al-Awlaki, al-Qaida Cleric and Top US Target, Killed in Yemen," *The Guardian* September 30, 2011, available at < http://www.guardian.co.uk/world/2011/sep/30/anwar-al-awlaki-killed-yemen> accessed October 28, 2011.

[118] Jason Ryan, 'License to Kill? Intelligence Chief Says U.S. Can Take Out American Terrorists', ABC News website, available at <http://abcnews.go.com/Politics/license-kill-intelligence-chief-us-american-terrorist/story?id=9740491> accessed October 28, 2011.

[119] Scott Shane, "U.S. Approves Targeted Killing of American Cleric," *New York Times*, April 6, 2011, available at < http://www.nytimes.com/2010/04/07/world/middleeast/07yemen.html> accessed October 28, 2011.

not know of any American who was approved for targeted killing under the former president."[120]

Abdul-Rahman al-Awlaki, son of Anwar al-Awlaki, also met his demise in Yemen a scant two weeks after his father's death, on October 15, 2011; the modality again was drone launched missile strike, killing the younger al-Awlaki, the Egyptian-born AQ media chief Ibrahim al-Bana, and six other militants.

To the acclaim of governments around the world and the relief of the Libyan people, Colonel Muammar Qaddafi's rule came to a decisive end on October 20, 2011, through a demise facilitated, but not directly accomplished, by a drone strike attempting a targeted killing in conjunction with a NATO aircraft strike on his convoy near Sirte, Libya.[121] Injured during the strike, Qaddafi was then captured by Libyan National Transitional Council (NTC) rebels and later killed along with his son Muatassim.[122]

Finally, at the time of writing, another U.S. drone strike on October 27, 2011 killed Hazrat Umar, a brother of the Pakistani Taliban commander, Maulvi Nazir, Khan Muhammad, another top commander in the group, and two other aides in Pakistan's northwestern region.[123] Hours later, five missiles hit the militant hideout near North Waziristan's town of Mir Ali, killing six men.[124] These latest targeted killings of AQ-affiliated militants has potentially created the conditions for regime change in Pakistan. Within a day of that strike, the cricketer-turned-politician Imran Khan led more than 2,000 tribesmen in protest at Parliament in Islamabad.[125] Khan condemned the "criminal silence" of non-governmental organizations, over the killings of civilians in drone attacks and has said that the

---

[120] Ibid.

[121] David Sperry, "Officials: US Drone Fired in Gadhafi Strike; Administration Looking Ahead to Libya's Future," *Washington Post* October 21, 2011, available at <http://www.washingtonpost.com/politics/congress/gadhafi-death-amounts-to-victory-for-obamas-approach-but-little-impact-likely-on-election/2011/10/21/gIQAxAGi2L_story.html> accessed October 28, 2011.

[122] Ibid.

[123] Salman Masood, "Drone Strike in Pakistan Kills Brother of Militant Commander," *New York Times,* Oct 27, 2011, available at < http://www.nytimes.com/2011/10/28/world/asia/drone-strike-in-pakistan-kills-brother-of-taliban-fighter.html?_r=1&emc=eta1> accessed October 28, 2011.

[124] AP, "US Drone Strikes Kill Prominent Militant Commander, 10 Others in NW Pakistan," *Washington Post,* October 27, 2011, available at <http://www.washingtonpost.com/world/asia-pacific/bomb-explodes-in-food-market-in-northwest-pakistan-city-of-peshawar-injuring-11-people/2011/10/27/gIQALBooKM_story.html> accessed October 28, 2011.

[125] "Pakistani Tribesmen Rally Against US Drone Strikes," *Daily News* and *Analysis India* website, available at <http://www.dnaindia.com/world/report_pakistani-tribesmen-rally-against-us-drone-strikes_1604371> accessed October 28, 2011. Note: Khan is a common surname of Central Asian origin, primarily found in Afghanistan, Bangladesh, India and Pakistan, and Imran Khan is no relation to the previously mentioned Tareq Khan or Samir Khan. See Sir Henry Yule, Hobson-Jobson, *A Glossary of Colloquial Anglo-Indian Words and Phrases, and of Kindred Terms, Etymological, Historical, Geographical and Discursive* (new edn edited by William Crooke, B.A. London: J. Murray, 1903), Digital Dictionaries of South Asia Website, available at <http://dsal.uchicago.edu/dictionaries/hobsonjobson/> accessed October 28, 2011.

"government should quit if it could not take action in this regard."[126] As a follow-on consequence impacting U.S.-coalitional operations in Afghanistan, sitting protesters in various places in Peshawar suspended the vital NATO supply chain of vehicles.[127]

Not limited to governmental agencies, this targeted killing as customary national security policy has also led to the opportunity for some increased "privatized" efforts in targeted killing operations. An offshoot of the former Blackwater International/Xe private military company (PMC),[128] now called "Select PTC," has allegedly been involved in classified clandestine activities in countries around the world, including Pakistan, Afghanistan, Iraq, Syria and the Philippines, and the same unit was also purportedly awarded a classified contract to assist U.S. government assets in targeted killing of AQ leaders around the world.[129] "There are skills we don't have in government that we may have an immediate requirement for," General Michael V. Hayden, who ran the CIA from 2006 until early 2009, said during a panel discussion on the privatization of intelligence and alluding to a foundational need for contractors to fill needs inherent to successful targeted killing planning and execution.[130] Quoting one government official familiar with the CIA program and the role of contractors in targeted killing, "[t]he actual pulling of a

---

126 Ibid.

127 "Imran Khan starts his Two Day Protest Against Drone Attacks," Latest BBCNews website, available at <http://www.latestbbcnews.com/imran-khan-starts-his-two-day-protest-against-drone-attacks.html> accessed October 28, 2011.

128 With respect to mercenarism and Private Military Firms/Private Military Corporations, see, e.g., P.W. Singer, *Corporate Warriors: The Rise of the Privatized Military Industry* (Cornell: Cornell University Press, 2003) 8, and see Kevin H. Govern and Eric C. Bales, "Taking Shots at Private Military Firms: International Law Misses its Mark (Again)" (2008) 32 *Fordham Int'l L.J.* 55, and Louise Doswald-Beck, *From Mercenaries to Market: The Rise and Regulation of Private Military Companies* (Oxford: Oxford University Press, 2007) ch. 7. These authors significantly distinguish between and among those categories of legal versus illegal actors subject to national and international criminal law, and the laws of war/international humanitarian law.

129 "Same Blackwater, Different Names," ABC News website, available at <http://abcnews.go.com/Blotter/blackwater-names/story?id=9634372&page=2> accessed October 28, 2011. According to a 2009 report in The Nation, JSOC, in tandem with Blackwater/Xe, has an ongoing drone program, along with "snatch and grabs" of high-value targets, along with targeted killing operations based upon "plans developed in part by Blackwater," with operations based in Karachi and conducted both in and outside of Pakistan. See Jeremy Scahill, "Blackwater's Secret War in Pakistan," *The Nation*, 23 November 2009, available at <http://www.thenation.com/article/secret-us-war-pakistan> Accessed October 28, 2011. Note: this is not to be confused with the similar-sounding "PTC Select," whose "highly trained network support engineers build, upgrade, secure and maintain computer network through scheduled visits." See PTC Select website, available at <http://www.ptcselect.com/> accessed October 28, 2011.

130 "CIA Said to Use Outsiders to Put Bombs on Drones," *NY Times.com*, available at <http://www.nytimes.com/2009/08/21/us/21intel.html> accessed October 28, 2011. By way of caveat, the article goes on to say "General Hayden, who succeeded Mr. Goss at the agency, acknowledged that the CIA program continued under his watch, though it was not a priority. He said the program was never prominent during his time at the CIA, which was one reason he did not believe that he had to notify Congress. He said it did not involve outside contractors by the time he came in."

trigger in some ways is the easiest part, and the part that requires the least expertise...It's everything that leads up to it that's the meat of the issue."[131]

Following the United States' lead in hiring "privatized" support to targeted killing, the crown prince of Abu Dhabi, Sheik Mohamed bin Zayed al-Nahyan has hired former president of Blackwater/Xe, Erik Prince, to build an 800-member battalion of foreign troops nicknamed "Reflex Responses" (R2) for the United Arab Emirates (UAE).[132] The private force's intended purpose is "to conduct special operations missions inside and outside the country, defend oil pipelines and skyscrapers from terrorist attacks and put down internal revolts."[133] The crown prince of Abu Dhabi also intends for such troops to deploy if they are confronted with pro-democracy uprisings such as similarly situated Arab countries have experienced in 2011,[134] and as part of such internal defense missions, that battalion may well be called upon to conduct targeted killing of key insurgent or insurrection leaders.

As apparent validation of the above-mentioned emergent "political acceptance" of targeted killing, the U.S. predator drone strike the week of June 20, 2011 against senior members of al Shabab in Somalia reportedly ensued from "growing concern within the U.S. government that some leaders of the Islamist group are collaborating more closely with al-Qaeda to strike targets beyond Somalia."[135]

This most recent airstrike makes Somalia "at least the sixth country where the United States is using drone aircraft to conduct lethal attacks, joining Afghanistan, Pakistan, Libya, Iraq and Yemen," with reports indicating that the CIA is "expected to begin flying armed drones over Yemen in its hunt for al-Qaeda operatives."[136] Targeted killing is a "growth industry" as far as modern warfare is concerned. The difficulty that stems from the need to justify the rejection of the traditional rule of capture in just war theory, and in international humanitarian law, poses a significant challenge to establishing its legitimacy.

Few if any nations, groups, or individuals outside of those allied or sympathizing with AQ have chosen to challenge the targeted killing of bin Laden by moralizing the acts of those who might be wrongfully identified for assassination or targeted killing. Even so, some academics challenge the legitimacy of the targeted killing, or the potential targeted killing of some other AQ operatives.[137] That is to say,

---

[131] Ibid.

[132] Ibid.

[133] Ibid.

[134] Mazzetti, *supra* n. 19.

[135] Greg Jaffe and Karen DeYoung, "U.S. Drone Targets Two Leaders of Somali Group Allied with al-Qaeda, Official Says," *Washington Post*, June 29, 2011, available at <http://www.washingtonpost.com/national/national-security/us-drones-target-two-leaders-of-somali-group-allied-with-al-qaeda/2011/06/29/AGJFxZrH_story.html> accessed October 28, 2011.

[136] Ibid. See also Afsheen John Radsan and Richard Murphy, "Measure Twice, Shoot Once: Higher Care For Cia-Targeted Killing," *University of Illinois Law Review*, Vol. 2011, 1201 *et seq.*

[137] See, e.g., Doebbler, *supra* n. 85, and Ryan P. Alford, "The Rule of Law at the Crossroads: Consequences of Targeted Killing of Citizens, March 7, 2011, *Utah Law Review*, forthcoming,

those targeted may have had justifiable cause to lead, follow, order or act as individuals, or on behalf of groups, organizations, or nations.[138] Still, one might return to think upon the time-tested, and oft-emulated logic, espoused by St Augustine, that nation-states are themselves "large-scale terrorist gangs:" "Because I do it with one small ship, I am called a terrorist. You do it with a whole fleet and are called an emperor."[139] By implied, dualistic effect under such logic, and taken to its extreme end, mercenaries, pirates, terrorists, and insurgents could gain the same legal and moral status—and liability—as nations.[140]

What is the propriety, and preference, from a moral standpoint, of capturing adversaries to bring them to justice instead of illicit assassination or licit targeted killing? From a non-legal perspective, the House of Commons Library Report also considered the present-day philosophical and pragmatic rationales that would support capturing terrorists, compared or contrasted to making them the subject of targeted killing. Quoting A.C. Grayling, professor of philosophy at the University of London:

> It would have been preferable to do that [capture bin Laden rather than kill him]—not because it would have been easier and not because it would have saved other lives in future—but because in the ideal, if we were to live up to the principles of our civilization (sic) (or the ones we claim anyway) it would have been the right thing to do. But practicality makes very, very different demands.[141]

What cannot be denied about targeted killing, regardless of the calculations of the cost-to-benefit ratio, is that there is a growing trend of nations seeking the assassination of adversaries and, with it, increasing legitimacy of targeted killing in any given case, depending on the norms and particular details under those norms

Targeted killing can and should be only one of a series of politico-military strategies for national security and homeland defense, neither solely within the purview of governmental agencies, nor contracted out entirely to PMCs and others. As a

available at SSRN: <http://ssrn.com/abstract=1780584> accessed October 28, 2011, and Chibli Mallat, "The Geneva Conventions and the Death of Osama bin Laden," *JURIST*—Forum, August 4, 2011, available at <http://jurist.law.pitt.edu/forum/2011/08/chibli-mallat-bin-laden.php> accessed October 28, 2011, and see also Afsheen, *supra* n. 136, and Robert Chesney, "Who May Be Killed? Anwar al-Awlaki As a Case Study in the International Regulation of Lethal Force," 13 *Y.B. Int'l Humanitarian L.* (forthcoming).

[138] See Christian Bueger, Jan Stockbruegger and Sascha Werthes, "Pirates, Fishermen and Peacebuilding: Options for a Sustainable Counter-Piracy Strategy in Somalia," *Contemporary Security Policy* Vol. 32, No. 2 (2011).

[139] Augustine of Hippo, *De Civitate Dei* (400), IV, 4, as quoted in Christopher Kirwan, *Augustine* (1989).

[140] See, e.g., Govern and Bales, *supra* n. 128.

[141] Ibid. at 8, citing with authority "Osama bin Laden's Death—Killed in a Raid or Assassinated?," *The Guardian*, May 6, 2011, available at <http://www.guardian.co.uk/world/2011/may/06/osama-bin-laden-death-assassination> accessed October 28, 2011.

model for such a balanced approach, we might look to the United States' most recent counterterrorism strategy released on June 29, 2011.[142]

But counterbalancing the weight of strategy, our inquiring into the legitimacy of targeted killing must include an investigation into the relationship between targeted killing and a set of core values, including rule of law and the privacy, civil rights, and civil liberties of all citizens.[143] The nation must employ every means and methodology at its disposal, including intelligence, military, homeland security and law enforcement, and securing much-needed cooperation from others. A crucial aspect of securing that cooperation is to establish fair and lawful terms of cooperation. The practice of targeted killing is not merely a philosophical debate, or an academic exercise regarding the conflict of laws in abstraction; this emergent method of fighting wars has risen to prominence as our primary strategy in the war on terror. Unless carefully theorized, and squarely addressed in real-world application, actual people around the globe who may be legally entitled—and might have the physical opportunity—to surrender under IHL may have not just their rights marginalized, but their lives cut short with or without justification by the developing trend towards kill rather than capture.

Nations that want to ensure their own security must also build partnerships with international institutions and partners so that they can counter threats where they begin when they begin.[144] The United States, in particular, "partners best with nations that share [its] common values, have similar democratic institutions, and bring a long history of collaboration in pursuit of our shared security,"[145] while "recognizing and working to improve shortfalls in cooperation with partner nations,"[146] lest adversaries exploit those shortfalls first.

The United States' Joint Special Operations University recently assessed the span of U.S. and foreign military operations throughout history, finding that the "[h]unting for persons of national interest and high value targets has been emblematic of U.S. operations—direct action—whereas indirect methods such as foreign internal defense should have been seen as the main effort."[147] Effectively planning

---

[142] The National Strategy for Counterterrorism, June 2011, available at <http://www.white-house.gov/sites/default/files/counterterrorism_strategy.pdf> accessed October 28, 2011.

[143] Ibid. at 4.

[144] Ibid. at 2.

[145] Ibid. at 6.

[146] Ibid. at 4.

[147] George A. Crawford, "Manhunting: Counter-Network Organization for Irregular Warfare," JSOU Report 09-7 (Hurlburt Field, Fl : The JSOU Press, 2009) vii, available at <http://www.bib-liotecapleyades.net/archivos_pdf/manhunting.pdf> accessed October 28, 2011. Foreign Internal Defense is defined by the U.S. DoD as "Participation by civilian and military agencies of a government in any of the action programs taken by another government or other designated organization to free and protect its society from subversion, lawlessness, insurgency, terrorism, and other threats to its security. Also called FID." U.S. Joint Publication JP 1-02, *supra* n. 21, 145.

for and executing national security and homeland security in the manner outlined above will likely mean fewer *in extremis*[148] requirements for direct action/targeted killing of persons such as bin Laden. Future efforts to "free and protect [societies] from subversion, lawlessness, insurgency, terrorism, and other threats to ... security" will increase demand for highly trained, culturally astute, superbly disciplined uniformed service members such as SOF "operators" to promote and maintain a vigilant and active peace. In this manner, rather than targeting the symptomatic expressions of terror, the United States will instead prescriptively promote the rule of law abroad as one of many measures to eliminate the root causes of terrorism, while maintaining the capability to deliberately and carefully tailor uses of authorized, licit force around the world.

Finally, in the spirit of the best offense being a good defense, the United States must aid other nations in fostering proactiveness, "to deter and interdict threats without resorting to the expense and turbulence associated with deployment of major military formations,"[149] and should sustain a "culture of preparedness and resilience" that will allow them "to prevent or—if necessary—respond to and recover successfully" from threats posed to their security.[150] Understanding the origins of AQ and bin Laden's leadership of that organization, and the operational, legal, and moral aspects behind bin Laden's targeted killing, will become key to developing sound future U.S. strategies, policies, and programs against AQ and its successors-in-interest.[151] Such multidisciplinary approaches to future national security matters should, have, and will involve (re-)considering some tested-and-true methods of mastering present and future destiny by principled action, not merely idle, amoral ambition or convenience of choice.

---

[148] Ibid. at 22 says " 'In-extremis' refers to a situation of such exceptional urgency that immediate action must be taken to minimize imminent loss of life or catastrophic degradation of the political or military situation."

[149] Crawford, *supra* n. 147, 40.

[150] National Strategy, *supra* n. 142, 8.

[151] Rollins, *supra* n. 2, i.

14

EFFICIENCY *IN BELLO* AND *AD BELLUM*: MAKING THE USE OF FORCE TOO EASY?

Kenneth Anderson

I. Introduction

Targeted killing by means of drone warfare has been the subject of much criticism over the past decade, particularly as the United States has increased its pace, intensity and geographic range since the Obama Administration took office in 2009. The criticisms range widely in their complaints. They include claims that civilian deaths are excessive and disproportionate; "blowback" and resentment in Pakistan and other places produces more terrorists and fighters in the future; drone warfare "de-humanizes" warfare and creates a "Playstation" mentality toward killing; targeting decisions lack transparency and legal standards, particularly with regard to strikes undertaken by the CIA; secret strikes in Pakistan, Yemen and beyond violate international law; targeted killing outside of a conventional battlefield constitutes extrajudicial execution and violates international human rights law; and many more.

Some of these criticisms are essentially factual in nature, while others are normative claims from law or morality. The claim of excessive civilian deaths—a claim that figures centrally in many of the normative arguments—depends upon facts that are highly contested. Some observers, especially European activists, say that the civilian deaths run in the hundreds or even thousands. The CIA and the U.S. government, by contrast, insist that the civilian death toll amounts to scores over all the years of targeted killing using drones in Afghanistan and Pakistan, and that the rate of civilian deaths continues to decline, year by year, even as the number of strikes increases, due to improved technology and intelligence. The activists and campaigners look for their numbers in local reports from the remote and inaccessible (to Western outsiders) places in Pakistan's border regions. The U.S. government responds that those reports are uncorroborated by Western journalists, typically exaggerated or wrong, and sometimes manipulated by Taliban or Pakistani military intelligence.

Beyond that factual argument, a general criticism can be leveled against the U.S. government for refusing to be more forthcoming about its targeted killing and drone warfare programs. The U.S. government says (frequently in leaks to the press that preclude effective public discussion) that its claims of extraordinary precision and low collateral damage levels should be believed, but then offers no independent proof on which to do so. The U.S. government (were it not in the position of offering no official comment) could reply that even apparently innocuous revelations on collateral damage amounts to handing the Taliban, Al Qaeda, and other hostile groups invaluable intelligence on how the United States conducts these operations. Broadly speaking, even the arguments over transparency and accountability, however, come down mostly to factual questions. If the United States is right regarding collateral damage, that says one thing. If the activist critics are right, it says another. But these are largely arguments about facts on the ground.

In this chapter, I propose to set aside these factual arguments and instead take certain factual premises by assumption. My purpose is to focus instead upon an argument over targeted killing using drones in which, importantly, the form of argument itself is at issue. The bare-bones argument is the following. Targeted killing using drone warfare is immoral because, by removing the personal risk to those carrying out these operations, the drone-wielding actor has no, or much reduced, disincentives against using force. Using force when your own people are not at risk in the operation makes using force "too easy" an option.

The argument comes in several different forms, with levels of detail, sophistication, and formality. Perhaps the simplest version is that offered by a campaigning lawyer, who said, "The problem with drones is that they remove the burden of having to fight one's way on the ground to the target, and so remove the constraints of geography and personal risk in warfare, so increasing the temptation to make war." Another version says that, since such attacks cause civilian casualties, reducing the personal risk to the drone-using forces increases civilian casualties that would not otherwise occur—even if they are still relatively small—and this is unjust. Still another version goes so far as to accept that drones might reduce, rather than increase civilian casualties—but the very fact of decreasing civilian casualties increases the propensity to use force in the first place, and this is a bad idea.

Versions of this general argument about drones are widely circulated in the press and literature about U.S. counterterrorism; those of us who participate in academic and policy conferences about drones and targeted killing find them to be an oft-repeated trope. Many of the references appear to trace back to comments in Brookings scholar Peter Singer's path-breaking book, *Wired for War*, and later a widely noticed 2009 article by *New Yorker* writer Jane Mayer. The prominent British computer scientist Noel Sharkey also brought these arguments to public awareness in articles in *The Guardian*. Versions of them were repeated in a recent U.K. Ministry of Defence report on robotics and drone warfare. Whatever precisely the version of the argument, however, or by whomever offered, the final conclusion is typically that drones make war "too easy."

The factual and normative claims are often closely associated with criticisms of drones based on affective claims, claims about the *emotions* of drone operators and targeters, on the one hand, or those in the targeting zone, whether targets or civilians, on the other. The affective criticisms include the supposed de-personalization of war by drones and a supposed de-sensitization toward violence on the part of drone operators. This is a claim about the affective consequences of the *remoteness* of the weapon platform and its operators from the place of killing, and not only solely the lack of personal *risk* for the operators. This was vividly spelled out in a *Newsweek* Article in which a CIA officer describes how he would watch these killings live on a monitor while sitting comfortably in his office.[1] Sometimes these criticisms lead to a different kind of criticism. Virtuous warfighters are somehow obligated to view each death, including those of acknowledged enemies, who threaten American soldiers or as terrorists, Americans generally, as "regrettable." So, in that case, it would be unseemly for U.S. personnel to cheer a drone attack upon a fleeing terrorist, because that would show callous indifference to human life; the proper attitude is regret even in killing an enemy who might, if not killed, be engaged in killing Americans.

The attitude of "remoteness" that is called for in the name of virtue seems to me quite morally unjustified. Indeed, it is *that* form of remoteness, the idea that one refuses to address the question of "sides" in war in the name of pure abstraction, which seems to me a much more problematic form of "remoteness," not remoteness in launching the missile from a physically remote place. But the proper balance of attitude and affect in the honorable and just warrior, as between the emotions of partiality and impartiality, carry us far afield into questions of virtue ethics that I will not address here.

Affective arguments often hint, nonetheless—even if inchoately— that war without personal risk is unchivalrous and dishonorable. It is a point that has featured in "blowback" criticisms—critiques of targeted killing using drones that argue it is counterproductive because of the resentment it produces among populations in Pakistan and elsewhere. As a psychological proposition, it is perhaps unsurprisingly featured in fictional literature about the war on terror—perhaps most

---

[1] Tara McKelvey, "Inside the Killing Machine," *Newsweek*, February 13, 2011, available at <http://www.thedailybeast.com/newsweek/2011/02/13/inside-the-killing-machine.html> accessed November 4, 2011.

prominently in *Blood Money*, the recent thriller written by *Washington Post* columnist David Ignatius.[2] It has been raised by many pundits—*LA Times* columnist Doyle McManus, for example[3]—and is a core critique for counterinsurgency experts such as Andrew Exum or David Kilcullen, who believe that targeted killing using drones is an affectively wrong strategy because anonymous, invisible, and impersonal "death from above," as it were, works against winning hearts and minds of local populations on the ground.[4]

The surface framing of these many and jumbled versions of the "too easy" argument hints at buried premises. This chapter proposes to examine some of these buried premises. At bottom, however, I want to urge that there is something wrong with the conceptual form of this argument, in which a successful strategy in war turns out to be immoral, not because of the damage it causes achieving its success, but because success itself increases the propensity to do it too much. The problem is not with the argument that even a successful strategy can lead to unintended consequences of its own success—including the tendency to overuse it. True, one ought to view such criticisms of success with considerable skepticism—does one really want to proceed from a heuristic of "Whatever you do, avoid success because you might overdo it?" It seems better to acknowledge that, at most, such criticism is a "second-order" problem, if a problem at all. The fundamental problem with this argument does not lie there.

It lies instead with the fundamental idea that drones make the resort to force and violence—war—"too easy." Attractive on the surface, it is not a coherent notion as applied in war. The most interesting and important version of the argument goes so far as to frame this as a matter of creating an "inefficient" level of disincentive to use of force on account of insufficient risks to one's own forces in so doing—appealing deliberately to the apparatus of welfare-maximization and cost–benefit analysis. That there is an "inefficient" level of incentive to use violence presumes, however, that there is in principle an "efficient" one. I will argue that this is conceptually faulty.

I believe this to be a bad argument, not so much on account of faulty factual premises about drones and targeted killing, but primarily on account of faulty reasoning about the place and role of "efficiency" in thinking about the resort to force. But whether I am right or wrong on this point, the argument is nonetheless of intrinsic interest because it involves an important and overlooked intertwining

---

[2] David Ignatius, *Blood Money* (W.W. Norton Publishing, 2011).

[3] Doyle McManus, "U.S. Drone Attacks in Pakistan 'Backfiring,' Congress Told," *LA Times*, May 03, 2009, available at <http://articles.latimes.com/2009/may/03/opinion/oe-mcmanus3> accessed November 3, 2011.

[4] David Kilcullen and Andrew McDonald, "Death From Above, Outrage Down Below," *NY Times*, May 16, 2009, available at <http://www.nytimes.com/2009/05/17/opinion/17exum.html> accessed November 3, 2011.

of two strands of the ethics of war, the rules governing the conduct of war (*jus in bello*) and the rules governing the resort to force (*jus ad bellum*). There is intrinsic interest to the argument that the "efficiency" of *jus in bello* might create "inefficiency" of *jus ad bellum*.

To be clear at the outset, the argument criticized here is the universal argument that makes claims about either morality or efficiency for all parties taken together—the two acknowledged sides as well as the civilians on both sides. It needs to be distinguished from a distinct debate over targeted killing using drones that is essentially strategic and runs to one side's interests only. David Ignatius, for example, has been arguing in a series of influential columns in the *Washington Post* that the United States is "addicted" to drones because they make it "too easy" to decide to attack in many places.[5]

This sounds very much like the argument that this chapter critiques, but Ignatius and others making this assertion are not making a claim about the morality or efficiency of drones on a universal ground. The claim, rather, is that considered only with respect to its own strategic interests, the United States overuses drones. Ignatius' claim is roughly that, as a matter of U.S. counterterrorism strategy (morality or universal welfare efficiency aside, just as a matter of U.S. strategy), the problem with drones is that they are tactically precise, but strategically incontinent. I believe that claim is incorrect, but it is essentially a factual question, and not the argument under consideration here.

The order of discussion is as follows. First, I set out several key factual assumptions about drone warfare, precision targeting, and civilian collateral damage. These assumptions are set against a background discussion of the nature of the drone campaign and targeted killing as currently conducted by the United States. The key descriptive point is to disentangle the technology of drone warfare from the practice of targeted killing; the two are not always linked, and are not the same thing or always aimed at the same strategic goal. Second, I set out the form of the argument that I propose to critique in what—given the factual assumptions—I take to be its most plausible, but also most sophisticated and interesting conceptual form. The essential task here is to unpack the intuition lying behind the oft-heard phrase in this context—drones make war "too easy." Third, I critique the web of conceptual assumptions that underlie the very idea that there is a coherent way to talk about drones making war "too easy"—which is to say, some notion of an "efficient" level of war that could make sense of saying that it is either "too easy" or "too hard." Fourth, assuming that the critique offered of the notion of an "efficient" level of the resort to force—war—is good, I finally turn to offer a speculative and

---

[5] David Ignatius, "The Price of Becoming Addicted to Drones," *Washington Post*, September 22, 2011, available at <http://www.washingtonpost.com/opinions/the-price-of-becoming-addicted-to-drones/2011/09/21/gIQAovp41K_story.html> accessed November 3, 2011.

incomplete account of why that would be so. Here, I will argue that war turns on the nature of "sides" that do not share commensurable grounds that would allow the commonality required to find an "efficient" point in a universal welfare sense.

II. Disentangling targeted killing and drone warfare

Although targeted killing and drone warfare are often closely connected, they are not the same and are not always associated with each other. We need to disaggregate the practices of targeted killing from the technologies of drone warfare.

Targeted killing consists of using deadly force, characterized by the identification of and then strike against an individual marked to be killed. It is distinguished, among other things, by making an individualized determination of a person to be killed, rather than simply identifying, for example, a mass of enemy combatants to attack as a whole. Since it is a practice that involves the determination of an identified person, rather than a mass of armed and obvious combatants, it is a use of force that is by its function integrated with intelligence work, whether the intelligence actors involved are uniformed military or a civilian agency such as the CIA.

Targeted killing might (and does) take place in the course of conventional warfare, through special operations or other mechanisms that narrowly focus operations through intelligence. But it might also take place outside of a conventional conflict, or perhaps far from the conventional battlefields of that conflict, sufficiently so operationally, to best be understood as its own operational category of the use of force—"intelligence-driven," often covert, and sometimes non-military intelligence agency use of force, typically aimed at "high value" targets in global counterterrorism operations. It might be covert or it might not—but it will be driven by intelligence, because of necessity it must identify and justify the choice of target (on operational grounds, because resources are limited; or legal grounds; or, in practice, both).

Targeted killing might use a variety of tactical methods by which to carry out the attack. The method might be by drones firing missiles—the focus of discussion here. But targeted killing—assassination, generically—is a very old method for using force and drones are new. Targeted killing in current military and CIA doctrine might, and often does, take place with covert civilian intelligence agents or military special operations forces—a human team carrying out the attack, rather than a drone aircraft operated from a distance. The bin Laden raid exemplifies the human team-conducted targeted killing, of course, and in today's tactical environment, the United States often uses combined operations that have available both human teams and drones, to be deployed according to circumstances.

Targeted killing is thus a tactic that might be carried out either by drones or human teams. If there are two ways to do targeted killing, there are also two functions for the use of drones—targeted killing as part of an "intelligence-driven" discrete use of force, on the one hand, and a role (really, roles) in conventional warfare. Drones have a role in an ever-increasing range of military operations that have no connection to "targeted killing." For many reasons ranging from cost-effectiveness to mission-effectiveness, drones are becoming more ramified in their uses in military operations, and will certainly become more so. This is true starting with their fundamental use in surveillance, but it is also true when they are used as weapons platforms.

From the standpoint of conventional military operations and ordinary battlefields, drones are seen by the military as simply an alternative air weapons platform. One might use an over-the-horizon manned aircraft—or, depending on circumstances, one might instead use a drone as the weapons platform. It might be a missile launched from a drone by an operator, whether sitting in a vehicle near the fighting or farther away; it might be a weapon fired from a helicopter 20 miles away, but invisible to the fighters; it might be a missile fired from a U.S. Navy vessel hundreds of miles away by personnel sitting at a console deep inside the ship. Future air-to-air fighter aircraft systems are very likely to be remotely piloted, in order to take advantage of superior maneuverability and greater stresses endurable without a human pilot. Remotely piloted aircraft are the future of much military and, for that matter, civil aviation; this is a technological revolution that is taking place for reasons having less to do with military aviation than general changes in aviation technology.

Missiles fired from a remotely piloted standoff platform present the same legal issues as any other weapons system—the law of war categories of necessity, distinction and proportionality in targeting. To military professionals, therefore, the emphasis placed on "remoteness" from violence of drone weapons operators, and presumed psychological differences in operators versus pilots, is misplaced and indeed mystifying. Navy personnel firing missiles from ships are typically just as remote from the fighting, and yet one does not hear complaints about their indifference to violence and their "Playstation," push-button approach to war. Air Force pilots more often than not fire from remote aircraft; pilots involved in the bombing campaign over Serbia in the Kosovo war sometimes flew in bombers taking off from the United States; bomber crews dropped their loads from high altitudes, guided by computer, with little connection to the "battlefield" and little conception at what they—or their targeting computers—were aiming. Some of the crews in interviews described spending the flights of many hours at a time, flying from the Midwest and back, as a good chance to study for classes they were taking—not Playstation, but study hall. In many respects, the development of new sensor technologies make the pilots, targeters, and the now extensive staff involved in a decision to fire a weapon from a drone far more aware of what is taking place at the target than other forms of remote targeting, from Navy ships or high-altitude bombing (but presumably the bombers did not drop their loads until they were over the battlefield, although they were very high over it).

Very few of the actors on a technologically advanced battlefield are personally present in a way that makes the destruction and killing truly personal—and that is part of the point. Fighting up close and personal, according to the critics' psychological theories, seems to mean that it has greater significance to the actors and therefore leads to greater restraint. That is extremely unlikely and contrary to the experience of U.S. warfighters; lawful kinetic violence is more likely to increase when force protection is an issue and overuse of force is more likely to increase when forces are under personal pressure and risk. The U.S. military has known since Vietnam at least that increased safety for fighting personnel allows them greater latitude in using force, encourages and permits greater willingness to consider the least damaging alternatives, and that putting violence at a remove reduces the passions and fears of war and allows a coolly professional consideration of what kinds, and how much, violence is required to accomplish a lawful military mission. Remote weapon systems, whether robotic or simply missiles launched from a safe distance, in U.S. doctrine are more than just a means for reducing risk to forces—they are an integral part of the means of allowing more time to consider less harmful alternatives.

This is an important point, given that drones today are being used for tasks that involve much greater uses of force than individualized targeted killing. Drones are used today, and with increasing frequency, to kill whole masses of enemy columns of Taliban fighters on the Pakistan border—in a way that would otherwise be carried out by manned attack aircraft. This is not targeted killing; this is conventional war operation. It is most easily framed in terms of the abstract strategic division of counterinsurgency from counterterrorism (though in practice the two are not so distinct). In particular, drones are being deployed in the AfPak conflict as a counterinsurgency means of going after Taliban in their safe haven camps on the Pakistan side of the border. A fundamental tenet of counterinsurgency is that the safe havens have to be ended, and this has meant targeting much larger contingents of Taliban fighters than previously understood in the "targeted killing" deployment. This could be—and in some circumstances today is—being done by the military; it is also done by the CIA under orders of the President, partly because of purely political concerns; much of it today seems to be a combined operation of military and CIA.

Whoever conducts it and whatever legal issues it might raise, the point is that this activity is fundamentally counterinsurgency. The fighters are targeted in much larger numbers in the camps than would be the case in "targeted killing," and this is a good instance of how targeted killing and drone warfare need to be differentiated. The targets are not individuated, either in the act of targeting or in the decision of who and where to target: This is simply an alternative air platform for doing what might otherwise be done with helicopters, fixed-wing aircraft, or ground attack, in the course of conventional counterinsurgency operations. But it also means that the numbers killed in such operations are much larger, and consist often of ordinary fighters who would otherwise pile into trucks and cross back into Afghanistan, rather than individualized "high value" targets, whether Taliban or Al Qaeda.

Disentangling targeted killing (whether by drones or human teams) from drone warfare (whether for targeted killing or conventional warfare) is important because the argument upon which this chapter focuses goes to the category of targeted killing by means of drones. It depends upon a factual assumption about the civilian consequences of targeted killing using drones; upon a further fact about the reduced risk to U.S. personnel in such operations; and about a supposed implication for the incentives or, more precisely, supposedly reduced disincentives to resort to violence under those two conditions. But it is therefore *not* about targeted killing using human teams; and it is likewise *not* about drones used for conventional warfare.

III. An assumption about civilian casualties and collateral damage

The undefended factual assumption of this argument is that targeted killing using drones results in significantly—vastly—less collateral damage and civilian deaths than other forms of attack. The alternatives include other forms of attack from manned attack aircraft, or attack by human special operations teams on the ground. It is true that there would presumably be no collateral damage if no attack were carried out at all, but that alters the fundamental question beyond recognition. This chapter takes that assumption as given and does not defend it, but it is worth saying something as to why this is a plausible and, at this date, the best assumption regarding civilian harm from targeted killing using drones.

The main approaches to collateral damage from targeted killing using drones in Afghanistan and Pakistan are three: first, various European campaigning groups purport to report using local sources, such as Pakistani newspapers and local media or governmental statements. Second, two American groups—with notably distinct political tendencies, the generally liberal New America Foundation and the generally conservative Long War Journal[6] (Bill Roggio of the Foundation for the Defense of Democracies)—have each been estimating strikes and apparent

---

[6] Available at <http://www.longwarjournal.org/pakistan-strikes.php> accessed November 3, 2011.

civilian casualties since the mid-2000s. Third, although the U.S. government does not comment openly on CIA operations or other secret strikes, senior officials have made anonymous comments to reporters, but more recently directly on the record, on what the U.S. claims are the levels of civilian casualties.

The general lines of those three, at this writing, can be summarized thus. The European campaigning groups suggest hundreds to thousands of civilian casualties over the decade that the United States has been engaged in such strikes. The New America Foundation[7] and the Long War Journal have separately estimated civilian casualties in the various hundreds; their evaluations today suggest that despite sharply escalating levels of strikes, the rate of civilian casualties has been declining in the past two years. The U.S. government has offered estimates, nearly all off the record, of a hyperbolic "zero" to civilian casualties in the two (sometimes said to be low two) digits.[8] Some important notes on what counts in these attempts at tabulation are required. First, outsiders do not have direct, ground-level access to strike locales, and so casualty counts are very much a function of local reports, which everyone grants carry much possibility of exaggeration or propaganda manipulation. It is not even clear the extent to which U.S. intelligence has access to on-the-ground reports; it seems to rely heavily on continued Predator drone air surveillance to see what happens on the ground following a strike to determine who was killed, though it might well have intelligence assets on the ground as well.[9]

In my opinion as an informed (though entirely outside the government) observer, the truth of the matter is likely higher than the U.S. government says, and unquestionably higher than its lowest (zero) estimate—but at most in the low hundreds, if not high two digits. If that is so, certainly I would endorse what former CIA director Leon Panetta has said about this technology—"It is the most accurate weapon system in the history of warfare." That is so, frankly, even if the numbers are the higher, earlier estimates given by the American monitors. (For what it is worth, I do not give much credence to the European campaigners' estimates, though they are politically influential in various quarters, but even those estimates, compared to the history of civilian deaths in war, represent a very considerable improvement. This is not intended as a legal judgment as to proportionality, which would require many separate considerations. The point, rather, is that these technologies are making targeting in war more precise on any historical measure, and criticizing them on a snapshot basis—your technology killed civilians, it's another war crime—rather than on their historical trend line, the horrors of urban battles in the Second World

---

[7] Available at <http://counterterrorism.newamerica.net/drones> accessed November 3, 2011.

[8] Available at <http://www.guardian.co.uk/commentisfree/cifamerica/2011/aug/11/civilian-victims-cia-drones> accessed November 3, 2011.

[9] For more on the trustworthiness of these numbers, see Gregory McNeal, "Are Targeted Killings Unlawful? A Case Study in Empirical Claims Without Empirical Evidence" in this Volume, ch. 12.

War as a baseline, seems to me morally indefensible. One should be encouraging improvements that will necessarily be incremental and over a long time.)

Second, understanding the separate roles of drones in targeted killing of individually identified terrorist targets as part of counterterrorism, on the one hand, and conventional counterinsurgency warfare targeting cross-border safe havens, camps, and columns of mass groups of Taliban fighters, on the other, is important in interpreting any of these estimates. The groups attempting to estimate numbers do not seek to disaggregate these roles, and thus total numbers killed might well go up or down significantly as a function of conventional combat in Afghanistan, not as a result of counterterrorism operations. Targeted killing using drones in the sense meant in this discussion is illustrated by an attack upon an Al Qaeda commander in the Pakistan border areas, not necessarily connected to Afghanistan Taliban operations or the safe haven camps for fighters but instead, for example, a person with a planning role for operations to be carried out abroad. But with respect to counting casualties, that Al Qaeda counterterrorism target is more likely to be surrounded with civilians, whether explicitly as human shields or not, than fighters in the camps or in transit across the Afghan border. The ratio of civilians to Al Qaeda target killed might be high, even though the total number of people is small in absolute terms; by contrast, an attack upon a camp might easily have no genuine civilian killed, but may kill large numbers of fighters in absolute terms. Add to that a third dimension of the value of the target—high value taken as an individual in the targeted killing of the Al Qaeda commander in counterterrorism; low value taken individually in the case of any individual Taliban fighter, but high value taken altogether as a fighting force in counterinsurgency.

These considerations indicate that the aggregate numbers of killed, civilians or targeted persons, for drone operations sometimes reported in the press and by monitors such as Long War Journal or the New America Foundation, do not tell us everything about casualty numbers that we need to know, particularly as the uses of drones ramify—as these monitors would be the first to agree (they have been admirably transparent as to the limitations of the methodology). Reporting on casualties from drone warfare is not the same as reporting on casualties from targeted killing as such. It is unclear whether the leaked statements about casualties from the CIA refer only to CIA strikes, and only to strikes carried out as genuine targeted killing. This is a very significant ambiguity in the statements, of course. Hence the granular differences matter.

The assumption of this chapter, therefore, is that targeted killing using drone technologies is significantly more discriminating and sparing of collateral damage to civilians and their property than alternative uses of force to the same end would be. That is so whether the actor is the military in conventional operations, military special forces, the CIA, or combined special operations. I happen to think that proposition is true and that it is becoming more so over time—an indication of the importance of allowing incremental improvements in weapons systems, rather than smothering the technological baby at birth. I also think the perception of greater precision leading to fewer civilian casualties is increasing even among skeptics of targeted killing using drones, including some of the human rights monitors, who today appear to be hanging back from full-on criticism of the technology and its possibilities. The fact of NATO having urgently requested, and received, Predator drones as attack platforms in the Libya conflict has also apparently had an effect. After the outbreak of the NATO air war, Qaddafi's forces quickly abandoned their tanks and heavy equipment, as NATO promptly targeted them with conventional aircraft, to mingle with civilians in ways that made locating them much more difficult.

Drones were first used to help identify targets in Libya—the surveillance role for which Predators were originally designed, with long loiter times over the battlefield (hours compared to precious minutes). But NATO quickly determined that it was both more effective and safer for civilians if the drones undertook the strike as quickly as possible, rather than waiting for manned aircraft to arrive. This role of drone aircraft in a "humanitarian" war seems to have put drones in a somewhat different light from how they appear—"anonymous death from the skies"—to their critics in Afghanistan and Pakistan, though without any particularly logical reason why it should be so, and appear to have done something to "bless" drones as more acceptable than they were. It has not escaped attention that drones are a near-perfect weapon of humanitarian intervention if there is an associated force on the ground—one's own troops are not at risk, and yet, at least in Libya, the war is not entirely an (oft-indecisive) air war, either. Of course, consonant with the burden of this chapter, what might be seen as a "feature" of drones—they do not put risk-averse humanitarian interveners at risk—might just as easily be seen as the "bug" of this chapter—they make armed humanitarian intervention "too easy."

Speaking to the broad future of the technology, however, and given the direction of technology and cost, it appears inevitable that drones will take on many more operational roles over time, whether in conventional war, special operations, and what has here been called generically "intelligence-driven uses of force." Drones will likely evolve—as aircraft, as well as in the weapons and sensor systems they bear—into many specialized types. They will get both bigger and smaller than they are now, for example, and they will surely evolve into those specialized for surveillance and those specialized to fire weapons. And they will also surely evolve into those specialized in high-value, "intelligence-driven" targeted killing of individuals and those that are suited to conventional operations. Bearing in mind these increasingly varied uses is essential to understanding, when it comes to targeted killing and/or drone warfare, that one-size-fits-all legal analysis is not sufficient.

One last background observation on the nature of targeted killing through drone warfare. Beyond technology, success in Afghanistan and Pakistan, and anywhere beyond, depends crucially upon on-the-ground intelligence long before any Predator is launched. It is an underappreciated point—very underappreciated. The United States has invested many years in the past decade of war in Afghanistan in establishing its own intelligence network on the ground that is able to supply information with respect to both counterinsurgency operations on both sides of the border, as well as with counterterrorism activities and targeting inside Pakistan. This has taken years, and, particularly during the past five years, the CIA has been the lead agency. This is a reason why the CIA, rather than the military, is tasked with much of the drone use in the border areas of Pakistan; it has the intelligence networks. This is also a source of irritation to the Pakistani government, which is no longer able to steer US targeting and intelligence activities.

But the precision of strikes with respect to civilian casualties, and also the ability to determine who the United States should target and ensure that this is the person actually being targeted by a drone, is a function of the CIA's intelligence capabilities on the ground, integrating a human network together with signals intelligence. This was the background that led to the successful bin Laden raid in 2011—and a key source of the Pakistani government's chagrin, that the United States did not need it and would possibly have been compromised in the operation. It is also instructive to compare the difficulties of the Libya air campaign, even with weaponized drone aircraft, with the U.S. capabilities in Afghanistan and Pakistan. The mere fact of drone technology in Libya helped targeting considerably, in the actual moment of fighting, but simply having drone capability could not make up for a lack of ground-level intelligence networks. Afghanistan, by contrast, after 10 years of high-technology war, is one of the most thoroughly mapped spaces in the world, ironically, even as it remains one of the least governable—mapped in natural, built, and social terms with respect to targeting and selection of least harmful weapons systems, as Gregory McNeal has observed.[10]

Ground-level intelligence operations are a vital part of making precision weapons precise; drone technology cannot make up for that capability, just as reliance upon pure signals intelligence is insufficient to direct targeting. All must be integrated. The drone is the sharp tip of a spear. But behind the sharp tip is the thin tail (to employ mixed metaphors) of intelligence operations that constitute the bulk of activities. Drones are only as useful as their supporting intelligence, and the only kind that works over the long run, as Libya teaches in one direction and Afghanstan in the other, are dense ground-level networks of human intelligence integrated with signals intelligence and long-running drone surveillance.

---

[10] Ibid.

What this points to, however, is that a view of drone warfare sometimes offered, of roving drones that observe from the sky, gather information, and then attack—globally roving birds of prey, so to speak—is simply wrong. A large part of this is intelligence required for useful and accurate targeting. But drones also require infrastructure—runways, bases, repair and maintenance, refueling, and the personnel to support all of that. The fact that they might be piloted from the United States does not change the very considerable physical infrastructure required to support them, relatively close to actual operations and, of course, not in Nevada or Langley. Drones are better understood, though not as "global," but instead as aircraft flown from, but finally tethered to, a (metaphorical) aircraft carrier—roving with a certain range, but always strictly tethered and entirely dependent upon a base. Far from being free-roving global birds of prey, they are instead the last kinetic step in a long, dense, and intensely *local* intelligence and infrastructure operation.

IV. The argument that drones make resort to war "too easy"

The preceding two sections aim at giving some practical background of targeted killing and drone warfare, and particularly in disentangling the two. They also aim to provide at least some background for why I regard the fundamental, but undefended, factual assumption of this chapter to be not just plausible, but likely correct and likely to be more correct over time. That assumption is that, in fact, targeted killing using drone technologies significantly reduces civilian casualties and civilian harms in comparison to alternative means of using force. This assumption assumes certain other background assumptions, raised in the earlier discussion, that intelligence resources are available to direct the targeting toward intended targets; the precision in the weapon as a whole system is more than simply technological precision; it is an integrated process of "intelligence-driven" uses of force.

In addition, the argument assumes something that is not disputed—the use of remotely piloted drones removes the personal risk to one's own forces. For these purposes, we will ignore reports that those who fire weapons from drones, even when located safely in the United States and as far from the kinetic battlefield as can be, suffer from psychological stress similar to that of pilots and others much closer to the battlefield. Those reports raise important issues, and would appear to run contrary to suggestions of a "Playstation" mentality toward killing using drone technologies, but for our purposes, harm to civilians and risk to own-forces will be taken as purely physical.

The most interesting version of the argument runs thus (I will refer to the argument that links a *jus in bello* consideration to a *jus ad bellum* one as the "overall" or "general" argument):

- Given that targeted killing removes personal risk to the attacker's forces; and

- even if targeted killing using drones reduces civilian harms and collateral damage;

- the use of drones in targeting killings is nonetheless (at least possibly) undesirable because those very factors (might possibly) lower the disincentives to the attacker resorting to force, (possibly) to an inefficient equilibrium with respect to the propensity of an attacker to resort to force.

Let us break this down piece by piece. The argument has two opening conditionals, the first undisputed and the second taken by assumption: removing personal risk to attackers and reducing civilian harm. These two each fall under the general heading in the law and ethics of war of "*jus in bello*"—the rules governing the conduct of hostilities. The *jus in bello* assumptions are striking, on their own, because they essentially say that military technology has lowered both the risk to one side's military combatants and to noncombatants. From the standpoint of the conduct of hostilities, *jus in bello*, this is a good thing.

It is, however, more than just a good thing—it is a double-plus good thing, so to speak. After all, ordinarily the problem in the conduct of hostilities is that what is good for one side's military operations is bad not just for the other side but for civilians as well. This leads to the famous "proportionality" calculus for military operations and collateral damage: "The benefits of a military operation must be weighed against the civilian harms, and the civilian harms cannot be 'excessive' in relation to the military benefits." The trouble with the proportionality calculus in *jus in bello*, however, is that it notoriously seems to pit apples against oranges, incomparable values of one side winning versus civilian harm. Everyone agrees that in some gross manner, judgments must be made, but the judgment not only lacks clear criteria in the law, it is far from evident that conceptually it can be done save by purely casuistical means—we did this in that case and believed it acceptable, and this case is more or less like that case, and so on.

The conceptual problem that I find in the overall argument about targeted killing using drone technology is not based upon the famously difficult problem of a calculus of proportionality necessarily involving incommensurables. On the contrary, one intriguing element of this version of the argument is that it sidesteps that proportionality issue altogether. Or, rather, if the facts ascribed to the technology are correct, technology provides a *deus ex machina* and an escape from the *jus in bello* proportionality trap. After all, everything in the *jus in bello* category here works together, not against each other. The technology provides force protection to (one side's) combatants; it provides greater protection to civilians through precision targeting. What's not to like? No weighing up of perplexing values need to take place, because everything is on the plus side, win-win.

The bite of the overall argument, however, assuming it is correct, is that precisely these virtues on the *jus in bello* side make the technology a vice on the side of the resort to force, *jus ad bellum,* or, more exactly, a vice with regard to the *propensity* to resort to force, *jus ad bellum.* The idea that making war itself more humane—including by creating legal codes for the conduct of war—has always given rise to arguments that humanizing war reduces the disincentives to engage in it. Florence Nightingale, for example, put the matter brusquely in a letter to the founder of the International Committee of the Red Cross as an objection (though later she was to become a strong supporter of the Red Cross movement):

> because first, such a Society...would relieve (governments) of responsibilities which really belong to them which they only can properly discharge...and *being relieved of which would make war more easy.*[11]

The greatest moral opprobrium for the use of drones, however, is generally focused, not upon the assumption that they spare civilians, but instead upon the proposition that they spare the attackers from personal risk. Most of those who make this general form of argument against drones—"too easy"—probably do not believe or discount the "greater civilian protection" assumption. That ultimately comes down to facts, but the argument as I have given it above is more illuminating because it holds out the possibility that even if the civilian safety assumption is true, the weapon system is still morally flawed, wrong even, because of the evils of making resort to force "too easy."

That is, the problem with drones is that they pit the benefits of technological advances in *jus in bello* against the relaxation of disincentives to use force in *jus ad bellum.* This is quite apart from any special supposed wickedness in a side reducing the personal risks of combat in relation to civilian harm. The special problem with drones that eliminate personal risk to a side's forces is, instead, not only harm in a deontological moral sense, but a special form of anti-social inefficiency. We might call it "wickedness" or "wrongfulness" in an imprecise sense, and we might indulge ourselves in essentially affective objections to unchivalrous ways of waging war. But the objection is to both wickedness and inefficiency. What we mean is not solely injustice—it is also social inefficiency, the special harm in a suboptimal welfare equilibrium sense arising from granting to yourself and your side the privilege of making war without risk to yourself. War becomes, or at least *might* become, "too easy," in relation to what is otherwise the "efficient" level of the resort to force.

---

[11] See Kenneth Anderson, "First in the Field: The Unique Mission and Legitimacy of the Red Cross in a Culture of Legality," *Times Literary Supplement,* July 31, 1998 (reviewing Caroline Moorhead, *Dunant's Dream: War, Switzerland and the History of the Red Cross*), available at <http:// papers.ssrn.com/sol3/papers.cfm?abstract_id=935781> accessed September 7, 2011 (emphasis added).

V. Personal risk

Surely this is over the top. It seems doubtful that anyone actually talks about the wrongs or harms of war by invoking language, less still arguments, of "suboptimal welfare equilibrium" or "disincentives to the propensity to use force to inefficient levels arising from insufficient personal risk to the attacker's personnel." Or, if this kind of language is used, surely it is merely students sampling the joys of applying an abstract apparatus to the real world; to a student newly equipped with the Coase Theorem, all situations look like opportunities for Coase bargaining to efficient outcomes. But this argument is one that I have heard offered in various meetings and conferences by professors, students, policy analysts, and journalists, and with admirable seriousness by academics whose intellectual commitments compel them to find welfare-based, apparently rational (in social science terms) ways of expressing a sentiment that might otherwise seem to be about the morality of taking no risks in targeting, or at least the unsportingness of it all, in the only language of value available to them, that of net social welfare and efficiency.

The professors are right to offer a more apparatus-laden way of talking about "too easy," however. "Too easy" captures a loose idea, one that has some intuitive appeal, but making sense of it—or concluding, alternatively, that it does not make sense—requires a more sophisticated statement of it. It merits unpacking. The unpacking can go in the direction of normative moral judgments set within the ethics of war. Or it can go in the direction of seeking to make a neutral judgment that if the criterion for optimal resort to force is x, then changes in the costs and benefits of certain ways of using force can alter the incentives to resort to force, and the resulting equilibrium might be above or below the optimal level, considered on its own. They are right to look to the apparatus of Coasean bargaining to the efficient point, in order to ask what is meant by moving from saying that the existence of these new drone technologies and precision targeting does not simply make the resort to force "easier" but "too easy."

And yet—there is a certain demurral, drawn from (though it will not be pursued here) virtue ethics. The military and those associated with it find this way of expressing the objection to drone warfare particularly objectionable—at least when expressed by itself, in a vacuum, as though this were the only relevant analysis to bring to bear. I both share their sentiment and believe it merits explicit recognition, not because this kind of apparent social-science framing should not be used—but because, when conjoined with an explicit discussion of its *affect*, it forces to the surface a debate over whether this apparent cool, rational, neutral observation is quite as neutral or rational as it seems. They see through the apparently "neutral" expression of "suboptimal equilibrium for the resort to force" and see instead two casual, contemptuous moral judgments lying just beneath the apparently rational surface: you're trigger-happy and you're cowards.

The anodyne expression of a point on a graph of efficiency where *jus in bello* benefits are outweighed by *jus ad bellum* costs, and the proposal that the personal risks taken by U.S. warfighters are "insufficient" and "suboptimal"—the apparently bloodless and disengaged analysis conceals, one is tempted to think, a viciousness and a callousness exhibited by those who take the sacrifices of others not gifted with professorships at leading universities a little bit too much for granted. The professional military in the United States are far too careful and, well, professional to say this aloud, even when they appear on exactly the same panels. I have no such qualms. Affect matters because it can help enunciate what we value.

But what lies beneath the anger at these entirely distanced and abstract attitudes toward the risks that are to be imposed on U.S. personnel? Partly, it is because this view of the role of personal risk is simply mistaken, factually wrong. I have already noted that one of the enormously important reasons why drones reduce risk to civilians is precisely that personnel are not at risk. Strikes can be considered with all the coolness possible when one's forces are not at risk—and not under pressure to strike at the moment, to take the shot because the human team cannot linger for hours, days, or weeks to find a better moment. It reveals a profound ignorance of professional military planning—and an arrogant assumption that professors can assume, based on their entirely abstract notions of self-interest, how in fact operational planning takes place. Reducing risk to one's own forces allows greater planning to reduce the harms and effects of military operations.

But it might be said that this misses the point. It might be true, after all, that reducing risk to one's own forces indeed reduces the risk of harm to civilians and reduces overall the damage caused by military operations—this would be an effect of technology, among other things. It would require, too, a military that cared about the harms of military operations. Very well; accepted. But the issue is not that reducing personal risk allows for reductions of risk to civilians; the issue is that reducing personal risk reduces the disincentives to using force at all. Resort to force is the issue here.

Here too, however, the actual experience of U.S. war-planners suggests something quite different. The United States reaches the decision to use force—military levels of force—on a basis that takes risks to troops seriously, but always starts from and is guided by imperatives of national security. Sometimes they will argue in favor of using force; other times they will counsel against. The responsibility for risks to U.S. personnel is always a grave consideration for military and political leadership; it does not follow, however, that this constraint acts as a veto on military actions that otherwise would be taken. The political, strategic, legal, and other disincentives to the use of force in the world are far greater than this argument would credit.

Indeed, there is only one circumstance where, realistically, the ability to avoid casualties altogether by the use of drones would make a serious difference in the calculation of whether to go to war. Ironically, that is the matter most desired by some of those who would otherwise argue in favor of increasing personal risk in order to deter making war—humanitarian intervention. Libya is the poster child for a new model of humanitarian intervention in which proxy ground forces combine with remotely piloted air forces to drive the dictator from power. That is the only realistic circumstance in which avoidance of own-force casualties is a sufficiently large concern to be decisive in the use of force or not; everything else obeys a much more stringent test of national security interests.

Armed altruism, ironically, is the one area in which the use of armed drones, because they avoid risk to personnel and so lower the disincentive to resort to force, is likely to be a decisive argument. Even that, to judge by Libya, is a hard sell, because war has many other disincentives besides personal risk, including the billions of dollars spent on the Libya campaign, the depletion of weapons stores, uncertainties of result, and the "you broke it, you bought it" problem after the immediate fighting ends. If drones were pioneered in the follow-on engagement to Charlie Wilson's War, they become a decisive weapon for risk-averse NATO powers in Samantha Power's War.

It is, however, quite likely that the development of technologies that allow for more discrete and targeted uses of force *will* incentivize more of them. One might call it "intelligence-driven uses of force" —a less felicitous, but perhaps more accurate, alternative phrase to "covert action." Drones *are* likely to increase those uses of force—not so much on account of lessened personal risk to forces, as on account of the precision in the weapon and the ability to engage in long-run intelligence gathering so to strike the target precisely as one wishes, and when. The trade-off will be between human special ops strike teams that can gather laptops, paper, other intelligence materials—and conceivably, should the United States ever return to the practice, capture and interrogate people—and drones that, unlike most human teams, wait for exactly the opportune moment to strike, but which cannot collect the left-overs.

One can say, certainly, that this increases the propensity to resort to force—and in practical terms, looking not just to the United States but also to other countries, as these technologies inevitably cheapen and become widely available, they will allow more instances of the use of force on the cheap and often with at least some deniability. There will be more assassinations and more assassination attempts, and much greater temptations to settle international affairs through apparently discrete, and occasionally even discreet, uses of force in this way. Again, however, we must be aware of the limits already discussed. Drones as a means of doing this are not some stealthy bird of prey, free-floating and alone; they require considerable infrastructure and, above all, on-the-ground intelligence. State actors who fear such interventions will quickly develop means of detection and counters, some kinetic and some not; the primary utility is likely to remain non-state actors of various kinds; Qaddafi's error, by this calculus, apart from not having a nuclear deterrent, was to have invited attack too soon, before counter-drone technologies have become widely available to states.

I have argued elsewhere that the development of these capabilities calls for the development of new legal standards that are neither law enforcement rules nor conventional armed conflict rules to govern these "intelligence driven uses of force."[12] But it would be an analytic mistake to assume that because there are more such interventions, that it's sufficient to say that they are too easy or too many. After all, uses of force need to be measured not just by their number, but also by their intensity. In any case, drones and targeted killing open a new chapter, but emphatically do not settle, the long-standing debate over whether opportune covert action can head off greater trouble and conventional war ahead—or instead compound the unpleasantness and tend to lead to war that is wider, more intense, or undertaken more often down the road.

This leaves the argument, however, back where it began with the anger of professional military over the entirely removed, neutral, distanced, and abstract argument over whether drones remove too much personal risk from the forces under command. In part the anger is directed at the way in which its supposed objectivity allows American professors to remove themselves in their criticism from the community of people who are part of a side. The academic critics benefit from the protection of the community, but then stand arrogantly outside the terms on which it is protected and discount the sacrifices of those who provide that protection. I will return to this consideration of the moral role of "sides" in a conflict briefly in the conclusion.

But there is a narrower and more specific ground of anger and objection on the part of professional military and warfighters here. It lies from a profound sense that the lives of soldiers are being treated as mere means, to another end, by critics who have no moral warrant from the community to do so. This might initially seem odd, as we have been instructed by Walzer on the ways in which the "War Convention" is about the implicit social contract of war by which soldiers are treated as means, material in war.[13] Nothing new about men as cannon fodder. But this misses the point of the anger. Soldiers accept that they are material of war, to be used as means and sacrificed on the altar of military necessity, and that sometimes the agreed-upon rules of conduct that protect civilians will involve risks to them that might be avoided by acting however one liked. The "War Convention," as Walzer describes it, is a pact within *jus in bello*—a pact about the conduct of war, and the agreement that combatants are indeed mere means to the ends of military necessity.

---

[12] Kenneth Anderson, "Law and Order: Targeted Killing is Legitimate and Defensible," *The Weekly Standard*, June 6, 2011, available at <http://www.weeklystandard.com/articles/law-and-order_571630.html> accessed November 3, 2011.

[13] Michael Walzer, *Just and Unjust Wars: A Moral Argument with Historical Illustrations* (Basic Books Press, 1977).

The critics' insistence on personal risks as against riskless drones, however, uses soldiers as means in quite a distinct sense. When it comes to the resort to force, whose decisions matter? The actors in that case are not the soldiers themselves, but instead the political leadership that makes the decisions of *jus ad bellum*, resort to force. The demand to put soldiers at risk is not actually to influence their behavior—but instead the behavior of their political leadership. The force of the demand to expose personnel to personal risks rather than use drones is not intended to influence their behavior, but instead to use them as hostages against the decisions of their leadership. This is to use them as "mere" means in a moral sense—and one that is distinctly different, and not morally covered by, the way in which the War Convention allows soldiers to be treated as means and material of war.

VI. The general argument is coherent

So perhaps the two *jus in bello* assumptions are plausible, and perhaps even more than plausible. In that case, what about protecting one's forces from personal risk through the use of drones? The alleged moral and non-moral imperative of putting one's forces at personal risk should *not* be seen as unexceptionable, admirable as a sentiment, or beyond criticism. That said, however, we must nonetheless acknowledge that the general argument, the overall argument, is coherent. This merits explicit acknowledgment, particularly given that I have sharply challenged some of the assumptions made in support of it.

It is possible—it cannot be ruled out *a priori*—that the resort to force might be "too easy." If a coherent basis could be offered for saying what the proper propensity of the resort to force should be, then we might be able to assess whether the effects of reducing the harms of how war is conducted have so great an effect in encouraging the resort to force that two things follow. One is that there is, on its own terms, "too much" resort to force; more than would be otherwise optimal in the absence of these altered incentives that, however ironically, result from reduced harms from war. The second is that there might be "too much" resort to force in another sense; not only relative to the "efficient" propensity to use force, but also relative to all the harms caused both by resort to force (the *jus ad bellum* consequences) and the harms caused to innocents in the conduct of war despite the more limited nature of harms from drones (the *jus in bello* consequences). These seem unlikely to me, but they cannot be ruled out *a priori*. The consequences from "too easy" resort to force might turn out to be far worse than the benefits conferred in a total-welfare sense, assuming, of course, that we could determine the "efficient" level of resort to force against which to assess any of this.

Framed as a general observation, although it is ironic that changes in war that make it less harmful to civilians and more protective of fighters might also have the unintended consequence of making resort to force "too easy," it might nonetheless be so. It cannot be ruled out *tout court*. Indeed, it might qualify as "tragic" in Isaiah Berlin's criteria of tragedy arising from the inability to bring about a unity of the good: plural goods and values that cannot be reconciled, in this case perfect conduct in war but optimal resistance to engaging in it.

VII. "Too easy"?

We have accepted that setting out the sophisticated version of the general argument (the one that unpacks the notion of "too easy" into its surprisingly complicated parts) is important in order properly to evaluate it. We have also accepted that the general argument is logically coherent. The question, then, is whether we accept the coherence of the notion of "too easy" in the context of *jus ad bellum*. This is to say, yes, the development of new ways of fighting that bring about positive changes in matters of *jus in bello* can have the effect, at least in principle, of making the resort to force, *jus ad bellum*, easier. The question is whether it is coherent to go from "easier" to "too easy."

"Too easy" demands comparison to something, some standard of what resort to force should be. How would one know when one was resorting to force at the optimal point? What would that mean? Let us stipulate all such measurements are inherently imprecise and difficult to make. The problem is to determine whether there is, even in principle, an optimal social welfare-maximizing point for the resort to force. I do not believe there is, at least not in the neutral, mere cost—benefit analysis way in which this proposition of "efficiency" proposes to separate itself from purely moral criteria.

Efficiency proposes that we extract the net benefits over costs.[14] As a proposition of social welfare in which there are multiple parties, the notion of welfare-maximizing efficiency starts from the idea that all costs and benefits are internalized in order to reach the point of net maximum social welfare for society as a whole. So-called Coase bargaining asks what happens when we have two (or more) parties with conflicting interests, conflicting costs and benefits; the classic example is "farmers" and "ranchers." The parties bargain to the efficient point, through payoffs between the parties. If the farmers and ranchers, with their conflicting requirements, were all part of the same enterprise, presumably the heads of that enterprise would make a rational choice that would internalize costs and benefits for the ranchers and the farmers taken together, and reach an efficient point of how much grain and how many cattle.

Where ranchers and farmers are not part of a common enterprise that will do this cost—benefit "netting" internally, Coase substitutes the market, with money

---

[14] This discussion leaves aside a more technical (though quite interesting) framing by reference to Pareto efficiency and Kaldor-Hicks efficiency concepts.

payoffs, to do the same thing. The market in this acts as a social mechanism that, even without making everyone part of the same enterprise, allows costs and benefits to be set against each other. But there must still be a mechanism of commonality, and for the farmers and ranchers, it is money. In order to bring about the net social welfare position, there has to be a common currency, by which payoffs can be made to bring the conflicting parties to the efficient point. Ranchers and farmers can pay each other. But what about war?

There are *some* wars for which that is true. It is particularly true of those that are mostly about extended banditry, war-lordism, control of diamond mines, and so on (leaving aside the many problems of parties keeping promises, defecting from bargains, etc.). In some of those cases one might in effect bribe parties away from resort to war. The losers in one sense might still count themselves the winners in another: equilibrium at last.

But many conflicts are not that way, and certainly not the historically most important. War in our historical world is not merely organized theft. The conflicts in which the United States engages are not that way; whatever its national security interests, if it has reached the point of war, it cannot be bought off by money or any other market "commonality" substitutes between the parties, and most of the time the party on the other side cannot be, either. The conflicts that matter to the United States involve sides that have interests, desires, ideologies, fears, motives, and reasons for fighting that are not only opposed to the other side—they will be unreachable by bargaining because there is no common currency, expressing a common framework of costs and benefits, and a "net" social welfare function, between them. Sides matter. Because sides matter, there is no ability to avoid the normative moral problem by trying to convert it into a merely neutral, technocratic problem of winners and losers paying each other off to reach the point of net social welfare.

Why does not efficiency *jus in bello* face the same problem? Perhaps it does, if one goes beyond military necessity as merely means to prior ends and treats the problem as Walzer's "importance of winning." It might or might not be coherent to do as the law of war does and confine the argument over military necessity to something that is limited to the situation on the concrete battlefield, connected perhaps to an overall strategic military aim, but not the political grand strategy of "winning." It is easier to see ways to weigh up seeming incommensurables of civilian harm and military necessity when military necessity is limited and made at the most concrete level in which "means to ends" is more obvious. Why this should be so remains a difficult and unresolved question of proportionality in *jus in bello*.

The peculiarity here is in part that the prong of *jus in bello* proportionality one might initially think is most connected to justice is civilian harm, rather than military necessity. After all, necessity of military means to military ends might seem like a merely technocratic, rational choice exercise—cost—benefit analysis par excellence, whereas civilian harm seems like an "excused injustice" done in the course of militarily necessary operations—excused yet still fundamentally a question of justice. Yet civilian harm, understood in another sense, turns out to be the least difficult as a category and far more closely related to cost—benefit analysis and concepts of net social welfare. Why? Because it is not so much about "justice" as it is about what it says, "harm"—for which, all things being equal, less is better. Harm to civilians might be about justice *simpliciter*, but it might well equally be regarded as "superior non-moral consequences." They come to the same thing in this case. However, this *cannot* be said of winning or losing the war as such because, well, one side *wins* and the other side *loses*. That makes them different, and incomparable in the sense of what each side will recognize as acceptable.

Moreover (and this is a slightly different point), what they each win or lose is not actually the same kind of thing or value. Winning is a different quality, when it comes to war, than losing, in the special sense that they are not simply opposites. We are used to thinking of winning and losing as the opposite sides of a coin, or the up and down sides of a single quality, laid out on a graph. That is misleading. The experience of what a side in war gains by winning is a distinctly different kind of experience and quality from that of the side that loses. Think about societies in war, either state-to-state wars, or civil wars—the winning and the losing are largely about different kinds of things.

Thus the ability to compare or "buy off" in Coasean bargaining to reach the efficient point in resort to force is not really there. Determining the net social welfare for when to resort to force would require a set of common grounds between parties of conflict that does not exist unless, perhaps, in the mind of God.

VIII. Conclusion: social welfare that turns out to be justice

The notion of efficiency in the resort to force thus turns out to be incoherent because there is no common ground of social welfare between the sides that would allow them to agree upon the efficient point, or a common currency that would allow them to bargain their way to it and pay each other off. They fight instead.

Not having available a common social criterion by which to define the efficient point of resort to force has the perhaps peculiar, perhaps unsurprising consequence of forcing the debate back to moral questions—the oldest question of *jus ad bellum* of all: which side is right? Which side has just cause? The interesting and important questions of "efficient" resort to force turn out to be the moral questions, the questions of the justice of the sides, and the notion of an efficient resort to force simply says the resort to force is efficient when force is resorted to justly. It is a disguised way, under concealing if comforting rubrics of maximizing social welfare, of asking exactly the same moral questions about just cause in war. The two sides do not agree on the answers, but there is no neutral way of answering the question of whether one side or the other has resorted to force "too easily" without answering the question of the justness of the cause.

Note that this is *not* simply an invocation of some form of moral relativism—the two sides cannot agree, because there is no objective moral answer as to the just or unjust side—and therefore there is no basis for determining common social welfare, either. After all, the fact of moral disagreement is typically used as an argument in *favor* of appealing to neutral non-moral facts about benefit and harm to settle the question. In the case of sides in war, however, that form of argument is incoherent. But it is not because there cannot be, in principle, a moral answer; there might well be. The moral answer might be contested by the two sides; the problem for the efficiency argument, by contrast, is that it is genuinely incoherent, and not merely contested. Of course the sides disagree, with the result that any neutral or common answer to the question is itself a moral position, a question of justice and just cause. The apparently neutral, non-moral welfare criterion turns out to be an irreducibly moral one. And even if the resulting moral claim is contested, and indeed unknowable, that is not a claim of moral relativism.[15]

The same applies for the idea of "too easy" resort to force over a series of uses of force. The proper answer for whether a party finds it "too easy" to use force is to ask about the justice—including the economy of means and methods to minimize harms—of each individual intervention in the series. If each is just (applying here the full criteria of just war for simplicity, including necessity), then the level of use of force is correct; if some or all is unjust, then it is incorrect. But because the sides have fundamentally incommensurable ideas of social welfare in winning and losing, they lack a common currency by which, even in principle, they could bargain by payoffs to some efficient common end. To say that they can, in principle, is simply to insist upon rather cryptic language, in the circumstances, of non-moral social welfare for what, in fact, depends essentially upon moral evaluations. Resort to force is "too easy" if it results in unjust interventions; otherwise not.

This is a roundabout way to what is finally an uncomplicated point. The discussion has walked through a perhaps unnecessarily overstated version of the "too easy" argument in order to get at the distinct notions of efficiency *jus in bello* and efficiency *jus ad bellum*, and to show that the latter, in particular, is incoherent unless it is understood to simply recapitulate and depend utterly upon evaluations

---

[15] I believe that this is approximately the position that Lincoln takes in the final paragraph of the Second Inaugural Address, in which he attempts to thread the needle between a moral absolutism, on the one hand, and moral relativism, on the other. Hence his abjuration to "finish the work we are in," with firmness in the right—but as God gives us to see the right. It is a marvelously subtle phrasing, seeking to find a way through without collapsing into either position, whether philosophically successful or not.

from morality and justice, not simply non-moral social welfare criteria with which, presumably, rational people could not disagree. Rational people do disagree, and those disagreements in war amount to sides. To the extent that one can talk about net welfare in arguments over resorting to force, they will be determined by the evaluation of the arguments made by the sides resorting to force, which is to say, an irreducible appeal to the justness of each side's cause.

This is not to deny that changes in the technology of war—drones and precision targeting—with which this discussion began do not have an effect upon the propensity to make war. As armed humanitarian intervention in Libya suggests, and is likely to be repeated, the decision to resort to war can be made "easier" by means of warfare that reduce civilian harm and spare one's own forces. If there is a social science prediction that emerges from this chapter, it is that if there are more humanitarian interventions by the advanced militaries (that is, the sole advanced military) of the West, drones are very likely to figure at the center of intervention strategy: a local partner fighting on the ground backed up by drones in the sky.

But the number of interventions must also be modified by intensity; it might turn out to be that the ability to engage in more covert actions, intelligence-driven uses of force, against non-state actors especially, means fewer, much less intense, and much shorter conventional wars waged to try and destroy non-state terrorist groups. The ability to reach non-state terrorists taking haven in a failed or hostile state without having to fight one's way to it on the ground, and to attack it with precision, is on balance a good thing—even from the standpoint of reducing the amount of conventional war fighting that might otherwise occur. In any case, the question of the resort to force does not start from a common social welfare framework, and so finally the questions of efficiency are simply re-enactments of assertions of justice made by sides to a conflict that have incommensurable positions on winning and losing.

Drones can make the decision to resort to force "easier;" that is not the same, however, as making it "*too* easy."

PART V

UTILITARIAN TRADE-OFFS AND DEONTOLOGICAL CONSTRAINTS

15

TARGETED KILLING IN WAR AND PEACE: A PHILOSOPHICAL ANALYSIS

Fernando R. Tesón[1]

I. Introduction

On May 2, 2011, a special unit of the U.S. Navy killed Osama bin Laden in Pakistan. Many (this writer included) rejoiced at this development and felt that justice had been served.[2] However, emotion is no substitute for dispassionate moral analysis. In this chapter I examine the morality of targeted killings in general. I address the killing of bin Laden, but my discussion goes beyond that: it probes the morality of *all* targeted killings by liberal governments. It applies to targeted killings by the United States as well as other liberal regimes, and it explores the justification of the practice in wartime and in peacetime. Given that the United States and Israel have announced that they will continue to kill named targets, and given that not all contemplated targets are as villainous or dangerous as bin Laden, a moral evaluation of the practice is especially required.

The deliberate killing of another human being is presumptively a deeply immoral act. Targeted killings are deliberate killings, so any discussion must start with a strong moral presumption against those acts. However, the prohibition has some exceptions: killing in war, self-defense, and law enforcement of various kinds.[3] This chapter examines whether targeted killing (which is a species of assassination) can be one of those exceptions.

---

[1] Simon Eminent Scholar, Florida State University. I thank my colleague Dan Markel and the participants in the conference that led to this volume, held at the University of Pennsylvania Law School on April 2011, and especially Andy Altman, for their helpful comments.
[2] A sentiment echoed by the President of the U.S. See the President's speech in "Osama Bin Laden Dead," available at <http://www.whitehouse.gov/blog/2011/05/02/osama-bin-laden-dead> accessed November 3, 2011.
[3] This chapter is about the morality of targeted killing, not about its lawfulness under international or domestic law.

First, some definitions are in order (these are conventional stipulations for expository purposes; no substantive issue turns on them). I define targeted killing as *the extrajudicial intentional killing by the state of an identified person for a public purpose.* This chapter will examine only those targeted killings conducted by a liberal democracy. The definition calls for some clarification. The word "extrajudicial" excludes from the definition all instances where someone is killed in execution of a lawful sentence (whether this is morally justified or not I will not address). The word "intentional" means that the assassin *directly* intends to kill the victim. It excludes from the definition all killings that are *incidental* to combat in war or revolution (serious as those are). Thus, it excludes not only unforeseen deaths, but also foreseen yet unintended deaths.[4] In a targeted killing the victim is precisely identified: the lethal action is directed at him. The requirement that the victim be identified is necessary to distinguish targeted killing from the anonymous intentional killing of enemy combatants in war. Killing an enemy soldier on the battlefield is not a targeted killing in our sense. Finally, I use the expression "public purpose" loosely, to exclude private purposes such as revenge or personal gain. A public purpose is still normatively neutral: it may or may not be morally justified.

In this chapter I examine the various forms of targeted killing. I proceed on the premise that the moral rules that govern killing in peacetime are very strict but that they are relaxed during wartime. Section II addresses peacetime situations; that is, the strict moral rules governing a liberal government's resort to targeted killing outside the war context. I then turn in section III to targeted killing in conventional war, where the central question becomes whether the more permissive moral rules governing lethal force in war relax the strict rules that govern targeted killing in peacetime. Section IV begins the examination of the targeted killing of terrorists.[5] I focus on the question of whether such killing must be analyzed under the stricter peacetime framework, or under the more permissive wartime framework, or under a third framework that borrows from the other two. The conclusions of this section are *presumptive.* I try to show that there are moral arguments in favor of these admittedly repulsive acts. Section V presents several objections to targeted killings and examines whether the force of those objections should make us revise our presumptive conclusions. At the very least, these objections show that targeted killings are troubling, even accepting the force of arguments in their favor.

---

[4] The distinction between intended outcomes and unintended yet foreseen outcomes has a crucial role in the morality of war, and is captured by the famous doctrine of double effect. See, *inter alia,* R.G. Frey, "The Doctrine of Double Effect" in R.G. Frey and C. H. Wellman (eds), *A Companion to Applied Ethics* (Blackwell, 2003); Joseph Boyle Jr, "Toward Understanding the Principle of Double Effect" in P.A. Woodward (ed.), *The Doctrine of Double Effect: Philosophers Debate a Controversial Moral Principle* (Notre Dame University Press, 2001) 12; and M. Walzer, *Just and Unjust Wars: A Moral Argument with Historical Illustrations,* 4th edn (Basic Books, 2006) 128.

[5] I avoid the term "asymmetrical war" because it prejudges the issue by deciding that the conflict with terrorists is sufficiently close to conventional war.

II. Targeted killing in peacetime

I start with the general concept of targeted killing, the extrajudicial intentional killing by a liberal government of a person for a public purpose. It will be convenient to start with targeted killing in peacetime, because clarifying that concept will help us analyze targeted killing in wartime and targeted killing of terrorists. During peacetime, the state can use lethal force only in very limited circumstances, mostly in self-defense or to protect persons from deadly threats. Beyond that, a suspected criminal is entitled to due process and may not be killed except in execution of a lawful sentence pronounced by a court of law after a finding of guilt (and this assuming, controversially, that the death penalty is justified). The liberal state's *moral* obligation not to kill a person without due process includes foreigners, even if they are not entirely protected by domestic constitutional guarantees. Foreigners have a right to life, which is universal. However, I would like to make a *prima facie* case for the occasional permissibility of targeted killing in peacetime, leaving for later whether such presumptive case may be defeated by the general objections against targeted killing. Because the moral presumption entailed by the right to life is strong, a targeted killing in peacetime can only be justified, if at all, under very stringent conditions. I provisionally suggest the following four conditions.[6] The conditions are individually necessary and jointly sufficient for the legitimacy of targeted killing in peacetime, again, disregarding for now the general objections discussed at the end of this chapter.

(a) The targeted killing will save many lives, including many innocent lives.

(b) The public purpose of the targeted killing is just.

(c) The target of the killing is morally culpable, a villain.

(d) There are no non-lethal alternatives available, such as diplomatic threats or capture.

(a) Saving lives

Targeted killing in peacetime can only start to make moral sense if it is likely is to spare the lives of a significant number of innocent persons.[7] In general, this happens when the targeted killing avoids war or a similar catastrophe such as genocide. Several examples come readily to mind; the most obvious is the morality of killing Hitler *before* the Second World War: arguably, that act would have spared the world terrible ordeals. Notice that killing Hitler in early 1939 would have been a targeted killing in peacetime. If the contemplated target, vile as he may be, is not

---

[6] In addition to the condition that the author must be a liberal government, which I do not discuss.

[7] See Andrew Altman and Christopher Heath Wellman, *A Liberal Theory of International Justice* (Oxford University Press, 2009) 116.

threatening innocent lives, then he may not be permissibly killed; the default prohibition against murder resurfaces. Let's set up two imaginary examples, both of which involve targeted killing in the form of assassinating a political leader.

Genocide in Rhodelia: Rhodelia is ruled by Caligula, a vicious dictator who is perpetrating genocide[8] against his own population. His neighbor, Freeland, is a liberal democracy with the military capability to stop the atrocities. The government of Freeland can do one of three things. It can do nothing; it can invade Rhodelia and fight a predictably successful war of humanitarian intervention; or it can kill Caligula and thus end the genocide. Let us assume that doing nothing is morally problematic. Invading Rhodelia to stop the atrocities, while predictably successful, will result in significant collateral deaths of civilians,[9] deaths of combatants on both sides, and physical destruction. However, sending a special operations team to kill Caligula will end his crimes and restore peace without any of these consequences. What should the government of Freeland do?

Planned aggression in the Chosen Kingdom: King Vlad, a charismatic absolutist monarch with delusions of grandeur, rules over The Chosen Kingdom, a militarily powerful nation. Against his advisers' best judgment, Vlad is planning a massive invasion of his neighbors, all liberal democracies, who are dreading the impending catastrophe. The government of Sunland, the most powerful of these democracies, is considering action. It can do three things: wait for the aggression and then react defensively; invade preemptively; or send a sniper to kill Vlad and predictably avoid the war. Again, the impending war is likely to have terrible costs in blood and treasure, whether started by the Kingdom or by Sunland's preemptive strike. What should the government of Sunland do?

These examples show why a blanket prohibition of targeted killing in peacetime is, on closer inspection, too quick. Moral considerations may favor targeted killing over war. Targeted killing, a *prima facie* immoral act, may appear as preferable because it will avoid genocide or war while placing the cost on a culpable person. Many people die in war. Those who bear arms to resist unjust attacks against themselves or others put their lives at risk for a just cause. Every one of those deaths is murder because inflicted by an unjust warrior.[10] Importantly, war also brings about the incidental deaths of civilians. As is well known, this is a highly problematic aspect of war. One important pacifist objection is that any war, no matter how "clean," will bring about the deaths of civilians. These persons have not given up their right to life, so starting a war that predictably will kill them is morally problematic, even if the country that initiates it has a just cause. Maybe this worry can be addressed by a properly

---

[8] I use the word "genocide" loosely, to denote mass murder.
[9] I use the term "civilians" to denote innocent noncombatants.
[10] As Jeff McMahan has convincingly argued. See J. McMahan, *Killing in War* (Oxford University Press, 2009) esp. chs 1 and 2. See the discussion below. I use the word "murder" as meaning prohibited killing.

formulated version of the doctrine of double effect, but the worry persists nonetheless, because even if one reluctantly thinks that bringing about those collateral deaths is permissible under the right circumstances, surely achieving the *same* results with no deaths is morally preferable. In the Rhodelia example, killing Caligula will save Caligula's present victims, plus the innocent lives (both just combatants and civilians on both sides) that would be lost should Freeland decide to start a war. It will also avoid the terrible physical destruction that war typically causes. In the Chosen Kingdom example, killing Vlad would have similar effects: it would avoid the terrible losses that the impending aggression would cause. The difference between these two peacetime cases is that Caligula is not threatening his neighbors yet killing his own citizens, while Vlad is not killing its own citizens yet threatening its neighbors.

(b) Just cause

However, saving lives, even in large numbers, does not suffice to justify targeted killing in peacetime. The government that orders the killing must itself not be on the wrong side of a conflict. The public purpose that defines targeted killing must be a normatively compelling just purpose in the sense of the just war tradition.[11] In the hypothetical examples discussed above, killing Caligula is justified because Caligula is committing a crime against humanity; and killing Vlad is justified because he is about to unleash a war of aggression, another major crime. In these cases, this condition is identical to the first: the just cause is preventing the humanitarian catastrophe. However, the two conditions must be carefully distinguished. Suppose that country A has decided to unlawfully attack country B. The leader of country B will predictably resist. On learning this, the government of A, the aggressor, decides to kill the leader of B, on the grounds that doing so will avoid the impending war and save many lives. This targeted killing is murder, notwithstanding the fact that it will save many lives. The reason is that A, as the aggressor, lacks a just cause. To take a real-life example, in 1939 Hitler knew, or should have known, that Winston Churchill would lead Britain to war if Germany invaded Poland. Suppose Hitler would have ordered the killing of Churchill on the grounds that it would have forced Britain to compromise and thus avoid the impending war. This would have been murder because Germany was the aggressor. So while saving lives may be a just cause for a targeted killing, not all targeted killings that save lives have a just cause. Determining what causes are just exceeds the confines of this chapter. Suffice it to say here that a just cause for war is *only* the defense of persons and liberal institutions against unjustified threats or attacks against them. National glory, economic gain, strategic advantage, redress of non-lethal wrongs, or territorial expansion never constitute just cause.[12]

---

[11] The literature on the just war tradition is extensive. See generally A. Bellamy, *Just Wars: From Cicero to Iraq* (Polity Press, 2006).

[12] This account of just cause is proposed by L. Lomasky and F.R. Tesón, *Justice at a Distance* (unpublished manuscript).

(c) Moral culpability

The object of targeted killing must be *culpable of having created the threat to, or destruction of, human lives in the first place*. In most cases he will be a villain.[13] In peacetime, a liberal government intentionally targets someone to avoid a war (either a defensive war or a humanitarian intervention). By doing so, the liberal government prevents the deaths of many combatants (its own and the enemy's) and civilians. As we saw, just combatants and civilians are not culpable. Even if one thinks that not all enemy combatants are free of blame for fighting an unjust war, surely they are less culpable than their leader who sends them to fight. Targeting the villain instead of targeting those who fight at his behest places the cost on the morally culpable person. This is ostensibly preferable to an alternative that, we know, will bring about the deaths of many persons who had nothing to do with the critical situation that forced the liberal government to act. Targeted killing, then, performs a double task: it reduces the number of victims to one, and it inflicts lethal force on the blameworthy individual.

The target *must* be the person responsible for creating the unjust threat or inflicting unjust violence. The targeted killing cannot be justified by the result alone. In the examples presented, imagine that the liberal government knows that by killing the *children* of Caligula or Vlad (or a few randomly chosen civilians, or equally non-culpable targets) it will avert the impending catastrophe. Such action is morally impermissible by straight application of general deontological principles that forbid *using* innocent persons to achieve a morally justified end.[14] The liberal government is not allowed to target someone affiliated with the enemy if that person is not sufficiently culpable (but it may target a sufficiently culpable henchman). Notice that this condition is distinct from the just cause condition, although they may sometimes overlap. The government may have a just cause but unjustifiably kill an innocent person to pursue that cause. In the examples above, Freeland's government has a just cause (stopping genocide), yet it is not allowed to target an innocent person in the pursuit of that cause, even if that killing would stop the genocide.[15] Likewise, Sunland's government has a just cause (preventing aggression) but may not target, say, the Queen instead of the King.

The requirement that the target be culpable adds a retributivist ingredient to the justification of targeted killings.[16] The just warrior is moved by the imperative of saving many lives in the context of a just fight. Any alternative he chooses will impose costs on someone. Given this, it is morally preferable to impose the cost on the person culpable for the lethal threat than on non-culpable persons. Yet moral guilt is a

---

[13] I say "in most cases" because one can think of the rare case of someone who created the threat of war in a non-culpable manner.

[14] This is an extraordinarily difficult problem which I cannot examine here. See, *inter alia*, J. Thomson, "The Trolley Problem," 94 *Yale Law Journal* (1985) 1395.

[15] I leave aside even more extreme circumstances where this prohibition may collapse.

[16] See S. David, "Israel's Policy of Targeted Killing," 17 *Ethics & International Affairs*, (2003) 111.

necessary condition for justification, not a sufficient one. The liberal government does not tell the victim: "We kill you *because* you deserve it." Rather, it tells him: "We must stop these deaths. We have several ways to do this, but the least costly way *in a moral sense* is to kill you, who are responsible for this predicament. Any alternative action will bring about the deaths of many innocent persons." Requiring culpability avoids killing innocent persons and, in a sense, "punishing" them for the misdeeds of another. The paradox is that assassination, a morally repulsive notion, is more in accordance with the liberal traditions of the criminal law because it requires a sort of *mens rea* on the part of the target of lethal force. This seems preferable to the rather illiberal practice of killing anonymous soldiers who, for all we know, have, if at all, diminished responsibility for the impending or ongoing disaster.

(d) Lack of non-lethal alternatives

These three conditions (saving innocent lives, having a just cause, and targeting a villain) are still insufficient to justify targeted killing in peacetime. In addition, the liberal government must lack non-lethal alternatives to resolve the crisis. In the Rhodelia example, suppose that the government of Freeland can credibly threaten Caligula with major destruction if he does not relent. This threat is preferable to killing Caligula, as are all other diplomatic maneuvers to get Caligula to desist.[17] The same reasoning is available in the Chosen Kingdom hypothetical: if Sunland has non-lethal alternatives to prevent the impending war, then it must use them.

Now why is this so? If part of the reason that makes targeted killing palatable is that the victim is culpable, then the government who avoids the killing through these diplomatic moves is getting the villain off the hook. Killing him would not only give him his due, but would also prevent him from ruling despotically and making the lives of everyone around him miserable, not to mention the probability that he will pose a similar threat in the future. In this case, forgoing the targeted killing may be worse in the long run. This happened when the Coalition decided not to kill Saddam Hussein in the 1991 Gulf War. Yet these alternatives to killing are preferable for two reasons. First, although the target is culpable, the killing deprives the target of the due process that would have ensued after capture. Most non-lethal alternatives at least preserve that possibility; and capture ensures it. To be sure, as we shall see in the discussion of targeted killing of terrorists, process is not due in *all* cases; in particular, it is not due when capture is impossible. But when capture is possible, it always precludes the permissibility of killing. Second, the prohibition of intentional killing is partly grounded in *agent-relative* reasons. (I return to this topic below.) By choosing alternatives to the killing, the governments of Freeland and Sunland avoid *being* killers. They avoid the state of affairs where *they* deliberately kill someone in cold blood.

---

[17] Interestingly, Freeland's government's threat must be credible, and this depends on Caligula's not realizing that Freeland's government is threatening him to avoid killing him! Caligula, in other words, must believe that Freeland's government is as callous as he is.

Punishing Caligula or Vlad (the retributivist impulse) is not a reason compelling enough to outweigh the immorality of *their* killing those villains, of getting their hands dirty with the deliberate extrajudicial killing of another human being.

We can imagine, however, that some would prefer the targeted killing over these alternatives. A strong *retributivist* would insist that the villain get his due. On the opposite end, a strong *consequentialist* would insist that the government weigh costs and benefits and proceed with the killing if, all things considered, it would cause more good than the alternatives. These positions are dubious, however. In response to the retributivist, giving people their due may perhaps be a necessary condition for the legitimacy of criminal punishment (outside of war), but it cannot alone justify *extrajudicial* killing. In most cases, a targeted killing based *only* on the culpability of the target, where capture and prosecution are possible, amounts to vigilantism or revenge. The answer to the consequentialist is well known. The morality of action cannot be determined *only* by their net benefit. There are immoral ways to produce beneficial consequences, and deliberate killing is surely a likely candidate. This does not mean that targeted killing is never permissible, but it does mean that the threshold for permissibility is high. If the liberal government can avert the humanitarian catastrophe that alone would justify the targeted killing in the first place by resorting to non-lethal alternatives, then it must do so, even if it means the survival of the villain. A non-lethal alternative to killing the villain is, of course, capturing him and bringing him to justice. This alternative is not simply *preferable* to killing: killing is prohibited when low-cost capture is possible (I return to the issue of capture in the discussion of targeted killing of terrorists, below).

III. Targeted killing in conventional war

As is widely recognized, these strict conditions for the legitimacy of targeted killing are significantly relaxed in wartime. Consider a conventional war scenario. Two armies are facing each other. One of them is the aggressor, so it lacks a just cause; the other is resisting aggression, so it has a just cause. Let us stipulate (although this is contested)[18] that in a conventional war only the combatants on the side that has a just cause have a moral license to kill enemy combatants. Further, all the deaths brought about by just combatants are legitimate only if they comply with the morality of war, including an appropriate version of the doctrine of double effect as reflected largely in the Geneva Conventions, in particular the principle that obligates belligerents to discriminate between combatants and civilians.[19]

---

[18] The position in the text largely follows McMahan, *supra* n. 10, but see n. 22 below. The classic *locus* for the view that McMahan opposes, the "moral equality of combatants," is Walzer, *supra* n. 4, 34–41. See also L. May, "Killing Naked Soldiers: Collective Identification in War," 19 *Ethics and International Affairs* (2005) 39.

[19] See *Protocol Additional to the Geneva Conventions of August 12, 1949, Relating to the Protection of Victims of International Armed Conflicts (Protocol I)* June 8, 1977, arts 51–54. I assume without

Can the government on the right side of a war target a named enemy for killing? Consider first a targeted killing *in the battlefield*. Notwithstanding the claims of some authors,[20] identifying the victim in advance does not alter the general permission to kill in combat.[21] A commander says to a soldier: "There behind the machine-gun is Colonel Sanders, the enemy's battalion commander. With his great skill he is decimating our troops and making our lives miserable, so make sure you take him out." Here the victim is identified by name and individually targeted, yet I take it most people would regard this killing as justified under the laws of war. The commander permissibly targets Sanders because Sanders, in the pursuit of an unjust cause, is *taking an active part in combat*. He is an unjust enemy combatant and as such may be permissibly killed, named or unnamed.

So let us consider targeted killing of an enemy combatant who is *not* on the battlefield. The guiding principle is that a *targeted* killing in war is justified only if it is sufficiently close, in a moral sense, to *standard* killing in war. If the killing is instead morally removed from that category, then it will be evaluated under the more restrictive standard of killing in peacetime. Stating this principle, however, is easier than applying it, so some elaboration is in order.

In war, the moral framework for targeted killing is more permissive. The first condition for peacetime, that the targeted killing must save many innocent lives, must be relaxed. In a just war, a necessary condition for the permissibility of a targeted killing is that the soldier should reasonably believe that it *will increase the chances of victory*. For in wartime it is permitted to kill enemy *combatants* for just that reason, assuming a just cause. Some may object that the rationale for killing enemy soldiers is self-defense, not a mere increase in the chances of victory. Even if the general rationale for killing in war is self-defense, this does not mean that the just warrior must feel threatened every time he faces an enemy combatant. I take it that those writers who claim self-defense as the proper rationale for war are thinking about the *overall* justification of the war, and not as a reason that applies in every individual case of combat. In other words, the aggressor has forced us to fight in self-defense. That is the reason why we, the just army, are fighting. We are defending ourselves from the aggressor. But that does not mean that in every case where I face the enemy soldier, an agent of the aggressor, I must feel threatened in order for my firing to be justified. The right way to look at this is to say that a soldier on the right side of a just war may permissibly kill an enemy soldier if that will increase the chances of victory (*a fortiori* he may kill the enemy soldier if his life is threatened).

argument that, with respect of *jus in bello*, the laws of war generally track the morality of war, with the already noted exception that unjust warriors lack permission to kill.

[20] See the Francis Lieber Code [1863], available at <http://www.civilwarhome.com/liebercode.htm> accessed November 3, 2011.

[21] See also C. Finklestein, "Targeted Killing as Preemptive Action," in this Volume, ch. 6.

The second condition applicable to targeted killing in peacetime, that the victim must be personally culpable, disappears in wartime, when it comes to the killing of a combatant who is on the battlefield and fighting for an unjust cause. This combatant is a piece in the war machine of a government or group that is fighting for an unjust cause, so he is liable to lethal attack by the enemy even if he is not *personally* culpable.[22] The rationale is the same for not requiring culpability as a condition for killing (without targeting) the combatants fighting on the unjust side. The soldier on the right side of a just war is facing an unjustified threat posed by the enemy. Whether the enemy soldiers are individually culpable or not, they are armed agents of the unjust enemy bent on destroying us (now or later). If this is correct, then it is correct also for the targeted killing of an unjust enemy combatant, as in the Colonel Sanders example above.

However, the concept of combatant is vague. Is it confined to combatants *in the battlefield*, or does it also it also include (i) combatants not in the battlefield; or (ii) non-military leaders of the enemy? Consider first enemy soldiers who are not in the battlefield. Again, two situations are possible. Colonel Sanders, the enemy's battalion commander, is not currently in the battlefield but is resting in his military headquarters. Some may object to this killing on the grounds that Sanders is not posing any threat. However, I think most people would say this killing is justified under the laws of war. The reason is, I believe, that the Colonel is simply restoring his strength to go back to the battlefield and continue his aggression (remember he is fighting for an unjust cause). Sanders and his subordinates are engaged in a continued unlawful fight, so the fact that he is resting now is irrelevant to the general justification for killing unjust enemies in war.[23] We can say that Colonel Sanders is in *combat*, although not in the battlefield. Again, Lieber's worry is not applicable here. Colonel Sanders is not killed because he is an outlaw, but because he is a piece in the unjust lethal machinery that the unjust enemy has mounted against us.

The second situation occurs when the enemy combatant is geographically removed from combat altogether—not just from the battlefield, but from any military installation such as a barrack (but not wounded, as different principles apply). He is in a private setting. Imagine Colonel Sanders is on vacation. Is the liberal government justified in killing him, for example, by a sniper gunshot? Daniel Statman has argued that there is no moral distinction between killing an enemy soldier while he is in his military headquarters and when he is on vacation. In neither case is he participating in active combat, so to make the legitimacy of the killing depend on location is arbitrary. As Statman points out, this is even

---

[22] I tend to depart from McMahan's views on *individual* culpability of soldiers fighting an unjust war. Average foot soldiers fighting an unjust war should not be held individually culpable, even though, as McMahan says, each one of their killings is an unjustified killing. See Lomasky and Tesón, *supra* n. 12.

[23] See J. McMahan, "War as Self-Defense," 18 *Ethics & International Affairs* (2004) 75.

clearer with respect to high-ranking officers, as they rarely pose an immediate threat.[24]

Yet I believe there is a moral difference between killing Colonel Sanders when he is in a combat role and killing him while on vacation. The distinction comports with a central purpose of the laws of war: to minimize deaths by confining as much as possible the destruction to the theater of operations. If the war conventions are in place, and those conventions prohibit killing enemies while on vacation, then killing him is *morally* impermissible on those grounds alone. Moreover, there are reasons to prohibit targeted killing of enemy combatants removed from the theater of operations, even conceiving the theater of operations quite broadly. This is a close call, but I think, contrary to Statman's claim, that the geographical location matters, for a couple of reasons. First, there is a *general* (not just conventional) obligation to minimize deaths in war where possible. Second, recall that in war the individual culpability of the victim (beyond the fact that he fights for an unjust cause) is not required for the permission to kill. If Colonel Sanders is commanding his troops or even resting in the barracks for next day's battle, he is participating in the war machine that threatens us. If he is on vacation he has removed himself from the war machine. Given that he may not be culpable, the default prohibition should re-emerge and assassinating him should be prohibited. These two reasons, plus the two general objections I will examine below, tip the balance against targeted killing in this case. The (admittedly tenuous) difference between killing Sanders while he is in the barracks and killing him while he is on vacation is that in the first case he is *in combat*, broadly conceived. In contrast, while on vacation Sanders has provisionally shed the role of combatant; he is truly acting in his civilian capacity. Given the longstanding conventional prohibition against this kind of targeted killing, and given the strong presumptive reasons against these kinds of acts, I think the scale should be tipped against permissibility (but the killing may be still justified under the stricter standard of targeted killing in peacetime examined above).

We turn now to the targeted killing in wartime of someone who is *not* formally a member of the enemy's army displayed on the battlefield. Here the situation changes and, again, there are two cases. The first is the case of the political leader of the enemy. Call it the Qaddafi case. As I write these lines, a civil war has just ended in Libya with Qaddafi's death.[25] Were the rebels, aided by NATO, justified in targeting Qaddafi? If we view the Libyan conflict as one where NATO assists justified revolutionaries against a tyrant, then Qaddafi was a legitimate target in the war to liberate Libya.[26] The reason is that Qaddafi was the commander-in-chief

---

[24] See D. Statman, "Targeted Killing," 4 *Theoretical Inquiries in Law: Targeted Killing* (2004) 179, 196.

[25] See K. Fahim, A. Shadid and R. Gladstone, "Violent End to an Era as Qaddafi Dies in Libya," *New York Times*, October 20, 2011, available at <http://www.nytimes.com/2011/10/21/world/africa/qaddafi-is-killed-as-libyan-forces-take-surt.html?pagewanted=all> accessed November 3, 2011.

[26] An analogous case is the assassination of Reinhard "The Hangman" Heydrich, ordered by the Czech government in exile in 1942. See R.C. Jaggers, "The Assassination of Reinhard Heydrich,"

of the unjust enemy forces. He *was* a combatant, even though for a while he sat in his comfortable Tripoli palace while his loyalists troops fought the rebels. The misgivings in Qaddafi's case arise, not because he was not a justified target in the civil war, but because apparently he was shot after he had surrendered.[27] But aside from that difficulty, the assassination of Qaddafi is not morally different from the assassination of Hitler *during* the Second World War, and not very different from killing any enemy combatant in war. The leaders are part—indeed, the essential part—of the enemy's military structure. A combatant is a person who is part of the logical chain of agency leading to the unjust threat.[28] The political leader is a crucial link in that chain. Moreover, the leader is culpable because he fully endorses the unjust cause and also sends others to die for that unjust cause. Most likely, he *invented* the unjust cause. His high position in the chain of agency in the pursuit of a criminal enterprise (since an unjust war is a criminal enterprise) is decisive. the killing of the political leader of an unjust enemy is, in a sense, morally *overdetermined*: The leader is morally culpable for unleashing and endorsing an unjust war, and he is an enemy combatant in the sense of *jus in bello*. He is a *culpable* enemy combatant. By the same token, it is not enough to claim, as a justification for a targeted killing, that the killing will avert the threat or win the war. For example, targeting Qaddafi's s relatives was impermissible, even if that act would have eliminated the threat or helped to achieve victory (because Qaddafi would collapse, or whatever) because those persons are not culpable.[29] The just warrior cannot target just anyone whose death he reasonably thinks will help him win. Here as elsewhere, the doctrine of double effect applies, so one can think of cases where the incidental deaths of civilians could be justified en route to killing the villain.

The second case involves a high-ranked government official who is not the commander-in-chief and is not otherwise part of the enemy's military structure. Here, as in the previous case, the culpability condition applies. Suppose that a cabinet minister of the Third Reich is an important piece in the war effort. Killing him, the Allies think, will considerably improve chances of victory. Call this the Albert Speer case. Albert Speer, a civilian architect, was the Minister of Armaments during

---

CIA's declassified document, available at <https://www.cia.gov/library/center-for-the-study-of-intelligence/kent-csi/vol4no1/html/v04i1a01p_0001.htm> accessed November 3, 2011.

[27] See D. Bentley, "Call for Inquiry into Gaddafy Death," *The Independent*, London, October 20, 2011, available at <http://www.independent.co.uk/news/world/africa/call-for-inquiry-into-gaddafi-death-2373545.html> accessed November 3, 2011. If that was indeed the case, then killing him was impermissible.

[28] See J.G. Murphy, "The Killing of the Innocent" in *Retribution, Justice, and Therapy* (Reidel 1979) 6–9.

[29] Thus, the strike by NATO forces on April 30, 2011 that killed three of Qaddafi's grandchildren is highly problematic. See MSNBC News, "Gadhafi's Youngest Son, Grandkids Killed in NATO Attack," available at <http://www.msnbc.msn.com/id/42829913/ns/world_news-mideast_n_africa/t/gadhafis-youngest-son-grandkids-killed-nato-attack/> accessed November 3, 2011.

the Third Reich.[30] Would the Allies have been justified in killing him? I would think the answer is yes, provided that the stipulated conditions apply (killing him would increase the chances of victory; Speer is culpable; there are no non-lethal alternatives). However, the more removed the official is from the war effort, the less acceptable the killing will be. Speer is a relatively easy case, but what about, say, the German Undersecretary of Public Parks at the time? The weaker the connection with the war, the less probable will be that the killing will comply with the required conditions, and the closer the killing will be to terror killing; that is, killing someone solely to demoralize the enemy. This is why the culpability condition must hold in the case of a targeted killing of someone who is not part of the enemy's armed forces. If the victim is sufficiently removed from the war effort, then targeting him comes dangerously close to using an innocent person to achieve legitimate war objectives. This case differs importantly from targeting a combatant, because in the latter case the victim has voluntarily identified himself, by wearing the real or symbolic uniform, as a permitted target. The person who does not belong to the military, does not participate in combat, and is sufficiently removed from the war effort is morally immune to targeted killing, even if the killing will increase the chances of victory.

IV. Targeted killing of terrorists

(a) Two views

Most of the literature on targeted killings has centered on whether the practice is acceptable to combat terrorism.[31] There are essentially two camps. Those in the first camp (the law enforcement view) claim that confronting terrorism is no different from confronting crime generally. The liberal state has at its disposal enough tools to respond to this kind of crime.[32] Thus, the government can arrest a terrorist when it has probable cause and prosecute him in court where it must convince a jury of his guilt beyond a reasonable doubt. If convicted, he can be sentenced to the penalties stipulated by the criminal law. True, terrorists pose special, large threats. The liberal state can counter them, however, in a number of ways: it can

---

[30] For Speer's own version of his role, see A. Speer, *Inside the Third Reich* (New York: Simon & Schuster, 1997). For a challenge to Speer's account, see G. Sereny, *Albert Speer: His Battle with Truth* (Vintage Books, 1996).

[31] See, in addition to the works already cited, M. L. Gross, *Moral Dilemmas in Modern War*, (Cambridge University Press, 2010) 100; T. Meisels, "Combatants—Lawful and Unlawful," 26 *Law & Philosophy* (2007) 31; A. Plaw, *Targeting Terrorists: A Licence to Kill?* (Ashgate, 2008); S. Miller, *Terrorism and Counter-Terrorism: Ethics and Liberal Democracy* (Oxford: Blackwell, 2009) 139.

[32] See, *inter alia*, D. Luban, "Eight Fallacies about Liberty and Security" in R. Ashby (ed.), *Human Rights in the "War on Terror"* (Cambridge University Press, 2005) 242. The position in international law is analyzed in N. Melzer, *Targeted Killing in International Law* (Oxford University Press, 2009). See also Jens Ohlin, "Targeting Co-belligerents," in this Volume, ch. 2.

increase the penalties for terrorist crimes or invest in improved techniques of crime detection, prevention, and apprehension. Above all, by using these standard tools to deal with terrorists the liberal state preserves the integrity of the liberal system, and especially of its constitutional guarantees. As the Supreme Court of the United States said in the celebrated *Milligan* case:

> The Constitution of the United States is a law for rulers and people, equally in war and in peace, and covers with the shield of its protection all classes of men, at all times and under all circumstances. No doctrine involving more pernicious consequences was ever invented by the wit of man than that any of its provisions can be suspended during any of the great exigencies of government. Such a doctrine leads directly to anarchy or despotism, but the theory of necessity on which it is based is false, for the government, within the Constitution, has all the powers granted to it which are necessary to preserve its existence.[33]

Those in the law-enforcement camp, then, claim to take the liberal constitution more seriously than their opponents, and they reject the idea that confronting terrorism requires departing from the Constitution.

Those in the second camp (the just-war view) claim that the nature of the terrorist threat is such that the only rational and effective way of confronting it is to use the tools of war making.[34] Terrorist crimes are not common crimes, for two reasons. First, the harm threatened by terrorism is so grave that the ordinary tools of the criminal law are insufficient. Terrorists will target innocent persons in large numbers using weapons with indiscriminate destructive power. Second, the terrorist threat is particularly ubiquitous. Terrorist networks usually operate in foreign nations whose governments sometimes protect and even encourage them. And whether they operate here or abroad, terrorists live normal lives as civilians, thus significantly decreasing the chances of capture. All of these facts became painfully evident on September 11, 2001, and they are equally evident in the frequent terrorist attacks that Israel experiences. For these reasons, the liberal state must defend itself by declaring war, as it were, on terrorism. The main consequence of doing this is that the liberal state has a broader moral permission to use lethal force against terrorists than the law-enforcement view would countenance. On the just-war view, the terrorist is an enemy combatant; in fact, he is an *unlawful* enemy combatant, because he is at war with the liberal state without overtly wearing the enemy uniform. The law-enforcement view unduly ignores the fact that, by his own admission, the terrorist is at war, yet he has chosen not to identify himself as a combatant, thus preventing the laws of war to operate normally.[35] The terrorist has an unfair advantage because whereas a conventional combatant can either be killed or captured, a terrorist (under the law-enforcement view) can only be

---

[33] Ex *Milligan*, 71 U.S. 2 (1866).
[34] See the works by, Gross, Meisels, and Miller, *supra*, n. 31.
[35] See Gross, 104–9; and Miller, *Terrorism and Counter-Terrorism*, 139–45, *supra* n. 31.

captured and brought to justice. He is just another criminal suspect. Worse, the terrorist claims combatant license to kill others (he regards himself at war with us) yet claims civilian immunity when the army is looking for him. This seems unacceptable. The just-war account solves this problem by treating targeted killing of a terrorist as *the functional equivalent of killing in combat*. The just-war view also claims to take the liberal constitution seriously. Doing so requires interpreting the liberal principles in a way that allows citizens to defend those very same principles.

The consequences of this debate for targeted killing are straightforward. If the law-enforcement camp is right, the liberal state is absolutely prohibited from intentionally killing a terrorist without affording him due process of law, except in the narrow set of situations in which the police may kill a terrorist under the same rules that apply to the use of lethal force in peacetime: they may kill the terrorist who fires at them or imminently threatens others, and so on. The government may try to arrest the terrorist or obtain his extradition, but it may not dispatch a sniper team to kill him. If the just-war camp is right, the liberal state may permissibly kill known terrorists on sight, just as it can kill enemy soldiers in conventional war. As in any war, in the "war on terror" the liberal state may not violate the *jus in bello* rules, but it does not have an obligation to afford the terrorist due process.

(b) What is a terrorist?

Before taking sides in this debate, we need to explore the concept of terrorism. Defining terrorism has proven especially daunting. The main reason is that it is impossible to provide a definition that is not condemnatory. The word "terrorism" has strong negative connotations. No one says "I'm a proud terrorist." The definitions offered by writers and legal documents differ, but they converge on two factors: the *method* of violence chosen by the terrorist, and his *purposes*.[36] Whatever else he does, the terrorist targets innocent persons in order to further, actually or symbolically, a political cause.

I will accept the pejorative connotation of the concept and provide a definition that reflects that condemnation. A terrorist, I stipulate, is someone who (1) *does not identify himself as a combatant*, (2) *uses immoral violent means (the deliberate killing of civilians)*, (3) *in the pursuit of an unjust political cause*. Someone who uses violence

---

[36] Bruce Hoffman's definition is typical: "Terrorism is...political violence in an asymmetrical conflict that is designed to induce terror and psychic fear...through the violent victimization and destruction of noncombatant targets." B. Hoffman, *Inside Terrorism*, 2nd edn (Columbia University Press, 2006) 34. See also the complex definition offered by S. Miller, *Terrorism and Counterterrorism: Ethics and Liberal Democracy* (Oxford: Blackwell, 2009) 53–4. Legal definitions of terrorism focus on the *method* of terrorism, not its purposes. For a sample, see S. Dycus et al., *National Security Law* (Aspen Publishing, 2007) 465–9.

in the traditional war context is a belligerent, not a terrorist. A belligerent who violates *jus in bello*, for example by deliberately targeting civilians, is a war criminal, but not a terrorist. If he pursues an unjust cause while abiding by the laws of war he is an unjust belligerent, but neither a war criminal nor a terrorist. Someone outside the traditional war context who pursues a *just* cause in violation of *jus in bello*, for example by targeting civilians, may be considered a freedom fighter who is also a criminal,[37] but not a terrorist. Finally, someone outside the war context who pursues an *unjust* cause with *moral* means is using illegitimate violence but is not a terrorist. I believe that this definition captures the two elements that explain why terrorism is so wrong. Terrorists are wrong on *two* counts. They are wrong because they use immoral means (they target civilians) *and* because they attempt to further an unjust political cause. In the case of Al Qaeda and similar religious extremists, the unjust cause is the desire to impose divine governance in accordance with the Koran.[38] Their immoral means consist in targeting the innocent in pursuit of that cause. Symbolic objectives are also encompassed by the unjust cause. When the violent immoral act conveys the message that the West is corrupt and should submit to divine governance, it communicates an unjust cause, even if the act makes no causal contribution to that objective.

The attackers of September 11, 2001, then, were doubly wrong. They were wrong because they targeted and killed civilians. This is enough, of course, to condemn them. However, they were also wrong because they pursued an unjustified political objective. If those groups decided to impose divine governance by war but respected *jus in bello*, for example by targeting only military objectives, they would be unjust enemies deserving of defeat, but not terrorists. Conversely, if a group pursues a *just* cause by immoral means they are criminals, but not terrorists under my definition. For consider: a commando attack by the French Maquis during the German occupation of France that blows up a school killing innocent children is, under my definition, a crime. But under my definition the Maquis were not terrorists, because their cause was just. Of course, this is a purely verbal question, but I want to reserve the term "terrorist" for persons who use violence meeting these two conditions. It clarifies issues better and separates terrorists from freedom fighters who commit crimes; that is, those who fight for a just cause with immoral means.

There is another reason that supports my suggestion that a terrorist should be defined by his advancement of an unjust cause, in addition to his targeting of civilians. A typical terrorist is a *principled* evildoer.[39] A theory of evil must distinguish

---

[37] I do not want to say here "war criminal" because I do not want to prejudge the issue whether anti-terrorist action is war.

[38] See J. Kelsay, *Arguing the Just War in Islam* (Harvard University Press, 2007) chs 3 and 4.

[39] I introduced the distinction in my essay "Enabling Monsters: A Reply to Professor Miller," 25 *Ethics & International Affairs* (2011) 165. There I compared different kinds of despots; here I compare different kinds of criminals.

between *opportunistic* evil and *principled* evil. Most criminals are opportunistic; they act in self-interest. Their goal is to gain something for themselves: wealth, power, or whatever. The ordinary murderer for monetary gain is in this category. But other criminals are principled. They do evil, not out of selfish motives, but because *they act out of evil maxims*. Terrorists such as Osama bin Laden belong in this category. These persons are typically fanatic and immune to corruption or other temptations. Here, being principled is a vice, not a virtue, because the value of fidelity to principle is entirely parasitic on the value of the principle. Because the terrorist has an unjust cause, his tenacious efforts to impose divine governance (to advance his unjust cause) count, morally, *against* him. The terrorist's fearlessness (shown by his willingness to die for his cause) and perseverance make him particularly objectionable, fearsome, and difficult to confront. Al Qaeda's proud admission of their crimes and their firm attachment to the principles in the name of which they commit them make them morally *worse* than if they acted for personal gain. Some may think the opposite, that the fact that they do these things sincerely in the name of Islam makes them less open to criticism. Perhaps, the argument goes, that is part of a culture that we Westerners do not fully understand. I suggest exactly the opposite: there are stronger reasons to fight principled criminals than opportunistic criminals, both because their maxim is evil and because they cannot be bribed or persuaded. The only way to stop principled evildoing is by the sword.

This intentional attachment to an evil maxim is a crucial feature of terrorists. By focusing almost exclusively on the terrorist's desire to *terrorize*, the mainstream literature has missed an important feature of this very dangerous political phenomenon.[40] It matters *why* the terrorist kills innocents. The account offered in this chapter assumes that the terrorist's reason for his killings is objectionable. If instead someone kills innocents in the pursuit of a justified aim, he should still be held accountable as a criminal, but an analysis other than the one suggested here would be required, one that would have to account for the killer's just cause. Defining the terrorist as a principled evildoer allows us to make room for his particular form of moral culpability.

(c) Peacetime and wartime settings

This analysis, however, still leaves open *which* violence the liberal state is entitled to use against terrorists. We must examine the morality of targeted killing of terrorists in two quite different settings. The first case is killing a terrorist in a setting that is *sufficiently close to a war theater*. An example would be killing a terrorist in a war zone in Afghanistan. The second and more problematic case is killing a terrorist in a setting that is *sufficiently close to a peacetime setting*. An example would be the United States' government targeting a known terrorist leader who lives in

---

[40] See the various definitions of terrorism in n. 36 above.

the United States or in a foreign country not at war—say, the United Kingdom or Saudi Arabia. I suggest that the liberal state's killing of a terrorist in a wartime setting is subject to the permissions and restrictions of killing in war, whereas the liberal state's killing of a terrorist in a peacetime setting is permissible only when necessary to avert a terrorist threat, and never if the terrorist can be captured at acceptable cost.

My proposal requires distinguishing between a wartime setting and a peacetime setting. I said something about this in my discussion of the concept of combatant in a conventional war (Section III). Here I must specify the distinction further because it is pivotal for the legitimacy of targeted killing of terrorists. To distinguish the two settings I use a *geographical-institutional* criterion. A wartime setting is a territory where the ordinary tools of crime control cannot operate because (1) rival political groups stake opposing claims to political supremacy, or (2) there are no claims to political supremacy whatsoever. A wartime setting is metaphorically a no-man's land. In contrast, a peacetime setting is a territory where, while there may be violence, there is an actual sovereign with undisputed claim to political supremacy who, for that reason, can use the standard tools of crime control. Thus Afghanistan and parts of Somalia are wartime settings; Paris, the United States, and Saudi Arabia are peacetime settings. To be sure, there are difficult cases (some of which I discuss in the next section), but this is the general line that must be drawn. If law and order reign, then the tools of crime control will presumptively apply; if instead law and order have broken down because of war, revolution, or anarchy, then the tools of war will presumptively apply.[41]

(d) Targeted killing of terrorists in a theater of war (counterinsurgency)

The analysis of targeted killing in conventional war (Section III above) applies equally to the targeted killing of a terrorist in a war theater, such as Afghanistan. There, the Western coalition is facing Taliban insurgents who use terrorist methods and have encouraged and protected Al Qaeda terrorists. This is a wartime setting as defined in the previous section, and therefore the coalition may kill insurgents because they are morally equivalent to enemy combatants. The Taliban members are terrorists to the extent that they meet the three conditions I stipulated: they do not identify themselves as combatants, they pursue an unjust cause, and they target civilians in the pursuit of that cause. They are close enough to enemy

---

[41] On September 16, 2011, John Brennan, the President's senior advisor on counterterrorism and homeland security, delivered a speech at the Harvard Law School clarifying the current Administration's security policy, including targeted killing. There he expressly rejected the geographical distinction in the text, and reaffirmed the long-standing view that the U.S. is at war with Al Qaeda. This means that, subject to a number of considerations such as "respect for a state's sovereignty and the laws of war," the U.S. is entitled to kill members of Al Qaeda regardless of location. The speech can be found at <http://www.lawfareblog.com/2011/09/john-brennans-remarks-at-hls-brookings-conference/> accessed November, 3, 2011(hereinafter *Brennan Speech*).

combatants and thus the liberal state may kill them in combat, just as it may kill enemy combatants—subject, of course, to *jus in bello* restrictions.[42] The just war view is right, I think, to deny civilian status to terrorists *in a wartime setting.* The restrictions on targeted killing in combat discussed in Section III apply, however. Just as the government may not kill Colonel Sanders while he is on vacation, it cannot kill a Taliban member sufficiently removed from the theater of operations. Also, compiling a list of terrorists in a wartime setting is not objectionable (just as it is not objectionable in regular war; see section III). The list is the substitute for the uniform and puts the terrorist on notice that he is a fair target.[43]

The difficulty with this approach is that the line between a peacetime setting and a wartime setting is often difficult to draw. I said that the distinction rests on the ability of the regular tools of crime control to operate; thus, Paris is a peacetime setting, whereas Afghanistan is a wartime setting. Other cases are not clear, however. I believe it was permissible for the Colombian government to treat terrorist organizations (or drug cartels) as enemies and target their members individually—as they targeted Pablo Escobar for assassination.[44] The Colombian government could reasonably treat the territory occupied by drug cartels and extremist groups as a wartime setting. But many settings where terrorists operate defy classification. Terrorists typically perpetrate sporadic attacks on civilians without mounting a full-blown insurrection. Can the government target them for killing? Or what about a territory that is formally at peace (in the sense that no military combat is taking place there) but where the local government harbors terrorists?[45] Again, all one can say is this: if the magnitude of the threat is sufficiently generalized to resemble an insurrection where the only plausible response is to use the armed forces, then the war paradigm will apply and targeted killings are permitted under the conditions I suggested above. If, however, the threat can be contained by law enforcement officials, then targeted killings are prohibited. I will say at once that I do not regard the present threat in the United States or in any European country as justifying treating their territories as wartime settings and thus enabling Western governments, without more, to conduct targeted killings there. (In the next section I specify when governments may target terrorists in a peacetime setting.) But I do regard the situation in Afghanistan as justifying the killing of insurrectionists, by application of the normal rules that apply to insurrections. (The right way to look at

---

[42] The laws of war distinguish between lawful and unlawful combatants, see Article 4, Third Geneva Convention, Relative to the Treatment of Prisoners of War. This distinction has been much debated in the literature; however, the argument in the text is agnostic about the moral justification of those distinctions. The distinction does not bear on the morality of targeted killing, except for the fact that the failure of the terrorist to openly identify himself as combatant contributes to the magnitude of the terrorist threat.

[43] See Gross, *supra* n. 31, 108–9.

[44] See M. Bowden, *Killing Pablo: The Hunt for the World's Greatest Outlaw* (London: Atlantic Books, 2001).

[45] For Pakistan and bin Laden, see below, Section V.

the situation in Afghanistan is that the western Coalition assists the local government in suppressing an unjust insurrection).[46]

(e) Targeted killing of terrorists in a peacetime setting

Defenders of the just-war view allow the targeted killing of terrorists in peacetime settings, such as the territories of the United States or Europe. Their argument is as follows. Terrorists do not wear uniforms and therefore they do not identify themselves as combatants. They live amongst the general population where they hide while they plan their next attack, in the assurance that the liberal state will not fire indiscriminately. Targeted killing is necessary because, as Daniel Statman says, "tanks, jets, and submarines are helpful when confronting other tanks, jets, and submarines, not hijackers carrying knives or terrorists wearing explosive belts."[47] On this view, it is not the political purpose of the terrorists that brings the conflict closer to the war paradigm: it is the nature of the threat. If this is correct, should the Mafia or a drug cartel pose a threat of similar magnitude, the government could resort, perhaps, to targeted killing. If a society becomes utterly paralyzed by drug wars, frequent street gun battles and so forth, perhaps the government can permissibly kill named criminals, even though they are not strictly terrorists but persons who kill for personal gain.[48] On the just-war view, the government can identify the possible targets. If the government *knows* who the terrorists are, it can announce publicly that these persons are enemy terrorists at war with the state, and therefore vulnerable to targeted killing. This can be done in two ways. The government may publish a *list* of known terrorists, and thus put them on notice that they can be lawfully targeted. The list performs a role analogous to the uniform in conventional war, and the publication of the list amounts to a *declaration of war* against terrorists.[49] The second method is to identify the terrorists by their membership in a terrorist organization. The government can simply announce that it is at war with Al Qaeda and that all present or future members are henceforth vulnerable to killing. This announcement would also operate as a declaration of war against Al Qaeda. For the just-war camp, either of these public acts (a list of individual names or the criterion of membership) solves the problem of identification. The liberal state is at war with the terrorists and knows who they are. Just as the liberal state can kill

---

[46] I examine some aspects of the morality of the war in Afghanistan in Tesón, *supra* n. 39.

[47] Statman, *supra* n. 24, 179.

[48] For the current situation in Mexico, see "Mexico Under Siege: The Drug War at Our Doorstep," *LA Times*, April 4, 2011, available at <http://projects.latimes.com/mexico-drug-war/#/its-a-war> accessed November 3, 2011.

[49] Curiously, this method is consistent with Lieber's aversion to assassination, *supra* n. 20. Lieber, let us recall, abhorred declaring a regular enemy soldier an outlaw and targeting him for assassination. The terrorist, however, is not a lawful enemy combatant but an *unlawful* enemy combatant, because his chosen method, targeting civilians, is immoral. Therefore, it is perfectly appropriate for the state to declare him an outlaw.

unjust enemies in a conventional war, so it can kill terrorists (who, by definition, are unjust enemies) in this war.

This argument must be rejected. The state cannot unilaterally repeal the strict moral and legal restrictions on state killing by just *declaring* war on terrorists. On the facts, the choice of the war paradigm may or may not be justified, but certainly it cannot be established by a mere statement from the government. Otherwise, the government could declare war on the Mafia, compile a list of *Mafiosi*, and announce that from now on the government will shoot them on sight. Sexual predators are especially repulsive. Why not allow the government to declare war on known sexual predators, compile a list, and start killing them? The prohibition of intentionally killing persons cannot magically disappear by the government's unilaterally declaring war on the persons it intends to kill. The criterion of membership does not fare any better, as it is overinclusive. Persons may be loosely affiliated with criminal organizations, yet in peacetime liberal principles require more than that to even *prosecute* them, let alone kill them. While in a liberal democracy we tend to trust our government, the experience with declared "wars" on terrorists and "subversives" in other societies should give us pause before abandoning the strict prohibition on deliberate killing.[50] If the named terrorist is an outlaw criminal, then it is hard to explain why the state should not treat him just like it treats any other outlaw criminal.[51] The state must in principle try to arrest and prosecute him.

Yet, while the just-war view fails to justify a broad permission to kill terrorists in peacetime, it has enough weight to prompt reconsideration of the law-enforcement paradigm. The weakness of the latter is its failure to recognize the special threat that terrorists pose, especially those whose centers of command are overseas. In particular, the dual nature of terrorists as individuals who claim license to kill indiscriminately but seek simultaneously the protection afforded by civilian status, strongly suggests that the solution to this problem must be *sui generis*.

(f) A *sui generis* standard for terrorism

In line with the conditions I set forth for targeted killing in peacetime, I propose a third solution for confronting terrorism: the liberal state may kill a targeted terrorist in peacetime *only when necessary to prevent the deaths of a substantial number of innocent persons—typically, when necessary to foil a deadly plot or a broader plan to conduct terrorist activities.* I hasten to add that the other three conditions for targeted killing in peacetime must hold as well: the contemplated target must be culpable, the liberal state must have a just cause, and capture should be impossible or prohibitive. I insist on

---

[50] A poignant example is Argentina's "dirty war" in the 1970s, where the regime targeted and killed thousands of persons that the government called terrorists and "subversives." See the chilling account in Comisión nacional sobre la desaparición de las personas, *Nunca Más* (Buenos Aires, 1985).

[51] See Gross, *supra* n. 31, 107.

this point because the existence of the threat is a necessary but not a sufficient reason to justify a targeted killing in peacetime. In addition, the liberal state must have a just cause (which, by the above definition of terrorism, it has) and the contemplated target must be morally responsible, both in the sense of endorsing the unjust cause and being causally responsible for posing the threat. A typical terrorist will often meet these conditions, but the threat alone does not suffice to justify a targeted killing. The liberal state is not justified to kill someone anytime it is necessary to avert a threat. Thus, killing innocent persons is always banned, even if necessary to suppress a threat.

A targeted killing of a terrorist (as defined above) is justified when necessary to avert a specific terrorist attack that is reasonably believed to be likely to cause the deaths of many innocents or to foil a broader plan to conduct such terrorist attacks. Notice that this condition is analogous to the first condition I specified for targeted killing in peacetime. The condition is somewhat relaxed here, however, because the number of deaths averted by killing the terrorist need not be as great as in the other peacetime cases. Recall that the normal justification for targeting a person in peacetime is to avert either a genocide or an impending war of aggression. The targeted killing of a terrorist need not avert as many likely deaths as genocide or aggressive war threaten to cause. This standard is more permissive than the normal standard for targeted killings in peacetime, yet not as permissive as the standard for state killings in a just war, where any combatant on the unjust side is permissibly targeted, regardless of how many persons he is likely to kill. This is why the treatment of terrorism is *sui generis*: it does not fall neatly into the law-enforcement camp or the just-war camp. Because the terrorist threat is ubiquitous, the threatened harm is great, and the terrorist is committed as a matter of principle to perpetrating the harm, the law-enforcement standard does not suffice. However, this does not mean that the liberal state should adopt the just-war standard, which would allow killing the terrorist on sight. The reasons supporting restraint in *peacetime* are powerful enough, I believe, to ban the killing of a terrorist merely because he is a known terrorist, or he has committed crimes in the past, or he is a member of a terrorist organization. The liberal state must protect its citizens from terrorist threat, but must also observe the restraints on the use of deadly force in peacetime, even when the temptation to take out a known enemy is great. The standard I suggest, then, mediates between the law-enforcement and just-war positions by trying to address the main concerns of each. It rejects the law-enforcement view that terrorists are just like any other criminals, by allowing the targeted killing of a terrorist who threatens to kill innocents. It likewise rejects the just-war view that known terrorists are enemy combatants who can be killed on sight regardless of the threat they actually pose.

As I indicated, the liberal state fulfills the just cause requirement by definition of what it is to be a terrorist: we saw that a terrorist pursues an unjust cause. In contrast, someone who targets innocents in pursuit of a *just* cause, for example because the government is a human rights violator and the perpetrator seeks restoration of

424

human rights, is not a terrorist. This chapter does not address that difficult situation; for our purposes, terrorists always have an unjust cause. If on reflection, citizens of the liberal state become convinced that the perpetrators of attacks against civilians have a just cause, a different analysis would be required. The requirement that the target must be culpable, or morally responsible, is also satisfied. The terrorist is culpable in a double sense: he endorses the unjust cause in the name of which he kills, and he contributes causally to the threat that the liberal state attempts to suppress. Therefore, the condition of culpability (or moral responsibility) that I required for killing in peacetime fully applies in the case of the terrorist. Here too, the condition prohibits the liberal state to kill innocent persons (such as the terrorist's family) even if the state reasonably thinks that would avert the terrorist threat.

The final condition also applies to the killing of a terrorist in peacetime: the government may not kill the terrorist without giving him the chance to surrender (subject to certain exceptions discussed below).[52] Often, if the special operations team can reach their victim they can apprehend him too. Now, either the terrorist surrenders or he resists arrest. If he surrenders, then it is morally impermissible to kill him; his captors should bring him to justice. If, on the other hand, the terrorist resists arrest, then the state agents can permissibly kill him under the rules applicable to resistance to justified arrests. Killing a person, no matter how culpable, without giving him a chance to surrender is morally impermissible.

A critic may challenge this requirement. He may argue that the onus of surrender should be on the terrorist. After all, he could have decided to surrender to the authorities at any time.[53] Because he has failed to surrender, the terrorist is now a fair target, and the liberal state does not have an obligation to give him the opportunity he himself disdained. This criticism, however, is a simple return to the war paradigm, where the just warrior can kill the enemy on sight without giving him the chance to surrender (although, of course, if the enemy does surrender he is *hors de combat* and cannot be killed). Here, however, we are in a peacetime setting and thus outside the war paradigm, and so the governing rule is the standard rule that operates in that setting. When the police encircle a common criminal, they do not kill him on sight. This is true even if the criminal, like the terrorist, failed to surrender voluntarily to the authorities. In a peacetime setting, state action against a terrorist is subject to a similar constraint. When the agents of the state encircle the terrorist they must order him to surrender before shooting. The fact that the criminal is a terrorist and not a common criminal does not make a moral difference here.

---

[52] The policy of the current U.S. Administration seems close to the view in the text, but it is not quite the same: "Whenever it is possible to capture a suspected terrorist, it is the unqualified preference of the Administration to take custody of that individual so we can obtain [vital] information," *Brennan speech, supra* n. 41. While this view is better than the view that terrorists can be freely killed without trying to capture them, it is still wanting, because it makes capture a *preferred* alternative, whereas I suggest capture is morally *required* unless impossible or morally prohibitive.

[53] I owe the point to Andy Altman.

However, there are complications. Capture may be *physically* impossible or *morally* prohibitive. Suppose the target is unreachable. The only way to kill him is shooting from afar or using drones or similar devices. In that case the condition is satisfied because the government cannot physically capture the terrorist, and killing the terrorist is permissible. (Recall that the main necessity condition applies.) Suppose, however, that the team *can* capture the terrorist but at the cost of the lives of five of its members. Killing him from afar would avoid these casualties. It is problematic to sacrifice five innocent persons (by our earlier definition of innocence, these are just warriors) just to spare the life of the terrorist. Perhaps one can say that the particular job description of the capturing team contemplates that they will risk their lives for these purposes: they would have given their lives to apprehend the terrorist. One *raison d'etre* for these special teams is precisely that they will risk their lives to protect innocents. Like police officers, SWAT teams are supposed to put their lives on the line to protect the public, so perhaps it is appropriate to pay that price for capturing the terrorist in these kinds of cases.

Now let us suppose instead that the terrorist can be captured but at the cost of the lives of five *civilians*. Here the job description rationale does not apply: these are innocent persons, and killing the terrorist instead of attempting capture would save them. This puzzle raises the question of collateral deaths in *peacetime*. What is the right way to think about these issues? Are deaths of bystanders during a police raid (regretfully) justified? If the answer is no, then the same is true in the case of capturing the terrorist, and an attempt to capture the terrorist might well be prohibited if it is likely to cause these collateral deaths. In those cases, killing the terrorist is morally preferable to attempting capture: better for him to die than the civilians.

But what if the liberal state has located a terrorist who is armed and willing to resist in a place where, the state reasonably knows, any attempt to *kill* him (he has sworn not to be taken alive) will bring about deaths of civilians? Here (unlike the previous case where the issue was capture and not killing) bringing about the deaths of civilians may be justified under some version of the doctrine of double effect. I cannot develop this complex matter here, but here is, in concise form, the view of double effect I discuss elsewhere. The deaths of civilians brought about by the state en route to killing a terrorist will be justified only if the threat to be averted is *serious enough* relative to the seriousness of bringing about those collateral deaths (and additional conditions are satisfied).[54] By the same token it is prohibited, in a peacetime setting, to bomb the terrorist's home without regard for his family or other innocent persons. The principles that apply to this situation are complex and problematic, to be sure, but not more so than those that apply to killing in conventional war.

The upshot, then, is this. The insight that terrorism calls for a *sui generis* response is correct. The law-enforcement view is wrong to claim that targeted killing of

---

[54] I discuss the doctrine of double effect in war in Lomasky and Tesón, *supra* n. 12.

terrorists in peacetime is never justified. The just war view is wrong to claim that targeting known terrorists in peacetime is justified as the functional equivalent of killing in war. The moral framework for killing terrorists is close to the one for targeted killing in *peacetime*, but not identical, because the threat in the case of the terrorist need not be as massive as the threat that would justify killing a political leader in peacetime. The permission to kill in conventional war, then, is inapplicable to terrorists outside a war zone. Because the license to kill is morally problematic even in conventional war, it should be strictly confined to that setting. Any extension to peacetime must be in principle avoided. The moral prohibition of deliberate killing is too strong to set aside every time the criminal threat increases. The liberal government should not be in the business of killing people except in extreme situations such as conventional war. However, because the terrorist scourge is *sui generis*, the government may kill a terrorist if necessary to prevent a terrorist crime, as explained. Targeted killing of a terrorist would then be, *mutatis mutandi*, the functional equivalent of killing Hitler in 1939, rather than the functional equivalent of killing an enemy combatant in conventional war.[55]

Critics may variously object. Some will say that my standard is too permissive because it does not require *imminence* of the threat. For example, Phillip Heymann and Juliette Kayemm suggest that killing a terrorist is justified only when "it is necessary to prevent a greater, *imminent* harm, or in defense against a reasonably *imminent* threat to the lives of the targets of the planned terrorist attack."[56] The idea is to restrict as much as possible this troubling practice. Targeted killing would not be available against terrorists who are planning a deadly attack that will take place some time in the more distant future, even if the killing is the only way to foil it. I am unpersuaded, however, because the requirement of imminence is clearly under inclusive, especially in this context.[57] Terrorists are ubiquitous and often engage in long-term planning. For that reason, the liberal state cannot easily forgo chances to foil their plot in the hope that it will be able to act effectively later when the threat is imminent. More generally, the requirement of imminence is in tension with the rationale for targeted killing, which lies in the legitimate interest of the liberal state to effectively protect its citizens from terrorist threats. Should imminence be required, then in some cases the state will forgo its only chance to protect civilians from deadly attack. I cannot see what can be gained by adding imminence as a requirement when the state reasonably knows that acting now may be its only chance to avert a terrorist strike.

---

[55] The argument here is strictly confined to targeted killing. It does not address other areas of disagreement between the two camps, such as whether terrorists should be tried by regular courts or military commissions.

[56] P.B. Heymann and J.N. Kayyem, *Protecting Liberty in an Age of Terror* (MIT Press, 2006) 66 (my emphasis).

[57] See R. Christopher, "Imminence in Justified Targeted Killing," in this Volume, ch. 9. Christopher makes the point that imminence may be useful as an evidentiary guideline, but it must not be confused with the underlying moral principle which, more plausibly, requires necessity.

As several criminal law scholars have argued in the context of individual self-defense, the reason to require imminence is to ensure that the defensive action is necessary.[58] Conceptually, imminence is subservient to necessity.[59]

The debate about imminence in other contexts is only marginally relevant to targeted killing. First, in international law many observers require imminence for lawful self-defense because (among other things) the harm done by a defensive *war* is catastrophic.[60] That worry does not apply to the much less harmful targeted killing of terrorists. Second, criminal law scholars who require imminence in individual self-defense are dealing with a different setting: in a targeted killing the "defender" is the liberal state, and the "attacker" is a terrorist. Importantly, in individual self-defense scholars require imminence because usually the victim has available other forms of redress. She has a background obligation not to respond with deadly force and summon the police instead. In contrast, in a targeted killing there is no one to summon. The action by the liberal state is its only chance to save innocents. And finally, in individual self-defense the attacker poses a threat to the victim, but not a larger threat to innocent third parties. The terrorist threat is typically more serious.

In short, in peacetime the liberal state may kill a terrorist only when the killing is necessary to avert a terrorist plot and capture is not physically or morally possible. Even though the government operates under a more permissive standard for using force when it confronts a terrorist than when it confronts a common criminal, the standard is far from licensing the government to treat the terrorist as a sub-human creature that can be hunted down and killed on sight.

V. The killing of Osama bin Laden

On May 1, 2011, an elite team of United States Navy SEALs killed Osama bin Laden, leader of Al Qaeda and responsible for the attacks of September 11, 2001, at a compound in Abbottabad, near Islamabad, Pakistan. According to early reports, bin Laden was shot in the head "while resisting."[61] In a speech minutes after the

---

[58] In the words of Paul Robinson: "If a threatened harm is such that it cannot be avoided if the intended victim waits until the last moment, the principle of self-defense must permit him to act earlier—as early as is required to defend himself effectively." P. Robinson, *Criminal Law Defenses* (West, 1984) § 131(c)(1), 78.

[59] The current U.S. Administration likewise rejects a strict concept of imminence. See *Brennan Speech,* supra n. 41.

[60] A summary of the debate can be found in T. Rheinold, "State Weakness, Irregular Warfare, and The Right to Self-Defense Post-9/11," 105 *American Journal of International Law* (2011) 244.

[61] See BBC News, May 2, 2011, available at <http://www.bbc.co.uk/news/world-us-canada-13256676> accessed November 3, 2011; CBS News, May 2, 2001 at <http://www.cbsnews.com/stories/2011/05/01/national/main20058777.shtml> accessed November 3, 2011; "Bin Laden is Dead, Obama Says," *New York Times,* May 2, 2011, available at <http://www.nytimes.com/2011/05/02/world/asia/osama-bin-laden-is-killed.html?pagewanted=all> accessed November 3, 2011.

operation, President Obama (who had made the capture of bin Laden a priority) said that bin Laden had been killed "after a firefight."[62] Shortly thereafter, how-ever, the official account changed. Apparently, bin Laden was unarmed when con-fronted by the Navy SEALs, although it is hard to know if the fatal shot was made in cold blood or upon some semblance of resistance.[63] John Brennan, the White House counter terrorism adviser, said that the United States would have captured bin Laden alive, "should it have had that opportunity."[64]

How does this targeted killing, the most important of all in the "war on terror," fare under the analysis presented here? The factual uncertainties are such that I cannot presume to issue a verdict here. The rationale that most people, including President Obama, endorse, that killing bin Laden was a lawful execution, an act of justice, is unavailable for the reasons I explained above. A person is not morally vulnerable to being killed on sight *only* because he committed heinous crimes in the past. Liberal principles do not condone extrajudicial execution of even the worst criminals.

The first step, then, is to determine whether Abbottabad, Pakistan, was at the time a wartime setting or a peacetime setting. If the former, then the United States had a right to kill bin Laden, an enemy combatant. If the latter, the United States could only kill him if it was necessary to avert a terrorist threat, and this only if bin Laden was given the chance to surrender (if surrender was physically possible at a relatively low cost). This incident shows how hard it can be to determine the nature of the setting. Paris is clearly a peacetime setting; Afghanistan is clearly a wartime setting. But a suburb of Islamabad, where the terrorist is hiding, according to all indica-tions, under the protection of segments of the Pakistani army, is in between the two. So if the notion of wartime setting extends to this kind of theater, where the local government is harboring terrorists, then the killing was justified as akin to killing in combat. This is a close call, but on reflection I think the concept of wartime setting

---

[62] See "Full text of Obama's Speech on Bin Laden's Death," available at <http://www.cbsnews.com/8301-503544_162-20058783-503544.html?tag=contentMain;contentBody> accessed November 3, 2011.

[63] Jim Miklaszewski, "Bin Laden 'Firefight': Only One Man Was Armed," NBC News, May 5, 2011, available at <http://www.msnbc.msn.com/id/42906279/ns/world_news-death_of_bin_laden/>. Here is a "senior official's" description of the killing: "Then, without hesitation, the same commando turned his gun on Bin Laden, standing in what appeared to be pajamas, and fired two quick shots, one to the chest and one to the head. Although there were weapons in that bedroom, Bin Laden was also unarmed when he was shot." One the most detailed accounts of the incident also reports that bin Laden was unarmed. See N. Schmidle, "Getting bin Laden," *The New Yorker*, August 8, 2011, available at <http://www.newyorker.com/reporting/2011/08/08/110808fa_fact_schmidle?currentPage=all>. The *New York Times* gives a different account: "When the commandos reached the top floor, they entered a room and saw Osama bin Laden with an AK-47 and a Makarov pistol in arm's reach. They shot and killed him, as well as wounding a woman with him." *New York Times* Topics, "The Death of Osama Bin Laden," available at <http://topics.nytimes.com/top/refer-ence/timestopics/people/b/osama_bin_laden/index.html>.

[64] See <http://www.cbsnews.com/8301-503544_162-20058913-503544.html> accessed November 3, 2011.

should be interpreted narrowly. Otherwise, the state would have a license to kill the terrorist anywhere whenever the liberal government thinks there is some local support for him. This is extending the notion of wartime setting too far.

Assuming, then, that the correct standard is the one that applies in peacetime, the next step is to determine if killing bin Laden was necessary to avert a terrorist threat. Although there is room for some doubt here, it was reasonable for the United States to believe that killing bin Laden would foil ongoing terrorist plots. After all, bin Laden's *mission* in life was to plot killings of civilians to further his political goals. Based on what he had done and what he had announced he would do, the United States could reasonably believe that killing bin Laden would avert terrorist threats, and so the killing of bin Laden, given the information we have, satisfied the necessity condition.

The real doubt arises with the question of capture. As I indicated, when capture is possible at acceptable cost killing the terrorist is morally prohibited. The crux of the issue is whether the person who killed bin Laden could reasonably have thought that bin Laden was resisting. Unfortunately, I have no way of knowing exactly what happened. As we saw, some credible reports say that bin Laden was unarmed; other equally credible reports say that he had weapons at hand. So I will put the conclusion in conditional form. If the officer who killed bin Laden reasonably thought that bin Laden was about to fire or was searching for a weapon, then the killing was permissible. But if the officer shot bin Laden while he was unarmed and not resisting, then the killing was impermissible: the officer had an obligation to capture him alive. The fact that the President's instructions were secret prevents us from establishing one crucial fact: did he order the commandos to execute bin Laden, or did he order them to capture him alive if possible? Perhaps some day we will know. The standard I propose in this chapter is incompatible with an instruction to execute a named person.

VI. General objections to targeted killings

I now turn to two objections to targeted killings. These objections may make us revise the conclusions reached above.

(a) The epistemic objection

In every instance where targeted killing is presumptively permitted, the liberal government must assess whether or not the permissibility conditions exist. In the case of Rhodelia above, the government must be sure that a genocide is afoot, that the target is culpable, and, most important, that the killing will save many innocent lives. This is seldom certain. Perhaps there is no genocide but a revolution with casualties on both sides. Perhaps the leader whose death the government is planning has nothing to do with those events. And perhaps killing him will make things worse. Governments do not have a particularly good record of making assessments of this kind. The same epistemic difficulties arise in the case of targeted killing in wartime. Here the government must ascertain even murkier facts. Is the enemy's government official in question involved in the war? Is Colonel Sanders really on vacation? Will the targeted killing really increase our chances of victory? And finally, the difficulties in ascertaining the permissibility conditions before killing a terrorist are daunting. In addition to getting the right person (identity mistakes are not uncommon), the liberal government must determine, first, if the theater is a wartime or a peacetime setting. Second, the government must determine that killing this person is necessary to avert a terrorist crime. And third, it must make sure that the operation will have acceptable collateral costs. These are unusually high epistemic barriers. While we should allow for the fact that sometimes the evidence on the ground will be clear to anyone, these barriers should give us pause before enacting a legal permission of targeted killing.

(b) The objection from virtue

Why are targeted killings morally repulsive even when they give villains their due and lead to highly beneficial consequences? One reason is the *heightened intentional focus* that characterizes targeted killing. The law assigns varying degrees of blameworthiness for outcomes. The criminal law teaches us that killing someone in self-defense is (perhaps) not blameworthy at all; killing someone as a result of negligence is somewhat blameworthy; killing someone in a rage of passion is blameworthy; and killing someone for monetary gain is very blameworthy.[65] When Colonel Sanders is commanding his troops, his unjust threat to us is imminent and proximate. Our soldiers kill him, even naming him, knowing who he is, in a situation that is quite close (though perhaps not identical) to individual self-defense.[66] The more removed he is from that situation of direct threat, the less defensible the targeted killing will be, because killing him requires *more planning*. In the law of homicide, the more *premeditated* the killing the more blameworthy it will be. However, premeditation is an aggravating circumstance when the killing is wrongful in the first place. If the killing is otherwise justified, can premeditation make it wrongful? Perhaps not, but targeted killings that are justified on the merits can still be morally troubling, even if that worry does not suffice to make it wrongful.[67]

This troubling aspect can be illuminated by reference to the idea of moral philosophers that each person has *agent-relative* reasons to refrain from killing, and not simply impersonal or agent-neutral reasons. Consider a *prima facie* justified case of targeted killing: killing the political leader of a nation that has perpetrated

---

[65] See Model Penal Code, sections 210.1–210.4.

[66] For a criticism of this assimilation, see David Rodin, *War and Self-Defense* (Oxford University Press, 2003) esp. ch. 5.

[67] Perhaps this premeditated planning is what makes the death penalty objectionable. On the other hand, one can say that the state would be blameworthy if it did not carefully plan executions.

aggression against us, where the killing will predictably end the war. All of these good consequences are *agent-neutral* reasons to kill; that is, impersonal considerations to kill the aggressor. Yet targeted killing involves detailed planning, a sure hand, cunning behavior, and nerves of steel. A morally sensitive person has reasons not to be so cold-blooded as to be able to perform such a killing or to undertake the necessary preparatory acts for it. He agrees that it would be a good thing, due to the consequences, should the villain *be* killed, but does not want to create the state of affairs where *he* kills. (This is not to say that in moral deliberation the agent-relative reasons will always prevail over the agent-neutral reasons, the good consequences.) There is an important difference between the sentences "it is a good thing that bin Laden died" and "it is a good thing that *I* killed bin Laden."

Can agent-relative reasons apply to the government? Possibly yes. The idea is that liberal governments should attempt to behave in accordance with values and virtues for which they stand.[68] This includes rejecting self-help, revenge, and random violence in favor of lawful coercion, coercion under the rule of law. This excludes assassination of any sort. The prohibition on assassination is an expression of the values embedded in the liberal social contract. Targeted killing would perhaps be understandable in the state of nature, but not in civil society, where due process and the rule of law reign supreme. Call this the *political virtue* argument. I think this argument, while not conclusive, has some weight. In considering the morality of targeted killing we must weigh not only the goodness of the villain's death, but the badness of *our government's* killing. These considerations may collapse in the face of supreme emergency, but they certainly carry substantial weight.

(c) Are the objections conclusive?

These objections carry considerable weight. The fact that governments will often err about the existence of the permissibility conditions, and the fact that the *modi operandi* of targeted killings are (arguably) troubling, point, perhaps, to one conclusion: targeted killing in peacetime should be, in principle, *legally* prohibited.[69] Not every morally permissible practice ought to be legally permitted. The law has its own logic and creates its own specific incentives. Given the proven tendency of governments to err—the many instances of government failure—it seems salutary

---

[68] I suggested this argument in my article "International Abductions, Low-Intensity Conflicts, and State Sovereignty: A Moral Inquiry," 31 *Columbia Journal of Transnational Law* (1994) 584–5. Altman and Wellman, in their excellent book on international justice, take me to task for wrongly conceiving assassination of a tyrant as punishment without due process, as opposed to suppression of a threat. While I was not altogether clear, my emphasis was not so much on the villain's due process, but on the government as assassin. I wrote: "agents of a liberal democracy must conduct themselves in a way that honors the civic virtues for which they stand." Ibid.

[69] Thus I concur with Jeremy Waldron's conclusion that targeted killings should not be legally allowed. Jeremy Waldron, "Justifying Targeted Killing With a Neutral Principle?", in this Volume, at ch. 4.

in a liberal democracy to prohibit the government from killing persons outside of war. Given how important it is for the state to stop terrorism, however, I think the highest authority in the land should have the power to waive the prohibition in cases where killing the terrorist is indeed necessary to avert a deadly terrorist attack, as I have specified in this chapter. The government should fully explain to the citizenry his reasons for waiving the prohibition. The secrecy that surrounds these operations in current liberal democracies does not help to ascertain their justification. It is important for the citizenry to understand the reasons why their government has resorted to an act as serious as a targeted killing—why the default rule against killing has been waived in a particular case. The justification for secrecy is the desire not to help the enemy; perhaps, then, the government should explain its reasons publicly after the fact. But secrecy should not serve as a way to hide from the state's *own* citizens the fact that these killings were, after all, summary executions.

VII. Concluding thought

A legitimate function of the liberal state is to protect persons from one another and from foreign enemies. In extreme cases, the state protects citizens against foreign enemies by waging war. But custom and morality have confined war, and the license to kill that it entails, to cases where the liberal state faces an organized enemy. The license to kill in war can plausibly be extended to situations where the liberal state faces commandos or terrorists in the battlefield. But the licence does not extend beyond those cases, so the state may not declare war against individuals. If the state's institutions function normally, it is bound by the strictures of the rule of law. One of the central precepts of the rule of law is the prohibition against killing anyone without due process, should that process be available. In times of peace due process is available, so the default rule is that the state may not conduct extrajudicial killings. This prohibition extends to foreigners, even if they have committed crimes. Nonetheless, I have argued that the terrorist threat justifies a departure from the prohibition when killing a terrorist is necessary to avert a crime that is likely to kill many innocents, even if the crime is not imminent. The permission to kill a terrorist in peacetime is an exception to a fundamental prohibition of state violence and must be interpreted strictly. In particular, the state must give the terrorist the chance to surrender if that option is available at an acceptable cost. These constraints reflect the fact that in a liberal democracy the morality of state coercion is not determined solely by the blameworthiness or dangerousness of bad persons, but by the values, goals, and purposes of the liberal state itself. The terrorist is a public danger and a moral monster, but those facts do not exhaust the relevant reasons for justifying state deadly violence. What *we* are, and what we may become, also matters. Perhaps that is what matters most.

16

TARGETED KILLINGS AND THE
MORALITY OF HARD CHOICES

Michael S. Moore

I. The moral topic to be examined here

Reasonably reliable sources indicate that the military attaché to the British Embassy in Berlin reported to the British government in 1938 that the SS guard around Hitler had gotten sloppy in one aspect of Hitler's security: Hitler apparently was reviewing troops within easy gunshot range for any marksman who located himself in the British mission.[1] The British officer, Colonel Noel Mason-MacFarlane, volunteered to assassinate Hitler personally, urging that doing so would forestall the calamity about to descend on the United Kingdom and the rest of Europe. Neville Chamberlain's government disapproved the assassination, reportedly with the comment that "it wouldn't be sporting."[2] My topic, roughly, is whether Chamberlain was right in not ordering an assassination of the leader of a country with whom the United Kingdom was not (yet) at war.

The echoes of Berlin in 1938 are, of course, all around us today. Israeli and American security forces regularly engage in "targeted killings" of individuals who intend to harm Israeli or American interests.[3] Such assassinations and killings do not easily fit under the rubric of wartime killings of enemy combatants, no more than would have the proposed assassination of Hitler in 1938. They thus raise the moral question that is the topic of my chapter.

---

[1] Roger Moorhouse, *Killing Hitler: The Plots, the Assassins, and the Dictator Who Cheated Death* (Random House, 2007) 190.

[2] Evan Thomas, "Assassination Is a Two-Edged Sword," Al Arabiya News, July 4, 2011.

[3] For a description of contemporary American practices, see Tara McKelvey, "Inside the Killing Machine," *Newsweek* (February 21, 2011) 34–7; for a description of recent Israeli practices, see Alan Dershowitz, *Pre-Emption: A Knife that Cuts Both Ways* (W.W. Norton, 2006) 121–40.

The topic that interests me here is purely a moral topic, as distinguished from related topics in law or in political philosophy. The topic is whether such targeted killings can ever be the morally right (permissible and perhaps even obligatory) thing to do. Such a moral question is distinct from: (a) the legal question of whether such killings violate present international or domestic law; (b) the question of political philosophy, whether such killings ought to be made illegal under international or domestic law, even if they are not already so; (c) another question of political philosophy, whether such killings ought to be publically *condemned* or even privately *believed* to be immoral/illegal by those who run our government or by those who advise (formally or informally from the academy) those who run our government. These other questions about the law we either have or ought to have, or about the conventional beliefs it would be good for our leaders to express or to hold, are important questions too, but they are different from the moral question that interests me.

What is morally right can diverge from what is (or ought to be) legally right because of a number of features of law as an institution.[4] For one thing, the law must necessarily speak in generalities, whereas morality can be as fine-grained in its resolution as the situation demands. For another thing, the law has certain formal requirements (such as clarity, prospectivity, and the like) needed for its notice-giving and administerability functions that have no analogues in morality. Also, the law is rightly concerned with the incentive effects of its rules, so its content may vary from what would be morally ideal in order to optimize desirable incentives for the actors to whom it is addressed.

What is morally right can also diverge considerably from the content of political philosophies when they are concerned with: appealing to an "overlapping consensus;" appealing to all "reasonable" points of view or to points of view that no one could "reasonably" reject; justifying beliefs even to those most disadvantaged by principles making up the contents of such beliefs; achieving neutrality or impartiality between competing conceptions of the good; etc.[5] These contemporary approaches to political philosophy also no doubt have their interest for some audiences, but they explicitly prescind away from the moral question that interests me. They each require a suspension of one's own considered moral judgments (in the name of some political ideal such as peace or agreement) in ways that rule out appeal to substantive moral theory. My own view is that such "political but not metaphysical" approaches overvalue peace and undervalue moral truth, but that is not something needing resolution here. It is enough to distinguish such political questions from the moral question to be examined here. Doing so, like

---

[4] For a discussion of some differences between legal and moral permissibility in this context, see Jeff McMahan, "Targeted Killing: Murder, Combat or Law Enforcement?" in this Volume, ch. 5.

[5] As an example of such questions of political philosophy, see Jeremy Waldron, "Justifying Targeted Killing With a Neutral Principle?," in this Volume, ch. 4.

distinguishing the legal questions too, brings into tighter focus the question of moral correctness about targeted killings that interests me.

The next clarification needed as a preliminary here has to do with the deontic nature of the question asked. The question is deontic in the sense that it asks what we should *do* in these situations. That is distinct from the aretaic question of how one should *feel* about what it is we should do. It has often and correctly been pointed out that difficult moral choices are often "no-win" situations for those who make them, in the sense that no matter which way such actors choose, they feel regretful, ashamed, and guilty.[6] Moreover, on some plausible theories of the virtues, people *ought* to feel these ways, even when they make the right choice.[7] But notice that such aretaic judgments need not affect the deontic truth about actions: it can be right to assassinate the next Hitler, no matter how guilty that makes one feel and no matter how virtuous it might be to feel such guilt.

Likewise, one must put aside considerations about what it might be politic to *say* about what one should do in such situations. For there are surely contexts in which it is impolitic, harmful, or even immoral to say what is morally true. Perhaps the recent torture debate is illustrative. I have long believed that torture is sometimes permissible to prevent significant harm in certain circumstances.[8] However, saying this to the wrong audiences can lead to impermissible abuses, Abu Ghraib being a case in point. So reasons to believe such moral truths as those about torture are not necessarily reasons to say publicly what one believes. Still, such (perhaps obligatory) restraint in expression does not touch on the truth of what is or is not expressed. And it is only the latter with which I am here concerned.

II. The generality of any plausible answer about the morality of targeted killings

What is needed to answer my moral query about targeted killings is something quite general. We need an ethical framework employable for many moral dilemmas besides that of targeted killings. For targeted killings scenarios are but an instance of what in

---

[6] Herbert Morris explores a variety of "non-moral guilt" feelings, of which this is a species, in his "Non-Moral Guilt" in F. Schoeman(ed.), *Responsibility, Character, and the Emotions* (Cambridge University Press, 1987).

[7] On the "emotional tail" people are thought virtuous to feel in these circumstances, see Bernard Williams, "Ethical Consistency," *Proceedings of the Aristotelian Society, Supp. Vol.*, Vol. 39 (1965) 103, 107–8.

[8] Michael S. Moore, "Torture and the Balance of Evils," *Israel Law Review*, Vol. 23 (1989) 280–344 reprinted in Moore, *Placing Blame: A General Theory of the Criminal Law* (Oxford University Press, 1997) ch. 17; Moore, "Patrolling the Borders of Consequentialist Justification," *Law and Philosophy*, Vol. 27 (2008) 35–96, reprinted in Moore, *Causation and Responsibility: An Essay in Law, Morals, and Metaphysics* (Oxford University Press, 2009) ch. 3.

general are usually categorized as moral dilemmas.[9] Such moral dilemmas are found whenever two or more quite plausible moral principles recommend diverging courses of action on particular occasions. Surely it is plausible, for example, to think that we are obligated not to murder people even when they say things that we do not like, as did Hitler. But it is also plausible that we should prevent the murders of millions of people, if we can do so. Such hard choices between conflicting moral principles are a familiar feature of our moral life. Well-known examples are to be found not only in contexts of assassinations and targeted killings, but also in questions of: triage in medical contexts, where medical resources are insufficient to save all;[10] jettison on the high seas, where planks or boats are insufficient to save all who need them;[11] rescue situations, where not all can be rescued; combat situations, where some must be sacrificed if others are to get through; starvation on the high seas or in remote regions, where the only available food is the flesh of others about to die anyway;[12] mountaineering situations, where ropes supporting some must be cut if others are to survive;[13] flame-outs and other crashing aircraft scenarios, where pilots must choose whether to redirect their aircraft from hospitals and schools to other, less populated locations; wartime choices of whether to warn civilian populations of impending attack where to do so would reveal one's penetration of the enemy's intelligence or communication systems;[14] wartime decisions about deliberate redirection of enemy rockets from more to less crowded civilian centers;[15] torturing terrorist suspects to reveal life-saving information;[16] transporting such suspects to other countries for torture impermissible in one's own, when such tortures will reveal life-saving information;[17]

---

[9] On the nature of moral dilemmas generally, see Michael Moore, "Moral Reality Revisited," *Michigan Law Review*, Vol. 90 (1992) 2423–533, 2463, reprinted in Moore, *Objectivity in Ethics and Law* (Ashgate, 2007).

[10] A famous example was described by *Life* magazine in 1958, where Seattle formed a "God Committee" to decide who should receive the then scarce respirators needed to live. (The Committee was so named because it attempted to rank potential recipients by the worthiness of their lives.) On triage generally, see Jonathan Glover, *Causing Death and Saving Lives* (Penguin Books, 1977) 203–27.

[11] As in *United States v. Holmes*, 26 Fed. Cas. 360 (Cir. Ct. F.D. Pa 1842), where some passengers were jettisoned from a sinking and overcrowded lifeboat.

[12] *Regina v. Dudley and Stephens*, 14 QBD 273 (1884) is the most famous murder/cannibalism case. For how common these were in the nineteenth century, see A.W.B. Simpson, *Cannibalism and the Common Law* (Oxford University Press, 1984).

[13] An example behind the Model Penal Code's Section 3.02 balance of evils provision. See *Model Penal Code and Commentaries* (American Law Institute, 1985). For a real-life example, see the well-told tale (recently made into a film) by Joe Simpson, *Torching the Void* (Harper Collins, 1988).

[14] William Stephenson, in his *A Man Called Intrepid: The Secret War* (The Lyon Press, 1976), describes a decision of this kind by Churchill during the Second World War with respect to the German bombing of Coventry.

[15] Another Churchill decision during the Second World War. Ibid. at 414. See also Jonathan Glover, *Causing Death and Saving Lives* (Penguin, 1977) 102.

[16] I discuss some Israeli cases of this in Moore, "Torture and the Balance of Evils," *supra* n. 8, and some American cases of this in Moore, "Patrolling the Borders" *supra* n. 8.

[17] The euphemistically labeled "extraordinary renditions" of the American Central Intelligence Agency (CIA) were an exempt of this. The CIA's practice in this regard is discussed in some detail in Jane Mayer, "Outsourcing Torture," *The New Yorker* (February 14, 2005) 106–23.

choosing whether to separate Siamese twins who otherwise will both die, when such separation will surely kill one of such twins;[18] choosing which child to save when one cannot save both;[19] shooting down civilian airliners when they are targeted at large civilian populations or crucial governmental or economic functions;[20] etc. The sad fact is that the world is full of such moral dilemmas, the general form of which is the same. To resolve any of them adequately demands recourse to something equally general, viz., something no less general than our overall deontic framework for all obligatory/permissible actions.

III. The possibility of finding objective answers to such questions of pure morality

There are a number of skepticisms about this enterprise that need to be defused for those otherwise inclined towards them. One stems from a general skepticism about morality itself. Common forms of such skepticism are:[21] relativism, where there are moral truths but these are relative to the conventional moral beliefs prevalent in a given society; subjectivism, where moral truth is relativized to each individual's subjective moral beliefs; non-cognitivism, where moral expressions are interpreted as serving exclusively non-descriptive functions and thus lacking any truth value, being neither true nor false; and cognitivist error theories, according to which moral statements do not lack truth values but such statements are always false because what such statements say exists (such as justice, fairness, etc.) never in fact exists.

I have elsewhere urged that general moral skepticisms such as these are the disease of our age because they demotivate all moral enquiries, this one included. I have accordingly devoted considerable effort elsewhere to showing such skepticisms to be false.[22] My general take on all such skepticisms is that they do not correspond to anyone's actual, lived moral experience. None of us experience moral choices as arbitrary and not mattering; none of us experience ourselves as incapable of moral error, either in our individual or in our collective judgments as a society. Recapitulating any detailed refutation of such skepticisms is a task beyond the present chapter, however. What can be done here is to look at more particular skepticisms about there being solutions to moral dilemmas that are not based in some more general skepticism about morality.

---

[18] See *In re A* [2001] Fam. 147, when the court faced the issue of whether to separate Mary from Jodie, when to do so would kill Mary but when not to do so would allow both to die.

[19] The choice in the film, *Sophie's Choice*, Dir. Alan J. Pakula, Incorporated Television Company, 1982.

[20] President Bush's choice regarding United Flight No. 93 on September 11, 2001, had the passengers on that flight not taken matters into their own hands.

[21] I survey a variety of general moral skepticisms in Moore, "Moral Reality," *Wisconsin Law Review*, Vol. [1982] 1061–156, reprinted in Moore, *Objectivity in Ethics and Law, supra* n. 9.

[22] Moore, "Moral Reality" *supra* n. 21; Moore, "Moral Reality Revisited" *supra* n. 9.

One of these more particular skepticisms is to think that moral reasons are incommensurable, so that when they conflict (as they do in moral dilemmas) there is no weighing up to be done. Alternatively, one might think that conflicting moral reasons are often equally weighty and thus in equipoise in their recommended action. In either case the results for rational decision-making would be unhappy. There would be two possibilities: either we are not obligated either way, meaning we are free to do either action, or each obligation still applies to us with undiminished force, so that whatever we do, we act immorally.

The first of these possibilities is one interpretation of the old saying (of Cicero, Aquinas, Kant, Bacon, Holmes, and others) that "necessity knows no law."[23] On this view, such irresolvable conflict of moral reasons takes us "beyond morality" to a realm where we must do what we must do, for whatever mysterious reason as may move us.[24] Morality, on this view, is only for simpler situations; when the going gets tough, it has nothing to say and we must navigate as best we can by our own lights.

The second of these possibilities is what Kant described as "inconceivable;"[25] namely, we are damned if we do and damned if we don't, because all possible courses of action (or inaction) are forbidden to us. Kant was surely offering up a bit of hyperbole when he said that such a morality was inconceivable; yet conceivable or not, such a morality would surely be unfair. Morality, on such a view, would become a kind of joke on the human race, the sort of thing some not-so-benevolent Greek God would foist off on us.

These more particular skepticisms about moral dilemmas make morality either ridiculously non-constraining (the first possibility) or ridiculously unfair (the second) in its condemnations. It is implausible that conflict frees us of all constraints (the first possibility), and equally implausible that conflict guarantees us moral failure (the second).The morality most of us experience looks nothing like either of these possibilities.

---

[23] O.W. Holmes, *The Common Law* (Little, Brown, 1881) 47; I. Kant, *The Metaphysical Elements of Justice*, J. Ladd, trans. (Bobbs-Merrill, 1965) 41–2; Sir Francis Bacon, *Maxims*, reg. 25; Bacon is excerpted in Shedding, Ellis and Heath, *The Works of Francis Bacon* (Parry and McMillan, 1859) 343.

[24] The late Bernard Williams' well-known views. Williams "Utilitarianism: Against" in J.J.C. Smart and Bernard Williams, *Utilitarianism, For and Against* (University of California Press, 1973) 92:

> there are certain situations so monstrous that the idea that the processes of moral rationality could yield an answer in them is insane: They are situations which so transcend in enormity the human business of moral deliberation that from a moral point of view it cannot matter any more what happens.

I discuss these views in Moore, "Torture and the Balance of Evils" *supra* n. 8, in *Placing Blame,supra* n. 8, 729–30.

[25] Kant, *supra* n. 23, 25.

Two remaining skepticisms are different. They assume that morality may deliver up answers to the most difficult of moral dilemmas, answers that are both objectively true and epistemically accessible to us. Yet for one reason or another, morality's answers are not the ones we should use when we act to resolve such dilemmas. Something else, it is thought, "trumps" morality when it comes to deciding what to do.

The first skepticism here is that the law is what makes morality irrelevant. The idea is that law obligates obedience by its subjects, so that what the law condemns, morality cannot condone, and what the law condones, morality cannot condemn. This view surfaces, for example, in the arguments of those who regard treaty obligations as decisive of what is morally permissible in the international arena; it also surfaces in the arguments of those who excuse any who obey lawful orders in the military, no matter how outrageous the actions such orders require of their subjects.

Such a conclusive role for law in our practical reasonings would certainly render irrelevant enquires such as this, divorced as they are from the law. Yet law surely has no such conclusive normative force, no matter what may be its pretensions to the contrary. Immoral but lawful military orders are not conclusive of what those subject to them should do; treaty-based and other international legal obligations are not conclusive of what our political leaders should do in targeting terrorists for killing, torture, or anything else. It is debatable whether the law even prima facie obligates citizens or official obedience;[26] however that debate is resolved, it surely is not plausible to cede law *conclusive* moral authority. The question of what it is morally right to do is open, no matter what the law may say on the subject.

A second thought (about what may "trump" morality) is more diffuse and difficult to pin down. Yet it surfaces in some form in all discussions of moral dilemmas between academics and those "in the field." Put simply, it is that morality is too impractical, too idealistic, too unrealistic, to be used in actual practice. It is *academic*, in a pejorative sense of that term. Morality on this view is said to be "trumped" by common sense, or practical realities, or some such thing.

Yet what exactly is this thought? Can it really be the claim that there are reasons for action more important than moral reasons? That morality, like the law, is just one more consideration among others, and not always the most important one to boot? One might well so regard *conventional* morality; that is, the practices and beliefs of a people with whom one only partly agrees. But can any of us so regard his or her own best thoughts about what morality really requires?

---

[26] Some of the now classic discussions of the "new anarchists" are M.B.E. Smith, "Is There a *Prima Facie* Reason to Obey the Law?," *Yale Law Journal*, Vol. 82 (1973) 950–76; Joseph Raz, *The Morality of Freedom* (Oxford University Press, 1986) chs 2–4; Heidi Hurd, "Sovereignty in Silence," *Yale Law Journal*, Vol. 99 (1990) 945–1028, 1007; Hurd, "Challenging Authority," *Yale Law Journal*, Vol. 100 (1991) 1611–77.

Again, we all experience some weakness of will. We all know that, like St Paul in Romans vii, we can know the good but do the bad. We may even excuse such akrasia in ourselves. But that is worlds apart from thinking it *right* to do the morally *wrong* thing because common sense, practical realities, or whatever, so dictate.

I conclude that the only sense to be made of this common enough skepticism is the epistemic sense. Surely the idea only amounts to this: abstract moral theory often glosses over important nuances of particular moral choices, and insofar as it does so, such abstract theory is to be corrected or even ignored. Yet what makes nuances important is nothing other than another moral theory—a better, because more nuanced, moral theory—but moral theory nonetheless. There is no higher standard for determining what we ought to do than a moral standard—recognizing that that has to be as nuanced, as context-sensitive, as responsive to real interests, as moral correctness demands.

IV. The desirability of finding objective answers to such questions of pure morality

To say that a thing is possible to do is not, of course, to say that such a thing is desirable to do. I have yet to answer why anyone should care about my moral question as I have defined and clarified it. Motivational questions are usefully divided up by those who are asking them. Consider first those actors within the American and Israeli intelligence community who are now making, will make, or have made, such decisions about targeted killings. For those presently making such decisions, or those who will do so in the future, what could be more relevant than assessing the morality of their prospective actions? Once one puts aside the skepticisms just mentioned, such actors have to ask and answer my moral question in order to decide rationally what to do.

Even for actors who made such decisions in the past but are no longer making them (such as John Rizzo of the CIA),[27] there is reason to ask and answer my question of moral assessment. Like all of us, such actors should want to be "in session with themselves"[28] to assess whether they acted in a morally proper way or not. Even when no corrective actions are possible, each of us should want to know how it stands with our moral ledger. We want to ask Harry Truman's kind of retrospective question (about his decision to bomb Hiroshima and Nagasaki),[29] Earl Warren's

---

[27] Rizzo's role in targeted killings is described in McKelvey, *supra* n. 3.

[28] Edmund Cahn's phrase, in describing Learned Hand reflecting on questions of good moral character and the like. Edmund Cahn, *The Moral Decision* (Indiana University Press, 1955).

[29] Truman's thoughts in this regard are described in David McCullough's *Truman* (Simon and Schuster, 1992).

kind of question (about his decisions regarding the Japanese interments during the Second World War),[30] the Shin Bet's kind of question about whether they did the right thing in beating two terrorists to death after they had taken the 300 Bus in the Sanai in the 1980s.[31] We all want to assess how we have done in this life, and our resolutions of moral dilemmas (where there was something to be said for the choice we did not make) can be a critical part of this assessment.

Most of those reading this chapter will not, of course, be persons who have ordered or themselves performed targeted killings, nor will they do so in the future. The morality of targeted killings thus does not affect their moral ledgers directly one way or the other. Yet we all should be concerned about the morality of our government's actions when that government acts in our name. One of Abraham Lincoln's favorite quotations was of John Winthrop, early governor of the Massachusetts Bay Colony. Winthrop famously told those early Americans that they should create a "new City upon a Hill for the eyes of the world were upon their efforts."[32] Few governmental actions speak for us as loudly as those of our military and intelligence services. The stakes are high, the temptations severe, the measure of who we are clearly visible for all to see. If our military or intelligence communities behave badly, they do so in our name and we are ashamed; whereas if they behave well in such circumstances, they make us proud. We all thus have an interest and a stake in the morality of governmental actions such as targeted killings.

For those in positions of power—legal policymakers—the interest in this question is even more direct. I earlier distinguished my moral question from the legal question of what current law provides. I also separated the moral question from the political philosophy question of what the law ought to provide. Yet even while reaffirming these distinctions, we should see that the moral question is not irrelevant to the question of what the law does or should provide in regards to targeted killings. Criminal law, for example, largely punishes only when it can blame, and on any plausible theory of punishment, criminal law should only punish those who are morally blameworthy.[33] Being morally blameworthy, in turn, requires one to have done something morally wrong, either in fact or at least in one's own mind. Whether an act (such as targeted killings) is morally wrong thus enters into both the criminal law we have and the criminal law we ought to have, even though an act's moral status is not by itself determinative of that act's legal status.

---

[30] Earl Warren's later reflections on his Japanese internment decision are described in G. Edward *Earl Warren: A Public Life* (Oxford University Press, 1982).

[31] Three Shin Bet lawyers participated in these decisions, one of whom, at his retirement recently, said he had no regrets about those decisions.

[32] John Winthrop, "A Modell of Christian Charity" (1630), reprinted in *Hanover Historical Texts Project* (Massachusetts Historical Society, 3rd Series 1838).

[33] See Moore, *Placing Blame, supra* n. 8.

V. Two straightforward but unsatisfactory views of when any action is morally right

There are two attractively simple views about what morality demands of us and what it permits us to do. One is usually termed a consequentialist (or "agent-neutral") view,[34] of which the most familiar variant is utilitarianism. A consequentialist believes two things: first, that the basic kinds of things that are valuable are states of affairs, second, that right action consists in maximizing good states of affairs, and minimizing bad states of affairs.

Consequentialism thus consists of two theories. The first is a theory of the (intrinsic) good. Such a theory marks out some state(s) of affairs as intrinsically good, others (perhaps but not necessarily derivatively) as intrinsically bad. All other states of affairs can be judged instrumentally good or bad, depending on how they contribute causally to what is intrinsically good or bad.

Utilitarianism usefully illustrates this first aspect of consequentialism.[35] Utilitarians believe that only one thing is intrinsically good: human welfare. Exactly what such welfare consists of varies within utilitarian theory: Bentham equated human welfare with pleasure, John Stuart Mill with the broader notion of happiness, the post-Paretian economic utilitarians with preference-satisfaction (which may or may not give pleasure or make one happy). Normative (or "objective") utilitarianism equates human welfare with identifiable human *needs*, rather than desires. But however fleshed out, the general idea is that human welfare is intrinsically good and all other states of affairs are instrumentally good insofar as they contribute to such human welfare, bad insofar as they detract from it.

The second theory needed by consequentialists is a theory of right *action*. On the plausible supposition that if something is good, more of that thing is better, the consequentialist theory of right action is a maximizing theory: right action maximizes intrinsically good states of affairs and minimizes intrinsically bad states of affairs. For a utilitarian-consequentialist, thus, actions are morally right when but only when they maximize human welfare. Each person's welfare counts equally in doing such utilitarian calculations; that is, your happiness gets no extra weight when it is you doing the calculation, just because that happiness is yours. Utilitarianism is not a kind of rational egoism, in other words.

The radically different but equally simple view of the deontic part of ethics is usually termed the deontological (or "agent-relative," or "non-consequentialist")

---

[34] For an introduction to these terms, see the classic essays on this topic collected in Samuel Scheffler, *Consequentialism and Its Critics* (Oxford University Press, 1988).

[35] An overview of utilitarianism is supplied in Anthony Quinton, *Utilitarian Ethics*, 2nd edn (Duckworth, 2007).

view.[36] Being rational and moral on this view does not consist in doing those actions that maximize good states of affairs and minimize bad ones; states of affairs are not the locus of value at all, on deontological views. Rather, it is actions themselves that are either intrinsically right or intrinsically wrong to do. Right action consists in conforming to moral norms that either permit or require that certain kinds of actions either be done or not be done. Such norms do not direct agents to maximize the satisfaction of such norms; rather, they are personally directed ("agent-relative") norms categorically telling each agent either to do, or not to do, certain actions. They say to each moral agent, "Don't you do some action A" (such as torture), not even when A-ing on this occasion would minimize A-ing overall in the long run.

Two examples may help make plain the distinction between consequentialist and deontological views of morally right action. The first comes from the waning days of the Soviet Union. Middle Eastern terrorists had captured four Soviet diplomats. They then made certain demands on the Soviet Union accompanied by threats to kill the diplomats if the demands were not met.[37] The terrorists then killed one of the diplomats to show they were serious in their demands. The KGB knew who the terrorists were but were powerless to attack them directly. So the KGB killed an innocent relative of one of the terrorists, a relative who had had nothing to do with the kidnapping or killing of the Soviet diplomats, and let it be known that they (the KGB) would kill every relative of the terrorists in the Middle East if the remaining three Soviet diplomats were not released unharmed. Believing the KGB, the terrorists released the three Soviet diplomats, and no further kidnappings of Soviet officials again took place in the Middle East.

On the plausible view that the killing of innocents is bad, a consequentialist should approve of the KGB's action of killing the one innocent relative of the terrorists. The KGB caused one bad state of affairs, to be sure, but that same act prevented three other equally bad states of affairs from taking place, namely, there were no killings of the three remaining Soviet diplomats. On the consequentialist view, it does not matter that it was the KGB that did some killing, or that the killings prevented would not have been by the KGB—for consequentialism is "agent-neutral" in the sense that the identity of the agent does not matter. What matters is that three bad states of affairs were prevented by bringing into existence one bad state of affairs; the world is better off by a net gain of two bad states of affairs that do not exist.

A deontologist sees the case much differently. The relevant moral norm says, "Don't you kill an innocent." That other killings (by you or by others in the future) will be prevented

---

[36] For an introductory overview of deontological ethics, see Larry Alexander and Michael Moore, "Deontological Ethics" in Edward N. Zalta (ed.), *The Stanford Encyclopedia of Philosophy* (Fall 2008 edition), available at <http://plato.stanford.edu/archives/fall2008/entries/ethics-deontological/> accessed November 3, 2011.

[37] See Ihsan A. Hijazi, "Beirut Captors Free 3 Russians After a Month," *New York Times,* October 31, 1985, A-1; Charles Chi Halevi, "A Hard United Line on the Mideast," *Chicago Tribune,* August 22, 1989, 17.

by the killing of an innocent here and now, is neither here nor there for a deontologist. The norm is personal and absolute: no matter what, "Thou shalt not kill."

I customarily raise this KGB example in my criminal law classes to illustrate the difference between consequentialist and deontological ethics. One year at the University of Virginia a burly male student at the back of my class interrupted my presentation by proclaiming that he was a former KGB Colonel who regularly taught this case in his teaching of KGB officers in Moscow. I asked him how he taught the case; his reply was pure consequentialism: "big success—one dead Arab, innocent to be sure, but three not-dead Soviet diplomats who were equally innocent." To test his deontological intuitions I asked, "But what about human rights?" His reply was again pure consequentialism, but of a non-utilitarian kind: "Rights? You want to talk about rights? One right violated in order to prevent three equally important rights from being violated. Net gain, two rights not violated." I concluded with a reminder of what many find compelling about deontology: "Amnesty International must have given you guys their annual award for human rights protection. Or did you miss something essential about rights (and their correlative duties): that they categorically are not to be violated, even in the name of minimizing rights-violations?"

The second example is self-defense. Except for a few Quakers and others, everyone concedes that each of us does no wrong in killing an attacker when necessary to save our own life. Most people also agree that it is permissible to kill an attacker who threatens some evil less than our own death, an evil such as rape, other forms of sexual assault, or kidnapping; most also think that we may kill as many attackers as it takes to save our own (one) life.[38] These moral conclusions should be problematic for a consequentialist. For in these cases we seemingly cause a worse state of affairs to exist in order to prevent a less bad state of affairs from existing. This remains true even if we discount the lives of aggressors; at some point the harm threatened by them should become small enough, or the harm done to a large enough number of them great enough, that any consequentialist-based permission to kill them evaporates. The deontological intuition is that our right of self-defense never evaporates in these ways, that for example, we can kill without limit all who are trying to kill us.

There are deep problems for each of these two simple views of morality. Among other things, consequentialism seems strikingly out-of-tune with moral intuitions that are very difficult to give up. Paradoxically, consequentialism's illness of fit has two opposed dimensions: consequentialism is both too demanding of us, and it does not demand enough of us. It is too demanding of us when it requires us to lay down our own life, for example, when our only way to save ourselves is to kill many culpable agressors who are out to kill us. It is not demanding enough, for example, when it permits us to kill one innocent in order to deter the killings of three other innocents by others.

---

[38] The Model Penal Code's conclusions, e.g., reflecting what I take to be the common moral view. *Model Penal Code and Commentaries*, Section 3.04.

Likewise, the simple deontological view I have sketched has deep problems, of which I shall mention three. (Most of these three have to do with such a simple deontological view being too demanding of us.) The first has to do with the content of the absolute (or categorical) norms of deontological morality. "Thou shalt not kill," for example, is only a start at specifying when morality forbids us to kill. If one has only one stone tablet with which to work, fair enough, this is an important start. But in a modern criminal code with between 7,000 and 15,000 prohibitions, surely we can (and must) more completely specify the content of the norm against killing. "Thou shalt not kill, unless in self-defense, in defense of others, in effecting a lawful arrest of a fleeing and dangerous felon, in fighting a just war...etc.," comes closer to what we intuitively think can rightly be demanded of us.

The second problem has to do with the force—the "absoluteness" or "categorical" nature—of deontological moral norms. Kant, a well-known proponent of deontological ethics, once proclaimed that it was better that the Heavens fall and the human race should perish than that an injustice be done.[39] This rightly strikes many people as absurd, a bit of hyperbole that cannot literally be true. If the only way to find and defuse a nuclear bomb planted by a terrorist somewhere in New York City is by torturing to death his child in front of him I, like many others, think you torture the child to death if necessary. Allowing the catastrophe of millions of deaths to occur because one innocent's rights must be violated gives too strong a force to those rights (and correlative duties) to be plausible.

The third problem for a simple deontological view of ethics lies in the potential for conflict between our absolute obligations. Kant perceived the problem, and proclaimed that a conflict of such obligations was "inconceivable."[40] Like the protagonist in the film, *The Princess Bride*, I do not think Kant means what we mean by "inconceivable." For surely such conflict of obligations is not only conceivable; it is seemingly quite possible. If I am categorically obligated to save you, and equally obligated to save another, and both you and she are in peril and I cannot save both, I seem to be in a no-win situation: whatever I do, I do wrong. This is not inconceivable; but it is surely unfair. If a view of morality gives us no chance of moral success because of such conflict of obligations, that is a reason to reject such a view.

These problems of under-and-over demandingness keep me from accepting either of these simple views of ethics, a pure consequentialism or a pure deontology. Yet I raise these simple theories not just to reject them, but to learn from them. They each have their intuitive tugs, do they not? The trick is to combine them into an overall view of ethics that accommodates our intuitions better than can either simple view.

---

[39] Kant, *supra* n. 23, 100.
[40] Ibid. at 25.

VI. The three-level analysis of ethics

My own long-held view of the deontic part of ethics is best unpacked in terms of three levels of analysis.[41] The basic picture is of an omnipresent consequentialism, one that is nonetheless subject to two kinds of deontological restrictions, those of strong permissions and of stringent obligations. These restrictions themselves are subject to an override in situations of moral catastrophe. Let me examine this picture, one level at a time.

Most of what we do is governed by consequentialist reasons. I sometimes put this as a slogan: "Man cannot live by deontology alone." Rational decision-making for most of our daily decisions is rational and moral, not because the actions decided upon instantiate categorical norms of permission or obligation, but rather because such actions produce good states of affairs or prevent bad states of affairs. Take the decision as to when a law school should begin its classes for the fall semester. Plausible reasons for choosing one date rather than another are considerations of faculty convenience, maximizing student summer employment opportunities, coordinating with the start dates of other units on campuses, etc. Implausible would be an argument of deontology, such as one I heard many years ago: "Whatever the balance of consequences in favor of moving the start date, it cannot be moved because faculty coming to the school have the right to the start date in place when they came."

In general, it is extremely plausible, is it not, that the right thing to do is the action that produces the best consequences, on the whole? Whatever one's theory of the good, surely it is usually rational and moral to choose actions productive of more of that good rather than less. We thus operate in an omnipresent, background sea of consequentialist reasons. Such reasons always bear on our actions, even in cases where they lose out because of deontological considerations. The omnipresence of such consequentialist reasons is what makes the kinds of life-and-death decisions earlier mentioned so hard and so problematic. It is this omnipresence of consequentialism that gives rise to moral dilemmas of the kind I want here to examine.

The force of consequentialist reasons can become so compelling that such reasons can constitute moral obligations. These are non-deontological obligations, to be sure, but genuine obligations nonetheless. We each have reason, for example, to rescue strangers from perils when we can do so at little risk or inconvenience to

---

[41] Explored by me in Moore, *Causation and Responsibility*, *supra* n. 8, 36–41. The three-level analysis is far from universally accepted, although it is getting some adoptions by other ethicists. See, e.g., Jeffrey Brand-Ballard, who regards the analysis as being an "illuminating framework for thinking about the relationship between deontological and consequentialist reasons." Brand-Ballard further "recommends [this framework] to deontologists. It seems as internally consistent and plausible as any deontological position with which I am familiar." "Moral Emotions and Culpability for Resultant Harm," *Rutgers Law Journal* 2012, forthcoming.

ourselves. Unlike the libertarians, I take this to be obligatory: we do wrong when we omit to help others in such circumstances. Yet the wrong we do is a consequentialist-based wrong, not one based in deontology. We can see this by seeing the ease with which we can justify apparent violations of this duty by good consequentialist reasons: I can easily justify omitting to save one if I instead save two, in situations where I cannot save all. Being based on good consequences, our duty to rescue evaporates when those consequences are not, on balance, as good as they could be. Whereas if our duty of rescue is deontological (as I think it is for our children, for example), such good consequences (as saving two rather than one) would not justify the omitting to save one.

This gets us to my second level of analysis: deontological suspensions of consequentialist reasons. There are two kinds of such suspensions: deontological permissions and deontological obligations. Sometimes we are permitted to do actions (such as self-defense) even when they are not productive of the best consequences on the whole; sometimes we are obligated not to do actions (such as the KGB's action of killing an innocent Arab) even though such actions would be productive of the best consequences on the whole. The right way to see these restrictions is as a kind of overlay, or "side-constraint," on consequentialist reasons. In such cases our deontological reasons do not outweigh our consequentialist reasons; rather, our deontological permissions and obligations preempt the consequentialist reasons from having their normal sway in determining what is rational and moral to do.

It is a long-standing puzzle in ethics just why or how consequentialist rationality can be preempted in these two ways.[42] I have no new solution to that puzzle to lay before you here. Yet it is very intuitive, is it not, that we are permitted to lead our lives in ways not always productive of the best consequences? How could one justify, for example, a good dinner out on the town if one was required to maximize good consequences (as by giving the money for the dinner to those more in need of basic sustenance)? How could one justify, as another example, refusing to have bone marrow extraction if that was the only way to save another (whose DNA uniquely matches your own) from death? A pure consequentialism never preempted by deontological permissions is a saintly mode of being that is not required (and, to my way of thinking, is not always even virtuous). Likewise, the KGB's killing of one innocent to save three would be justified by true consequentialists; yet it (and thousands of examples like it) flies in the face of what most of us think is moral to do. I cannot take your property, your spouse, your children, your bone marrow, or your life, just because doing so will make them and others better off more than doing so makes you worse off. Our rights-based duties have a stickiness to them that rejects as irrelevant consequentialist justifications such as these.

---

[42] See the survey of possibilities in Scheffler, *supra* n. 34.

We have then, deontological permissions (such as the right to defend ourselves against wrongful aggressors), and deontological obligations (such as the duty not to torture or kill) that exist even though doing or omitting to do these actions is not productive of net good consequences. Such permissions and obligations operate as overlays on omnipresent consequentialist reasons, overlays that preempt such reasons from having their normal determinative effect on rational choice.

Merely combining consequentialism and deontology in this way so far only alleviates the problems besetting a pure consequentialism. (It does this by making such a side-constrained consequentialism neither too lenient nor too demanding.) It does not alleviate the three problems of deontology I earlier alluded to, problems largely having to do with the seeming over-demandingness of deontology. So I need to say more about how this three-level analysis of ethics is not subject to these three problems.

The first problem was that of content. "Thou shalt not kill," while short and snappy and nicely fitting onto one stone tablet, misses all the situations where killing seems permissible to almost all of us. The existence of deontological permissions can help here, for they can supply the content to the exceptions deontological norms of obligation need in order to be plausible. If our deontological permission to defend ourselves, for example, supplies an exception within the content of the deontological obligation not to kill, the full statement of the obligations is not, "Don't kill," but rather, "Don't kill except in self-defense, except in . . . ," etc.

Not all exceptions to deontological norms of obligation need be deontological permissions. The exceptions for killings necessary to protect other people who are strangers, and killings necessary to stop fleeing felons, for example, might well not be based on deontological permissions. If so, such exceptions only remove such killings from the content of a deontological obligation; they do not by themselves make such killings right. Such killings are still subject to our consequentialist reasons, and become right only when productive of net good consequences.

The distinction between exceptions based on deontological permissions and those that are not, illustrates an important fact about permissions. There are two kinds of permissions: those that make an action right irrespective of that action producing net good consequences (deontological permissions); and those that make an action right only if that action produces net good consequences. I call the first of these, the deontological ones, *strong* permissions, and the second *weak* permissions.[43] Weak permissions are simply the absence of deontological obligations; such absence returns one to the "background, omnipresent sea" of the unrestricted consequentialist calculus determinative of right action.

These two kinds of exceptions, based on either strong or weak permissions, are needed to make plausible a not-too-demanding deontology. The simple absolutes

---

[43] Moore, *Causation and Responsibility, supra* n. 8, 39–40.

we teach our children can only be heuristics for the more complicated norms of deontological obligation, completed as these norms must be by numerous exception clauses. As long as such exception clauses do not include things like, "unless productive of net good consequences on the whole," I see nothing problematic for a more sophisticated deontology that regards such exceptions as an integral part of the content of its norms of obligation.

The distinction between weak and strong permissions just introduced in my discussion of the first problem of deontology will also help with the third problem. The third problem was that conflict between deontological obligations, while not inconceivable, was unfair and therefore problematic for the truth of any moral theory generating much of such conflict. Once one sees the existence of weak permissions by virtue of some exceptions in the content of norms of obligation, one should also see the possibility of there being weak permissions of a more general sort. And the generality of these latter weak permissions might help alleviate the potential for conflict between the deontological norms of obligation.

To explain, what makes conflict between deontological obligations widespread and inevitable would be the broad scope of such obligations. If they apply generally to omissions to save as well as actions that kill, known riskings of death as well as intending of deaths, causings of death as well as allowings of death, etc., then conflicts of obligation will be endemic. If the KGB, for example, was deontologically obligated not to *omit* to save the three Soviet diplomats as much as it was so obligated not to *kill* the one innocent Arab, then its choice was inevitably a conflict-ridden one. Whereas if its obligation to save its diplomats was only a consequential one, whereas if its obligation not to kill the Arab was deontological, there is no conflict of *deontological* obligations.

What might these conflict-reducing scope distinctions look like, and from whence do they spring? I have elsewhere charted in some detail six main distinctions here.[44] They are: (1) the distinction between intending and foreseeing. I may consequentially justify causing a harm that is merely foreseen when I could not consequentially justify causing that harm when I intend to do so. The most famous example of this medieval distinction is the killing of noncombatants in a just war: I can justify killing such noncombatants by the justness of the war only if I foresee that my bombing of strategic targets will surely kill them; I cannot justify the killing of noncombatants by the justness of the war if I intend their deaths as a means to winning the war (say, by dispiriting the enemy population so that they sue for peace). (2) The distinction between action and omission. I can consequentially justify failing to prevent some evil, whereas I cannot consequentially justify acting so as to cause such evil to come about. Thus, I can omit to save one drowning person when

---

[44] The six is a simplification of the larger number of such distinctions: ibid. at 42–76; Moore, *Placing Blame, supra* n. 8, 689–703.

I use the only rope I have to save two; but I may not save the two by drowning one who is saving himself with the only available rope. A famous historical example is Churchill's decision not to alert the citizens of Coventry about the bombing of their city intended by the Germans during the Second World War.[45] Saving them by alerting them would have tipped off the Germans that MI-6 had penetrated the German code system, thus lengthening the war and even putting its outcome in jeopardy. Imagine if Churchill had tried to keep secret the MI-6 success in breaching German communications in a more active way: he had all the civilian population of Coventry killed, because an unidentified one of their number was about to tell the Germans of MI-6's success. Surely Churchill could justify *not saving* the citizens of Coventry by good consequences in a way that he could not justify *acting* so as to cause the deaths of those same citizens. (3) The distinction between doing and allowing. I can consequentially justify allowing someone to die, whereas I cannot consequentially justify killing that same person. This medieval distinction is often illustrated by the difference between active and passive euthanasia: if medical equipment is needed to save others, I can remove it from the patient for whom it is doing less good, even though I know that he will die without the equipment; whereas I cannot actively kill that same patient in order to free up the equipment that can then be used to save others. In the first case I *allow* nature to take its course by removing a defense to that course that I earlier provided, and thus prevent something from preventing death (which is why these cases are commonly called cases of "double prevention"); whereas in the second case I cause death (by an injection of poison, say). Morally the first case is easier to justify by good consequences than is the second. (4) The distinction between causing and aiding. I can consequentially justify aiding another to cause some harm even when I cannot consequentially justify causing that harm myself. The British duress cases illustrate this distinction. Under British law, one cannot justify killing an innocent because of the duress of threats by another. But (for a time, at least) one could justify aiding another to kill an innocent, if such aid were the only way to avert threatened harm to oneself or one's family. Thus, in one well-known case, the defendant could justify driving the IRA killers to where they could kill a British policeman by the threats of the IRA otherwise to kill the defendant's family; but averting such threats could not justify the defendant in actually killing the policeman himself.[46] A more contemporary use of this distinction was by the CIA in its program of "extraordinary renditions": one could justify flying terrorist suspects to other countries such as Egypt for torture there by those countries' police, by the good consequences of extracting life-saving information,[47] whereas one could not justify torturing those suspects oneself by those same good consequences. (5) The distinction between initiating a

---

[45] As described in Stephenson, *supra* n. 14.
[46] *Director of Public Prosecutions for Northern Ireland v. Lynch* [1975] AC 653.
[47] Mayer, *supra* n. 17.

threat and redirecting a threat initiated by others. One can consequentially justify redirecting a threat initiated by others when one cannot consequentially justify initiating such a threat to others oneself. Philosophers have long illustrated this distinction by the example of a switchman who must choose whether to turn a runaway trolley onto one track or another, when each track has some trapped workman on it who will be killed by the trolley.[48] A more real-life example is provided by another of Churchill's wartime decisions, this one having to do with the V-1, V-2 rocket barrage of London.[49] The German targeting of their rockets depended on spies calling in the hits; MI-6 had penetrated the German spy network, so by deliberate mis-information Churchill's agents were able to redirect the German rockets from more populated areas of London to less populated suburbs. The rockets were going to kill some; Churchill's redirection decision caused them to kill less rather than more. The American Model Penal Code provides yet another example of this distinction in its licensing of the blowing of a dike and thereby diverting a flood about to inundate an entire village, even when the diverted flood will kill a farmer and his family. (6) The distinction between causing a harm not about to occur anyway, and merely accelerating a harm about to happen without one's contribution. One can consequentially justify accelerating an inevitable harm even when one could not justify causing such a harm when it was not inevitable that it would occur. Thus, when all mountaineers on a rope are about to die, some may cut the rope saving themselves, even though this means the others will die a little sooner than they otherwise would have.[50] When two Siamese twins are attached in such a way that both will die within the space of a year or two, doctors may sever the two, saving one, even at the cost of accelerating the death of the other.[51] When a Nazi officer cruelly threatens a mother with the death of both of her children unless she chooses one over the other, she may choose to save her son (as in the film) or the daughter, even though that condemns the other child to death.[52] And in cases of shipwrecks, when all will die unless one is pushed off the plank that's insufficient

---

[48] The "trolley discussion" in philosophy begins with Philippa Foot, "The Problem of Abortion and the Doctrine of Double Effect," *Oxford Review*, Vol. 5 (1967) 5–15. There is now a considerable literature.

[49] Stephenson, *supra* n. 14, 414.

[50] As the Model Penal Code too concludes. See Model Penal Code and Commentaries Section 3.02. Such practice also seems accepted within the contemporary mountaineering community (Joe Simpson, *supra* n. 13), although it was not the norm in the nineteenth-century British mountaineering community. Thus, the Whymper party disaster on the descent of the first climb of the Matterhorn in 1865 led to an extensive investigation as to whether the rope holding four fallen climbers to three remaining climbers had been cut or had simply broken, the assumption being that if it was cut that would have been improper (despite the then inevitable death of all seven climbers).

[51] As the court concluded in *In re A* [2001] Fam 147.

[52] As in the film, *Sophie's Choice, supra* n. 19. That the mother is (perhaps virtuously) racked with guilt, does not mean that she was not justified in saving one of her children when otherwise both would die.

to support all,[53] or some are thrown from the sinking lifeboat,[54] or some are eaten to sustain the rest[55]—in such cases, such actions can be justified by the net good consequences of saving some.

Intuitive as these distinctions are to many people, they cry out for some explanation as to why they mark the line of permissible consequentialist justification. Why are we weakly permitted to allow or omit to prevent harms we cannot cause, foresee harms we cannot intend, aid others to cause harms we cannot ourselves cause, redirect or accelerate harms we cannot ourselves initiate? Why is the scope of our deontological obligations limited in these ways, rather than other, equally conflict-reducing ways?

The answer lies in the general shape of our deontological obligations. Not only do particular obligations have exceptions to them specific to such obligations—see above—but there is a general shape to the content of our deontological obligations that limits their scope and thus their potential for conflict. That shape is dictated by the four major determiners of desert that exist in morality: act, cause, intent, and counterfactual dependence. We are most responsible, most blameworthy, most deserving of punishment, for our *acts*[56] (rather than omissions) that *cause*[57] (rather than fail to prevent, allow, redirect or aid) harms to others, when those harms are *intended*[58] (rather than foreseen or risked) and when those harms *counterfactually depended* on our acts[59] (rather than being such as were going to happen anyway). It is these four desert-determiners that dictate the general shape of our most stringent duties, which are our deontological norms of obligation.

To say that we are weakly permitted to fail to prevent or allow harms to others, to aid others or nature to cause harms, to foresee or risk harms, or to cause harms about to occur anyway is not, of course, to say that we are (bottom line) right or justified to do any of these things. Such weak permissions betoken no more than an absence of deontological obligation (because we are outside the scope of such obligations). That means that we are back in the land where consequentialism holds full sway. Such

---

[53] That either person on a plank sufficient to float only one, can throw off the other to his death, has been concluded by Cicero, Aquinas, Bacon, Kant, Holmes, and Glanville Williams. See the citations in Moore, *Placing Blame, supra* n. 8, 693 fn. 53.

[54] The conclusion of the court (in dictum) in *United States v. Holmes*, 226 Fed Cas. 360 (3rd Cir. 1842)

[55] Although the court came out the other way in *Regina v. Dudley and Stephens*, 14 QBD 273 (1884), as Brian Simpson documents in his *Cannibalism and the Common Law*, the custom of nineteenth-century mariners was to sanction the killing and eating of some when the alternative was for all to die.

[56] See Michael Moore, *Act and Crime: The Implications of the Philosophy of Action for the Criminal Law,* 2nd edn (Clarendon Press, 1993, 2010).

[57] Moore, *Causation and Responsibility, supra* n. 8, ch. 2; Moore, *Placing Blame, supra* n. 8, ch. 5.

[58] Moore, *Placing Blame, supra* n. 8, chs 9, 11; Michael Moore, "Intention as a Marker of Moral Responsibility and Legal Punishability" in Antony Duff and Stuart Green (eds), *The Philosophical Foundations of Criminal Law* (Oxford University Press, 2011).

[59] Moore, *Causation and Responsibility, supra* n. 8, ch. 18.

weakly permitted actions or omissions will be right and justified only if such actions or omissions produce the best consequences overall. Weak permissions, in other words, do not permit actions as such; rather, they permit consequentialist reasons to do their justifying work, if any such justifying consequentialist reasons exist.

The existence of these general kinds of weak permissions, which are part and parcel of the general shape of the deontological norms of obligation, reduces but does not eliminate the potential for conflict between such obligations.[60] It thus reduces the force of the third objection to deontology considered above. Yet we so far have said nothing about the second objection to deontology's seeming over-and underdemandingness. This was the moral catastrophe objection. It seems very counterintuitive that the Heavens should fall or that the human race should perish, rather than a deontological obligation be violated.

Enter the third layer of the analysis. I have urged that consequentialist reasons are omnipresent in the determination of rational and moral action (the first layer); further, that the force of those consequentialist reasons can be suspended by either strong permissions or deontological obligations (the second layer). Now see that those deontological overlays can themselves be overridden by consequentialist reasons whose force exceeds some threshold of moral weight. This so-called "threshold-deontology" is the subject of the third layer of analysis.

Threshold deontology answers the second objection to deontology directly; such a threshold deontology denies that we are obligated not to torture an innocent in situations where such torture will save the planet, save a city, preserve a culture, etc. It also denies that we may exercise any of our permissions (such as our strong permission to defend ourselves) if such action will have these catastrophic consequences. Threshold deontology restricts the operation of strong permissions and deontological obligations to the normal world most of us face throughout our daily lives, a world where no such huge catastrophes loom before us.

Threshold deontology, popular though it is amongst philosophers who are deontologists in their ethics, is largely supported by intuition alone. Deontology becomes too counterintuitive without interposing some such threshold for overriding deontological permissions and obligations. Some find this kind of intuitive support disquieting (although the older one gets, the shorter the argument chains one finds acceptable). Others find the lumpiness of threshold deontology queer: consequentialists reasons do not count, and then all of a sudden they do if they are weighty enough. Others find the vagueness of where any such threshold might be located troubling, accompanied by a disquieting sense of arbitrariness if a precise threshold is specified.[61]

---

[60] See G.E.M. Anscombe, "War and Murder" in Walter Stein (ed.), *Nuclear Weapons: A Catholic Response* (Sheed and Ward, 1962).

[61] See, e.g., Larry Alexander, "Deontology at the Threshold," *San Diego Law Review*, Vol. 37 (2000) 893–912.

I do not find any of these worries sufficiently worrisome as to abandon threshold deontology. Indeed, if anything were to be abandoned in the face of moral catastrophe kinds of examples, it would be deontology itself. Deontology without thresholds, á la Kant, would be too implausible to be accepted.

This third level of analysis provided by threshold deontology can be seen as a kind of skewed consequentialism. This characterization will be accurate if one adopts what I call "sliding scale threshold deontology." What slides on this view is the threshold: more serious moral wrongs require a higher threshold of bad consequences averted than do less serious moral wrongs. This is not the normal consequential balance, but a skewed one whereby the doing of a single moral wrong by the agent doing the calculation is equated (at the threshold) to a large measure of bad states of affairs not due to one's agency that would be averted by the doing of that wrong.

The three-level analysis just sketched invites the following sorts of questions about practices such as that of targeted killings. One can think of these seven questions, in the order presented below, as a kind of ordered decision procedure, one amongst others possible that yield a rational way to proceed. First question: is there a strong permission to engage in the action (say, a particular targeted killing)? If the answer is yes, that requires that one ask a second question: is this strong permission nonetheless overridden by the catastrophic consequences of its being exercised? If this answer is no, then one is justified in doing the action without asking further questions; if this answer is yes, then one is not justified in doing the action without asking further questions. If the answer to the first question is no—that there is no strong permission to engage in the action—then ask a third question, the question of general consequentialist balancing: will the action produce more net good consequences than its alternative(s)? If the answer to this third question is no, then one is not justified in doing the action without asking any further questions. But if the answer to this general consequentialist question is yes, then one must ask a fourth question: is the action prohibited by a deontological obligation, at least prima facie? If the answer is no—there is no deontological prohibition—then one is justified (given that the action is productive of net good consequences) in doing the action without asking further questions. But if the answer is yes, that the action prima facie instantiates a deontologically prohibited act-type, then ask a fifth question: is there nonetheless a weak permission to do such action embedded as an exception within the content of the deontological norm of obligation? If there is such a weak permission, and since the action also is productive of net good consequences, then one is justified in taking the action without asking further questions. But if the answer is no, then ask a sixth question: is there nonetheless a weak permission to do the action because the general nature of the action (or omission) falls outside the scope of all deontological prohibitions, this one included? Is it a merely foreseen or risked action rather than an intended act? Is it not an act at all, but an omission? Is it a mere allowing or an aiding or redirecting or accelerating? If the answer to this sixth question is yes, then one is justified (given that the action is productive of net good consequences) in doing the action without asking further questions. But if the answer here is no—that there is no weak permission to do an act deontologically prohibited to one—then ask a seventh and final question: is the act nonetheless necessary to prevent some moral catastrophe that is over the threshold of one's threshold deontology? If the answer to this last question is no, then one may not do the action; if the answer is yes, then one may (and indeed, must) do the action.

Since this is a complicated decision procedure, I have schematized it on the following decision tree:

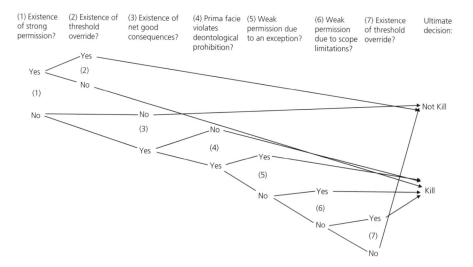

Admittedly this decision procedure has a bit of a mechanical feel to it, something akin to painting-by-numbers. But this is because it is algorithmic and ploddingly methodical in making plain the connections between the different questions, and because it is complete. Much of what we know here is intuitive, so that (like much of our inference-drawing in many areas) in practice we can be elliptical.In cases of horrendous consequences looming on one side or the other (nodes (2) and (7) above), for example, these will in practice be so salient that we may well focus on them first or even exclusively, determinative as they are of our decisions if they exist. The same may be said for the existence and application of a deontological norm of prohibition (nodes (4), (5) and (6)): the application of such a norm may be sufficiently clear, and the absence of strong permissions or threshold overrides so obvious, that we focus our decision on this alone.

I thus do not pretend that the decision procedure schematized above will always or even often be the actual psychological process a rational actor should go through explicitly and consciously. Still, the schema organizes all of the questions potentially relevant in assessing the morality of a given action or practice, and is useful for that reason. That is how I intend to use it in the discussion of targeted killing that follows.

VII. The three-level analysis applied to targeted killings

I shall here sketch the relevant variables to assess the morality of targeted killings. I make no attempt to be definitive; my purpose is to illustrate *how* one should decide this question more than it is to decide it. I shall proceed using the seven-question decision procedure outlined in the last section.

First question: is there a strong permission to kill terrorists about to engage in violence against us? One obvious strong permission to invoke here as that of self-defense, as a number of papers prepared for the Penn conference anticipated.[62] I am not concerned with the technical legal notions of self-defense of either domestic criminal law or the international law of war. Sticking to the moral question relieves us of any need to abide by these legal doctrines (such as the imminence requirement) except insofar as they capture or reflect some underlying moral truth.

In morality the privilege to defend oneself is but an instance of a more general principle.[63] When someone attacks us meaning serious harm, and when the only way to prevent such harm is by our own use of harm-causing force, the attacker has made it inevitable that someone be harmed, either himself or his intended victim. The general moral principle behind self-defense (and defense of others) is that he who culpably causes the necessity of some harm being visited on somebody, is himself the right person to be made to suffer such harm. And this is true, without regard to whether the harm inflicted on the attacker is greater or lesser than the harm he would inflict on his intended victims.

Such a principle has support in rather robust intuitions of fairness and appropriateness. When someone has tried to harm another, and yet the harm he has put in motion comes back to him rather than his intended victims, we often recognize such outcomes as peculiarly fitting as a kind of "divine justice." Think of the would-be murderer's bullet that kills him instead of his intended victim. Such sense of fittingness carries over to situations where we must initiate a new force, rather than

---

[62] See Phillip Montague, "Defending Defensive Targeted Killings;" Russell Christopher, "Imminence in Justified Targeted Killing," in this Volume, chs 10 and 9, respectively; see also Peter Vallentyne, "Enforcement Rights Against Non-Culpable Non-Just Intrusion," forthcoming, *Ratio*.

[63] I have long relied on Phillip Montague's notion of self-defense, as first laid out in Montague, "Self-Defense and Choosing Among Lives," *Philosophical Studies*, Vol. 40 (1981) 207–19. See also Moore, "Torture and the Balance of Evils," *supra* n. 8, in *Placing Blame*, 712–17. That the Bush Administration also adopted this theory of self-defense (in the Yoo-Bybee memoranda on torture) does not dissuade me from its correctness.

redirect the wrongdoer's old one, as in Philippa Foot's well-known example:[64] a fat man has wedged himself, face outward, in the only opening to a cave filled with people and rising water. He had done this to drown all inside.Surely we may use dynamite to blow him out of the cave's entrance, since it was his act that made it necessary that either he or the group die. (Notice this same act of blowing open the cave seems permissible if there's only one who is trapped, and a large group blocking the entrance in their attempt to drown the one.)

As applied to targeted killings, the strong permission (to turn the hard end of a hard choice on he who culpably caused the necessity of such choice) would seem to apply to killings of those terrorists who otherwise would visit harm on us. The only interesting questions here are factual, not moral: how certain is it that the terrorist targeted will in fact do serious harm if not assassinated? Bomb-makers, suicide bomb-carriers, those who plan such things, seem easy examples of justified targeting, even if there will also be harder cases of less certainty.

More difficult moral questions are faced when the threat emanates from an innocent source. In domestic criminal law we call these "innocent aggressor" cases.[65] The child who does not know what a gun is but who will shoot you with it unless you shoot her first, the insane (and thus not blameworthy) attacker,[66] the coerced or duped assassin, the man whose body will fall on you unless you disintegrate it,[67] etc., are innocent aggressors. In the international arena, think of bin Laden's amused comment on video that some of the 9/11 hijackers were ignorant of what was in store for them; or think of those couriers ignorant of the deadly peril in what they carry. Can these too be killed, if necessary to prevent the harms they threaten, however innocently? I think the standard answer—and the right answer—is "yes" domestically, and it should be "yes" internationally. Whether these are justified killings, or only excused ones, is a close question, but here too I think morality makes such killings right and not merely wrong but excusable.

A second deontological permission possible here has to do with retributive punishment. According to retributivists (in which I include myself),[68] we are obligated to punish those culpable wrongdoers who deserve it. Such categorical obligation to punish carries with it an equally categorical permission: we are permitted to punish the guilty, even when doing so is not conducive to achieving the best consequences on the whole. Such obligation-cum-permission will justify targeted killings

---

[64] See Foot, *supra* n. 48.

[65] The modern discussion of the innocent aggressor issue begins with George Fletcher," Proportionality and the Psychotic Aggressor: A Vignette in Comparative Criminal Law Theory," *Israel Law Review*, Vol. 8 (1973) 367–90.

[66] The example of Fletcher, "Psychotic Aggressor," and of the Model Penal Code and Commentaries §3.04.

[67] The example of Robert Nozick, *Anarchy, State, and Utopia* (Oxford University Press, 1974).

[68] My main defense of there being a kind of justice that is retributive in nature (as opposed to corrective or distributive), is in Moore, *Placing Blame, supra,* n. 8, chs 2–4.

whenever those killings are of terrorists whose past acts merit a sentence of death. The justification here is backward-looking and punitive, not forward-looking and preventative, as in self-defense.[69]

Examples here that come to mind include the 2011 U.S. Navy SEAL killing of Osama bin Laden, as well as the decision of Golda Meir to kill the terrorists who had killed Israeli athletes at the 1972 Olympics in Munich. To my mind, these were unproblematically justifiable killings on this retributive ground alone. True, the process for determining guilt was a bit abbreviated and informal in that no court ever passed on the guilt of those executed. Yet when capture and trial is not feasible for one reason or another, better these executions of deserving wrongdoers than no punishment at all.

Second question: if there is such strong permission, is it nonetheless not available because the consequences of preemptively killing terrorists are so horrendous that they override the permission? The consequences that come to mind here are those brought forward by liberal political theorists: law and order on the international scene will disappear, no one will trust or respect any country that engages in such practices, terrorism against us will only be heightened and prolonged by such practices, etc. Conceivably such kinds of consequences could reach a magnitude that could override a nation's right of self-protection.[70] Witness the sacrifice the French and British governments asked of the Czechs in 1938, giving up the only defensive line the Czechs had with which to exercise their right of self-defense against German aggression, in the name of avoiding the horrendous consequences of world war. Yet as in 1938, the question is an empirical one: will these bad consequences really be averted if targeted killings do not take place? Equivalently, will the international order generally, trust or respect of America specifically, or the self-restraint of terrorists up to now, disappear or even be much diminished if America and Israel continue their practices of targeted killings? I doubt this very much. The only thing that makes a horrendous level of these consequences seemingly plausible is the confusion of empirical likelihood with a kind of formal postulate of political philosophy. The postulate is that we should only do what we would allow others to do, or what we could give reason to them to accept what we do, or what some neutral observer stripped of any beliefs in the justness of our cause versus theirs, would accept. These postulates (that I put aside earlier) are no substitute for the needed empirics. The empirical questions are not, for example, whether everyone should

---

[69] I raised the punishment of the deserving as a possible exception to the norm against torture, but only as a partial exception because of torture's general impermissibility as a mode of punishment. Moore, "Torture and the Balance of Evils", *supra* n. 8 in *Placing Blame*, 717–19. Targeted killings, by contrast, utilize a permissible mode of punishment, viz., death.

[70] Kevin Govern examines such questions in "Operation Neptune Spear: Was Killing Bin Landen a Legitimate Military Objective?," in this Volume, ch. 13.

be allowed to do what we do;[71] rather, it is whether they *will* do what we do. And the answer to this empirical question seems to be rather clearly no.

Third question: are the consequences of targeted killing on the whole good? This is a large question. We need to introduce some distinctions to make it more manageable. The first is a distinction I have intentionally suppressed until now. This is the distinction between justifying an individual decision to target a particular terrorist for assassination, on the one hand, and justifying the general practice of targeted killings, on the other.

To use this distinction here is not to return to the much-rejected idea that there is a kind of indirect, or two-step consequentialism, often called, "rule-consequentialism." Such a form of consequentialism has long been known to be incoherent, collapsing as it does either into act-consequentialism or irrational rule-worship.[72] Rather, the consequentialism urged here is always an act-consequentialism; that is, a calculus which one uses to decide how to act on particular occasions. It is just that some actors, because of their institutional roles, have a choice set that is limited to the enactment of general rules. As Rawls pointed out years ago,[73] legislators, for example, can only decide on the enactment of statutory rules; they cannot make individual decisions under those rules because that is not their institutional role. Similarly here, policymakers within the CIA and elsewhere in government are not themselves in the business of deciding whether and when to target particular terrorists. Their choice set consists of general policies defining the practice of targeted killing that they think will produce the best consequences on the whole.

It might be thought that the consequentialist calculation (about the general practice of targeted killings) has at least the potential to preempt any calculation of consequences by CIA officers doing the targeting. As long as the general rule is not, "use your discretion," in other words, it might be thought that individual CIA decisions are wholly governed by the general policies decided upon and not by any further consequentialist calculation. Yet this is not so, because (among other things) the normative viewpoint of the officer in the field is not the same as the viewpoint of those making general policies. There is always a "gap" between the viewpoints of those who make rules, and those who apply them.[74] As much as the former like to pretend that their general decisions fully govern the particular decisions of officers in the field, in fact those officers have to make their own consequentialist

---

[71] If this universalizability principle were in issue, notice that what it is we *do* is open to a detailed description allowing only those who, like us, are in the right, to do targeted killings.

[72] The *locus classicus* of this argument is in David Lyons, *The Forms and Limits of Utilitarianism* (Clarendon Press, 1975).

[73] John Rawls, "Two Concepts of Rules," *Philosophical Review*, Vol. 64 (1955) 3–32. Rawls himself did not always carefully distinguish the *role*-relativity of different institutional actors' choice sets, from the incoherent *rule*-utilitarianism that is not in any way role-dependant.

[74] See Larry Alexander, "The Gap," *Harvard Journal of Law and Public Policy*, Vol. 14 (1991) 695–701.

calculations. Thus we have two consequentialist balances to assess: one, does the practice of targeted killings produce net good consequences, and two, does some particular targeted killing produce net good consequences?

Separate as these two questions are, there is an impact that the answer to each has on the answer to the other. The field officer, when calculating the consequences of a particular targeting, should take into account those long-term consequences (such as precedential effect, reputational injury to his country, disbelief in international law, etc.) to which his individual action may contribute.[75] Similarly, the policy-maker when calculating the consequences of some general policy on targeted killings, should take into account that his policy will be imperfectly applied by those in the field. The latter's calculation, in other words, should not be, "What would be the best rule to enact if universally followed?" Rather, it should be, "What is the best rule to enact in light of how I predict it will actually be applied in the field?" Despite these interactions, we still have two separate consequential calculations to consider.

Consider first the general practice of targeted killings, as say it is currently being carried out by the intelligence communities in the United States and Israel. Are these practices producing better consequences than their conceivable alternatives (such as a flat ban on such killings, or an expansion of them)? Now the considerations of political philosophers mentioned above in discussion of Question Two can come into their own, pitched perhaps at a less hysterical level. It does cost America's reputation something, does it not, to kill people around the world that it alone judges to be a threat to its interests, when those people are not combatants in any declared war? The damage done to America's reputation by the Bush Administration's well-publicized practices of torture illustrates how serious a harm this can be.

On the other side of the balance, of course, is the intended benefit of targeted killings: They are intended to prevent great harms to America, Americans, and the citizens of our allies. Whether much of such benefit is achieved by the practice of course depends on the accuracy of the targeting, a matter difficult to assess from public information. In principle it is certainly possible that these gains in security and safety outweigh the costs to reputation (and respect for law) that are also consequences of the practice.

The consequentialist calculations of officers in the field are even more difficult to assess from the armchair. For everything depends on the details of individual cases. We are told that the CIA has levels of review on proposals to assassinate given terrorists, and that numerous candidates proposed for assassination are declined by this higher order review.[76] Both Israeli and American targeting also make efforts

---

[75] Nicely explored in Heidi Hurd, *Moral Combat* (Cambridge University Press, 1999).
[76] McKelvey, *supra* n. 3.

to avoid "collateral damage," the euphemism for killing or injuring those near those targeted but who have no culpable connection with them.[77] If this works as it should, it is plausible that net good consequences are produced in some (many, most?) cases of targeted killings as currently practiced.

Even in cases where mistakes are made—the one targeted turns out not to have been a threat to U.S. or Israeli interests—those decision-makers assessing their own responsibility need to distinguish the question of whether they did the right thing from the question of whether they were culpable in doing the wrong thing. As the criminal law extending from Aristotle to the current Model Penal Code reflects, these are two distinct moral questions.[78] Acts of mistaken targeting in fact do the wrong thing, but if such targetings are reasonably believed to be necessary to prevent serious injury by those who do or order them, culpability is lacking. For those like John Rizzo "in session with himself," regret at wrong choices would be appropriate (and aretaically, demanded), but guilt would not.

There is an interesting skewing question about doing the consequentialist calculation at either level, that of general practice or of particular targeting. Before, I noted that a sliding scale threshold deontology could be seen as a skewed consequentialism, skewed by the great but not infinite weight each actor should give to the fact that it is his or her agency that is involved in causing some harm or evil to exist. Now consider skewing the consequentialist calculation by the identities of the victims, not the agents. Standard consequentialisms follow Bentham's dictum that "each is to count for one, but only one." A consequentialism skewed by the identities of victims and beneficiaries, by contrast, might weight the interests of the "near and dear" greater than those of strangers.

As applied to the present situation, such a skewed consequentialism might weight the lives of U.S. citizens more heavily than the lives of non-U.S. citizens. Consider as an example of such skewing the decision about the altitude at which bombers should fly prior to the introduction of "smart bombs." Suppose the facts are these: the numbers of innocent noncombatants killed varies directly with the altitude of the bombers (viz., the higher the planes, the greater civilian casualties because of the lesser accuracy of the bombs). Suppose further that the number of airmen killed varies inversely with the altitude, because the higher the plane the less vulnerable it is to anti-aircraft fire. Assume (contrary to fact, but to simplify) that the accuracy in hitting the intended targets does not change with altitude.

A standard consequentialism, where each noncombatant life is equal to one airman's life despite their different citizenship, would recommend bombing at that altitude where one airman will be lost for each noncombatant killed, whereas a victim-skewed

---

[77] Ibid.; see also Dershowitz, *supra* n. 3, 121–40.
[78] Moore, *Placing Blame, supra* n. 8, 45, 191–3, 403–4.

consequentialism would recommend a somewhat higher altitude, valuing a U.S. airman's life as the equivalent of some large number of noncombatant, non-U.S. citizen lives. A radically skewed consequentialism would not count noncombatant, non-U.S. citizen lives at all in assessing the proper level of risk to U.S. airmen.

One of the features we like about the use of unmanned drones to do our targeted killings, of course, is that we eliminate the risks to U.S. airmen that would exist if we used manned aircraft. If this substitution were at the cost of increased civilian casualties, we would be facing the same question of differential weighting as in my older bombing scenario.

My own sense is that some skewing of the consequentialist calculus is appropriate in military contexts such as these. Putting our own airmen at risk up to the level equal to the risk imposed on innocent noncombatants seems too idealistic; ignoring the interest of the latter entirely seems too heartless. We have a vague-by-degree privilege to prefer our own in making such consequentialist balances, difficult as that is to quantify.

Fourth question: are we prima facie debarred from achieving whatever balance of net good consequences as can be achieved by targeted killings, because of a prima facie deontological duty prohibiting such killings? As long as we recognize the work done by "prima facie" here (in putting aside momentarily the possibilities of strong or weak permissions or threshold overrides), surely the answer to this question is in the affirmative. Targeted killings are intentional killings of human beings.[79] As the contemporary electronic commentary on the proposed 1938 assassination of Hitler notes, "Assassination is hard to justify when you're not at war—it is generally called 'murder'."[80]

We have seen two possible exceptions to this deontological norm (in the form of strong permissions to defend ourselves and to punish past culpable wrongdoing) that, if they exist, would render this prima facie prohibition idle. Yet at this stage of our decision procedure we should assume that these permissions do not exist. In which case, the prima facie deontological prohibition threatens to override the consequentialist balance in favor of such killings. More pertinent at this stage in our deliberations would be the existence of weak permissions, as those exist either in the form of further exceptions to the deontological norm against murder, or in the form of scope limitations on all such deontological norms. I shall examine these possibilities in the fifth and sixth questions below.

Fifth question: are there further exceptions to the norm prohibiting murder beyond self-defense and retributive punishment that are relevant here? Few come to mind.

---

[79] As further defended in Fernando Teson, "Targeted Killing in War and Peace: A Philosophical Analysis," in this Volume, ch. 15.

[80] Available at <http://www.imdb.com/title/tt0360715/> accessed November 3, 2011, for *Killing Hitler* (TV 2003).

Perhaps if terrorists forfeit their rights (to life and bodily integrity, among others) by engaging in acts of terrorism threatening those rights in others, that constitutes a (weak) permission to kill them, a permission exercisable only if net good consequences are produced by such killings. Such rights-forfeiture ideas are the basis for one of the extant theories about the moral basis for self-defense.[81] Yet neither in that context, nor in this, are such forfeiture theories plausible.

Sixth question: are some ways of arranging for the deaths of terrorist suspects outside the scope of deontological obligations generally, and thus weakly permitted? Most targeted killings are central cases of *acts* (not omissions), strongly *causing* (not merely aiding, allowing, or redirecting) the deaths of terrorists who are *not about to die anyway* (versus mere accelerations of inevitable deaths) where those deaths are *intended* (not merely foreseen or risked). Such central cases of targeted killings cannot thus avail themselves of what I earlier called the scope limitations common to deontological obligations generally.

There are some less central cases, however, where these distinctions may have some bite. One of these has to do with the killing of noncombatants, typically spouses, children, and other relatives of a targeted terrorist. In cases where the killing of the terrorist himself is (strongly or weakly) permitted by an exception (such as extended self-defense or retributive punishment), the justifiability of the action that also kills non-involved others will depend on whether their killings were deontologically prohibited. Here the doctrine of double effect may do some work, for in such cases the intelligence services can truly say that they did not intend the death(s) of those relatives of the terrorist who were at the wrong place at the wrong time. Indeed, in one well-known case, that of the killing of the Hamas military commander Salah Shehada by Israeli forces in 2002, the Israelis not only did not intend, they did not even know that they would also kill Shehada's14-year-old daughter as well as several other relatives and neighbors.[82] While they did know that his wife always accompanied him, and did knowingly accept her death as inevitable, they no more than risked the deaths of the others. In which case the Israeli forces were weakly permitted to kill Shehada where and when they did, if such killing at that time was necessary to prevent even greater evil than was the death of Shehada's relatives and neighbors. (Remember, a weak permission only permits the consequentialist balance to be made; the action itself is permitted only if in addition that consequentialist balance favors that action.)

More occasionally, the omitting, allowing, aiding, and redirecting distinctions may have some bearing on the morality of a terrorist's deaths. In the taking of Al Qaeda's one-time chief of security, Abu Zubeida, for example, he was thrice wounded before capture. One could imagine justifying omitting to provide life-

---

[81] On self-defense as an instance of rights forfeiture, see Judith Jarvis Thomson, "Self-Defense," *Philosophy and Public Affairs*, Vol. 20 (1991) 283–310.

[82] Recounted in Dershowitz, *supra* n. 3, 132.

saving medical treatment (or discontinuing any already begun) in a situation where his death was necessary to prevent even worse consequences.[83] Likewise, where U.S. intelligence knows of a planned Israeli assassination, or vice versa, and could stop it, the omission to prevent such targeted killings by others is surely open to consequentialist justification. Likewise, the sharing of information and other minor forms of aiding targeted killings by others is also open to consequentialist justification, as would be redirecting other nations' targetings from less to more useful targets.

Suicide bombers and those who, willingly or unwillingly, accompany them to their deaths, present an easy example of justified targeting. Such individuals are about to die anyway, and even if they are coerced into doing what they are doing or are acting in ignorance, the fact of their inevitable death licenses a consequentially justified killing of them. Accelerating the inevitable is open to consequentialist justification in a way that killing someone not under pre-existing threat is not. This is even true of decisions that many of us would find difficult psychologically to make, such as shooting down a passenger airliner commandeered by terrorists in order to prevent destruction of national monuments and the deaths of those who occupy them. Psychologically difficult as these decisions would be to make, morally these are not hard cases.

In these kinds of cases, intelligence and military services may act or fail to act in ways that are not subject to deontology's prohibition on murder. Like all weak permissions, however, that only means that action or inaction in such cases may be justified by the good consequences produced or allowed; the actions/inactions are themselves permissible only if such net of good consequences are actually in the offing.

Seventh question: are some targeted killings justified simply by the catastrophic consequences thereby avoided, without regard to any other permission, exception, or scope limitation? Surely the answer to this last question is sometimes, "yes." The 1938 proposed assassination of Hitler is to my mind of this character. If that assassination would have prevented the Second World War and the Holocaust, it would have been justified and permissible on this basis alone. The only room for quibbling here might be on epistemic grounds: did Chamberlain's government in 1938 know enough about Hitler and his plans to ground a sufficiently certain prediction as would warrant Hitler's murder? The British colonel in Berlin, Colonel MacFarlane, surely thought so, and of course Winston Churchill had seen the danger for some time. But however much one wants to quibble on these epistemic grounds, isn't the substantive moral principle clear? Hitler would have been justifiably assassinated in light of the horrendous consequences of his survival.

---

[83] The facts are only imagined. The actual facts were that medical treatment was delayed in order to get Zubeida to talk, not to allow him to die. *LA Times,* March 6, 2003.

In our own times there are equally clear cases "beyond the threshold." Should a targeted killing be necessary to prevent the detonation or even acquisition of nuclear weapons or of biological weapons of mass destruction, that killing too would be justified on this ground. For most deontologists with whom I am familiar (to a person, threshold deontologists), the hard questions do not lie in these clear cases. They lie in the borderlands. Israel's preemptive strike on the Iraqi nuclear facilities in 1981 come to mind in this regard, as does any similar action the United States might yet take against North Korea or Iranian nuclear capabilities. Or consider the Israeli assassination of Gerald Bull, an expert in barrel ballistics who was assisting the Iraqis under Saddam Hussein in developing a supergun capable of hitting Israel from Iraq.[84] If such guns (three were planned) were only capable of firing conventional warheads in Iraqi hands, are such bad consequences enough to cross the threshold of moral permission?

VIII. Conclusion

My topic has been the morality of targeted killings. It has not been about their legality, either under present law or under better law that ought to exist. Even if one agrees with each of my moral conclusions, it would be a mistake to think that one should then simply write them into law. By way of example of the need for caution here, consider the seventh and last point in the preceding section, that of threshold deontology. I meant what I said there: over the threshold, one's duty is to do what it takes—kill innocents, torture, etc.—to prevent true moral catastrophes. Yet quite good reasons might yet stay the hand of the judge or legislator from writing a threshold override into law, for its potential for misapplication may be both large as well as asymmetrical: intelligence agents may well overpredict catastrophe and undervalue non-citizen lives if they were directed by law to apply such a standard. Plus, one suspects, often those acting in such extreme circumstances do not need the law's encouragement to do what they need and ought to do. In which case, one may well not want the law to say explicitly what is morally true.

Still, for the reasons given earlier, it matters how morality stands with respect to practices like targeted killings. It matters to those who do such things, and it matters to those of us in whose name those things are done. My aim in this chapter has not been to be definitive on this question; only to get those who order or execute such decisions to see the possibility of ordered, rational analysis of such issues, and to take seriously the implications of that analysis for the morality of what they do. Such thoughtfulness about morality is not pie-in-the-sky, ivory tower academics; it is where decent people live.

---

[84] Dershowitz, *supra* n. 3, 122–3.

17

TARGETED KILLING AND THE STRATEGIC USE OF SELF-DEFENSE

Leo Katz

Although governments that engage in targeted killing will usually invoke self-defense as a primary justification, they often seem on thin ice in doing so. We frequently have the sense that there is something very strategic and dishonest in the way self-defense is utilized in such cases. The most obvious example is the case in which the government uses an *agent provocateur* to induce a potential terrorist to take actions for which it then proceeds to kill him—in "self-defense." In this chapter I will examine a series of such strategic situations and will suggest that, appearances notwithstanding, there is in fact nothing illegitimate about using self-defense in such strategic ways. That is not to say that our persistent unease about what governments are doing in such cases is without significance. But its significance turns out to lie mostly in what it teaches us about certain counterintuitive features of legal and moral rules, which is another issue I aim to explore here.[1]

I. Take no prisoners

Consider the following scenario. Our government has learned that a long-sought major terrorist is holed up in a secret compound on the territory of a friendly power. With that other government's assent, we send a special forces unit into the compound to "take him out." We do not expect him to surrender. More importantly, we do not really *want* him to surrender, because bringing him back home and putting him on trial is going to mean major legal headaches, in addition to the danger of terrorist reprisals.[2] To this end, the President actually vetoes an initial

---

[1] Obviously, this chapter only takes on a thin slice of the self-defense problems raised by targeted killings. For an encyclopedic look at the subject, see Nils Melzer, *Targeted Killings in International Law* (Oxford University Press, 2008).

[2] As explored more fully in Jeff McMahan, "Targeted Killing: Murder, Combat or Law Enforcement?" in this Volume, ch. 5.

proposal that would have had us land in the target's compound with such over-whelming force as to possibly intimidate him into surrender. Instead, the President sends in a much smaller elite unit, which our target is likely to try to resist, thus justifying our shooting him on the spot. Let us suppose that things turn out exactly as planned: the target resists and gets shot. The government invokes the self-defense rights of legitimate government enforcement agents to justify what it did. Others, however, have suggested that there is something improper when the need for such self-defense has been strategically contrived by sending in a smaller force than would have been required to bring him in alive. After all, if the President had simply told his men to take no prisoners, that would surely have been illegitimate; but isn't what he actually did the functional equivalent, and therefore not really permissible either? Or so the critics' argument goes.

What should one make of this criticism? Standard self-defense doctrine holds that you forfeit your right of self-defense if you provoke the attack against which you are defending. Walking into a bar, goading your worst enemy with everything you can think of until he loses his self-control and lunges at you, and then finishing him off—that is the kind of case where we generally do not want to view the person acting in self-defense as justified. Isn't this what the government has done when it sends in a smaller-than-optimal special forces unit that then serves as something akin to an *agent provocateur*?

Provoking an attack to use one's right of self-defense is a particular instance of a phenomenon sometimes described as contriving to create the condition of your own defense. German criminal law calls this the problem of the *actio libera in causa*—an "action free in its origins." What is being referred to are cases in which someone deliberately, or maybe even just recklessly, creates situations in which he then finds a need to commit an act that would ordinarily be considered justified or excused by reason of necessity, or duress, or insanity, or lack of a voluntary act, or innumerable other potential defenses, but inasmuch as he deliberately contrived to create the situation, or just impermissibly risked its coming about, he no longer seems entitled to invoke those defenses. His actions being "free in their origin," though no longer entirely "free in their execution," deserve to be punished just as though he had no defense to begin with. That at least is the standard view.[3]

---

[3] The problem of the *actio libera in causa* has received surprisingly little attention in the English language literature. The exceptions include Miriam Gur-Arye, *The Actio Libera in Causa* (Harry Sacher Institute for Legislative Research and Comparative Law, 1984); Paul H. Robinson, "Causing the Conditions of One's Own Defense: A Study in the Limits of Theory in Criminal Law Doctrine," 71 *Va L Rev* 1, 3 (1985); Larry Alexander, "Reconsidering the Relationship Among Voluntary Acts, Strict Liability, and Negligence in Criminal Law," 7 *Social Philosophy and Policy* 84 (1990); Douglas Husak and Brian McLaughlin, "Time Frames, Voluntary Acts, and Strict Liability," 12 *Law and Philosophy*, 95 (1992); Michael S. Moore, *Act and Crime: The Philosophy of Action and its Implications for the Criminal Law*, (Oxford University Press, 1993), 35–6; Leo Katz, "Proximate Cause in Michael Moore's Act and Crime," 142 *U. Penn. L.Rev.* 1513 (1994); Leo Katz, *Ill-Gotten Gains* (University of Chicago Press, 1996); Claire Finkelstein, "Involuntary Crimes, Voluntarily Committed" in *Criminal Law Theory: Doctrines of the General Part*, Stephen Shute and A.P. Simister

But why exactly is that? Why should contriving to create the conditions of one's own defense deprive one of the right to make use of that defense? One line of argument that has been offered to explain why that should be so goes something like this. Consider the case in which a storeowner contrives to create a situation of necessity so as to be able to do damage to his closest competitor's storefront without having to fear criminal liability. To this end, he starts driving at breakneck speed down the narrow alleyway where he knows the rival's store to be located. He anticipates that when he gets close to the store, there will probably be a cluster of people congregating in front of it, and that he will then face the choice of either running into them or veering to the side and damaging his rival's storefront instead. Naturally he would do the latter, thus getting to inflict the desired damage on his rival with impunity by invoking the law of necessity. Clearly he should not by this subterfuge be able to avoid liability. But how exactly should this kind of situation be analyzed? On what grounds could we actually deny him the necessity defense? What the most thoughtful commentators of this situation have said is that we should think about the matter in the following way. There is no doubt that the defendant acted rightly when, at the moment of encountering the cluster of people, he decided to veer into the storefront instead, and he should not on that account be held liable. He really did have a valid necessity defense at that moment. However, he did not have a valid claim to a necessity defense when he inaugurated the chain of events that led to this denouement—in other words, at the moment at which he first began hurtling down the alleyway. All that liability requires is that the prosecution be able to identify a moment in time at which he committed an act that constituted the forbidden actus reus of damaging another person's property, and that he did not at that time have a valid defense for that act. Therefore, when causing his car to hurtle down the alleyway, what the defendant did could probably be described as the first step of damaging another person's property, and for that step he did not have a justification. Necessity certainly did not require him to race down the alleyway. It only required him to swerve once he was already doing so. Ergo, he is liable.[4]

(eds) (Oxford University Press, 2002), 147; Claire Finkelstein and Leo Katz, "Contrived Defenses and Deterrent Threats: Two Facets of One Problem," 5 *Ohio Law Journal* 479 (2008). The German language literature, however, abounds with in, depth studies of this problem. Here is a sampling—with a preference for overviews to guide the curious: Michael Hettinger, *Die Actio Libera in Causa: Strafbarkeit wegen Begehungstat trotz Schuldunfaehigkeit? Eine historisch-dogmatische Untersuchung* (Duncker & Humblot, 1988); Joachim Hruschka, *Strafrecht nach logisch-analytischer Methode* (de Gruyter, 1983); U. Neumann, *Zurechnung und Vorverschulden* (Duncker & Humblot, 1985); Dorothee Sydow, *Die Actio Libera in Causa nach dem Rechssprechungwandel des Budgerichtshofs* (Lang, 2002); Hubert Stuehler, *Die Actio Libera in Causa de lege lata und de lege ferenda: Eine Analyse von Rechtsprechung und der Literatur verbunden mit einem Gesetzgebungsvorschlag* (Ergon 1999); Rene Zenker, *Actio Libera in Causa: Ein Paradoxon als oeffentlicher Strafanspruch in einem vom Schuldprinzip geprageten Rechststaat* (LIT Verlag 2003).

4 See, e.g., Robinson, *supra* n. 3, 4–8, and Moore, *supra* n. 3, 35–6.

Possibly an even more compelling way to make this point is the following example. A person jumps out of a window, so as to land on top of his intended victim, whom in this fashion he kills. He then claims the involuntary act defense, because at the moment at which his body made contact with his victim's he was not committing a voluntary act. We would deny him the defense because we would view the involuntariness of his landing on his victim's head as irrelevant: he engaged in a voluntary act when he threw himself out of the window and that voluntary act qualifies as the actus reus required by a homicide—"causing another person's death."

Interestingly enough, however, this argument against the legitimacy of contrived defenses does not work all that well when applied to contrived self-defense. The problem has to do with proximate causation. We are going to feel uneasy saying about the defendant who goaded his victim into an ill-considered attack, to which the defendant then responds with lethal force, that he (the defendant) inaugurated a chain of events at the end of which he may have had a legitimate right of self-defense but at the beginning of which he did not. The reason we feel uneasy is that the chain of events he inaugurated did not *proximately* trigger the victim's death. It did not do so because the victim's response seems like the kind of *intervening act* ordinarily considered to break the chain of proximate causation, thereby negating liability. To be sure, the matter is far from clear-cut. Whether the provoked victim's actions qualify as an intervening act is an uncertain matter under the usual understanding of the intervening cause doctrine. The arch-typical intervening act is one in which the intervening actor intends to bring about the consequence he brings about. Since the victim here quite obviously was not trying to bring about his own death, he is not an arch-typical intervening actor. On the other hand, if the provoked attacker had succeeded in killing the provoker, we would clearly not judge the provoker to have proximately caused his own death (inasmuch as in that case the intervening actor would in fact have brought about the intended consequences of his actions). But inasmuch as the provoked attacker's death is the result of an action by him that would be considered a non-proximate consequence of the provoker's actions—the attempt to kill the provoker—we seem to have pretty strong grounds for considering the provoker's action to be a break in the chain of proximate causation, even if the end result is not the provoker's but the provoked attacker's death.

One might, however, try an entirely different tack altogether to argue for the impermissibility of the provoking defendant's making a legitimate self-defense claim. Self-defense is legitimate if it is truly necessary for the defendant to save his life. But if he provoked the victim, was it truly necessary? Could he not simply have saved his life by not provoking him, rather than by provoking and killing him?

The difficulty with this argument becomes apparent if we try to make the time period involved in the process of goading a very extended one. Suppose a woman embarks on a relationship with a man who has some track record in starting to behave abusively toward his partners many months, or even years, into the relationship. She is well aware of this. Do we want to say that she loses her right of self-defense on the ground that she could have avoided the whole problem by not entering into the relationship with him in the first place? What this brings out is an important ambiguity in the notion of necessity as it enters into the definition of self-defense. We do not really mean that you are only entitled to self-defense if that is logically necessary in some absolute sense. Necessity is relative to background circumstances. And we are surely willing to restrict the background circumstances that we allow as being relevant, most especially by only focusing on recently developed background circumstances. So for instance if our elite special forces units are kept generally small, in part with the thought that that might invite victims to engage in ill-considered resistance which might then justify killing them, it is hard to believe that anyone would want to seriously argue that they were not entitled to kill in self-defense because it was not strictly speaking necessary to do so, if one only took enough of a long-range view of the matter.

A third way to argue for depriving the special forces unit of their right of self-defense is to say that what we have here is a form of entrapment. In a literal sense, we arguably do, but in a legal and moral sense, the situation is far from clear. What we are talking about here certainly is not the entrapment defense in the strictly legal sense—where it is simply an argument someone is allowed to raise against being convicted of a crime into which the government entrapped him. This is not a case of a government seeking to punish someone for something they entrapped him into doing, for the simple reason that they killed him before the issue of punishment even arose. Moreover, if they had tried to arrest and prosecute him, he would have had trouble making a doctrinally sound entrapment defense because it is usually restricted to non-violent crimes, and putting even that technical issue aside, he might have had trouble proving the lack of predisposition that the entrapment defense requires. But more important than any of these slightly formalistic points is the fact that the entrapment defense is hardly an uncontroversial moral principle. In fact, its moral footing continues to be much debated and is if anything more widely questioned than the restriction of the right of self-defense with regard to provoking agents. In a similar vein, one might try to make some sort of estoppel argument against the special unit's claim of self-defense. But estoppel arguments are on an even less sound footing than entrapment, from which in this case they seem barely distinguishable.

But rather than continuing with what I have been doing so far—which is to answer individually every separate argument that has been raised against allowing a provoker to raise the claim of self-defense—it is perhaps more effective to respond in a more general way to the skepticism regarding the provoker's right of self-defense. But that will require some stage-setting.

Elsewhere I have argued—in a joint paper with the economist Alvaro Sandroni— that all rule-based decision-making produces certain kinds of cycles and that these cycles necessarily invite maneuvers of the kind that the provoking agent is engaged in. Let me here give a very brief sketch of that argument.[5]

First, a bit of background. Sandroni, who constructed the model on which our argument builds, had been interested in the kind of cyclical choices that psychologists often hold up as the hallmark of human irrationality. Here are two telling examples.

(1) When someone is given the choice between watching movie X and watching movie Y, he chooses to watch movie Y. When given the choice between watching movie Y by himself or with a handicapped person, he chooses to watch it with a handicapped person. But when given the choice between watching movie Y with a handicapped person or movie X, without a handicapped person, he chooses movie X. In other words, his choices are cyclical. Why is that? What he is doing seems bizarre and irrational, at least from a purely formal point of view. Informally, it is not so hard to make out what is going on here. The person would be embarrassed to admit to not wanting to watch a movie in the presence of a handicapped person, which is why he chooses to watch it *with* him rather than *without* him. But given the opportunity to escape doing so by watching an entirely different movie, which he has the option of watching all by himself, he has no trouble doing so, because he can say that he happened to prefer that movie, though of course we know the opposite to be true, since we know that given the opportunity he would choose Y over X.

(2) When someone has to choose between staying in the office and working, or going home to relax instead, he would opt for going home. When given the choice between going home to relax or visiting a sick friend in the hospital, he would opt for visiting his friend. Alas, when given the choice between staying in the office and working, or visiting a sick friend, he would choose staying in the office. Once again we have a cycle, which at least on a formal level seems strange and perplexing. Of course, informally we find nothing strange and perplexing about it. The person is too embarrassed to admit that he would rather stay away from the hospital, and since he can only do so if he has work as an excuse, he chooses to stay at the office.

Sandroni pointed out that a natural way to describe, or model, what is going on here is to think of the chooser as maximizing his preferences subject to the requirement that he respect, first, the usual feasibility constraint (also known as the budget constraint)—that is, only choose something that is actually available to him—and second, and this is where Sandroni's interesting innovation comes in, the constraint that one's choice be "rationalizable," his term for a choice that can be justified in terms of applicable legal or moral rules. That extra constraint somewhat unexpectedly gives rise to cycling. The cycling in turn gives rise to the possibility of

---

[5] Alvaro Sandroni and Leo Katz, *Why Law Breeds Cycles* (2010), manuscript on file with authors; Vadim Cherepanov, Timothy Feddersen, and Alvaro Sandroni, *Rationalization* (2009) manuscript on file with authors.

certain strategic actions that allow one to attain a seemingly forbidden objective by being manipulative. One is supposed to visit his friend, but one can avoid doing so by making sure not to be home but in the office. One is supposed to not discriminate against a handicapped person, but one can nonetheless do what comes to the same thing, by choosing a movie different from the one the handicapped person is going to be watching, and so on.

As we point out in our joint paper, these situations have ready analogues in the law, most especially in the law of criminal law defenses. Consider the law of duress. If I am threatened with torture, unless I have committed a rather serious crime, including something as serious as killing several people, I might well qualify for the duress defense if I submit: the law cannot expect me to be a hero, the explanation would presumably run. By contrast, if I were threatened with the destruction of a manuscript I have devoted my life's work to, unless I commit the identical crime—killing several people—I naturally will not qualify for the duress defense if I submit. Now suppose that I have in the past endured significant torture just to save the manuscript. Then it seems we just landed in another cycle, this time a legal one. As between suffering the destruction of the manuscript or being tortured, I would rather be tortured. As between torture and committing several killings, I would rather carry out the killings. Yet as between committing several killings and suffering the destruction of my manuscript, I would rather allow my manuscript to be destroyed (because I will do what's necessary to avoid doing something illegal). This cycle too gives rise to possibilities of circumvention, like the psychological cycles considered earlier.

For instance, imagine that I am able to protect myself against the people who are threatening the destruction of my manuscript (unless I do what they want) by borrowing a lot of money from a loan shark which I then use to hire people to safeguard my manuscript. When it comes to paying off the loan shark, I do not have the funds, as a result of which he threatens to torture me unless I commit several killings in his behalf. Now I am likely to qualify for the duress defense. If one tried to create doctrines that made such exploitation of legal cycles impossible, they would turn out to be tantamount to the most extreme and unyielding kind of utilitarianism—the sort that would inflict punishment every time I choose to do anything at any moment in time that does not maximize overall social utility, more or less understood in traditional Benthamite ways. (If there are other ways to block the exploitation of legal cycles, they are going to be at least equally unappealing.)

There are entirely uncontroversial examples of this kind of cycle in the law of self-defense. Suppose a robber says to me "Your money or your life." I stand fast and refuse to give him my money, whereupon he attacks me, whereupon I kill him, which would, of course, be perfectly legitimate on my part. Hidden within this simple interaction is the exploitation of a cycle much like the one involved in duress. Given the choice between killing a thief and losing my money, I am required by law to lose my money. Given the choice between losing my money and losing my life, I am free to lose my life. Given the choice between losing my life and taking the attacker's life instead, I am free to kill my attacker. The result is that if I want to get around the prohibition against choosing my money over my attacker's life, I can do so by first choosing to put my life at risk for the sake of my money, and then saving my life by killing the attacker. Obviously, something analogous is really being done when I contrive to create the circumstances of self-defense by putting an *agent provocateur*—the special forces unit—in the victim's vicinity.

II. Redirected self-defense

Let us now turn to a different type of targeted killing case, raising a different set of questions about the strategic use of self-defense. Let us suppose that there lives on the territory of a generally unfriendly foreign power a peaceable holy man who has inspired a fanatical, violence-prone following. Members of his movement are in the process of preparing a violent attack upon us. It would solve our problems if we could eliminate the holy man with a targeted killing. But he is not actually doing anything to deliberately foment acts of aggression against us. In fact he is not only opposed to such actions, he strongly counsels against them. But it does no good. Those who like his spiritual message are led, in significant numbers, to regard our nation as the devil and to plan on violent actions against us.

It would be convenient for us to get rid of him, but it seems we cannot. Neither self-defense nor necessity, as conventionally understood, would seem to allow us to do anything to bring him down. There is no ground for self-defense because he is not actually attacking anyone. And to kill him on grounds of necessity would be a classic case of killing one innocent to save a larger number, which the defense of necessity, without more, would not usually be held to permit. The excuse of duress, I suppose, might fare a little better, but not much: first, because its scope might not reach that far, since we are not quite in the classic duress situation where someone tells us to do something lest he injure us (admittedly, this is a somewhat controversial restriction on the duress defense), and second, and more importantly, because of the interesting fact that excuses are not the kind of defense a government can readily invoke. (To be sure, there is something mysterious and perplexing in this which seems worth exploring, but I will not concern myself with it here.)

Now suppose that the holy man's followers are indeed about to launch their long-planned attack against us. They will do so from a place in which they are surrounded by many innocent civilians. We are considering a preemptive attack upon them that would take out the attackers and their weapons just as they are about to strike. It has the unfortunate drawback of costing the lives of many innocent civilian bystanders, but given that we are essentially responding to an attack by another country upon us, we would be well within our rights. Suppose further, however, that all of this could be prevented, if instead of preempting the attack along such conventional lines, we simply arranged for the death of the innocent holy man. Would that be legitimate? Notice that in doing so we are not simply saving some innocents who are about to die by taking the life of some other innocent. Rather, we are choosing to substitute for the deaths of several innocents whom we are entitled to kill, despite their innocence, the death of another innocent whom we are not entitled to kill.

But will this in fact work? Such an argument is usually dismissed because it sounds at first indistinguishable from the standard utilitarian claim that it is all right to do whatever achieves a net saving of lives, which many would dismiss by drawing the analogy to organ-harvesting doctors and lynch-mob-appeasing prison wardens. But in fact our situation is different in some crucial respects, and the net saving of lives argument here is on much stronger, even if not entirely unassailable, ground.

To see why, let's begin by adapting the infamous trolley example to our kind of situation. Imagine that we could take preemptive action against would-be attackers by building a long ramp, an incline, down which we could chase a trolley which would run over, and kill, the innocents that happen to surround our would-be attackers and in due course would kill our would-be attackers as well. This is something we are obviously entitled to do.[6]

Now add the familiar second track to this incline, such that if we were turn the trolley, it would run into our holy man instead, killing him, sparing the innocents, and stopping in their tracks the attackers who depended on the sustenance they drew from his message. Would it not be perfectly acceptable to turn the trolley here, just as it is in the standard trolley case?

To be sure, we cannot ordinarily use this kind of a trolley arrangement to liquidate just anyone by setting things up in such a way that we take aim at one group of innocents and then avoid hitting them by turning the trolley onto a second track. But that is because we are ordinarily not entitled to take aim at a group of innocents in the first place. Here things are different, because we are entitled to take aim at them, in the course of exercising our right of self-defense. Turning the trolley now seems an entirely different matter.

---

[6] Philippa Foot, "The Problem of Abortion and the Doctrine of the Double Effect" in *Virtues and Vices* (University of California Press,1978); Judith Jarvis Thomson, "Killing, Letting Die, and the Trolley Problem," 59 *The Monist* 204–17 (1976); Judith Jarvis Thomson, "The Trolley Problem," 94 *Yale Law Journal* 1395–1415 (1985); Francis Myrna Kamm, "Harming Some to Save Others," 57 *Philosophical Studies* 227–60 (1989); *Morality, Mortality, Vol. 1: Death and Whom to Save From It* (Oxford University Press, 1993); *Morality, Mortality, Vol. 2: Rights, Duties, and Status* (Oxford University Press, 1996).

Most of the details of the trolley arrangement are surely inessential for this argument to work. If we simply directed a strike against the holy man, that seems just as permissible as engaging in the trolley maneuver—once one has registered that it is not essentially different from the trolley case. And so it would seem that at least in a context in which we are entitled to take innocent lives in the course of defending ourselves—and probably for other reasons as well—we will often be entitled to cash in that chit for other innocent lives, in this case for a targeted killing.

Some people are going to find my analysis here too coarse-grained. There are many situations in moral theory in which chits like this just do not work—you really cannot cash them in, however Pareto-optimal it would be if you could. A good illustration is what one might call the problem of delayed self-defense: take an ordinary case of self-defense, in which rather than killing my attacker outright I allow myself to be injured by him, hoping to survive his attack without having to kill anyone. Having been injured badly, however, it turns out I can only survive with a heart transplant, for which he is the only potential donor. Can I avail myself of his heart? Can I claim that this is a kind of extended self-defense? Some people might say yes (Michael Moore has so argued); most, however, would say no. Not killing him in the first place did not give me a chit I can cash in later on, however mutually beneficial it would be for him and me alike if I could.[7]

Some people would claim that my holy man case is just such a case where the logic of chits fails, where the right to commit one killing cannot be exchanged for the right to commit a different killing that happens to have fewer victims. They might invoke the famous fat man example posed originally by Judith Jarvis Thomson in one of her well-known articles on the trolley problem. She asks us to consider the following variation of the trolley case: "As before, a trolley is hurtling down a track towards five people. You are on a bridge under which it will pass, and you can stop it by dropping a heavy weight in front of it. As it happens, there is a very fat man next to you—your only way to stop the trolley is to push him over the bridge and onto the track, killing him to save five. Should you proceed?" The widely shared intuition about this case is that doing so is off limits. The natural question to then ask about my holy man case is whether killing him to spare those innocent civilians is not rather like killing the fat man to spare the five on the track?

My own sense is that the holy man scenario differs in some crucial ways from that of the fat man. To see this, consider a variation of the fat man case that is rather closer to the holy man case. Suppose that, as in the original trolley problem, we can spare the five by diverting the trolley onto another track. But let us also suppose that on that other track there is not just one potential victim, but two.

---

[7] Michael Moore, "Torture and the Balance of Evils," 23 *Isr. L. Rev.* 280, 323 (1989). For a more general exploration of this type of issue, see Claire Finkelstein, "A Contractarian Argument Against the Death Penalty," 81 *N.Y.U. L. Rev.* 1283 (2006).

Finally, suppose that we only push the fat man onto that second track once we have diverted the trolley toward those two victims. My own intuitions about this case would permit us to do this. By diverting the trolley, we are choosing to target two innocents to save the life of five other innocents. We did so permissibly, of course, but that does not change the fact that we are actually *killing* those two, rather than merely letting them die. If we can spare those two innocents by substituting some smaller number of innocents, then that seems to me acceptable because we are no longer simply saving some innocents, in whose death we had no active part; rather, we are choosing to avoid actively killing a certain number of innocents by killing some other smaller number of innocents, a small but significant difference.

III. A back-up argument: minimizing rights violations

A standard argument for a targeted killing is the following. If we do not eliminate the potential attacker, or for that matter the holy man, on the grounds that we would be violating their rights if we did, we are thereby facilitating a much greater number of rights-violations down the road. To begin with, there are the rights violations carried out by the would-be attacker and by the followers of the holy man, but those are not the only ones to worry about. There are also the rights-violations that are likely to be carried out by our own side in the course of any conflict: unjustified detentions of suspicious aliens, abrogation of civil rights in the interest of national security and so on. Not that we think we are justified in engaging in such conduct—if we were, they would not be rights-violations—it is just that we can statistically predict that there will be many of those, whether we like it or not. That is just how it is. If one cares about rights, surely one should prefer a single rights-violation now in lieu of many more later on.

This kind of argument is what Robert Nozick called a utilitarianism of rights, and he viewed it as one which an advocate of rights, or at least a deontologist, would generally reject.[8] If one is a deontologist, one ought to respect rights, not seek to minimize rights-violations. That means, somewhat paradoxically, that one ought to avoid violating a right here and now, such as the right not to be the victim of an unjustified targeted killing, even if the person or governmental entity that is respecting that right would be causing more rights-violations in the long run, such as more individuals being the victim of unjustified killing.

I am willing to go along with that. What I am not willing to go along with is a conclusion usually drawn from it: namely that it would be better if one did not violate a right than if one did. "Would be better" turns out to have several possible senses, and while it might well be better not to carry out the targeted killing *in the*

---

[8] Robert Nozick, *Anarchy, State and Utopia* (Perseus Book Group, 1974) 28–9.

sense that it is what one ought to do, it turns out, on reflection, not to be better in some other, equally important sense—namely in the sense that one might well be less blameworthy if one were willing to engage in such a violation here and now. In other words, if someone were to review the moral ledger of someone who decided to respect a certain right here and now at the expense of violating many more such rights later on, and compared that to the moral ledger of someone who ignored that self-same right here and now, so as to forestall having to commit many more rights-violations later on, this last person might well end up with the better moral ledger.

To see this more clearly, let's consider for a moment the venerable *Regina v. Dudley and Stephens*, the lifeboat case in which Thomas Dudley decides to kill the youngest of the sailors, Richard Parker, so that he and the other two sailors, Stephens and Brooks, would have a shot at survival by feeding on his remains.[9] Let us suppose, not implausibly, that Dudley had acted with criminal recklessness in taking a comparatively slight boat like the Mignonette on an ocean voyage to Australia—so criminal in fact that if Parker, Stephens and Brooks had all died in the resulting shipwreck, he would be guilty of their murder. Finally, let us suppose that we agree with the court's judgment that Dudley's killing of Parker was wrong, that it was too much like the classic utilitarian horror stories in which killings that achieve net savings of lives are nevertheless impermissible, like those I alluded to earlier: the organ-harvesting surgeon who saves five people one of whom needs a heart, two of whom need kidneys, and two of whom need lungs, by killing a fifth; or the prison warden who surrenders a prisoner to a lynch mob so as to avert a riot in which many more innocent lives would be lost.

Let us now compare what would have happened if Dudley had done the right thing, and abstained from killing Parker, and what would have happened if he had done what he actually did, killed him. In the first case, he would have been guilty of three murders—that of Stephens, Brooks and Parker. In the second case, he would only be guilty of what he actually was found guilty of: the murder of Parker. In short, Dudley's legal position is improved by doing the wrong thing.

What I am imagining here is not as unusual as it might sound. After all, all we really need to construct this kind of scenario is to take any one of the classical utilitarian dilemmas—like the organ-harvesting case or the lynch mob case—and to imagine someone who has wrongfully inflicted some kind of serious harm that he could mitigate if he engaged in one of these unpalatable utilitarian trade-offs. Imagine, for instance, a ruler who first whips up the frenzy of the crowd against an innocent prisoner, but then wants to backtrack. He will minimize his blameworthiness by agreeing to the execution of the innocent prisoner, so as to prevent the lynch mob from doing even worse things, for which he could otherwise be blamed, given his role in whipping them up.[10]

---

[9] *Regina v. Dudley and Stephens* [1884] 14 QBD 273 DC.
[10] As in Nozick, *supra* n. 8, 28–9.

What this means for a government engaged in targeted killings is that even if we consider those killings illegitimate, either because the arguments I have put forward in earlier sections regarding their legitimacy are not persuasive, or because they do not fall within the range of situations to which my arguments would apply, they might well serve to improve the moral position of the government engaging in them. By engaging in such killings, even if they are illegitimate, the government might well be reducing the overall amount of illegitimate conduct it will end up being guilty of. That does not mean that it did the right thing, not by any stretch. Only that it will end up with a better moral ledger, as it were, than if it *had* done the right thing!

This is without a doubt a very paradoxical situation for the government to be in. It means that if they were to ask God what he would recommend they do, he would tell them not to commit the targeted killing. But if they then proceeded to ask him whether they would be more likely to enter the pearly gates if they engaged in the targeted killing than if they did not, he would tell them that targeted killings are the way to go.

IV. Root causes

I have laid out in this chapter three lines of argument for certain defensive uses of targeted killings. Each of them has something strange and paradoxical about it. But what exactly makes them so strange and paradoxical? What makes them that, in my opinion, is that they reveal features of legal rules and legal reasoning that we would regard as irrational in the course of ordinary decision-making.

Start with the strategy of provoking intense resistance to an arrest so that the special forces can then simply take out the intended target, rather than having to arrest him. The legitimacy of this strategy depends on the ubiquity of cyclical, or intransitive, choices in a legal system, something which many would regard as the hallmark of an irrational person, if an individual decision-maker were to exhibit it.

The strategy of killing the holy man as an alternative to killing other innocents in the course of self-defense violates what is sometimes called the principle of independence of irrelevant alternatives. The standard joke used to illustrate this particular principle of rationality is the man in a restaurant who, having chosen to order steak rather than chicken, then learns that he overlooked that there was also fish on the menu, and promptly changes his order to chicken. Absurd, of course, yet something analogous is going on in our evaluation of the holy man scenario. As between killing the holy man or letting a lot of innocents be killed as a result of the pernicious influence of his teachings, we are ordinarily inclined to opt for the latter and reject the option of killing the holy man. But if a third option—that of killing other innocents in the course of self-defense—is introduced, then suddenly the killing of the holy man becomes acceptable. That third option plays the same role as the fish alternative in the restaurant and it is thus bound to seem strange that it should affect the outcome.

Finally, the strategy of minimizing rights-violations goes against a desirable feature of rational decision-making that decision theorists like to call non-monotonicity. We expect sound moral and legal choices to have the basic property that if we choose to do the right rather than the wrong thing, we end up in a legally and morally better position than someone who chooses to the wrong rather than the right thing. (We expect moral choices to be monotonically related to overall moral status.) It just happens not to be true.

There is in fact nothing accidental about the fact that legal reasoning violates these canons of rational decision-making. It has long been known that collective decision-making routinely violates these canons. Those are the familiar paradoxes of social choices—the impossibility theorems of Arrow, Sen and others. It has also come to be accepted that individual decision-making, if it seeks to reflect a multiplicity of judgmental criteria, closely resembles collective decision-making and produces analogous paradoxes. But that is exactly what legal decision-making is: individual decision-making based on a multiplicity of criteria. This fact is sometimes disguised by the fact that we are applying rules, but the rules themselves are a device for aggregating a multiplicity of criteria into a decision-making device. Legal decision-making thus cannot avoid those paradoxes either. Our paradox-fraught assessment of targeted killings is just a special case of all that.

What I have so sweepingly asserted in this last paragraph is really a mouthful. I certainly do not consider it to be obviously right—though I do consider it to be right, else I would not have asserted it, just not *obviously* right. Indeed, I have made the defense of this thesis the subject of an entire book called *Why the Law Is So Perverse*.[11] This larger claim about the root causes of the dissonance between the *actual* solidity and the *apparent* feebleness of the arguments for targeted killings is thus one the reader has to either take on faith—or read the book.

---

[11] Leo Katz, *Why the Law is So Perverse* (University of Chicago Press, 2011).

INDEX

References such as "178–9" indicate (not necessarily continuous) discussion of a topic across a range of pages. Wherever possible in the case of topics with many references, these have either been divided into sub-topics or only the most significant discussions of the topic are listed. Because the entire work is about 'targeted killing' the use of this term (and certain others which occur constantly throughout the book) as an entry point has been minimised. Information will be found under the corresponding detailed topics.